ATTENTION, MEMORY, AND EXECUTIVE FUNCTION

This book is printed on recycled paper.

ATTENTION, MEMORY, AND EXECUTIVE FUNCTION

edited by

G. Reid Lyon, Ph.D.

and

Norman A. Krasnegor, Ph.D.

Human Learning and Behavior Branch
National Institute of Child Health and Human Development

·P·A·U·L·H·
BROOKES
PUBLISHING C°

Baltimore • London • Toronto • Sydney

Paul H. Brookes Publishing Co.
Post Office Box 10624
Baltimore, Maryland 21285-0624

Attention, memory, and
executive function

Typeset by Brushwood Graphics, Baltimore, Maryland.
Manufactured in the United States of America by
The Maple Press Company, York, Pennsylvania.

Library of Congress Cataloging-in-Publication Data
Attention, memory, and executive function / edited by G. Reid Lyon,
    Norman A. Krasnegor.
        p.   cm.
    Includes bibliographical references and index.
    ISBN 1-55766-198-7
    1. Attention.   2. Memory.   3. Cognition.   I. Lyon, G. Reid,
1949–   .   II. Krasnegor, Norman A., 1939–
    [DNLM: 1. Mental processes—physiology.   2. Attention—
physiology.   3. Memory—physiology.   BF 441 A883 1996]
QP405.A866   1996
612.8'2–dc20
DNLM/DLC
for Library of Congress   95-2540
                                                             CIP

British Library Cataloguing-in-Publication data are available from the
British Library.

CONTENTS

Contributors...ix
Preface..xv
Acknowledgments...xvii

I   INTRODUCTION TO THE CONCEPTUAL,
    MEASUREMENT, AND METHODOLOGICAL ISSUES........................1

   1   The Need for Conceptual and Theoretical Clarity in
       the Study of Attention, Memory, and Executive
       Function
       G. Reid Lyon...3

   2   Relationships and Distinctions Among the Concepts
       of Attention, Memory, and Executive Function:
       A Developmental Perspective
       Robin D. Morris 11

   3   Conceptual and Methodological Issues in Construct
       Definition
       Jack M. Fletcher, David J. Francis, Karla K. Stuebing,
       Bennett A. Shaywitz, Sally E. Shaywitz,
       Donald P. Shankweiler, Leonard Katz, and
       Robin D. Morris 17

II ATTENTION...43

   4   Critical Issues in Research on Attention
       Russell A. Barkley...45

   5   A Theory of Attention: An Information Processing
       Perspective
       Joseph Sergeant..57

   6   Disorders of Attention: A Neuropsychological
       Perspective
       Allan F. Mirsky 71

   7   Attention: A Behavior Analytical Perspective
       William J. McIlvane, William V. Dube, and
       Thomas D. Callahan 97

   8   Conceptualizing, Describing, and Measuring
       Components of Attention: A Summary
       Jeffrey M. Halperin..119

III   MEMORY 137

    9   From Simple Structure to Complex Function: Major
        Trends in the Development of Theories, Models, and
        Measurements of Memory
        Richard K. Wagner 139

  10   A Model of Memory from an Information Processing
        Perspective: The Special Case of Phonological
        Memory
        Joseph K. Torgesen 157

  11   Multiple Memory Systems: A Neuropsychological
        and Developmental Perspective
        Jocelyne Bachevalier, Ludise Malkova, and
        Mario Beauregard 185

  12   Attention and Memory in Relation to Learning:
        A Comparative Adaptation Perspective
        Duane M. Rumbaugh and David A. Washburn 199

  13   Conceptualizing, Describing, and Measuring
        Components of Memory: A Summary
        Kimberly Boller 221

IV   EXECUTIVE FUNCTION 233

  14   Theories, Models, and Measurements of Executive
        Functioning: An Information Processing Perspective
        John G. Borkowski and Jennifer E. Burke 235

  15   A Theory and Model of Executive Function:
        A Neuropsychological Perspective
        Martha Bridge Denckla 263

  16   Relational Frame Theory and Executive Function:
        A Behavioral Approach
        Steven C. Hayes, Elizabeth V. Gifford, and
        L.E. Ruckstuhl, Jr 279

  17   Linkages Between Attention and Executive Functions
        Russell A. Barkley 307

  18   Executive Functions and Working Memory:
        Theoretical and Measurement Issues
        Bruce F. Pennington, Loisa Bennetto, Owen McAleer,
        and Ralph J. Roberts, Jr 327

19 Addressing Problems in Attention, Memory,
    and Executive Functioning: An Example from
    Self-Regulated Strategy Development
    Steve Graham and Karen R. Harris 349

20 Conceptualizing, Describing, and Measuring
    Components of Executive Function: A Summary
    Paul J. Eslinger 367

V   SUMMARY AND CONCLUSIONS 397

21 Critical Issues and Future Directions in the
    Development of Theories, Models, and Measurements
    for Attention, Memory, and Executive Function
    H. Gerry Taylor 399

Index 413

CONTRIBUTORS

The Editors

G. Reid Lyon, Ph.D., Psychologist, Human Learning and Behavior Branch, National Institute of Child Health and Human Development, National Institutes of Health, 6100 Executive Boulevard, Room 4B05D, Bethesda, MD 20892. Dr. Lyon is responsible for the development and management of research programs in learning disabilities, language development and disorders, and disorders of attention in children.

Norman A. Krasnegor, Ph.D., Chief, Human Learning and Behavior Branch, National Institute of Child Health and Human Development, National Institutes of Health, 6100 Executive Boulevard, Room 4B05, Bethesda, MD 20892. Dr. Krasnegor is a physiological and experimental psychologist whose current research interests lie in developmental behavioral biology, learning, and cognitive development.

The Chapter Authors

Jocelyne Bachevalier, Ph.D., Associate Professor, Department of Neurobiology and Anatomy, MSB 7.046, University of Texas Medical Center, 6431 Fannin, Houston, TX 77030. Dr. Bachevalier is Associate Professor in the Department of Neurobiology and Anatomy at The University of Texas Health Science Center in Houston. Her research interest focuses on the ontogenetic development, maturation, and decline of learning and memory in the monkey as well as on the underlying neurobiological mechanisms.

Russell A. Barkley, Ph.D., Professor, Department of Psychiatry, University of Massachusetts Medical Center, 55 Lake Avenue, North, Worcester, MA 01655. Dr. Barkley is Director of Psychology and Professor of Psychiatry and Neurology in the Department of Psychiatry at the University of Massachusetts Medical Center. His research interests are in attention deficit hyperactivity disorder and its associated conditions, etiology, developmental course, and treatment.

Mario Beauregard, Research Fellow, Cognitive Neuropsychology Laboratory; Lady Davis Institute, Department of Clinical Neurosciences, Jewish General Hospital, 3755 Chemin de la Cote Ste. Catherine, Montreal, Quebec H3T 1EZ, CANADA. Dr. Beauregard is Research Fellow at Jewish General Hospital.

Loisa Bennetto, M.A., Department of Psychology, University of Denver, 2155 South Race Street, Denver, CO 80208. Loisa Bennetto's research interests include the neurocognitive bases of developmental disorders, particularly autism and fragile X syndrome.

Kimberly Boller, Ph.D., Fellow, Human Learning and Behavior Branch, National Institute of Child Health and Human Development, National Institutes of Health, Executive Building, Room, 4B05, 6100 Executive Boulevard, MSC 7510, Bethesda, MD 20892. Dr. Boller, a Fellow at the National Institute of Child Health and Human Development (NICHD), is trained in cognitive and developmental psychology and has studied memory development in human infants.

John G. Borkowski, Ph.D., Professor, Department of Psychology, University of Notre Dame, Hagger Hall, Notre Dame, IA 46556. Dr. Borkowski holds a Ph.D. degree in experimental psychology. Following a postdoctoral year of studies with Arthur Benton, a neuropsychologist, he became Assistant Professor of Psychology at Oberlin College. For the past 27 years he has been at the University of Notre Dame, where he holds the Andrew J. McKenna Family Chair of Psychology.

Jennifer E. Burke, A.B., Department of Psychology, University of Notre Dame, Hagger Hall, Notre Dame, IA 46556. Jennifer E. Burke is pursuing a Ph.D. degree at the University of Notre Dame in developmental psychology, specializing in adolescent parenting and developmental delay.

Thomas D. Callahan, B.S., Behavioral Sciences Division, Eunice Kennedy Shriver Center, 200 Trapelo Road, Waltham, MA 02254. Thomas D. Callahan is Research Coordinator in the Behavioral Sciences Division, Eunice Kennedy Shriver Center for Mental Retardation.

Martha Bridge Denckla, M.D., Kennedy Krieger Institute, Suite 501, 707 North Broadway, Baltimore, MD 21205. Dr. Denckla is Professor of Neurology and Pediatrics at The Johns Hopkins University School of Medicine and Director of the Department of Developmental Cognitive Neurology at the Kennedy Krieger Institute. She is also the principal investigator and director of a center devoted to research on learning disabilities ("Neurodevelopmental Pathways to Learning Disabilities," P50 HD 25806).

William V. Dube, Ph.D., Associate Scientist, Behavioral Sciences Division, Eunice Kennedy Shriver Center, 200 Trapelo Road, Waltham, MA 02254. Dr. Dube is Associate Scientist in the Behavioral Sciences Division, Eunice Kennedy Shriver Center for Mental Retardation; and Clinical Associate Professor, College of Pharmacy and Health Sciences, Northeastern University. Dr. Dube's research is in the area of stimulus control and discrimination learning in individuals with mental retardation.

Paul J. Eslinger, Ph.D., Associate Professor, Division of Neurology, College of Medicine, Pennsylvania State University, P.O. Box 850, Hershey, PA 17033. Dr. Eslinger is Associate Professor in the Departments of Medicine (Division of Neurology) and Behavioral Science in the College of Medicine, Pennsylvania State University, and the Milton S. Hershey Medical Center. He directs the clinical, teaching, and research programs in the Laboratory of Clinical Neuropsychology and Cognitive Neuroscience and is Consulting Neuropsychologist to the University Hospital Rehabilitation Center.

Jack M. Fletcher, Ph.D., Psychologist and Professor, Department of Pediatrics, MSB 3.136, The University of Texas Medical School at Houston, 6431 Fannin, Houston, TX 77030. Dr. Fletcher's research has focused on the classification of reading disabilities and on the development of children with different types of brain injuries.

David J. Francis, Ph.D., Associate Professor, Department of Psychology, University of Houston, Houston, TX 77030. Dr. Francis's research focuses on the measurement of change in behavior over time and structural equation modeling.

Elizabeth V. Gifford, Department of Clinical Psychology, University of Nevada, Reno, NV 89557-0062. Elizabeth V. Gifford is a doctoral student in clinical psychology at the University of Nevada at Reno. Her research interests include functional analyses of language and their implications for the assessment and treatment of problems in human functioning.

Steve Graham, Ph.D., Professor, Department of Special Education, University of Maryland, 1308 Benjamin Building, College Park, MD 20742-1121. Dr. Graham is Professor at the University of Maryland. He conducts research on writing and writing instruction with children with learning difficulties. He previously taught at Purdue University and Auburn University.

Jeffrey M. Halperin, Ph.D., Professor, Department of Psychology, Queens College, City University of New York, 65-30 Kissena, Flushing, NY 11367-0904. Dr. Halperin is Professor in the department of psychology, Queens College of the City University of New York and the Neuropsychology Doctoral Program of the Graduate School and University Center of the City University of New York. He is also a professorial lecturer in the Department of Psychiatry of the Mount Sinai School of Medicine. He has published extensively on cognitive, neuropsychological and neurochemical aspects of attention and attention deficit hyperactivity disorder.

Karen R. Harris, Ph.D., Professor, Department of Special Education, University of Maryland, 1308 Benjamin Building, College Park, MD 20742-1121. Dr. Harris is Professor at the University of Maryland. Her research involves the study of effective means for integrating affective, behavioral, cognitive, developmental, and social models in the teaching–learning process.

Steven C. Hayes, Ph.D., Professor, Department of Psychology, University of Nevada, Reno, NV 89557-0062. Dr. Hayes is Nevada Foundation Professor and Chair in the Department of Psychology at the University of Nevada. An author of more than a dozen books and nearly 200 scientific articles, his interests cover basic research on language pragmatics, rule governance, and semantic relations; applied research on verbal regulatory processes; and work on contextualism as a philosophy of science. Dr. Hayes is currently President of the American Association of Applied and Preventive Psychology.

Leonard Katz, Ph.D., Professor, Department of Psychology, University of Connecticut, Box U-20, Storrs, CT 06268. Dr. Katz is Professor in the Department of Psychology at the University of Connecticut.

Ludise Malkova, Ph.D., Visiting Fellow, Laboratory of Neuropsychology, National Institute of Mental Health, Building 49, 9000 Rockville Pike, Bethesda, MD 20892. Dr. Malkova is Visiting Fellow in the laboratory of neuropsychology at the National Institute of Mental Health. She is a behavioral neuroscientist, who for the last 6 years has been examining the neurobiological substrate of learning and memory and socioemotional behavior in rhesus monkeys. Her research has concentrated on long-term effects of selective early brain lesions on memory and socioemotional behavior.

Owen McAleer, master's student, Department of Biology, University of Denver, Denver, CO 80208.

William J. McIlvane, Ph.D., Director, Mental Retardation Research Center, Behavioral Science Division, Eunice Kennedy Shriver Center, 200 Trapelo Road, Waltham, MA 02254. Dr. McIlvane is Director of the Mental Retardation Research Center at the Eunice Kennedy Shriver Center for Mental Retardation, Inc. He holds current academic appointments at the Massachusetts General Hospital, Harvard Medical School, and Northeastern University. Dr. McIlvane's research interests concern the experimental and theoretical analysis of both human and nonhuman behavior, with a primary emphasis on processes involved in discrimination learning and formation of stimulus classes.

Allan F. Mirsky, Ph.D., Chief, Section on Clinical and Experimental Neuropsychology, Laboratory of Psychology and Psychopathology, National Institute of Mental Health, National Institutes of Health, Building 10, Room 4C110, 9000 Rockville Pike, Bethesda, MD 20892. Dr. Mirsky is Chief of the Section on Clinical and Experimental Neuropsychology of the Laboratory of Psychology and Psychopathology of the National Institute of Mental Health, and Adjunct Professor in the Departments of Mental Hygiene and Psychiatry of the Johns Hopkins University. He was previously Professor of Psychiatry (Neuropsychology), Neurology and Psychology at Boston University, where he was the recipient of a Research Scientist Award from the National Institute of Mental Health.

Robin D. Morris, Ph.D., Professor and Chairman, Department of Psychology, Georgia State University, University Plaza, Atlanta, GA 30303. Dr. Morris's research has focused on the classification of learning and attention disorders, developmental neuropsychology, and the effects of various interventions on children with acquired brain injuries.

Bruce F. Pennington, Ph.D., Professor, Department of Psychology, University of Denver, 2155 South Race Street, Denver, CO 80208. Dr. Pennington is Professor of Psychology at the University of Denver. He worked as a school teacher and started an alternative school in the Brookline, Massachusetts, public schools. He has been doing research on children's disorders for over 17 years. He currently holds both a Research Scientist Award and a MERIT Award from the National Institute of Mental Health.

Ralph J. Roberts, Jr., Ph.D., Associate Professor, Department of Psychology, University of Denver, 2155 South Race Street, Denver, CO 80208. Dr. Roberts is Associate Professor of Psychology at the University of Denver. His research is in developmental cognitive neuropsychology, with a focus on attention, working memory, and the interaction between controlled and automatic processes.

L. E. Ruckstuhl, Jr., Department of Clinical Psychology, University of Nevada, Reno, NV 89557-0062. L. E. Ruckstuhl is a doctoral student in clinical psychology at the University of Nevada at Reno. His research interests are behavior-analytically derived clinical and community-based interventions.

Duane M. Rumbaugh, Ph.D., Professor, Language Research Center, Georgia State University, 3401 Panthersville Road, Atlanta, GA 30034. Dr. Rumbaugh is Regents' Professor of Psychology and Biology and Director of the Language Research Center, Georgia State University. His comparative research programs since 1958 have emphasized the biopsychological roots of human competence as defined in the processes of learning, cognition, and language skills of primates. He initiated the LANA (chimpanzee) Language Project in cooperation with the Yerkes Primate Center, Emory University, and led development of Georgia State University's Language Research Center.

Joseph Sergeant, Ph.D., Chair, Department of Clinical Psychology, University of Amsterdam, Roetersstraat 15, 1018 WB Amsterdam, THE NETHERLANDS. In 1975, Professor Sergeant joined the Groningen Laboratory in The Netherlands and began his research on the attentional problems of hyperactive children. This research has concentrated on identifying the specific information processing deficit of hyperactive children. In 1985 he was appointed to the chair of clinical psychology at the University of Amsterdam, where he has continued his research in hyperactivity.

Donald P. Shankweiler, Ph.D., Professor, Department of Psychology, University of Connecticut, Box U-20, Storrs, CT 06268. Dr. Shankweiler is Professor in the Department of Psychology at the University of Connecticut, and a member of the research staff of Haskins Laboratories, New Haven. His research is concerned with the intersection of reading and writing with the primary language and with the origin and interpretation of reading difficulties. Much of his recent work concerns the role of working memory in disorders of comprehension.

Bennett A. Shaywitz, M.D., Professor and Chief of Pediatric Neurology, Yale University School of Medicine, Department of Pediatrics, 333 Cedar Street, New Haven, CT 06510. Dr. Shaywitz's primary and long-standing research has focused on the neurobiological influences in learning and attention disorders. His most recent area of investigation involves the nosology and classification of learning and attention disorders.

Sally E. Shaywitz, M.D., Director, Learning Disorders Unit, and Professor, Yale University School of Medicine, Department of Pediatrics, 333 Cedar Street, New Haven, CT

06510. Dr. Shaywitz is particularly interested in utilizing epidemiological and biological strategies to more clearly elucidate the nature of learning and attention disorders.

Karla K. Stuebing, Ph.D., Adjunct Assistant Professor, Department of Pediatrics, University of Texas Health Science Center, 6431 Fannin, Houston, TX 77030. Dr. Stuebing's research interests are in the measurement of human abilities and applied statistical analyses.

H. Gerry Taylor, Ph.D., Associate Professor of Pediatrics, Case Western Reserve University, Cleveland OH 44106. H. Gerry Taylor is Associate Professor of Pediatrics at Case Western Reserve University School of Medicine and Director of Pediatric Psychology at Rainbow Babies and Children's Hospital, Cleveland, Ohio. He received his Ph.D. from the University of Iowa in child behavior and development. His research interests include the neuropsychological consequences of childhood brain injuries and cognitive and social antecedents of children's learning problems.

Joseph K. Torgesen, Ph.D., Professor, Department of Psychology, Florida State University, Tallahassee, FL 32306. Dr. Torgesen is Professor of Psychology at Florida State University. He is a member of the professional advisory board of the Learning Disabilities Association of America, and he is the editor of a recent volume titled *The Cognitive and Behavioral Characteristics of Children with Learning Disabilities*. His research interests include the cognitive characteristics of children with reading disabilities and instructional methods for reading disabilities.

Richard K. Wagner, Ph.D., Professor, Department of Psychology, Florida State University, Tallahassee, FL 32306. Dr. Wagner is Professor of Psychology at Florida State University. His major area of research interest is the acquisition of complex cognitive knowledge and skills in the domains of reading and human intelligence.

David A. Washburn, Ph.D., Language Research Center, Georgia State University, 3401 Panthersville Road, Atlanta, GA 30034. Dr. Washburn conducts research at Georgia State University's Sonny Carter Life Sciences Laboratory. He has published widely on research conducted with the Language Research Center's Computerized Test System (LRC-CTS), an important system developed in cooperation with Duane M. Rumbaugh and others for NASA's space program.

PREFACE

An explosion of research activity in attention, memory, and executive function has occurred since the mid-1980s. Unfortunately, the literature relevant to these domains is so voluminous that important converging trends in the data are sometimes difficult to identify and to apply to development and learning in children. This difficulty is exacerbated by the application of divergent theories, methodologies, and vocabularies that are used to identify and describe normal and atypical development in attention, memory, and executive function.

For this reason, Dr. Norman Krasnegor and I organized a January 1994 working conference to bring to the National Institutes of Health leading researchers in the fields of cognitive psychology, neuropsychology, developmental psychology, experimental and behavioral psychology, educational psychology, special education, neurology, and pediatrics to discuss what is currently known about attention, memory, and executive function, to amalgamate these findings, and to map out directions for future research.

Within this context, and in collaboration with a conference planning committee composed of Dr. Russell Barkley, Dr. Jack Fletcher, Dr. Norman Krasnegor, Dr. Robin D. Morris, Dr. Judy Rumsey, Dr. Joseph Torgesen, and myself, it was decided to examine the domains of attention, memory, and executive function from the perspectives of information processing and cognitive theories, neuropsychological theories, and behavioral theories. These frames of reference were selected as organizational scaffolding because of the prominence of these theories in guiding empirical research in child development and disorders over the past decade. Thus, we felt that, given these perspectives, the majority of studies addressing attention, memory, and information processing could be identified, analyzed, discussed, and then applied to future research efforts.

No doubt, this undertaking was ambitious. The domains of attention, memory, and executive function contain unwieldy constructs with fuzzy conceptual boundaries. However, we did find that some consensus was achieved with respect to the interpretation of findings and the planning of future investigations by identifying common themes that permeated the research methodologies inherent in the scientific arenas of information processing, neuropsychology, and behavioral psychology. One significant point of agreement that was achieved during this 3-day conference was that, in any study or scientific discussion of attention, memory, and executive function, a series of questions must be posed and answered if valid interpretations of the data are to be expected. These questions are as follows:

1. What theoretical context and theoretical model guide your conceptual view of attention or memory or executive function?
2. What are the primary constructs within the model?
3. How can the model and the constructs be operationalized? For example:

   • What instruments, tests, and/or procedures are used to measure the model and the constructs?
   • What are the criteria that are used to select and/or develop the instruments, tests, or procedures?
   • What populations are most relevant in testing the model?

4. What are the critical hypotheses that provide an opportunity for disconfirmation of the model, and what specific experimental design(s) and experiments should be developed and applied?

The chapters within this book reflect an attempt by each of the authors to address these complex issues that constantly must be dealt with in the study of attention, memory, and executive function. Certainly, we have only scratched the surface in our attempts to organize, interpret, and apply current research findings to ongoing and future investigations of children. However, the efforts discussed in this book provide a strong foundation for emerging scientific and clinical inquiries in the domains of attention, memory, and executive function.

This book is intended for a wide range of audiences including researchers, clinicians, psychologists, physicians, educators, and methodologists. It is hoped that the inclusion and exploration of information processing, neuropsychological, and behavioral perspectives vis-à-vis the study of attention, memory, and executive function will provide the reader with a unique breadth and depth or information relevant to these areas.

G. Reid Lyon, Ph.D.
Bethesda, Maryland

ACKNOWLEDGMENTS

The editors wish to thank Dr. Russell Barkley (University of Massachusetts), Dr. Jack Fletcher (University of Texas Medical Center), Dr. Robin Morris (Georgia State University), Dr. Judy Rumsey (National Institute of Mental Health), and Dr. Joseph Torgesen (Florida State University) for both their leadership and their efforts in helping to plan and design the framework and content of this volume. Their substantial experience and contributions to the fields of cognitive psychology, neuropsychology, and developmental psychology served as the foundation for much of what is presented in this book. We also wish to acknowledge the vibrant and prescient leadership of Dr. Duane Alexander, Director of the National Institute of Child Health and Human Development. His persistent dedication to the blending of biological and behavioral sciences to address complex developmental issues continues to serve as a guiding light to those who strive to improve the health and well-being of children.

Finally, the information presented in this book would not be available to the public without the tremendous guidance and support provided by the fine professionals at Paul H. Brookes Publishing Co. We are indebted to Melissa Behm for initiating and continuing to encourage and support the collaborative efforts between the NICHD and Paul H. Brookes Publishing. Elaine Niefeld deserves a special note of thanks for her talented and tireless editorial support and feedback, as does Lynn Weber for shepherding this book through the complicated production process. In addition, many thanks are extended to Chris Muldor for the many hours of copyediting required before going to press.

In memory of my fellow paratroopers and helicopter pilots in the 82nd and 101st Airborne Divisions, who made the ultimate sacrifice when they were so very young during battles that took place in Hue, Phu Bai, Chou Chu, the Ashau Valley, Quang Tri, Cu Chi, the Iron Triangle, and Tay Ninh, South Vietnam, during 1968 and 1969. They played no angles, they sought no refuge, they sold no souls, they told no lies, and they died so their brothers in combat could live.

—G. Reid Lyon

To My Father, Abraham J. Krasnegor.

—Norman A. Krasnegor

ATTENTION, MEMORY, AND EXECUTIVE FUNCTION

I

INTRODUCTION TO THE CONCEPTUAL, MEASUREMENT, AND METHODOLOGICAL ISSUES

There is no doubt that an understanding of the constructs of attention, memory, and executive function is critical to our understanding of human cognition and learning. Our ability to define these constructs in a rigorous manner is a fundamental prerequisite to our ability to measure the components of attention, memory, and executive function; to communicate about them in a reliable fashion; and to develop accurate assessment methodologies. Within this first section of the book, the case is made for the importance for studying attention, memory, and executive function and for delineating the conceptual, theoretical, methodological, and measurement issues and conditions that must be addressed if progress in research and clinical practice is to be achieved. In Lyon's chapter, the central importance of attention, memory, and executive function in development, learning, and behavior is underscored. In Chapter 2, Morris addresses the complex interactions and overlap among the constructs of attention, memory, and executive function and the need to develop measurement systems that are capable of assessing these interactions. In Chapter 3, Fletcher and his associates explain the importance of construct validation and the steps that need to be taken to define and validate the constructs that are the central theme of this book.

1

THE NEED FOR CONCEPTUAL AND THEORETICAL CLARITY IN THE STUDY OF ATTENTION, MEMORY, AND EXECUTIVE FUNCTION

G. Reid Lyon

Human learning and behavior are dependent upon the ability to pay attention to critical features in the environment; retain and retrieve information; and select, deploy, monitor, and control cognitive strategies to learn, remember, and think. Without these abilities, we could not plan, solve problems, or use language. Likewise, being absent of the capacity to attend, remember, and organize and structure data within our world, we would be incapable of modifying our behavior when confronted with new situations. More directly, it would be impossible to generalize what we already know to novel situations and to acquire new concepts and strategies in coping with current, anticipated, and forthcoming events if we were not vigilant and attentive, if we could not remember the relevant cues in the environment that led to previous reinforcement, and if we were not strategic in our efforts. Thus, attention, memory, and executive function (mental control processes) play a central role in thinking, problem solving, and other complex symbolic activities involved in oral language, reading, writing, mathematics, and social behavior.

Our understanding of the development of attention, memory, and executive function take on added importance when one considers that deficits in any of these three processes typically result in difficulties succeeding in school and in the work force. The impact of attentional disorders on learning and behavior is significant. Youngsters manifesting the characteristics of attention deficit hyperactivity disorder constitute the largest number of children now referred for diagnostic evaluations (see Chapter 4). Moreover, it is known that defective attentional mechanisms have long-term serious implications for children's development of memory strategies as well as intellectual and cognitive functions, including executive function (Douglas, 1980). Unfortunately, our ability to chart the specific relationships between attention, memory, and executive function has been hampered by fuzzy definitions of these domains and competition among theories and models to explain their development or lack of development.

More specifically, the central importance of attention, memory, and executive function in our development, learning, and behavior begs for a more complete theoretical and conceptual understanding of these domains. While each of the domains has a rich history and literature, knowledge about each remains limited and fragmented. This is primarily because scientists exploring these areas approach their investigative tasks with widely divergent basic assumptions, questions, and methodologies. Researchers studying attention frequently use a variety of vocabularies and employ different theories to test their hypotheses. A review of research on memory processes reveals enormous differences in how memory is conceptualized and studied. Likewise, the study of executive function is confounded significantly by variations in definitions and confusions with other cognitive processes.

Given the substantial debate and confusion about how best to conceptualize, operationalize, and assess the domains of attention, memory, and executive function, the National Institute of Child Health and Human Development (NICHD) sponsored a working conference to produce a state-of-the-art review about current thinking in these areas and the application of this knowledge to our understanding of child development in general and learning disabilities in particular. In order to accomplish this review, the NICHD relied heavily upon the expertise of Dr. Russell Barkley (University of Massachusetts), Dr. Jack Fletcher (University of Houston), Dr. Robin Morris (Georgia State University), Dr. Judy Rumsey (National Institute of Mental Health), and Dr. Joseph Torgesen (Florida State University) to assist the editors of this book in planning and designing a conference format that would 1) bring together leading researchers in attention, memory, and executive function; 2) provide the conference participants with the setting and time necessary to identify and discuss critical theoretical and conceptual issues; and 3) stimulate in-depth discussions of several paradigms that could serve as candidates for organizing, interpreting, and explaining research in attention, memory, and executive function. In line with our previous NICHD initiatives (see Lyon, Gray, Kavanagh, & Krasnegor, 1993; Lyon, 1994), this conference was convened with the express purpose of reviewing our ongoing research programs in learning disabilities, language disorders, and disorders of attention and suggesting future research directions.

The chapters in this book summarize the topics that were discussed in detail throughout the 3-day NICHD Conference on Attention, Memory, and Executive Function. Readers will note that each of the three domains is addressed from the perspective of three major scientific paradigms. Specifically, development and disorders within the domains of attention, memory, and executive function are each viewed through the lens of an information processing paradigm, a neuropsychological paradigm, and a behavioral paradigm. Our decision to construct the conference and this book according to this three-paradigm scaffolding was predicated on Torgesen's (1986, 1994) seminal reviews of literature, which indicated that the lion's share of research in attention, memory, and executive function can be organized and interpreted in a relatively clean fashion if one employs these three overarching superordinate categories. Simply put, we felt that this structure would afford us with the opportunity to provide the field with an initial theoretical and conceptual analysis of the major issues, measurement domains, and types of behaviors that should be identified and studied if one's goal is to increase their understanding of attention, memory, and executive function and the relationship of these issues to the study of learning and learning disabilities.

In inviting scientists to participate in the NICHD Conference on Attention, Memory, and Executive Function and to contribute to this volume, we asked each author to consider four sets of questions:

1. What theoretical context and theoretical model guide your conceptual view of attention, or memory, or executive function?
2. What are the primary constructs within the model?
3. How can the model and the constructs be operationalized?
   A. What instruments, tests, and/or procedures can be used to measure the model and the constructs?
   B. What are the criteria that are used to select and/or develop the instruments, tests, and/or procedures?
   C. What populations are most relevant in testing the model?
4. What are a series of testable hypotheses that can provide an opportunity for disconfirmation of the model, and what specific experimental designs and experiments would be designed and conducted?

To answer these questions, we brought together theorists and researchers in the fields of cognitive psychology, experimental psychology, neuropsychology, educational psychology, applied behavior analysis, special education, pediatrics, and neurology to represent each of the three major paradigms that guided discussions. In the chapters that follow, the four sets of questions are addressed at different levels of complexity and completeness. This is because the corpus of information available from the study of attention, for example, may presently be more plentiful and robust than the data currently available for executive function. Nevertheless, the chapters considered individually and collectively should provide the reader with a comprehensive and in-depth analysis of current theory and research in developmental aspects related to attention, memory, and executive function.

OVERVIEW OF THE BOOK

The book is organized into four sections. The first section (Chapters 1, 2, and 3) provides an overview of the conceptual, measurement, and methodological issues critical to an understanding of current research directions in attention, memory, and executive function. In Chapter 2, Robin D. Morris points out that improved measurement will be critical if we are to ever understand the multivariate constructs of attention, memory, and executive function and how these constructs can inform our grasp of the cognitive mechanisms that are related to learning and learning disabilities. Morris goes on to provide clear and compelling discussions about the need to understand the theoretical overlap of attention, memory, and executive function and the developmental considerations that must be addressed if one is to derive powerful measures of these constructs. In Chapter 3, Jack M. Fletcher and his colleagues from the University of Houston Learning Disabilities Intervention Project and the Yale Center for the Study of Learning and Attention bring to bear their substantial theoretical and methodological expertise on the task of delineating the steps that should be taken to define and validate the constructs of attention, memory, and executive function. This conceptual and methodological road map for establishing construct validity must be read in detail if advances in our understanding are to be expected.

Section II is devoted to the subject of attention. In Chapter 4, Russell A. Barkley sets the stage for the following discussions of attention from information processing, neuropsychological, and behavioral perspectives by providing a rich overview and analysis of critical issues in attention research. In Chapter 5, Joseph Sergeant describes attention from an information processing perspective with an eye toward explaining individual differences in cognitive functioning as well as delineating the role of attention in developmental psychopathology. His discussion demonstrates the critical relationship that must exist between the articulation of a theoretical model and a theoretical construct and the measurement of the construct. In Chapter 6, Allan F. Mirsky addresses the construct of attention and the development of attentional mechanisms from the perspective of a research neuropsychologist. Like Sergeant, Mirsky discusses the roles and relationships between theory, experimental methods, measurement, and research. In Chapter 7, William J. McIlvane, William V. Dube, and Thomas D. Callahan discuss the construct of attention from a behavioral perspective and the conceptual and empirical assumptions for their position. They also elucidate the conditions that must be in place in order to demonstrate that a behavioral analytic conceptualization of attention can predict and explain how one does or does not attend to critical cues and features in their environment. In Chapter 8, Jeffrey M. Halperin summarizes the information processing, neuropsychological, and behavioral views on attention that were provided in Section II. His comparison and contrast of the three different theoretical constructs and theoretical models of attention speak to the tremendous complexity of attention and the need to amalgamate different perspectives and theories to enhance understanding and treatment of disorders of attention.

Section III focuses on the extraordinarily complex topic of memory. To set the stage for the discussion in this section, Richard K. Wagner, writing in Chapter 9, reviews the major issues in memory research that influence theory, models, and measurement. Wagner's excellent chapter can stand alone as a valuable contribution to existing literature on short-term memory and its measurement. In Chapter 10, Joseph K. Torgesen uses his knowledge of phonological processing and memory to exemplify how information processing models can make a substantial contribution to the study of individual differences in memory functions. Particularly relevant to this book, and our overall goals in the NICHD Learning Disabilities Research Program, Torgesen demonstrates how the information processing paradigm can explicate the relationship between deficits in phonological representation in memory and difficulties developing early reading skills. In Chapter 11, Jocelyne Bachevalier and her associates from the University of Texas and the National Institute of Mental Health take a direction different from that proposed by Torgesen and address various forms of memory with an emphasis on their neural organization. To accomplish this, Bachevalier, Malkova, and Beauregard review data related to neuropsychological studies to demonstrate how this scientific paradigm can shed light on the existence of multiple memory systems and memory disorders. In Chapter 12, Duane M. Rumbaugh and David A. Washburn provide a fascinating discussion of how comparative studies of chimpanzees and rhesus monkeys, conceived, designed, and conducted from the perspective of a behavioral paradigm, can inform our understanding of memory development and disorders in children. In Chapter 13, Kimberly Boller takes on the daunting task of summarizing the major points made in Chapters 10, 11, and 12. Boller not only highlights the critical issues and points relevant to research on memory raised by each of the authors, but brings her own research and experience to a wise analysis of these points.

In Section IV, seven chapters are devoted to analysis and discussion of executive function. This section is necessarily longer than the preceding sections on attention and memory for two reasons. First, as in the sections on attention and memory, three chapters are devoted to a discussion of executive function from the perspectives of information processing, neuropsychology, and behavioral theories, respectively. However, given the relatively young literature in the area of executive function and the significant interrelations that are hypothesized to exist among attention, memory, and executive function, additional chapters are provided to explicitly address these linkages and their influence on the development of strategies for learning. In Chapter 14, John G. Borkowski and Jennifer E. Burke provide a well-organized and well-written account of the emergence of the construct of executive function in cognitive and developmental psychology. Within this context, they clarify the role of executive function as it is currently described in psychological theories and articulate the major issues that must be addressed if studies of executive function are to inform current understanding of cognitive development and learning. Martha Bridge Denckla follows in Chapter 15 with a neuropsychological perspective on executive function. Her discussion highlights the need to conceptualize executive function as composed of control processes that undergird our ability to orient, plan, program responses, and verify and modify our performance. In Denckla's view, these control processes are intimately intertwined with brain function, and thus the relations between complex executive behaviors and neurological functioning should be identified and explained. In their discussion in Chapter 16 of a behavioral theory that can explain different executive functions, Steven C. Hayes, Elizabeth V. Gifford, and L.E. Ruckstuhl address the critical issue of the definition of executive function. To our benefit, they also discuss the problems that arise when constructs such as executive function are linked, possibly prematurely, to specific regions of the brain. The authors also provide a significant contribution to our understanding via their clear description of candidate tests for a theory of executive function. In Chapter 17, written by Russell A. Barkley, and in Chapter 18, written by Bruce F. Pennington and his associates from the University of Denver, the linkages between executive function, attention, and memory are explored in detail; these chapters explore our conceptualization of executive function as a complex process capable of mediating and modifying what we pay attention to and what we can retain and recall. In Chapter 19, Steve Graham and Karen R. Harris discuss how principles derived from several perspectives on attention, memory, and executive function can serve as a foundation for developing powerful instructional methodologies to enhance academic learning; the chapter also demonstrates how theory can be directly applied to teaching in practical settings. In Chapter 20, Paul J. Eslinger provides a detailed and informative summary of the major issues that were discussed relative to executive function.

Finally, in Section V, H. Gerry Taylor applies his substantial theoretical, experimental, and clinical knowledge to the job of bringing coherence to the diverging perspectives on attention, memory, and executive function provided throughout this book. His evaluation of where we have been, where we are now, and where we need to go with respect to research in attention, memory, and executive function provides the guidance for our future scientific endeavors in these domains.

The chief objective of this book is to present the most current information on the theoretical, conceptual, and measurement issues that are critical to our understanding of attention, memory, and executive function, and the deficits and disorders that are associated with each of these clinical and research domains when development is less than optimal. We are hopeful that the following chapters will positively and intelligently influence future efforts in research and clinical practice.

REFERENCES

Douglas, V.I. (1980). Higher mental processes in hyperactive children: Implications for training. In R.M. Knights & D.J. Bakker (Eds.), *Treatment of hyperactive and learning disordered children: Current research* (pp. 65–92). Baltimore: University Park Press.

Lyon, G.R. (Ed.). (1994). *Frames of reference for the assessment of learning disabilities: New views on measurement issues.* Baltimore: Paul H. Brookes Publishing Co.

Lyon, G.R., Gray, D.B., Kavanagh, J.F., & Krasnegor, N.A. (Eds.). (1993). *Better understanding learning disabilities: New views from research and their implications for education and public policies.* Baltimore: Paul H. Brookes Publishing Co.

Torgesen, J.K. (1986). Learning disability theory: Its current state and future prospects. *Journal of Learning Disabilities, 19*, 399–407.

Torgesen, J.K. (1994). Issues in the assessment of executive function. In G.R. Lyon (Ed.), *Frames of reference for the assessment of learning disabilities: New views on measurement issues* (pp. 143–162). Baltimore: Paul H. Brookes Publishing Co.

2

RELATIONSHIPS AND DISTINCTIONS AMONG THE CONCEPTS OF ATTENTION, MEMORY, AND EXECUTIVE FUNCTION

A Developmental Perspective

Robin D. Morris

Over the years, there has been a trend in the field of learning disabilities for its measurement models to be overly influenced by sociopolitical considerations and its measures to be of limited psychometric specifications or quality (Lyon, 1994). In addition, the measures frequently used to study children with learning disabilities have not been developed for children, but have been adapted from work with adults with little regard for their differences. Typically, only age-linked norms on a particular test are used as evidence for its validity with a particular population. There has also been little consideration of the assessment needs of children with various disabilities or for the potential of such children to show different relations among the constructs being measured by any particular set of measures. The need for increased science-driven investment in our measurement models and tools is critical for improving our understanding of the developmental progression of children with and without learning and related disabilities (Morris, 1994).

Measurement tools can be considered as the ultimate "translators" of our verbal/linguistic concepts and constructs into the scientific language of numbers, which can then be investigated using the tools of mathematics. The act of translating our verbal concepts into numerical values through the use of standardized tests and measures has at its core the assumption that the "language" of numbers and the tools of mathematics have much greater credibility and consensus among scientists than do the ideas we express verbally. This is because the number system has clear definitions of meaning and the mathematics that acts upon it has consensus rules that guide its use. Therefore, researchers are able to test and evaluate their data, or those of others, by following a translation that uses consensual means widely available to the scientific community, regardless of theoretical bent or bias. Until such a translation occurs, we are not able to easily compare, manipulate, or evaluate the "reality" of our verbal constructs, their usefulness in our specific investigations, or their relation to presumably similar or overlapping constructs measured by other investigators.

Why do we need such test-derived translations? We need them because verbal labels and definitions are, owing to the limited specificity of language in general, not clearly delineated at the level necessary for evaluation within a scientific enterprise. These limitations are frequently observed when scientists who come from similar or different frameworks are not able to clearly communicate and describe the same phenomenon even though they are using the same labels or words. This appears to be the case when researchers discuss the common concepts of attention, memory, and executive functions in the field of learning disabilities. Many scientists in the field use these terms frequently and with authority. Such use has led others in the field to conclude that we understand these concepts, that there are commonly agreed upon definitions, and that scientists in the field have a consensus view regarding their interrelationships. Of even more concern is the prevalent view that we can measure attention, memory, or executive functions reliably and that our available measures have not only been validated for children with a variety of different disabling conditions, but have also been validated for a wide range of age groups and developmental levels. The recent acknowledgment of these widely held views as fiction has led to a renewed interest in the basic scientific processes involved in defining such concepts, detailing their relationships, and developing more valid measures for their operationalization (Morris, 1994).

STATUS OF ATTENTION, MEMORY, AND EXECUTIVE FUNCTION CONSTRUCTS WITHIN THE FIELD OF LEARNING DISABILITIES

Unfortunately, as a number of previous reviews and analyses of definitional and measurement issues have highlighted (Lyon, 1994; Lyon, Gray, Kavanagh, & Krasnegor, 1993), the field of learning disabilities has historically forged only limited conceptual or measurement linkages between researchers. Scientists and clinicians working in the field are a community of researchers without clear "community standards." That is, each of us has our own constructs and measurement models for our particular areas of interest and focus. Rarely do we link these models to other related areas of study or to the work of other researchers in the field. Because of this situation, a test or measure that is used by one researcher as a measure of attention may be used by another as a measure of executive function.

To serve as a context for a discussion of this lack of clarity among researchers and clinicians, six well-respected journals that frequently publish articles related to learning disabilities were selected for a survey of measures commonly used for attention, memory, and executive functions. All volumes for a 5-year period of *Brain and Language, Child Development, Educational Psychology, Journal of Clinical and Consulting Neuropsychology, Journal of Learning Disabilities,* and *Learning Disability Quarterly* were reviewed. A review of the articles within these journals indicated that there were over 25 different measures described as attentional in nature, 15 different measures of memory and learning, and over 20 different measures of executive functions (typically described as problem-solving skills) for the individualized assessment of school-age children.

Attentional measures included paper-and-pencil cancellation tests, the Coding and Digit Span subtests from the Wechsler Intelligence Scale for Children–Revised (Wechsler, 1974), computerized continuous performance tests (CTP) with a wide variety of task demands and parameters, the Stroop test (Stroop, 1935), the Trail Making Tests (Reitan & Wolfson, 1985), various behavioral checklists, the Paced Auditory Serial Addition Test (Gronwall & Sampson, 1977), various dichotic listening tasks, central–incidental learning tasks (Lane & Pearson, 1982), the Matching Familiar Figures Test (Kagan, Rosman, Day, Albert, & Phillips, 1964), the Embedded Figures Test (Witkin, Oltman, Raskin, & Karp, 1971), chronometric measures of attention (i.e., reaction- and decision-time tasks), event-related potential (ERP) measures of attention, and a number of less commonly used measures for measuring attention. Interestingly, many of these same measures were found listed as measures of executive functions within the same journals. These included the Trail Making Tests, the Stroop test, CPT, ERP, and a number of other less common measures. There was also overlap between measures of attention and memory. For example, the Digit Span subtest was frequently used as a measure of both attention and memory.

Besides the striking amount of overlap among the measures used to assess the reportedly different constructs of attention, memory, and executive functions, there was an additional concern raised when each task was carefully analyzed for the component behaviors required to complete it. For example, although cancellation tasks are frequently used to assess selective and sustained attention, they also require some minimal learning and memory abilities to help maintain the target stimulus in memory. In addition, they require the elaboration of a strategy (planning), the execution of a sequence of planned responses, and the maintenance of a behavioral set, all representing executive functions. Such analysis suggested that a majority of the tests described as measuring a single construct were actually multidimensional in nature.

In our recent review of the measurement of attention in children (Cooley & Morris, 1990), it was evident that there has been little focus on partitioning behavioral assessment tasks and paradigms into those factors relevant to the construct of attention versus those that are related to other cognitive constructs such as memory or executive functions. Almost all of the available measures of attention appear to represent a mixture of various perceptual and cognitive abilities. Therefore, some children may perform poorly on a reported attentional task, not because their attentional system is deficient, but because one or more of their perceptual, memory, or executive function systems are deficient.

THEORETICAL OVERLAP OF ATTENTION, MEMORY, AND EXECUTIVE FUNCTIONS

The reason for such complexity and overlap among the various tests used to measure attention, memory, and executive functions is partly due to some of the basic theoretical issues surrounding their relationships. For instance, Gibson and Rader (1979) have argued that there is no easy way to separate attention from basic perceptual processes. Such theoretical discussion has fostered questions such as, When does attention cease and perception or cognitive processes begin? Can one encode information into memory without adequate attention or without an adequate strategy (i.e., executive functions)? Theoretical measurement models in the literature also show significant overlap, adding to the confusion. For example, Mirsky, Anthony, Duncan, Ahearn, and Kellam (1991) developed a neuropsychological model of attention, defining four components of attention (*focus/execute, sustain, encode,* and *shift*). The Mirsky team used eight traditional measures of attention in a factor-analytical study that addressed the question of construct measurement. At about the same time, Daigneault, Braun, and Whitaker (1992) defined six components of prefrontal or executive functions (planning, execution, self-regulation, maintenance, spatiotemporal segmentation, and sustained mental productivity) using a similar methodological approach. Of particular interest was that over 50% of the tests used to assess their model were identical to those used by Mirsky et al. Therefore, two different research teams, focused on understanding the measurement of two different constructs, but using highly similar batteries of tests, found sets of factors that they labeled differently. Are they really different constructs, or just labeled differently? Through the use of available statistical methods, their redundancy or concordance could be directly tested.

There are many such examples of diverse theoretical formulations being supported through the use of many of the same measures and analysis methods as evidence. Such results lead one to question whether there is a useful difference between the concepts of attention, memory, and executive functions or whether the measures being used are inadequate for the purposes being described. These are questions that can be systematically addressed using available construct validation approaches as described in Chapter 3.

DEVELOPMENTAL CONSIDERATIONS

Because the field of learning disabilities is mostly concerned with the development of these abilities, there are additional complexities in defining and measuring these attention, memory, and executive functions because of their changing nature over time. In many of these domains, the data suggest that children's attentional, memory, and executive functions improve with age. As children develop, they become more accurate, they process information more quickly, and they are better able to handle information of increasing complexity in an increasingly automatized manner. Are these changes related to the development of specific subcomponents of attention, memory, and executive functions or the development of higher-order executive systems that impact their ability to coordinate the lower attentional and memory systems, inhibit irrelevant information flow, and provide system adaptability? Such developmental questions, which address the sequence in which various abilities unfold, their rate of change, and how such changes affect other related functions, all must be considered in any discussion of the measurement of the constructs of attention, memory, and executive functions. Because of these concerns, it is critical that researchers develop measures designed to be sensitive to the developmental changes within these domains of interest.

The need to derive developmentally sensitive measures of attention, memory, and executive functions is based on the critical need to understand the changes that occur within these abilities and their relations to academic struggles or success in children with learning disabilities. Many researchers in the field consider these constructs to be of critical importance in understanding the nature of the deficits in these children. Therefore, unless the field is better able to define and measure these constructs, investigate their interdependency, and understand those factors that affect their development, there will continue to be gaps in our knowledge of children with learning disabilities.

CONCLUSIONS

Based on this survey and the issues identified, it appears that the concepts of attention, memory, and executive functioning are best considered to be superordinate constructs with multifactorial attributes. Without adequate construct validation, however, their attributes will continue to be poorly defined and understood, and the similarities and differences between them will continue to be confused. This will most likely result in many researchers in the field of learning disabilities using measures that are poorly understood. Poor construct validation will also preclude the necessary replication of important results, which could provide the field with a more solid scientific foundation. The need for improved measurement development is critical in order to address core issues and debates in the field of learning disabilities. The constructs of attention, memory, and executive functions represent some of the least well-defined and operationalized abilities within the field. Nevertheless, these constructs hold significant promise in furthering our understanding of children with learning disabilities. Therefore, the need to focus on their development and measurement is critical.

REFERENCES

Cooley, E.L., & Morris, R.D. (1990). Attention in children: A neuropsychologically based model for assessment. *Developmental Neuropsychology, 6*(3), 239–274.

Daigneault, S., Braun, C.M.J., & Whitaker, H.A. (1992). An empirical test of two opposing theoretical models of prefrontal function. *Brain and Cognition, 19*(1), 48–71.

Gibson, E., & Rader, N. (1979). Attention: The perceiver as performer. In G.A. Hale & M. Lewis (Eds.), *Attention and cognitive development* (pp. 10–21). New York: Plenum.

Gronwall, D.M., & Sampson, H. (1977). *The psychological effects of concussion.* Auckland, New Zealand: Auckland University Press.

Kagan, J., Rosman, B.C., Day, D., Albert, J., & Phillips, W. (1964). Information processing in the child: Significance of analytic and reflective attitudes. *Psychological Monographs, General and Applied, 78,* 1–27.

Lane, D.M., & Pearson, D.A. (1982). The development of selective attention. *Merrill-Palmer Quarterly, 28,* 317–337.

Lyon, G.R. (Ed.). (1994). *Frames of reference for the assessment of learning disabilities: New views on measurement issues.* Baltimore: Paul H. Brookes Publishing Co.

Lyon, G.R., Gray, D., Kavanagh, J., & Krasnegor, N. (Eds.). (1993). *Better understanding learning disabilities: New views from research and their implications for education and public policies.* Baltimore: Paul H. Brookes Publishing Co.

Mirsky, A.F., Anthony, B.J., Duncan, C.C., Ahearn, M.B., & Kellam, S.G. (1991). Analysis of the elements of attention: A neuropsychological approach. *Neuropsychology Review, 2*(2), 109–145.

Morris, R.D. (1994). A review of critical concepts and issues in the measurement of learning disabilities. In G.R. Lyon (Ed.), *Frames of reference for the assessment of learning disabilities: New views on measurement issues* (pp. 615–626). Baltimore: Paul H. Brookes Publishing Co.

Reitan, R.M., & Wolfson, D. (1985). *The Halstead-Reitan Neuropsychological Test Battery.* Tucson: Neuropsychology Press.

Stroop, J.R. (1935). Studies of interference in serial verbal reactions. *Journal of Experimental Psychology, 18,* 643–662.

Wechsler, D. (1974). *Wechsler Intelligence Scale for Children–Revised.* New York: Psychological Corporation.

Witkin, H.A., Oltman, P., Raskin, E., & Karp, S. (1971). *Manual for the Children's Embedded Figures Test.* Palo Alto, CA: Consulting Psychologists Press.

3

CONCEPTUAL AND METHODOLOGICAL ISSUES IN CONSTRUCT DEFINITION

Jack M. Fletcher, David J. Francis,
Karla K. Stuebing, Bennett A. Shaywitz,
Sally E. Shaywitz, Donald P. Shankweiler,
Leonard Katz, and Robin D. Morris

This chapter discusses some of the issues involved in defining and operationalizing psychological processes or *constructs*. Whenever an assessment device is developed, there are presumptions about what attributes and processes are actually measured by the assessment device. The process of validating these presumptions is called *construct validation.*

NATURE OF CONSTRUCT VALIDITY

In the classic treatment of this problem, Cronbach and Meehl (1955) stated that "Construct validation is involved whenever a test is to be interpreted as a measure of some attribute or quality which is not operationally defined. The problem faced by the investigator is 'What constructs account for variance in test performance?'" (p. 282).

Construct validity issues are central for measuring psychological processes such as attention, memory, and executive functions. Unfortunately, little construct validation research has been completed on these constructs. To illustrate, the assessment devices used to measure each of these three constructs often over-

Preparation of this chapter was supported in part by National Institute of Child Health and Human Development Grants P01 HD21889, "Psycholinguistic and Biological Mechanisms in Dyslexia," and P50 HD2582, "Center for Learning and Attention Disorders."

lap, but they are labeled differently depending on the theoretical perspective of the investigator. From the viewpoint of construct validation, individuals working with a particular assessment device should not assume that the construct has been adequately operationalized or that the assessment device measures the construct in the absence of formal construct validation research. The tendency to give an assessment construct validity that is greater than the criteria against which it is validated has been termed a "bootstraps effect" (Cronbach & Meehl, 1955). If the validation criterion carries considerable credence, the construct becomes valid solely by lifting itself by the "bootstraps" of the criterion.

A more contemporary approach to construct validation asks what *latent variables* underlie performance on an assessment device. If the underlying construct is clearly operationalized, which is often the case when principles of behavior analysis are employed, there is little difference in the observed performance of the subject and the latent variables or constructs. However, if the latent variable is inferred on the basis of some observed behaviors that are presumed to reflect an underlying construct, observed performance on the assessment device does not fully operationalize the latent variable. For example, a subject's score on a continuous-performance test is not what attention theorists intend to be fully interchangeable with the construct of *sustained attention*. This is because the score only imperfectly reflects the construct of sustained attention (Cook & Campbell, 1979). One problem is *surplus construct irrelevancies*, which means that test performance also reflects the joint influence of other variables, such as motivation, focused attention, and the environment in which performance occurs. The second problem is *construct underrepresentation,* which means that a single index does not fully represent the underlying construct. Hence, there is excess variance in the measurement caused by other constructs as well as excessive variance in the construct that is not fully reflected in the test (Cook & Campbell, 1979).

The task of construct validation research is to determine the degree to which a test or assessment device measures the construct of interest. Tests are never pure measures of a particular construct. Although performance on a test is often treated in this fashion, there are few tests that are pure measures of single constructs. Unfortunately, there is a clear tendency to treat test performance and latent variables synonymously, without the careful work on construct validation necessary to specify the degree to which an assessment device measures the latent variables presumed to underlie performance. One of the consequences of relying on observed variables is that the error associated with imperfect measurement may be correlated, leading to overestimates of the relationships among variables.

The process whereby the validity of constructs is established is of central importance to any psychological experiment. Problems with construct validity represent a major threat to the internal validity of a study. *Internal validity* is the process whereby a set of independent and dependent variables are causally related. If an experiment is completed, the investigator typically wants to conclude that a manipulation of an independent variable *caused* a change in a particular dependent variable. Underlying the capacity of an investigation to establish these relationships is the scientist's ability to indicate that the independent and dependent variables are true measures of some constructs. If either the independent or dependent variables also measure other unknown constructs or simply fail to adequately specify the hypothesized construct, the internal validity of the experiment will be jeopardized (Maxwell & Delaney, 1990). In other words, some construct other than those presumably measured in the experiment is responsible for the relationship of the independent and dependent variable. In these circumstances, the investigator is not able to generalize the results to another context. As Cook and Campbell (1979) indicated, the fundamental problem in construct validity is "that the operations which are meant to represent a particular cause or effect construct can be construed in terms of more than one construct . . ." (p. 59).

Another way in which bootstraps validation is apparent is the attachment of a measurement device that is difficult to operationalize to one that is easier to operationalize. For example, there are many measures of phonological awareness, a construct which is clearly related to another construct, reading decoding ability. The latter is relatively easy to measure, largely because different assessment devices are very highly correlated. Operationalizing the former can be difficult. Hence, there are many tests for assessing phonological awareness skills. The relationship of these tests to the criterion skill varies depending on the age of the child and the manner in which the construct of phonological awareness is measured by the device.

An essential assumption of construct validation research is that assessment devices have surplus variability. In other words, the device measures more than one construct and measures all of the underlying constructs imperfectly. Consequently, it is just as important to specify how well an assessment device measures the construct of interest as it is to show the extent to which the device measures other constructs. This objective requires careful consideration of the construct dimensions of a device *prior* to beginning an experiment. Attention, memory, and executive functions are clearly multidimensional concepts that subsume multiple operations at behavioral, psychological, and other levels. These operations are not perfectly correlated. A single index of the overarching construct may distort the relationship of the construct with some external criterion (Maxwell & Delaney, 1990, pp. 30–31). Often it is assumed that a single measure of these skills is adequate, when the construct may be better specified by examining shared variance across multiple measures. This problem, which assumes that a single dependent variable assesses a latent construct, was described by Cook and Campbell (1979) as "mono-operation bias."

In the remainder of this chapter, the process of validating constructs is examined at the theoretical and empirical levels. Different steps involved in establishing construct validity are discussed. Methods for exploring construct validity are summarized. An example of how construct validity can be assessed is presented.

VALIDATING CONSTRUCTS

In an excellent discussion of construct validity, Nunnally (1978, p. 98) defined three aspects of construct validity:

1. Specify the domain of observables related to the construct.
2. Determine the extent to which the observables tend to measure the same thing, several different things, or many different things (based on research and statistical analyses).
3. Perform studies of individual differences and/or controlled experiments to determine the extent to which supposed measures produce results that are predictable from highly accepted theoretical hypotheses concerning the construct.

Unfortunately, as Nunnally (p. 99) indicated, "These steps are seldom, if ever, purposefully planned and undertaken by an investigator or group of investigators . . . this order is seldom, if ever, followed. More likely, psychologists will develop a particular measure that is thought to partake of a construct; then they will leap directly to aspect 3 and perform a study relating the supposed measure of the construct to measures of other constructs . . . other investigators will develop other particular measures of the same construct, skipping aspects 1 and 2, and move directly to aspect 3."

Indeed, investigators all too commonly participate in a process that might be termed *consensual validation.* In this approach to validity, a group of investigators will simply engage in highly reinforced verbal behavior in which a group of people agrees that the theorist knows the content area; the measurement is valid because the expert says so and it relates to some other construct that has wide acceptance.

There is clearly insufficient attention in neurobehavioral research to construct validity issues. This lack of attention has hampered research on cognitive processes in children with developmental disabilities. There is a persistent tendency for investigators to compare children with and without disabilities on a single test, find a difference, and conclude that the difference "causes" the disability (Doehring, 1978; Satz & Fletcher, 1980). The problems with this approach are multiple (Campbell & Stanley, 1963), but two are most relevant for this chapter. First, children with a particular disability usually vary along more than one dimension. For example, many children with reading disabilities have pronounced phonological awareness difficulties. However, the phenotypical profile shows differences across multiple dimensions of cognition (Fletcher et al., 1994; Stanovich & Siegel, 1994). Phonological awareness measures may account for the lion's share of variability in one particular outcome (reading skills), but the academic achievement and overall adjustment of children with reading disabilities can also be significantly (but less robustly) accounted for by whatever is measured by tests of attention, memory, and executive functions. Indeed, virtually any single test of cognitive skills will show significantly lower performance in a group of children with reading disabilities relative to children without such disabilities if the sample is large enough.

This finding leads to the second problem, which is the degree to which performance on a particular test is correlated with performance on another test. For example, measures of phonological awareness typically correlate highly with indices of the size of receptive vocabulary skills. This result does not mean that phonological awareness skills and receptive vocabulary skills cannot be measured separately, only that any attempt to measure either skill will reflect the degree to which these two latent variables are correlated and measured imperfectly. Investigators who measure phonological awareness skills without taking into account vocabulary development have no better grounds for concluding that phonological awareness skills "cause" reading disability than they do for concluding that vocabulary size "causes" either reading disability or phonological awareness skills, or even that reading proficiency "causes" performance on both language tests (Doehring, 1978; Satz & Fletcher, 1980).

A central component of construct validity is the specification of not only the nature of the latent variables but also the interrelationship of these variables to each other *and* to the outcome of interest. The former refers to *construct validity*, but the latter refers to *predictive* or *discriminant validity*. These forms of validity require good specification of construct validity *prior* to making causal inferences from a particular study, regardless of the degree to which the experimental design permits causal inferences (Campbell & Stanley, 1963).

Table 3.1 provides in more detail some of the essential steps involved in defining and validating constructs. As this table shows, the first step is always to articulate a theoretical model, framework, or context for the construct of interest. What is generally most appropriate is the selection of some type of theoretical model that generates testable hypotheses about the relationship of the constructs to each other. This model can be taken from the literature or developed independently, depending on the goals of the research project. As part of this theoretical model, the major constructs should be clearly defined. Exactly what the investigator intends by the different constructs should be articulated as fully as possible.

Table 3.1. Steps in defining and validating constructs

1. Articulate a theoretical model, framework, or context for the constructs of interest.
2. Define the major constructs in the model.
3. Outline (hypothetical) relationships among the constructs and in relationship to external criteria.
4. Operationalize the model and constructs.
   • Approach to measurement
   • Scaling
   • Item/response content
   A. What instruments, tests, or procedures are used to measure the constructs?
   B. What are the criteria used to select and/or develop the instruments, tests, or procedures?
   C. What populations need to be sampled in order to develop and evaluate the model?
   D. What statistical approaches are best suited to evaluating the model?
5. Develop a series of testable hypotheses that provide an opportunity for disconfirmation of the model.
6. Outline specific experimental design(s) and experiments that would be applied and conducted.

The investigator then should outline hypothesized relationships among the constructs and in relationship to external criteria. Redundancy of measurement is inevitable in cognitive and behavioral research; the sources of redundancy should be specified on an a priori basis and articulated as fully as possible.

The operationalization of the model should represent an attempt to address some of the measurement issues involved in validating constructs. Of utmost importance is to carefully consider the approach taken to measurement. Is the approach based on psychometrical assessment, the application of principles of behavioral analysis, observational assessment, or some other approach to measurement? This description should give some idea about the units of measurement that will be obtained when the constructs are operationalized.

Careful attention to issues involving scaling and item/response content should be made. Scaling issues are often underemphasized. In particular, there is a need to consider the relationship of the items to the construct. Applications of methods such as item response theory may be needed, which can help address scaling issues. For example, if the goal is to study how a construct changes over time, measurement techniques that yield continuously distributed variables should be used. The scaling approach should be represented on an interval scale so that the difference in difficulty level across items is known. Finally, the items must have content validity and must represent the domain of interest.

When the steps shown in Table 3.1 are taken, specific decisions can be made concerning the instruments, tests, or procedures used to measure the constructs. Different criteria based on measurement issues as well as the hypotheses under investigation can then be applied to select the instruments, tests, and procedures. The types of populations in whom the constructs need to be measured can then be designated. Based on the approach to scaling, decisions concerning statistical approaches for evaluating the hypothesized measurement model can be developed. The ultimate goal is a series of testable hypotheses that provide an opportunity for disconfirmation of the measurement model. Through this process, clear specification can be made of the capacity of the measurement model to delineate the latent variables and metrics. In addition, hypotheses concerning the relationship of the latent variables can be tested. This process should lead to a set of specific experiments in which the measurement model can be applied to address the overarching hypotheses.

EVALUATING MEASUREMENT MODELS

In the past, construct validity was generally evaluated by analyzing redundancy among the variables of interest. Methods for the analysis of correlational matrices, such as factor analysis, were often used. One of the major problems with the application of these correlational techniques is that they are exploratory and have little relationship to the hypothesized measurement model. More recently, a set of hypothesis-oriented methods commonly known as *confirmatory factor analysis* or *structural equations analysis* have been developed. These methods are different from exploratory techniques because they impose a hypothetical model on the data. The relationship of the measures to the latent variables is operationalized on an a priori basis. In addition, specific tests are performed to determine whether the hypothesized model reproduces the data. These techniques represent the most significant advance in construct validation research since Cronbach and Meehl (1955).

Redundancy

A fundamental advantage of any approach to the creation of measurement models, whether the model is exploratory or confirmatory, is the capacity of these methods to indicate areas of redundancy in the data set, which allows the investigator to reduce the data to a smaller number of meaningful variables. Analyzing the redundancy of large data sets is preferable to the collection of small data sets because the constructs of interest are rarely captured reliably by any single variable. In some instances, when multiple measures of the same construct are aggregated into a single index, the composite measure has greater reliability and validity than the individual measures that make up the composite measure. The decision of whether to use a composite or a single indicator depends on the reliability of the measures, the hypothesis under investigation, and the statistical technique being used. In any event, it is important to understand how any particular variable relates to other variables in the data base.

Data Reduction

An advantage of attempts to evaluate measurement models in terms of latent variables is the reduction of the number of variables requiring analysis in the predictive or discriminant validity phase of the study. Data reduction is necessary for at least two reasons. First, the use of many outcomes necessitates that procedures be implemented for Type I error control. Adjustment based on the entire set of measures is likely to lead to substantial reduction in power. By employing latent variable techniques, the size of the set of outcome measures can be substantially reduced to allow better balance between control of Type I and Type II errors. Second, by aggregating measures that share information, more reliable measures can be created than is possible through the elimination of some measures from the study, which in turn enhances power for detecting group differences and change over time. In addition to allowing the creation of more reliable composites, redundant measures should be proposed in order to link findings from the present investigation with those from previous research at different laboratories.

Exploratory versus Confirmatory Methods

There are many advantages of confirmatory models for the analysis of redundancy and data reduction. It is common to use exploratory methods such as principal component analysis (PCA), because the principal components are variance maximizing and do not require estimation from the data. However, when PCA is completed, communalities for all variables are set equal to 1.0. Thus, principal components combine common, specific, and error variance, so that it is not possible to separate these sources of variability. Consequently, the component loadings are influenced by multiple sources of variability. Moreover, there is no guarantee that the resultant composite indicators will represent meaningful constructs (Guertin & Bailey, 1970). Uninterpretable but predictive components are not desirable; rather, the goal should be to derive meaningful indicators of specific constructs so that the constructs can be related to the hypotheses of the experiment.

Common factor analyses, such as principal axis (R-type) and alpha factor analyses of correlational data, are time-honored methods for analyzing redundancy. However, these methods are often poorly suited to studying the latent structure of cognitive tests, such as those used to measure attention, memory, and executive functions, because these methods require that all relationships among measures be accounted for through the factor loadings and factor correlation matrices. This assumption is frequently not met with instruments in psychology. Thus, these methods may aid researchers in the generation of potential models and the exploration of potential relationships, but they are inadequate for hypothesis-guided data reduction to a small number of psychologically meaningful indicators. There are also major problems with estimating communalities, determining the size of factor loadings, deciding on the number of factors, and rotating factors to enhance interpretability. Perhaps most important, common factor analysis, like PCA, is strictly heuristic, with no statistical relationship to theory.

Confirmatory factor analysis (CFA), on the other hand, requires the imposition of a definite model on the data from the outset. The factor loadings, uniqueness and factor correlations of this particular model are then estimated with statistical tests to determine whether the model adequately reproduces the data. Unlike the exploratory common factor methods mentioned above, CFA does not require either an estimation of communalities before estimating factor loadings or an angle through which to rotate the solution. Variables are constrained to measure only certain factors, and all other factor loadings are forced to be zero. In other words, the researcher specifies the factor pattern in advance and tests whether the hypothesized pattern accurately reproduces the variability in the data. Forming models takes time and thought but is essential to the process of developing measurement models for statistical analysis.

The data are used to estimate the parameters and determine the adequacy of the hypothetical model. If the model fits the data well, composites can be created for use in subsequent data analysis. The use of composites increases power in subsequent analyses by ensuring more favorable subject-to-variable ratios and increased reliability of measurements. Furthermore, the use of composites facilitates interpretation of results because the focus of discussion is on a set of global measures with general meaning, as opposed to many individual measures, each with its own test-specific interpretation.

The CFA method of analysis is extremely flexible and allows the researcher to test specific hypotheses regarding the psychometrical properties of variables prior to forming composites. As a result, the potentially biasing effects of measures with undesirable psychometrical properties can be reduced or removed from hypotheses of substantive interest. Other advantages of CFA include the ability to fit factor models that are constrained over time. This allows the temporal stability of the psychometrical properties of the instruments to be tested and taken into account in tests of subsequent hypotheses. CFA allows more precise formulation of measurement models and can be used to determine if such models are invariant across populations of interest (Cole & Maxwell, 1986; Joreskog & Sorbom, 1986). Factorial invariance over populations is essential to the meaningful comparison of different populations on any set of variables. If variables measure constructs differently in different populations, differences on those variables do not unambiguously reflect between-group differences on the underlying constructs. There is no exact test of factorial invariance across time or groups in exploratory factor analysis, and it is not possible to specify and test forms of equivalence that are less stringent than full equivalence. CFA can be used to accomplish all of these goals before forming composites for use in later analyses.

In any psychometrical factor model, the errors of measurement indicate that not all of the variability in a particular observed measure is explained by the underlying factor or factors. Errors of measurement indicate that the variables are not perfect measures of their factor(s). Indeed, these errors are the very reason why collection of multiple measures and the use of data reduction strategies are recommended. The error variance in a particular variable may be systematic or random from the standpoint of the model under investigation, so that the errors may or may not represent potentially explainable variation in the psychological tests. Application of exploratory factoring methods assumes that error variance is unrelated to all other variables in the data set. However, in CFA, the assumption of unrelated errors is testable and can be relaxed when theoretically and empirically supported (Francis, 1988). This assumption is frequently untenable with psychological test measures, in which pairs of tests frequently share method variance. The assumption of uncorrelated errors is also suspect when data are collected over time.

Application of CFA

Making practical use of confirmatory factor models requires several steps. These steps include the following: 1) data screening for outliers, influential data points, nonnormality, and nonlinearity; 2) model specification; 3) parameter and model identification; 4) parameter estimation and hypothesis testing; 5) assessment of model fit; 6) model modification; and 7) estimation of factor scores. Steps 2 through 6 are outlined in detail in Francis (1988). Methods for completing Step 1 have been detailed in Chambers, Cleveland, Kleiner, and Tukey (1983). Finally, Step 7 has been described in Gorsuch (1983), Lawley and Maxwell (1971), and MacDonald (1985).

Table 3.2 summarizes the process. Briefly, Step 1 involves the use of uni-variate and multivariate graphical data analysis tools (e.g., stem and leaf, quartile, bivariate scatter, influence, bubble and density plots, mid-summaries, and data transformation techniques) to enhance symmetry in individual measures, and to enhance linearity among measures of the same construct.

Model specification, Step 2, is the attempt to develop a model for the relationships among the individual measures. These relationships are expressed in terms of the measures themselves, the constructs they measure, the relationships among the constructs, and the errors of measurement. It is essential that the model draw on information from at least three areas: substantive theory, experimental design, and measurement theory. This process leads to hypothetical measurement models and the construction of different assessment tools. These models are fairly explicit in terms of variable selection and the measurement dimensions of the various tests.

Parameter and model identification, Step 3, is a complex issue that concerns the estimability of the model parameters and the testability of the model. Basically, identification means that a unique solution exists for the parameters in the model or for the model as a whole. If a parameter is identified, there is a single estimate for it that, given the model and the data, will maximize the fit of the model to the data. The model is said to be identified only if all parameters in the model are identified (Joreskog & Sorbom, 1986). It is possible that the model as a whole can be tested, even if all parameters in the model have not been identified. Kenny (1979, p. 38) provides an example of such a model. When a parameter is not identified, some constraint can often be placed on the parameter in order to gain identification of the parameter and the model as a whole.

In CFA models, three indicators per factor are sufficient to guarantee that each factor is just-identified, provided that no correlated errors are specified. Four indicators per factor guarantee that each factor is overdetermined, which allows each factor to be tested for single-factoredness of its indicators. If factors are correlated, then it is possible to identify factor loadings with two indicators per factor, and sometimes one indicator for some of the factors. However, this state of identification is not optimal because it can lead to factors that are poorly defined as well as problems of empirical underidentification.

Step 4 is parameter estimation, which simply refers to how numerical values come to be assigned to the parameters in the model. There are many ways to esti-

Table 3.2. Steps in the application of confirmatory factor analysis

1. Examination of the form and distribution of individual data
2. Model specification: Relationships of the measures
3. Parameter and model identification: Specification of model parameters and the testability of the model
4. Parameter estimation: Assignment of numerical values to the model parameters
5. Model assessment: Evaluation of local and global indices of fit
6. Modifications of the model
7. Creation of composites and factor score estimation

mate parameters in CFA, but no one method is optimal under all conditions. The most important differences among the various methods concern the distributional theory on which the estimates are based (e.g., multivariate normal, elliptical, or arbitrary distribution theory). There has been some empirical work that examines the robustness of certain estimators to violations of their distributional assumptions (Boomsma, 1982; Muthen, 1984). This research generally shows that maximum-likelihood estimators perform well, provided that variable distributions are symmetrical. Bentler (1985) provides some guidelines for choosing an appropriate method of estimation, as do Joreskog and Sorbom (1986). Joreskog and Sorbom provide considerably less detail because LISREL only provides normal theory estimates, whereas Bentler's structural equation program, EQS, estimates parameters under elliptical and arbitrary distribution theory as well as under normal theory.

Regardless of the method of estimation chosen, it is most important to keep in mind that one is always trying to assign a numerical value to the same structural parameter. Changing the method of estimation does not change the parameter, only the estimate of its true value. The best estimate will be obtained when the variable distribution conforms to the distribution theory on which the estimator is based, but reasonable estimates are likely even when the distributional assumptions are not met. However, these distributional assumptions form the basis for making statistical statements (inferences) about the parameters, and these statements may be inappropriate when the assumptions are not met. With these caveats in mind, it is important to make use of the results from Step 1 to guide the selection of an optimal estimation process. When no clear-cut choice emerges on the basis of Step 1, the influences of estimates under differing sets of assumptions should be made.

Step 5 is model assessment. There are many pieces of information that contribute to the assessment of model fit, and each provides a slightly different view of where the model fits well and where it fits poorly. The indices that assess model fit can be characterized as either global or local. Global indices reflect how well the model as a whole reproduces all of the relationships among the variables, whereas local indices reflect more specific aspects of model fit. In assessing model fit, it is important to consider both types of information. It is possible for a model to fit well on the whole and yet poorly reproduce some important relationships among variables. On the other hand, if a model fits poorly in a general sense, global indices do not aid in detecting the source of the problem. The global and local indices often used in assessing model fit are summarized by Francis (1988) and Joreskog and Sorbom (1986).

Assessment of model fit must include a comprehensive examination of the model, not just a global assessment of the properties of the model. This assessment involves examination of local indices, such as the normalized residuals, which identify specific relationships between variables that are poorly reproduced by the model. In addition, the acceptability of all parameter estimates must be examined. If a model contains unacceptable parameter estimates (e.g., estimated factor correlations that exceed 1.0) or negative error variances, it is likely that the model has misspecified certain relationships. Similarly, it is important to compare parameter estimates to their standard errors to determine whether proposed relationships in the model are contributing significantly to model fit. Large standard errors relative to the size of the corresponding parameter estimates suggest that those parameters may not be contributing to model fit. However, in order for significance tests of specific parameters to be valid, the sample size should be large, analysis should be based on the covariance matrix (Browne, 1982), and the multivariate distribution of the variables must conform to the theoretical distribution associated with the estimation procedure. Very large standard errors may signal multicollinearity among parameter estimates, which may indicate problems in identification—that is, problems in obtaining unique estimates for those parameters. This situation is frequently encountered in modeling longitudinal data.

An important aspect of any model is how well each variable is explained by the model. The squared multiple correlations provided by LISREL VII indicate the proportion of variance in each variable that is explained by the proposed model. Variables with small squared multiple correlations are not well-explained by the model and suggest areas where the model might be improved. However, a small squared multiple correlation can indicate that the variable does not intercorrelate highly with other variables in the data matrix. Model modification will not improve the explanation of such variables unless additional variables are added to the data matrix. A quick check against this explanation for small squared multiple correlations is provided by an examination of the matrix of residual covariances. If the residuals for a variable are all small, the model is adequately explaining that variable's relationships in the particular data matrix, regardless of the size of the squared multiple correlation. Of course, the question remains as to why the variable is not well-related to other variables in the data.

If the model does not adequately reproduce the data, modification is indicated (Step 6). Certain pieces of information regarding model fit are helpful in determining where the model might be changed in order to provide a more adequate fit to the data. Specifically, the Modification Indices, LaGrange, and Wald tests (which are multivariate extensions of the Modification Index, expected parameter change statistics, and the absolute and normalized residuals) (Francis, 1988) are particularly helpful at this stage of model development. Any changes made to the model must be theoretically defensible. Also, modifying the model changes the inferential process from confirmatory to exploratory and, as such, may lead to a model that is unduly influenced by sample-specific characteristics. Model modification gives an overly optimistic view of model adequacy, much like the failure to adjust for shrinkage in multiple regression or discriminant analysis. When model modification is anticipated, make sure that the available subject pool is sufficiently large to allow for cross-validation.

Finally, Step 7 involves data reduction. Our group uses two approaches to data reduction. First, measures are grouped based on conceptual subdivisions provided by investigators familiar with each general domain of interest. For example, language measures might be grouped into measures of phonology, syntax, and semantics. These subdivisions are then evaluated empirically using CFA (Francis, 1988; Francis, Fletcher, & Rourke, 1988; Francis, Fletcher, Rourke, & York, 1992). A second approach is to select key variables instead of composites from a construct identified through conceptual subdivision of the data or CFA.

Factor scores can be estimated in CFA. However, as with the common factor model, it is not possible to calculate factor scores. Rather, one must estimate the scores. There are various approaches to factor score estimation (Gorsuch, 1983). However, there tends to be a high degree of consistency across these methods. Factor score estimates produced by LISREL are regression-based estimates that allow for estimation of nonstandardized factor scores, which is an important consideration in the use of composite variables for studying developmental phenomena.

There are problems with factor scores. Important information is carried in the variances of variables as well as in the variable means. If all variables are standardized prior to studies of change, time-dependent changes in the variance of instruments will be lost. Similarly, normalized scores can mask the presence of subtypes, so that factor scores are not useful for methods such as cluster analysis. If composites are used, z scores can be computed and averaged to address this problem.

AN EXAMPLE: YALE CENTER FOR
LEARNING AND ATTENTION DISORDERS

The steps outlined in the section on CFA, including a priori development of a hypothetical measurement model, were followed as part of a large study addressing the classification of children with learning disabilities (Shaywitz et al., 1991). The goals of this study were to address the definition and classification of children with reading disabilities and to evaluate hypotheses about the cognitive mechanisms underlying reading disability.

In order to accomplish these goals, it was necessary to obtain a large sample of children with reading and other disabilities and measures of cognitive skills presumed to be related to these disabilities. The approach to measurement was based on the long history of theory and research on language, reading, and reading disability emanating from the Haskins Laboratory over the past 20 years (Brady & Shankweiler, 1991; Liberman, 1973; Liberman, Shankweiler, Fischer, & Carter, 1974; Shankweiler & Crain, 1986). In terms of reading disability, this research indicates that the cognitive mechanisms underlying both reading proficiency and reading disability are largely language-based. In particular, the phonological component of language appears central to the initial origin of word decoding ability as well as to the deficiencies in word decoding abilities that are the principal characteristics of children with reading disabilities. There is considerable support for the hypothesis that, in order to learn to read, children must become aware of the parts of the word in order to connect oral and written language, thereby developing the capacity to use an alphabetical system to read and spell (Shankweiler & Crain, 1986; Stanovich, 1988; Vellutino, 1991). Children with reading disabilities appear impaired in the capacity to deal with the phonological component of language. Hence, difficulties in decoding words, segmenting spoken words using the phonological code, rapid automatized naming, and verbal short-term memory may represent a syndrome describing the language impairments of children with reading disability. These deficiencies may all have their origins in phonological language impairments.

In order to adequately evaluate this hypothesis and provide a general measurement framework for assessing children with reading disabilities, two batteries of tests were developed. The first battery (Level I) consisted of reading, spelling, and math measures. The second battery (Level II) was based on the hypothesized relationship of language and reading, as well as on more general models of language and cognition in relation to academic achievement. Emphasis was placed on the assessment of phonological awareness skills because of their theoretical relevance for reading disability. Because children with reading disabilities may have other more general language problems, measures of morphological awareness, vocabulary development, naming skills, speech perception, and syntactic comprehension were also developed. Whenever possible, comparable nonlanguage tasks were also developed to parallel the language-based tasks. Finally, in order to determine the extent to which reading disability resided in the language area, measures of other cognitive skills were also obtained, including verbal and nonverbal short-term memory, focused attention, and visual–spatial ability.

A specific goal of both test batteries was to ensure redundant measurement of various constructs in order to allow adequate specification of the latent variables. To address classification issues and to ensure that the cognitive processes that were being measured were not general characteristics of children with reading disabilities, other contrast groups were also included. For example, children with problems in mathematics but not in reading were identified as a comparison group. Because many children with reading disabilities also have attention deficit hyperactivity disorder (ADHD), a contrast group of children with ADHD and no learning disability was included. Because of the controversy over the role of IQ scores in the identification of children with learning disability, children were selected who met both discrepancy and low-achievement definitions of reading and mathematics disability. Finally, a contrast group of children with lower intelligence test scores who did not meet the selection criteria of a Verbal IQ or Performance IQ of 80 on the Wechsler Intelligence Scale for Children–Revised (WISC–R)(Wechsler, 1974) was also included. This selection resulted in a sample of 378 children in 9 different groups: reading disability, mathematics disability, and both reading and mathematics disability. These children were selected according to both discrepancy and low-achievement definitions, making 6 groups of children with learning disabilities. In addition, contrast groups of children with ADHD and no learning disability, intelligence test scores below 80, and children with no disabilities were included.

The cognitive measures included over 30 different tests of cognitive skills. Obviously, analyzing all of the data a variable at a time could lead to serious problems with Type I errors as well as difficulty relating the results of individual measures across this large sample. However, the sample was constructed in a way that would permit the application of CFA to the analysis of the redundancy across variables and the reduction of the data into a set of meaningful composites.

The steps outlined in Table 3.1 were then followed. For example, Step 1 was addressed by examining the distributional characteristics of all of the variables. The results of this process indicated the presence of one subject who was an outlier across virtually all variables. This subject, who had an extremely low IQ, tended to score much higher on many of the cognitive tasks. Eliminating this subject was important because it reduced the influence of this single subject on the results of any statistical analysis. Similarly, some measures were not found to have particularly desirable characteristics. Most of the methods used for statistical analysis are robust to violations of normality. In a sample that is predominantly composed of children with disabilities, normal distributions would not be expected. In fact, virtually all measures were significantly positively skewed. In some instances, the amount of skew was so severe that the measure could not be used. These measures were eliminated because of their psychometrical characteristics. For example, the rhyme generation task used by Olson, Wise, Conners, Rack, and Fulker (1989) in a sample of children much older than the children in this study had a floor effect and was not modeled.

For both Level I and Level II measures, a set of hypothetical measurement models was developed (Step 2). These models generally began by hypothesizing that the latent structure of the data set could be captured by a single factor. For example, for the achievement measures, this hypothesis would be tantamount to assuming that the achievement tests measured only a single factor (achievement) and that differentiations into reading, math, and spelling were not possible. The overall model hypothesized that six dimensions were measured: real word decoding, pseudoword decoding, spelling, reading comprehension, listening comprehension, and mathematics. To go from the single-factor model to a six-factor model, the measures were nested and tested in a successive manner. Consequently, a two-factor model was developed that simply separated the arithmetic measures from all other measures. The three-factor model included measures of decoding/spelling, listening/reading comprehension, and arithmetic. The four-factor model included measures of decoding ability, listening/reading comprehension, spelling, and arithmetic. For the five-factor model, decoding real words and pseudowords were separated. The six-factor model separated the measures of listening and reading comprehension.

A similar process was followed for the Level II (cognitive) measures. The single-factor model simply indicated that only one dimension was measured by the test battery. The two-factor model separated measures into those that were presumed to measure language skills versus nonlanguage skills. The three-factor model proposed a separate memory factor. This process proceeded up to a nine-factor model, which included dimensions of lexical/vocabulary measures, nonverbal/visual–spatial measures, visual attention, verbal memory, nonverbal memory, phonological awareness, speech production, rapid naming, and syntax. The syntax measures had extremely low relationships with all other measures in the test battery. Including them in the model yielded inadequate fit indices, reflecting this complete lack of redundancy. It was necessary to remove the syntax measures in order to examine the other dimensions in the model.

An important characteristic of this model was that virtually all factors had at least four indicators. In the present data set, this assumption could be somewhat more relaxed because of the inflation of correlational relationships that occurred, reflecting nature of the sample (comprising predominantly persons with disabilities). Samples of this sort typically produce correlational relationships that are much higher than those that would be observed in an unselected population. For example, the relationship of IQ and reading achievement is approximately .6 in a population-based sample; it was approximately .85 in this sample, depending on what indices of IQ and reading achievement were selected. In this situation, it becomes much harder to actually fit the model because of the amount of redundancy among the measures. This redundancy has more to do with the way the sample was created than with the true redundancy of the constructs in the state of nature. Hence, in completing the third step (parameter model identification), we had concerns about overidentification of the factors.

The next step was to estimate the parameters (Step 4) and assess the fit of the models (Step 5). The models were fit using the LISREL VII program and were based on maximum likelihood methods of estimation. Assessment of model fit included both global and local indices. The results of the model assessment phase were used to suggest alternative models in instances in which the data were not adequately reproduced (Step 6). The indices of model fit from LISREL VII provide indications of exactly what variables do not fit the model well and also suggest guidelines for alternative models in order to increase the fit.

For Step 7, composites were created in order to enhance the reliability of the assessment. Factor scores were not created because of the possibility of masking subtypes within the sample.

Table 3.3 summarizes the factor loading of the best achievement model, and Table 3.4 summarizes the fit statistics across the different models for the cognitive measures. As Table 3.4 shows, the five-factor model had a chi-square of approximately 298 with 84 degrees of freedom, which was significant. However, chi-square tests are commonly inflated in large samples. Another rule of thumb for global fit is to look at the goodness-of-fit index. Models that fit at a level of approximately .9 are commonly considered to reproduce the latent structure fairly well. As Table 3.4 shows, each successive model led to improvement in both the chi-square estimates and the goodness-of-fit estimate. The chi-squares for differences in each model were always significant, and the five-factor model clearly best approximates the data. The six-factor model did not lead to a signifi-

Table 3.3. Factor loadings for the five-factor model for the achievement data

Factor	Loading	Observed variable
Real words	.97	Wide Range Achievement Test (WRAT) Reading Recognition (Jastak & Jastak, 1978)
	.95	W–J Word Identification (Woodcock & Johnson, 1977)
	.93	Decoding Skills Test–Real Words (Richardson & DiBenedetto, 1985)
	.87	GORT–R Passages (Wiederholt & Bryant, 1986)
Nonsense words	.92	Decoding Skills Test–Pseudowords
	.87	W–J Word Attack
Listening/reading	.93	W–J Passage Comprehension
	.84	Formal Reading Inventory (FRI) Silent Reading Comprehension (Wiederholt, 1986)
	.83	GORT–R Comprehension
	.56	FRI Listening Comprehension
Spelling	.94	Test of Written Spelling–Predictable Words (Larsen & Hammill, 1976)
	.92	Test of Written Spelling–Unpredictable Words
	.92	WRAT Spelling
Arithmetic	.88	W–J Calculations
	.87	WRAT Arithmetic
	.81	W–J Applied Problems

W–J, Woodcock-Johnson Psychoeducational Test Battery; GORT–R, Gray Oral Reading Test–Revised.

Table 3.4. Model fit statistics for each of five models in the achievement data

Model	Fit statistics[a]					Difference from previous model		
	Chi-square	df	p<	GFI	AGFI	Chi-square dif	df dif	p<
1 Factor	808	94	.0001	.78	.68	NA	NA	NA
2 Factor	481	93	.0001	.85	.79	326.74	1	.00001
3 Factor	457	91	.0001	.86	.80	23.46	2	.00001
4 Factor	378	88	.0001	.89	.83	78.95	3	.00001
5 Factor	298	84	.0001	.91	.86	80.10	4	.00001

[a]GFI, goodness-of-fit index; AGFI, adjusted goodness-of-fit index; dif, difference.

cant increment in chi-square nor did the fit indices improve. This may be because only one measure of listening comprehension was available and may reflect underidentification of the latent construct.

It is very important to recognize that many of these factors are highly correlated (see Table 3.5). For example, decoding real words and nonsense words should be very highly correlated. This is clearly the case, with the correlation of real words and nonsense words standing at .97. In fact, all the reading and spelling measures showed correlations above .90. In contrast, the arithmetic measures have much lower correlations. One of the true advantages of this approach is the ability to specify the relationship of constructs even when they are highly intercorrelated. Whether specification of highly intercorrelated factors is of any practical significance is questionable. In this situation, there were no obvious differential relations of the reading decoding and spelling measures with other cognitive skills.

Table 3.5. Correlations of the five achievement factors

	RW	PW	Comp	Spelling
Real words (RW)				
Pseudowords (PW)	.97			
Reading/listening comprehension (comp)	.98	.92		
Spelling	.94	.97	.94	
Arithmetic	.72	.70	.75	.74

Table 3.6 shows the factor loadings of the LISREL analysis for the eight-factor model. Table 3.7 provides the fit statistics for the eight-factor model as well as a model that was subsequently fit, which allowed for eight specific factors and one general factor. As Table 3.7 shows, there was a tendency for each successive approximation to result in improved fit indices. The eight-factor model is clearly superior to the other models. However, the chi-square value is large, and the adjusted goodness-of-fit index is relatively low. Examination of local fit indices also revealed a number of problems. Consequently, another model was fit that included the eight factors as well as a general factor. In this model, all variables loaded on the general factor, but the general factor was uncorrelated with the specific factors.

Table 3.8 provides the factor loadings for this model. It is important to note that all the factor loadings are much lower, reflecting the extent to which the individual variables loaded on the general factor. The most significant reductions of factor loadings between Table 3.6 and Table 3.8 occur on the lexical/vocabulary factor. Whereas in Table 3.6 the Boston Naming Test (Goodglass & Kaplan, 1983) and the Peabody Picture Vocabulary Test–Revised (Dunn & Dunn, 1981) load the highest on the lexical/vocabulary factor, these measures have the lowest loadings on this factor in Table 3.8. This is because these two measures are the best indicators of the general factor. Most measures load to some extent on the general factor, and the extent of this loading can be gauged by comparing Tables 3.6 and 3.8. Perhaps more important is the significant increment in the adjusted goodness-of-fit as well as the reduction in chi-square that occurred when the model was fit with a general factor.

Another influence of including a general factor can be seen in Table 3.9, which presents factor correlations for both models. As this table shows, there are high relationships among several of the factors when the general factor is not included. For example, the phonological awareness and lexical/vocabulary factor correlate at .88. There is a general tendency for the language-based factors to correlate more highly with each other than with other measures. In contrast, the correlations in parentheses show the significant reduction in the redundancy of these measures when the general factor is included.

In summary, two different measurement models have been developed, tested, and found to be adequate for reproducing the latent structure of the data. One of these models involves achievement data, whereas the second involves cognitive data. Because the goal of this process was to produce a smaller number of variables in order to relate the achievement and cognitive measures, the next

Table 3.6. Factor loadings for the eight-factor model for the cognitive data

Phonological awareness	Lexical/ vocabulary	Speech production	Rapid naming	Verbal memory	Nonverbal memory	Visual-spatial	Visual attention
	.87 Peabody Picture Vocabulary Test–Revised	.85 Tongue Twisters—easy (Olson, Kliegl, Davidson, & Foltz, 1985)			.92 Corsi Blocks—ordered (Milner, 1971)		.76 Underlining—3 (Doehring, 1968)
	.83 Boston Naming Test	.84 Speed of Articulation			.85 Corsi Blocks—unordered		.53 Underlining—2
	.79 WISC–R Vocabulary	.83 Speed of Articulation					.50 Underlining—8
	.71 WISC–R Similarities	.80 Tongue Twisters—hard					.39 Underlining—4
	.64 WISC–R Comprehension						
.89 Morphological Awareness (Shankweiler et al., in press)			.82 Rapid Naming 1 (Katz, 1986)	.79 Word String Recall—nonrhyme (Shankweiler, Liberman, Mark, Fowler, & Fischer, 1979)		.76 WISC–R Block Design	
				.70 WISC–R Digit Span			
.77 Auditory Analysis Test (Rosner & Simon, 1971)			.78 Rapid Naming 2			.71 Judgment of Line Orientation (Lindgren & Benton, 1980)	

(continued)

Table 3.6. (continued)

Phonological awareness	Lexical/ vocabulary	Speech production	Rapid naming	Verbal memory	Nonverbal memory	Visual-spatial	Visual attention
			.78 Rapid Naming 3			.67 Developmental Test of Visual-Motor Integration–Revised (Beery, 1989)	
.64 Embedded Phonemes-Neutral Foils (Haskins Laboratory, New Haven, CT)			.78 Rapid Naming 4	.79 Sentence Repetition		.63 Embedded Figures (Satz, Taylor, Friel, & Fletcher, 1978)	
.51 Embedded Phonemes-Spelling Foils				.59 Word String Recall—rhyme		.61 WISC–R Object Assembly	

36

Table 3.7. Model fit statistics for the nine models used with the cognitive data

	Fit statistics[a]					Difference from previous model		
Model	Chi-square	df	p<	GFI	AGFI	Chi-square dif	df dif	p<
1 Factor	2278	456	.0001	.689	.640	NA	NA	NA
2 Factor	1986	455	.0001	.718	.673	297	1	.00001
3 Factor	1883	453	.0001	.732	.687	103	2	.00001
4 Factor	1896	450	.0001	.731	.684	NA	NA	NA
5 Factor	1857	446	.0001	.730	.681	39	4	.00001
6 Factor	1553	441	.0001	.761	.714	304	5	.00001
7 Factor	1031	435	.0001	.857	.822	522	6	.00001
8 Factor	722	428	.0001	.891	.865	309	7	.00001
8 Specific / 1 general	545	396	.0001	.920	.893	177	32	.0001

NA indicates that the model was not tested.

[a]GFI, goodness-of-fit index; AGFI, adjusted goodness-of-fit index; dif, difference.

question was how to create composites. In order to create the composites, the two measures with the highest factor loadings were converted into z scores and averaged. However, since the eight-factor model also includes a general factor, we decided to create cognitive measures that were either adjusted or not adjusted for the general factor. Again, composites were created based on the two variables with the highest factor loadings. The advantage of adjusting and not adjusting for the general factor is the ability to understand the influence of this general factor on the ultimate outcomes of interest, which include relationships of cognitive skills and academic abilities as well as group contrasts across these dimensions. In this sample, the general factor largely appears to be a measure of vocabulary size. Hence, analyses that involve the factors adjusted for the general factor may be analogous to adjusting scores for verbal IQ. This is important because children with reading disabilities generally have lower verbal IQs than children without reading disabilities. Adjusting for this general factor provides an excellent approach to understanding the influence of general language skills on the cognitive performance of children with reading and other learning disabilities. These results are also preliminary. We are presently attempting to evaluate more complicated models. In addition, we will eventually develop a structural model that relates the achievement and cognitive measures. However, as opposed to models with over 30 variables, we will be able to work with a much smaller set of more reliable measures that should permit accurate estimates of unique relationships among the constructs. The ultimate test of the validity of the constructs is their ability to predict theoretically relevant relationships within the data. This is the next step in the process of construct validation.

CONCLUSIONS

Construct validity issues are at the heart of psychological research. Although the examples used in this chapter involved areas in which the authors have their prin-

Table 3.8. Factor loadings for the cognitive data

Phonological awareness	Lexical/ vocabulary	Speech production	Rapid naming	Verbal memory	Nonverbal memory	Visual-spatial	Visual attention
	.40 WISC–R Vocabulary	.79 Speed of Articulation			.86 Corsi Blocks— ordered		.71 Underlining –3
	.27 WISC–R Similarities	.76 Speed of Articulation					.55 Underlining –2
	.24 WISC–R Compre- hension	.74 Tongue Twisters— easy			.79 Corsi Blocks— unordered		.43 Underlining –8
	.18 Boston Naming						
	.16 Peabody Picture Vocabulary Test– Revised	.68 Tongue Twisters— hard					.33 Underlining –4
						.59 WISC– Block Design	
						.57 Developmental Test of Visual– Motor Integration– Revised	
.65 Auditory Analysis Test			.77 Rapid Naming 1	.68 WISC–R Digit Span		.57 Judgment of Line Orientation	
.55 Embedded Phonemes– Neutral Foils			.71 Rapid Naming 2	.53 Word String Recall— Nonrhyme		.52 Embedded Figures	
						.47 WISC–R Object Assembly	
.47 Embedded Phonemes– Spelling Foils			.70 Rapid Naming 3	.36 Word String Recall—Rhyme			
.30 Morphological Awareness			.67 Rapid Naming 4	.33 Sentence Repetition (Mann, Liberman, & Shankweiler, 1980)			

Note: The model has eight specific factors and one general factor.

Table 3.9. Factor correlations for the eight-factor models

	Phonological awareness	L/V	SP	RN	VM	NVM	V-S
Lexical/vocabulary (L/V)	.88						
	(.28)						
Speech production (SP)	.49	.44					
	(.27)	(2.07)					
Rapid naming (RN)	.55	.41	.40				
	(.37)	(.04)	(.24)				
Verbal memory (VM)	.80	.73	.43	.46			
	(.58)	(.27)	(.19)	(.27)			
Nonverbal memory (NVM)	.47	.39	.17		.50		
	(.30)	(.15)	(.02)	(.28)	(.37)		
Visual-spatial (V-S)	.72	.65	.38	.33	.60	.63	
	(.50)	(.38)	(.16)	(.12)	(.37)	(.55)	
Visual attention (VA)	.39	.35	.33	.50	.32	.39	.49
	(.09)	(.12)	(.21)	(.42)	(.14)	(.30)	(.38)

Note: The numbers in parentheses are the correlations for the model with a general factor.

cipal expertise, namely the relationship of language and learning disabilities, the results easily generalize to studies of other cognitive processes. It is clear that theoretical models of attention, memory, and executive functions overlap. A measure that is conceptualized as an index of selective attention in a model of attention, such as the Stroop test (Stroop, 1935), can be conceptualized as a measure of disinhibitory control in a model of executive functions. Similarly, the "encoding" factor in the Mirsky model of attention is also very prominent in many models of memory (see Chapter 6). Hence, there is considerable overlap in the nature of these models. When the constructs in these models are measured, the tests that are used can be redundant and may have surplus variability. There are certainly examples where exploratory factor analytical models have been used, but these models are simply out of date and do not possess the same utility as confirmatory models. For example, a major problem with exploratory factor analyses of data from memory, attention, and executive functions tasks is method variance. Factors emerge simply because subtests of a particular measure are so highly intercorrelated with each other that they load on a single factor. Confirmatory models can be used to address this problem because of the ability to specify correlated errors of measure.

More generally, the rationale behind the use of CFA and structural equation modeling, which forces investigators to superimpose a hypothetical model on a data set, encourages investigators to form hypotheses about construct dimensions on an a priori basis. Investigators simply should not assume that single indicators of a particular construct are adequate. In addition, it should not be assumed that the measure reproduces only one dimension. By engaging in the process of construct validation and applying methods such as CFA, the assumptions that investigators make when designing experiments can be assessed. In addition, more refined measurement models can be developed. The relationship of measurement models under attention, memory, and executive functions will become clearer. Perhaps most important, the nature of the cognitive deficits related to various types of disabilities will become more apparent and eventually more susceptible to intervention.

REFERENCES

Beery, K.E. (1989). *Developmental Test of Visual-Motor Integration–Revised.* Chicago: Follett.

Bentler, P.M. (1985). *Theory and implementation of EQS: A structural equations program.* Los Angeles: BMDP Statistical Software.

Boomsma, A. (1982). The robustness of LISREL against small sample sizes in factor analysis models. In K.G. Joreskog & H. Wold (Eds.), *Systems under indirect observation: Causality, structure, prediction* (Part I, pp. 149–173). Amsterdam: North Holland.

Brady, S.A., & Shankweiler, D.P. (Eds.). (1991). *Phonological processes in literacy: A tribute to Isabelle Y. Liberman.* Hillsdale, NJ: Lawrence Erlbaum Associates.

Browne, M.W. (1982). Covariance structures. In D.M. Hawkins (Ed.). *Topics in applied multivariate analysis* (pp. 72–141). London: Cambridge University Press.

Campbell, D.T., & Stanley, J.C. (1963). *Experimental and quasi-experimental designs for research.* Chicago: Rand McNally.

Chambers, J.M., Cleveland, W.S., Kleiner, B., & Tukey, P.A. (1983). *Graphical methods for data analysis.* Belmont, CA: Wadsworth.

Cole, D.A., & Maxwell, S.E. (1986). Multitrait-multimethod comparisons across populations: A confirmatory factor analytic approach. *Multivariate Behavioral Research, 20,* 389–417.

Cook, T.D., & Campbell, D.A. (1979). *Quasi-experimentation: Design and analysis issues for field settings.* Chicago: Rand McNally.

Cronbach, L.J., & Meehl, P.E. (1955). Construct validity in psychological tests. *Psychological Bulletin, 52,* 281–302.

Doehring, D.G. (1968) *Patterns of impairment in specific reading disability.* Bloomington: Indiana University Press.

Doehring, D.G. (1978). The tangled web of behavioral research in developmental dyslexia. In A.L. Benton & D. Pearl (Eds.), *Dyslexia: An appraisal of current knowledge* (pp. 123–138). New York: Oxford University Press.

Dunn, L.M., & Dunn, L.M., (1981). *Peabody Picture Vocabulary Test–Revised.* Circle Pines, MN: American Guidance Service.

Fletcher, J.M., Shaywitz, S.E., Shankweiler, D.P., Katz, L., Liberman, I.Y., Fowler, A., Francis, D.J., Stuebing, K.K., & Shaywitz, B.A. (1994). Cognitive profiles of reading disability: Comparisons of discrepancy and low achievement definitions. *Journal of Educational Psychology, 85,* 1–18.

Francis, D.J. (1988). An introduction to structural equation models. *Journal of Clinical and Experimental Neuropsychology, 10,* 623–639.

Francis, D.J., Espy, K.A., Rourke, B.P., & Fletcher, J.M. (1991). Validity of intelligence test scores in the definition of learning disability: A critical analysis. In B.P. Rourke (Ed.), *Validity issues in learning disabilities* (pp. 12–40). New York: Guilford Press.

Francis, D.J., Fletcher, J.M., & Rourke, B.P. (1988). Discriminant validity of lateral sensorimotor test in children. *Journal of Clinical and Experimental Neuropsychology, 10,* 779–799.

Francis, D.J., Fletcher, J.M., Rourke, B.P., & York, M.J. (1992). A five-factor model for motor, psychomotor, and visual-spatial tests used in the neuropsychological assessment of children. *Journal of Clinical and Experimental Neuropsychology, 14,* 625–637.

Goodglass, H., & Kaplan, E. (1983). *Boston Naming Test.* Philadelphia: Lea & Febiger.

Gorsuch, R.L. (1983). *Factor analysis* (2nd ed.). Hillsdale, NJ: Lawrence Erlbaum Associates.

Guertin, W.H., & Bailey, J.P. (1970). *Introduction to modern factor analysis.* Ann Arbor, MI: Edwards Brothers, Inc.

Jastak, J.F., & Jastak, S. (1978). *The Wide Range Achievement Test: Manual of instructions.* Wilmington, DE: Jastak Associates.

Joreskog, K.G., & Sorbom, D. (1986). *LISREL: Analysis of linear structural relationships by the method of maximum likelihood. User's guide* (4th ed.). Mooresville, IN: Scientific Software.

Katz, R. (1986). Phonological deficiencies in children with reading disability: Evidence from an object naming task. *Cognition, 22,* 225–257.

Kenny, D.A. (1979). *Correlation and causality.* New York: John Wiley & Sons.

Larsen, S.C., & Hammill, D.D. (1976). *The Test of Written Spelling–Revised.* Austin, TX: PRO-ED.

Lawley, D.N., & Maxwell, A.C. (1971). *Factor analysis as a statistical method.* London: Butterworth.

Liberman, I.Y. (1973). Segmentation of the spoken word. *Bulletin of the Orton Society, 23,* 65–77.

Liberman, I.Y., Shankweiler, D.P., Fischer, F.W., & Carter, B. (1974). Explicit syllable and phoneme segmentation in the young child. *Journal of Experimental Child Psychology, 18,* 201–212.

Lindgren, S.D., & Benton, A.L. (1980). Developmental patterns of visuospatial judgment. *Journal of Pediatric Psychology, 5,* 217–225.

MacDonald, R.P. (1985). *Factor analysis and related methods.* Hillsdale, NJ: Lawrence Erlbaum Associates.

Mann, V.A., Liberman, I.Y., & Shankweiler, D.P. (1980). Children's memory for sentences and word strings in relation to reading ability. *Memory and Cognition, 8,* 329–335.

Maxwell, S.E., & Delaney, H.D. (1990). *Designing experiments and analyzing data: A model comparison perspective.* Belmont, CA: Wadsworth.

Milner, B. (1971). Interhemispheric differences in the localization of psychological processes in man. *British Medical Bulletin, 27,* 272–277.

Muthen, B. (1984). A general structural equation model for dichotomous, ordered categorical, and continuous latent variable indicators. *Psychometrika, 49,* 115–132.

Nunnally, J.C. (1978). *Psychometric theory* (2nd ed.). New York: McGraw-Hill.

Olson, R.K., Kliegl, R., Davidson, B.J., & Foltz, G. (1985). Individual and developmental differences in reading disability. In G.E. MacKinnon & T.G. Waller (Eds.), *Reading research: Advances in theory and practice* (Vol. 4) (pp. 1–64). San Diego, CA: Academic Press.

Olson, R.K., Wise, B., Conners, F., Rack, & Fulker, D. (1989). Specific deficits in component reading and language skills. *Journal of Learning Disabilities, 22,* 339–348.

Richardson, E., & DiBenedetto, B. (1985). *Decoding skills test.* Parkton, MD: York Press.

Rosner, J., & Simon, D. (1971). The Auditory Analysis Test: An initial report. *Journal of Learning Disabilities, 4,* 384–392.

Satz, P., & Fletcher, J. (1980). Minimal brain dysfunctions: An appraisal of research concepts and methods. In H.E. Rie & E.D. Rie (Eds.), *Handbook of minimal brain dysfunctions: A critical review* (pp. 669–714). New York: John Wiley & Sons.

Satz, P., Taylor, H.G., Friel, J., & Fletcher, J.M. (1978). Some developmental and predictive precursors of reading disability: A six-year follow-up. In A.L. Benton & D. Pearl (Eds.), *Dyslexia: An appraisal of current knowledge* (pp. 457–501). New York: Oxford University Press.

Shankweiler, D.P., & Crain, S. (1986). Language mechanisms and reading disorder: A modular approach. *Cognition, 24,* 139–168.

Shankweiler, D.P., Crain, S., Katz, L., Fowler, A.E., Brady, S.A., Fletcher, J.M., Stuebing, K.K., Shaywitz, S.E., & Shaywitz, B.A. (in press). Dissociation of children's language skills in dyslexia: Deficits in phonological processing with sparing of syntax. *Psychological Science.*

Shankweiler, D.P., Liberman, I.Y., Mark, L.S., Fowler, C.A., & Fischer, F. (1979). The speech code and learning to read. *Journal of Experimental Psychology: Human Learning and Memory, 5*, 531–545.

Shaywitz, B.A., Shaywitz, S.E., Liberman, I.Y., Fletcher, J.M., Shankweiler, D.P., Duncan, J., Katz, L., Liberman, A., Francis, D., Dreyer, L., Crain, S., Brady, S., Fowler, A., Kier, L., Rosenfield, N., Gore, J., & Makuch, R. (1991). Neurolinguistic and biological mechanism in dyslexia. In D.D. Duane & D.B. Gray (Eds.), *The reading brain: The biological basis of dyslexia* (pp. 27–52). Parkton, MD: York Press.

Stanovich, K.E. (1988). Explaining the differences between the dyslexic and the garden-variety poor reader: The phonological core variable difference model. *Journal of Learning Disabilities, 21*, 590–604.

Stanovich, K.E., & Siegel, L.S. (1994). Phenotypic performance profile of children with reading disabilities: A regression-based test of the phonological-core variable difference model. *Journal of Educational Psychology, 86*, 24–53.

Stroop, J.R. (1935). Studies of interference in serial verbal reactions. *Journal of Experimental Psychology, 18*, 643–662.

Vellutino, F.R. (1991). Introduction to three studies on reading acquisition: Convergent findings on theoretical foundations of code-oriented versus whole language approaches to reading instruction. *Journal of Educational Psychology, 83*, 437–443.

Wechsler, D. (1974). *Wechsler Intelligence Scale for Children–Revised.* New York: Psychological Corporation.

Wiederholt, J.L. (1986). *Formal Reading Inventory.* Austin, TX: PRO-ED.

Weiderholt, J.L. & Bryant, B.R. (1986). *Gray Oral Reading Tests–Revised (GORT-R).* San Antonio, TX: The Psychological Corporation.

Woodcock, R.W., & Johnson, M.B. (1977). *Woodcock-Johnson Psychoeducational Test Battery.* Boston: Teaching Resources.

II

ATTENTION

A ttention is a complex and multivariate psychological construct that has received substantial attention in the research and clinical literatures. Despite its importance and its ubiquitous nature in cognition and learning, the topic of attention and its components has been the subject of considerable debate. The purpose of the chapters within this section is to identify, organize, and discuss conceptualizations, definitions, and theories of attention according to three major frames of reference detailed in Chapter 1. In Chapter 4, Barkley reviews the major issues that pervade the study of attention. This is important because the study of attention has a long history of using competing models and methods to understand the construct. In Chapter 5, Sergeant begins the discussion of these different perspectives by outlining and discussing attention from an information processing frame of reference. In Chapter 6, Mirsky takes a different tack and explores the definition, conceptualization, and componential nature of attention through the lens of a neuropsychological perspective. In marked contrast, McIlvane, Dube, and Callahan in Chapter 7 focus on attention from a behavioral view. These divergent points of view are eloquently compared and contrasted by Halperin in Chapter 8. His overarching summary underscores the tremendous complexity inherent in the study of attention and the translation of research findings into clinical practice.

4

CRITICAL ISSUES IN RESEARCH ON ATTENTION

Russell A. Barkley

This chapter briefly examines critical issues in research on attention as an introduction to the three more detailed chapters on this topic that follow. All subsequent chapters in this section discuss the different theoretical models used in the research on various components or aspects of attention, so that we may see the manner in which attention is viewed from the perspective of information processing, neuropsychological, and behavioral models. Each chapter thus provides information on the theoretical assumptions and constructs of the different models, how these constructs may be operationalized and measured, and what populations may be the best to study in order to test the models. Of considerable importance is whether or not these models can generate experimental tests that would potentially falsify or disconfirm the model if certain results were to be obtained. It may be that some of the models to be discussed here are not sufficiently elaborated and operationalized to permit such high-level theory testing.

The aims of this section on attention speak to a critical issue within this field of research: the need to examine competing models of attention for their heuristic value in better understanding the nature of attention and their ability to guide our future research on this concept. Each of the perspectives described in this section has produced a substantial body of literature, and each is likely to continue to do so as long as it retains the loyalty and respect of the current generation of active scientists in this realm. This would be fine in a world of infinite resources. We do not live in such a world, however, and so each perspective must compete with the others for a share of the funding and other resources needed to carry out the research. In the marketplace of scientific ideas, we have a right to challenge the value of each in explaining current research findings and in directing avenues of future research that will prove fruitful.

CRITICAL ISSUES AND TRENDS IN THEORY

We also need to examine whether sufficient research exists within each area suggesting lines of convergence into common notions, processes, and constructs.

Such areas of consensus may point to basic or fundamental truths about the nature of human attention and its disorders and may help to link it to other literatures in psychology, such as those dealing with memory and executive functions. A current example from the study of attention deficit hyperactivity disorder (ADHD) may help to show the potential value that such lines of convergence might hold. Each model of attention has served as the basis for studying children with ADHD, using diverse methodologies. Yet all are now converging on the common notion that ADHD most likely does not represent a disturbance in selective or sustained attention, as its name implies. Instead, it is a deficiency in response inhibition and the capacity to delay responding (Barkley, 1994b). This represents a fundamental shift in our thinking about ADHD—as fundamental as the shift from viewing ADHD as representing hyperkinesis, or excessive motor activity for one's mental age, to the view that attention and impulse control are prominently involved in the disorder. The implications of this shift in perspective are quite profound.

The fields of developmental neuropsychology and developmental psychology have been studying response inhibition and delayed responding for some time. There have been common findings that these processes are related to working memory, or what the late philosopher/mathematician Jacob Bronowski once called prolongation (Bronowski, 1977). Inhibition and delayed responding are also linked in ways not yet fully understood to other important and uniquely human brain functions, often called the executive functions (see Section IV). These functions include the following: 1) the senses of time, hindsight, and forethought; 2) self-awareness; 3) the internalization of language and its governance over behavior; 4) the separation of affect from content in responding to events, or objectivity; 5) the regulation of affective and motivational states in subservience to goal-directed behavior; and 6) reconstitution, or the dissembling of events and messages from others, the progressive redistribution of their components to parallel brain systems for processing of their particulars, and their reconstruction into novel messages or responses. As Fuster (1989) has recently noted, these executive functions have as an overarching purpose the cross-temporal organization of behavior: behavior that is future-oriented and goal-directed and that links events substantially disparate in time. These executive functions are inherently self-organizing and self-regulating.

More will be said about these functions and their link to attention later. An important point, however, should be noted here. A joining of ideas in the field of ADHD, such that the disorder is viewed as one of inhibition and delayed responding, points immediately to its convergence with other areas of psychology. These areas of overlap suggest that ADHD also ought to involve impairments in the executive functions related to response inhibition discussed above. If so, ADHD is not merely a disorder of attention but of self-regulation and the cross-temporal organization of behavior. Thus, future research into the integrity of these executive functions related to delayed responding should find that these functions are deficient and demonstrate a developmental lag in those with

ADHD. No research, in the thousands of studies on ADHD to date, directly addresses most of these matters. The little research that does exist suggests that the new perspective on ADHD and its predictions fit the facts very nicely. If these scientific perspectives are indeed correct, entirely new directions for promising research into the nature of ADHD will be opened up, with enormous implications for the clinical evaluation and management of this disorder.

Another critical issue regarding the study of attention is the need to more adequately operationalize the concept. The concept of attention has been difficult to grasp in one unifying definition; not surprisingly, then, the definitions of attention offered up by past theorists have been quite diverse, as Cooley and Morris (1990) have indicated. Others have avoided defining the concept at all, dismissing it as a mentalism or circular concept with little explanatory value (Skinner, 1953). Several examples will attest to this diversity of opinion.

History of Theories of Attention

William James defined attention as "the taking possession by the mind, in clear and vivid form, of one out of what seem several simultaneously possible objects or trains of thought. Focalization, concentration, of consciousness are of its essence. It implies withdrawal from some things in order to deal effectively with others, and is a condition which has a real opposite in the confused, dazed, scatter-brained state which in French is called distraction, and *Zerstreutheit* in German. . . . One principal object comes then into the focus of consciousness, others are temporarily suppressed" (James, 1898, pp. 261–262). To James, attention and interest were inseparable, as one's interests defined to what one will attend. He went on to identify the "varieties of attention" as being either objects of sense (sensorial attention) or ideal or represented objects (intellectual attention). Intellectual attention is separable into immediate and derived categories. It is immediate when the topic or stimulus is interesting in itself, without relation to anything else; derived, when it owes its interest to association with some other immediately interesting thing.

Attention may also be passive (reflexive, nonvoluntary, effortless) or active and voluntary. James further characterized the latter as sustained attention; it is dependent upon repeated redirection of effort to the focus of attention and the resistance to attractions that coexist in the process. The threads of these ideas continue to be seen in contemporary models of attention, as in Posner's (1988) concept of automatic activation versus conscious strategies in determining attentional performance, and in Fuster's (1989) concept of inhibition of interference in his neuropsychological model of executive functions. Other recent models of attention include notions of selective, divided, focused, and sustained attention by Sergeant (Chapter 5) and Mirsky (Chapter 6); the behavioral notions of stimulus control, discrimination, and equivalence by McIlvane and colleagues (see Chapter 7); and the neuropsychological concepts of working memory summarized by Pennington and colleagues (Chapter 18). The use of the terms *effort* and *interest* by James (1898) clearly shows the link of attention with motivation noted by so many throughout the history of research on attention. Obvious, too, is the overlap of attention with executive functions.

Pavlov dealt with the involuntary aspects of attention in his research on the orienting, investigatory, or "What is it?" reflex.

> It is this reflex which brings about the immediate response in man and animals to the slightest changes in the world around them, so that they may immediately orientate their appropriate receptor organ in accordance with the perceptible quality in the agent bringing about the change, making full investigation of it. (Pavlov, 1927)

Titchener (1924) discussed attention as follows: "Consciousness in attention is patterned or arranged into focus and margin, foreground and background, centre and periphery. And the difference between the processes at the focus and the processes in the margin is, essentially, a difference of clearness: the central area of consciousness lies clear, the more remote regions are obscure. In this fact we have, indeed, the key to the whole problem of attention" (p. 267). However, the issue has not seemed that simple over the 70 years since this definition was rendered.

Skinner (1953) defined attention as a functional relationship between stimuli and responses. Important here was the notion that attention is not a thing, entity, or a mental function but a shorthand term for a set of relations between stimuli or events and responses to them—a correlation, if you will. The correlation varies in strength and is not so important as the determination of the factors of which these correlations are a function. These factors, Skinner seemed to believe, are the same as those determinants of stimulus discrimination and control and, as James also noted, have much to do with the immediate consequences associated with responding to any stimulus and the ontogenetic or learning history of the organism and the phylogenetical history of that species.

Gibson and Rader (1979) later defined attention as "perceiving in relation to a goal, internally or externally motivated" (p. 2). Others have proposed definitions influenced heavily by information processing theories.

And no less an authority on consensual definitions of terms as Merriam-Webster's dictionary (1967) defined attention as "applying the mind to an object of sense or thought" and a "selective narrowing or focusing of consciousness and receptivity" (p. 57).

This brief historical tour was intended only to show that we seem no closer now to a universal, consensual, or operational definition of the construct of attention than did our forebears. It is obvious why many of them abandoned the search for a definition of the general construct and adopted a multidimensional view, about which we will hear more in the chapters to follow. Yet, while the concept of attention has died many deaths, it continues to be sighted again and again in our literature. We are stuck with the notion, as Michael Gordon (personal communication, August 14, 1993) once said, that there is a glue that binds behavior to the environment: This glue we call attention. It is to be found in our responsiveness, broadly construed as both external and internal reactions, to our environment. And, perhaps, it is this general responsiveness or capacity to react that is the best agreement we can currently reach regarding the meaning of the term *attention*.

However, as both James and Titchener wrote, to admit this is to concede that attention incorporates the whole of psychology.

The move from a unidimensional to a multidimensional view represents one of the major trends in theories on attention. As noted above, we will see this in the work of those who follow this chapter. It is a trend that has allowed for greater clarification of terms, specification of measurement, and testability of ideas through experiment. Haunting this trend has been the ghost of method variance, which says that many of the components or factors of attention identified in multimethod studies may reflect as much method variance as real dimensions of attentional performance. Mirsky (Chapter 6) has addressed this problem in his research on the components of attention. More evidence of the kind that he marshals in support of his multidimensional model is to be encouraged.

A second trend, implicit in many efforts to develop theories of attention, has been the borrowing of new metaphors, analogies, or models from other areas of science and technology to guide our model building. Witness the borrowing of the concept of selection by consequences from evolutionary theory in biology in the behavioral views of attention and learning, or the extrapolation of information processing models from the design of computers to comparable models of human nervous system functions. As other areas of science continue to advance, we can expect to see new metaphors appear in our literature, perhaps in attempts to apply chaos theory or punctuated evolutionary theory to the understanding of attention. Such metaphors have always helped us reframe or reconceptualize our understanding of our piece of nature's turf, human behavior, see new relations among findings that previously went unnoticed, and design new studies to test our hypotheses regarding these new relations. They are, however, only metaphors and are therefore only approximations of explanations for the events we study, tools for furthering our explorations of events rather than definitive accounts of the events themselves. Their measure of success is how effectively they serve in guiding our search for understanding the nature of attention before their inevitable abandonment for a better theory or metaphor. This, in part, is what we have attempted to do in this book.

A third detectable trend in our research on attention, as noted earlier in the example from research on ADHD, has been the awareness of lines of convergence among different literatures, the very fact of which is attested to by the aims of this book (Chapter 1). We are all contributors to this book because each of us realizes the significance of recent developments in research on memory and executive functions that are converging on our own models of attention, as well as the potential importance of the points of intersection among different theoretical perspectives.

A fourth trend in our theories of attention has been the tacit recognition that animal, particularly primate, models or analogues of attention, memory, and executive functions, although contributing substantially to our understanding of these processes, have serious limitations as well. For instance, the capacity of humans to utilize rule-governed behavior and turn language on the self, as Hayes,

Gifford, and Ruckstuhl address in Chapter 16, dramatically influences our capacity for sustained attention, response inhibition, executive function, cross-temporal organization of adaptive behavior, and moral development. Using animal models to approximate these aspects of human cognition will prove as unsatisfactory as using primate analogues for building models of the aphasias. The elements of the models are certainly present in primitive forms in other primates, and are instructive in this regard, but will hardly offer complete accounts of the phenomena we wish to study in humans. To go further, we must rely on our uniquely human capacities for imagination and reconstruction, both of which are powerful tools in the realm of our executive functions.

ISSUES AND TRENDS IN THE MEASUREMENT OF ATTENTION

The staggering range of measures used to assess attention has been limited principally by the creativity of the investigators, the available technology, and the particular theoretical models driving the research (Barkley, 1994a). Among the more commonly used measures have been variations on reaction time tasks, continuous performance or vigilance tests, information processing paradigms, particular tests or subgroups of tests from intelligence test batteries, maze completion tests, and, more recently, direct observations of attending behaviors in natural field or analogue settings. Behavior rating scales have also proven ubiquitous, particularly in the study of the attention deficit disorders. What trends might be apparent from a cursory review of the dependent measures being employed in research on attention?

One that will become immediately obvious from Sergeant's chapter (see Chapter 5) has been the refinement of existing measures to permit closer examination and classification of the error patterns evident in traditional tests of attention. The view that response variability in reaction time and vigilance tests may be an important measure, sensitive to aspects of sustained attention or resource allocation, is but one example of this. Previously, the standard deviation of the subject around its own mean across trials on the tasks was viewed as error variance to be averaged out or disregarded entirely. This view has been replaced by the notion that the standard deviation may be as important, or even more important, than the mean of the individual in evaluating certain types of attention, inhibition, or response regulation, or in understanding certain disorders of attention, such as ADHD. Recognition of this situation has encouraged several marketers of commercially available continuous-performance tests (CPTs) intended for use in the clinical evaluation of ADHD children to include such scores in the output of these devices and heavily weigh their interpretation.

Another example has been the elegant work of Halperin, Wolf, Greenblatt, and Young (1991) in breaking down the types of errors demonstrated on the CPT beyond the customary d' and β scores and examining the correlates of these error patterns (see also Chapter 8). Halperin et al. identified four subtypes of commission errors and found that the reaction times associated with them differ significantly. Only some error patterns reflect impulsivity, whereas others do not, explaining some of the inconsistency in past studies attempting to use CPTs to measure response inhibition. On the traditional AX paradigm, where the target for responding is the letter A followed by the letter X, Halperin et al. have demonstrated that A-only and A-not-X error types reflect impulsivity, or the fast-guess definition of impulsivity. X-only errors are more likely to reflect inattention to the letter preceding the X, much as complete omission errors likely reflect inattention. This clarification of response patterns has helped to further clarify the nature of ADHD as a disorder of response inhibition and may help to distinguish this type of attention deficit disorder from those with the disorder who are not hyperactive-impulsive.

In a related vein of measurement advancement, van der Meere and Sergeant (1988a, 1988b, 1988c) have used reaction time tasks and information processing paradigms to study the influence of errors made by the subject on the subsequent responding of these subjects in the next trial. Such studies have helped to demonstrate that typical subjects use this feedback to increase their focus of attention and slow down subsequent responding, whereas subjects with ADHD do not seem to do so.

Progress has also been made in the further study of various aspects of stimulus parameters in laboratory tasks, such as CPTs, to assess their influence on attentional performance and response inhibition. These stimulus factors were reviewed recently by Corkum and Siegel (1993); their review demonstrated that stimulus type, complexity, duration, rate, and sensory modality, as well as overall task length, all influence to some degree the results obtained on the CPT. Similarly, Conners, March, Fiore, and Butcher (1994) have recently shown that variations in the interstimulus interval greatly determine the extent of errors on the CPT and the nature of the effects of stimulant drugs on the CPT performance of children with ADHD. Short interstimulus intervals (ISIs) of up to 2 seconds, which result in faster presentation rates, were much less likely to provide error responses than longer ISIs of 2–4 seconds. Moreover, shorter ISIs did not demonstrate any deleterious effects of high doses of stimulant medication, whereas ISIs over 2 seconds demonstrated a decrease in sensitivity, or d', at these doses. Such studies clearly increase the yield that is possible from traditional measures of attention and lead to a clarification of those variables affecting attentional performance.

Various studies have also examined variations in response formats of CPT tasks on task performance. For instance, traditional CPTs require subjects to withhold responding on most trials and respond only to trials where a particular target stimulus appears. Conners et al. (1994) have reversed this format in their CPT version so that the children respond to every trial but inhibit the response to the target. Similarly, Schachar, Tannock, and Logan (1993) have used a stop-signal paradigm within a reaction time task to create a priming of the subject to respond to each trial. Such priming may increase the sensitivity of the tasks to impulsiveness in the subjects when the target signal appears. Early results suggest that such paradigms may be more sensitive to dose effects of stimulant medication on sustained attention and impulse control and to differences between children with ADHD and those without the disorder. Another creative twist on the response format of a traditional CPT paradigm was the measurement by Shaw and Giambra (1993) of task-unrelated thoughts during CPT performance in college students with and without a history of ADHD. Subjects were randomly prompted to disclose whether or not they were thinking about the CPT task during their CPT performance. The results indicated that adult subjects with a prior history of ADHD reported more task-unrelated thoughts than those without such a history, implying that the disturbance in inhibition does not simply involve motor responding but also cognitive responding. Continued exploration of creative variations on response formats with traditional tasks is to be encouraged, considering the illuminating results of this sample of studies.

Past research has also shown that various parameters of the setting in which the task is performed may also affect attentional performance (Corkum & Siegel, 1993). Whether or not the experimenter stays in the room during the CPT performance, and the nature of the instructions given with the CPT, significantly affect the likelihood of error rates on the task. Such studies suggest that aspects of motivation influence attentional performance as much as the nature of the stimulus and response formats of the task. Likewise, the presence and type of distractors in the setting, and even the time of day, seem to significantly affect task performance. Such a trend to broaden the focus of research from the parameters of the traditional CPTs to the context in which they are given is likely to continue; it will probably enrich our understanding of the impact of the contextual factors on attention.

Converging Trends in Research

The trend for convergence among diverse literatures on the concepts of attention, not to mention memory and executive functions, was noted earlier. This trend has brought with it the recognition that methods used to study these functions in one body of literature, such as developmental psychology, may be fruitful for their study from a different perspective, such as developmental neuropsychology. Welsh and Pennington (1988) made this point in their review of the intersection of these two literatures in the study of prefrontal lobe functions in children, and the same point will be stressed in the study of such executive functions in ADHD (Chapter 17). Developmental psychologists have created variations on the delayed-response task, so well exploited in primate studies of developing brain–behavior relationships, in order to study the development of executive functions in young children. As Welsh and Pennington note, developmental neuropsychologists could likewise benefit from borrowing the procedures in developmental psychology for the study of attention and self-regulation.

Research over the past two decades has greatly expanded our knowledge of how various subject factors influence performance on attention tasks. The sex, age, and IQ of the subjects are important, as are diagnostic grouping, etiology, and site of central nervous system (CNS) injury within neuropsychological studies of clinical populations in determining task performance. There is every reason for this type of research to continue in the future in order to clarify the knowledge of attentional mechanisms and their CNS substrates.

This leads to another inescapable line of research that is sufficiently prolific as to hardly be considered a trend any longer. This is the study of neurological substrates associated with various aspects of attention and inhibition. Early lesion studies with animals, as well as studies of brain injury or surgical lesions in humans, have been part of the armamentarium for the study of neuropsychological functions for over a century. The works of Posner (1988), Mirsky (Chapter 6), and Goldman-Rakic (1987) have yielded a quantum increase in our knowledge of brain mechanisms and sites related to attention and inhibition. In addition to these traditional sources of information, there have been sophisticated psychophysiological measures of brain electrical functioning along with peripheral measures of autonomic functioning, such as heart rate changes and galvanic skin response (GSR) parameters. The more recently developed neuroimaging technologies are producing remarkable discoveries concerning the substrates of attentional components. An example of the application of these modern technologies to the study of attention was the recent study of Rezai and colleagues (Rezai et al., 1993) at the University of Iowa. This study correlated changes in cerebral blood flow, as measured by single photon emission tomography, with simultaneous performance on a CPT, the Tower of London task, the Wisconsin Card Sorting Test (WCST) (Heaton, Chelune, Talley, Kay, & Curtiss, 1993) and the Porteus mazes (Porteus, 1965). Different regions of the frontal cortex were found to be activated during different tasks: CPT and Tower of London performance were most closely associated with bilateral mesial region activation, whereas performance on the WCST was associated with left dorsolateral activation. Advances within these technologies, such as the recent addition of fast-MRI (magnetic resonance imaging) capability to many regional medical centers, are likely to only further our appreciation of CNS correlates of the components of attention and inhibition.

In the 1990s, we have begun to witness studies on the genetic contributions to attentional performance. A number of studies have demonstrated a remarkable degree of heritability for the disorder of ADHD (Barkley, 1990), with ratios of genetic to environmental influences on variation in this behavior pattern ranging from 5:1 to 12:1, depending on the study methods and populations evaluated. Similarly, Brandt and colleagues (Brandt et al., 1993) at Johns Hopkins University have shown that, among four cognitive factors they assessed, the factor comprised of language/attention items had the highest degree of heritability among nearly 4,500 twin pairs examined in the study. This trend of studying the genetic contributions to attentional performance will most certainly continue.

There has also been increasing acknowledgment of the limitations of laboratory-type tasks and paradigms for the study of attention and related functions. The utility and ecological validity of many of the traditional laboratory measures of attention (i.e., how well they relate to or predict attentional performance in natural settings, such as classroom academic performance) has recently been challenged (Barkley, 1992; Barkley, Grodzinsky, & DuPaul, 1992). Our reviews found that making direct behavioral observations of children while they perform laboratory tasks may greatly augment the generalizability of the results to more natural settings, as may the use of repeated administrations of these laboratory tests or test batteries. Making such behavioral observations in the natural settings of children may be even more satisfactory, as it eliminates any leaps of inference that must be made from the laboratory to the natural setting when laboratory measures are employed. The strong trend toward incorporating such observational procedures in research on children with ADHD is to be encouraged in studies of attention in other populations as well (Barkley, 1994a).

Related to the issue of using direct observations as measures of attentional performance have been the recent creative uses of more natural tasks for the study of attention. The vast majority of us are not required to sit around performing CPT-like tasks in our daily occupations or lives, and so our performance on such tasks may reflect poorly or not at all on how well we attend to events in our everyday world. Recognizing this, several investigators have been using procedures such as television viewing, performance of classroom tasks, video games, and driving performance as means of studying attention and its deficits in various groups of children and young adults. Although often more time consuming and expensive to utilize than traditional laboratory tasks, such procedures employ more ecologically valid methods for evaluating attention that may yield greater generality of their results as a consequence.

No doubt there are many other trends that can be discerned in the literature on measuring the components of attention and the factors affecting them. From the appearance of those trends elucidated here, however, the study of attention is likely to remain vigorous despite the problems with definitions and theory building discussed earlier. It is the aim of the second section of this book to reduce some of these definitional and theoretical problems while seeking convergence in the paradigms now driving the study of attention.

REFERENCES

Barkley, R.A. (1990). *Attention deficit hyperactivity disorder: A handbook for diagnosis and treatment.* New York: Guilford Press.

Barkley, R.A. (1992). The ecological validity of laboratory and analogue assessment methods of ADHD symptoms. *Journal of Abnormal Child Psychology, 19,* 149–178.

Barkley, R.A. (1994a). The assessment of attention in children. In G.R. Lyon (Ed.), *Frames of reference for the assessment of learning disabilities: New views on measurement issues* (pp. 69–102). Baltimore: Paul H. Brookes Publishing Co.

Barkley, R.A. (1994b). Delayed responding and attention deficit hyperactivity disorder: Toward a unified theory. In D.K. Routh (Ed.), *Disruptive behavior disorders in children: Essays in honor of Herbert Quay* (pp. 11–57). New York: Plenum.

Barkley, R.A., Grodzinsky, G., & DuPaul, G. (1992). Frontal lobe functions in attention deficit disorder with and without hyperactivity: A review and research report. *Journal of Abnormal Child Psychology, 20,* 163–188.

Brandt, J., Welsh, K., Breitner, C., Folstein, M., Helms, M., & Christian, J. (1993). Hereditary influences on cognitive functioning in older men. *Archives of Neurology, 50,* 599–603.

Bronowski, J. (1977). Human and animal languages. In J. Bronowski (Ed.), *A sense of the future* (pp. 104–131). Cambridge, MA: MIT Press.

Conners, C.K., March, J.S., Fiore, C., & Butcher, T. (1994). *Information processing deficits in ADHD: Effect of stimulus rate and methylphenidate.* Unpublished paper, Duke University, Durham, NC.

Cooley, E.I., & Morris, R.D. (1990). Attention in children: A neuropsychologically based model for assessment. *Developmental Neuropsychology, 6,* 239–274.

Corkum, P.V., & Siegel, L.S. (1993). Is the continuous performance task a valuable research tool for use with children with attention-deficit-hyperactivity disorder? *Journal of Child Psychology and Psychiatry, 34,* 1217–1239.

Fuster, J.M. (1989). A theory of prefrontal functions: The prefrontal cortex and the temporal organization of behavior. In J.M. Fuster (Ed.), *The prefrontal cortex: Anatomy, physiology, and neuropsychology of the frontal lobe* (pp. 157–196). New York: Raven Press.

Gibson, E., & Rader, N. (1979). Attention: Perceiver as performer. In G. Hale & M. Lewis (Eds.), *Attention and cognitive development* (pp. 1–22). New York: Plenum.

Goldman-Rakic, P.S. (1987). Development of cortical circuitry and cognitive function. *Child Development, 58,* 601–622.

Halperin, J.M., Wolf, L., Greenblatt, E.R., & Young, G. (1991). Subtype analysis of commission errors on the continuous performance test in children. *Developmental Neuropsychology, 7,* 207–217.

Heaton, R.K., Chelune, G.J., Talley, J.L., Kay, G.G., & Curtiss, G. (1993). *Wisconsin Card Sorting Test manual: Revised and updated.* Odessa, FL: Psychological Assessment Resources.

James, W. (1898). *Principles of psychology.* Chicago: University of Chicago (Britannica Great Books).

Merriam-Webster (1967). *Webster's Seventh New Collegiate Dictionary.* Chicago: G & C. Merriam and Co.

Pavlov, I.P. (1927). *Conditioned reflexes.* Oxford: Oxford University Press.

Porteus, S.D. (1965). *Porteus mazes.* San Antonio, TX: Psychological Corporation.

Posner, M. (1988). Structures and function of selective attention. In M. Dennis, E. Kaplan, M. Posner, D. Stein, & R. Thompson (Eds.), *Clinical neuropsychology and brain function: Research, measurement, and practice* (pp. 169–201). Washington, DC: American Psychological Association.

Rezai, K., Andreasen, N., Alliger, R., Cohen, G., Swayze, V., & O'Leary, D.S. (1993). The neuropsychology of the prefrontal cortex. *Archives of Neurology, 50,* 636–642.

Schachar, R.J., Tannock, R., & Logan, G. (1993). Inhibitory control, impulsiveness, and attention deficit hyperactivity disorder. *Clinical Psychology Review, 13,* 721–739.

Shaw, G.A., & Giambra, L. (1993). Task-unrelated thoughts of college students diagnosed as hyperactive in childhood. *Developmental Neuropsychology, 9,* 17–30.

Skinner, B.F. (1953). *Science and human behavior.* New York: Macmillan.

Titchener, E.B. (1924). *A textbook of psychology.* New York: Macmillan.

van der Meere, J., & Sergeant, J. (1988a). Focused attention in pervasively hyperactive children. *Journal of Abnormal Child Psychology, 16,* 627–640.

van der Meere, J., & Sergeant, J. (1988b). Controlled processing and vigilance in hyperactivity: Time will tell. *Journal of Abnormal Child Psychology, 16,* 641–656.

van der Meere, J., & Sergeant, J. (1988c). Acquisition of attention skill in pervasively hyperactive children. *Journal of Child Psychology and Psychiatry, 29,* 301–310.

Welsh, M.C., & Pennington, B.F. (1988). Assessing frontal lobe functioning in children:
Views from developmental psychology. *Developmental Neuropsychology, 4,* 199–230.

5

A THEORY OF ATTENTION
An Information Processing Perspective

Joseph Sergeant

This chapter provides a brief description of the concept of attention and its application to developmental psychopathology. It is intended to provide an initial introduction on the subject with a view to stimulating research in developmental psychopathology. It should be clear from the outset that the term *attention* is a multidimensional concept involving both cognitive and psychophysiological variables (see Chapter 4). It is an area that has received considerable research effort as part of the cognitive revival, as can be witnessed in the large number of series and journals dedicated to this concept.

Viewed simply from an information processing point of view, one might illustrate the diversity of attentional constructs by distinguishing selective from sustained attention. Selection may be said to focus attention at a particular point in contrast to dividing attention between two simultaneous inputs. Sustained attention is the (in)ability of the subject to maintain performance over time. These terms give some indication of the variety of usages of the term *attention*.

The intention here is to limit the scope of this construct. The functions associated with attention are presented in this chapter within the context of a cognitive-energetic model of information processing. Attention, as will become apparent, cannot be separated from memory, since the definition of selective attention used here places the locus of the attention limitation in working memory. Similarly, the control functions associated with the cognitive-energetic model are exactly those that are attributed to executive functions. Hence, the constructs that are the primary concern of this book are interrelated and cannot be considered as "pure" constructs or as independent from one another. It may be useful to sketch briefly some historical factors that have influenced current conceptions of attention.

BRIEF HISTORICAL REVIEW

Interest in attention began with von Helmholtz (1850), who considered that attention was concerned with *where* processing should be directed. This contrasted with James (1890), who considered that the function of attention was to answer "*what* has to be processed." Both of these positions have their merits and may be considered as complementary. Another traditional use of attention is that of the "attentional set" of a person, which means attending either to a specific cluster of incoming stimuli or to a subset of response alternatives (Lange, 1888). This is often associated with the use of attention as a means for preparing the subject for a specific reaction. Early European research into attention was concerned with the psychophysical properties of the information processing system. The Dutch physiologist Donders (1868) argued that it was possible to measure the rate of attentional processes by using reaction time. He proposed that, by measuring the reaction time to one task variable and then subtracting this time from the time required to process a second task variable, it would be possible to infer the duration of the added task variable. This was called the subtractive method. This method was soundly criticised by Wordsworth (1938), and the use of reaction time to discover mental processes fell into disrepute for a period of time. This state of affairs changed when Sternberg (1969) proposed that the rate of information processing could be determined by using the additive factor method (AFM), described in detail below. At this point, another historical influence should be noted.

Broadbent (1958, 1971) argued that the purpose of selective attention was to enable the system to overcome its limitations in capacity: "Selection takes place in order to protect a mechanism of limited capacity." This structural assumption was that the capacity of human information processing was inherently limited. In order to protect the limited capacity system from being overloaded, it was postulated that there was a filter, which protected the central processing mechanism from overload. Broadbent placed the filter immediately before the system of limited capacity. Broadbent (1971) reviewed the literature on attentional processing and concluded that there was a body of evidence suggesting that selection occurs at the input side and that a second cluster of studies indicated that some stimuli could be fully processed by the system of limited capacity and that selection occurs at the response side of the system. Thus, the "early" selection hypothesis was enlarged to incorporate the "late" selection hypothesis proposed by Deutsch and Deutsch (1963). A third hypothesis is that selection is required because of the *rate* at which information could be processed in working memory, which is essentially the system of limited capacity (Shiffrin & Schneider, 1977). More recently, Allport (1990) has argued that selectivity should not be related to a discussion of the locus and limitations of human capacity, since from a connectionist point of view the information contained in long-term memory is virtually limitless. Connectionists suggest that selectivity should be associated with how information is weighted and switched between processes or given a priority. In this sense, the selection function of attention is associated with planning and control of behavior. This view contrasts with the more structural view of selective attention. These functions are generally associated with what in neuropsychology is thought to be the executive functions of the frontal lobes (see Section IV).

A neuropsychological approach to attention was emphasised by Hebb (1949), who stressed that human behavior is organized, coordinated, and planned. Hebb associated attentional functions with the neurophysiology of the human system known at that time. In addition, Hebb emphasized the role of physiological activation of the human organism, which was considered to play an important role in the regulation of behavior. This theme will be returned to later under the topic of cognitive energetics.

From this brief historical review, it is evident that the term *attention* has had a checkered career and, in all probability, will continue to have one. What is required at this point is not so much a discussion of the pros and cons of the various definitions of attention but rather an understanding of how attention may be operationalized and measured.

OPERATIONALIZATIONS OF ATTENTION

Attention is, as already noted, a multidimensional construct. It can be measured at various levels of inquiry: ethological, cognitive, psychophysiological, and biochemical. Here the operationalizations of attention will be limited to two levels: the cognitive and the psychophysiological. The cognitive approach has emphasized the processes that operate between stimulus input and response output. Information processing models of human cognition postulate three general stages:

ENCODING   CENTRAL PROCESSING   RESPONSE ORGANIZATION

This postulation is not new. What *is* new is the method by which psychologists have been able to operationalize these stages and develop a taxonomy of task variables that may be associated with these stages. This method is the additive factor method (AFM), first outlined by Sternberg (1969). He suggested that, in contrast to Donders (1868), it would be possible to discover the stages of information processing by examining how task variables were independent or interactive. The AFM states that when two task variables are found to be statistically independent they are operating upon two independent stages of processing. If two task variables are found to significantly interact, it is said that they are acting upon a common stage. Sternberg (1975) reviewed the evidence for this assumption and marshalled a considerable body of evidence in its support. Nevertheless, exceptions to the taxonomy of task variables were found (Sanders, 1977). The taxonomy of task variables is briefly outlined in Table 5.1. For fuller accounts of task variables and their relation to processing stages, the reader is referred to Sanders (1977, 1983).

As indicated in Table 5.1., encoding is generally examined by variables such as stimulus intact versus stimulus degradation. Reaction time and errors are measured in both conditions, and the extra time required to process the degraded stimuli compared with the intact stimuli is used as a measure of encoding. A higher form of encoding involves the reaction time to words requiring the meaning to be used as the basis of a decision. Memory search and display search are

Table 5.1. A brief taxonomy of task variables

Encoding	Central processing	Response organization
	Processing Load:	
Feature extraction	Memory search	Motor adjustment
Signal quality: Stimulus intact Stimulus degraded	Display search	Muscle tension
Signal intensity	Stimulus similarity	
Semantic association	Stimulus evaluation Context updating Decision making	Foreperiod S-R frequency S-R compatibility/incompatibility Time uncertainty More decision time

manipulated by the number of items that the subject is required to retain in memory or the number of items on a display. *Processing load* is the product of both memory and display load. *Decision making* is the time required to place items in one set rather than another. Motor organization was classically measured by making response output more difficult (muscular exertion) or increasing the number of response choices (e.g., from two to four). *Motor decision time* (also called response or motor selection) is the difference in reaction time for responses that are isomorphic to the stimulus (stimulus left side–response left side; stimulus right side–response right side) compared with reaction time to the reversal (stimulus left–right response). This manipulation is referred to as stimulus-response compatibility. Another task variable used to examine the motor output side of the system is response preparation. Response preparation involves varying the period of time between warning a subject that an imperative signal is about to appear and the actual time that the imperative signal appears. This period is known as the foreperiod. Preparation can also be manipulated by using a constant foreperiod and giving the warning stimulus a signal function.

When two task variables that operate on the same stage of processing are used in a study, the prediction is that an interaction between them will be found. Variables chosen from two separate stages should never show a significant interaction. Hence, experimenters can assess whether their manipulations operate according to the assumptions of the AFM. The primary dependent variable used in the AFM is reaction time. Stage duration is estimated not only by the partitioning of means of reaction time but also by examining the variance of reaction times associated with the task variables.

The AFM makes specific predictions of how reaction times should be related to errors. It is obvious that task errors will be made when subjects are required to process the information as quickly as possible. Pachella (1974) pointed out that the stage model assumes that speed is not traded for accuracy. If this were the case, the measure of processing, reaction time, would be confounded with accuracy. The opposite situation, in which the subject makes no errors, is also undesirable. If no errors were made in a task, it would be disputable whether the subject had worked as fast as possible and thus whether reaction time measured the processing time. These two situations (known as macro-tradeoffs) can be detected by inspecting the data. No errors indicate a reflective strategy; the data cannot be corrected for this strategy. When errors are made and the correlation between frequency of errors and correct reaction times is negative, accuracy has been traded for speed. This can be corrected by predicting accurate reaction times from the error rates of the subject, using regression analysis. Should errors and correct reaction times be correlated positively, then the attentional task variable may be said to have operated both on the speed and the quality of processing. This requires no further data treatment prior to analysis.

The AFM has generated, among other things, considerable interest in psychophysiology. This has led to the development of cognitive psychophysiology and the cognitive-energetic model, which has replaced the cold cognitions of the information processor's black box. However, at this stage, the reader may be wondering how the thinking behind the AFM is related to attention. This is covered in the following sections on selective and sustained attention.

Selective Attention

The link between the AFM approach and selective attention was inherently present in the assumption that reaction time could be manipulated by well-defined task variables, in that selective attention refers to selective processing of information. However, this only became explicit following the publications of Schneider and Shiffrin (1977) and Shiffrin and Schneider (1977). They distinguished between controlled and automatic information processing. The former was characterized as being capacity limited, serial, and effortful. The latter was described as unlimited, parallel, and effortless. The controlled/automatic distinction has been criticized (see, among others, Ryan, 1983). These authors proposed that selective attention was required because human capacity was limited in the *rate* at which processing could occur. Hence, they localized selective attention effects in working memory. They further distinguished between two types of selective attention deficits: divided attention deficits and focused attention deficits. Divided attention deficits occurred when the system was unable to allocate resources to multiple simultaneous inputs. Focused attention deficits appeared when the subject, although fully knowing what was required to be processed, allocated processing resources to irrelevant stimuli. These two deficits were operationalized in visual search tasks of the type described above. An important contribution by Schneider and Shiffrin (1977) was to give quantitative indications of the processing time for divided attention and the variances associated with a divided attention deficit. The resource model stands in contrast to this structural model of selective attention.

The resource model of selective attention conceives attention as a general pool of energy that is limited but can be distributed over simultaneous demands (Gopher & Navon, 1980; Norman & Bobrow, 1975; Wickens, 1984). This model emphasizes the concept of concentration. Tasks require effort for them to be performed, and resources are allocated according to the demands that they place upon the central resource pool. Priority assignment to and between tasks, their planning, and their coordination have become recognized as important functions of the attentional system. This is sometimes referred to as *economy of processing* (Gopher & Navon, 1980). The type of task used to study attentional processing from this point of view has been the dual task. In the late 1970s, a somewhat simple conception of double tasks existed: Merely requiring the subject to process two tasks simultaneously was thought to be a valid procedure. The idea was that one could give the subject a primary task and measure the processing requirements of this task. A secondary task required that the remaining resources be allocated to process this task. An example of this methodology was presented by Posner and Boies (1971). In the probe task, the subject was given a primary task in which cognitive load was exerted. In addition to the primary task, the subject was required to respond to a simple tone. This probe was administered at various points before, during, and after the primary task stimulus was administered. Obviously, when the probe was heard prior to or after the stimulus, reaction time to the probe was fast. When the probe was administered immediately before or during the primary task stimulus, reaction time was slowed considerably. The experimenter could then plot the reaction time to the various probe administrations and observe the diminishment of resource allocation to the secondary probe. This was considered to be a measure of processing capacity.

In the 1980s, several comments appeared on the validity of dual tasks. The first concerned whether the subject perceived the tasks as two separate tasks or managed the two tasks in such a way that they were handled as one large task. The ability of the subject to use a time-sharing strategy might influence results. A second concern was whether the primary task was considered by the subject as primary. It was conceivable that the subject assigned priorities to the task other than those the experimenter thought had been assigned. A third issue arose out of neuropsychological research. It was pointed out that careful selection of tasks was required for dual tasks: Lateral specialization of the brain for verbal and spatial tasks might favor parallel processing without interference (a verbal and nonverbal task), whereas two verbal or two nonverbal tasks would have greater interference due to shared neuropsychological structures (Shallice, 1988).

Gopher and Navon (1980) argued that the dual task methodology could be substantially improved by studying the tradeoff between two tasks. They proposed that the experimenter instruct subjects so that the priority given to one task be manipulated, holding the second task constant. Following manipulation of the priority to the first task, the priority given to the second task was varied and the first task held constant. By plotting the performance to the first and second tasks at various levels of priority, it is possible to see a curve of resource allocation to the two tasks.

The resource model has added priority allocation as one of the functions in the list associated with attention. Clearly, this is a sense of the word *attention* different from either concentration or energetic allocation. Priority allocation and control has a much more managerial function. In this sense, attention becomes intimately associated with executive functioning. In order for confusion not to arise in the field, it will be necessary for researchers to state very clearly their definition and operationalization of the term. The following section briefly examines the sustainment of attention.

Sustained Attention

Vigilance research began with the study of the decline in performance of radar operators over time. The two vigilance measures, perceptual sensitivity (d') and response bias (β), can be plotted over time. Decline in perceptual sensitivity with time-on-task is the classic index of a failure in sustained attention (Warm, 1984). Many clinical researchers have used only the false-positive rate as a measure of sustained attention. This is in fact an incorrect procedure, because the false-positive rate in itself may be the product of either perceptual sensitivity or response bias. Therefore, no conclusions can be drawn *solely* on the basis of the false-positive rate. Similarly, a false positive cannot be considered as a measure of impulsivity without inspection of the latency of such a response (Halperin et al., 1988). Depending upon which model of attention one is using, it might be argued that false negatives (failures to detect targets) have more validity as indices of failures of attention. However, this argument suffers from the same objection noted above concerning use of only false positives. It is, consequently, of considerable importance to the field of experimental psychopathology that the correct measures be used and their analysis over time reported to establish sustained attention effects.

An alternative approach to sustained attention has been proposed within the controlled/automatic distinction. A sustained attention deficit has been defined as a decline in controlled processing over time (Fisk & Schneider, 1981). Thus, these authors conceive of sustained attention as a skill of maintaining controlled processing performance over time. From this point of view, increases in the slope functions for divided attention over time would be evidence of a sustained attention deficit.

Since every task administered must be performed over time, it is inevitable that a potential confound for a divided or focused attention task could be a sustained attention deficit. In other words, group interactions with the task thought to measure divided or focused attention could actually reflect differences in sustained attention. Unfortunately, the separation of the sustained attention effect from the selective attention demands is seldom reported. If claims of selective attention effects are to be sustained, experimenters need to examine the sustained attention effect and partial this out from any selective attention effects. This procedure is needed if more than lip service is to be paid to the multidimensional character of attention.

Cognitive Energetics

The black box model of information processing became energized with the introduction of the concept of *effort* by Kahneman (1973). *Effort* was conceived of as the energy needed to meet the demands of a task. This concept was used by Pribram and McGuiness (1975) as one of three energetic pools—arousal, activation, and effort. *Arousal* was associated with the mesencephalon, reticular formation, and the amygdala. Arousal was specifically associated with phasic responding and is time-locked to a stimulus. The activation pool was identified with the basal ganglia and corpus striatum. Tonic changes of physiological activity were thought to represent the operation of the *activation* pool. The *effort* pool was identified with the hippocampus. Kahneman originally proposed that effort was best measured by pupil dilation: the greater the dilation, the more effort applied to the task. Later work by psychophysiologists has suggested that heart rate deceleration, respiratory sinus arrhythmia, and event-related desynchronization (ERD) may reflect the operation of this pool. These constructs are *state* concepts; that is, they reflect the energy or activity of the processing system. They do not refer to a structural process such as encoding or memory search. They describe the current state or energy that is allocated to meet a task or that is the result of drug administration or a stressor such as sleep deprivation or noise. It is evident that state concepts are amenable to psychophysiological investigation and relevant to clinical research.

Sanders (1983) reviewed the performance literature and related task variables of the AFM type to these three energetic pools. Typical variables that influence arousal are signal intensity and signal novelty (i.e., orienting). Activation was suggested to be affected by task variables such as preparation, alertness (sleep state), time-of-day, and time-on-task. Variables such as cognitive load affected effort. Sanders assigned to effort the function of both exciting and inhibiting the other two energetic pools. Specifically, effort was said to be required when the current state of the organism did not meet the state required to perform a task.

Sanders also argued that encoding affected the arousal pool and that motor factors affected the activation pool. The stage model described earlier was thus specifically related to the three energetic pools. Two important indices of the arousal and activation pools were the vigilance measures perceptual sensitivity (d') and response bias (β). The former was argued to be a measure of arousal and the latter of the activation pool. The interested reader is referred to the original paper for a full review of the evidence supporting this part of the model.

In response to earlier findings in vigilance research, the cognitive-energetic model was designed by Sanders to include a management or evaluation mechanism. Vigilance researchers had shown that knowledge of results enabled the subject to adjust and improve performance. Rabbitt (1982) showed that correction of errors took place more quickly than normal correct responding. Furthermore, the detection of an error by the subject had the effect that, on the following trial, the subject took more time to ensure that a correct response was made (Rabbitt & Rodgers, 1977). The addition of a management component to the model placed the cognitive-energetic model squarely in the class of top-down models. This feature made it a much more interesting model for experimental psychopathologists than the structural models because control was not adequately localized in such models. The management component immediately made it possible for neuropsychological studies of attentional processing to be related to traditional cognitive information processing (Kinsbourne & Hicks, 1978). This paved the way for neuropsychologists to relate the functioning of the brain to information processing (Shallice, 1988) and selective attention (Posner, Inhoff, Friedrich, & Cohen, 1987). The relation between neuropsychological concepts such as executive functioning and memory are treated elsewhere in this volume (see Section IV). This work reflects the degree of integration that is gradually appearing in psychology in the current decade.

More recently, the ability to inhibit responding (Logan, 1980) has been recognized as an important function of the information processing system. These functions may be attributed to the management stage placed in the upper section of the energetic model. As the reader will appreciate, the addition of a management function to the cognitive-energetic model makes the model a top-down one in which control passes from the upper to the lower levels. This is in contrast to the stage model, which is a data-driven model. The resource model of attention strongly contrasts with the stage model and AFM approach to attention.

Because clinical research necessarily involves work with psychopharmacological substances, a model of attention that incorporates drug effects has a considerable heuristic advantage. The cognitive-energetic model offers some indications of the locus of the effects of drugs. Frowein (1981) published a thesis in which the logic of the AFM was used to suggest with which task variables barbiturates and amphetamines interacted. The logic was the same as described earlier. If a drug was found to be independent of a task variable, it is said that the task variable and drug operated on different stages of processing. Should the task variable and drug interact, it is said that they operated upon a common stage. Frowein showed a highly consistent pattern of interactions for both barbiturates and amphetamines. Barbiturates were shown to interact with task variables whose locus was at the encoding stage. Amphetamines were demonstrated to act with task variables that operated upon the motor organization stage. Subsequent research by Klorman and colleagues has shown that a widely used amphetamine, ritalin, has its locus between central processing and response selection (Brumaghim, Klorman, Strauss, Lewine, & Goldstein, 1987). Global attention enhancement effects can therefore become specifically localized. This is clearly a considerable advantage in specificity. It further enables predictions at both a psychophysiological and psychopharmacological level to be made with a greater degree of differentiation. This in turn can assist in improving the chance of discovering supportive evidence from other convergent operations.

DEVELOPMENT AND ATTENTION

It is evident from this brief review that there are a wide variety of usages and operationalizations of the term *attention*. This diversity may be considered an unworkable situation; or it may be considered a fact of life that adds greater validity to psychological inquiry. At this point it may be useful to make a few general remarks with respect to the application of attention in clinical child psychopathology.

The first concerns the issue of development. Sergeant and Mulder (1979) reviewed studies using memory search paradigms in typical and atypical children. They concluded that the overall difference between such children was located at the encoding or motor stage of processing. Similarly, Enns and Cameron (1987) reported that the search slopes for typical children age 4–7 years were parallel, suggesting that in that age range no difference in search rate could be found. However, clear slope differences could be discerned in that study between children and adults. This suggests that rate differences change with development early and reach an asymptote. Kail (1990) calculated the processing slopes for mental addition, mental rotation, name retrieval, visual search, memory search, and addition for individuals age 8 to 22 years. He showed that there was a change in the rate of processing between ages 8 and 12, the degree of which was greatest for mental addition. Between ages 12 and 22, there were virtually no differences for any type of processing. These results suggest that the magnitude of change in cognitive functioning is greatest at stages of processing associated with reaction time intercept (i.e., encoding and/or motor functioning). Differences at central processing are small, rapidly disappear with development, and may be associated with processing such as mental arithmetic that require greater effort.

These results suggest that developmental psychopathologists should be careful concerning which cognitive processes may be "late" or "ripe." The differences in central processes between adults and children is rather small and only significant because of the small variation in these processes. The greatest differences are to be found at the input and output stages. Consequently, assessment of developmental effects could be better directed toward these stages.

A critical problem for the application of attentional tasks to childhood disorders is the lack of good psychometric data for a large number of the tasks used by cognitive psychologists. An urgent point for the research agenda is the establishment of norms for these tasks (see Lyon, 1994). Until such norms become available clinical practice will be forced to resort to psychometrical tests.

The traditional psychometric test, although often available with norms for specific populations, has another type of disadvantage. Tests have two products: latency and errors. As will be appreciated following the above review, these products can be the output of a wide variety of processes. They may be the result of a speed–accuracy tradeoff. This makes the use of classic tests a hazardous undertaking in making statements on attention. It will be necessary for psychometricians to reevaluate tests with these objections in mind before they may be considered valid indices of attention.

The event rate of a task can also have profound effects upon task performance. The event rate is the speed at which signals are presented within a given period of time. Posner (1978) argued that the event rate influenced two systems. A slow event rate leads to poorer motor preparation and alertness, whereas a fast event rate leads to declines in arousal (van Winsum, Sergeant, & Guze, 1984). More critical for the stage analysis of reaction time is the fact that manipulation of event rate induces a strategy effect (van der Meere, Vreeling, & Sergeant, 1992). Consequently, differences between studies using attentional tasks may not reflect simply a process effect but a strategy difference or energetic effect (or combination of both). Differences between studies may be more apparent than real.

It is important not to simply take attentional paradigms and apply them without careful evaluation of the pathology for which they are being purported to measure. Furthermore, merely to contrast a clinical group with a control group and discover group differences on a task adds no information to the fact that the groups were known to differ in the first instance. The objective of attentional research is to *explain* what the differences are between such groups. This requires that differentiation of effects be established in order to be specific about which deficits are associated with which groups. In this way, a taxonomy of task deficits can be established with some degree of specificity.

CONCLUSIONS

This paper briefly reviewed the variety of terms used in the information processing approach to attention. It traced the development of models of attention and indicated the diversity of associated views found in the literature. From the point of view of developmental psychopathology, the current models have not been designed to account for developmental processes or psychopathological functioning. This is not a failure on the part of cognitive psychologists, but a lacuna that has to be filled in by developmental psychopathologists. The area described here is rich in its constructs, has well-developed operationalizations, and can be shown to have relations with neuropsychological and psychophysiological functioning. The details of these relations have yet to be provided, but the rough sketch is present in the current literature. Developmental psychopathologists must begin to integrate this work within their own area. Attention, although a concept that can mean all things to all people, is a fruitful one for further study.

REFERENCES

Allport, A. (1990). Visual attention. In M. Posner (Ed.), *Foundations of cognitive science* (pp. 631–682). Cambridge, MA: MIT Press.

Broadbent, D.E. (1958). *Perception and communication.* London: Pergamon Press.

Broadbent, D.E. (1971). *Decision and stress.* New York: Academic Press.

Brumaghim, J.T., Klorman, R., Strauss, J., Lewine, J.D., & Goldstein, M.G. (1987). Does methylphenidate affect information processing? Findings from two studies on performance and P3b latency. *Psychophysiology, 24,* 361–373.

Deutsch, J.A., & Deutsch, D. (1963). Attention: Some theoretical considerations. *Psychological Review, 70,* 80–90.

Donders, F.C. (1868). Die Schnelligkeit psychische Prozesse. *Archiv für Anatomie und Physiologie, 8,* 657–681.

Enns, J.T., & Cameron, S. (1987) . Selective attention in young children: The relations between visual search, filtering, and priming. *Journal of Experimental Child Psychology, 44*, 38–63.

Fisk, A.D., & Schneider, W. (1981). Control and automatic processing during tasks requiring sustained attention. *Human Factors, 23*, 737–750.

Frowein, H.W. (1981). *Selective drug effects on information processing.* Enschede: Sneldruk Boulevard.

Gopher, D., & Navon, D. (1980). How is performance limited: Testing the notion of central capacity. *Acta Psychologica, 46*, 161–180.

Halperin, J.M., Wolf, L.E., Pascualvaca, D.M., Newcorn, J.H., Healey, J.M., O'Brien, J.D., Morganstein, A., & Young, J.G. (1988). Differential assessment of attention and impulsivity in children. *Journal of the American Academy of Child and Adolescent Psychiatry, 27*, 326–329.

Hebb, D.O. (1949). *Organisation of behavior.* New York: John Wiley & Sons.

Helmholtz von, H. (1850). Messungen über den zeitlichen Verlauf der Zuckung animalischer Muskeln und die Fortpflanzungsgeschwindigkeit der Reizung in den Nerven. *Archiv für Anatomie, Physiologie und Wissenschaftliche Medicin*, 276–364.

James, W. (1890). *The principles of psychology.* London: Dover.

Kahneman, D. (1973). *Attention and effort.* Englewood Cliffs, NJ: Prentice Hall.

Kail, R. (1990). More evidence for a common, central constraint on speed of processing. In J.T. Enns (Ed.), *The development of attention: Research and theory* (pp. 159–173). Amsterdam: Elsevier.

Kinsbourne, M., & Hicks, R.E. (1978). Functional cerebral space: A model for overflow, transfer and interference effects in human performance. A tutorial review. In J. Requin (Ed.), *Attention and performance VII* (pp. 345–362). Hillsdale, NJ: Lawrence Erlbaum Associates.

Lange, L. (1888). Neue Experimente über den Vorgang der Einfachen Reaction auf Sinneseindrüke. *Philosophische Studien, 4*, 479–510.

Logan, G.D. (1980). Short-term memory demands of reaction-time tasks that differ in complexity. *Journal of Experimental Psychology: Human Perception and Performance, 6*, 375–389.

Lyon, G.R. (Ed.). (1994). *Frames of reference for the assessment of learning disabilities: New views on measurement issues.* Baltimore: Paul H. Brookes Publishing Co.

Norman, D.A., & Bobrow, D.G. (1975). On data-limited and resource-limited processes. *Cognitive Psychology, 7*, 44–64.

Pachella, R.G. (1974). The interpretation of reaction time in information processing research. In B. Kantowitz (Ed.), *Human information processing: Tutorial in performance and recognition* (pp. 41–82). Hillsdale, NJ: Lawrence Erlbaum Associates.

Posner, M.I. (1978). *Chronometric explorations of mind.* Hillsdale, NJ: Lawrence Erlbaum Associates.

Posner, M.I., & Boies, S.J. (1971). Components of attention. *Psychological Review, 78*, 391–408.

Posner, M.I., Inhoff, A.W., Friedrich, F.J., & Cohen, A. (1987). Isolating attentional systems: A cognitive-anatomical analysis. *Psychobiology, 15*, 107–121.

Pribram, K.H., & McGuiness, D. (1975). Arousal, activation and effort in the control of attention. *Psychological Review, 82*, 116–149.

Rabbitt, P.M.A. (1982). Sequential reactions. In D. Holding (Ed.), *Human skills* (pp. 153–174). London: John Wiley & Sons.

Rabbitt, P., & Rodgers, B. (1977). What does a man do after he makes an error: An analysis of response programming. *Quarterly Journal of Experimental Psychology, 29*, 727–743.

Ryan, C. (1983). Reassessing the automaticity-control distinction: Item recognition as a paradigm case. *Psychological Review, 90,* 171–178.

Sanders, A.F. (1977). Structural and functional aspects of the reaction process. In S. Dornic (Ed.), *Attention and performance VI* (pp. 3–25). Hillsdale, NJ: Lawrence Erlbaum Associates.

Sanders, A.F. (1983). Towards a model of stress and performance. *Acta Psychologica, 53,* 61-97.

Schneider, W., & Shiffrin, R.M. (1977). Controlled and automatic human information processing: I. *Psychological Review, 84,* 1–66.

Sergeant, J., & Mulder, G. (1979). Psychofysiologische aspecten van de cognitieve ontwikkeling. (Psychophysiological aspects of cognitive development.) In W. Koops & J.J. van der Werf (Eds.), *Overzicht van de ontwikkelingspsychologie* (pp. 63–89). Groningen: Wolters Nordhoff.

Shallice, T. (1988). *From neuropsychology to mental structure.* Cambridge: Cambridge University Press.

Shiffrin, R.M., & Schneider, W. (1977). Controlled and automatic human information processing: II. Perceptual learning, automatic attending, and a general theory. *Psychological Review, 84,* 127–190.

Sternberg, S. (1969). Discovery of processing stages: Extensions of Donders' method. In W.G. Koster (Ed.), *Attention and performance II* (pp. 276–315). Amsterdam: North Holland.

Sternberg, S. (1975). Memory scanning: New findings and current controversies. *Quarterly Journal of Experimental Psychology, 27,* 1–32.

van der Meere, J.J., Vreeling, H.J., & Sergeant, J.A. (1992). A motor presetting study in hyperactives, learning disabled and control children. *Journal of Child Psychology and Psychiatry, 34,* 1347–1354.

Warm, J.S. (1984). *Sustained attention in human performance.* New York: John Wiley & Sons.

Wickens, C.D. (1984). *Engineering psychology and human performance.* Columbus, OH: Charles B. Merrill.

Winsum, W., van, Sergeant, J.A., & Guze, R. (1984). The functional significance of event-related desynchronization of alpha rhythm in attentional and activating tasks. *Electroencephalography and Clinical Neurophysiology, 58,* 519–524.

Wordsworth, R.S. (1938). *Experimental psychology.* New York: Holt, Rinehart & Winston.

6

DISORDERS OF ATTENTION
A Neuropsychological Perspective

Allan F. Mirsky

The scientific study of attention has been enriched greatly by a consideration of the symptoms shown by patients suffering from seizure disorders. Epileptologists have always viewed alterations in consciousness associated with seizures as an important sign in the diagnosis and treatment of seizure disorders. However, the writings of Penfield and Jasper (1954) placed increased emphasis on the importance of the loss of consciousness associated with petit mal epilepsy and provided a theoretical-anatomical basis for the *absence* attack (and for consciousness itself) associated with this form of seizures. Their work stimulated many investigators, including the present author, to investigate the neuropsychological mechanisms underlying consciousness and—by extension—alterations in attention. We consider that attention represents a highly articulated form of consciousness that has been shaped and modified by learning and experience. However, without consciousness there can be no attention, and to understand attention we must have some basic understanding of the nature of consciousness itself. We therefore study patients with seizure disorders to enhance our understanding of the normal mechanisms of attention, just as we study patients with disorders of speech to understand the normal mechanisms underlying the reception and articulation of speech.

The following quotation is from the classic work of Penfield and Jasper, *Epilepsy and the Functional Anatomy of the Human Brain* (1954):

> In a petit mal seizure there is a loss of consciousness which may be associated with no other outward manifestation than a blank stare, an arrest of what one might call voluntary activity. The return of consciousness may likewise be without sign except for the resumption of his previous train of thought as shown by speech or action. The patient himself may have no knowledge of the gap unless he perceives that his position has changed or his surroundings have altered [. . .] . Thus, the clinician is brought to a consideration of consciousness and unconsciousness, in spite of himself and however insecure he may feel, when forced to pass over so much deep water on the thin ice of his own psychological insight. (p. 480)

THE THEORETICAL CONTEXT AND MODEL
UNDERLYING THE CONCEPTUAL VIEW OF ATTENTION

The Evolutionary Perspective

The theoretical context guiding the author's conceptual view of the neuropsychology of attention presented here is, broadly speaking, evolutionary-developmental. That is to say, the basic neural *anlage* for attention is a brain stem system that has existed for millions of years and is still present and functioning quite adequately in the brains of modern reptiles.

The model is based, in part, on the concept of the "triune brain" as delineated by MacLean (1990). According to this theory, the brain of higher mammals consists of three layers corresponding to major evolutionary leaps. The oldest of these layers is the *reptilian* or R-complex. Overlaid upon this is the *paleomammalian* or limbic system layer. The highest developmental layer, manifest in the great augmentation in the size of the forebrain in higher mammals (and especially primates) is the *neomammalian*. These layers are illustrated in Figure 6.1.

The R-complex, or reptilian brain, is depicted in black and consists of masses of gray matter at the center of the cerebrum. The basal ganglia are included (caudate, putamen, globus pallidus, and their connections to the thalamus, tegmental, and pontine regions of the brain stem). The R-complex is overlaid by the paleomammalian (cross-hatched) brain, which includes the limbic system

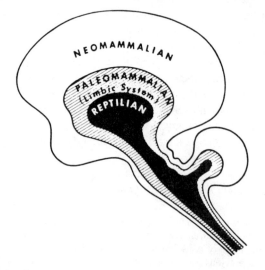

Figure 6.1.   The "triune brain." In its evolution the human forebrain expands along the lines of three basic formations that anatomically and biochemically reflect an ancestral relationship, respectively, to reptiles, early mammals, and late mammals. The three formations are labeled at the level of the forebrain that constitutes the cerebral hemispheres comprised of the telencephalon and diencephalon. (From MacLean, P.D. [1990]. *The triune brain in evolution: Role in paleocerebral functions,* p. 9. New York: Plenum; reprinted by permission.)

(amygdala, hippocampus, cingulate gyrus, and related structures) and more primitive (paleo-) cortex. The neomammalian brain (open area in the diagram) is comprised primarily of the phylogenetically newer neocortex and the thalamic structures to which it is connected.

MacLean (1990) has pointed out that the brain of the reptile consists of little more than a brain stem and several ganglia; the paleomammalian and neomammalian "brains" are represented only in rudimentary form in the brain of the reptile. Nevertheless, the reptilian brain supports a complex series of behaviors, including many of the attention functions discussed below in our model. From the point of view of evolution, therefore, it is clear that the capacity for sustained attention behavior is present in many species in which there is no more than a rudimentary forebrain or telencephalon. MacLean's (1990) analysis of the R-complex within the human brain leads to the view that this "clump of ganglia," which constitutes virtually all of the reptilian brain, can support a variety of behaviors that could be characterized as sustained and attentive. The following passage, which describes the case of a giant Komodo lizard lying in wait to ambush a deer, illustrates this most dramatically:

> He proceeds to a favored ambush site . . . Well camouflaged by his own colors and the surrounding herbage, he hides himself about 1 m from the trail where he can lunge forward and grip the deer . . . he remains so motionless that one might think that he was asleep or dead . . . Finally the moment arrives! . . . (he) lunges forward, grabbing a large stag by the hind leg. (MacLean, p. 131)

Figure 6.2 is a photograph of a free-ranging giant Komodo lizard taken on the island of Komodo.

Figure 6.2. Photograph of free-ranging Komodo lizard. (Courtesy of Professor Elkhonon Goldberg.)

As evolution progressed to other species, the brain developed additional complexity and volume. Additional capacity for attentive behavior was thus overlaid on the more primitive, although in many aspects thoroughly adequate, brain stem system of the reptile. Therefore, although the system for maintenance of attentive behavior in the human (or higher primate) includes limbic and neocortical components, the brain stem remains a key component and, possibly, the keystone of the entire system. A related observation is the capacity of the newborn human for sustained visual attention well before the neocortex is fully myelinated (see review by Lipsett & Eimas, 1972). Therefore this capacity appears to be heavily dependent upon subcortical structures in the paleomammalian and reptilian portions of the human brain.

Penfield and Jasper—Contributions from the Study of Epilepsy

The writings of MacLean (1990) have emphasized the critical role of deep subcortical structures in the maintenance and elaboration of numerous behaviors, including, as we have pointed out, vigilance or sustained attention. A similar conclusion could have been reached on the basis of an entirely different line of evidence, namely, the consideration of the behavioral and electrophysiological signs associated with various types of seizure disorders, particularly as manifest in the clinical phenomena of absence epilepsy.

As background, it should be noted that Hughlings Jackson (1931, cited in Penfield & Jasper, 1954) enunciated the principle of three levels of differentiation or integration of functioning of the central nervous system. The first two levels were concerned, respectively, with representation of body parts and coordination of movements or sensations. The highest level of integration was a functional rearrangement of sensory and motor behavioral components that constituted the neural basis of consciousness. Although Jackson suggested that this highest level might reside in the frontal lobes, Penfield and Jasper proposed instead that it was localized deep within the brain stem. A central integrating mechanism existed in that region of the brain (the "centrencephalic" system) for coordinating and regulating the activities of the two cerebral hemispheres. The central integrating mechanism would ensure that information from the lower centers in the spinal cord, brain stem, and thalamus reached the appropriate targets in the cerebral cortex, including both hemispheres, at approximately the same time. Figure 6.3 illustrates the centrencephalic system.

This concept was supported by the results of numerous experimental studies of the electrical activity of the brain in animals, which pointed to a major coordinating role for midline brain stem structures. Penfield and Jasper (1954) maintained, furthermore, that petit mal (absence) seizures provided an example of a *disorder* of the centrencephalic system: The primary symptom is a brief interruption of consciousness or attention that occurs in conjunction with bilaterally symmetrical electroencephalographic (EEG) discharges of a characteristic nature. These seizures were "centrencephalic" in origin, and they could properly be called "highest level seizures." Penfield and Jasper proposed that the diagnostic

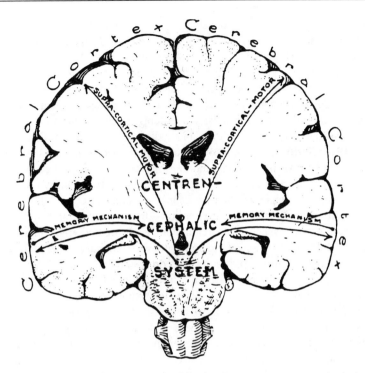

Figure 6.3. The centrencephalic system may be defined as that neuron system, centering in the higher brain stem, which has been up to the present, or may be in the future, shown to have equal functional relationships with the two cerebral hemispheres. It forms the chief central integrating mechanism for various areas of the cortex. (From Penfield, W., & Jasper, H.H. [1954]. *Epilepsy and the functional anatomy of the human brain,* p. 475. Boston: Little, Brown & Co.; reprinted by permission.)

label *petit mal* epilepsy be replaced with *centrencephalic* epilepsy. In their theorizing, therefore, consciousness was either localized in or regulated by deep brain stem structures, and the symptom of the absence was the behavioral manifestation of the disturbance of the centrencephalic system.

Localization of Attention Functions in the Brain—The Brain Stem and Beyond

Lest one gather the impression that there are no functions concerned with attention localized dorsal to the third ventricle, it is important to add that there has been extensive research conducted over the past two decades that indicates a major role of limbic and neocortical structures in the support of attention. However, the functions of attention have become differentiated and articulated as the brain has developed over evolution.

Evidence is rapidly accumulating to indicate that mental operations involved in various types of cognitive processing are localized in distinct regions of the brain and that task performance requires coordination of these operations into a system (Heilman, Watson, Valenstein, Damasio, 1983; Mesulam, 1987;

Posner, 1988). Some years ago the suggestion was made (Mirsky, 1987) that attentive functioning results from the coordinated action of several elements linked into such a system (Figure 6.4).

This multicomponent view of attention is in keeping with information processing studies that identify a variety of functions linked to attention such as selectivity, focusing, sustaining concentration or vigilance, switching attention, distractibility, modulating the intensity of attention, and attention to memorial processes such as rehearsal, retrieval, and coding (Parasuraman & Davies, 1984; Posner, 1978; Shiffrin, 1988). In order to begin to bridge the gap between this work from cognitive psychology and neuropsychology, my colleaguges and I proposed a *restricted taxonomy of attentive functions,* based in part on Zubin's (1975) attempt to categorize attentive deficits in schizophrenia. Zubin proposed that there are three "elements" of attention—focus, sustain, and shift—which represent significant aspects of the regulation of information processing.

Focus refers to the capacity to concentrate attentional resources (to use the term favored by cognitive psychologists) on a specific task and to be able to screen out distracting peripheral stimuli. In our attempts to isolate tests that are dependent on this capacity, we were unable to separate focusing from the task demand of rapid response. As a result, we have used the term *focus/execute* in an attempt to capture the essence of this aspect or element of attention. The part of attention referred to by Zubin as *sustain* entails being able to stay on task in a vigilant manner for an appreciable interval—not missing designated targets, re-

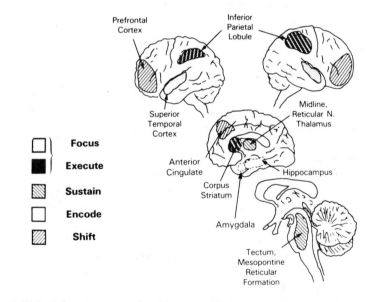

Figure 6.4. Semischematic representation of the proposed brain attention system with tentative attributions of functional specialization to distinct brain regions. (From Mirsky, A.F., Anthony, B.J., Duncan, C.C., Ahearn, M.B., & Kellam, S.G. [1991]. Analysis of the elements of attention: A neuropsychological approach. *Neuropsychology Review, 2,* 109–145; reprinted by permission.)

sponding briskly to them, and inhibiting responses to nontargets. The third piece of the triad proposed by Zubin concerns the capacity to *shift* attentional focus from one aspect of a stimulus complex to another in a flexible, efficient manner.

Our research and statistical analyses aimed at discovering tests conforming to these elements or factors of attention have repeatedly identified a fourth type of skill or function: a mnemonic capacity to hold information briefly in mind while performing some action or cognitive operation upon it. This function has been tentatively labeled as *encode*. Most recently, Tatman (1992) and Tatman, Fantie, and Mirsky (1995) gathered evidence suggesting that there may be a fifth element or factor that is related to the reliability or *stability* of attentional effort. The relationship between the two models of attention—the four- and five-factor models—is shown in Table 6.1.

Elements such as these are, in fact, targets of extensive research in cognitive psychology and, to a lesser extent, neuropsychology. Our work suggests that it is useful to consider attention as a multifaceted process or capacity, different components of which may be sensitive to different agents, rather than as a single monolithic trait.

The Primary Constructs within the Five-Factor Model

The primary constructs may be summarized as follows:

- Attention is a complex process or set of processes. It can be subdivided into a number of distinct functions, including *focus/execute, sustain, stabilize, shift,* and *encode.*
- These functions may be supported by different brain regions, which have become specialized for this purpose and are organized into a system.
- The system organization allows for shared responsibility for attentional functions, which implies that the specialization is not absolute and that some structures may substitute for others in the event of injury.
- The function of *focusing* on environmental events is shared by superior temporal and inferior parietal cortices as well as by structures that comprise the corpus striatum.
- The *execution* of responses must depend heavily on the integrity of inferior parietal and corpus striatal regions (see discussion in Mesulam, 1987).
- *Sustaining* a focus on some aspect of the environment is the major responsibility of rostral midbrain structures, including the mesopontine reticular formation and midline and reticular thalamic nuclei. We suspect that the function tentatively labeled as *stabilize* may also be dependent upon midline–thalamic and brain stem structures.
- The capacity to *shift* from one salient aspect of the environment to another is supported by the prefrontal cortex, including the anterior cingulate gyrus.
- *Encoding* of stimuli is dependent upon the hippocampus and amygdala.
- Damage or dysfunction in one of these brain regions can lead to circumscribed or specific deficits in a particular attention function.

Table 6.1.   Comparison of four- and five-factor solutions attention "elements"

Four-factor solution[a]	Five-factor solution[b]
1. Focus/execute	1. Scan/focus/speed
2. Shift	2. Shift/be flexible
3. Sustain	3. Arouse/exert
4. Encode	4. Encode/retain
	5. Stabilize/steady[c]

[a]Adapted from Mirsky et al. (1991).
[b]Adapted from Tatman (1992).
[c]Continuous Performance Test (X and AX tasks) Reaction Time Variance, AX task Commission Errors.

Theories of the Etiology of Attention Disorders in Children

The general view espoused here is that the etiology of disordered attention in children is as varied and complex as the manifestations of attention disorders themselves. The mechanism responsible for the disorder may be genetic-familial, as is presumed to be the case with schizophrenia (Mirsky et al., 1992), certain metabolic disorders (e.g., phenylketonuria) (Anderson, Siegal, Frisch, & Wirt, 1969), attention deficit hyperactivity disorder (ADHD) (Gillis, Gilger, Pennington, & DeFries, 1992), and absence epilepsy (Levav, unpublished doctoral dissertation). There is a class of noxious agents injurious to typical brain development that tends to be associated with impoverished living conditions. These conditions, which include malnutrition, lead poisoning, and parasitic infection, may affect hundreds of millions or, possibly, billions of persons the world over. The effects of these agents are probably in large measure preventable. The agent may exert its effect during the intrauterine period, as is the case with ethanol use by pregnant women (Streissguth et al., 1994), or in the perinatal period (as would be the case with asphyxia neonatorum).

Were we to understand the action of these agents on the developing nervous system, we would have a complete taxonomy concerning the etiology of attention disorders in children; at present, we can only offer theory and some informed speculation. Moreover, the etiology of some disorders is essentially unknown. In Table 6.2, we have listed some of the neuropsychiatric disorders of children in which impairment of attention has been reported.

Models of the Brain's Attention System

The Pribram and McGuinness Model   Pribram and McGuinness (1975) proposed arousal, activation, and effort as essential factors or elements in the control of attention. Arousal, according to these authors, is more or less defined by the orienting response to sensory input, which is generated by a "core system of neurons . . . from the spinal cord through the brainstem reticular formation, including hypothalamic sites . . ." (p. 123). In their conception, this is the core, or possibly the primordial, attention system that mediates the action of an effective external stimulus. Forebrain control over this system is exerted by the amygdala and portions of the frontal cortex, which regulate arousal (a phasic or short-

Table 6.2. Neuropsychiatric disorders in children in whom impairment of attention has been reported

- Disorders related to familial/genetic factors
  - Attention deficit disorder—with or without hyperactivity
  - Seizure disorders, especially absence epilepsy
  - Prodromal sign of later psychotic disorder
  - Metabolic disorders, including phenylketonuria
- Disorders associated frequently with poverty
  - Sequelae of exposure to lead, fetal alcohol, other toxins
  - Malnutrition, effect of specific nutrient deprivation
  - Parasite infection of the brain (neurocysticercosis)
  - Cultural, educational deprivation
- Disorders related to injury or infection
  - Asphyxia neonatorum
  - Head injuries
  - Infectious diseases affecting the brain
- Disorders of unknown etiology
  - Developmental disorders (e.g., autism, Tourette's)

lasting effect), and by the basal ganglia, which regulate activation (a tonic or long-lasting effect). The system that coordinates arousal and activation is centered in the hippocampus.

Although the structures discussed by Pribram and McGuinness (1975) are included within the system we have proposed, the assignment of functional specialization differs from theirs. We would include arousal and activation within the *sustain* element; in addition, our model does not deal with the concept of effort, although we have recognized the eventual necessity of discussing automatic versus effortful *processing*. Pribram and McGuinness do not deal with this issue either. These differences aside, the present model is more concerned with an articulation of clinical neurobehavioral issues. This might be expected in view of the fact that the database that gave rise to the present model, that is, neuropsychological data from neuropsychiatric patients, differs considerably from the orientation of Pribram and McGuinness, which has been primarily directed toward animal research. Moreover, the information accumulated during two decades of research since 1975 (particularly, but not limited to, the functions of parietal and temporal cortices) would require an update of their treatment.

The Posner and Petersen Model   The conception proposed by Posner and Petersen (1990) is based upon a consideration of "three major functions that have been prominent in cognitive accounts of attention: (a) orienting to sensory events; (b) detecting signals for focal (conscious) processing, and (c) maintaining a vigilant or alert state" (p. 26). These authors suggest, furthermore, that the attention system of the human brain is comprised of two major loci. One of these is a posterior attention system that lies in the dorsal visual pathway and has its primary cortical projection area in V1, extending into the parietal lobe. This system has the responsibility for the process of orienting. (Note the difference in the treatment of orienting by these authors and by Pribram and McGuinness.) The second major locus is the anterior attention system, which seems to be in the anterior cingulate gyrus and supplementary motor cortex (both of which are midline frontal lobe structures). This system has the responsibility for signal detection. The function of alertness (or maintaining vigilance) is not quite so clearly defined anatomically by these authors, but the structures involved seem to comprise, at a minimum, the norepinephrine innervation system, extending from the locus ceruleus of the brain stem rostrally to the posterior attention system, particularly of the right hemisphere.

There is at least a correspondence between some of the structures comprising the Posner–Petersen model and those included within the one proposed here (i.e., prefrontal cortex, parietal cortex, selected brain stem structures). There is clearly not total agreement between the two models as to the definition of the essential elements of attention; nevertheless, there appears to be considerable overlap in conception between what we have referred to as *focus/execute* and as *sustain,* and the Posner–Petersen elements of *orient/detect* and *maintaining vigilance.* (The combining of the two elements of orienting and detection into one is our proposal, not that of Posner & Petersen.) There is a difference in the neural basis proposed for shift behavior. Posner and Petersen (1990) link this to the superior colliculus and surrounding structures and therefore to their posterior attention system. In our model, based on the Wisconsin Card Sorting Task (WCST) (Grant and Berg, 1948), this behavior is linked to the dorsolateral prefrontal cortex. The difference is obviously a function of whether shifting is defined in terms of movement of the eyes (Posner & Petersen) or the shifting of sorting concepts (the present model).

The Heilman et al./Mesulam Model   Studies of the symptom of neglect have led to a neural system view of spatial selective attention. This symptom, described originally by Geschwind and colleagues as a consequence of damage to the right posterior and, most often, parietal cortical regions (Heilman et al., 1983), involves the reported lack of awareness of visual, auditory, or somatosensory stimuli from one half of space. The neglect symptom may also occur following damage to portions of the cingulate gyrus, thalamus, and the corpus striatum (Healton, Navarro, Bressman, & Brust, 1982). Heilman et al. and Mesulam (1987) have linked these findings to the concept of a cortico-limbic-reticular circuit, damage to which underlies the neglect symptom (see Figure 6.5).

Although it is attractive to think of attention as dependent upon a system (as opposed to a single focus supporting a specific behavior), the behavioral concept of neglect—although a powerful and impressive symptom—seems too narrow to support all that is implied by attention impairment.

The Mirsky et al. Model   In comparison to the model that we have developed there are similarities and differences among the several proposals for the brain's attention system. Perhaps the one that resembles our own most closely is the Heilman-Mesulam model. The differences among the models notwithstanding, there is a fundamental similarity in the assignment of what we have referred to as sustain, what Posner and Petersen (1990) have called maintaining vigilance, and what Pribram and McGuinness (1975) term core arousal. Structures in the brain stem and medial thalamus support this attentional function.

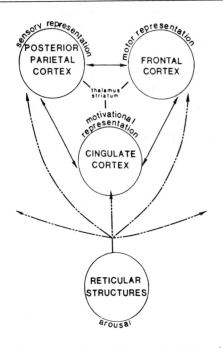

Figure 6.5. A network involved in the distribution of attention to extrapersonal targets. (From Mesulam, M.M. [1987]. Attention, confusional states and neglect. In M.M. Mesulam [Ed.], *Principles of behavioral neurology* (pp. 157). Philadelphia: F.A. Davis; reprinted by permission.)

From this brief review of three other models of an attention system in the brain, it would appear that the nature of the neuropsychological model of attention depends upon the behavioral data used to generate it. Since all these conceptions deal with fundamentally the same database, there is a fair degree of commonality among them. The differences seem to be a function of the part of the database that particular authors have chosen to emphasize.

METHODS USED FOR ATTENTION ASSESSMENT IN CHILDREN

Instruments, Tests, or Procedures Used to Measure the Mirsky Model and the Constructs

The tests used in the Mirsky model are commonly used neuropsychological measures. They were selected initially from a larger list of tests and measures used in neuropsychological assessment. Unlike the other two models discussed above, the Mirsky model was stimulated by and informed by neuropsychological test data derived from clinical practice.

The *focus/execute* element is tapped by a group of tests that capture the ability to identify salient task elements and perform motor responses under conditions of distraction. There may be considerable conceptual overlap between impairment on this attention element and the neurological symptom referred to as "neglect." In our research, the tests used to measure this aspect of attention include the Digit Symbol Substitution Test from the Wechsler Adult Intelligence Scale–Revised (WAIS-R) (Wechsler, 1981), the Stroop test (Stroop, 1935), the Trail Making Test (Parts A and B) from the Halstead–Reitan Scale (Reitan & Davidson, 1974), and the Talland Letter Cancellation Test (Talland, 1965).

The *encode* function, as we have defined it, includes sequential registration, recall, and mental manipulation of numeric information. This is tapped by the Digit Span and Arithmetic Subtests of the WAIS–R. Note the mnemonic function included here.

The capacity to *shift* from one stimulus quality or aspect to another is measured by the Wisconsin Card Sorting Test (WCST) (Grant & Berg, 1948). This is the paradigmatic method of testing this capacity. This time-honored test is the Americanized version of the Goldstein-Scheerer-Weigl color-form sorting test (Goldstein & Scheerer, 1941).

The capacity to *sustain* a focus of attention for an appreciable interval of time is assessed by scores derived from the Continuous Performance Test (CPT) (Rosvold, Mirsky, Sarason, Bransome, & Beck, 1956). Specifically, the data collected include correct responses to targets, correct nonresponses to nontargets, and reaction time.

Stability of response in an attention task is measured by the variability of reaction time on the CPT and by erroneous responses to targets in the AX version of the CPT.

The Criteria Used to Select and/or Develop the Instruments, Tests, or Procedures

Data in support of the Mirsky model were derived initially from neuropsychological test scores obtained from two samples, the first consisting of 203 adult neuropsychiatric patients and typical control subjects and the second consisting of a sample of 435 second-grade schoolchildren (an epidemiological sample) ranging in age from 7 through 9 years. Independent principal components analyses of test scores from these two populations yielded similar results: a set of independent elements of attention that are assayed by different tests.

The results of the analysis of the data from the schoolchildren are presented in Tables 3, 4, and 5. Table 3 lists the tests of the attention battery used with the children; Table 4, the descriptive variables and the attention test scores; Table 5, the results of the principal components analysis applied to the test scores. These results have been replicated on six independent samples of adult and adolescent subjects, including both typical and neuropsychiatric populations. The test methods used have varied sufficiently from sample to sample to rule out—or at least substantially disconfirm—the objection that the principal components analysis is essentially reflecting method variance (see the discussion of this issue in Mirsky, Anthony, Duncan, Ahearn, & Kellam, 1991).

Table 6.3. Tests of the attention battery: Child sample

Test	Scores used
Digit Cancellation[a]	Completion time (seconds)
	Omission errors
Wisconsin Card Sorting Test	Percentage of errors
	Number of categories achieved
Coding Test[b]	Number correct
Arithmetic Test[b]	Number correct
Digit Span Test[b]	Number correct
Continuous Performance Test[c]	Mean percentage correct responses, X task
	Mean percentage commission errors, X task ("commissions")
	Mean reaction time to X

[a]This test was in place of the Talland Symbol Cancellation Test, which was used in the adult sample.

[b]Subtests of the Wechsler Intelligence Scale for Children–Revised. The Coding Test was used in place of the Digit Symbol Substitution Test (Adult Sample); they are designed to be equivalent.

[c]This task was identical to that used in the Adult Sample, except that only the X task was employed, the stimulus duration was 100 milliseconds, and the allowable response time to register a correct response was 800 milliseconds.

Table 6.4. Descriptive variables and attention test battery scores: Child sample

Measure	Mean	SD
Descriptive variable		
Age (Months)[a]	95.3	5.6
Peabody Picture Vocabulary Test–Revised[b]		
(Dunn & Dunn, 1981)	87.1	16.0
Attention test scores		
WISC–R Digit Span	9.3	2.6
WISC–R Arithmetic	9.2	3.2
WISC–R Coding	10.9	3.3
Digit Cancellation completion time	72.8	18.8
Digit Cancellation omission errors	3.4	2.9
CPT Correct Responses (%)	80.3	14.4
CPT Commission Errors (%)	2.2	2.5
CPT Reaction Time (ms)	610.6	55.1
WCST % Correct	48.9	14.6
WCST # Categories	2.9	1.8

Note: WISC-R, Wechsler Intelligence Scale for Children–Revised; WCST, Wisconsin Card Sorting Test; CPT, Continuous Performance Test.

[a]Of the 435 children, 380 were in the second grade and 55 in the first grade at the time of testing. There were 217 males, mean age 95.5 months ($SD = 6.0$) and 218 females, mean age 95.2 months ($SD = 5.2$).

[b]This test yields scores roughly equivalent to verbal IQ. The mean score for the males was 88.9 ($SD = 17.3$); for the females it was 85.4 ($SD = 16.1$).

Psychophysiological Methods

While doubtless of relevance to the topic of the neuropsychology of attention, it is beyond the scope of this chapter to review in detail the psychophysiological methods that have been employed for this purpose. These methods have included assessment of variables such as heart rate, skin conductance, and pupillary dilation (Zahn, Frith, & Steinhauer, 1991) and measures of brain electrical activity derived from the scalp EEG.

Table 6.5. Rotated factor patterns: Child sample

	Factor 1	Factor 2	Factor 3	Factor 4
CPT correct responses	−.03	−.19	.85	.01
CPT commission errors	.01	−.35	.52	−.13
CPT reaction time	−.14	.27	.65	.35
Digit Cancellation completion time	−.12	−.07	.14	.80
Digit Cancellation omission errors	−.27	−.16	.18	−.57
Coding (WISC–R)	.06	.38	−.11	−.58
Arithmetic (WISC–R)	.22	.74	−.16	.01
Digit Span (WISC–R)	.03	.75	−.04	−.12
WCST % correct	.95[a]	.10	−.03	−.01
WCST # of categories	.95	.11	−.06	.01
Variance explained[b]	19.7%	15.3%	15.1%	14.5%
Proposed identity of factor	Flexibility	Numerical-mnemonic	Vigilance	Perceptual–motor speed
Element of attention	Shift	Encode	Sustain	Focus/execute

Note: CPT, Continuous Performance Test; WCST, Wisconsin Card Sorting Test.

[a]Italicized values are the highest loadings within a column and were used in the interpretation of the identity of the factor.

[b]The total variance accounted for by the four factors was 64.6%.

Earlier investigators studying the electrophysiological correlates of attention examined such EEG-derived measures as amount of alpha activity (Lindsley, 1960). More recently, the emphasis has been on assays of what are referred to as event-related brain potentials (ERPs). These assays depend upon computer-assisted analysis of brain electrical activity and are based on the assumption that there is a small but reliable signal (ERP) produced in the brain in response to environmental events. These events may be as simple as the repeated occurrence of a noise or a light, requiring no overt attention from the subject; the event may require close attention, such as evaluating a stimulus in comparison with some internal template and making a decision as to whether or not to perform a motor response. This brain signal—the ERP—can be extracted from the noise of the EEG by averaging techniques; moreover, the ERP grows in complexity (i.e., new "components" appear) and richness as a function of the question being posed. Computer methods permit one to measure the ERP latency, amplitude, composition, and distribution over the scalp.

One of the earliest ERP components identified that was related to attention was the Contingent Negative Variation (CNV) (Grey Walter, 1969; McCallum, 1969). The CNV is a negative electrical signal recorded on the scalp and elicited by a particular task; it is one of a class of components identified as "endogenous" in nature. These components are viewed as related to some cognitive operation performed on a stimulus, rather than an obligatory ("exogenous") response to a sensory event such as a tone or light flash. The endogenous component referred to as the P300, in particular, has been widely used as a method of assaying attention. This component is a positive electrical signal that occurs about 300 milliseconds after the onset of an attention-demanding stimulus. The studies by Klorman and associates in recent years have established the utility of the P300 component for measuring attentive capacity in children with ADHD and in assessing the beneficial effects of drugs such as methylphenidate (e.g., Klorman et al., 1990). Other good examples of the use of P300 in the study of neuropsychiatric disorders include Duncan-Johnson and Donchin (1977) (a classic paper on the P300 metric); Duncan (1988) (evaluation of the attention status of patients with absence epilepsy); Duncan (1990) (a discussion of P300 research in schizophrenia, with emphasis on the difference between the processing of visual and auditory information in the disorder); and Duncan et al. (1994) (P300 findings in adult dyslexia, with emphasis on the role of early attention deficit disorder in some of the probands).

THE APPLICATION OF ATTENTION ASSESSMENT METHODS IN CLINICAL RESEARCH

Using The LPP-NIMH Attention Battery

Attention Profiles in Seizure Disorders   Two recent investigations have included assessment of attentional capacities in individuals with differing types of seizure disorders. In one of the studies, we compared the attentional profiles of several groups of patients, including those with absence seizures, complex partial seizures, closed head injuries, and a group of typical control subjects. The rationale for this comparison was this: Because the two seizure groups have differing types of presumed cerebral pathology, their patterns of attentional deficit (if any) should differ as well. The pathology in the complex–partial group would likely involve frontotemporal cortical regions, whereas that in the absence group would be expected to implicate (at least in part) subcortical structures in the midline thalamus–brain stem reticular formation axis. In keeping with the results of prior investigations (Lansdell & Mirsky, 1964; Mirsky et al., 1960), we found that persons with absence seizures performed more poorly than controls and patients with complex partial seizure disorders on tests measuring the *sustain* attentional factor (i.e., the CPT). However, patients with complex partial seizures showed the reverse effect; that is, they were impaired relative to absence patients (and controls) on tests of the *shift* and *focus/execute* attention factors. This reverse or double-dissociation result, which is illustrated in Figure 6.6, is consistent with the tenets of the attention model explicated above and as depicted in Figure 6.4 (Mirsky et al., 1991). Figure 6.6 shows the average standard or *z* score for the tests in each of the elements for the four groups of subjects referred to above.

Another investigation involving patients with seizure disorders had as its focus the question of familial–genetic factors in the symptom of impaired attention (Levav, 1991). It is well known that certain forms of absence seizures are strongly genetic (Anderson & Hauser, 1988). In this study, the emphasis was on the assessment of the behavioral symptoms of absence epilepsy (using the atten-

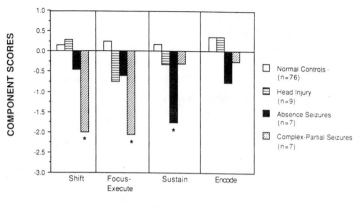

Figure 6.6. Component scores extracted by principal components analysis of attention tests on normal control subjects and three groups of neuropsychiatric patients. The asterisks appearing below the columns indicate that the group so designated differed significantly from all other groups on that component at $p < 0.05$ or better (Student-Newman-Keuls post hoc test). (From Mirsky, A.F., Anthony, B.J., Duncan, C.C., Ahearn, M.B., & Kellam, S.G. [1991]. Analysis of the elements of attention: A neuropsychological approach. *Neuropsychology Review, 2,* 109–145; reprinted by permission.)

tion battery described above) in persons with the disorder (probands) and in their first-degree relatives.

Significant impairment of the probands (in comparison with their unaffected siblings) was found on the CPT. This result is seen in Figure 6.7, which summarizes the mean standard or *z* scores on the four versions of the CPT (Visual X, AX, and Degraded X, Auditory X) used in the study. The scores presented are mean reaction time (top bar graph) and percentage of correct responses (bottom bar graph). Data for four groups of subjects (individuals with absence epilepsy, siblings, parents, and adult controls) are presented separately by sex. Females with the disorder tended to be more affected than males, and mothers tended to perform more poorly on the CPT than fathers. This result was not found in the siblings or in the group of adult controls. Greater impairment in the female than the male proband was reported earlier by Lansdell and Mirsky (1964).

Levav's (1991) finding of no impairment in the siblings of individuals with the disorder is consistent with the results of earlier genetic studies summarized by Anderson and Hauser (1988): The prevalence of absence epilepsy in both members of dizygotic twin pairs is significantly lower than the comparable figure for monozygotic twin pairs. The finding of low CPT scores in the mothers is consistent with previous reports that point to a maternally transmitted susceptibility to epilepsy (Ottman, Annegers, Hauser, & Kurland, 1988).

These data are preliminary. However, they suggest that measures of attention provide additional markers of vulnerability to the disorder of absence epilepsy that may enhance and enrich the sensitivity of genetic investigations.

Prediction of Schizophrenia Spectrum Disorders The results discussed here were obtained in a study concerned (in part) with the prediction of adult di-

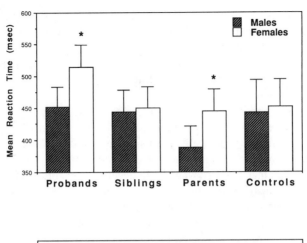

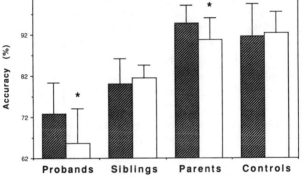

Figure 6.7. Mean Continuous Performance Test (CPT) scores (average z scores from four CPT tasks) of probands with absence epilepsy, unaffected siblings, parents of the probands, and adult control subjects. Top portion, reaction times; bottom portion, percentage accuracy. Note that the female probands scored significantly lower than the male probands, and the mothers of the probands performed significantly more poorly than the fathers.

agnostic outcomes in a group of genetically vulnerable children on the basis of their scores on an attention test when they were 11 and 17 years old. The data were collected as part of a long-term follow-up of 50 children with a schizophrenic parent and 50 matched typical controls (Mirsky, Kugelmass, & Ingraham, 1995). Reported here are analyses of two sets of digit cancellation test scores. The test procedure, described fully in Lifshitz, Kugelmass, and Karov (1985), required the subject to cross out two target digits under nondistraction conditions and then while listening to auditory distraction tapes. The task is very similar to the Talland Letter Cancellation Test (Talland, 1965), which is used to assess the *focus/execute* element of the Attention Battery described above. The categorization of scores was based upon neuropsychiatric diagnoses derived from the SADS–L interview schedule, administered twice, once in 1981 and once in 1989–1991, when the subjects' average age was 25 and the mid-30s, respectively.

The subjects' omission error scores at ages 11 and 17, categorized by later diagnoses, are presented in the form of bar graphs in Figure 6.8. The diagnostic categories included Schizophrenia Spectrum Disorders, Affective Spectrum Disorders, Other Diagnoses, and No Diagnosis. In this figure, the higher the bar, the poorer the performance; the results of within-group analyses of variance are also included in the figure.

The results in general support the proposition that, in a group of vulnerable children, scores on this test of attention at age 11 were predictive of psychiatric diagnosis in adulthood. Specifically, those children who would receive a diagnosis of Schizophrenia Spectrum Disorder in young adulthood performed more poorly on this test than children who would develop other (or no) diagnoses.

The results also suggest the following tentative conclusions: 1) performance under distraction conditions was somewhat more predictive of diagnostic outcome than performance under nondistraction conditions, 2) the test scores at 11 years of age predicted the later (1991) diagnoses better than the earlier (1981) diagnoses, and 3) the discriminating power of the cancellation task diminished from age 11 to age 17. The latter outcome may be due to the fact that the task was not demanding enough for the 17-year-old subjects. Thus, the proportion of subjects who made two or fewer errors on the nondistraction version of the task (i.e., at least 98% correct target detections) rose from 10% at age 11 to 32% at age 17; for the distraction version of the task, the proportion rose from 11.1% to 27.3%.

These results suggest that measures of attention, particularly under conditions of distraction, may be useful prognostic indicators in programs that seek to provide aid and beneficial interventions to vulnerable children.

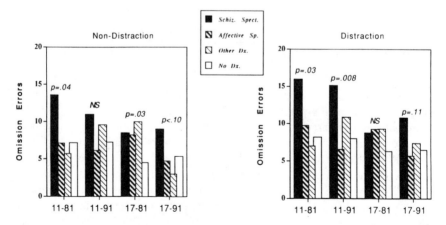

Figure 6.8.   Scores on a digit cancellation task at ages 11 and 17 predict DSM–III–R (American Psychiatric Association, 1987) diagnoses at ages 25 and mid-30s. At the left, scores under nondistraction conditions; at the right, scores under distraction conditions. The poorest scores at age 11 were obtained by children who would later be diagnosed as Schizophrenia Spectrum Disorder. Predictions based on scores at age 17 were less successful, possibly because the test was not demanding enough for 17-year-olds. From Mirsky, Kugelmass, and Ingraham (in press). NS = not significant.

Fetal Alcohol Exposure   Streissguth and colleagues have been following, with repeated neuropsychological assessments, a unique group of 500 children from birth through late adolescence. They are unique in that precise records were kept of the alcohol consumption of the mothers of these children during pregnancy. These were not alcoholic mothers, but could be classified as "social drinkers." Streissguth et al. reported that scores derived from measures of sustained attention (i.e., various versions of the CPT) correlate more strongly with maternal alcohol consumption than other measures. Such correlations have been reported at age 4 (Streissguth et al., 1984), age 7 (Streissguth et al., 1986), and age 14 (Streissguth et al., 1994). A summary of the most statistically significant findings derived from the assessment conducted at age 14 is presented in Table 6.6.

As can be seen in the table, at age 14 the best correlate of maternal drinking was variability of reaction time on the CPT. In earlier assessments, omission or commission errors were found to be significant correlates of maternal drinking; by and large, this was not the case at the 14-year assessment. These results suggest that manifestations of the same fundamental problem with attention may have different expressions, depending on the age of the subjects at the time of assessment.

Johns Hopkins—NIMH Epidemiological Study   The Laboratory of Psychology and Psychopathology of the National Institute of Mental Health (NIMH) has been involved in a collaborative research project with the Prevention Research Center of the Department of Mental Hygiene at the School of Hygiene and

Table 6.6.   Maternal drinking during pregnancy—attention and short-term memory in 14-year-old offspring: a longitudinal prospective study

Deficits on measures of attention, related to prenatal alcohol exposure, were seen in this cohort of 462 14-year-old subjects. This population had been evaluated previously at ages 4 and 7, at which times significant positive correlations were found between maternal alcohol consumption and CPT errors of omission, commission, and reaction time (RT). At age 14, the strongest relationships with maternal alcohol consumption were with the following variables:

CPT:

Standard deviation, reaction time, X task

Standard deviation, reaction time, AX task

Standard deviation, reaction time, degraded X task

(In all cases, increased RT variability was associated with increased prenatal alcohol exposure)

Talland (Letter Cancellation):

Total correct

Errors of commission

(Poorer performance was associated with increased prenatal alcohol exposure)

Stepping Stone Maze:

Trials to first success

(Poorer performance was associated with increased prenatal alcohol exposure)

Adapted from Streissguth et al. (1994).

Note: CPT = Continuous Performance Test.

Public Health of the Johns Hopkins University. The goal of this project has been to discover the antecedents of maladaptive (e.g., abnormal aggressiveness and shyness, poor concentration) classroom behavior in an epidemiological sample of schoolchildren from East Baltimore. The intention is to provide beneficial interventions in an attempt to modify the outcome of children who show these maladaptive characteristics. In the absence of intervention, such children are likely to experience early academic failures and to exhibit increased incidence of neuro-psychiatric disorders (depression, drug abuse, antisocial behaviors) (Kellam, Branch, Agrawal, & Ensminger, 1975).

Our joint investigations have revealed that children rated as unusually aggressive or shy by their teachers are also likely to be rated as having poor concentration. In fact, it was unusual to find a child rated as abnormally shy or aggressive who was not also rated as impaired in concentration. When formal assessments of attention skills were made with neuropsychological tests (in a stratified sample of 435 children), it was found that the teacher rating of "poor concentration" was highly correlated with poor scores on our neuropsychological test battery. The tests (and component scores) comprising the attention battery are listed in Table 6.7. We also discovered that aggressiveness and shyness are associated with distinctive patterns of attention impairment (Figure 6.9, Anthony et al., submitted). As can be seen in the figure, the children rated by their teachers as having both poor concentration and abnormal shyness (the cross-hatched columns) were significantly worse than the control children (the open columns, labeled as "Adaptive" in the figure) on the score identified as *sustain/detect*. This was a measure of the number of omission errors on the CPT. In contrast, the children identified as impaired in concentration and abnormally aggressive tended to perform poorly on the *sustain/inhibit* measure (i.e., the tendency to make errors

Table 6.7.   Attention scores

CPT
Number of hits
Reaction time (> 1.5 SD)
Reaction time (< -1.5 SD)
Commission errors
WISC–R
Arithmetic
Digit span
Coding
WCST
Categories
Perseverative errors
Digit cancellation
Completion time
Omission errors

Note: CPT = Continuous Performance Test, WISC–R = Wechsler Intelligence Scale for Children–Revised, WCST = Wisconsin Card Sorting Test.

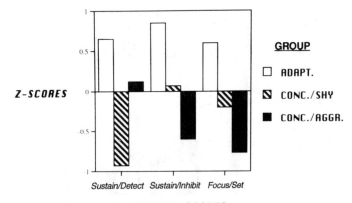

ATTENTION SCORES

Figure 6.9. Distinctive patterns of attention impairment shown by aggressive and shy children, in comparison with control children (i.e., the ADAPT. or Adaptive sample). Both Shy and Aggressive children in this cohort were also rated as poor in Concentration by their teachers, hence the designations CONC./SHY and CONC./AGGR. *Sustain/detect* refers to Detection (omission) errors (i.e., reduced number of hits) on the CPT; *sustain/inhibit* refers to failure of Inhibition (i.e., commission) errors on the CPT; *focus/set* refers to errors in the Coding subtest of the WISC-R (Wechsler, 1974). (From Anthony, B., Rebok, G., Pascualvaca, D., Jensen, P., Ahearn, M.B., Kellam, S.G., & Mirsky, A.F. [submitted for publication]. Epidemiological investigation of attention performance in children. II. Relationships to classroom behavior and academic performance. Reprinted by permission of the author.)

of commission on the CPT). They were also seen as impaired on the *focus/set* measure—the Coding score from the Wechsler Intelligence Scale for Children–Revised (WISC–R) (Wechsler, 1974).

Figure 6.10 (Pascualvaca et al., submitted) illustrates the relationship between performance on the California Achievement Test (CAT) and the number of attention scores (from the list in Table 6.7) that were classified as impaired. It can be seen that the greater the number of impaired attention scores a child has, the poorer the achievement on Reading, Mathematics, and Language subtests on the CAT. This last finding, in particular, helps to establish the ecological validity (i.e., relation to classroom performance) of the neuropsychological attention test scores.

CONCLUSIONS

This chapter has focused on theory, methods, and research related to disorders of attention in adults and children, as viewed from the perspective of neuropsychology. With respect to theory, the material reviewed included research bearing on the neuroanatomical substrate of attention. Attention is an articulated form of consciousness that has been shaped by learning and experience, and it is dependent in part on a phylogenetically ancient system in the brain, as well as the participation of limbic and cortical structures. The operation of this primitive (i.e., brain stem) part of the system is still evident in the behavior of modern reptiles and amphibians.

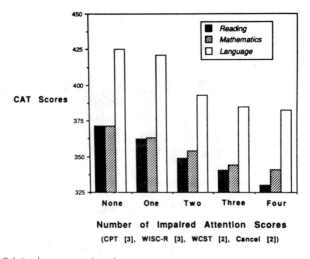

Figure 6.10.   Relation between number of attention test scores classified as impaired and performance on subtests of the California Achievement Test (CAT). CPT, continuous performance test (Rosvold et al., 1956); WISC-R, Wechsler Intelligence Scale for Children–Revised (Wechsler, 1974); WCST, Wisconsin Card Sorting Test (Grant & Berg, 1948); Cancel, Digit Cancellation test. (From Pascualvaca, D., Anthony, B., Arnold, L.E., Rebok, G., Ahearn, M.B., Kellam, S.G., Mirsky, A.F. [submitted for publication]. Epidemiological investigation of attention performance in children. I. The effect of gender, intelligence and age. Reprinted by permission of the author.)

The genetic, environmental, and congenital antecedents of disorders of attention were reviewed. Disorders that appear to have a prominent familial/genetic component include attention deficit disorder, absence epilepsy, psychosis (schizophrenia), and certain metabolic disorders such as phenylketonuria. There is a group of disorders associated often with poverty, including those that result from exposure to lead, maternal alcohol consumption, and other toxins. Other poverty-related conditions related to impaired attentional capacity include malnutrition, parasite infection, and cultural and educational deprivation. The agents that may produce impairment in attention also include injury, infection, and disorders of unknown etiology (autism, Tourette's syndrome).

Several models of the components or elements of attention, as seen by different authors, were compared, and the similarities and differences among the models noted. The model ("attention elements") presented in detail in this chapter is linked strongly to the clinical assessment of attention. Methods for assessment of attention were presented, with the emphasis on clinical neuropsychological techniques (i.e., the NIMH Attention Battery).

Specific examples of research using the NIMH Attention Battery were presented. These included studies of attention profiles in seizure disorders, in which the unique pattern of attentional deficits seen in different seizure disorders (absence epilepsy versus complex partial epilepsy) was noted. The use of attention measures in the successful prediction of schizophrenia spectrum disorders was described, in the context of a long-term followup study of children at genetic risk for the development of schizophrenia. The persistent core deficit in sustained attention, as measured by the Continuous Performance Test, was illustrated in the investigation of the long-term effects of maternal alcohol consumption during pregnancy. In addition, studies illustrating the pernicious effects of impaired attention on classroom adaptation were described in an epidemiological sample of school children.

REFERENCES

American Psychiatric Association. (1987). *Diagnostic and statistical manual of mental disorders* (3rd Ed., Rev.). Washington, DC: Author.

Anderson, V.E., & Hauser, W.A. (1988). Genetics of absence seizures and related epileptic syndromes. In M.S. Myslobodsky & A.F. Mirsky (Eds.), *Elements of petit mal epilepsy* (pp. 37–70). New York: Peter Lang.

Anderson, E.V., Siegal, F.S., Frisch, R.O., & Wirt, R.D. (1969). Responses to phenylketonuric children on a continuous performance test. *Journal of Abnormal Psychology, 74,* 358–362.

Anthony, B., Rebok, G., Pascualvaca, D., Jensen, P., Ahearn, M.B., Kellam, S.G., & Mirsky, A.F. (submitted for publication). Epidemiological investigation of attention performance in children. II. Relationships to classroom behavior and academic performance.

Duncan, C.C. (1988). Event-related potentials in absence epilepsy. In M.S. Myslobodsky & A.F. Mirsky (Eds.), *Elements of petit mal epilepsy* (pp. 341–364). New York: Peter Lang.

Duncan, C.C. (1990). Current issues in the application of P300 to research in schizophrenia. In E.R. Straube and K. Hahlweg (Eds.), *Schizophrenia: concepts, vulnerability, and intervention* (pp. 117–134). Berlin: Springer-Verlag.

Duncan, C.C., Rumsey, J.M., Wilkniss, S.M., Denckla, M.B., Hamburger, S.D., & Odou, M.A. (1994). Developmental dyslexia, attention deficit, and P300. *Psychophysiology, 31,* 386–401.

Duncan-Johnson, C.C., & Donchin, E. (1977). On quantifying surprise: The variation of event-related potentials with subjective probability. *Psychophysiology, 14,* 456–467.

Dunn, L.M., & Dunn, L.M. (1981). *Peabody Picture Vocabulary Test–Revised.* Circle Pines, MN: American Guidance Service.

Gillis, J.J., Gilger, J.W., Pennington, B.F., & DeFries, J.C. (1992). Attention deficit disorder in reading-disabled twins: Evidence for a genetic etiology. *Journal of Abnormal Child Psychology, 20*(3), 303–315.

Goldstein, K., & Scheerer, M. (1941). Abstraction and concrete behavior: An experimental study with special tests. *Psychological Monographs, 53,* 1–151.

Grant, D.A., & Berg, E.A. (1948). A behavioral analysis of degree of reinforcement and ease of shifting two new responses in a Weigl-type card sorting problem. *Journal of Experimental Psychology [Gen], 38,* 404–411.

Grey Walter, W. (1969). Can "attention" be defined in physiological terms? In C.R. Evans and T.B. Mulholland (Eds.), *Attention in neurophysiology: An international conference* (pp. 27–39). London: Butterworth.

Healton, E.B., Navarro, C., Bressman, S., & Brust, J.C.M. (1982). Subcortical neglect. *Neurology, 32,* 776–778.

Heaton, R.K., Chelune, G.J., Talley, J.L., Kay, G.G., & Curtiss, G. (1993). *Wisconsin Card Sorting Test manual: Revised and updated.* Odessa, FL: Psychological Assessment Resources.

Heilman, R.M., Watson, R.T., Valenstein, E., & Damasio, A.R. (1983). Location of lesions in neglect. In A. Kertez (Ed.), *Localization in neuropsychology* (pp. 319–331). New York: Academic Press.

Kellam, S.G., Branch, J.D., Agrawal, K.C., & Ensminger, M.E. (1975). *Mental health and going to school.* Chicago: University of Chicago Press.

Klorman, R., Brumaghim, J.T., Salzman, L.F., Strauss, J., Borgstedt, A.D., McBride, M.C., & Loeb, S. (1990). Effects of methylphenidate on processing negativities in patients with attention-deficit hyperactivity disorder. *Psychophysiology, 27,* 328–337.

Landsdell, H., & Mirsky, A.F. (1964). Attention in focal and centrencephalic epilepsy. *Experimental Neurology, 9,* 463–469.

Levav, M.L. (1991). *Attention performance in children affected with absence epilepsy and their first-degree relatives.* Unpublished doctoral dissertation, University of Maryland, College Park, MD.

Lifshitz, M., Kugelmass, S., & Karov, M. (1985). Perceptual-motor and memory performance of high risk children. *Schizophrenia Bulletin, 11,* 74–84.

Lindsley, D.B. (1960). Attention, sleep and wakefulness. In J. Field, H.W. Magoun, & V.E. Hall (Eds.), *Handbook of physiology* (pp. 1553–1593). Washington, DC: American Physiological Association.

Lipsett, L.P., & Eimas, P.D. (1972). Developmental psychology. *Annual Review of Psychology, 23,* 1–50.

MacLean, P.D. (1990). *The triune brain in evolution: Role in paleocerebral functions.* New York: Plenum.

McCallum, C. (1969). The contingent negative variation as a cortical sign of attention in man. In C.R. Evans & T.B. Mulholland (Eds.), *Attention in neurophysiology: An international conference* (pp. 40–63). London: Butterworth.

Mesulam, M.M. (1987). Attention, confusional states and neglect. In M.M. Mesulam (Ed.), *Principles of behavioral neurology* (pp. 125–168). Philadelphia: F.A. Davis.

Mirsky, A.F. (1987). Behavioral and psychophysiological markers of disordered attention. *Environmental Health Perspectives, 74,* 191–199.

Mirsky, A.F., Anthony, B.J., Duncan, C.C., Ahearn, M.B., & Kellam, S.G. (1991). Analysis of the elements of attention: A neuropsychological approach. *Neuropsychology Review, 2,* 109–145.

Mirsky, A.F., Ingraham, L.J., & Kugelmass, S. (1995). Neuropsychological assessment of attention and its pathology in the Israeli cohort. *Schizophrenia Bulletin, 21,* 183–192.

Mirsky, A.F., Lochhead, S.J., Jones, B.P., Kugelmass, S., Walsh, D., & Kendler, K.S. (1992). On familial factors in the attentional deficit in schizophrenia: A review and report of two new subject samples. *Journal of Psychiatric Research, 26,* 383–403.

Mirsky, A.F., Primac, D.W., Ajmone Marsan, C., Rosvold, H.E., & Stevens, J.A. (1960). A comparison of the psychological test performance of patients with focal and nonfocal epilepsy. *Experimental Neurology, 2,* 75–89.

Ottman, R., Annegers, J.F., Hauser, W.A., & Kurland, L.T. (1988). Higher risk of seizures in offspring of mothers than of fathers with epilepsy. *American Journal of Human Genetics, 43,* 257–264.

Parasuraman, R., & Davies, D.R. (1984). *Varieties of attention.* Orlando, FL: Academic Press.

Pascualvaca, D., Anthony, B., Arnold, L.E., Rebok, G., Ahearn, M.B., Kellam, S.G., & Mirsky, A.F. (submitted for publication). Epidemiological investigation of attention performance in children. I. The effect of gender, intelligence and age.

Penfield, W., & Jasper, H.H. (1954). *Epilepsy and the functional anatomy of the human brain.* Boston: Little, Brown & Co.

Posner, M.I. (1978). *Chronometric explorations of mind.* Hillsdale, NJ: Lawrence Erlbaum Associates.

Posner, M.I. (1988). Structures and functions in selective attention. In T. Boll & B.K. Bryant (Eds.), *Clinical neuropsychology and brain function* (pp. 169–202). Washington, DC: American Psychological Association.

Posner, M.I., & Petersen, S.E. (1990). The attention system of the human brain. *Annual Review of Neuroscience, 13,* 25–42.

Pribram, K.H., & McGuinness, D. (1975). Arousal, activation, and effort in the control of attention. *Psychological Review, 2,* 116–149.

Reitan, R.M., & Davidson, L.A. (1974). *Clinical neuropsychology: Current status and applications.* Washington, DC: V.H. Winston and Sons.

Rosvold, H.E., Mirsky, A.F., Sarason, I., Bransome, E.D., Jr., & Beck, L.H. (1956). A continuous performance test of brain damage. *Journal of Consulting Psychology, 20,* 343–350.

Shiffrin, R.M. (1988). Attention. In R.C. Atkinson, R.J. Herrnstein, G. Lindsay, & R.D. Luce (Eds.), *Stevens' handbook of experimental psychology (2nd ed.)* (pp. 739–812). New York: John Wiley & Sons.

Streissguth, A.P., Barr, H.M., Sampson, P.D., Parrish-Johnson, J.C., Kirchner, G.L., & Martin, D.C. (1986). Attention, distraction and reaction time at age 7 years and prenatal alcohol exposure. *Neurobehavioral Toxicology and Teratology, 8,* 717–725.

Streissguth, A.P., Martin, D.C., Barr, H.M., Sandman, B.M., Kirchner, G.L., & Darby, B.L. (1984). Intrauterine alcohol and nicotine exposure. Attention and reaction time in 4-year-old children. *Developmental Psychology, 20,* 533–541.

Streissguth, A.P., Sampson, P.D., Carmichael Olson, H., Bookstein, F.L., Barr, H.M., Scott, M., Feldman, J., & Mirsky, A.F. (1994). Maternal drinking during pregnancy: Attention and short-term memory performance in 14-year-old offspring: A longitudinal prospective study. *Alcoholism: Clinical and Experimental Research, 18,* 202–218.

Stroop, J.R. (1935). Studies of interference in serial verbal reactions. *Journal of Experimental Psychology, 18,* 643–662.

Talland, G.A. (1965). *Deranged memory.* New York: Academic Press.

Tatman, J.E. (1992). *Elements of attention and concentration in normal aging adults: Locus of decline.* Unpublished doctoral dissertation, American University, Washington, DC.

Tatman, J.E., Fantie, B.D., & Mirsky, A.F. (1995). *Five elements of normal and disordered attention: The performance of normal adults and neuropsychiatric patients on a battery of attention tests.* Manuscript in preparation.

Wechsler, D. (1974). *Wechsler Intelligence Scale for Children–Revised.* New York: Psychological Corporation.

Wechsler, D. (1981). *Wechlser Adult Intelligence Scale–Revised.* New York: Psychological Corporation.

Zahn, T.P., Frith, C.D., & Steinhauer, S.R. (1991). Autonomic functioning in schizophrenia: Electrodermal activity, heart rate, pupillography. In S.R. Steinhauer, J.H. Gruzelier, & J. Zubin (Eds.), *Handbook of schizophrenia, Volume 5: Neuropsychology, psychophysiology, and information processing* (pp. 185–224). Amsterdam: Elsevier.

Zubin, J. (1975). Problem of attention in schizophrenia. In S. Kietzman, S. Sutton, & J. Zubin (Eds.), *Experimental approaches to psychopathology* (pp. 139–166). New York: Academic Press.

7

ATTENTION
A Behavior Analytical Perspective

William J. McIlvane, William V. Dube, and Thomas D. Callahan

Discussion of the construct of attention from a behavioral perspective must begin by acknowledging two facts. First, there are many behavioral psychologies, and they have different scientific philosophies, fundamental assumptions, and experimental methods. Examples include the rich diversity reflected in Skinner's (1938, 1953) experimental analysis of behavior, Kantor's (1959) inter-behaviorism, Tolman's (1932) cognitive behaviorism, and the mechanistic stimulus–response (S–R) psychologies of Hull (1943) and Spence (1956). Second, even within any given behavioral subdiscipline, there is not unanimity of opinion on the usefulness of the construct of attention. Some take the position that attention is a poorly defined, even superfluous term. Terrace (1966), for example, wrote "*Attention* seems to be synonymous with *stimulus control* to the extent that failures to establish stimulus control are referred to as failures of attention" (p. 288). By contrast, Dinsmoor (1985), another prominent voice in the experimental analysis of behavior, has written more recently that observing behavior such as eye orientation and focusing may not be sufficient to explain the acquisition of stimulus control, and "to complete the picture I think we are obliged to consider analogous processes occurring further along in the sequence of events, presumably in the neural tissue, and commonly known as attention. The processes involved in attention are not as readily accessible to observation as the more peripheral adjustments, but it is my hope and working hypothesis that they obey similar principles" (p. 365).

In this chapter, written from a behavior analytical perspective, we adopt a position closer to Dinsmoor's than to Terrace's. We suggest that attention, or rather

The research program discussed in this chapter has been supported by NICHD Grants HD 25995, 25488, and 28141. We also acknowledge support from the Department of Mental Retardation of the Commonwealth of Massachusetts (Contract 100220023SC).

attending, is a multicomponent behavior that is similar in kind to other forms of behavior. Although attending often is a private event in the sense discussed by Skinner (1953), we suggest that attending can be observed and measured, directly or indirectly, given appropriate experimental methods and apparatus. We argue further that attending is influenced by its consequences and modifiable by arranging appropriate contingencies of reinforcement.

AN EXPERIMENTAL ANALYSIS OF ATTENDING

Our perspective on the analysis of attention is, we believe, consistent with contemporary thinking and research within the experimental analysis of behavior. Following Skinner (1953), we view the task of behavior analysis mainly as describing functional relations between behavior and its controlling variables. The approach to theory building is conservative, and there is an emphasis on experimental rather than statistical control of behavioral variability.

As the Terrace quote above suggests, behavior analysts have traditionally viewed the term *attention* with caution; the perception has been that the term is frequently used too broadly and often with insufficient scientific rigor. As the Dinsmoor quote suggests, however, the traditional view may be changing in the face of accumulating data and more rigorous definitions of attentional processes in cognitive psychology (e.g., Mirsky, Anthony, Duncan, Ahern, & Kellam, 1991; Parasuraman & Davies, 1984; Posner, 1978). Despite this movement, it seems appropriate to remain faithful to and consistent with both the past and current scientific language of behavior analysis. Where others might use the term *attention*, we discuss instead in terms of the establishment and maintenance of stimulus control and of attending to or observing features of the environment.

CONTINGENCY ANALYSIS OF STIMULUS CONTROL

"Control" by a given stimulus is shown when that stimulus influences some aspect of behavior. In the language of attention research, stimulus control shows that the subject "attends" or "pays attention" to it. In examining attending, behavior analysts use the method of contingency analysis, which at its most basic level concerns itself with three types of events: *antecedents* (stimulation caused by events both outside and within the skin); *behaviors* (e.g., listening, thinking, talking); and *consequences* (reinforcers, neutral events, and punishers). Each of these major classes of events is influenced by each other, and also by other variables related to remote ontogenic or/and phylogenic contingencies (Skinner, 1971)— the biological or constitutional determinants of behavior.

Figure 7.1 provides an overview that suggests some of the many variables that may influence stimulus control development. In addition to stimulus variables (e.g., complexity, modality), behavioral variables (e.g., type, duration), and consequential variables (e.g., type, schedule), note the potentially modulating effects of subject variables (e.g., age, sex, clinical diagnosis) and state variables (e.g., bio-

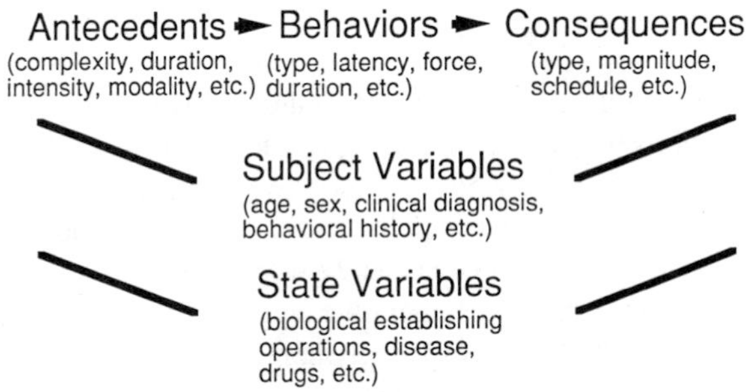

Antecedents ➤ Behaviors ➤ Consequences
(complexity, duration,   (type, latency, force,   (type, magnitude,
intensity, modality, etc.) duration, etc.)   schedule, etc.)

Subject Variables
(age, sex, clinical diagnosis,
behavioral history, etc.)

State Variables
(biological establishing
operations, disease,
drugs, etc.)

Figure 7.1. Variables that may influence stimulus control development.

logical establishing operations, disease, drug influence). In our view, studies of the effects of such modulating variables provide a natural path to multidisciplinary experimental analyses of behavior and a fully informed behavioral neuroscience.

THEORETICAL ANALYSIS OF STIMULUS CONTROL

Although behavior analysis does not yet offer a comprehensive, broadly validated theory of stimulus control (see Dinsmoor, 1985), it does make certain assumptions and assertions, some implicit, many of which have theoretical status. In the spirit of this volume, it seems appropriate to consider them formally here. While undoubtedly there are disagreements among behavior analysts, we suggest that the three general and seven specific statements in Table 1 provide a representative behavior-analytical perspective on the subject matter of attention research.

Table 7.1. Attention research from a behavior analytical perspective

General Assumptions

1. Stimulus control is a function of a number of interacting variables. Increasingly comprehensive contingency analysis leads to increasingly greater understanding of behavior and one's ability to influence it.
2. All purposeful behavior is under antecedent control and is influenced by its consequences.
3. Analytical units do not have a fixed "size." Unit size depends on the behavior being analyzed.

Assumptions Specific To Antecedent Stimulus Control

4. Control by an antecedent stimulus depends on observing/attending and reflects the aspect(s) observed.
5. Observing/attending is modifiable by altering contingencies.
6. Antecedent stimulus control must first occur before it can be influenced by consequences.
7. New topographies of stimulus control can be encouraged by altering contingencies.
8. Multiple stimulus control topographies co-occur under identical stimulus conditions. Individual topographies may be isolated by altering contingencies.
9. Direct experimental analysis and control of observing/attending is increasingly possible and necessary for some purposes.
10. Observing/attending may constitute a "generalized response class."

General Assumptions

Statement 1 follows directly from our preceding discussion. The behavior analyst believes that contingency analysis is necessary to understand fully the critical elements of behavior (see following section on Evaluating Behavior Analytical Assumptions about Stimulus Control). This does not mean, of course, that one cannot use other methods (e.g., statistical analyses of groups of subjects) to discover important facts about behavior. Rather, the suggestion is that explicit, or at least implicit, contingency analysis is especially helpful for understanding, predicting, and influencing the behavior of individual subjects.

Statement 2 follows directly from its predecessor. The behavior analyst believes that, with diligent contingency analysis, one will be able to identify or infer the environmental events that occasion all purposeful (operant) behavior and the consequences that maintain it. No such behavior is "uncontrolled," even in environments explicitly arranged to minimize environmental variation (Ray & Sidman, 1970). An important element of the behavioral perspective is that the behaving individual need not understand (e.g., be able to describe) the antecedents that occasion behavior and the consequences that maintain it. Contingencies may have their influence outside the individual's awareness. This automatic action of contingencies has been demonstrated many times, for example, by Hefferline's classic studies of conditioning of imperceptible muscle movements (Hefferline, Keenan, & Harford, 1959; Hefferline & Perera, 1963).

Statement 3, a general statement about contingency analysis, is pertinent to the extraordinarily varied and complex subject matter addressed by attention researchers. Studies of selective and sustained attention, for example, focus on behavioral episodes of brief and protracted duration, respectively. From a behavior analytical perspective, the fundamental units of analysis need not change with the subject matter. Figure 7.2 presents a series of everyday examples to make this point. It diagrams contingency analyses of multielement, extended antecedents, responses, and consequences. For example, driving to work is analyzed as an extended behavioral chain; target detection in a vigilance task is analyzed as a series of smaller behavioral units embedded in a larger one, and each of these behaviors is influenced by current values and variations in subject and state variables. On the basis of criticisms that appear in the literature from time to time (e.g., Mahoney, 1989), scientists from other disciplines sometimes appear to confuse behavior analysis with mechanistic S–R psychologies that do not have this scope and inherent flexibility. Behavior analysts in turn have trouble defining the scope, core methodology, and analytical units of other disciplines (e.g., Sidman, 1986).

Assumptions Specific to Antecedent Stimulus Control

Statement 4 indicates that behavior analysts, like many other behavioral scientists, differentiate between behavior that merely occurs in the presence of an antecedent and behavior controlled by that antecedent (Ray, 1969). Environmental

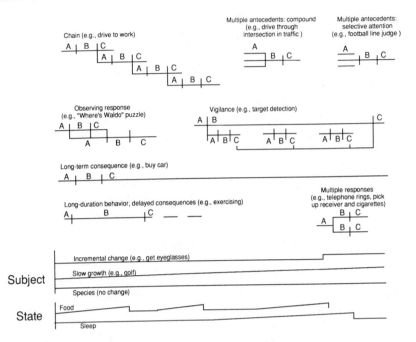

Figure 7.2.   Examples of contingency analyses. A, B, and C refer to antecedent stimuli, behaviors, and consequences, respectively. Time flows from left to right; the passage of time is merely suggested, on a relative scale. The examples are described from the upper left of the figure. In a response chain, stimuli serve the dual functions of conditioned reinforcers for the behavior they follow and discriminative stimuli for the behavior they precede. Multiple antecedents may control behavior as a compound or they may set the occasion for selective attention. An observing response may itself be analyzed in terms of antecedent, behavior, and consequence. In vigilance tasks, a series of observing responses may be analyzed within the behavior term of a larger contingency. Long-term consequences follow some behaviors; long-duration behavior may have relatively short antecedents and immediate consequences but also delayed consequences. Multiple responses may be controlled by the same antecedent. The time lines for subject and state variables suggest ways in which changes in these variables may modulate contingencies. Some subject variables change incrementally, some slowly, and some not at all. State variables may change cyclically.

events are viewed as complex, with many different aspects that the subject may attend to and, in turn, that may come to control behavior (Ray & Sidman, 1970). Elsewhere, we have suggested use of the term "stimulus control topography" to refer to the stimulus aspects or relations that do control (McIlvane & Dube, 1992; Ray, 1969); stimulus control topography appears to be the closest behavior analytical parallel to "representation" in cognitive psychology.

In general, behavior analysts share the assumption that controlling stimuli are selected from complex environments. Perhaps the main difference is that behavior analysts typically emphasize that attending is behavior to be explained; typically avoided are causal statements such as "the stimulus did not control behavior *because* the subject did not attend to it" or "the student is having trouble *because* she does not pay attention in class."

Statement 5, asserting the malleability of stimulus control/attention, is a perspective that seems emphasized in behavior analysis relative to other disciplines.

In certain cognitive theories, for example, attention is a fixed, scarce resource that limits the subject's ability to select relevant aspects of complex environments (Merrill, 1990; Shiffrin & Schneider, 1977). From the perspective of behavior analysis, difficulty attending to aspects of complex environments can be managed by altering contingencies to direct attending to relevant stimuli. The frequent successes of this tactic suggest that certain attending problems may be modifiable and perhaps correctable (e.g., Allen & Fuqua, 1985; Schreibman, Charlop, & Koegel, 1982).

Statement 6 addresses a logical problem that confronts contingency analysis: Where do new forms of stimulus control come from? For example, how does the subject notice the manner in which two novel stimuli differ for the first time? This "problem of the first instance," as Skinner (1935) called it, has been recognized for decades, although few behavior analysts pursue it in their scientific agenda.

We believe that our genetic endowment, itself a result of phylogenetic contingencies, provides us with the basic equipment necessary to detect stimulus change, notice stimulus differences, and determine the relations among environmental events (cf. Gibson, 1979). In general, however, behavior analysis does not yet have a well-advanced answer to the problem of the first instance. This topic, in particular, seems to be an obvious area for fruitful multidisciplinary collaborative studies.

Statement 7 permits a contingency analysis approach to go forward in the absence of a solution to the problem of the first instance. Although we do not know how to "force" the first occurrence of stimulus control, there are powerful and effective procedures for encouraging it. For example, there is an expanding technology of stimulus control shaping (McIlvane & Dube, 1992), which directly parallels powerful, effective procedures for shaping new response topographies (see the section on Stimulus Control Shaping).

Statement 8 represents a viewpoint that is not frequently articulated by behavior analysts, but it parallels directly the analogy that we have made with respect to response topography. Just as many response topographies may be emitted to fulfill the requirements of a programmed contingency (the operant response class; Skinner, 1935), many stimulus control topographies may control the response class (the operant stimulus class). In general, we suggest that the complexity inherent in all environmental events sets the stage for potential competition among multiple environment–behavior controlling relations.

Even when the experimenter seeks to minimize environmental variation, the subject's immediate experience, history, and current state provide sources of variation in the stimulus control topographies—even from moment to moment. Our assumptions here roughly parallel those of the cognitive psychologists interested in problems of interference, response competition, and inhibition of attention, as illustrated, for example, in attentional gating theory (Hasher & Zacks, 1988).

The problems of managing environmental complexity and behavioral variability are major reasons that statistical methods are used so widely in the behavioral sciences. We hope to go further. Our approach is to manage the complexity, to identify sources of variability, and thereby to establish direct experimental rather than statistical control of attending. Illustrative examples will be presented in the material that follows.

Statement 9 alludes to recently developed technologies that make it possible to conduct on-line, moment-by-moment analyses of attending. The capacity for doing these analyses seems essential for diagnosing and possibly remediating stimulus control problems in individual subjects. Behavior analysts' interests, experimental methods, and fundamental assumptions encourage studies with individual subjects that apply the knowledge gained by our own research and that of other disciplines.

Statement 10 asserts merely that general improvements in attending may be attainable through the right kind of training. When attention is viewed as a fixed resource, the improvement route is to teach the individual to allocate that resource more efficiently, that is, to improve executive functioning. Behavior analysts tend to assume that attending itself can be made more efficient—that the attentional resources can be expanded.

EVALUATING BEHAVIOR ANALYTICAL
ASSUMPTIONS ABOUT STIMULUS CONTROL

We present an extended example to address the issue of how behavior analytical assumptions are tested: Under development in our laboratories is a battery of behavioral test procedures designed to evaluate stimulus control development and maintenance. This multipurpose battery addresses a range of performances, including, for example, tests of symbolic processes, immediate and delayed remembering, and attending to both visual and auditory stimuli. The battery is intended to give us greater access to people with poorly developed communication skills: those with mental retardation, autism, or other intellectual disabilities. With members of this population, one cannot rely on syntactically complex verbal instructions.

Even relatively simple tests of attention, like the Stroop test (Stroop, 1935) or the Wisconsin Card Sorting Test (Heaton, 1981), may not be feasible. In their stead, we use behavior analytical procedures, some of which now are finding application in the developing field of behavioral neuroscience (Sahgal, 1993). These procedures meet one of our main criteria for testing procedures: They succeed with little or no verbal instruction. There are certain advantages to avoiding instructions, even with subjects who might understand them. Our experimental analysis of stimulus control development and maintenance would be complicated by extraexperimentally established instructional control. Did our procedures establish stimulus control or merely import it through instructions from the world outside the laboratory?

Another criterion (or rather a goal) is that our procedures succeed in establishing stimulus control with virtually every subject we test regardless of preexperimental capabilities. Although we have not yet fully achieved this goal, we rarely encounter subjects who are "untestable" by our methods. Our procedure choices and criteria reflect our commitment to make contact with individuals who may have the most severe attending problems. We see ourselves as building the capacity to determine the extent to which the manifest behavioral deficits are due to correctable deficits in attending behavior. By focusing on this very difficult population, we also hope to assure effective access to less impaired populations (e.g., individuals with attention deficit hyperactivity disorder [ADHD]), where behavior analysis may also prove useful and revealing.

For reasons of space, we give only an abbreviated, selective view of the methodology, emphasizing procedures that relate most closely to research on attending. Primarily visual stimuli will be featured in these examples, but they are not typically modality-specific. Our presentation follows Sidman's (1986) proposal that a contingency analysis framework could lead to the development of a worthwhile, defensible replacement for traditional psychometrical testing, particularly for populations that are difficult to test.

ASSESSING TWO-TERM CONTINGENCIES

Analysis at this level looks only at the frequency of occurrence of a given response or response class, perhaps a simple touch to a key. If touching produces reinforcers and all other responses do not, then a two-term (response–reinforcer) contingency is defined.

When the behavior of different subject groups is compared; an important consideration is to assure that reinforcing stimuli are comparable across the groups. Schedules of reinforcement are quantitative measures that may be used for this purpose. Schedules may also be useful in evaluating effects of state variables, for example, neurological dysfunction and disease. While certain schedules may not be very sensitive to such factors (cf. Pribram, 1991), others have proven very sensitive. Schedules that typically engender low rates of spaced responding, for example, appear to be excellent choices for screening for neurological dysfunctions that may be related to attending (e.g., frontolimbic damage; Kesner, 1991).

For assessing reinforcer effectiveness, one might employ a fixed-ratio schedule in which reinforcement depends upon a specified number of responses (Ferster & Skinner, 1957). One might compare, for example, response rate and/or length of acquisition to a given stability criterion. When stable response rates are achieved, one can discontinue reinforcement and examine the effects of an extinction contingency. Data in Figure 7.3, from a subject with mental retardation, show a response pattern that is consistent with effective consequences.

In the left portion of Figure 7.3, the rate of responding (button pressing) increased when each response produced a reinforcer (a penny). When reinforcement was discontinued (vertical line), a characteristic "burst" of responding was followed by a decrease in response rate. Reinstituting the reinforcement contingency (not shown in Figure 7.3) permits examination of reacquisition.

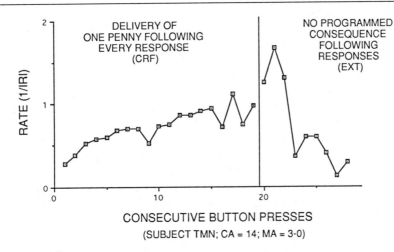

Figure 7.3.   Data from an assessment of reinforcer effectiveness in a subject with mental retardation. Response rate is expressed as the reciprocal of the interresponse interval (IRI) in seconds (i.e., 1/IRI).

Although extinction tests have the advantages of conceptual and procedural simplicity, they may pose implementation problems with some individuals with developmental disabilities; examples include emotional reactions to the aversive effects of extinction and a bias toward responding because of the demand characteristics of the experimenter (i.e., a teacher-like adult). We are now exploring an alternative to extinction tests that makes use of concurrent intermittent schedules of reinforcement.

THREE-TERM CONTINGENCIES

Our concurrent schedules are correlated with different, readily discriminable environmental events; three-term contingencies are thus defined. For example, when stimulus A is presented, two responses on average are required to produce a reinforcer. On other trials when stimulus B is presented, five responses are required. Then, the subject is given trials with a choice between A and B. More frequent selection of A than B is consistent with the schedule disparity. To complete the test, the rates of reinforcement for A and B when presented separately are changed so that, for example, only three responses are required for B but six are now required for A. After exposure to the new schedules, the choice test is repeated. If the subject now selects B more frequently than A, the change in stimulus preference indicates an effective reinforcement contingency and sensitivity to the difference in reinforcement schedules.

As we noted earlier, three-term contingency analysis defines the behavior analytical approach to the study of attending. Figure 7.4 presents examples of stimuli to which we ask the participants in our studies to attend. Some, like letters of the alphabet, are elements of communication systems that may or may not make contact with a given individual's communication repertoire. Others, like pictures, bring extraexperimentally established stimulus classes into the laboratory when that is our interest. Still others, like those shown at the bottom of Figure 7.4, are arbitrary and nonrepresentative; these stimuli are used to establish experimental isolation, insofar as that is possible.

Figure 7.5A illustrates a very basic procedure for evaluating stimulus control, which is modeled after the classic procedures of Sidman and Stoddard (1966). In a simultaneous discrimination procedure, a horizontal line is displayed on one of nine response keys and the subject must discriminate it from the blank keys. A touch to it tells us that the subject observes or attends to some aspect of the form. In the task shown in Figure 7.5B, the subject must discriminate the horizontal feature from the vertical feature common to both the positive and negative stimuli. Figure 7.5C presents a more demanding test for selective attending. The subject must observe the horizontal and vertical features and their respective locations, ignoring identical features in other spatial arrangements. Care in stimulus choices allows one to determine stimuli to which the subject attends—specific features, relations among specific features, or maybe the entire display (see McIlvane, 1992, for a discussion of the relevant techniques).

Three-term contingencies can establish behavioral baselines that permit one to evaluate several major aspects of attending. These aspects include the ability to sustain attending for protracted periods, to shift attending from one stimulus or modality to another, or to divide attending between two or more simultaneously presented stimuli. With respect to Figure 7.5A, for example, one can arrange a test of sustained attention merely by presenting a large number of trials and comparing earlier performance to later. One can also modify that task by presenting some trials without the positive stimulus (S+) and requiring the participant to engage in some other behavior when all of the choices are negative stimuli (S−); "rare stimulus" procedures, in which the target stimulus is infrequent, can be implemented by adjusting proportions of S+ and S− trials.

One can assess shifts of attention across modalities, for example, by establishing two successive discriminations, one involving visual stimuli, the other auditory (see Serna, Stoddard, & McIlvane, 1992, for a discussion of techniques for

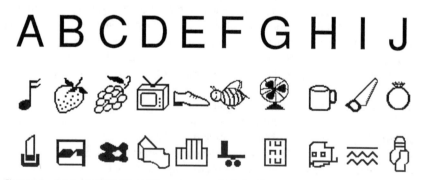

Figure 7.4.   Examples of stimuli used in our assessments of attending.

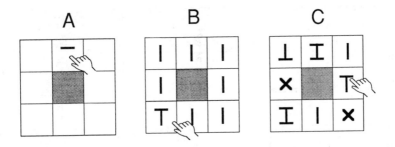

Figure 7.5. Stimulus displays for an assessment of stimulus control by a horizontal line (S+). Highly accurate performance with each type of display indicates attending to and stimulus control by different features of S+. Panel A: Control by any feature of S+ is sufficient. Panel B: S+ and S− have a vertical line in common; discrimination requires control by line orientation. Panel C: S+ is displayed with a variety of S−'s with various features in çommon; discrimination requires control by line orientation and location.

auditory discrimination training); successive stimulus presentation is necessary because auditory stimuli do not retain their intelligibility in simultaneous presentation. With appropriate training, it becomes possible to include individuals with severely limited language in neuropsychologically oriented studies of attending. An especially pertinent question is whether autism renders one especially prone to atypically narrow, restricted stimulus control (cf. Burke, 1991). Behavior analytical procedures allow one to begin evaluating, for example, whether deficits in the ability to shift attending between modalities (see Courchesne et al., 1994) may be due to damage, dysgenesis, or dysfunction in neocerebellar areas in this disorder (Bauman & Kemper, 1985; cf. Akshoomoff & Courchesne, 1992).

With appropriate pretraining (Dube, Iennaco, & McIlvane, 1993) or, sometimes, protracted, elaborate behavioral programming (Dube, Iennaco, Rocco, Kledaras, & McIlvane, 1992), it proves possible to teach individuals with severe learning disabilities a generalized identity matching-to-sample task that permits certain highly refined tests of attending.[1] Figure 7.6 illustrates three trials from an identity matching task that presents not one but two discrete forms as the sample stimuli. With this procedure, a form of "divided attention" test is conducted. After the subject touches the center key, which displays the two-element sample, the sample disappears and the comparison stimuli appear immediately. Control by individual elements can be assessed. For example, in the left sample display, does the subject observe the form on the top? If so, he or she may be able to report that observation by touching the form on the lower left key. Does he or she observe the X-like figure? Other trials test that possibility. Across many such trials, one can test all possible combinations of forms from a stimulus set to evaluate whether the individual attends to certain forms or form combinations better than others (Stromer, McIlvane, Dube, & Mackay, 1993).

With this divided attention task, we routinely find subjects who apparently come under the control of only one of the two elements of the complex sample

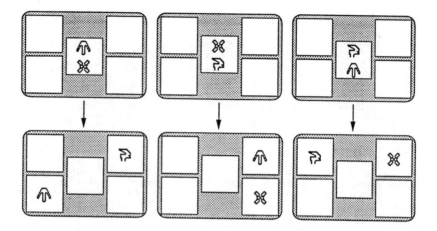

Figure 7.6. Examples of three trials from a "divided-attention" assessment using identity matching to sample with two-element sample stimuli. When the subject touches the sample (top row), it disappears and two single-element comparison stimuli appear (bottom row). Only one comparison element was displayed as a sample element; the specific element varies unpredictably from trial to trial. High accuracy scores indicate attending to both sample elements on every trial.

stimulus, even when the stimuli are representative and namable (e.g., Figure 7.4, center row). Can we arrange contingencies to broaden attending to both elements? One method that we have used is to require differential observing behavior to both elements to verify that they have in fact been observed (Stromer & Dube, 1994). This simple programming method teaches some subjects to attend to both, even when the differential observing responses are no longer explicitly required.

The complex sample procedure has certain disadvantages: It requires an identity matching baseline, and it requires the individual to both attend to and remember the two sample elements. Another procedure that requires the individual to attend to two stimuli simultaneously is the "transverse patterning" (Spence, 1956) (or "ambiguous cue") problem. In this procedure, two (sometimes more) trial types are intermixed. On one type, forms A and B are positive and negative stimuli, respectively; on the second, forms B and C are positive and negative, respectively. In order to make consistent correct selections, the individual must attend to both forms on each trial. Protracted difficulties acquiring this discrimination (which we have seen with a number of individuals with a lower level of functioning) may reveal developmentally related problems in selective attending (cf. Rudy, 1991).

Procedures for Establishing
Control by Three-Term Contingencies

Broadly viewed, there have been two different approaches to establishing stimulus control via three-term contingencies. In one type, the subject is exposed merely to simple differential reinforcement of the final discrimination performance. Responses to the positive stimulus are followed by reinforcers, and those to the negative stimulus are not. The typical dependent variable is trials to meet some prespecified criterion (e.g., responses to $\geq 85\%$ of S+ presentations and to $\leq 15\%$ of S− presentations). This procedure allows ample room for individual variation, but it may produce many failures to achieve stimulus control in individuals with severe learning disabilities (e.g., Zeaman & House, 1963).

Stimulus Control Shaping

The other approach is to provide a stimulus control shaping program to help the subject master the discrimination. From the behavior analytical perspective, stimulus control shaping is synonymous with shaping attending. Figure 7.7 presents an elementary stimulus control shaping technique used to teach a difficult form discrimination between an upright and inverted T. The starting point is an established discrimination between the upright T and seven vertical lines. Over successive trials, the bottom horizontal features of the negative stimuli become more prominent until ultimately they are identical in form to the feature on the top of the positive stimulus.

Methods like these are effective, we believe, for two reasons. First, they may help the subject to detect relevant stimuli. Second, the shaping may help to prevent stimulus control by irrelevant features like position per se, constant features like the key borders, or features common to both positive and negative stimuli. To illustrate the latter problem, we will briefly describe an ongoing program of research that seeks to (a) demonstrate problems of competing stimulus control and (b) develop procedures to reduce or eliminate the competition.

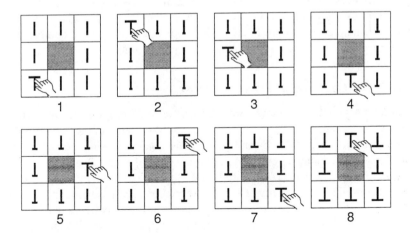

Figure 7.7. Examples of steps from a stimulus control shaping program to transform a T-vs.-I discrimination into a more difficult discrimination between an upright and inverted T. Gradual stimulus changes are programmed over successive trials.

STUDIES OF THE DELAYED S+ PROCEDURE

In one variant of the basic task, two to four identical forms are displayed, and the subject must select the one that differs from the others. The difference is obvious to individuals without developmental limitations; the form flashes, alternates with a black field, or appears on a desaturated color background (McIlvane, Kledaras, Dube, & Stoddard, 1989). Individuals with developmental limitations, however, often find the task extremely difficult, as one might predict from the results of early information processing work on field dependency (Witkin & Goodenough, 1981). Many adopt position preferences, while others show asymptotic, intermediate accuracy scores, perhaps only slightly above the scores that would be achievable by chance. Results of the latter type are most interesting to us. They challenge us to isolate the relevant stimulus control and perhaps to show that intermediate accuracy scores reflect competition from other stimulus control topographies.

The left portion of Figure 7.8 illustrates the analytical method. In Phase 1, every trial initiation response is followed by a display of the type just discussed. Selection of the positive stimulus is followed by a reinforcer and selection of the negative stimulus is not. As noted, the Phase 1 accuracy score may stabilize at levels above chance but short of perfection. In Phase 2, the contingencies are altered. Every trial begins with the presentation of negative stimuli on all keys (trial state 1, or TS1). The appropriate response is to wait a few seconds until one stimulus becomes different (TS2). Any failures to wait merely extend TS1.

Characteristic data are shown under Phase 2 in the rightmost portion of Figure 7.8. Provided that the subject does wait, selections in TS2 are nearly always correct. Over sessions, competing control—reflected in the TS1 responses—gradually declines as it is extinguished. Data of this general type have been obtained on a variety of tasks in our laboratory, and together they make a good case that certain apparent failures of attending occur when the teaching contingencies foster and maintain mixed topographies of stimulus control.

SHAPING GENERALIZED ATTENDING

Our final assumption in Table 1 was that generalized improvements in attending may be achievable through training.[2] One line of research in our laboratory has examined the potential for extending stimulus–control shaping methods to produce generalized attending behavior. Our measure of such behavior is *one-trial discrimination learning* (OTDL). In OTDL, the subject receives a series of two-trial discrimination problems. On the first trial of each problem, one stimulus (S+) is presented alone, and selecting it is reinforced. On the second trial, the S+ is presented again along with a different stimulus (S−), and selecting the S+ is again reinforced. Different stimuli, drawn from a large pool of nonrepresentational forms, are presented on every two-trial problem (cf. House & Zeaman, 1958; Moss & Harlow, 1947). Thus, the first trial of each problem is the subject's

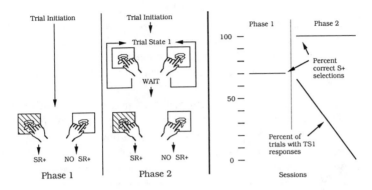

Figure 7.8. Left portion: Delayed S+ analytical method. In Phase 1, a trial-initiation response (e.g., button press) produces S+, a flashing form (denoted by diagonal lines), and S−, an identical but nonflashing form. Only selections of S+ are followed by reinforcers (SR+). In Phase 2, the trial-initiation response produces Trial State 1 (TS1), where two identical S− stimuli are displayed. Responses in TS1 have no effect other than to prolong TS1. TS1 continues until no responses have occurred for several seconds. In Trial State 2 (TS2), S+ is displayed (one form begins flashing), and reinforcement contingencies are as in Phase 1. Right portion: Characteristic data. In Phase 1, accuracy scores are intermediate (70%). When Phase 2 is initiated, accuracy scores immediately improve to near-perfect, and TS1 responses are frequent. TS1 responses gradually extinguish over successive sessions.

only opportunity to observe features of the S+ before being confronted with the forced choice between S+ and S− on the second trial. Highly accurate OTDL performance, therefore, demonstrates experimental control of attending on the first trial of each problem. Furthermore, the attending behavior is generalized in that it is displayed immediately with new stimuli.

The program to teach OTDL combines the methods of learning set research with those of programmed instruction (for a complete description, see Dube et al., 1992; McIlvane, Dube, Kledaras, Iennaco, & Stoddard, 1990). Initially, subjects are trained to perform a series of two-choice visual discrimination problems with a standard multitrial stimulus–control shaping procedure; often an intensity fading procedure is used (see Sidman & Stoddard, 1966, for examples of the technique).

In the OTDL program, the number of shaping steps used to train each discrimination problem is gradually decreased over a large number of different problems with different stimuli, a process we have termed "fading out the fading." As the number of fading steps decreases, the number of different discrimination problems per session increases. If all of the fading steps can be eliminated (except the first one that presents S+ alone) while maintaining highly accurate performance, the result is OTDL.

We have completed this "fading out the fading" program with a number of subjects who were unable to perform OTDL or similar matching tasks in pretests. With respect to attending behavior, the program seems to function like response shaping; more efficient, effective attending is established by reinforcing successively closer approximations to it. We have also encountered a few subjects with whom the last few fading steps could not be eliminated. One possibility in such cases is that the subject engages in various subsets of the responses necessary for adequate attending (orienting, focusing, examining all alternatives, etc.), but never completes all of the requirements within one trial. Because the OTDL procedure provides only an indirect measure of attending, this possibility must at present remain speculative.

More direct evidence that attending is shaped may be obtainable by recording observing–response topography during the OTDL program. Where does the individual look, and for how long? Does the form of observing behavior change with exposure to behavioral programming? A recently developed eyetracking system, appropriate for individuals with mental retardation, could help answer these questions and others (e.g., the question of whether differences in observing topography are associated with accurate vs. poor performance on the divided-attention task described earlier). The eyetracking apparatus incorporates miniature head-mounted video cameras that eliminate the need for the subject's head to remain immobile during recording. This apparatus will allow precise records of observing in subjects who would not tolerate a bitebar or similar requirements.

Furthermore, the apparatus produces real-time video images that track the subject's point of gaze moment-to-moment. This monitoring capability may allow us to do more than evaluate the effects of stimulus–control shaping procedures on observing. It may also allow us to modify observing behavior directly by arranging contingencies for specific observing responses. With this methodology, we hope to determine if good attenders have characteristic observing behaviors, and, if so, if those behaviors can be taught with benefit to poor attenders.

INSTRUCTIONAL CONTROL OF ATTENDING

Our presentation so far has focused mainly on our program of research with individuals who have mental retardation, autism, or some other profound learning disability. In doing so, we do not want to reinforce the misperception that behavior analysis speaks only to those who work with these or other populations with developmental limitations. To the contrary, we believe that contingency analysis can reveal important dimensions of the behavior that is the focus of studies in cognitive and developmental psychology and cognitive neuroscience. As one example, we briefly present the results of a study (Callahan, Deutsch, & McIlvane, 1993) that we conducted with a typical population without mental retardation and one of the now classic procedures of cognitive neuroscience.

In the "prepset" task (Posner, 1980), an arrow or similar instruction cues the subject that a stimulus will appear either left or right of a fixation point. Some instructions are valid; the stimulus appears in the cued location. Other instructions are not valid; the stimulus appears in the other, uncued location. The subject is required to depress a switch as soon as possible when the stimulus appears. Data of primary interest are reaction time differences between valid-cue and invalid-cue trials. Figure 7.9 presents prepset data from five high school student volunteers and Subject DEA, a newly employed, paid laboratory technician in our laboratory, who was unfamiliar with the prepset procedure.

In every subject's initial sessions, we replicated the valid–invalid reaction-time difference that has been widely reported in the cognitive neuroscience literature. Unlike most prepset studies, however, we intended to use the procedure for repeated evaluations of covert orienting. Each of our subjects had 16–18 test sessions. For every subject except DEA, the valid–invalid trial difference disappeared during the testing. At first, this finding puzzled us, but upon reflection we

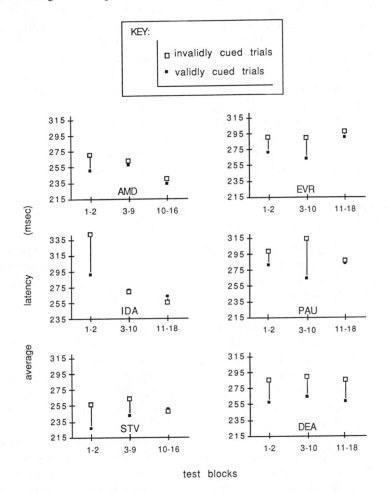

Figure 7.9.   Prepset data from five student volunteers and one paid laboratory technician (Subject DEA). In initial test blocks, response latencies are greater on invalidly cued trials (hollow points) than on validly cued trials (filled points) for all subjects. Only DEA continued to show the valid–invalid latency difference with repeated testing.

view it as perfectly consistent with findings reported in behavior analytical studies of instructional control and rule governance (Baron & Galizio, 1983).

Skinner (1974) pointed out that human behavior may be established quickly by rules or instructions but that such behavior may have different characteristics than that shaped by exposure to reinforcement contingencies. Instructional control may be lost when instructions do not reliably describe environmental contingencies (e.g., Galizio, 1979). On the basis of the data shown in Figure 7.9 and of other findings, we think that instructional control by our cues degraded because they did not reliably describe the locations in which stimuli would appear.

If our preliminary results hold up to further study, we may show that covert orienting is subject to contingency control. If that proves to be the case, that finding might suggest that failure to show "normal" attending in clinical entities like ADHD and autism might be due either to problems of attentional processes per se or to problems of maintaining contingency control. In the general case, the behavior analyst's close analysis of the contingencies may prove quite useful in helping to develop a more complete account of findings in information processing, cognitive neuroscience, and perhaps other disciplines. Our view is that these disciplines are not really in opposition to one another, as is sometimes portrayed. We believe rather that each examines important, often complementary aspects of a very difficult subject matter, and that each can contribute data and perspectives that will ultimately lead to developing scientific consensus.

CRITICAL ISSUES FOR THE BEHAVIOR
ANALYTICAL PERSPECTIVE ON ATTENDING

We conclude by considering the matter of how some of the basic assumptions of the behavior analytical perspective on attentional processes might be tested. First, it is reasonable to ask behavior analysts to define the limits of contingency control. Will one always be able to identify the consequences that maintain behavior? As a challenge, behavior analysts might take on the job of accounting for findings reported in the cognitive psychology literature. Studies of the negative priming phenomenon (Tipper, MacQueen, & Brehaut, 1988), for example, show that attending to a nontarget stimulus (i.e., one not to be responded to) tends to slow responding to a target stimulus that is presented immediately afterwards. No feedback or other explicit consequences are provided for responding. Can a contingency analysis framework accommodate these findings in terms of competing behavior and instructional control?

Second, the burden is on the behavior analyst to demonstrate that one can establish and maintain direct experimental control of attending. Furthermore, we must be able to show that control of attending behavior is in fact related to stimulus control development. We are now beginning studies that have these explicit goals.

Finally, the burden is on the behavior analyst to show that attentional functioning is as malleable as the limited data now available suggest. Our colleagues in other disciplines, particularly the neurosciences, might argue that adequate attentional functioning depends upon intact neural functioning. While this is obviously true, we are not proposing that attending in individuals with severe retardation and autism can be fully "normalized." Perhaps, however, such individuals can learn to attend more broadly than they do, to notice stimulus differences that might otherwise be ignored, and, by training for generalization, to bring improved capabilities to the world outside the laboratory.

ENDNOTES

[1]Stimulus control in conditional matching-to-sample procedures is exerted by both sample and comparison stimuli. For certain purposes, it proves useful to define a four-term reinforcement contingency: sample–comparison–response–consequence (McIlvane, 1992; Sidman, 1986).

[2]Our approach has certain parallels to cognitive theories that view discrimination learning as a two-stage process, an attentional response of selecting the correct stimulus dimension, followed by an instrumental response of selecting the correct value along that dimension (Zeaman & House, 1979). According to two-stage theories, one must first learn to attend to the relevant stimulus dimension before one can learn which stimulus within that dimension to select.

REFERENCES

Akshoomoff, N.A., & Courchesne, E. (1992). A new role for the cerebellum in cognitive operations. *Behavioral Neuroscience, 106*, 731-738.

Allen, K.D., & Fuqua, R.W. (1985). Eliminating selective stimulus control: A comparison of two procedures for teaching mentally retarded children to respond to compound stimuli. *Journal of Experimental Child Psychology, 39*, 55–71.

Baron A., & Galizio, M. (1983). Instructional control of human operant behavior. *The Psychological Record, 33*, 495–520.

Bauman, M.L., & Kemper, T.L. (1985). Histoanatomic observations of the brain in early infantile autism. *Neurology, 35*, 866–874.

Burke, J.C. (1991). Some developmental implications of a disturbance in responding to complex stimuli. *American Journal on Mental Retardation, 96*, 37–52.

Callahan, T.D., Deutsch, C.K., & McIlvane, W.J. (1993). Experimental control of covert orienting. *Experimental Analysis of Human Behavior Bulletin, 11*, 42–46.

Courchesne, E., Townsend, J., Akshoomoff, N.A., Yeung-Courchesne, R., Press, G.A., Murakami, J.W., Lincoln, A.J., James, H., Saitoh, O., Egaas, B., Haas, R.H., & Schreibman, L. (1994). A new finding: Impairment in shifting attention in autistic and cerebellar patients. In S.H. Broman, & J. Grafman (Eds.), *Atypical cognitive deficits in developmental disorders: Implications for brain function* (pp. 101–137). Hillsdale, NJ: Lawrence Erlbaum Associates.

Dinsmoor, J.A. (1985). The role of observing and attention in establishing stimulus control. *Journal of the Experimental Analysis of Behavior, 43*, 365–382.

Dube, W.V., Iennaco, F.M., & McIlvane, W.J. (1993). Generalized identity matching to sample of two-dimensional forms in individuals with intellectual disabilities, *Research in Developmental Disabilities, 14*, 457–477.

Dube, W.V., Iennaco, F.M., Rocco, F.J., Kledaras, J.B., & McIlvane, W.J. (1992). Microcomputer-based programmed instruction in generalized identity matching for persons with severe disabilities. *Journal of Behavioral Education, 2*, 29–51.

Ferster, C.B., & Skinner, B.F. (1957). *Schedules of reinforcement.* New York: Appleton-Century-Crofts.

Galizio, M. (1979). Contingency-shaped and rule-governed behavior: Instructional control of human loss avoidance. *Journal of the Experimental Analysis of Behavior, 31,* 53–70.

Gibson, J.J. (1979). *The ecological approach to visual perception.* Boston: Houghton-Mifflin.

Hasher, L., & Zacks, R.T. (1988). Working memory, comprehension, and aging: A review and a new view. In G.H. Bower (Ed.), *The psychology of learning and motivation* (Vol. 22, pp. 193–225). San Diego: Academic Press.

Heaton, R.K. (1981). *The Wisconsin Card Sorting Test manual.* Odessa, FL: Psychological Assessment Resources.

Hefferline, R.F., Keenan, B., & Harford, R.A. (1959). Escape and avoidance conditioning in human subjects without their observation of the response. *Science, 130,* 1338-1339.

Hefferline, R.F., & Perera, T.B. (1963). Proprioceptive discrimination of a covert operant without its observation by the subject. *Science, 139,* 834–835.

House, B.J., & Zeaman, D. (1958). Reward and nonreward in the discrimination learning of imbeciles. *Journal of Comparative and Physiological Psychology, 51,* 614–619.

Hull, C. (1943). *Principles of behavior.* New York: Appleton-Century-Crofts.

Kantor, J.R. (1959). *Interbehavioral psychology.* Granville, OH: Principia Press.

Kesner, R.P. (1991). Neurobiological views of memory. In J.L. Martinez, Jr. & R.P. Kesner (Eds.), *Learning and memory: A biological view* (2nd ed.) (pp. 499–548). Boston: Academic Press.

Mahoney, M.J. (1989). Scientific psychology and radical behaviorism: Important distinctions between scientism and objectivism. *American Psychologist, 44,* 1372–1377.

McIlvane, W.J. (1992). Stimulus control analysis and nonverbal instructional methods for people with intellectual disabilities. In N.W. Bray (Ed.), *International review of research in mental retardation,* Vol. 18 (pp. 55–109). San Diego: Academic Press.

McIlvane, W.J., & Dube, W.V. (1992). Stimulus control shaping and stimulus control topographies. *The Behavior Analyst, 15,* 89–94.

McIlvane, W.J., Dube, W.V., Kledaras, J.B., Iennaco, F.M., & Stoddard, L.T. (1990). Teaching relational discrimination to individuals with mental retardation: Some problems and possible solutions. *American Journal on Mental Retardation, 95,* 283–296.

McIlvane, W.J., Kledaras, J.B., Dube, W.V., & Stoddard, L.T. (1989). Automated instruction of severely and profoundly retarded individuals. In J. Mulick and R. Antonak (Eds.), *Transitions in Mental Retardation* (Vol. 4., pp. 15–76). Norwood, NJ: Ablex.

Merrill, E.C. (1990). Resource allocation and mental retardation. In N. W. Bray (Ed.), *International review of research in mental retardation* (Vol. 16) (pp. 51–88). San Diego: Academic Press.

Mirsky, A.F., Anthony, B.J., Duncan, C.C., Ahern, M.B., & Kellam, S.C. (1991). Analysis of the elements of attention: A neuropsychological approach. *Neuropsychology Review, 2,* 109–145.

Moss, E., & Harlow, H.F. (1947). The role of reward in discrimination learning in monkeys. *Journal of Comparative and Physiological Psychology, 40,* 333–342.

Parasuraman, R., & Davies, D.R. (1984). *Varieties of attention.* Orlando, FL: Academic Press.

Posner, M. I. (1978). *Chronometric explorations of the mind.* Hillsdale, NJ: Lawrence Erlbaum Associates.

Posner, M.I. (1980). Orienting of attention. The VIIth Sir Frederic Bartlett Lecture. *The Quarterly Journal of Experimental Psychology, 32,* 3–25.

Pribram, K.H., (1991). *Brain and perception: Holonomy and structure in figural processing.* Hillsdale, NJ: Lawrence Erlbaum Associates.

Ray, B.A. (1969). Selective attention: The effects of combining stimuli which control incompatible behavior. *Journal of the Experimental Analysis of Behavior, 12,* 539–550.

Ray, B.A., & Sidman, M. (1970). Reinforcement schedules and stimulus control. In W.N. Schoenfeld (Ed.), *The theory of reinforcement schedules* (pp. 187–214). New York: Appleton-Century-Crofts.

Rudy, J.W. (1991). Elemental and configural associations, the hippocampus and development. *Developmental Psychobiology, 24,* 221–236.

Sahgal, A. (Ed.). (1993). *Behavioural neuroscience, a practical approach* (Vol. I and II). Oxford: IRL/Oxford.

Schreibman, L., Charlop, M.H., & Koegel, R.L. (1982). Teaching autistic children to use extra-stimulus prompts. *Journal of Experimental Child Psychology, 33,* 475–491.

Serna, R.W., Stoddard, L.T. & McIlvane, W J. (1992). Developing auditory stimulus control: A note on methodology. *Journal of Behavioral Education, 2,* 391–403.

Shiffrin R.D., & Schneider, W. (1977). Controlled and automatic information processing: II. Perceptual learning, automatic attending, and a general theory. *Psychological Review, 84,* 127–190.

Sidman, M. (1986). Functional analysis of emergent verbal classes. In T. Thompson & M.D. Zeiler (Eds.), *Analysis and integration of behavioral units* (pp. 213–245). Hillsdale, NJ: Lawrence Erlbaum Associates.

Sidman, M., & Stoddard, L.T. (1966). Programming perception and learning for retarded children. In N. R. Ellis (Ed.), *International Review of Research in Mental Retardation* (Vol. 2, pp. 151–208). New York: Academic Press.

Skinner, B.F. (1935). The generic nature of the concepts of stimulus and response. *Journal of General Psychology, 12,* 40–65.

Skinner, B.F. (1938). *The behavior of organisms: An experimental analysis.* New York: Appleton-Century-Crofts.

Skinner, B.F. (1953). *Science and human behavior.* New York: Macmillan.

Skinner, B.F. (1971). *Beyond freedom and dignity.* New York: Alfred A. Knopf.

Skinner, B.F. (1974). *About behaviorism.* New York: Alfred A. Knopf.

Spence, K.W. (1956). *Behavior theory and conditioning.* New Haven, CT: Yale University Press.

Stromer, R., & Dube, W.V. (1994). Differential observing of complex sample stimuli and delayed matching performance: A brief report. *Experimental Analysis of Human Behavior Bulletin, 12,* 17–20.

Stromer, R., McIlvane, W.J., Dube, W.V., & Mackay, H.A. (1993). Assessing control by elements of complex stimuli in delayed matching to sample. *Journal of the Experimental Analysis of Behavior, 59,* 83–102.

Stroop, J.R. (1935). Studies of interference in serial verbal reactions. *Journal of Experimental Psychology, 18,* 643–662.

Terrace, H.S. (1966). Stimulus control. In W. K. Honig (Ed.), *Operant behavior: Areas of research and application* (pp. 271–355). New York: Appleton-Century-Crofts.

Tipper, S.F., MacQueen, G.M., & Brehaut, J.C. (1988). Negative priming between response modalities: Evidence for the central locus of inhibition in selective attention. *Perception & Psychophysics, 43,* 45–52.

Tolman, E C. (1932). *Purposive behavior in animals and man.* New York: Appleton-Century-Crofts.

Witkin, H.A., & Goodenough, D.R. (1981). *Cognitive styles: Essence and origin.* New York: International University Press.

Zeaman, D., & House, B.J. (1963). The role of attention in retardate discrimination learning. In N.R. Ellis (Ed.), *Handbook of mental deficiency, psychological theory and research* (pp. 159-223). New York: McGraw-Hill.

Zeaman, D., & House, B.J. (1979). A review of attention theory. In N.R. Ellis (Ed.), *Handbook of mental deficiency, psychological theory and research* (pp. 63–120). Hillsdale, NJ: Lawrence Erlbaum Associates.

8

CONCEPTUALIZING, DESCRIBING, AND MEASURING COMPONENTS OF ATTENTION
A Summary

Jeffrey M. Halperin

The previous three chapters described cognitive, neuropsychological, and behavior analytical approaches to studying attention. In past decades, proponents of different schools of thought were often antagonistic toward each other. However, in contrast to that tradition, these authors not only acknowledge the importance of varying approaches, but they also indicate ways in which these approaches complement each other. Furthermore, despite substantial differences in research strategies, there is considerable convergence with regard to the authors' overall conceptualization of attention.

In this chapter, the essential features of the three perspectives on attention are summarized, with a primary focus on points of convergence. Subsequently, an approach is offered for conceptualizing and studying attention by integrating cognitive, neuropsychological, and behavior analytical methodologies, and by placing them within a developmental perspective.

THE COGNITIVE APPROACH

Following a brief historical review of cognitive perspectives on attention, Sergeant (Chapter 5) presented a contemporary view based largely on Sternberg's (1969) additive factor model (AFM). The AFM provides a serially based framework for information processing, along with a methodology for measuring the various components of the model. Through the AFM, Sergeant described experimental and statistical procedures for distinguishing among encoding, central

---

The author would like to thank Kathleen E. McKay for her helpful comments on this manuscript.

processing, and response organization, each of which is viewed as a distinct stage of information processing.

Subsequently, through the addition of "cognitive–energetic" concepts, Sergeant developed a more dynamic model of attention. This latter model, which stresses the central role of effortful processing (Schneider & Shiffrin 1977; Shiffrin & Schneider, 1977), begins to integrate the constructs of arousal and activation with selective and sustained attention. Importantly, in this more elaborated conceptualization, attention is viewed as an active process with a dynamic "management function" that regulates the allocation of resources and plays a central role in determining what is selected for attention. Sergeant points out that this management function closely resembles what neuropsychologists often refer to as executive functions, which are presumed to be regulated by the frontal lobes.

Sergeant's cognitive model of attention is most commonly tested through the systematic manipulation of stimulus characteristics and task demands in nonreferred subjects. Within this paradigm, the primary measure of interest is the slope of the line representing the change in reaction time (RT) observed across experimental conditions. Differences in slope are seen as reflecting the difference in time necessary to process the target information. By differentially manipulating individual task components, one can ascertain the relative efficacy and independence of distinct elements of attention by comparing their slopes. Yet Sergeant cautions against the blind use of RT as a measure of processing speed without first evaluating the error rate. He points out that it is impossible to infer whether the subject is performing at maximal speed, or whether speed is reduced in order to maximize accuracy, without first evaluating the relationship between accuracy and RT. Sergeant argues that knowledge regarding this "speed–accuracy trade-off" is essential for interpreting data generated through most information processing paradigms.

Finally, Sergeant briefly reviews studies that assess developmental changes in cognitive/attentional ability. From the limited literature available, he concludes that most changes in cognitive development during middle childhood are related to encoding and motor output functions rather than to central processing per se. This conclusion is similar to that reached by Halperin, McKay, Matier, and Sharma (1994) in a recent review of the attentional literature. Furthermore, Sergeant points out that there may be additional developmental differences in the allocation of effort.

THE NEUROPSYCHOLOGICAL APPROACH

Mirsky's neuropsychological model (Chapter 6) is based largely on his evolutionary–developmental perspective, which highlights the fact that the ability to attend is not unique to humans. Rather, attention to the environment is a basic capacity required for survival of even the most primitive creatures. Although this capacity is most refined in humans and is enabled by phylogenetically higher brain regions, a substantial proportion of the neural mechanisms of attention must be mediated via phylogenetically older subcortical structures.

On the basis of data derived from performance on neuropsychological tests, Mirsky provides a model of attention, which, in its latest revision, has been expanded from containing four to five distinct elements. The first, *focus/execute*, refers to the capacity to allocate attentional resources to a specific task while screening out irrelevant stimuli. The second, *shift*, refers to the ability to move attentional focus efficiently across stimuli. The third, *sustain*, relates to the concept of vigilance or the ability to maintain performance over extended periods of time. The fourth, *encode*, relates to the capacity to hold information in mind for a brief period while utilizing or manipulating it. Finally, *stability*, the most recently (and tentatively) added factor, is believed to relate to the reliability or consistency of attentional effort over time.

Mirsky's *focus/execute* and *sustain* elements closely parallel the cognitive concepts of selective (or focused) and sustained attention. The *shift* element appears similar to Sergeant's management function and is closely associated with executive functions. Notably, the Wisconsin Card Sorting Test (Heaton, 1981), a key measure of Mirsky's *shift* element, is among the most sensitive neuropsychological instruments to frontal lobe dysfunction in man. In contrast, Mirsky's *encode* element is quite different from the stimulus encoding process described by Sergeant as part of the AFM. Mirsky's *encode* element appears more closely associated with central processing, as defined by the AFM, and is quite similar to what others would refer to as working memory. It is not yet clear how the tentatively defined *stability* element relates to cognitive models of attention. However, it may relate either to the concept of sustained attention or the ability to consistently allocate resources. The latter of these could be subsumed under the management function of the cognitive/energetic models.

It is important to note that Mirsky's elements of attention were identified through the use of factor analytical procedures that were applied to neuropsychological test data. Because random data can generate distinct factors, models derived from such analyses are often met with skepticism. The fact that Mirsky was able to replicate his original findings in diverse subject populations, however, provides additional support for the model.

After establishing the stability of his model across subject groups, Mirsky hypothesizes how each component of attention relates to the integrity of specific brain regions. The *focus/execute* element is associated with the integrity of the superior temporal and inferior parietal cortices, along with the corpus striatum. The *sustain* and *stability* elements are hypothesized to be subserved by the brain stem/midbrain reticular formation and some thalamic nuclei. The *shift* component is seen as relating to the function of the prefrontal cortex and anterior cingulate gyrus, and the *encode* to the hippocampus and amygdala. According to the model, these individual regions are linked to form an organized attentional system within the brain. These hypotheses, which are based upon data from a limited number of studies with animals and patients with known brain damage, must be considered tentative until further data are gathered. This is particularly true when considering the implications of these hypotheses for developmental theories of attention and the ontogenesis of the neural substrates that subserve these functions. Nevertheless, recent advances in neuroimaging technology may provide the means for adequately testing these hypotheses in the near future.

Another important aspect of Mirsky's model is the ease with which it can be applied to study various clinical groups. Chapter 6 highlights the application of the model for assessing attentional deficits in adults with epilepsy, as well as children at risk for schizophrenia spectrum disorders, fetal alcohol syndrome, shyness, and aggressive behavior. This model can just as readily be applied to a wide range of other disorders that purportedly result in attentional dysfunction, such as attention deficit hyperactivity disorder (ADHD), learning disabilities, closed head injury, and Tourette's syndrome, to name just a few.

THE BEHAVIOR ANALYTICAL APPROACH

Finally, McIlvane, Dube, and Callahan (Chapter 7) approach the construct of attention from a behavior analytical perspective. Clearly, less has been written about the construct of attention from this perspective when compared to the voluminous literature within the fields of cognitive psychology and neuropsychology. The reason for this relates to the view of some behavior analysts that attention is "a poorly defined, even superfluous term" (Chapter 7, page 97). Furthermore, attention is difficult to investigate from a behavior analytical perspective because it is not always readily accessible to direct observation. McIlvane et al. adopt the position that attention is synonymous with the establishment and maintenance of stimulus control. They view attention as similar to other behaviors in that it is influenced by antecedents and consequences and modifiable through the systematic application of reinforcement and/or punishment. Unlike other disciplines, which oftentimes use "attention" as a hypothetical construct to explain behavior (e.g., Joey got the answer wrong because he wasn't paying attention), McIlvane et al. emphasize the fact that attention is a behavior to be explained and/or manipulated (e.g., Joey wasn't paying attention because there were too many distractions in the room. How can we modify the environment and/or reinforce attentive behavior?).

Distinctions between selective and sustained attention common to cognitive and neuropsychological views of attention are somewhat less important from a behavior analytical perspective. Rather, attentional tasks are viewed as having either brief or protracted durations involving an extended behavioral chain (e.g., driving to work) or a series of small behavioral units embedded in a larger unit (e.g., a repetitive vigilance task). This latter view is not substantially different from that proposed by some neuropsychologists (Cooley & Morris, 1990), who have described sustained attention as the ongoing repetition of selective attention.

Through the use of three-term contingency analysis, McIlvane et al. demonstrate how behavioral procedures can be used to assess a wide array of attentional functions. Their procedure involves the presentation of positive (reinforced) and negative (nonreinforced) stimuli on each trial. Selective attention is demonstrated when a subject accurately selects and responds to the reinforced stimulus. Sustained attention can be evaluated by presenting a large number of trials and assessing whether a decrement in performance occurs as a function of time on task. Shifts in attention across modalities can be assessed via the use of both visual and auditory (or tactile) stimuli. Finally, divided attention can be assessed by requiring the subject to attend to multiple stimuli on a given trial. The authors suggest that these procedures may be more appropriate for assessing attention in severely impaired subject populations than the more typically used psychometrical tests, which have a multitude of problems when administered to individuals who are low functioning.

The most notable aspect of the behavior analytical approach is the belief that attention is malleable. Whereas cognitive psychologists measure distinct components of attention in order to understand the workings of the human psyche, and neuropsychologists assess the relationship of attentional elements to brain function in order to understand the nature of dysfunction in a wide range of patient groups, behavior analysts strive to *modify* attention with the hope of improving the functional capacity of the patient. Preliminary data in children with autism (Chapter 7) suggest that through the systematic application of behavioral principles this goal may be attainable. However, further research will be necessary to determine whether improved performance on these laboratory measures generalizes to greater attention in natural settings.

COMPARISON OF APPROACHES

Researchers from the disciplines of cognitive psychology, neuropsychology, and behavior analysis use distinct methodologies and often very different language when studying attention. Despite these differences, there is considerable agreement across these investigative approaches with regard to the basic structure of attention. Investigators from all three areas agree that attention is a multifaceted construct that is not readily captured by a single concept or measure. Additionally, all three distinguish between selective (or focused) and sustained attention. Although defined somewhat differently, the cognitive and neuropsychological approaches further elaborate upon distinct encoding and response organization (or outputting) processes. Although many investigators have maintained that response organization and output are distinct from attention, which is seen primarily as an inputting process, Sergeant (Chapter 5) and Mirsky (Chapter 6) appear to take a broad perspective and view selection of response (or output) and response modulation as requiring attentional resources.

The most notable difference across the three approaches is in regard to their test instruments and procedures. Proponents of the cognitive perspective frequently use computer-based assessments to evaluate changes in RT as a function of experimental manipulations. Changes in RT across conditions are then attributed to the manipulated variable. Thus, a main effect demonstrating a difference across conditions provides support for the construct validity of the manipulation. If two manipulations are used within a single paradigm, according to the AFM, it can be determined whether they are affecting the same or different stages of information processing by evaluating whether their combined impact is additive or interactive. Similarly, the relationship between task manipulation (or condition) and age group or patient status can be used to assess developmental changes or specific deficits, respectively. If the performance of one group relative to another differs consistently across all conditions (i.e., main effect for Group without a Group × Condition interaction), it would indicate that the function being manipulated does not account for the difference between the groups. In contrast, if the manipulation differentially affects the groups (i.e., there is a Group × Condition interaction), this may indicate that the manipulated variable accounts for the group differences. Again, an important consideration when using this approach is related to performance accuracy. Because RT, and not accuracy, is usually the primary measure of interest, low accuracy can have a substantial impact upon the validity of the data. It is difficult to interpret RT data in the context of poor accuracy. Thus, when using this approach to assess developmental changes or specific impairments in a patient group, one must be certain that all subjects can perform the task with a relatively high level of accuracy.

The behavior analytical approach of McIlvane et al. (Chapter 7) also utilizes direct experimental manipulations, allowing one to make causal inferences regarding alterations in performance. In addition to manipulating task stimuli and demands, these investigators also manipulate reinforcement contingencies. Within this framework, attention is seen as relating to stimulus discrimination, and performance is modified by reinforcing "attention" to selected stimulus features. Although the behavior analytical approach is less concerned with discriminating between the various components of attention, it may be possible to do so by differentially reinforcing hypothesized subcomponents of attention to determine their relative independence. Instead, McIlvane et al. focus their efforts on the treatment of presumed attention deficits. Although their data clearly indicate enhanced performance in children with autism, it is difficult to know with certainty what specific process is being reinforced and the extent to which behavior changes will generalize to nonlaboratory settings. Yet the implications for treatment of patients with attentional dysfunction are compelling, and this is clearly a worthy direction for future research.

The neuropsychological approach of Mirsky differs from the other two in that it is based primarily on correlative rather than experimental procedures. Direct manipulation of brain structures is a common research strategy in work with animals, but human neuropsychological research is obviously limited in this regard. Alternatively, human research focuses on differences in neuropsychological test performance in patients with different types of "naturally occurring" neurological dysfunction. This approach has yielded tremendous gains in our knowledge of brain–behavior relationships, particularly in the areas of language, perception, and motor output. Yet, when applied to the study of attention, this approach becomes more problematic. Performance on virtually all neuropsychological tests requires all components of attention, making pattern analysis vis-à-vis elements of attention difficult. Although one can argue that different tests require more (or less) of individual elements of attention, the differences across tests are not readably quantifiable. Furthermore, performance on most neuropsychological tasks involves a variety of processes other than attention (e.g., motor skills, language, memory, perception). Performance on any given task, which is typically represented by a single score, can only reflect the sum of all of these factors.

Mirsky deals with these difficulties by using multiple, well-normed measures that appear (based on factor analysis) to measure distinct constructs. Each factor is interpreted as reflecting a distinct element of attention. Inferences regarding the association of attentional functions to distinct brain regions are made by showing performance differences across patient groups. Yet the addition of cognitive tasks containing systematically manipulated conditions to his battery of well-standardized tests could boost confidence in the construct validity of his factors. For example, would performance decrements associated with systematically increasing the number of distractors on a cognitive task be correlated with (or load on) his *focus/execute* factor?

Not surprisingly, each of these approaches to studying attention has relative strengths and weaknesses. A primary purpose of this book is to provide communication and (it is hoped) integration across these differing schools. Below, components from the cognitive, neuropsychological, and behavior analytical perspectives are culled with the intention of generating a developmentally based approach for studying attention. This attempt at integration is not intended to be a conclusive answer to critical questions regarding the construct of attention and its relationship to human development. Rather, the goals are to raise questions, facilitate thought, and provide potential directions for future developmental research in the area of attention. In addition to using the ideas presented by the authors of the previous three chapters, this section borrows from, and further expands upon, previously published work (Halperin et al., 1994).

A DEVELOPMENTAL APPROACH TO UNDERSTANDING AND STUDYING ATTENTION

Components of Attention

Although there is no universally accepted definition for attention, most theorists agree that attention is not a unitary construct. A number of multifaceted theories have been developed, which typically divide attention into several components. Implicit in most theories of attention, including those described in the previous chapters, is the notion of arousal, which is characterized by a physiological readiness to perceive environmental stimuli. Presumably, extreme levels of arousal on either end of the continuum can impair attention (Yerkes & Dodson, 1908). Furthermore, level of arousal differentially affects performance as a function of task difficulty; high arousal tends to improve performance on easy tasks but interferes with performance on more difficult ones (Seltzer & Mesulam, 1988). This concept of arousal has been characterized by neuropsychologists as the regulator of "tone" (Luria, 1973) and by cognitive investigators as the underlying "matrix" or "state" function of attention (Mesulam, 1985). As suggested by the writings of both Sergeant (see Chapter 5) and Mirsky (see Chapter 6), arousal is closely associated with, but not identical to, the notion of sustained attention. It enables the maintenance of vigilance and focusing power that is necessary for efficient processing of information. Overall, arousal appears to be necessary, but not sufficient, for efficient attention and information processing.

Another important component of attentional functioning is the orienting response. The orienting response reflects physiological and behavioral changes that occur upon detection of a novel or significant stimulus (Ohman, 1979; Rohrbaugh, 1984; for review see Cowan, 1988). The orienting response can be involuntary, or it may be of a voluntary and effortful nature, such as when one actively directs attention to an interesting stimulus. Orienting, whether voluntary or involuntary, is a necessary precursor for selective attention and further information processing, although selective attention may subsequently involve the inhibition of the orienting response to irrelevant stimuli. The development of this ability to actively inhibit the orienting response may play an important role in the development of selective attention.

Selective attention refers to one's ability to focus on relevant stimuli while ignoring irrelevant information. In Chapter 5, Sergeant reviews several theories that have been proposed to explain this process of selectivity. Selective attention is also often seen as including divided attention or the ability to attend to multiple stimuli simultaneously. The difficulty encountered when attending to "two things at once" reflects what is referred to as the limited capacity of selective attention. Yet, as an individual moves from an effortful mode of processing, where attention is actively controlled, to automatic processing, which occurs without conscious awareness (Schneider, Dumais, & Shiffrin, 1984; Schneider & Shiffrin, 1977; Shiffrin & Schneider, 1977), the amount of information that can be processed increases. The way in which this occurs remains unclear, raising the question as to whether multiple stimuli are truly being attended to simultaneously or whether attention is being switched across stimuli very quickly. If attention is rapidly switching from one stimulus to the next, then the phenomenon can be explained via a single-channel mechanism. If, however, attention is truly focused on several stimuli simultaneously, then attention might best be described as a mechanism with multiple channels of selectivity. If this were the case, as learning occurs and tasks become more automatic, not only could the capacity of any given channel increase, but so could the number of channels.

Some investigators have suggested that the distinction between selective and sustained attention may not be useful and that sustained attention is just on-going selective attention (Cooley & Morris, 1990). Most investigators (including Sergeant and Mirsky), however, consider them to be at least partially distinct. Within this latter context, sustained attention is usually viewed as being more closely related to arousal and/or the maintenance of vigilance following the orienting response, whereas selective attention is more closely associated with information processing. However, the two components are not completely dissociable because the ability to sustain attention is usually measured by decrements in performance over time, which at least in part involves selective attention.

Yet preliminary data from my laboratory suggest that time-related decreases in performance (i.e., sustained attention) are not merely the result of changes in selective attention (Halperin et al., 1994). Children were administered a visual focused attention test (Sharma, Halperin, Newcorn, & Wolf, 1991) in which target and nontarget stimuli were presented in the presence of zero, two, or five randomly presented distractors. Selective attention was assessed by the increase in RT to the target stimulus as a function of the number of distractors, and sustained attention was measured by increases in RT as a function of time on task. However, there was no Distractor × Time interaction, suggesting that selective and sustained attention are distinct processes. Although further studies are required to elucidate the relationship between these aspects of attentional function, these findings raise the possibility that selective and sustained attention have distinct developmental trajectories, have distinct neural substrates, and are differentially impaired in different patient groups. Prior to addressing these possibilities, it is important to briefly review methodological issues in the assessment of attention.

Measurement of Attention

Within the clinical literature, the assessment of attention in children is dominated by the use of parent and teacher rating scales. Even among sophisticated psychometrical evaluations, one frequently sees detailed objective test data supporting contentions regarding intelligence, academic achievement, language, and perceptual functioning, whereas statements regarding attention are based upon clinical impressions or subjective observations.

Multiple difficulties plague these subjective approaches to assessing attention, including poor interrater reliability as well as the overrating of the prevalence of attentional problems, which appears to be due at least in part to halo effects. Studies have convincingly demonstrated that children who are disruptive are rated by teachers as inattentive even if they are not "off-target" more than their peers (Abikoff, Courtney, Pelham, & Koplewicz, 1993; Schachar, Sandberg, & Rutter, 1986). As a result, ratings of attention are confounded by disruptive behavior, making rating scales more appropriate for evaluating problematic behavior than for assessing attention. In fact, recent investigations have suggested that the overuse of rating scales may have led us astray and that many children diagnosed as having ADHD do not have attentional difficulties (Chapter 4; Halperin et al., 1990; van der Meere & Sergeant, 1988a; 1988b). Furthermore, outside of the clinical domain, rating scales cannot be used to delineate developmental aspects of attention because raters usually evaluate children relative to their age-matched peers, thus effectively removing the variance accounted for by age.

On the other hand, most clinical/research reports that use objective test data to support inferences about a child's attentional capacity use measures that lack specificity and have questionable construct validity (for a more thorough review, see Halperin et al., 1994). These procedures tend to assess aspects of attention, but they also measure a number of other cognitive processes. This problem, which is inherent to virtually all psychometrical measures of attention, is due to the fact that attention is primarily involved with early stages of information processing. Yet our tests only measure the final product or endpoint of a number of cognitive processes. Thus, poor performance on most purported measures of attention can be due to any of a variety of cognitive processes. As a result, an attentional difficulty may be erroneously diagnosed, or age-related changes may be inappropriately attributed to the development of attentional capacities. To infer more confidently that the process being assessed is attention, one must directly manipulate the attentional component of the task while maintaining equivalence across all other parameters (van der Meere & Sergeant, 1988a; 1988b). Then, differences in performance across conditions can be attributed to the attentional manipulation, and the magnitude of the difference can be used to assess individual differences in attention.

For example, to assess focused attention, one must have a series of tasks that differ in the number and/or salience of distractors but are identical in every other way, including their encoding/perceptual, mnestic, linguistic, cognitive, and motor demands. Then, the decrement in performance across tasks, which *must* increase as a function of the number of distractors, could be considered the measure of focused attention. Individual differences can be evaluated by comparing the impact of the distractors between subjects. When comparing index and control groups, a Group × Task interaction, rather than a main effect for Group, would be necessary to demonstrate a focused attention deficit in the index group. The distractors would need to have a greater impact upon the index group as compared to controls. Similarly, to evaluate age-related changes in focused attention, it would be necessary to demonstrate an Age × Task interaction. Using the same approach, if one wanted to measure sustained attention, performance decrements on a single task must be measured as a function of time on task, and a Group (or Age) × Time interaction would have to be demonstrated.

Clinicians and researchers are likely to gain by using this more precise approach, which is commonly used by cognitive psychologists to study attention. However, this approach is not often used because reliability of most measures has not been systematically assessed, there is a lack of adequate norms, and serious questions have been raised regarding the ecological validity of these measures (Barkley, 1991; see also Chapter 4). The development of well-standardized procedures for assessing attention, similar to those used by cognitive psychologists, is an important direction for future research.

Development of Attention

The degree to which developmental increases in cognitive abilities during childhood are attributable to growth in attentional mechanisms is unclear. In Chapter 5, Sergeant provides a brief review of the cognitive literature examining developmental progressions in attentional capacity in typical children, and more extensive reviews have been published elsewhere (Halperin et al., 1994; Taylor, 1980).

During early childhood, attention appears to be driven primarily by stimuli in the environment, with some stimuli being better able to elicit an orienting response than others. For the first 4 months of life, attention is drawn most consistently to objects with greater light–dark contrast, those with a moderate number of edges, and those that move (Fantz, 1966; Karmel, 1969; Salapatek & Kessen, 1966; for review see Taylor, 1980). Subsequent to this age, novelty becomes more important for directing attention as infants attend less, or "habituate," to repeated stimuli (Wetherford & Cohen, 1973).

Only later does the ability to orient one's attention voluntarily gradually develop. Vygotsky (as cited in Luria, 1973) suggests that the interaction between child and adult may be crucial to the development of the ability to direct attention voluntarily. He suggests that "from an external, socially organized attention [e.g., where an adult directs an infant's attention to stimuli of interest by altering the stimulus characteristics in some way] develops the child's *voluntary attention*, which . . . is an internal, self-regulating process" (p. 262). By about 4 years of age, children develop the ability to scan their environment actively, rather than being drawn by the novelty or salience of a stimulus. This internally driven attention is believed to be well established by 5 or 6 years of age.

Early studies assessing the development of selective attention indicated substantial age-related changes during childhood (Doyle, 1973; Maccoby, 1969; Strutt, Anderson, & Well, 1975). However, as suggested by Sergeant (see Chapter 5), as well as others (Shepp, Barrett, & Kolbet, 1987; Smith, Kemler, & Aronfreed, 1975), these data may reflect differences in perceptual ability (inputting) or motor output, rather than developmental growth in selective attention per se.

Relatively few studies have adequately examined the development of sustained attention. Rather, most have reported age-related increments in overall performance on vigilance tasks without evaluating performance changes over time. Thus, one can clearly state that the number of missed targets on a continuous performance test is highly age-dependent in children (Gordon, 1983; Halperin, Sharma, Greenblatt, & Schwartz, 1991; Levy, 1980). However, the extent to which these age-related changes are due to sustained attention, as opposed to other processes, is not clear. A child's overall performance on vigilance tasks can be poor because of selective attention deficits (i.e., he or she is distractible), sustained attention deficits (i.e., initial performance level cannot be maintained), or deficits in response organization (i.e., difficulty in organizing output), to name just a few possibilities.

Seidel and Joschko (1990) evaluated performance changes over time on a vigilance task in 6- to 10-year-old children. They reported significant reductions in accuracy over time only in 6- and 7-year-olds, suggesting developmental differences in sustained attention. More recently, McKay, Halperin, Schwartz, and Sharma (1994) systematically examined the development of attentional abilities by comparing the performance of children between the ages of 7 and 11 years, as well as adults, on a battery of cognitive tasks designed to measure focused attention, sustained attention, and response organization. The data from this study suggested that the capacity for focused attention is fully developed in nonreferred children by 7 years of age, whereas sustained attention continues to develop throughout adolescence. Finally, the ability to organize a motor output, which is a later stage of information processing and often considered to be an executive rather than attentional function, appears to develop primarily during middle childhood.

Neural Basis of Attention

As indicated by Mirsky (Chapter 6), data strongly suggest that specific regions at different levels of the neuraxis interact to form a neural system that is involved in the regulation of attention. Halperin et al. (1994) have partially outlined a neural system for visual attention that is based upon the work of several prominent investigators. This hypothesized neural system overlaps substantially with, but is not identical to, that proposed by Mirsky.

At the core of this attentional system is the locus coeruleus (LC), which is located in the brain stem and provides the bulk of the noradrenergic (NA) innervation throughout the brain. As described by Aston-Jones (1985), the discharge rate of neurons in the LC is highly dependent upon the degree to which the animal is attending to its environment. Low vigilance states are accompanied by a relatively low rate of discharge by LC neurons. However, when attention shifts to the external environment there is marked increase in LC activity. Postsynaptic NA release that results from LC firing appears to enhance the "signal-to-noise" ratio for target cells so that neurons respond preferentially to their most significant inputs (Aston-Jones, 1985; Foote & Morrison, 1987; Oades, 1985). In this manner, the NA neurons of the LC may "set the stage" for selective attention.

Rostral to the LC are three areas that receive dense NA innervation and have enhanced neuronal activity when subjects attend to visual stimuli. These areas are the posterior parietal lobe (Mountcastle, 1978; Wurtz, Goldberg, & Robinson, 1980), the pulvinar nucleus of the thalamus (Petersen, Robinson, & Morris, 1987), and the superior colliculus (Morrison & Foote, 1986; Posner & Petersen, 1990). Injury to any of these areas leads to a disruption in attention, although the nature of the deficit varies depending upon the region affected. Damage to the posterior parietal lobe results in difficulty disengaging attention from the location that was being attended to (Posner, Walker, Friedrich, & Rafal, 1984), damage to the pulvinar nucleus causes difficulty engaging attention in another location (Petersen et al.), and injury to the superior colliculus causes impairment in the movement of attention across locations (Gouras, 1985; Posner & Petersen).

Furthermore, the posterior parietal lobes have elaborate limbic connections that run through the cingulate gyrus and the hippocampal formation. These connections may account for the fact that visually responsive posterior parietal neurons fire most rapidly when the stimulus has behavioral (or affective) significance for the subject (Goldman-Rakic, 1988). Finally, the posterior parietal lobes are systematically connected with prefrontal regions, which, in turn, are intricately interconnected with a number of thalamic, sensory, and motor nuclei (Goldman-Rakic, 1988). The interplay between these regions appears to provide the "on-line" modulation of attention, which varies in response to environmental alterations as well as in response to the individual's ongoing behaviors.

Thus, the LC, posterior parietal lobes, pulvinar nucleus of the thalamus, superior colliculi, and frontal cortex appear to constitute a neuroanatomical system that regulates visual attention. It is likely that stimuli in other sensory modalities are processed through at least partially distinct neural networks (Cooley & Morris, 1990). The fact that virtually all medications that improve attention in children affect NA metabolism (Zametkin & Rapoport, 1987) provides support for the hypothesis that the regions in this attentional network interact primarily, although not exclusively, through a NA-mediated system.

Limited data are available regarding the ontogenesis of these regions. The LC, which is associated with level of arousal and the orienting response to external stimuli, is probably fully functional prior to or just after birth, and it is likely that the thalamic structures mature very shortly thereafter. The superior colliculi, which are involved in the eye movements necessary to redirect attention, have been shown to reach adult levels of synaptic density well before cortical regions (Cooper & Rakic, 1983). Studies (Goldman-Rakic, 1987) in monkeys suggest that peak synaptic density in the parietal and frontal cortices occurs at about 4 months of age, which is believed to be equivalent to about 2 years of age in the human child. Following this, there is an extended period of synapse elimination, but it is not yet clear whether this latter process differs temporally across cortical regions. Yet it is likely that the development and refinement of cognitive functions are partially dependent upon this synapse elimination, which appears to continue at a slower rate into early adulthood.

Clinical Diagnosis and Attention in Children

Despite the fact that attentional difficulties are purported to be a primary characteristic of children with a wide array of psychiatric and neurological disturbances, strikingly little is known regarding the precise nature of these deficits. Using his neuropsychological model, Mirsky (Chapter 6) has begun to examine differences in the nature of the attentional dysfunction between several different groups of patients. This approach not only elucidates distinctions between his hypothesized elements of attention, but it also allows him to make specific statements beyond the fact that patients perform worse than controls. For example, Mirsky found that patients with absence seizures performed poorly on his *sustain* factor relative to both normal controls and patients with partial–complex seizures, whereas those with partial–complex seizures performed worse than the other two groups on measures of his *shift* and *focus/execute* factors. Using a similar approach, he found differences in the nature of attentional dysfunction between aggressive and shy children. Furthermore, prospective studies using his paradigm to assess attention in children with fetal alcohol exposure (Streissguth et al., 1994) have raised the intriguing question as to whether the nature of attentional dysfunction within a single patient group may vary at different times in development.

Yet studies such as these are not the norm. As stated previously, most clinical investigations of attention in patient groups have relied upon rating scales to measure attention. These studies tell us little about the nature of the attentional deficit. In addition, several investigators, including the author (Halperin et al., 1993), have used a single continuous performance test to assess attention in various patient groups. However, without systematic manipulations, even this "more objective" procedure provides only limited information regarding the nature of the deficit.

Nevertheless, some studies have systematically assessed selective and sustained attention in groups of children with different diagnoses. Although results have not always been consistent, some studies suggest that selective attention deficits are associated with reading disabilities (RD), whereas sustained attention deficits may be more closely associated with ADHD (Douglas & Peters, 1979; Dykman, Ackerman & Oglesby, 1979; Seidel & Joschko, 1990). Van der Meere, van Baal, and Sergeant (1989) found evidence for inputting difficulties in children with learning disabilities, whereas children with ADHD showed evidence of response organization deficits. Yet these preliminary dissociations may be further complicated by the frequent comorbidity between learning problems and ADHD. Preliminary data from my laboratory (Hall, Halperin, Matier, Schwartz, & Newcorn, in review) suggest that among children with ADHD, those with and without RD differ such that children with ADHD + RD show evidence of sustained attention deficits, whereas those with ADHD alone have response organization difficulties.

Finally, among patient groups, intervention strategies targeting attentional dysfunction are quite common. Currently, stimulant medication appears to be the most effective short-term treatment for improving attention in children, irrespective of diagnosis (Rapoport et al., 1980). Yet medication does not appear to improve long-term outcome, and improved attention does not transfer to the unmedicated state. McIlvane et al. (Chapter 7) described a behavior analytically oriented procedure for treating attentional difficulties in children with autism. It remains to be seen whether improved attention evident in the laboratory will transfer to the natural environment and have a lasting impact. Other investigators (Barkley, 1990; Pelham, 1989; Swanson, 1992) have been using behavior analytical procedures to treat children with a higher level of functioning (primarily those with ADHD) in settings that more closely approximate the natural environment. These latter intervention programs, which target a wide range of behavioral difficulties including inattention, have had at least partial success. Yet it is still unclear whether improved attention resulting from these treatments will generalize to nontreatment settings and remain effective beyond the termination of treatment.

CONCLUSIONS

Future research should systematically evaluate individual components of attention, in multiple modalities, in distinct subgroups of children, at varying points in development. This approach can then be used 1) in combination with modern neuroimaging and/or electrophysiological techniques to elucidate further the neural substrates of attention; 2) in nonreferred children, both prospectively and cross-sectionally, to clarify the developmental progression of attention and its relationship to cognitive development; and 3) with a wide range of patient groups to clarify the functional nature of their impairment as well as potential predictors and/or mediators of outcome. Once the multifaceted components of attention are more clearly delineated, we will be in a better position to design well-targeted interventions for ameliorating these all-too-common and debilitating difficulties in children. Currently, stimulant medication is commonly used as a short-term intervention for improving attentional difficulties in children. However, with more precise measurement and delineation of attentional problems, particularly at an early age, the treatment of attentional difficulties will become more accessible to behavior analytical interventions that may have greater promise for producing lasting effects.

REFERENCES

Abikoff, H., Courtney, M., Pelham, W.E., Jr., & Koplewicz, H.S. (1993). Teachers' ratings of disruptive behavior: Influence of halo effects. *Journal of Abnormal Child Psychology, 21*, 519–534.

Aston-Jones, G. (1985). Behavioral functions of locus coeruleus derived from cellular attributes. *Physiological Psychology, 13*, 118–126.

Barkley, R.A. (1990). *Attention deficit hyperactivity disorder: A handbook for diagnosis and treatment.* New York: Guilford Press.

Barkley, R.A. (1991). The ecological validity of laboratory and analogue assessment methods of ADHD symptoms. *Journal of Abnormal Child Psychology, 19*, 149–178.

Cooley, E.L., & Morris, R.D. (1990). Attention in children: A neuropsychologically based model for assessment. *Developmental Neuropsychology, 6*, 239–274.

Cooper, M.L., & Rakic, P. (1983). Gradients of cellular maturation and synaptogenesis in the superior colliculus of the fetal rhesus monkey. *Journal of Comparative Neurology, 215*, 165–186.

Cowan, N. (1988). Evolving conceptions of memory storage, selective attention and their mutual constraints within the human information processing system. *Psychological Bulletin, 104*, 163–191.

Douglas, V., & Peters, K.G. (1979). Toward a clearer definition of the attentional deficit of hyperactive children. In G.A. Hale & M. Lewis (Eds.), *Attention and the development of cognitive skills* (pp. 173–247). New York: Plenum.

Doyle, A.B. (1973). Listening to distraction: A developmental study of selective attention. *Journal of Experimental Child Psychology, 15*, 100–115.

Dykman, R.A., Ackerman, P.T., & Oglesby, D.M. (1979). Selective and sustained attention in hyperactive, learning-disabled and normal boys. *Journal of Nervous and Mental Disease, 167*, 288–297.

Fantz, R.L. (1966). Pattern discrimination and selective attention as determinants of perceptual development from birth. In A.H. Kidd & J.J. Rivoire (Eds.), *Perceptual development in children* (pp. 143–173). New York: International Universities Press.

Foote, S.L., & Morrison, J.H. (1987). Extrathalamic modulation of cortical function. *Annual Review of Neuroscience, 10*, 67–95.

Goldman-Rakic, P.S. (1987). Development of cortical circuitry and cognitive function. *Child Development, 58*, 601–622.

Goldman-Rakic, P.S. (1988). Topography of cognition: Parallel distributed networks in primate association cortex. *Annual Review of Neuroscience, 11*, 137–156.

Gordon, M. (1983). *The Gordon diagnostic system*. Dewitt, NY: Gordon Systems.

Gouras, P. (1985). Oculomotor system. In E.R. Kandel & J.H. Schwartz (Eds.), *Principles of neural science* (pp. 571–583). New York: Elsevier.

Hall, S.J., Halperin, J.M., Matier, K., Schwartz, S.T., & Newcorn, J.H. (in review). Behavioral symptomatology and information processing among children with attention-deficit hyperactivity disorder and reading disabilities.

Halperin, J.M., McKay, K.E., Matier, K., & Sharma, V. (1994). Attention, response inhibition, and activity level in children: Developmental neuropsychological perspectives. In: M.G. Tramontana & S.R. Hooper (Eds.), *Advances in child neuropsychology* (Vol. 2, pp. 1–54). New York: Springer-Verlag.

Halperin, J.M., Newcorn, J.H., Matier, K., Sharma, V., McKay, K.E., & Schwartz, S.T. (1993). Discriminant validity of attention-deficit hyperactivity disorder. *Journal of the American Academy of Child and Adolescent Psychiatry, 32*, 1038–1043.

Halperin, J.M., Newcorn, J.H., Sharma, V., Healey, J.M., Wolf, L.E., Pascualvaca, D.M., & Schwartz, S. (1990). Inattentive and non-inattentive ADHD children: Do they constitute a unitary group? *Journal of Abnormal Child Psychology, 18*, 437–449.

Halperin, J.M., Sharma, V., Greenblatt, E., & Schwartz, S.T. (1991). Assessment of the continuous performance test: Reliability and validity in a nonreferred sample. *Psychological Assessment: Journal of Consulting and Clinical Psychology, 3*, 603–608.

Heaton, R.K. (1981). *Wisconsin Card Sorting Test manual*. Odessa, FL: Psychological Assessment Resources.

Karmel, B.Z. (1969). The effect of age, complexity and amount of contour on pattern preferences in human infants. *Journal of Experimental Child Psychology, 7*, 338–354.

Levy, F. (1980). The development of sustained attention (vigilance) and inhibition in children: Some normative data. *Journal of Child Psychology and Psychiatry, 21*, 77–84.

Luria, A.R. (1973). *The working brain*. New York: Basic Books.

Maccoby, E.E. (1969). The development of stimulus selection. In J.P. Hill (Ed.), *Minnesota symposium on child psychology* (Vol. 3, pp. 68–96). Minneapolis: University of Minnesota Press.

McKay, K.E., Halperin, J.M., Schwartz, S.T., & Sharma, V. (1994). Developmental analysis of three aspects of information processing: Sustained attention, selective attention and response organization. *Developmental Neuropsychology, 10*, 121–132.

Mesulam, M. (1985). Attention, confusional states and neglect. In M. Mesulam (Ed.), *Principles of behavioral neurology* (pp. 125–168). Philadelphia: F.A. Davis.

Morrison, J.H., & Foote, S.L. (1986). Noradrenergic and serotonergic innervation of cortical, thalamic, and tectal visual structures in old and new world monkeys. *Journal of Comparative Neurology, 243*, 117–138.

Mountcastle, V.B. (1978). Brain mechanisms of directed attention. *Journal of Research in Social Medicine, 71*, 14–27.

Oades, R.D. (1985). The role of noradrenaline in tuning and dopamine in switching between signals in the CNS. *Neuroscience and Biobehavioral Reviews, 9*, 261–282.

Ohman, A. (1979). The orienting response, attention and learning: An information processing perspective. In H.K. Kimmel, E.H. Van Olst, & J.F. Orlebeke (Eds.), *The orienting reflex in humans* (pp. 443–471). Hillsdale, NJ: Lawrence Erlbaum Associates.

Pelham, W.E. (1989). Behavior therapy, behavioral assessment, and psychostimulant medication in the treatment of attention deficit disorders: An interactive approach. In L. Bloomingdale & J.M. Swanson (Eds.), *Attention deficit disorder IV*. New York: Pergamon Press.

Petersen, S.E., Robinson, D.L., & Morris, J.D. (1987). Contributions of the pulvinar to visual spatial attention. *Neuropsychology, 25*, 97–105.

Posner, M.I., & Petersen, S.E. (1990). The attention system of the human brain. *Annual Review of Neuroscience, 13*, 25–42.

Posner, M.I., Walker, J.A., Friedrich, F.J., & Rafal, R.D. (1984). Effects of parietal lobe injury on covert orienting of visual attention. *Journal of Neuroscience, 4*, 1863–1874.

Rapoport, J.L., Buchsbaum, M.S., Weingartner, H., Zahn, T.P., Ludlow, C., & Mikkelsen, E.J. (1980). Dextroamphetamine: Cognitive and behavioral effects in normal and hyperactive boys and normal men. *Archives of General Psychiatry, 37*, 933–943.

Rohrbaugh, J.W. (1984). The orienting reflex: Performance and central nervous system manifestations. In R. Parasuraman & D.R. Davies (Eds.), *Varieties of attention* (pp. 323–372). New York: Academic Press.

Salapatek, P., & Kessen, W. (1966). Visual scanning of triangles by the human newborn. *Journal of Experimental Child Psychology, 3*, 155–157.

Schachar, R., Sandberg, S., & Rutter, M. (1986). Agreement between teacher ratings and observations of hyperactivity, inattentiveness, and defiance. *Journal of Abnormal Child Psychology, 14*, 331–345.

Schneider, W., Dumais, S.T., & Shiffrin, R.M. (1984). Automatic and control processing and attention. In R. Parasuraman & D.R. Davies (Eds.), *Varieties of attention* (pp. 1–27). Orlando, FL: Academic Press.

Schneider, W., & Shiffrin, R.M. (1977). Controlled and automatic human information processing: I. Detection search and attention. *Psychological Review, 84*, 1–66.

Seidel, W.T., & Joschko, M. (1990). Evidence of difficulties in sustained attention in children with ADDH. *Journal of Abnormal Child Psychology, 18*, 217–229.

Seltzer, B., & Mesulam, M. (1988). Confusional states and delirium as disorders of attention. In F. Boller & J. Grafman (Eds.), *Handbook of neuropsychology* (Vol. 1, pp. 165–174). New York: Elsevier.

Sharma, V., Halperin, J.M., Newcorn, J.H., & Wolf, L.E. (1991). The dimension of focused attention: Relationship to behavior and cognitive functioning in children. *Perceptual and Motor Skills, 72*, 787–793.

Shepp, B.E., Barrett, S.E., & Kolbet, L.L. (1987). The development of selective attention: Holistic perception vs. resource allocation. *Journal of Experimental Child Psychology, 43*, 159–180.

Shiffrin, R.M., & Schneider, W. (1977). Controlled and automatic human information processing: II. Perceptual learning, automatic attending, a general theory. *Psychological Review, 84*, 127–190.

Smith, L.B., Kemler, D.G., & Aronfreed, J. (1975). Developmental trends in voluntary selective attention: Differential effects of source distinctiveness. *Journal of Experimental Child Psychology, 20*, 352–362.

Sternberg, S. (1969). Memory-scanning: Mental processes revealed by reaction-time experiments. *American Scientist, 57*, 421–457.

Streissguth, A.P., Sampson, P.D., Carmichael, O.H., Bookstein, F.L., Barr, H.M., Scott, M., Feldman, J., & Mirsky, A.F. (1994). Maternal drinking during pregnancy: Attention and short-term memory performance in 14-year-old offspring: A longitudinal prospective study. *Alcoholism: Clinical and Experimental Research, 18*, 202–218.

Strutt, G.F., Anderson, D.R., & Well, A.D. (1975). A developmental study of the effects of irrelevant information on speeded classification. *Journal of Experimental Child Psychology, 20*, 127–135.

Swanson, J.M. (1992). *School-based assessments and interventions for ADD students.* Irvine, CA: K.C. Publishing.

Taylor, E. (1980). Development of attention. In M. Rutter (Ed.), *Scientific foundation of developmental psychiatry* (pp. 185–197). London: Heinemann Educational.

van der Meere, J., & Sergeant, J. (1988a). Controlled processing and vigilance in hyperactivity: Time will tell. *Journal of Abnormal Child Psychology, 16*, 641–655.

van der Meere, J., & Sergeant, J. (1988b). Focussed attention in pervasively hyperactive children. *Journal of Abnormal Child Psychology, 16*, 627–639.

van der Meere, J., van Baal, M., & Sergeant, J. (1989). The additive factor method: A differential diagnostic tool in hyperactivity and learning disability. *Journal of Abnormal Child Psychology, 17(4)*, 409–422.

Wetherford, M.J., & Cohen, L.B. (1973). Developmental changes in infant visual preferences for novelty and familiarity. *Child Development, 44*, 416–424.

Wurtz, R.H., Goldberg, M.E., & Robinson, D.L. (1980). Behavioral modulation of visual responses in monkeys. *Progress in Psychobiology, Physiology and Psychology, 9*, 42–83.

Yerkes, R.M., & Dodson, J.D. (1908). The relation of strength of stimulus to rapidity of habit formation. *Journal of Comparative Neurology and Psychology, 18*, 459–482.

Zametkin, I.A., & Rapoport, J.L. (1987). Neurobiology of attention deficit disorder with hyperactivity: Where have we come in 50 years? *Journal of the American Academy of Child and Adolescent Psychiatry, 26*, 676–686.

III

MEMORY

The chapters within this section focus on memory. In line with the design of this book, the chapters are organized to address memory from an information processing, neuropsychological, and behavioral perspective. Even with the breadth of these three frames of reference, the topic of memory is far too broad and complex to conceptualize and define in any neat way. Consider that any discussion of memory may include reference to short-term and long-term memory, verbal and spatial memory, episodic and semantic memory, procedural and declarative memory, and a number of additional subdivisions of memory processes that are made more complicated by a discussion of memory stages to include coding, storage, and retrieval. It is this complexity that Wagner addresses in Chapter 9. His discussion of the major issues in memory research sets the stage for Torgesen's examination of phonological memory in Chapter 10, which serves as an example of how an information processing paradigm can be applied powerfully in memory research. In Chapter 11, Bachevalier and colleagues demonstrate the utility of a neuropsychological perspective in fractionating different types and levels of memory. In Chapter 12, Rumbaugh and Washburn provide excellent examples of how a behavioral paradigm can be employed to develop hypotheses and construct experiments to get at basic forms of memory. Boller concludes this section with a well-organized and informative summary of memory research in Chapter 13.

9

FROM SIMPLE STRUCTURE TO COMPLEX FUNCTION
Major Trends in the Development of Theories, Models, and Measurements of Memory

Richard K. Wagner

Perhaps the single most important trend in the study of memory is a shift in the dominant research paradigm. The paradigm has shifted from within-discipline testing of relatively simple theories and models of memory structure to interdisciplinary investigation of complex theories and models of memory function. This is a most welcome and promising development. Whereas memory has been of keen interest to both scientists who study behavior and those who study brain function, never before has there been so much fertile ground for interdisciplinary interchange.

A potential pitfall to avoid in such interdisciplinary exchanges is the tendency to accept at face value constructs and findings from sister disciplines (at least when they support one's own findings!). For whatever reason, the results seem more clear-cut and the conclusions more compelling the further one is from the messy center of the empirical activity in question. According to ancient wisdom, prophets are shunned in their own towns. We should be alert to the possibility that, in some instances, the hometown crowd may have it right.

Consider the case of short-term memory, the kind of memory that you use when you attempt to remember a phone number from the time you looked it up in a phone book until you have finished dialing. Short-term memory has been studied by researchers in the field of cognitive psychology for many decades, and the results of this effort are disseminated widely.

In an extraordinarily well-done and informative recent review of neuropsychological studies of memory phenomena, Squire, Knowlton, and Musen (1993) began a section on short-term memory in the following way: One of the oldest and most widely accepted ideas about memory is that short-term memory (STM) can be usefully distinguished from long-term memory (LTM) [Glanzer & Cunitz, 1966; James, 1890; Waugh & Norman, 1965] (p. 444). This statement, and the nature of the coverage typically given to short-term memory in introductory texts in general psychology and cognitive psychology, would lead one to believe that our understanding of short-term memory is one of the rock-solid contributions of modern psychology.

But compare this view to that of some contemporary psychologists. In an article titled "The Demise of Short-Term Memory," Crowder (1982) wrote the following:

> The first wave of modern research on short-term memory was preoccupied with its existence as a valid system of memory. One subsequent development has been the application of the short-term/long-term distinction to the study of individual and subject-population differences (aging, amnesia, and so on). . . . These efforts have now faltered, badly, in response to changing conceptions of human memory and unwelcome data. (p. 291)

These two positions present quite a contrast. Crowder is not alone in his pessimistic view of traditional conceptions of short-term memory. The Annual Meeting of the Psychonomic Society is a major annual meeting for cognitive psychologists. The conference consists almost exclusively of paper presentations and posters. An occasional symposium is allowed, however, when there appears to have been a critical development in the field. One such symposium 3 years ago, titled "Short-Term Memory: Where Do We Stand?," concerned a critical development, namely, a sobering account of the ways in which the traditional view of short-term memory was off the mark. Given these kinds of discrepancies between views on basic constructs such as short-term memory, it would seem that memory is a prime candidate for the kind of reflective, multiperspective examination that is the hallmark of this book.

The present chapter is divided into four parts. The first part reviews the modal model of short-term memory and some evidence that has supported this view. The second part discusses the challenge to the modal view. The third part sketches a contemporary account of short-term memory. The fourth and final part addresses measurement issues.

A MODAL VIEW OF SHORT-TERM MEMORY

Memory obviously is involved in any observable performance that one can imagine. Anything that is learned requires memory. But what is the basic nature of human memory? Research activity in the field of memory exploded in the second half of the present century. The decades of the 1960s and 1970s were characterized by debate about whether there were one or two basic memory stores and the characteristics of a second memory store if one existed. The origin of this debate was a series of groundbreaking studies reported by Broadbent (1958), Brown (1958), and Peterson and Peterson (1959). This work supported the existence of a second, temporary, or short-term memory store to go along with primary or long-term memory.

The Modal View

What has become known as the modal view of memory had its origin in influential accounts by Waugh and Norman (1965) and Atkinson and Shiffrin (1968), with some revision thereafter. Perceptual processing of auditory and visual stimuli leads to very brief storage of the stimuli in sensory stores. If the stimuli undergo additional processing, aided by representational codes available for many sensory stimuli (e.g., phonemes or sound-based codes for auditory information, letters or figural codes for visual information, and semantic codes for meaning), the representations reach short-term memory. Once in short-term memory, the information begins to decay unless it undergoes additional processing or rehearsal. The longer information resides in short-term memory, the better the chances that it will be kicked into the long-term memory system for permanent storage.

Evidence Supporting the Modal View of Short-Term Memory

Three kinds of evidence that support the modal view of short-term memory are briefly considered. The first consists of memory performance of normal subjects. The specific example to be used is that of the recency effect in free recall. The second kind of evidence is the presumed role of short-term memory in language comprehension. The third kind of evidence to be described is the memory performance of individuals who have suffered brain injury.

The Recency Effect in Free Recall   Here is a list of words for you to read and then, without looking back, try to recall them immediately:

dog, mirror, shoe, red, bulb, cannon, book, flag, tile, bus

Chances are that your performance was best on the last few words—bus, tile, and perhaps flag, as it has been for thousands of such lists given to thousands of subjects over the years. This empirical fact of superior performance for the most recent items that you are given is called the *recency effect.*

The standard explanation of the recency effect is that it represents improved performance for items that remain in short-term memory at the time recall is initiated. And, indeed, variables that presumably affect short-term memory, such as performing mental arithmetic immediately at the end of the list before recall begins, eliminate the recency effect but have no corresponding selective effect on performance for beginning or middle items. Conversely, variables that presumably affect long-term memory, such as the meaningfulness of the items or the age and intelligence of subjects, influence overall performance on the list items, including items at the beginning and middle of the list, but do not selectively alter the recency effect. The fact that some variables influence the recency effect but not performance on the beginning or middle items, whereas other variables influence performance overall but not the recency effect, provides support for the existence of two memory stores—short-term and long-term memory.

The Apparent Role of Short-Term Memory in Language Processing

What makes alternative views about short-term memory more than just interesting parlor conversation is the belief that short-term memory is instrumental in behavior that is vital to our species, such as language comprehension.

Short-term memory would seem to play a crucial role in listening and reading comprehension. When an individual is listening, acoustic information is processed by auditory perceptual mechanisms that then are deposited in a sensory store of very brief duration (milliseconds). If one were limited to a direct readout of the contents of the sensory store without the backup provided by short-term memory, comprehension of sentences such as the following would seem to be impossible:

> Jerry, who was known to be hot-tempered, was believed to bear the brunt of the blame for the argument, even if he had not started it in the first place.

If this sentence were spoken to you, you would have no trouble recognizing that the word "he" in the last third of the sentence clearly refers to Jerry. This feat of comprehension would seem to require short-term storage of the beginning of the sentence to resolve the meaning of the end. Presumably, short-term memory is used to provide as close to a verbatim record of the words as is possible while higher-level comprehension processes are applied to them.

The same logic applies to the case of reading. The traditional view has assumed that, as the reader works through a text, short-term memory provides a verbatim record of the last several words that can be accessed by higher-level comprehension processes (Crowder, 1982). Such a view is consistent with a phenomenon known as the eye–voice span. When reading aloud, a reader's eyes gaze about four words ahead of the word they are pronouncing. The lag in pronunciation, and presumably in comprehension, reflects the fact that such processes are operating on the contents of short-term memory, and some delay is involved between when a word is perceived and when it is available for additional processing in short-term memory.

The Memory Performance of Brain-Injured Individuals

For over 30 years, the careful study of brain-injured individuals has been carried out to further understand the nature of human memory. Consider two well-known cases, H.M. (Milner, 1966) and K.F. (Warrington & Shallice, 1972), whose performance appears to support the modal view of short-term memory. H.M. had a digit span in the normal range but showed a severe impairment in long-term retention of new information, as when attempting to learn lists of paired associates. Conversely, K.F. had a digit span of only one item but without an impairment in long-term retention of new information. K.F. had, for example, no trouble learning lists of paired-associates. The performance of these two individuals appears to support the modal model: H.M. had a normal short-term memory but an impaired long-term memory; K.F. had an impaired short-term memory but a normal long-term memory.

The existence of patients such as H.M. who perform normally on span tasks yet who show little long-term retention has been argued to provide the most compelling evidence for the distinction between short-term and long-term memory (Pashler & Carrier, in press). Because of their disorder, patients such as H.M. are unable to transfer the contents of an intact short-term memory into their long-term memory system.

THE DEMISE OF THE MODAL VIEW OF SHORT-TERM MEMORY

The title of this section has been taken directly from the article by Crowder (1982), mentioned at the beginning of this chapter, in which he reviewed the evidence against the modal view of short-term memory. This chapter draws liberally from this article and from more recent discussion about limitations of the modal view of memory (Baddeley & Hitch, 1993; Crowder, 1993; Shiffrin, 1993). The interested reader is strongly encouraged to consult these sources directly. It should also be pointed out that, although it is fair to say that acknowledgment of problems with the modal view of short-term memory is widespread, the demise of the modal view is not universal (see, e.g., Pashler & Carrier, in press).

Three areas of support for the modal view were mentioned in the last section. They included the recency effect in free recall, the presumed role of short-term memory in language comprehension, and the memory performance of brain-injured individuals. Each of these areas of support is revisited in turn.

The Recency Effect Revisited

Recall the empirical support for the modal view of short-term memory provided by the recency effect in free recall: Variables that should affect short-term memory influence the recency effect but not performance on the beginning or middle items, whereas other variables that should affect long-term memory influence performance overall but not the recency effect.

Although the empirical fact that performance for recently presented items is superior to performance for items occurring in the middle of a list remains unchallenged, what has been challenged is the belief that this effect is due to short-term memory. It had been assumed that performance for recent items was superior by virtue of the fact that the last couple of items remained stored in short-term memory at the time recall was initiated. The problem for this interpretation is that *recency effects are observed under situations in which short-term memory clearly is not involved.* For example, Crowder (1993) reported a recency effect for recall of presidents of the United States by undergraduates at Rice and Yale universities. Performance was high for the first several presidents (e.g., everyone recalled Washington), then declined through the middle (with the exception of Lincoln), and finally improved at the end in a recency effect for presidents such as Bush, Reagan, and Carter. The problem for the original interpretation of the recency effect is that recall of presidents is clearly a long-term as opposed to a short-term memory task. A similar long-term recency effect was re-

ported for bar patrons who were asked to name the teams that had played the local team during the past season (Baddeley & Hitch, 1977).

Granted, recall of presidents or opponents of one's home team involves information quite different from the verbal lists typically used in short-term memory experiments. However, research on long-term serial recall in which subjects
are asked to recall verbal lists after a delay of many minutes or even several
hours—plenty of time for the items to have been displaced from short-term memory—yielded results comparable to that seen in short-term memory experiments
(Nairne, 1992).

These results suggest that recency may be a general property of memory, including long-term memory, rather than being a marker variable for short-term
memory. The recency effect may represent a general temporal distinctiveness for
recent items that applies regardless of whether the items to be recalled were just
presented or must be retrieved from long-term storage (Crowder & Neath, 1991;
Glenberg & Swanson, 1986; Greene, 1986; Johnson, 1991). This temporal distinctiveness explanation also can account for the effects of distractor tasks on recall (e.g., the Brown–Peterson task; Brown, 1958; Peterson & Peterson, 1959),
which has been second only to the recency effect in free recall as an empirical
cornerstone of the modal view of short-term memory. A detailed account of this
view of recency effects is beyond the scope of this chapter, but the interested
reader could consult the sources just cited for further information.

Problems for the modal view of memory are not limited to the recency effect. The relation between speech rate and memory span provides a second example. Speech rate is known to be correlated with memory span performance; individuals with faster speech rates show better span performance. Hulme, Maughan,
and Brown (1991, cited in Cowan, 1993) found this typical result in their sample
of adults for both English words and nonsense words. However, the intercept
(i.e., measure of average performance) was higher for words than for nonwords.
This means that memory span performance was affected considerably by the lexical familiarity of the stimuli, and the lexical familiarity of a stimulus is a property of long-term memory.

An analogous result is that of superior performance on the digit span task.
When subjects are asked to repeat sequences of digits, the longest sequences typically recalled fall somewhere below 10 digits. However, two subjects who were
given hundreds of hours of practice achieved digit spans of over 80 digits, even for
digits presented at a fast pace (Chase & Ericsson, 1982; Staszewski, 1988). Analysis of their performance showed that they accomplished this feat by employing a
coding system that relied on long-term memory, such as a runner coding sequences
of digits as though they were times in a race. Thus, long-term memory once again
is implicated in a task that purports to measure the capacity of short-term memory.
Torgesen's studies (see Chapter 10) of span performance of children with learning
disabilities, which show span performance to be a function of the type of stimuli—
digits, words, or syllables—make the same point for children. These studies show
clear evidence of the effects of long-term memory on memory span.

Language Comprehension

Despite the questionable support of the modal view of short-term memory provided by the recency effect in light of alternative explanations, might this conceptualization of short-term memory still account for important aspects of language comprehension? Unfortunately for the modal view of short-term memory, at least the strong view of an important role of short-term memory in language comprehension appears to be false. Consider the results from "garden-path" experiments.

Carpenter and Daneman (1981) asked subjects to read aloud passages such as the following one while their eye fixations were being recorded:

> The young man turned his back on the rock concert stage and looked across the resort lake. Tomorrow was the annual one-day fishing contest and fishermen would invade the place. Some of the best bass guitarists in the country would come to this spot.

The garden path involves the word "bass" in the last sentence. The prior context provides a garden path to the fish-related word "bass" as opposed to the musical term that is spelled the same but pronounced as though it were spelled "base." What subjects did when they came to the word "guitarists" was to produce a longer eye-fixation, compared to a control condition lacking the garden path, and then change their pronunciation of "bass" to coincide with its interpretation as a musical term.

Frazier and Rayner (1982) reported a similar result for silent reading when subjects read sentences such as, "As she was sewing the sleeve fell off her lap." When you reach the word "fell," a reinterpretation of the sentence is necessary in which the first clause is seen to consist of the first four words as opposed to the first six words.

The crucial piece of information for present purposes from these studies is that changes in the interpretation of these sentences are made almost immediately, within about a quarter of a second after coming across the word that informs the reader that a previous interpretation was in error. If comprehension processes operated on the contents of short-term memory, subjects would delay recognition of the incongruity built into the garden-path sentences. Presumably, the contents of short-term memory would lag behind the eyes with a three- to four-word delay corresponding to the eye–voice span. Because recognition of incongruity in garden-path sentences essentially is immediate, comprehension clearly does not depend on short-term memory in the way that the modal view of short-term memory suggests that it should.

A Closer Examination of the Memory Performance of Brain-Injured Individuals

Martin (1993) has chronicled the role of the neuropsychological study of individuals with brain damage in furthering our understanding of the role of short-term memory in language comprehension.

Recall the patients H.M. (Milner, 1966) and K.F. (Warrington & Shallice, 1972), whose memory performance supported the modal view of short-term memory. H.M., with a digit span in the normal range, had a normal short-term memory but an impaired long-term memory. K.F., with a digit span of only one item, had an impaired short-term memory but a normal long-term memory.

The performance of H.M. indeed is consistent with the modal view of short-term memory. H.M.'s problem can be explained as an inability to transfer the contents of an intact short-term memory into his long-term memory system for some reason associated with brain injury. But consider two problems for the modal model presented by the performance of K.F., who had a profoundly impaired short-term memory but normal long-term retention of new information (Martin, 1993).

According to the modal model, the only way to deposit information in long-term memory is by transfer from short-term memory. Thus, the modal view would predict that an impaired short-term memory necessarily implies impaired long-term retention of new information. Yet K.F. was not impaired in a paired-associate learning task that required long-term retention of new information. The second problem for the modal view is that short-term memory was believed to be the memory system in which thinking and language comprehension were carried out. Yet K.F. showed no intellectual or comprehension deficits of the magnitude that would be expected with a memory span of one item.

Martin (1990, 1993) reports a careful investigation into the memory and comprehension performance of a new patient, E.A., whose memory deficit parallels that of K.F. The span performance of E.A. was about two words if they were presented auditorially, and three words if they were presented visually. One major purpose of Martin's analysis of the performance of E.A. was to determine if short-term memory might play a more limited, yet nonetheless important, role in comprehension. Specifically, short-term memory might be required for syntactic comprehension. For many sentences, pronouns occur at considerable distance from their referents. Short-term memory could be used to retain words in their phonological form to enable the listener to link pronouns with their appropriate referents.

In one experiment, E.A. listened to short, medium, and long sentences in which the pronoun either matched or did not match its referent. E.A.'s task was to indicate whether or not the sentences were acceptable. Examples of nonmatching sentences include:

Short: The girl hurt himself.
Medium: The first fell down the stairs and hurt himself.
Long: The girl fell down the stairs at least once a week and often hurt himself.

If short-term memory is required to link pronouns to their referents, then E.A. should perform worse than control subjects on this task, and the longer the sentence, the worse E.A.'s relative performance should be. However, the results were that E.A.'s performance was comparable to that of controls and consistent across the three sentence lengths.

Other investigations of E.A.'s syntactic processing ability yielded the same result. A severe short-term memory impairment does not limit syntactic comprehension. The fact that adequate syntactic processing occurs when short-term memory is impaired is consistent with the view presented earlier that comprehension is done for the most part "on-line," with an initial interpretation made soon after words are perceived.

It still is possible, however, that short-term memory comes into play *when the initial interpretation turns out to be incorrect*. Recall the garden-path experiments described previously, in which context was used to suggest one interpretation of a word that later would be shown to be incorrect (e.g., "bass" the fish rather than the type of guitar). When normal adult readers read a garden-path sentence and reach the point at which their error is obvious, they produce a longer fixation and then change their pronunciation to fit the correct interpretation. If short-term memory is required to notice garden-path errors, E.A. would be expected to miss them with greater frequency than control subjects. However, E.A.'s performance on garden-path sentences was comparable to that of control subjects.

E.A. did, however, demonstrate one significant area of language impairment, namely, verbatim recall of sentences. E.A. recalled only 1 of 30 sentences perfectly, compared to 29 or 30 out of 30 sentences recalled perfectly by control subjects. Fortunately for E.A., verbatim recall appears to be of little consequence for language comprehension. However, it is possible that, although impaired short-term memory does not affect language comprehension for adults to a marked degree, it might impair the acquisition of new vocabulary words. Acquiring new vocabulary involves linking a semantic representation to a stable pronunciation (and to a stable orthographic representation for the case of written language). A patient, P.V., whose impairment resembled that of E.A. (i.e., impaired span, nonimpaired long-term retention of new information), was tested on long-term retention of new information (Baddeley, Papagno, & Vallar, 1988). The measure of long-term retention of new information was learning paired associates (word pairs). As with the performance of E.A., P.V.'s paired-associate learning performance was normal *when the words to be paired were already in P.V.'s vocabulary*. However, P.V. was unable to learn paired associates when the pairs involved a known English word and its Spanish equivalent that was not in P.V.'s vocabulary. Presumably, P.V. had difficulty remembering the novel phonological string represented by the new Spanish vocabulary word with sufficient accuracy. Martin (1993) replicated this result in patient E.A. and also showed that E.A. was unable to even repeat accurately Spanish words longer than one syllable. E.A.'s performance at repeating nonwords also was impaired, with only 47% accuracy for two-syllable nonwords.

A CONTEMPORARY
CONCEPTUALIZATION OF SHORT-TERM MEMORY

The ultimate "demise" of the modal view of short-term memory does not mean that an individual's performance on a task such as reading is not constrained by memory limitations. In many contexts, it is essential that people retain information over brief periods of time. However, what is required is memory per se, not necessarily a dedicated system of processing that is distinct in its properties from other systems of processing (Crowder, 1993). What appears to be wrong is to conceptualize memory limitations as reflecting the operations of dedicated short-term stores.

Having said a lot about how short-term memory should not be conceptualized, how should we think about it? With regard to the structure of memory, short-term memory is best conceptualized as *that portion of long-term memory that is temporarily at a heightened state of activation at a particular moment in time* (Cowan, 1993; Shiffrin, 1993). This conceptualization reinforces two key characteristics.

First, short-term memory is not a separate, dedicated storage area that we might search for in some area of the brain or another. Rather, it involves activation patterns over a large number of neural circuits that are the same as those involved in both processing and long-term storage. This view rejects the spatial metaphor of memory and replaces it with a procedural one (Crowder, 1993), in the sense that temporary memory storage is a product of the processing that occurs in neural units that are implicated in long-term storage and other information processes. This, of course, resembles Hebb's (1949) view long ago that memory represented continued activity or reverberation of the neural cells involved in perception.

Second, the capacity for short-term storage is limited, which is implied by the idea that the heightened state of activation of a given portion of long-term memory is temporary (Shiffrin, 1993). As processing operations are carried out, new portions of long-term memory become activated, and previously activated portions of long-term memory decay to their former resting levels of activation.

With regard to the functions of short-term memory, of particular importance given the content of this book, it is crucial to note that short-term memory functions as the locus of cognitive control processes (see Section IV), including attention (see Section II) (Shiffrin, 1993). Examples of such control processes include determining where to direct peripheral attention, how to encode new inputs, and engaging the process of rehearsal.

Short-term memory also includes information beyond that which is the current focus of attention or of cognitive control processes. Evidence for the view that short-term storage extends beyond what is currently being attended to or operated on is provided by the phenomenon of priming, one of the most commonly studied effects in cognitive psychology. Priming refers to the situation in which having processed a stimulus previously makes processing of a new stimulus faster. For example, in a lexical decision experiment, words mixed with non-words are presented on a computer screen one by one. The subject's task is to indicate whether an item is a word or nonword by pressing one of two response keys (yes or no) as quickly as possible. Performance is measured in terms of latency to make a response. Priming is demonstrated when subjects make a yes response to *butter* faster when the previous item is *bread* than when it is some unrelated item. Countless studies have shown that items that have been attended to previously remain at a heightened state of activation for some time after they have left awareness.

This conceptualization of short-term memory is portrayed in Figure 9.1, which has been adapted from Cowan (1988, 1993). Short-term memory is shown to be an activated subset of long-term memory, with the focus of attention in turn being a subset of short-term memory. This conceptualization is intended to be a "bare-bones effort" that highlights key assumptions about the organization of memory. It makes no attempt to be complete with respect to a wide variety of important issues, such as whether there are multiple memory systems associated with different kinds of coding operations.

One attempt at a more "fleshed-out" functional account of short-term memory is provided by Baddeley's model of working memory (1986; see also Chapter 10). According to this view, working memory includes storage mechanisms such as a "phonological loop" that can be thought of as functioning like a short loop of recording tape that continuously stores a small amount of auditory information, as well as a "workspace" for processing information. This view of working memory handles the problem for the modal view of short-term memory that comprehension occurs despite limited span performance. Memory span tasks largely measure the efficiency of the phonological loop. However, language comprehension is supported primarily by the workspace as opposed to the phonological loop. Because language comprehension takes place in the workspace area outside the phonological loop, adequate language comprehension can coexist with poor span performance.

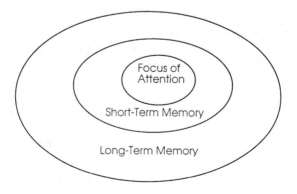

Figure 9.1.   The memory system. (Adapted from Cowan, 1988, 1993.)

Many investigations of short-term memory were designed to study its *capacity* and to determine how capacity affects cognitive performance. Capacity basically is what memory-span tasks were designed to measure, and researchers have been interested in knowing how individuals such as K.F., with a limited capacity short-term memory, perform on a wide variety of cognitive tasks such as language comprehension. A parallel interest has emerged in the case of working memory, with some researchers seeking to measure the capacity of working memory, especially that of the workspace in which comprehension is carried out. If comprehension is largely confined to working memory, then differences in working memory capacity ought to be predictive of differences in comprehension performance.

Daneman and Carpenter (1980) developed a task to measure the capacity of working memory during reading. The task involves reading sets of unrelated sentences. As the sentences are read, subjects answer comprehension questions about them, to ensure that the subjects will read for comprehension. Then, when the sentences have been completed, the subjects are asked to recall the last word of each sentence in the set. To get an idea of what this task is like, read and answer each of the following questions. When you get to the last one, without looking back, try to recall the last word of each sentence:

Do ducks swim?	(yes)
Do cats fly?	(no)
Are alligators blue?	(no)
Are dogs pets?	(yes)

The target words to be recalled were *swim, fly, blue,* and *pets.* To make the task more difficult, more sentences could be included in the list, and the sentences could be made longer and more difficult. Note how this measure of working memory capacity differs from the typical memory span task used to measure short-term memory capacity. Instead of merely listening to a set of unrelated items such as digits and then repeating them, this task requires you to comprehend sentences at the same time you are attempting to store at least the last word.

Daneman and Carpenter (1980) reported correlations of 0.5–0.6 between working memory performance on their task and performance on comprehension tests. Just and Carpenter (1992) suggest that comprehension differences between good and poor readers are primarily attributable to differences in working memory capacity. Good readers are presumed to have a greater total capacity of working memory than do poor readers. This allows the good reader to store more information in working memory than can be stored by the poor reader.

However, Ericsson and Kintsch (in press) have recently challenged the notion that general differences in working memory capacity underlie differences in comprehension performance. They argue instead that performance on working memory tasks reflects efficient storage of information in, and retrieval from, long-term memory. Furthermore, efficiency of storage and retrieval increases with practice and varies from one text to another as a function of the subject's prior knowledge of passage content.

For example, researchers have formed groups of subjects on the basis of reading ability (high or low) and knowledge of a specific content domain (high or low) such as baseball (Recht & Leslie, 1988) or soccer (Schneider, Korkel, & Weinert, 1989). Subjects then read passages about baseball or soccer and either were asked to recall them or to answer comprehension questions. Memory and comprehension performance were determined primarily by whether a subject was high or low in domain knowledge rather than by reading ability. Assuming that memory and comprehension performance reflect working memory capacity (Just & Carpenter, 1992), one is left to conclude that working memory capacity is not a general individual difference variable but rather varies as a function of the topic of the material being read.

These results do not challenge the idea of working memory as a useful conceptualization of the functions of short-term memory. Rather, they challenge an overly literal, structural interpretation of the model in which a workspace of some fixed size is presumed to exist apart from long-term memory. Note the parallel between these arguments regarding the origin of capacity differences in working memory and those discussed in the context of the modal view of short-term memory. In both cases, long-term memory processes appear to be involved in performance that had been attributed solely to short-term memory or working memory processes.

Because of limited space, the primary focus of this chapter has been on conceptions of short-term memory. However, the need to be cautious in embracing constructs from other domains also applies to constructs associated with long-term memory (e.g., implicit versus explicit learning, declarative versus procedural knowledge) as well as to constructs associated with topics such as attention and executive function (e.g., controlled versus automatic functioning). In each case, what can appear from afar as a clear-cut distinction becomes less distinct upon closer inspection.

MEASUREMENT ISSUES

The fact that short-term memory appears to be an integral aspect of long-term memory challenges researchers to move beyond simple questions about memory structure (e.g., one, two, or more memory stores?) to tackle complex questions about memory function in the context of ongoing cognitive operations. Behavioral data alone may be insufficient to meet this challenge (Schneider, 1993). What appears to be required is an interdisciplinary effort that is sensitive to constraints imposed by our knowledge of brain function and computation as well as by observed behavior. To be maximally effective, such an approach needs to be sensitive to measurement difficulties associated with variables associated with behavior and brain function.

An Example of Converging Evidence
from Studies of Brain and Behavior

A nice example of converging evidence from brain–behavior studies is provided by research on the problem of retrieving the correct meaning of a word from long-term memory when reading or listening. Many words have multiple meanings. In the sentence, "She got rid of the bugs," the word *bugs* could refer to insects, listening devices used by spies, or faulty computer code. The context in which a sentence is found somehow is used to pick the correct meaning, but how is this actually done? One approach would be to retrieve from memory all known meanings of a target word and then pick the best candidate as more information becomes available from the sentence context. Alternatively, context might be used as a source of search cues to zero in on the correct meaning, in which case memory retrieval might be postponed if enough cues were available to suggest that the probability of retrieving the correct meaning is sufficiently high.

Clever behavioral studies have employed a priming methodology to provide a chronology of how the correct meaning of a word is obtained. Swinney (1979) had subjects sit in front of a computer screen prepared to do the lexical decision task. As mentioned previously, the lexical decision task involves presenting a letter string on a screen and asking subjects to respond as quickly as possible by pressing one of two keys, indicating whether the letter string is a word or nonword. Of course, subjects can do the task quite accurately, so time to respond or response latency is the key variable of interest. While subjects were sitting in front of a computer screen prepared to do the lexical decision task, they also listened to spoken sentences such as the following one:

The man found several insects, spiders, and other bugs in the room.

For this sentence, the meaning of the word bugs is clear; it refers to creatures rather than to listening devices or faulty computer code. As subjects listened to the sentence, just after hearing the word *bugs*, a letter string was presented on the screen for subjects to make the lexical decision of whether the string was a word or nonword. Subjects saw one of three words: *ant*, which would be expected to be primed or facilitated by the creature meaning of *bugs*; *spy*, which would be primed by the eavesdropping meaning of *bugs*; or *sew*, which would receive no priming because it is unrelated to any meaning of "bugs." The results were that *bugs* initially primed *ant* and *spy* equally, even in sentences that favored one meaning over another. However, when the lexical decision task was delayed by about a quarter of a second, a priming effect was observed for *ant* but not for *spy*. In other words, readers initially activate all meanings of a word but, in about a quarter of a second, drop all but the meaning suggested by the context. The Swinney (1979) study involved listening comprehension, but similar results have been found for reading comprehension (e.g., Kintsch & Mross, 1985).

Turning to brain studies, Posner and McCandliss (1993) reviewed studies of retrieving the correct meaning of a word when reading; these studies used positron emission tomographic (PET) scans or evoked-related potentials to observe brain activity. Approximately a quarter of a second after a word has been read, diffuse activity is observed in frontal brain regions that are used for semantic processing. This appears to correspond with retrieval of multiple word meanings. Then, processing activity shifts to posterior areas and differs across hemispheres, which appears to correspond with the suppression of irrelevant word meanings and the integration of the meaning with the rest of the text. Although further study is needed before drawing definitive conclusions, the correspondence between behavioral and brain data is promising.

Measurement Difficulties

Perhaps the most important development in the area of measurement is the slowly growing appreciation of the complex nature of measurement and the need for caution in making inferences about theories of memory and brain function from performance. Two examples of such complexities are described briefly, one behavioral and the other physiological.

Young children's short-term memory for phonological information is commonly measured with a digit span task as well as span tasks involving words or other stimuli. Although researchers recognize that performance on any task is multidetermined, they routinely equate span performance with short-term memory functioning. We have carried out several studies that have addressed the nature of memory span performance in young children. One study involved 111 preschool children who were given memory span measures and multiple measures of other constructs as well, including phonological awareness (Wagner et al., 1987). Phonological awareness refers to a child's awareness of the sound structure of language, including such things as knowing that *cat* and *hat* rhyme and have the same number of sounds. A second study involved 95 kindergarten pupils who were given span tasks as well as measures of phonological awareness and other constructs (Wagner, Torgesen, Laughon, Simmons, & Rashotte, 1993). By obtaining multiple measures of each construct and using confirmatory factor analysis, the investigaters were able to estimate the correlations between constructs with more accuracy than is possible in the typical study with only one measure for each construct. The interesting finding for present purposes was that short-term memory and phonological awareness were perfectly correlated with one another. In other words, the two purportedly different kinds of tasks in fact measured the same thing.

Turning to measures of brain function, until recently evidence had suggested that the locus of word priming effects is a word–form area in the left hemisphere (Tulving & Schacter, 1990). However, a growing body of data from PET studies now suggests the existence of at least 30 loci of priming affects distributed in cortical areas (Squire, Knowlton, & Musen, 1993). The extent of involvement of the different areas appears to depend on task demands and materials used. The implication of these findings and others that show complex relations between behavior and brain function is that strong assumptions about the effects of specific lesions are naive and likely to be falsified as our knowledge of brain function becomes more complete.

CONCLUSIONS

The challenges faced by participants in interdisciplinary investigations into memory function are considerable, but not insurmountable, and are dwarfed by the promise of such an approach. The following chapters provide a glimpse of where such investigations are leading us.

Torgesen (Chapter 10) focuses on working memory and reports investigations that have begun to address the possibility that an impaired phonological loop, implied by poor span performance, limits the acquisition of children's reading skills. Recall that patients with impaired short-term memory could learn new paired associates when the words to be associated were already in their vocabularies but could not learn paired associates consisting of new words such as Spanish equivalents of English vocabulary. The problem appeared to be a difficulty in remembering the novel phonological string represented by the new Spanish vocabulary word with sufficient accuracy. In fact, they were unable even to repeat individually presented two-syllable Spanish words or pronounceable nonwords. Imagine the consequences of a comparable inability in young children who are faced with the task of expanding their oral language vocabularies and building a new reading vocabulary. Studies of such children are reviewed in Chapter 10.

Bachevalier, Malkova, and Beauregard (Chapter 11) provide a neuropsychological perspective on brain structures that might be primarily responsible for different kinds of *long-term memory*. Differences between implicit and explicit learning and between declarative and procedural information have been the topics of intense empirical investigations. Chapter 10 provides a review of a comparably intense investigation into the neurological underpinnings of these behavioral findings.

Rumbaugh and Washburn (Chapter 12) provide a fascinating comparative perspective on memory through their review of studies of the cognitive abilities of chimpanzees and rhesus monkeys. Increasing interest in the brain structures that support memory has resulted in increased interest in animal models of memory performance (e.g., Roitblat & von Fersen, 1992).

REFERENCES

Atkinson, R.C., & Shiffrin, R.M. (1968). Human memory: A proposed system and its control processes. In K.W. Spence & J.T. Spence (Eds.), *The psychology of learning and motivation* (Vol. 2, pp. 89–195). New York: Academic Press.

Baddeley, A.D. (1986). *Working memory*. New York: Oxford University Press.

Baddeley, A.D., & Hitch, G. (1977). Recency reexamined. In S. Dornic (Ed.), *Attention and performance* (Vol. 6, pp. 647–667). Hillsdale, NJ: Lawrence Erlbaum Associates.

Baddeley, A.D., & Hitch, G. (1993). The recency effect: Implicit learning with explicit retrieval? *Memory & Cognition, 21,* 146–155.

Baddeley, A.D., Papagno, C., & Vallar, G. (1988). When long-term learning depends on short-term storage. *Journal of Memory & Language, 27,* 586–595.

Broadbent, D.E. (1958). *Perception and communication.* New York: Pergamon.

Brown, J. (1958). Some tests of the decay theory of immediate memory. *Quarterly Journal of Experimental Psychology, 10,* 12–21.

Carpenter, P.A., & Daneman, M. (1981). Lexical retrieval and error recovery in reading: A model based on eye fixations. *Journal of Verbal Learning & Verbal Behavior, 20,* 137–160.

Chase, W.G., & Ericsson, K.A. (1982). Skill and working memory. In G.H. Bower (Ed.), *The psychology of learning and motivation* (Vol. 16, pp. 1–58). New York: Academic Press.

Cowan, N. (1988). Evolving conceptions of memory storage, selective attention, and their mutual constraints within the human information processing system. *Psychological Bulletin, 104,* 163–191.

Cowan, N. (1993). Activation, attention, and short-term memory. *Memory & Cognition, 21,* 162–167.

Crowder, R.G. (1982). The demise of short-term memory. *Acta Psychologica, 50,* 291–293.

Crowder, R.G. (1993). Short-term memory: Where do we stand? Memory & Cognition, 21, 142–145.

Crowder, R.G., & Neath, I. (1991). The microscope metaphor in human memory. In W. E. Hockley & S. Lewandowsky (Eds.), *Relating theory and data: Essays on human memory in honour of Bennet B. Murdock, Jr.* (pp. 111–125). Hillsdale, NJ: Lawrence Erlbaum Associates.

Daneman, M., & Carpenter, P.A. (1980). Individual differences in working memory and reading. *Journal of Verbal Learning & Verbal Behavior, 19,* 450–466.

Ericsson, K.A., & Kintsch, W. (in press). Long-term working memory. *Psychological Review, 102.*

Frazier, L., & Rayner, K. (1982). Making and correcting errors during sentence comprehension. *Cognitive Psychology, 14,* 178–210.

Glanzer, M., & Cunitz, A.R. (1966). Two storage mechanisms in free recall. *Journal of Verbal Learning & Verbal Behavior, 5,* 351–360.

Glenberg, A.M., & Swanson, N.C. (1986). A temporal distinctiveness theory of recency and modality effects. *Journal of Experimental Psychology: Learning, Memory, & Cognition, 12,* 3–24.

Greene, R.L. (1986). A common basis for recency effects in immediate and delayed recall. *Journal of Experimental Psychology: Learning, Memory, & Cognition, 12,* 413–418.

Hebb, D.O. (1949). *Organization of behavior.* New York: Wiley.

Hulme, C., Maughan, S., & Brown, G.D.A. (1991). Memory for familiar and unfamiliar words: Evidence for a long-term memory contribution to short-term memory span. *Journal of Memory & Language, 30,* 685–701.

James, W. (1890). *Principles of psychology.* New York: Holt, Rinehart & Winston.

Johnson, G.J. (1991). A distinctiveness model of serial learning. *Psychological Review, 98,* 204–217.

Just, M.A., & Carpenter, P.A. (1992). A capacity theory of comprehension. *Psychological Review, 99,* 122–149.

Kintsch, W., & Mross, E.F. (1985). Context effects in word identification. *Journal of Memory and Language, 24,* 336–349.

Martin, R.C. (1990). Neuropsychological evidence on the role of short-term memory in sentence processing. In G. Vallar & T. Shallice (Eds.), *Neuropsychological impairments of short-term memory* (pp. 390–427). Cambridge, England: Cambridge University Press.

Martin, R.C. (1993). Short-term memory and sentence processing: Evidence from neuropsychology. *Memory & Cognition, 21*, 176–183.

Milner, B. (1966). Amnesia following operation on the temporal lobes. In C. Whitty & O. Zangwill (Eds.), *Amnesia* (pp. 109–133). London: Butterworth.

Nairne, J.S. (1992). The loss of positional uncertainty in long-term memory. *Psychological Science, 3*, 199-202.

Pashler, H., & Carrier, M. (in press). Structures, processes and the flow of information. In E.L. Bjork & R.A. Bjork (Eds.), *Handbook of perception and cognition* (Vol. 10). San Diego: Academic Press.

Peterson, L.R., & Peterson, M.J. (1959). Short-term retention of individual items. *Journal of Experimental Psychology, 61*, 12–21.

Posner, M.L., & McCandliss, B.D. (1993). Converging methods for investigating lexical access. *Psychological Science, 4*, 305–309.

Recht, D.R., & Leslie, L. (1988). Effect of prior knowledge on good and poor readers' memory of text. *Journal of Educational Psychology, 80*, 16–20.

Roitblat, H.L., & von Fersen, L. (1992). Comparative cognition: Representations and processes in learning and memory. *Annual Review in Psychology, 43*, 671–710.

Schneider, W. (1993). Varieties of working memory as seen in biology and in connectionist/control architectures. *Memory & Cognition, 21*, 184–192.

Schneider, W., Korkel, J., & Weinert, F.E. (1989). Domain-specific knowledge and memory performance: A comparison of high- and low-aptitude children. *Journal of Educational Psychology, 81*, 306–312.

Shiffrin, R.M. (1993). Short-term memory: A brief commentary. *Memory & Cognition, 21*, 193–197.

Squire, L.R., Knowlton, B., & Musen, G. (1993). The structure and organization of memory. *Annual Review in Psychology, 44*, 453–495.

Staszewski, J.J. (1988). Skilled memory and expert mental calculation. In M.T. Chi, R. Glaser, & M.J. Farr (Eds.), *The nature of expertise* (pp. 71–128). Hillsdale, NJ: Lawrence Erlbaum Associates.

Swinney, D.A. (1979). Lexical access during sentence comprehension: (Re)consideration of context effects. *Journal of Verbal Learning and Verbal Behavior, 18*, 645–659.

Tulving, E., & Schacter, D.L. (1990). Priming and human memory systems. *Science, 247*, 301.

Wagner, R.K., Balthazor, M., Hurley, S., Morgan, S., Rashotte, C., Shaner, R., Simmons, K., & Stage, S. (1987). The nature of prereaders' phonological processing abilities. *Cognitive Development, 2*, 355–373.

Wagner, R.K., Torgesen, J.K., Laughon, P., Simmons, K., & Rashotte, C.A. (1993). Development of young readers' phonological processing abilities. *Journal of Educational Psychology, 85*, 83–103.

Warrington, E.K., & Shallice, T. (1972). Neuropsychological evidence of visual storage in short-term memory tasks. *Quarterly Journal of Experimental Psychology, 24A*, 30–40.

Waugh, N.C., & Norman, D.A. (1965). Primary memory. *Psychological Review, 72*, 89–104.

10

A MODEL OF MEMORY FROM AN INFORMATION PROCESSING PERSPECTIVE
The Special Case of Phonological Memory

Joseph K. Torgesen

The goal of this chapter is to discuss an aspect of the human memory system in a way that will contribute to the understanding of its impact on individual differences in acquiring important academic/intellectual skills. Along the way, questions about the conceptualization and measurement of this component of the human memory system will also be addressed. In order to identify the relationship of the kind of memory to be discussed here with other types of memory abilities, an overview of the human memory system is first presented. This overview also provides some idea of the extent of our knowledge about human memory and gives a perspective on the narrowness of the focus of this chapter. Both the larger conceptualization of human memory described here, as well as the narrower model of a specific aspect of memory discussed in more detail, derive from the extensive empirical work on memory conducted within the information processing paradigm extending over the last 30 years.

Although it is possible to characterize the human memory system in a number of different ways, the diagram in Figure 10.1 is helpful in organizing most of what is currently known about the functions of human memory. This diagram should be viewed as a representation of the functional, rather than structural, properties of the human memory system. That is, the division of human memory into three broad areas does not imply that these kinds of memories are necessarily located in different areas of the brain or that they are supported by au-

The research reported in this chapter was supported by grants no. HD29663-01 and HD23340 from the National Institute of Child Health and Human Development.

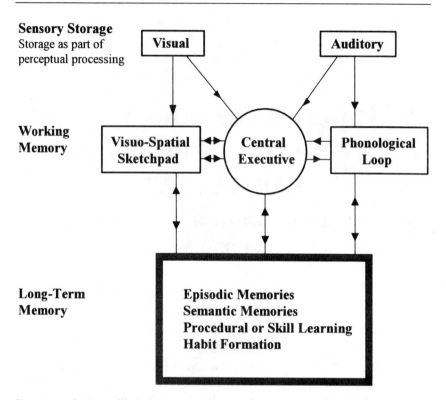

Figure 10.1. Overview of the human memory system.

tonomous memory systems. Rather, the diagram is simply meant to summarize the broad range of memory phenomena that have been studied from the information processing perspective (see Chapter 9 for a more complete discussion of the distinction between the functional and structural properties of human memory).

It is clear, for example, that a very brief form of memory storage is associated with perceptual processing in at least the visual and auditory senses and very likely the other senses as well. This very brief storage of visual information is usually referred to as *iconic* memory (Sperling, 1967), whereas very brief retention of auditory information is usually referred to as *echoic* memory (Efron, 1970). The duration of this type of storage is a matter of milliseconds, rather than seconds, and it is best regarded as a prolongation of the original stimulus trace in order to allow time for recognition and further processing to take place.

If information in sensory storage undergoes additional processing (some form of representational code is activated), it becomes a more durable memory. The relative durability of this memory trace depends upon the nature of the representational codes that are activated. In Figure 10.1, these activated memory representations are designated by the portion of the diagram labeled "working memory." Procedures or representational codes for the brief storage of visual and auditory material form the visuospatial sketchpad and the phonological loop, although, in the case of auditory information, this is admittedly too narrow a conceptualization of this stage of processing. For example, the phonological loop is specialized for storage of speech-based information, and we clearly have short-term storage of other kinds of auditory information such as music, nonverbal sounds, and rhythmic patterns.

The entire middle part of Figure 10.1 actually represents the working memory system that has been so well described and studied by Baddeley (1986). We will return to this system again, as it involves the kind of memories on which this chapter will focus most closely.

Finally, it is clear that we also retain information for very long periods of time in what is usually referred to as long-term memory. Long-term memory is not a unitary storage system but is a very complex one that appears to follow somewhat different rules for different types of memories. The labels within the long-term memory box suggest one way of thinking about the different types of information that is stored in long-term memory (Baddeley, 1991).

Although this chapter presents no detail about concepts or models having to do with long-term memory, this form of memory is important in human information processing. The task of explaining learning is, to a significant degree, the task of understanding how the contents of long-term memory are changed by various kinds of experience. We know that different types of brain damage can produce a striking array of isolated effects on the ability to store and retrieve various kinds of information from long-term memory (Baddeley & Wilson, 1986; Meltzer, 1983; Parkin, 1982), so that the study of individual differences in patterns of long-term memory performance is potentially a very interesting one.

With that brief overview, we now return to a more detailed discussion of the working memory system.

DESCRIPTION OF THE WORKING MEMORY SYSTEM

As was mentioned earlier, the conceptualization of working memory discussed here derives from the work of Baddeley (1986, 1992). In this conceptualization, working memory contains a controlling system referred to as the central executive, which is a limited capacity work space that can be devoted to a variety of processing activities, including executive routines and decision making. Pennington (in press) has recently referred to this part of the system as a "computational arena, in which information relevant to a current task is both maintained on-line and subjected to further processing" (p. 21).

In Baddeley's conceptualization, the central executive coordinates a number of slave systems. The two that have been studied most extensively are the visuospatial sketchpad and the phonological loop. The sketchpad is responsible for generating and storing visual images, and the phonological loop is responsible for the manipulation and storage of speech-based information.

There is, at present, some controversy as to whether the central executive and the two slave systems should actually be considered parts of the same memory system. Pennington (in press), in his recent conceptualization of working memory, indicates that working memory (the central executive in Baddeley's system) should be considered a completely separate system from the short-term auditory and visual storage systems. Swanson (1994) has suggested the same idea, based on evidence that performance on measures tapping functions of the central executive is only weakly correlated with measures of short-term auditory memory. There is actually relatively solid evidence that the functions of the central executive (working memory) are empirically dissociable from those of auditory short-term memory (Brainerd & Kingma, 1985; Klapp, Marshburn, & Lester, 1983; Morris & Jones, 1990), so that it is probably more accurate to think of them as separate memory systems rather than as components of the same system. Thinking of them as separate memory systems does not mean, however, that they do not interact with one another. It is fundamental to this discussion that working memory, in its role as the primary "computational space" for decision making and action selection (Pennington, in press) will draw upon extra storage support during complex information processing tasks that have particularly pressing storage demands.

This chapter does not further address the characteristics and functions of the central executive, or working memory. It is considered part of the human memory system because it maintains representations of past, present, and even future events on-line, but its primary functions involve things like action selection, planning, and decision making. These behaviors are discussed in this book under the heading of executive function. The narrow segment of the memory system that this chapter focuses on is the phonological or, as it is sometimes called, the articulatory loop.

THE PHONOLOGICAL LOOP

The phonological loop provides a means for the brief, verbatim storage of verbal information using a code that represents the distinctive phonological features of the material to be remembered. *Item coding* refers to the process of translating sensory input into a representational form that can be efficiently stored in memory. Most descriptions of coding processes suggest that codes for specific items are gradually constructed as the items are processed on repeated occasions. Thus, more familiar or frequently processed items are easier to represent in memory. The phonological codes used in the phonological loop are well adapted for representing order, as well as item information (Drewnowski & Murdock, 1980).

As it is currently conceptualized, the phonological loop is composed of two components. The *phonological store* holds speech-based (phonological) information for a brief period. Unless the memory trace, or coded representation, is refreshed, it will decay from this store in about 2 seconds. An *articulatory control process* refreshes, or establishes, the memory trace in the phonological store through activation of central speech–motor programs. If verbal material needing to be briefly stored is presented visually, the articulatory control process is engaged to establish representations of the material that is maintained in the phonological store. If the material is presented auditorally, it can be directly represented in the phonological store. In this case, the articulatory control process can be used to enhance or refresh the representation in the phonological store.

The conceptualization of the phonological loop outlined above explains a truly impressive array of experimental effects. These effects include the following.

The Phonological Similarity Effect

Immediate serial recall of sequences of verbal items is impaired when the items are similar to one another in the way they sound (Baddeley, 1966; Conrad, 1964). Thus, the letter sequence *v, t, z, g, e, b* is more difficult to recall than the sequence, *r, h, s, c, f, o*, regardless of whether the sequence is presented aurally or visually. This same effect does not occur if the items to be remembered are visually rather than aurally similar. The phonological similarity effect presumably occurs because items like *v, g,* and *b* share more phonological features than do items like *r, s,* and *o*. Because items in the phonological loop are represented in terms of their distinctive phonological features, the more features that are shared between items, the more confusable they are in recall.

The Unattended Speech Effect

The recall of visually presented verbal sequences can be disrupted by background noise, if that noise contains words of phonological structure similar to those being remembered (Colle & Welsh, 1976; Salame & Baddeley, 1987, 1989). The background words do not have to be meaningful, but they do need to be phonologically similar to those being remembered. This effect does not occur for background noise that is not speech. The effect occurs presumably because the unattended speech gains involuntary access to the phonological store. Again, the effect occurs only if the unattended material is similar in phonological structure to the material to be remembered.

The Word Length Effect

The length of verbal sequence that can be recalled verbatim is powerfully affected by the spoken duration of the words to be remembered (Baddeley, Thompson, & Buchanan, 1975). Thus, it is much easier to remember a sequence of words like *ham, big, up, go, dog, knife* than to remember a sequence like *alligator, constitutional, frequently, association, diligent, opportunity*, even when the words are matched for concreteness, meaningfulness, and frequency of occurrence in language. Furthermore, the length of digit sequences that can be recalled in different languages varies directly with the time it takes to articulate the digits in each language (Hoosain & Salili, 1988; Naveh-Benjamin & Ayres, 1986). In addition, developmental increases in performance on digit span tasks vary directly with the rate at which children can articulate digits (Hulme, Thomson, Muir, & Lawrence, 1984). This effect is interpreted as indicating the ubiquity of some sort of articulatory process in refreshing the memory trace in the phonological store. The articulatory process takes time to operate, and the time required to articulate individual items determines how many can be refreshed in a given period of time.

The Articulatory Suppression Effect

Requiring a subject to continually pronounce a simple word like *the* while a sequence of verbal items is being presented for recall (either visually or aurally) significantly affects the number of items that can be recalled correctly (Baddeley, Lewis, & Vallar, 1984). This effect does not occur if the subject is asked to perform an alternative simultaneous task such as tapping a table while the material for recall is being presented. The effect is interpreted as arising from interference with the articulatory control process caused by the requirement to continually reinstate the speech–motor program for the word that is being continuously pronounced.

Recent work involving individuals with dysarthria, who have lost the capacity to control their articulatory muscles through damage to their brains, suggests that the articulatory processes involved in operation of the phonological loop are very central. That is, they do not involve peripheral aspects of speech–muscle control. The articulatory control process does not involve subvocal speech as we normally think of it, but rather some form of speech–motor program that is run at a central level. Acquired dysarthria does not appear to have a noticeable impact on the operation of the phonological loop in adults (Logie, Cubelli, Della Sala, Alberoni, and Nichelli (1992). In addition, a recent study (Biship & Robson, 1989) of children with dysarthria from birth showed that they had relatively normal memory spans; they showed both the phonological similarity effect and the word length effect. Both of these findings suggest that they were able to use articulatory control processes in a normal manner.

The experimental effects outlined above are all consistent with a conceptualization of the phonological loop as a system that provides a means for the brief, verbatim storage of verbal material (both information about the items themselves and about their order in a sequence) using a code, or representation, that consists of the distinctive phonological features of the material to be remembered. Material can be activated in the phonological store either directly, in the case of auditory information, or through the use of an articulatory control process, in the case of visually presented material.

MEASUREMENT OF FUNCTIONAL
CAPACITY OF THE PHONOLOGICAL LOOP

Even on a task with as simple a structure as the digit span task, which is the most commonly used measure of ability to store information in the phonological loop, performance differences can arise from a number of different causes (Dempster, 1981, 1985). Such things as high levels of anxiety, inattention, and lack of motivation can all influence performance on digit span tasks. In addition, it is possible to enhance performance on span tasks through the use of such cognitive strategies as *chunking* (grouping digits into meaningful or rhythmic patterns) or *cumulative rehearsal* (overt repetition of parts of the sequence as it is being presented). How then can we have confidence that any given measure assesses processes unique to the phonological loop, such as efficiency of phonological representation, rather than more general performance factors or the operation of specific, consciously organized, mnemonic strategies?

One way to narrow the range of possible interpretations of performance differences in this area is to apply a number of specific constraints to tasks that are used to assess functioning of the phonological loop. Given the present conceptualization of this memory system, tasks used to assess its functioning should present verbal material (i.e., words, digits, pronounceable nonwords, letters, objects that are easily named) for immediate verbatim recall. Recall should be immediate in order to reduce the likelihood of performance differences caused by differences in the use of consciously applied rehearsal (repetition) strategies between presentation and recall. Furthermore, if items are presented as a sequence, the presentation rate should not be slower than one item per second. When items are presented at this rate, there is good evidence that children, at least up to the age of about 12, do not use consciously organized cumulative rehearsal strategies to enhance performance (Huttenlocher & Burke, 1976). On the other hand, if items are presented more slowly than this rate, performance differences can be heavily influenced by variability in the use of mnemonic strategies, such as rehearsal, to enhance performance (Torgesen & Houck, 1980).

Tasks used to assess functioning of the phonological loop should not involve any manipulation of the material to be remembered. The phonological loop is a passive storage system, designed simply to provide brief and accurate storage of sequences of verbal information. A task like the digit span task of the Wechsler Intelligence Scale for Children, Third Edition (Wechsler, 1991), violates this constraint because half the task requires that the sequence of digits *be reversed* before it is recalled. The reversed recall portion of the task requires active manipulation of the material to be remembered through some sort of special recall strategy, so that it depends on factors other than simple representational efficiency in the phonological loop (Torgesen, Rashotte, Greenstein, & Portes, 1991).

Finally, special attention needs to be given to the reliability of measures used to study functioning of the phonological loop. When measures of digit span are included on IQ tests, they are usually one of the least reliable subtests (Sattler, 1992). In our experience, acceptable reliability for these tasks requires multiple presentations of the task, with careful attention to standardization of measurement conditions. For example, we recently reported split-half reliabilities for an auditory digit span task for kindergarten, first-grade, and second-grade children of .84, .88, and .86, respectively (Wagner, Torgesen, & Rashotte, 1994).

Even if tasks are chosen to follow all of these constraints, multiple causes of variability in performance will still operate for any given sample of children or adults. Only experiments that systematically manipulate aspects of the tasks in theoretically meaningful ways can hope to isolate the specific causes of performance differences on them.

Listed below are tasks that meet the criteria outlined above for measures to assess functioning of the phonological loop. All of these tasks have been used previously in research related to phonological memory.

Forward Digit Span

On this task (Torgesen & Wagner, 1995), sequences of randomly arranged digits are presented for immediate verbatim recall. The task can be given as a series of increasingly longer sequences, where the task is discontinued after the subject makes errors on a specified number of sequences; or it can be given as a prespecified number of sequences of two or three different lengths. Digits are not repeated within a given sequence. Typically, in order to receive credit for a response, the subject must recall the entire sequence in the correct order. In our research, we have employed a scoring system that gives some credit for partially correct responses (Torgesen & Houck, 1980).

Forward Word Span

This task (Torgesen & Wagner, 1995) is given in a manner similar to the digit span task, except that common single-syllable words are used instead of digits. On a word span task in which different words were used for each span sequence, Torgesen, Wagner, and Rashotte (1994) found correlations between word and digit span measures ranging between .66 and .72 for children in kindergarten through fifth grade.

Forward Digit Span with Visual Presentation

This task (Wagner, Torgesen, & Rashotte, 1994) is the same as the auditory span task, except that the digits are presented visually. They are presented one at a time on a computer screen at a rate similar to those presented auditorally. It is critical that the digits be presented one at a time, rather than simultaneously, as the latter presentation condition makes available a number of different encoding strategies that are not present when the items are presented one at a time in sequence (Torgesen, Bowen, & Ivey, 1978). Visually presented digit span is very difficult for many children in kindergarten, but by second grade scores between auditory and visual presentations are much more comparable (Wagner et al., 1994).

Nonword Repetition

On this task (Torgesen & Wagner, 1995), subjects are asked to immediately repeat a nonword after it is presented to them auditorally. Typically, the nonwords are arranged in order of increasing difficulty (i.e., easy item: *frachet,* hard item:

morfaglationustically), with the task being discontinued after a given number of errors. Torgesen et al. (1994) found correlations between this task and forward digit span of .47, .43, .31, .40, .47, and .46 for children in kindergarten through fifth grade, respectively.

Sentence Repetition

This task (Woodcock & Johnson, 1989) requires subjects to listen to meaningful sentences of various lengths and then to repeat them verbatim. This task can be viewed as a measure of phonological memory only if the verbatim recall of all words in their correct order is required in order for a response to be considered correct. Even with this scoring convention, this task probably also depends to a greater extent than other phonological memory measures on semantic and syntactic language skills. Wagner et al. (1994) obtained correlations between sentence and digit span tasks of .46, .56, and .58 for a large sample of children measured in kindergarten, first grade, and second grade.

Repeated Trials, Nonword Learning, and Free Recall

In this task (Vellutino, Scanlon, & Tanzman, 1994), six phonologically similar nonsense syllables are presented for free recall over eight trials. On each trial, the child's task is to correctly repeat as many of the nonsense syllables as possible, without regard to order. The total score is the number of items correctly recalled over eight trials. Although this task does not require memory for the order of items, because it involves repeated opportunities to recall initially novel verbal stimuli, it may assess, in a way that span tasks with familiar material do not, ability to form distinctive phonological representations of words. Vellutino et al. report that the task is highly reliable across a broad age range.

With the exception of the last task, which was included because of its potentially novel contribution to the assessment of functional capacity of the phonological loop, these are the most commonly used measures of phonological short-term memory. Torgesen et al. (1994) and Wagner et al. (1994) found through the use of confirmatory factor analysis that at least forward digit span, word span, nonword repetition, and sentence memory are coherent enough to be considered measures of the same construct. Taken together, they provide a solid foundation for the assessment of individual differences in the functional capacity of the phonological loop.

CONCEPTUALIZING PHONOLOGICAL MEMORY PROBLEMS IN CHILDREN WITH READING DISABILITIES

Since the early 1960s, many different studies of children with specific reading disabilities have reported that poor performance on forward digit or word span tasks is one of the most common cognitive characteristics of these children (see Heulsman, 1970; Hulme, 1988; Jorm, 1983; and Torgesen, 1978, for reviews). Two relatively recent studies of subtypes within heterogeneous samples of children with learning disabilities (Lyon, 1985; Speece, 1987) found that significant proportions (15%–20%) of these children showed serious difficulties on span tasks. In addition, severely impaired digit span performance has been a characteristic of all of the subjects who have been examined in detailed case studies of developmental phonological dyslexia (Campbell & Butterworth, 1985; Snowling & Hulme, 1989; Temple & Marshall, 1983).

Over the years, a variety of explanations have been proposed for these performance problems, but the most widely accepted current idea is that they result from subtle speech processing problems that produce degraded or less distinct phonological codes for verbal material (Brady, 1991; Liberman & Shankweiler, 1991; Torgesen, 1988). These codes, or representations, are a permanent part of the child's auditory or speech–motor long-term memory and are activated for storage in the phonological loop either directly by auditory material or through articulatory processes for visual material. In this explanation, there is something wrong with the phonological codes that are available for use in the phonological store.

Given the present conceptualization of the phonological loop, another explanation for the performance problems of children with reading disabilities on verbal memory span tasks arises from the role of articulatory processes in this system. For example, the articulatory loop may operate less efficiently because articulation processes are slowed, or it may be that children with reading disabilities are less likely, for some reason, to employ articulatory processes on memory tasks. Either of these conditions would result in difficulty refreshing memory traces in the phonological store, and the second one would also produce special difficulties coding visual material in that store.

There is actually relatively good evidence that children with reading disabilities may not be able to use the articulatory loop as efficiently as children who learn to read normally. For example, a number of studies have shown that children with reading disabilities are deficient in articulatory speed when compared to typical children (Rudel, Denckla, & Broman, 1978; Spring & Perry, 1983; Wolf & Goodglass, 1986). Although these deficits in articulation speed involve articulation processes at the peripheral, or overt speech, level (and the articulatory loop utilizes very central speech–motor processes), there is at least the suggestion that children with reading disabilities may be deficient in the speed-dependent processes used to maintain activation of phonological memory codes prior to recall (Hulme et al., 1984).

The data reported in Figure 10.2 appear to rule out the possibility that severe problems on verbal short-term memory tasks in children with developmental reading disabilities are caused by a simple failure to employ articulatory processes on verbal short-term memory tasks. In this figure (Torgesen et al., 1991), the LD-S group are children with learning disabilities who had severe problems on verbal memory span tasks, the LD-N group are children with learning disabilities but without memory span problems, and the N group are a group of average learners. This graph presents standard scores for performance on a short-term memory task for visual material that is not easily labeled (and thus might depend heavily on the visuospatial sketchpad), a long-term memory task involving the use of semantic codes, and four verbal short-term memory tasks. The major point of the graph is to show that the children with severe span problems were no more impaired when verbal material was presented visually than when it was presented auditorally. This suggests that their problem is not limited simply to lack of availability of articulatory processes to activate codes in the phonological store.

In addition to the possibility of deficiencies in speed-related processes in the articulatory loop, there is also evidence that children with reading disabilities are deficient in phonological coding processes that do not involve articulation. First, techniques that interfere with articulation (during presentation of items) or that force articulation do not eliminate performance differences between typical children and children with reading disabilities (Baddeley, 1982; Torgesen & Houck, 1980). Second, recall differences between children with reading disabilities and

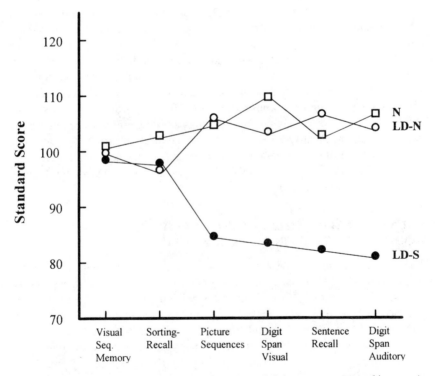

Figure 10.2. Relative performance of children with severe verbal short-term memory problems on six memory tasks (N = children with normal academic achievement; LD-N = learning disabled who performed in average range on Digit Span Subtest; LD-S = learning disabled with short-term memory deficits). (Adapted from Torgesen, Rashotte, Greenstein, & Portes, 1991.)

typical children have emerged when information is presented rapidly enough (eight items/second) to preclude coarticulation of the stimuli as these are being presented (Cohen, 1982).

The data reported in Figure 10.3 are typical of those upon which the hypothesis of a phonological coding deficit for children with reading disabilities has been developed. They were obtained in another experiment with different groups of children selected in the same manner as those in the experiment outlined above (Torgesen & Houck, 1980). The children were required to recall three different types of material: digits, familiar words of the same phonological complexity as digits, and consonant-vowel-consonant pronounceable nonwords. The results show that the absolute size of the performance deficit of the LD-S group is affected by the familiarity of the material to be recalled. This deficit is largest for the most familiar material, next largest for the next most familiar, and smallest for material for which there is no readily available, unitary code to enable efficient representation of the material in phonological memory.

The clearest explanation for this familiarity effect involves the idea that the larger absolute difference for digits over words arises from the fact that all children have had more experiences processing and pronouncing digits as individual verbal stimuli than words. At least for the two groups with learning disabilities, we can assume that their experience with digits has been roughly similar, as these groups did not differ on math achievement. The children with typical recall (the LD-N and N groups) have used their experience with digits to construct highly efficient representational codes for these items, while the LD-S group constructed less efficient codes from the same experience. The difference in recall for words is not as large, because the smaller frequency of these words in the children's experience has not produced as large a coding efficiency difference between the groups. Finally, the absolute size of the recall difference for nonwords is very small, because the groups that are more able to develop useful representations of verbal material (the N and LD-N groups) have not had the opportunity to do so for these novel stimuli.

CAUSAL RELATIONSHIP OF PHONOLOGICAL CODING DEFICIT TO READING DISABILITIES

The conceptualization of difficulties experienced by children with reading disabilities on verbal short-term memory tasks outlined above suggests a plausible theoretical connection between deficiencies on these tasks and difficulties acquiring early reading skills. For example, inadequate representations of phonological units in long-term memory should affect all learning tasks that involve pairing a visual stimulus with a verbal response, such as learning letter-sound correspondences, or learning "sight" words. Godfrey, Syrdal-Lasky, Millay, and Knox (1981) point out that

> Any such abnormality in the long-term stored "image" could be expected to adversely affect reading processes that involve the transformation of script to phonetic units of

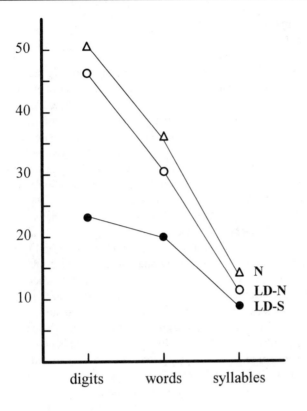

MATERIAL RECALLED

Figure 10.3. Memory span performance with three different types of stimulus materials. (N = children with normal academic achievement; LD-N = learning disabled who performed in average range on Digit Span Subtest; LD-S = learning disabled with short-term memory deficits). (From Torgesen, J.K., & Houck, G. [1980]. Processing deficiencies in learning disabled children who perform poorly on the digit span task. *Journal of Educational Psychology, 72,* 141–160; reprinted by permission.)

speech, as well as the ordering and combining of those units that make up words. (p. 420)

In their discussion of a single case of a boy with severe reading disabilities who also showed specific performance problems on verbal short-term memory tasks, Snowling and Hulme (1989) placed similar emphasis on the problems created by "impoverished" specification of phonological codes for words and letters. Specifically, children who perform poorly on verbal short-term memory tasks may find it difficult to perform the simultaneous or rapidly sequential identification, comparison, and blending processes that are required to identify words by phonological/analytical strategies. In fact, the special difficulties of children with reading disabilities in acquiring analytical decoding skills, in comparison to their whole-word identification skills, are now widely documented in the research literature

(Rack, Snowling, & Olson, 1992; Siegel, 1985; Stanovich, 1990; Vellutino & Scanlon, 1991).

Although there is a plausible theoretical relationship between phonological representation (coding) problems and difficulties acquiring early alphabetical reading skills, the empirical evidence thus far for a causal relationship between these two variables is relatively weak. Pennington, Van Orden, Kirson, and Haith (1991) identified five possible ways that phonological memory might be related to reading: 1) it might be a primary symptom, or a prerequisite for the development of reading disabilities; 2) it might be a contributing symptom, or a facilitator of reading problems; 3) it might be influenced by level of reading skill; 4) it might simply be a correlated symptom through its association with some other causal variable; and 5) it could both contribute to, and be influenced by, level of reading ability. Pennington et al. ruled out the possibility that verbal short-term memory problems are a primary symptom or prerequisite for reading disabilities, because comparisons of children with reading disabilities and typical children and adults have not *always* found individuals with reading disabilities to be significantly impaired in phonological memory. Furthermore, where differences in phonological memory do occur, they are not usually as large for verbal short-term memory tasks as for measures of other phonological skills, such as phonological awareness or rapid automatic naming of familiar verbal stimuli. This latter pattern of results was recently reported in a large scale definitional study of dyslexia (Fletcher et al., 1994). In this study, a carefully defined sample of children with reading disabilities 7.5–9.5 years old performed deficiently, in comparison to a sample of typical readers, on a wide variety of both verbal and nonverbal tasks including measures of verbal short-term memory. However, when the profile of scores was adjusted for "elevation" (average ability across all tasks), the differences between children with dyslexia and typical children on the phonological memory tasks were very small in comparison to those for phonological awareness, vocabulary/word finding, and rapid naming tasks. This same pattern of findings was also reported in another definitional study using a large random sample of first-grade children (Felton & Wood, 1990).

Although direct comparisons between samples of readers with and without disabilities cannot be used to establish causal relationships, findings of inconsistent or weak concurrent relationships between verbal short-term memory and word reading ability certainly weaken the hypothesis that there is a primary causal relationship between the two variables.

Pennington et al. (1991) also considered longitudinal correlational studies that have addressed the causal relationship between phonological memory and early word reading skill. In this research, a set of predictor variables (phonological skills, verbal intelligence, etc.) is measured at Time 1, and reading skills are measured at Time 2. The crucial question is whether individual differences in memory at Time 1 can explain individual differences in reading at Time 2, after reading and other important variables at Time 1 are held constant. Where this question has been directly evaluated using appropriate methodology (Wagner et al., 1994), the answer appears to be negative. An earlier study by Mann and Liberman (1984) did find that both phonological memory and phonological awareness made independent contributions toward explaining individual differences in later reading skill, but this study also reported an unusually weak relationship between phonological awareness and later reading ($r = .40$). The weakness of this relationship was probably due to the fact that the measure of phonological awareness was actually a measure of syllable rather than phoneme segmentation (Blachman, 1984).

A similar problem involving measurement of phonological awareness occurred in another study that investigated the relationships between phonological awareness, phonological memory, and reading in a sample of English 4- and 5-year olds (Gathercole, Willis, & Baddeley, 1991). This was not a longitudinal study, and relationships among these variables were investigated separately in the younger and older samples. A unique predictive relationship between verbal short-term memory and reading was found only in the 5-year olds. However, this relationship occurred only for one of the two measures of phonological memory, and the rhyme detection task used to assess phonological awareness is not usually as strongly related to reading as other measures of phonological awareness that might have been used (Stanovich, Cunningham, & Cramer, 1984).

The most extensive examination of causal relationships among phonological abilities and reading was recently reported by Wagner et al. (1994). In this study, multiple measures of each phonological skill were taken in kindergarten, first grade, and second grade for a randomly selected sample of 244 children. This allowed the use of structural equation models to study causal relationships between reading and the phonological skills, with all variables measured as latent variables. A latent variable represents the common variance among a set of measures and thus allows measurement of constructs relatively free of measurement error. The two measures used to represent phonological memory were forward auditory digit span and sentence span.

When causal relationships between phonological variables measured in kindergarten and word reading skill measured in first grade were estimated (with general verbal intelligence and kindergarten reading skills also in the model), Wagner et al. (1994) obtained the causal coefficients reported in Table 10.1. Analysis represents skill in identifying individual phonemes within orally presented words. Synthesis tasks required children to identify words that could be formed when individually presented phonemes were blended together, and serial naming tasks required children to rapidly name sequences of digits and letters presented on a card. Although memory had the weakest relationship with reading, it did have a significant causal effect on reading development when considered by itself. As can be seen from Table 10.1, once significant individual differences in reading skill emerge in first grade, the phonological variables contribute

Table 10.1. Causal relationships between early phonological skills and later word reading skills

	K–1	1–2
Analysis	.67***	.38***
Synthesis	.39***	.35***
Memory	.21***	.06
Serial naming	.37***	.24***

***$p < .001$.

less to the continuing emergence of further individual differences in reading, and the effect of memory differences becomes nonsignificant.

Further analyses (Wagner et al., 1994) showed that the causal influences of the phonological variables were redundant with one another, both in kindergarten and first grade. In a simultaneous causal model in which all phonological variables were included, phonological analysis captured all of the causally relevant variance in phonological skills during the period from kindergarten to first grade. In the first- to second-grade analysis, phonological synthesis emerged as the most powerful causal agent, with none of the other phonological variables contributing unique explanatory power to the model. In this study, then, the phonological skills measured by the memory tasks were completely redundant with skills measured by the phonological awareness tasks, in terms of their causal relationships to the emergence of individual differences in reading.

When the pattern of causal effects going the opposite way (from reading at Time 1 to phonological skill at Time 2) was examined, the results reported in Table 10.2 were found. Individual differences in reading at each Time 1 made a small causal contribution to emergence of further individual differences in phonological skills at each Time 2, except for phonological memory. Individual differences in reading appeared to exert no causal influence on the emergence of individual differences in memory, either in first or second grade.

These data showing small causal influences of reading skill development on subsequent phonological development are consistent with data that were also reported in this study showing the stability of these skills over the period of time from kindergarten to second grade. Stability coefficients for each of the phonological skills are reported in Table 10.3. As can be seen from this table, the phonological variables show a high degree of stability over this period of time, with phonological memory being particularly stable.

Table 10.2. Causal relationships between early reading skills and later phonological skills

	K–1	1–2
Analysis	.19***	.26***
Synthesis	.27***	.28***
Memory	.03	.05
Serial naming	.27***	.18***

***$p < .001$.

Table 10.3. Stability of phonological processing abilities

Latent variable	Time interval		
	K–1	1–2	K–2
Analysis	.87***	.92***	.66***
Synthesis	.71***	.81***	.49***
Memory	1.0***	1.0***	1.0***
Serial naming	.81***	.87***	.62***

Adapted from Wagner, Torgesen, & Rashotte (1994).
*** $p < .001$.

Torgesen et al. (1994) have recently obtained some cross-sectional data suggesting that the relationships between some aspects of word reading skill and performance on verbal short-term memory tasks might become stronger at later stages of growth in these skills. Multiple measures of three different phonological skills (phonological awareness, phonological memory, rapid automatic naming) were given to 100 randomly selected children during the second semester in each of the grades from kindergarten through fifth. Latent variables were constructed for each of these three constructs, and Figure 10.4 shows their relationships to children's ability to read nonwords (alphabetical reading skill) at each of the grade levels. It is apparent from this figure that the relationship between memory performance and reading increases substantially with age. The average correlation for grades kindergarten through second was .36, whereas that for third through fifth grade was .52.

Of course, this is cross-sectional data, so we cannot say anything about causal directions in these relationships. However, there is a good possibility that reading skill might be influencing performance on the memory variable because this increasingly strong relationship was primarily the result of one of our measures of phonological memory, nonword repetition.

Table 10.4 presents the correlations between nonword reading ability and all the memory measures, along with those for one of the phonological awareness tasks (phoneme elision) and naming rate for digits. As this table shows, the largest increase in relationship with reading skill among the memory measures was with nonword repetition. Performance on this task might be influenced by reading experience and skill because the more difficult multisyllabic nonwords on the test (i.e., *perplisteronk, structerempible, conflaturationist*) usually contained some syllables that are also found in real words. The broader reading experience of the better readers may have allowed them to establish better representations of these syllabic elements in long-term memory, thus making parts of the nonword stimuli more familiar to them. As can be seen, there was a much smaller increase in relationships between reading skills and standard digit and word span measures.

In summary, the data from Torgesen et al. (1994) and Wagner et al. (1994), as well as that from other longitudinal and cross-sectional research (Pennington et al., 1991), do not support the hypothesis that deficiencies in phonological coding efficiency are a powerful and unique cause of individual differences in word

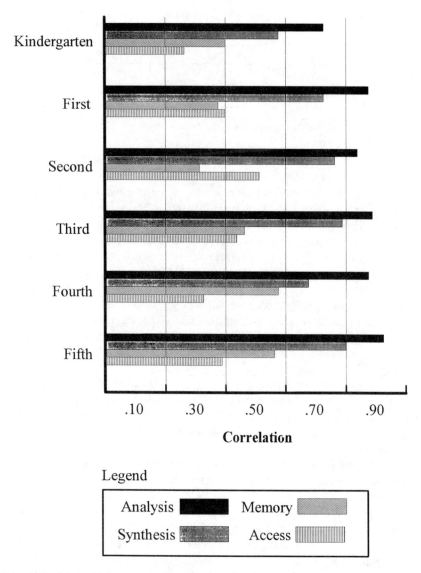

Figure 10.4. Relationship between phonological processing latent variables and alphabetical reading skill at six grade levels.

reading skill in young children. Problems on verbal short-term memory tasks do appear to be correlated with difficulties in acquiring alphabetic reading skills. However, this correlation is relatively weak in comparison to that between word reading ability and other phonological skills, so that verbal short-term memory tasks do not appear to be the best index of the kind of individual differences in phonological skill that are causally related to individual differences in the growth of early word reading skills.

Table 10.4. Correlations between selected phonological variables and alphabetical reading skill across six grade levels

Grade	Phoneme elision	Digit span	Word span	Nonword repetition	Naming speed
K	.65	.28	.34	.34	.47
1	.70	.27	.19	.43	.53
2	.69	.23	.25	.44	.53
3	.71	.25	.31	.56	.40
4	.69	.36	.34	.59	.30
5	.75	.38	.42	.61	.35

RELATIONSHIPS AMONG PHONOLOGICAL VARIABLES

Although phonological coding deficiencies, as measured by performance on verbal short-term memory tasks, do not appear to play an important unique causal role in difficulties acquiring early word reading skills, they may influence reading growth by their impact on the growth of phonological awareness in young children. The ability to easily compare groups of words or word segments simultaneously in working memory (aided by effective storage in the phonological loop) may contribute importantly to acquisition of phonological awareness. In support of this speculation, there is good evidence that span performance and phonological awareness are highly correlated with one another in preschool (Wagner et al., 1987) and kindergarten (Wagner, Torgesen, Laughon, Simmons, & Rashotte, 1993) children. In fact, both of these studies used confirmatory factor analysis to test models of the structure of covariance among a large set of phonological variables and found that the best models included verbal short-term memory tasks and phonological analysis tasks as measures of the same construct for pre-school and kindergarten children. The abilities do appear to become more differentiated with development (Wagner et al., 1994).

Since representational efficiency in short-term memory may be a more basic or early emerging skill than phonological awareness, it is clearly possible that early differences in phonological memory may play an important role as one factor causing differences among children in growth of phonological awareness skills prior to the beginning of reading instruction. A recent study by Torgesen and Davis (in press) provided a fairly direct test of this hypothesis. This study examined which cognitive abilities best predicted growth in phonological analysis and synthesis skills as a result of a 12-week training program. Sixty kindergarten children received approximately 20 hours of training designed to enhance growth in phonological analysis and synthesis as oral language skills. Performance on analysis and synthesis tasks was assessed three times during the training, and hierarchical linear modeling techniques were used to construct individual growth curves in analysis and synthesis for each child. Hierarchical linear modeling procedures were used to obtain standardized regression coefficients describing the relationship between these growth curves and four different classes of predictor variables: 1) general verbal ability, 2) pretest levels of analysis and synthesis skill, 3) basic phonological processing skills (phonological memory and naming rate for familiar verbal stimuli), and 4) beginning reading/spelling skills. Table 10.5 reports the standardized regression coefficients for the predictor variable from each class (except that coefficients for both memory and naming rate are reported), with the strongest relationship to growth in analysis and synthesis skills. It is clear from this table that we obtained no support for the hypothesis that individual differences in children's phonological memory skills predict response to training in either analytical or synthetic phonological awareness. The best model for predicting growth in analytical awareness involved a measure of invented spelling plus verbal IQ. However, this model only predicted about 30% of the reliable differences in growth. The best model for blending involved invented spelling and naming rate, and this model predicted almost all of the reliable differences in growth in this skill.

In contrast to the lack of evidence that memory is somehow a more fundamental phonological skill than phonological awareness, there are some pilot data available (A. Alexander, personal communication, April 21, 1993) suggesting that a certain kind of intensive training in phonological awareness can have quite marked effects on the verbal short-term memory performance of children with reading disabilities.

The training program involved is the *Auditory Discrimination in Depth* program (Lindamood & Lindamood, 1984), which involves explicit attempts to increase children's awareness of the articulatory movements associated with each of the phonemes in the English language. This is coupled with intensive practice in using this newly acquired awareness to track sequences of phonemes within both nonwords and real words. In these tracking exercises, children are encouraged to both "feel" and "hear" the sounds in words.

Table 10.6 presents case study results from five children who received approximately 80 hours of this training. Pre- and posttests were given approximately 6 months apart, and the children ranged in age from 9 to 12 years old. The tests given were taken from the Clinical Evaluation of Language Fundamentals–Revised (Semel, Wiig, & Secord, 1987) and included 1) *oral directions*, which assesses children's ability to follow arbitrarily constructed directions such

Table 10.5. Pretest variables as predictors of growth rate in segmenting and blending skills

	Segmenting		Blending	
	Coefficient	Standard error	Coefficient	Standard error
Analysis				
(sound matching)	1.98*	.86	2.29**	.81
Synthesis (blending)	1.68*	.89	0.24	.86
Naming rate	1.36	.89	2.21*	.85
Digit span	1.31	.89	1.16	.82
Invented spelling	2.48**	.82	2.81*	.77
Verbal IQ	2.34**	.85	1.91*	.85

Adapted from Torgesen & Davis (1994).
*$p < .05$.
**$p < .01$.

as, "point to the first black square"; 2) *recalling sentences*, which was scored for verbatim retention of all the words in the sentence; and 3) *listening to paragraphs*, in which children answered content questions after listening to short paragraphs. In Table 10.6, standardized percentile scores are given for each measure before and after training. The most consistent effects of the training were on recalling sentences and listening comprehension. Of course, this latter test is not a direct measure of verbal short-term memory, but individual differences in phonological memory have been linked to language comprehension by a number of investigators (Baddeley, 1991). The less consistent effects on oral directions are troublesome, but at present the relationship between this task and other measures of verbal short-term memory are not well understood.

If this effect can be replicated on a broader variety of phonological memory measures and is not just a general attentional effect, it could contribute importantly to our understanding of individual differences in performance on tasks that assess the functional capacity of the phonological loop. For example, it might suggest that accuracy of recall on verbal short-term memory tasks could be enhanced if children are trained to supplement their use of the strictly phonological features of words with more active processing of their articulatory features as well. In this interpretation, the training might not have a direct effect on the actual quality of the codes used to represent information in the phonological loop, but rather would facilitate recall by providing a broader basis for distinguishing

Table 10.6. Pilot data on response to intensive training in speech-motor and phonological awareness

	Pretraining (%)	Posttraining (%)
Child 1		
OD	5	25
RS	16	75
LS	5	63
Child 2		
OD	50	37
RS	9	37
LS	16	95
Child 3		
OD	5	5
RS	8	75
LS	63	84
Child 4		
OD	95	63
RS	25	75
LS	2	84
Child 5		
OD	25	84
RS	12	84
LS	23	84

Note. Pre- and posttraining percentages reflect standardized percentile scores for each measure and each child before and after training.

OD, oral directions; RS, recalling sentences; LC, listening comprehension.

among items. Alternatively, this training might actually enhance the quality of representational codes by encouraging more active and precise coarticulation of items as they are being presented in the first place. Because the training places such a premium on "feeling" the phonemes in words by attending to the articulatory gestures that produce them, it may help children to compensate for their weakness in phonological coding by inducing more active articulatory processing. If this is true, then the growth in oral/motor awareness that appears to support and stimulate the development of phonological awareness in young children (Lindamood & Lindamood, 1984) might play a similar role in increasing the quality of phonological representations in verbal short-term memory.

CONCLUSIONS

In this review, we have considered whether individual differences in children's ability to briefly store verbatim sequences of verbal information play an important role in causing differences in their ability to acquire early word reading skills. Such a causal connection is suggested by the many studies that have found differences between children with and without reading difficulties on tasks that measure verbal short-term memory skills. It is also suggested by the plausible theoretical role for short-term memory processes in many early reading tasks. However, the most comprehensive recent studies suggest that other phonological skills, such as phonological awareness and rapid automatic naming of familiar verbal stimuli, play a much more important role in causing individual differences in early reading skill than does phonological short-term memory. It is highly probable that early studies showing reliable differences between good and poor readers on verbal memory tasks would have found even larger differences on measures of phonological awareness and rapid automatic naming if those skills had been measured.

One plausible interpretation of the results reported here is that verbal short-term memory is simply correlated with reading disability because of its relationship to other variables like phonological awareness and rapid naming that are the actual causal agents. This is the interpretation favored by Pennington et al. (1991). In their words,

> . . . one deficit could be part of the final common pathway leading to deficits in reading and spelling, whereas other deficits could be variable by-products of the different etiologies leading to that final common pathway. Hence, these other deficits would be correlates of the primary deficit and could contribute to the development of the disorder. (p. 184)

The primary support for this conclusion comes from evidence that short-term memory skills do not account for unique variance in word reading ability when phonological awareness and rapid naming skills are in the same predictive equation. Although there have been scattered findings in which verbal short-term memory has been shown to play a unique predictive role for individual differences in word reading skill, methodological problems in these studies undermine the credibility of their results.

It is also possible to interepret the results reported in this review in a way that would preserve a limited causal role for verbal-short term memory deficits in reading disabilities. This interpretation starts with the finding that, although phonological awareness, verbal short-term memory, and rapid automatic naming tasks should be considered separate abilities, they are highly correlated with one another in development (Torgesen et al., 1994; Wagner et al., 1994). One possible reason these tasks are linked together in development is their common dependence on the functional intactness of the phonological component of children's "natural capacity for language" (Liberman, Shankweiler, & Liberman, 1989, p. 1). If this is the case, then phonological awareness and rapid naming tasks may be more strongly related to individual differences in word reading skill, either because they are more sensitive measures of this natural capacity or because the tasks used to assess them share more method variance with reading. Share and Stanovich (1995) have shown how phonological awareness tasks have many mental operations in common with early reading tasks, and Wolf and her colleagues (Bowers & Wolf, 1993; Wolf, 1991) have made a similar analyses of rapid automatic naming tasks, particularly those that involve serial naming. The idea that phonological awareness and rapid naming tasks share more mental operations with reading than do verbal short-term memory tasks is consistent with their more fully reciprocal causal relationships with reading. In the most comprehensive current analysis (Wagner et al. 1994), individual differences in reading ability have an impact on further growth of both phonological awareness and rapid naming skills, but not on phonological memory skills.

If, in fact, phonological awareness and rapid naming tasks are more sensitive to individual differences in the linguistic ability they measure in common with verbal short-term memory tasks, then they will consistently emerge as more important variables in causal models that contain all three variables. The same result would be produced if the two former tasks are more strongly related to reading because they share more mental operations with reading. Thus, the weaker causal relationship between verbal short-term memory abilities and early reading skill may be masked when it is included in the same prediction equation with phonological awareness and rapid naming. Although this masking hypothesis cannot be ruled out on the basis of current evidence, it must be remembered that the absolute size of the relationship between verbal short-term memory and word reading skill is small.

One possible reason for differences between studies of extreme cases (Gathercole & Baddeley, 1990; Snowling & Hulme, 1989; Torgesen, 1991) and studies involving large random samples (Felton & Wood, 1990; Wagner et al., 1994) in the importance assigned to verbal short-term memory deficits in accounting for reading disabilities is that variation in memory over normal limits may have little impact on early reading development. Although some degree of ability to represent phonological information in short-term memory is obviously required to perform many early reading tasks, the "tolerance" of these tasks to variance in memory skill may be quite large. In this sense, phonological memory skills may operate similarly to visual processing skills in relation to reading. They are intimately involved in learning to read, but they are not an important source of individual differences in reading because almost all children have at least "good enough" skills in them to learn to read. In both cases, extreme disabilities are required in order to have a noticeable impact on reading development.

REFERENCES

Baddeley, A.D. (1966). Short-term memory for word sequences as a function of acoustic and formal similarity. *Quarterly Journal of Experimental Psychology, 18*, 362–365.

Baddeley, A.D. (1982). Reading and working memory. *Bulletin of the British Psychological Society, 35*, 414–417.

Baddeley, A.D. (1986). *Working memory.* New York: Oxford University Press.

Baddeley, A.D. (1991). *Human memory: Theory and practice.* London: Allyn & Bacon.

Baddeley, A.D. (1992). Working memory. *Science, 255*, 556–559.

Baddeley, A.D., Lewis, V., & Vallar, G. (1984). Exploring the articulatory loop. *Quarterly Journal of Experimental Psychology, 36*, 233–252.

Baddeley, A.D., Thompson, N., & Buchanan, M. (1975). Word length and the structure of short-term memory. *Journal of Verbal Learning and Verbal Behaviors, 14*, 575–589.

Baddeley, A.D., & Wilson, B. (1986). Amnesia, autobiographical memory and confabulation. In D. Rubin (Ed.), *Autobiographical memory* (pp. 225-252). New York: Cambridge University Press.

Biship, D.V.M., & Robson, J. (1989). Unimpaired short-term memory and rhyme judgement in congenitally speechless individuals: Implications for the notion of "articulatory coding." *Quarterly Journal of Experimental Psychology, 41*, 123–141.

Blachman, B.A. (l984) Relationship of rapid naming ability and language analysis skills to kindergarten and first-grade reading achievement. *Journal of Educational Psychology, 76*, 610–622.

Bowers, P.G., & Wolf, M. (1993). Theoretical links between naming speed, precise timing mechanisms and orthographic skill in dyslexia. *Reading and Writing: An Interdisciplinary Journal, 5*, 69–85.

Brady, S.A. (1991). The role of working memory in reading disability. In S.A. Brady & D.P. Shankweiler (Eds.), *Phonological processes in literacy* (pp. 129–152) Hillsdale, NJ: Lawrence Erlbaum Associates.

Brainerd, C.J., & Kingma, J. (1985). On the independence of short-term memory and working memory in cognitive development. *Cognitive Psychology, 17*, 210–247.

Campbell, R., & Butterworth, B. (1985). Phonological dyslexia and dysgraphia in a highly literate subject: A developmental case with associated deficits of phonemic processing and awareness. *The Quarterly Journal of Experimental Psychology, 37*, 435–475.

Cohen, R.L. (1982). Individual differences in short-term memory. *International Review of Research in Mental Retardation, 11*, 43–77.

Colle, H.A., & Welsh, A. (1976). Acoustic masking in primary memory. *Journal of Verbal Learning and Verbal Behavior, 15*, 17–32.

Conrad, R. (1964). Acoustic confusions in immediate memory. *British Journal of Psychology, 55*, 75–84.

Dempster, F.N. (1981). Memory span: sources of individual and developmental differences. *Psychological Bulletin, 89*, 63–100.

Dempster, F.N. (1985). Short-term memory development in childhood and adolescence. In C. Brainerd & M. Pressley (Eds.), *Basic processes in memory development* (pp. 128–157). New York: Springer-Verlag.

Drewnowski, A., & Murdock, B. (1980). The role of auditory features in memory span for words. *Journal of Experimental Psychology: Human Learning and Memory, 6*, 315–332.

Efron, R. (1970). The minimum duration of a perception. *Neuropsychologia, 8*, 57-63.

Felton, R.H., & Wood, F.B. (1990). Cognitive deficits in reading disability and attention deficit disorder. In J.K. Torgesen (Ed.), *Cognitive and behavioral characteristics of children with learning disabilities* (pp. 89–114). Austin, TX: PRO-ED.

Fletcher, J.M., Shaywitz, S.E., Shankweiler, D.P., Katz, L., Liberman, I.Y., Stuebing, K.K., Francis, D.J., Fowler, A.E., & Shaywitz, B.A. (1994). Cognitive profiles of reading disability: Comparisons of discrepancy and low achievement definitions. *Journal of Educational Psychology, 86*, 6–23.

Gathercole, S.E., & Baddeley, A.D. (1990). Phonological memory deficits in language disordered children: Is there a causal connection? *Journal of Memory and Language, 29*, 336–360.

Gathercole, S.E., Willis, C.S., & Baddeley, A.D. (1991). Differentiating phonological memory and awareness of rhyme: Reading and vocabulary development in children. *British Journal of Psychology, 82*, 387–406.

Godfrey, J.J., Syrdal-Lasky, A.K., Millay, K.K., & Knox, C.M. (1981). Performance of dyslexic children on speech perception tests. *Journal of Experimental Child Psychology, 32*, 401–424.

Heulsman, C.B. (1970). The WISC subtest syndrome for disabled readers. *Perceptual and Motor Skills, 30*, 535–550.

Hoosain, R., & Salili, F. (1988). Language differences, working memory, and mathematical ability. In M.M. Gruneberg, P.E. Morris, & R.N. Sykes (Eds.), *Practical aspects of memory: Current research and issues, Vol. 2: Clinical and educational implications* (pp. 512–517). Chichester, England: John Wiley & Sons.

Hulme, C. (1988). Short-term memory development and learning to read. In M. Gruneberg, P. Morris, and R. Sykes (Eds.), *Practical aspects of memory: Current research and issues, Vol. 2: Clinical and educational implications* (pp. 234–271). Chichester, England: John Wiley & Sons.

Hulme, C., Thomson, N., Muir, C., & Lawrence, A. (1984). Speech rate and the development of short-term memory span. *Journal of Experimental Child Psychology, 38*, 241–253.

Huttenlocher, J., & Burke, D. (1976). Why does memory span increase with age? *Cognitive Psychology, 8*, 1–31.

Jorm, A.F. (1983). Specific reading retardation and working memory: A review. *British Journal of Psychology, 74*, 311–342.

Klapp, S.T., Marshburn, E.A., & Lester, P.T. (1983). Short-term memory does not involve the "working memory" of intellectual processing: The demise of a common assumption. *Journal of Experimental Psychology: General, 112*, 240–264.

Liberman, I.Y., & Shankweiler, D. (1991). Phonology and beginning reading: A tutorial. In L. Rieben & C.A. Perfetti (Eds.), *Learning to read* (pp. 3-18). Hillsdale, NJ: Lawrence Erlbaum Associates.

Liberman, I.Y., Shankweiler, D., & Liberman, A.M. (1989). The alphabetic principle and learning to read. In Shankweiler, D. & Liberman, I.Y. (Eds.), *Phonology and reading disability: Solving the reading puzzle* (pp. 1–33). Ann Arbor, MI: University of Michigan Press.

Lindamood, C.H., & Lindamood, P.C. (1984). *Auditory discrimination in depth.* Blacklick, OH: SRA.

Logie, R.H., Cubelli, R., Della Sala, S., Alberoni, M., & Nichelli, P. (1992). Anarthria and verbal short-term memory. In J. Crawford & D. Parker (Eds.), *Developments in clinical and experimental neuropsychology* (pp. 113–132). New York: Plenum.

Lyon, G.R. (1985). Identification and remediation of learning disability subtypes: Preliminary findings. *Learning Disabilities Focus, 1,* 21–35.

Mann, V.A., & Liberman, I.Y. (1984). Phonological awareness and verbal short-term memory. *Journal of Learning Disabilities, 10,* 592–599.

Meltzer, M.L. (1983). Poor memory: A case report. *Journal of Clinical Psychology, 39,* 3–10.

Morris, N., & Jones, D.M. (1990). Memory updating in working memory: The role of the central executive. *British Journal of Psychology, 81,* 111–121.

Naveh-Benjamin, M., & Ayres, T.J. (1986). Digit span, reading rate, and linguistic relativity. *Quarterly Journal of Experimental Psychology, 38,* 739–751.

Parkin, A.J. (1982). Residual learning capability in organic amnesia. *Cortex, 18,* 417–440.

Pennington, B.F. (in press). The working memory function of the pre-frontal cortices: Implications for developmental and individual differences in cognition. In M.M. Haith, J. Benson, R. Roberts, & B.F. Pennington (Eds.), *The development of future oriented processes.* Chicago: University of Chicago Press.

Pennington, B.F., Van Orden, G., Kirson, D., & Haith, M. (1991). What is the causal relation between verbal STM problems and dyslexia? In S.A. Brady & D.P. Shankweiler (Eds.), *Phonological processes in literacy: A tribute to Isabelle Y. Liberman* (pp. 173–186). Hillsdale, NJ: Lawrence Erlbaum Associates.

Rack, J.P., Snowling, M.J., & Olson, R.K. (1992). The nonword reading deficit in developmental dyslexia: A review. *Reading Research Quarterly, 27,* 29–53.

Rudel, R.G., Denckla, M.B., & Broman, M. (1978). Rapid silent response to repeated target symbols by dyslexic and nondyslexic children. *Brain and Language, 6,* 52–62.

Salame, P., & Baddeley, A.D. (1987). Noise, unattended speech and short-term memory. *Ergonomics, 30,* 1185–1193.

Salame, P., & Baddeley, A.D. (1989). Effects of background music on phonological short-term memory. *Quarterly Journal of Experimental Psychology, 41,* 107–122.

Sattler, J.M. (1992). *Assessment of children (Rev. 3rd ed.).* San Diego: Sattler Publishing.

Semel, E., Wiig, E.H., & Secord, W. (1987). *Clinical evaluation of language fundamentals (Rev. ed.).* Austin, TX: Psychological Corporation.

Share, D.L., & Stanovich, K.E. (1995). Cognitive processes in early reading development: A model of acquisition and individual differences. *Issues in Education: Contributions from Educational Psychology, 1,* 1–57.

Siegel, L.S. (1985). Psycholinguistic aspects of reading disabilities. In L. Siegel & F. Morrison (Eds.), *Cognitive development in atypical children* (pp. 45–64). New York: Springer-Verlag.

Snowling, M., & Hulme, C. (1989). A longitudinal case study of developmental phonological dyslexia. *Cognitive Neuropsychology, 6,* 379–401.

Speece, D.L. (1987). Information processing subtypes of learning disabled readers. *Learning Disabilities Research, 2,* 91–102.

Sperling, G. (1967). Successive approximations to a model for short-term memory. *Acta Psychologica, 27,* 285–292.

Spring, C., & Perry, L. (1983). Naming speed and serial recall in poor and adequate readers. *Contemporary Educational Psychology, 8,* 141-145.

Stanovich, K.E. (1990). Explaining the differences between the dyslexic and the garden-variety poor reader: The phonological-core variable-difference model. In J. Torgesen (Ed.), *Cognitive and behavioral characteristics of children with learning disabilities* (pp. 7–40). Austin, TX: PRO-ED.

Stanovich, K.E., Cunningham, A.E., & Cramer, B.B. (1984). Assessing phonological awareness in kindergarten children: Issues of task comparability. *Journal of Experimental Child Psychology, 38,* 175–190.

Swanson, H.L. (1994). Short-term memory and working memory: Do both contribute to our understanding of academic achievement in children and adults with learning disabilities? *Journal of Learning Disabilities, 27,* 34–50.

Temple, C.M., & Marshall, J.C. (1983). A case study of developmental phonological dyslexia. *British Journal of Psychology, 74,* 517–533.

Torgesen, J.K. (1978). Performance of reading disabled children on serial memory tasks: A review. *Reading Research Quarterly, 19,* 57–87.

Torgesen, J.K. (1988). Studies of children with learning disabilities who perform poorly on memory span tasks. *Journal of Learning Disabilities, 21,* 605–612.

Torgesen, J.K. (1991). Cross-age consistency in phonological processing. In S. Brady & D. Shankweiler (Eds.), *Phonological processes in literacy: A tribute to Issablle Y. Liberman* (pp. 187–194). Hillsdale, NJ: Lawrence Earlbaum Associates.

Torgesen, J.K., Bowen, C., & Ivey, C. (1978). Task structure versus presentation: A study of the construction validity of the visual-oral digit span test. *Journal of Educational Psychology, 70,* 451–456.

Torgesen, J.K., & Davis, C. (in press). Individual difference variables that predict response to training in phonological awareness. *Journal of Experimental Psychology.*

Torgesen, J.K., & Houck, G. (1980). Processing deficiencies in learning disabled children who perform poorly on the digit span task. *Journal of Educational Psychology, 72,* 141–160.

Torgesen, J.K., Rashotte, C.A., Greenstein, J., & Portes, P. (1991). Further studies of LD children with severe performance problems on the digit span test. *Learning Disabilities Research and Practice, 3,* 113–144.

Torgesen, J.K., & Wagner, R.K. (1995). *Comprehensive Test of Reading-Related Phonological Processing—Experimental Version.* Unpublished test, Florida State University.

Torgesen, J.K., Wagner, R.K., & Rashotte, C.A. (1994). *Relationships among measures of phonological processing and word reading skills in grades kindergarten through fifth.* Unpublished manuscript, Florida State University.

Vellutino, F.R., & Scanlon, D.M. (1991). The preeminence of phonologically based skills in learning to read. In S. Brady & D. Shankweiler (Eds.), *Phonological processes in literacy: A tribute to Isabelle Liberman* (pp. 237–252). Hillsdale, NJ: Lawrence Erlbaum Associates.

Vellutino, F.R., Scanlon, D.M., & Tanzman, M.S. (1994). Components of reading ability: Issues and problems in operationalizing word identification, phonological coding, and orthographic coding. In G.R. Lyon (Ed.), *Frames of reference for the assessment of learning disabilities* (pp. 279–332). Baltimore: Paul H. Brookes Publishing Co.

Wagner, R.K., Balthazar, M., Hurley, S., Morgan, S., Rashotte, C., Shaner, R., Simmons, K., & Stage, S. (1987). The nature of prereader's phonological processing abilities. *Cognitive Development, 2,* 355-373.

Wagner, R.K., Torgesen, J.K., Laughon, P., Simmons, K., & Rashotte, C. (1993). The development of young readers' phonological processing abilities. *Journal of Educational Psychology, 85,* 83–103.

Wagner, R.K., Torgesen, J.K., & Rashotte, C.A. (1994). The development of reading-related phonological processing abilities: New evidence of bi-directional causality from a latent variable longitudinal study. *Developmental Psychology, 30,* 73–87.

Wechsler, D. (1991). *Wechsler Intelligence Scale for Children* (3rd ed.). San Antonio, TX: Psychological Corporation.

Wolf, M. (1991). Naming speed and reading: The contribution of the cognitive neurosciences. *Reading Research Quarterly, 26,* 123–141.

Wolf, M., & Goodglass, A. (1986). Dyslexia, dysnomia, and lexical retrieval: A longitudinal investigation. *Brain and Language, 28,* 154–168.

Woodcock, R.W., & Johnson, M.B. (1989). *Woodcock-Johnson Psycho-Educational Battery–Revised.* Allen, TX: DLM/Teaching Resources.

11

MULTIPLE MEMORY SYSTEMS
A Neuropsychological and Developmental Perspective

Jocelyne Bachevalier, Ludise Malkova, and Mario Beauregard

It has been traditional in the history of cognitive psychology to separate psychological theory from neurobiological mechanisms. A trend of unification between these two disciplines appears to have emerged more recently, leading to new intellectual frameworks to examine various cognitive processes, such as perception, language, memory, and conscious awareness. A particularly fascinating example can be seen in the study of learning and memory and is considered in the present chapter. This discussion focuses on the characteristics of various forms of memory and how they are organized in the brain. The data reviewed here derive more specifically from neuropsychological studies of memory-impaired patients and related studies with experimental animals. Finally, how the notion of multiple memory systems has provided new ways to study the development of memory function and to think about the phenomenon of infantile amnesia is considered.

MULTIPLE MEMORY PROCESSES

The suggestion that memory might not be unitary was made at least as early as the 1940s by Hebb (1949), who speculated that memory might comprise a temporary trace (short-term memory) based on the reverberation of electrical circuits within the brain, coupled with a more durable form of memory (long-term memory) based on neuronal changes. This notion was supported by clinical findings indicating that amnesic patients with damage to the medial temporal region or the medial diencephalon typically show grossly impaired long-term learning capacity coupled with normal performance on immediate memory span (Milner, 1970;

The work discussed in this chapter was supported in part by NIMH Grant No. MH49728.

Victor, Adams, & Collins, 1971). This dichotomy between short- and long-term memory has received further support from investigation of the specific biological mechanisms underlying these two types of memory process. The results demonstrated the existence of a representation at the cellular level for each of the two types of memory processes (for review, see Kandel & Hawkins, 1992). Just as neuropsychological and neurobiological evidence indicated the need to abandon the idea that memory is a unitary process, it has now been proposed that both short-term and long-term memory can be further subdivided. Baddeley (for review, see Baddeley, 1986) has recently elaborated a model implicating a multi-component working memory concept subserving several forms of short-term storage. Thus, short-term memory has come to be viewed as a diverse collection of temporary capacities that are distributed across multiple, separate processing modules (see also Goldman-Rakic, 1987). In this way, auditory short-term memory is a temporary storage system only for auditory stimuli. Similarly, recent data have indicated the need to differentiate two forms of long-term memory subserved by separate neural circuits that are summarized in the following sections.

THE FRACTIONATION OF LONG-TERM MEMORY

It is now generally accepted that long-term memory can be divided into two separate components (Squire, 1987). One of these components involves the conscious awareness of newly acquired information and is termed *declarative or explicit memory*. This form of memory appears to be seriously impaired in amnesic patients, specifically because of damage within a system linking the medial temporal lobe, medial diencephalon, and medial prefrontal cortex. The other type of learning that appears to be intact in amnesic patients is often termed *procedural or implicit memory* and reflects the acquisition of skills, in which performance may steadily improve without any recollection of previous learning. This system represents the operation of several neural systems, one of which includes the basal ganglia (Mishkin & Appenzeller, 1987; Packard, Hirsh, & White, 1989).

Evidence that retention of the effects of experience proceeds according to two different principles, each served by a different neural system, has come mainly in the last decade from investigations of brain-damaged amnesic subjects. A particularly dramatic case study was published by Milner (1970). This patient (HM) had undergone an operation involving bilateral medial temporal lobe resection in an attempt to relieve intractable epilepsy. The operation involved the bilateral destruction of the anterior two thirds of the hippocampus and hippocampal gyrus, as well as the uncus and the amygdala, but spared the lateral neocortex. It left HM densely amnesic, but intellectually otherwise unimpaired. Memory for his early life was spared, but his capacity for most kinds of new long-term learning was severely impaired, although his immediate memory span remained normal. Despite the severe memory disorder, HM showed unimpaired learning on new tasks ranging from classic conditioning through perceptual learning to the solving of complex intellectual puzzles (Corkin, 1984). Since the report of HM, there have been numerous studies showing the ability of amnesic patients to learn despite their inability to remember (Brooks & Baddeley, 1976; Cohen & Squire, 1980; Warrington & Weiskrantz, 1968). The crucial feature of such spared learning is that it does not depend on the patient's capacity to recollect previous experience. In each case, the patient demonstrates learning by performing a task more efficiently, while at the same time typically denying ever having encountered the task before. In this way, amnesic patients have not necessarily lost the capacity to learn but rather have lost conscious access to such learning.

The global anterograde amnesia seen in HM has been described in patients with various types of neurological insult that affect different regions of the brain. These regions include the medial temporal lobe area, in patients with temporal lobe resections and herpes encephalitis (Lilly, Cummings, Benson, & Frankel, 1983; Penfield & Milner, 1958; Scoville & Milner, 1957); the medial diencephalic area in patients with Korsakoff's disease (Cermak, 1982; Mair, Warrington, & Weiskrantz, 1979; Squire, 1987; Victor, Adams, & Collins, 1971; Whitty & Zangwill, 1966); the ventral aspect of the prefrontal cortex in patients with aneurysms of the anterior communicating artery (Alexander & Freedman, 1984; Gade 1982; Talland, Sweet, & Ballantine, 1967); frontal lobe neoplasms (Angelergues, Hecaen, & De Ajuriaguerra, 1955) or prefrontal surgical removals (Whitty & Levin, 1960); and the basal forebrain in patients with Alzheimer's disease (Arendt, Bigl, Arendt, & Tennstedt, 1983; Candy et al., 1983; Whitehouse et al., 1982).

A number of studies conducted with nonhuman primates have demonstrated corresponding losses and hidden learning capacities in monkeys with brain damage similar to HM's (Mishkin, Malamut, & Bachevalier, 1984; Zola-Morgan & Squire, 1985). For example, when tested on a visual recognition task, such as delayed non–matching-to-sample or object–reward association,[1] each with trial-unique objects, monkeys with combined ablation of the medial temporal lobe structures[2] seem unable either to recognize an object they had seen just a minute or two earlier or to remember for even a few seconds whether or not the object had been baited (Mishkin, 1978; Spiegler and Mishkin, 1979). Paradoxically, the same monkeys are able to master a multiple-trial concurrent object discrimination task in which successive trials on a given pair are separated by 24-hour intertrial intervals (Malamut, Saunders, & Mishkin, 1984). As for the amnesic patients, the same pattern of memory failure despite normal learning is also present in monkeys with lesions of either the medial diencephalon, medial prefrontal cortex, or basal forebrain (Mishkin & Appenzeller, 1987).

The conclusion to which most investigators have arrived is that there are at least two different forms of memory process, only one of which is affected in amnesic subjects. One system supports gradual and incremental learning and is involved in the acquisition of habits or skills, whereas the other supports rapid one-trial learning and is necessary for forming new memories that represent specific situations and episodes. Furthermore, the fact that one system is dependent upon the integrity of the medial temporal lobe structures whereas the other is not has led Mishkin and Appenzeller (1987) and Mishkin et al. (1984) to propose that these two retention systems are in fact subserved by two independent neural circuits.

THE NEURAL CIRCUITS FOR MEMORIES AND HABITS

The detailed knowledge now available concerning the neuroanatomy of the medial temporal lobe structures and their interconnections with diencephalic, prefrontal, and basal forebrain areas, the pattern of physiological activity of neurons in these brain areas, as well as the memory loss described following lesion or neuropathology in these neural structures, have guided the formulation of a functional neural system for the formation of cognitive or representational memory (declarative memory). As shown for visual recognition memory, the neural model proposed by Mishkin and Murray (1994) postulates that visual information is processed sequentially along an occipitotemporal pathway (Figure 11.1). This ventrally directed chain of cortical visual areas (V1 to TEO) appears to extract

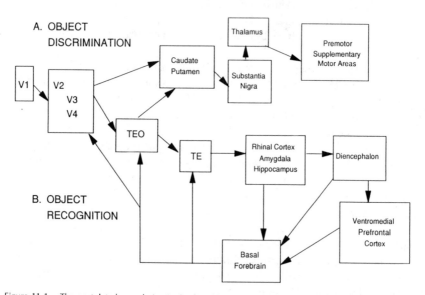

Figure 11.1. The postulated neural circuits for visual habit formation (a form of procedural memory) and visual object recognition (a form of declarative memory). The arrows schematize the flow of visual information originating in striate cortex (V1), passing through extrastriate areas (V2, V3, and V4), and then coursing ventrally into the inferior temporal cortex (areas TEO and TE). Visual information is next processed via two independent pathways, one coursing through the basal ganglia (caudate, putamen), substantia nigra, and thalamus to end onto the premotor supplementary motor areas, and the other coursing through the medial temporal lobe structures (rhinal cortex, hippocampus, and amygdala), the medial diencephalon, the ventromedial prefrontal cortex, and finally from the basal forebrain back to the cortical areas in which perception of an object has taken place.

stimulus-quality information, such as size, color, shape, and texture, from the retinal input reaching the striate cortex, until the final stations of the inferior temporal cortex (area TE) synthesize a complete representation of the object. Storage of the object's representation (and assignment of some meaning or association to it) is realized each time a perception formed in the final station of the visual cortical sensory system activates successively the medial temporal, medial diencephalic, and medial prefrontal areas. Each of these regions in turn sends signals to the basal forebrain which, through its widespread cortical projections, reaches back to the sensory cortical areas. It is postulated that the feedback action of these circuits on sensory and medial temporal areas strengthens synapses among active neurons and so perhaps stores the neural representation of the sensory event that had just taken place. Once established, this central representation can be reactivated whenever the same stimulus reappears in the field, yielding visual recognition. Furthermore, since all the sensory modalities appear to be represented centrally by a hierarchical arrangement from primary to higher processing areas (Turner, Mishkin, & Knapp, 1980; Van Hoesen & Pandya, 1975) and because the highest cortical levels in each modality appear to project to the medial temporal lobe structures, it is postulated that the same circuit that mediates recognition memory in vision does so in the other sensory modalities (Murray & Mishkin, 1983).

Systematic investigation of the effects of restricted lesions of different regions in the medial temporal lobe has now refined our understanding of the critical structures for stimulus recognition (see for review Mishkin & Murray, 1994). Although the earlier results (Mishkin, 1978) led to the conclusion that combined lesions of the amygdaloid complex and the hippocampal formation were necessary to produce the profound memory deficit, newer evidence indicates the need to review this interpretation. Damage restricted to the perirhinal and entorhinal cortices, a sheet of cortical tissue covering the medial aspect of both the amygdaloid complex and the rostral portion of the hippocampal formation, is sufficient to yield severe visual recognition loss (Meunier, Bachevalier, Mishkin, & Murray, 1993; Zola-Morgan, Squire, Amaral, & Suzuki, 1989). In addition, new ablation procedures using neurotoxins have permitted selective destruction of the amygdala and the hippocampus without damaging the surrounding rhinal cortex. Interestingly, such selective lesions had little or no effects on recognition memory (O'Boyle, Murray, & Mishkin, 1993). Similar results have now been reported in rodents (Mumby & Pinel, 1994; Mumby, Wood, & Pinel, 1992; Otto & Eichenbaum, 1992). These findings demonstrate that the rhinal cortex appears to play a crucial role in recognition memory.

As for the neural circuit that underlies the formation of visual habits (a form of procedural memory), here the evidence is still relatively sparse. Both clinical reports as well as experimental neuroanatomical and lesion studies indicate, however, that the striatum is the most likely candidate. The striatum receives projections from sensory processing areas of the cerebral cortex and sends projections to the globus pallidus, substantia nigra, and associated structures within the extrapyramidal system that control movements. Behavioral evidence also supports the view that the corticostriatal system serves noncognitive habit formation. For example, impairments in visual discrimination have now been demonstrated following lesions of either 1) the inferior temporal cortex (Mishkin, 1954; Phillips, Malamut, Bachevalier, & Mishkin, 1988); 2) the projections from the visual areas to the neostriatum (Horel, 1978; Zola-Morgan, Squire, & Mishkin, 1982); or 3) the striatal regions (Buerger, Gross, & Rocha-Miranda, 1974; Divac, Rosvold, & Szwarcbart, 1967; Wang, Aigner, & Mishkin, 1990). Furthermore, a deficit in procedural memory has been recently found in patients with either Huntington's disease (Martone, Butters, Payne, Becker, & Sax, 1984) or Parkinson's disease (Saint-Cyr, Taylor, & Lang, 1988), each of which results in a dysfunction of the basal ganglia.

For visual habit formation (Figure 11.1), the neural model proposed by Mishkin and colleagues (Mishkin & Appenzeller, 1987) postulates that information about objects is processed through a series of cortical visual areas, including striate and prestriate cortices and inferior temporal cortical areas TEO and TE. Through a series of connections from the striatum to the globus pallidus and substantia nigra, to the ventral thalamus, and, finally to the premotor cortex, cortically processed visual inputs could become associated with extrapyramidal generated motor outputs and so yield the stimulus–response bonds that constitute visual habits.

DEVELOPMENT OF MEMORY PROCESSES

The accumulating evidence that two memory systems do indeed exist has led to a renewed interest to investigate their ontogenetic development. In recent years, there has been impressive progress in this area. That is, using behavioral tasks that are known to be selectively sensitive to damage to the medial temporal lobe in adult subjects, studies in rodents (Castro, Paylor, & Rudy, 1987; Rudy, Stadler-Morris, & Alberts, 1987; Green & Stanton, 1989), monkeys (Bachevalier & Mishkin, 1984; Mahut & Moss, 1986), and humans (Diamond, 1990; Overman, 1990; Overman, Bachevalier, Turner, & Peuster, 1992), have suggested that the two memory systems discussed above are developmentally dissociable.

To trace the ontogenetic development of these two forms of learning and memory (Bachevalier & Mishkin, 1984), we first investigated the development of medial temporal lobe memory processes by testing infant monkeys between 3 months and 4 years of age on a visual recognition task (delayed nonmatching-to-sample [DNMS] with trial unique objects) that was used originally to demonstrate anterograde amnesia in adult monkeys with medial temporal lobe lesions (Mishkin, 1978). The results indicated that the youngest monkeys failed to solve the DNMS task until they were approximately 4 months of age. With further maturation, there was a gradual improvement in learning ability, yet it did not reach the adult level of proficiency even at 1 year. Only at about 2 years of age do monkeys master the recognition task as efficiently as adult animals. A similar delay in the maturation of abilities to solve the DNMS task was recently demonstrated in human infants (Overman, 1990; Overman et al., 1992). In both species, the data indicate that there is an age at which the DNMS task can first be solved and a considerably greater age at which it can be solved with full adult proficiency. This slow ontogenetic development of visual recognition memory was shown even more strikingly in the memory performance test in which the delays between the sample presentation and the choice test and the number of objects to remember were progressively increased. Average recognition memory scores declined systematically in inverse relation to the groups' age. Nevertheless, despite their poor recognition memory abilities, 3-month-old monkeys, like adult amnesic monkeys, were still able to learn, in as few trials as normal adults, to pick the baited object of two in a concurrent object discrimination task,[3] even though in this task the pairs of objects were presented after long intertrial intervals. These findings suggested that the two independent memory systems that were found to be separable in the adult monkeys were also developmentally dissociable. That is, the corticostriatal system that is preserved in adult subjects rendered amnesic by medial temporal lobe lesion seems to be present in very early infancy. In contrast, the corticolimbic memory system, which is severely impaired in adult monkeys with medial temporal lesions, develops later in infancy, presumably because the circuitry on which it depends undergoes a relatively slow ontogenetic development. These results led to the conclusion that one or more of the structures in the medial temporal lobe (Bachevalier & Mishkin, 1984), and perhaps more specifically the hippocampal formation (Rose, 1980; Nadel & Zola-Morgan, 1984; Schacter & Moscovitch, 1984), may not be fully developed at birth.

Data gathered since the early 1990s have cast serious doubts on this view (Bachevalier, 1990; Bachevalier & Beauregard, 1993; Diamond, 1990). One set of results emerged from a study of the effects of early lesions at different neural stations in the neural pathway underlying visual recognition memory (Figure 11.1). We began our behavioral investigation by preparing newborn monkeys with bilateral removals of the medial temporal lobe structures, including either combined damage to the amygdaloid complex, the hippocampal formation, and the adjacent cortical areas or separate damage to the amygdaloid complex or the hippocampal formation. The operated monkeys and their controls were then tested at different ages in a series of discrimination and recognition tasks. All behavioral data gathered up to now indicate that early combined damage to the structures in the medial temporal lobe yields a behavioral pattern strikingly similar to that found after late damage to the medial temporal lobe. That is, like large medial temporal lobe lesions in adulthood, those in infancy result in a global and long-lasting memory deficit, affecting not only memory for visual information (Bachevalier and Mishkin, 1994) but also memory for tactile stimuli and spatial locations (Malkova, Mishkin, & Bachevalier, in press). In addition, as with medial temporal lobe in adult monkeys, those in infant monkeys do not affect the ability to learn concurrent object discrimination (Bachevalier, Brickson, Hagger, & Mishkin, 1990). Together with recent clinical reports of profound memory loss in children who sustain medial temporal lobe damage (Ostergaard, 1987; Rossitch and Oakes, 1989; Tonsgard, Hardwicke, & Levine, 1987; Vargha-Khadem, Isaacs, & Watkins, 1992; Wood, Brown, & Felton, 1989), these findings indicate that the medial temporal lobe operates early to sustain memory and that other regions cannot assume this function even when the damage occurs neonatally. Furthermore, the recent demonstration that early damage to the hippocampal formation alone does not result in a severe loss of visual recognition (Beauregard & Bachevalier, 1993) adds to the notion that the neural structures in the medial temporal lobe more critical for recognition memory are not the hippocampal formation but rather the rhinal cortex adjacent to it (Meunier et al., 1993; Zola-Morgan et al. 1989; Suzuki, Zola-Morgan, Squire, & Amaral, 1993; Otto & Eichenbaum, 1992; Mumby & Pinel, 1994).

Another indication that the medial temporal lobe structures develop early in infancy came from an investigation of recognition memory in infant monkeys using a paired–comparison preferential viewing task (Bachevalier, 1990; Bachevalier, Brickson, & Haggar, 1993). In this task, originally designed to test recognition memory in human infants (Fagan, 1970; Fantz, 1964), recognition memory is inferred from the infant's tendency to look more at a novel than at a previously exposed target. Between 15 and 30 days of age, infant monkeys showed a strong preference for viewing novel objects at least for short periods of time (Bachevalier et al., 1993; Gunderson & Sackett, 1984). Moreover, this early developing recognition ability was absent after both early and late damage to the medial temporal lobe (Bachevalier, 1993; McKee & Squire, 1993; Saunders, Richards, & Bachevalier, 1991), indicating that the structures in the medial temporal lobe make a critical contribution to visual recognition memory, even at an early age (see also Nelson, 1993).

CONCLUSIONS

In the span of just a few years, the field of memory research has moved from a rather monolithic view of long-term memory to a view that distinguishes several kinds of memory. Thus, declarative memory requires the reciprocal anatomical connections that enable the neocortex to interact with the rhinal cortex and related structures in the medial temporal and diencephalic areas, and the neocortex is thought to be the final repository of declarative memory. Procedural learning depends on a corticostriatal system, among others, and permits stimulus–response bonds.

The discovery that these two forms of memory follow different developmental sequences provided a new way to explain the phenomenon of infantile amnesia. That is, why are our earliest memories so rare, evasive, and random, and why are we unable to recollect them? Although the new findings led to the idea that infantile amnesia was directly attributed to the late development of declarative memory and by implication to an immaturity of the medial temporal lobe structures, recent behavioral evidence from nonhuman primates suggests rather that it is the functional immaturity of the association areas of the cortex that is the limiting factor (Bachevalier et al., 1990; Bachevalier & Mishkin, 1994). Thus, in contrast to the severe memory loss found after neonatal lesion of the medial temporal lobe reported above, neonatal damage to area TE, an earlier station in the neural pathway for visual recognition memory (Figure 11.1), yields relative sparing of both habit formation and memory formation (as compared to the severe deficit in both functions seen in adults with the same lesions). This sparing of memory functions following early TE lesions indicates that association areas of the cortex appear to possess considerable plasticity at birth, implying a degree of functional immaturity (Bachevalier & Mishkin, 1994). These behavioral data are supported by direct neurobiological evidence of neocortical immaturity, reflected in the homogeneous distribution of opiatergic and cholinergic receptors (Bachevalier, Ungerleider, O'Neil, & Friedman, 1986; O'Neil, Friedman, Bachevalier, & Ungerleider, 1986), in the low level of metabolic activity in the inferior temporal cortex, resulting from visual stimulation (Bachevalier, Hagger, & Mishkin, 1991), as well as in the electrophysiological responses of TE neurons, which are substantially weaker, of longer latency, and more susceptible to anesthesia than those found in adult monkeys (for review, see Rodman, 1994). The limiting factor in the formation and persistence of declarative memory may be the gradual maturation of the neocortical areas, such as area TE, which are believed to be the repositories of long-term memory rather than the maturation of the medial temporal/diencephalic structures, necessary for the formation of declarative memory.

ENDNOTES

[1]The delayed non–matching-to-sample task requires the ability to recognize whether an object has been seen before. In this task, for each trial, the animal is first confronted with a baited object followed 10 seconds later by the presentation of the same object (this time unbaited) together with a new baited object. To perform on this task, the animal has to recognize the familiar object and to displace the new object to obtain the reward. The object–reward association task requires the ability to remember which of the two previously presented objects had been baited. In this task, for each trial the animal is confronted with two objects presented successively (one of the objects is baited, the other is not). Ten seconds later, the two objects are represented simultaneously. The animal's task is to respond to the previously baited object. These two tasks involve trial–unique objects in that new pairs of objects are used for each trial.

[2]In this report, the term *medial temporal lobe* refers to an ensemble of subcortical and cortical structures. It includes the hippocampal formation, the amygdaloid complex, and adjacent entorhinal cortex and parahippocampal gyrus.

[3]The concurrent object discrimination task requires the ability to discriminate between two objects. In this task, a list of 20 pairs of objects is presented one at a time to the animal, but only one object in each pair hides a food reward. The list is presented once every day, and the animal must consistently select the rewarded object for each pair.

REFERENCES

Alexander, M.P., & Freedman, M. (1984). Amnesia after anterior communicating artery aneurysm rupture. *Neurology, 34,* 752–757.

Angelergues, R., Hecaen, H., & De Ajuriaguerra, J. (1955). Les troubles mentaux au cours des tumeurs du lobe frontal (Mental disorders following frontal lobe tumors). *Annales de Médecine Psychologique, 113*, 577–642.

Arendt, T., Bigl, V., Arendt, A., & Tennstedt, A. (1983). Loss of neurons in the nucleus basalis of Meynert in Alzheimer's disease, paralysis agitans, and Korsakoff's disease. *Acta Neuropathology Journal, 61*, 101–108.

Bachevalier, J. (1990). Ontogenetic development of the habit and memory formation in primates. In A. Diamond (Ed.), *Development and neural bases of higher cognitive functions* (pp. 1–9). New York: New York Academy of Sciences Press.

Bachevalier, J., & Beauregard, M. (1993). Maturation of medial temporal lobe memory functions in rodents, monkeys, and humans. *Hippocampus, 3*, 191–202.

Bachevalier, J., Brickson, M., Hagger, C., & Mishkin, M. (1990). Age and sex differences in the effects of selective temporal lobe lesion on the formation of visual discrimination habits in rhesus monkeys. *Behavioral Neuroscience, 104*, 885–899.

Bachevalier, J., Brickson, M., & Hagger, C. (1993). Limbic-dependent recognition memory in monkeys develops early in infancy. *NeuroReport, 4*, 77–80.

Bachevalier, J., Hagger, C., & Mishkin, M. (1991). Functional maturation of the occipitotemporal pathway in infant rhesus monkeys. In N.A. Lassen, D.H. Ingvar, M.E. Raichle, & L. Friberg (Eds.), *Alfred Benzon Symposium No. 31: Brain work and mental activity, quantitative studies with radioactive tracers* (pp. 231–241) Copenhagen: Munksgaard.

Bachevalier, J., & Mishkin, M. (1984). An early and late developing system for learning and retention in infant monkeys. *Behavioral Neuroscience, 98*, 770–778.

Bachevalier, J., & Mishkin, M. (1994). Effects of selective neonatal temporal lobe lesions on visual recognition memory in rhesus monkeys. *Journal of Neuroscience, 14*, 2128–2139.

Bachevalier, J., Ungerleider, L.G., O'Neil, B., & Friedman, D.P. (1986). Regional distribution of [3H] naloxone binding in the brain of a newborn monkey. *Developmental Brain Research, 25*, 302–308.

Baddeley, A. (1986). *Working memory*. Oxford: Oxford University Press.

Beauregard, M., & Bachevalier, J. (1993). Long-term effects of neonatal hippocampal lesions on visual recognition memory. *Society for Neuroscience Abstracts, 19*, 1004.

Brooks, D.N., & Baddeley, A. (1976). What can amnesic patients learn? *Neuropsychologia, 14*, 112–122.

Buerger, A.A., Gross, C.G., & Rocha-Miranda, C.E. (1974). Effects of ventral putamen lesions on discrimination learning by monkeys. *Journal of Comparative and Physiological Psychology, 86*, 440–446.

Candy, J., Perry, R., Perry, E., Irving, D., Blessed, G., Fairnairn, A., & Tomlinson, B. (1983). Pathological changes in the nucleus of Meynert in Alzheimer's and Parkinson's diseases. *Journal of Neurological Science, 54*, 277–289.

Castro, C.A., Paylor, R., & Rudy, J.W. (1987). A development analysis of the learning and short-term memory processes mediating performance in conditional-spatial discrimination problems. *Psychobiology, 15*, 308–316.

Cermak, L.S. (1982). *Human memory and amnesia*. Hillsdale, NJ: Lawrence Erlbaum Associates.

Cohen, N.J., & Squire, L.R. (1980). Preserved learning and retention of pattern-analyzing skill in amnesia: Dissociation of "knowing how" and "knowing that." *Science, 210*, 207–209.

Corkin, S. (1984). Lasting consequences of bilateral medial temporal lobectomy: Clinical course and experimental findings in H.M. *Seminars in Neurology, 4*, 249–258.

Diamond, A. (1990). Rate of maturation of the hippocampus and the developmental progression of children's performance on the delayed non-matching to sample and visual paired comparison tasks. In A. Diamond (Ed.), *Development and neural bases of higher cognitive functions* (pp. 394–426), Annals New York Academy of Sciences, 608.

Divac, I., Rosvold, H.E., & Szwarcbart, M.K. (1967). Behavioral effects of selective ablation of the caudate nucleus. *Journal of Comparative and Physiological Psychology, 63,* 184–190.

Fagan, J.F. (1970). Memory in the infant. *Journal of Experimental Child Psychology, 9,* 217–226.

Fantz, R.L. (1964). Visual experience in infants: Decreased attention to familiar patterns relative to novel ones. *Science, 146,* 668–670.

Gade, A. (1982). Amnesia after operation on aneurysms of the anterior communicating artery. *Surgical Neurology, 18,* 46–49.

Goldman-Rakic, P.S. (1987). Circuitry of primate prefrontal cortex and regulation of behavior by representational memory. In V.B. Mountcastle, F. Blum, & S.R. Geiger (Eds.), *Handbook of physiology* (pp. 373–418). Bethesda, MD: American Physiological Association.

Green, R.J., & Stanton, M.E. (1989). Differential ontogeny of working memory and reference memory in the rat. *Behavioral Neuroscience, 103,* 98–105.

Gunderson, V.M., & Sackett, G.P. (1984). Development of pattern recognition in infant pigtailed macaques (*Macaca nemestrina*). *Developmental Psychology, 20,* 418–426.

Hebb, D.P. (1949). *The organization of behavior: A neuropsychological theory.* New York: John Wiley & Sons.

Horel, J.A. (1978). The neuroanatomy of amnesia: A critique of the hippocampal memory hypothesis. *Brain, 101,* 403–445.

Kandel, E.R., & Hawkins, R.D. (1992). The biological basis of learning and individuality. *Scientific American, 267,* 79–86.

Lilly, R., Cummings, J.L., Benson, F., & Frankel, M. (1983). The human Klüver-Bucy syndrome. *Neurology, 33,* 1141–1145.

Mahut, H., & Moss, M. (1986). The monkey and the sea horse. In R.L. Isaacson & K.L. Pribram (Eds.), *The hippocampus* (pp. 241–279). New York: Plenum.

Mair, W.G.P., Warrington, E.K., & Weiskrantz, L. (1979). Memory disorder in Korsakoff's psychosis. A neuropathological and neuropsychological investigation of two cases. *Brain, 102,* 749–783.

Malamut, B.L., Saunders, R.C., & Mishkin, M. (1984). Monkeys with combined amygdalohippocampal lesions succeed in object discrimination learning despite 24-hour intertrial intervals. *Behavioral Neuroscience, 98,* 759–769.

Malkova, L., Mishkin, M., & Bachevalier, J. (in press). Long-term effects of selective neonatal temporal lesions on learning and memory in monkeys. *Behavioral Neuroscience.*

Martone, M., Butters, N., Payne, M., Becker, J., & Sax, D.S. (1984). Dissociations between skill learning and verbal recognition in amnesia and dementia. *Archives of Neurology, 41,* 965–970.

McKee, R.D., & Squire, L.R. (1993). On the development of declarative memory. *Journal of Experimental Psychology: Learning, Memory and Cognition, 19,* 397–404.

Meunier, M., Bachevalier, J., Mishkin, M., & Murray, E.A. (1993). Effects on visual recognition of combined and separate ablations of the entorhinal and perirhinal cortex in rhesus monkeys. *The Journal of Neuroscience, 13,* 5418–5432.

Milner, B. (1970). Memory and the medial temporal regions of the brain. In K.H. Pribram & D.E. Broadbent (Eds.), *Biology of memory* (pp. 29–50). New York: Academic Press.

Mishkin, M. (1954). Visual discrimination performance following partial ablations of the temporal lobe: II. Ventral surface vs. hippocampus. *Journal of Comparative and Physiological Psychology, 47,* 187–193.

Mishkin, M. (1978). Memory in monkeys severely impaired by combined but not by separate removal of amygdala and hippocampus. *Nature (London), 273*, 297–298.

Mishkin, M., & Appenzeller, T. (1987). The anatomy of memory. *Scientific American, 256*, 421–446.

Mishkin, M., Malamut, B.L., & Bachevalier, J. (1984). Memories and habits: Two neural systems. In G. Lynch, L. McGaugh, & N.M. Weinberger (Eds.), *Neurobiology of learning and memory* (pp. 65–77). New York: Guilford Press.

Mishkin, M., & Murray, E.A. (1994). Stimulus recognition. *Current Opinion in Neurobiology, 4*, 200–206.

Mumby, D.G., & Pinel, J.P.J. (1994). Rhinal cortex lesions and object recognition in rats. *Behavioral Neuroscience, 108*, 1–8.

Mumby, D.G., Wood, E.R., & Pinel, J.P.J. (1992). Object-recognition memory is only mildly impaired in rats with lesions of the hippocampus and amygdala. *Psychobiology, 20*, 18–27.

Murray, E.A., & Mishkin, M. (1983). Severe tactual memory deficit in monkeys after combined removal of the amygdala and hippocampus. *Brain Research, 270*, 340–344.

Nadel, L., & Zola-Morgan, S. (1984). Infantile amnesia: A neurobiological perspective. In M. Moscovitch (Ed.), *Infant memory* (pp. 145–172). New York: Plenum.

Nelson, C.A. (1993). Neural correlates of recognition memory in the first postnatal year of life. In G. Dawson & K. Fischer (Eds.), *Human development and the developing brain.* New York: Guilford Press.

O'Boyle, V., Murray, E.A., & Mishkin, M. (1993). Effects of exitotoxic amygdalohippocampal lesions on visual recognition in rhesus monkeys. *Society for Neuroscience Abstracts, 19*, 438.

O'Neil, J.B., Friedman, D.P., Bachevalier, J., & Ungerleider, L.G. (1986). Distribution of muscarinic cholinergic receptors in the brain of a newborn monkey. *Society for Neuroscience Abstracts, 12*, 809.

Ostergaard, A.L. (1987). Episodic, semantic and procedural memory in a case of amnesia at an early age. *Neuropsychologia, 25*, 341–357.

Otto, T., & Eichenbaum, H. (1992). Complementary roles of the orbital prefrontal and the perirhinal-entorhinal cortices in an odor-guided delayed-nonmatching-to-sample task. *Behavioral Neuroscience, 106*, 762–775.

Overman, W. (1990). Performance on traditional match-to-sample, non-match-to-sample, and object discrimination task by 12 to 32 month-old children: A developmental progression. In A. Diamond (Ed.), *Development and neural bases of higher cognitive functions* (pp. 365–383). New York: New York Academy of Sciences Press.

Overman, W., Bachevalier, J., Turner, M., & Peuster, A. (1992). Object recognition versus object discrimination: Comparison between human infants and infant monkeys. *Behavioral Neuroscience, 106*, 15–29.

Packard, M.G., Hirsh, R., & White, N.M. (1989). Differential effects of fornix and caudate nucleus lesions on two radial maze tasks: Evidence for multiple memory systems. *Journal of Neuroscience, 9*, 1465–1472.

Penfield, W., & Milner, B. (1958). Memory deficit produced by bilateral lesions in the hippocampal zone. *Archives of Neurology and Psychiatry, 79*, 475–497.

Phillips, R.R., Malamut, B.L., Bachevalier, J., & Mishkin, M. (1988). Dissociation of the effects of inferior temporal and limbic lesions on object discrimination learning with 24-hr intertrial intervals. *Behavioral Brain Research, 27*, 99–107.

Rodman, H. (1994). The development of inferior temporal cortex in primates. *Cerebral Cortex, 5*, 484–498.

Rose, D. (1980). Some functional correlates of the maturation of neural systems. In D. Caplan (Ed.), *Biological studies of mental processes* (pp. 27–43). Cambridge, MA: MIT Press.

Rossitch, E., & Oakes, W.J. (1989). Klüver-Bucy syndrome in a child with bilateral arachnoid cysts: Report of a case. *Neurosurgery, 24*, 110–112.

Rudy, J.W., Stadler-Morris, S., & Alberts, P. (1987). Ontogeny of spatial navigation in the rat: Dissociation of "proximal" and "distal-cue-based" behaviors. *Behavioral Neuroscience, 10*, 62–73.

Saint-Cyr, J.A., Taylor, A.E., & Lang, A.E. (1988). Procedural learning and neostriatal dysfunction in man. *Brain, 111*, 941–959.

Saunders, R.C., Richards, R.S., & Bachevalier, J. (1991). The effects of neonatal limbic lesions on long-term recognition memory in the adult rhesus monkey. *Society for Neuroscience Abstracts, 17*, 133.

Schacter, D.L., & Moscovitch, M. (1984). Infants, amnesics and dissociable memory systems. In M. Moscovitch (Ed.), *Infant memory* (pp. 173–226), New York: Plenum.

Scoville, W.B., & Milner, B. (1957). Loss of recent memory after bilateral hippocampal lesions. *Journal of Neurology, Neurosurgery, and Psychiatry, 20*, 11–21.

Spiegler, B.J., & Mishkin, M. (1979). Associative memory severely impaired by combined amygdalo-hippocampal removals. *Society for Neuroscience Abstracts, 5*, 323.

Squire, L.R. (1987). *Memory and brain.* Oxford: Oxford University Press.

Suzuki, W.A., Zola-Morgan, S., Squire, L.R., & Amaral, D.G. (1993). Lesions of the perirhinal and parahippocampal cortices in monkey produce long lasting memory impairments in the visual and tactual modalities. *Journal of Neuroscience, 13*, 2430–2451.

Talland, G.A., Sweet, W.T., & Ballantine, H.T. (1967). Amnesic syndrome with anterior communicating artery aneurysm. *Journal of Nervous Mental Disease, 145*, 179–192.

Turner, B.H., Mishkin, M., & Knapp, M. (1980). Organization of the amygdalopetal projections from modality-specific cortical association areas in the monkey. *Journal of Comparative Neurology, 191*, 515–543.

Tonsgaard, J.H., Hardwicke, N., & Levine, S.C. (1987). Klüver-Bucy syndrome in children. *Pediatric Neurology, 3*, 162–165.

Van Hoesen, G.W., & Pandya, D.N. (1975). Some connections of the entorhinal (area 28) and perirhinal (area 35) cortices of the rhesus monkey. III. Efferent connections. *Brain Research, 95*, 39–59.

Vargha-Khadem, F., Isaacs, E.B., & Watkins, K.E. (1992). Medial temporal-lobe versus diencephalic amnesia in childhood. *Journal of Clinical and Experimental Neuropsychology, 14*, 371–372.

Victor, M., Adams, R.D., & Collins, G.H. (1971). *The Wernicke-Korsakoff syndrome.* Philadelphia: F.A. Davis.

Wang, J., Aigner, T., & Mishkin, M. (1990). Effects of neostriatal lesions on visual habit formation in rhesus monkeys. *Society for Neuroscience Abstracts, 16*, 617.

Warrington, E., & Weiskrantz, L. (1968). New method of testing long-term retention with special reference to amnesic patients. *Nature (London), 217*, 972–974.

Whitehouse, P., Price, D., Struble, R., Clark, A., Coyle, J., & DeLong, M. (1982). Alzheimer's disease and senile dementia: Loss of neurons in the basal forebrain. *Science, 215*, 1237–1239.

Whitty, C.W.M., & Levin, W. (1960). A Korsakoff syndrome in the postcingulectomy confusional state. *Brain, 83*, 648–653.

Whitty, C.W.M., & Zangwill, O. (1966). *Amnesia.* London: Butterworth.

Wood, F.B., Brown, I.S., & Felton, R.H. (1989). Long-term follow-up of a childhood amnesic syndrome. *Brain and Cognition, 10*, 76–86.

Zola-Morgan, S., & Squire, L.R. (1985). Complementary approaches to the study of memory: Human amnesia and animal models. In N. Weinberger, J. McGaugh, & G. Lynch (Eds.), *Memory systems of the brain: Animal and human cognitive processes* (pp. 463–477). New York: Guilford Press.

Zola-Morgan, S., Squire, L.R., Amaral, D.G., & Suzuki, W.A. (1989). Lesions of the perirhinal and parahippocampal cortex that spare the amygdala and hippocampal formation produce severe memory impairment. *Journal of Neuroscience, 9,* 4355–4370.

Zola-Morgan, S., Squire, L.R., & Mishkin, M. (1982). The neuroanatomy of amnesia: Amygdalo-hippocampus versus temporal stem. *Science, 218,* 1337–1339.

12

ATTENTION AND MEMORY IN RELATION TO LEARNING
A Comparative Adaptation Perspective

Duane M. Rumbaugh and David A. Washburn

This chapter offers a comparative perspective of attention and memory in order to foster a better understanding of these basic processes in the development, learning, and competence of the human child. It is common knowledge that deficits in these processes interfere with social as well as academic success and are very difficult to correct. Remediation is characteristically limited, both in scope and in its generalization to real-world situations.

Fortunately, comparative studies, particularly with chimpanzees (*Pan*) and rhesus monkeys (*Macaca mulatta*), have a great deal to tell us about attention, memory, and learning. Captive-born and -reared specimens are characteristically lacking in attention and prone to be both hyperemotional and hyperactive. Thus, they might be viewed as *natural* models for research intended to ameliorate these conditions.

By good fortune, our primate research of recent years reveals several ways whereby chimpanzees have become *highly* attentive, task-oriented, tenacious, and outstanding learners of language and video tasks. In addition, they have demonstrated substantial ability to *generalize* their skills to diverse test situations *and* contexts. Except for language skills, the same holds for rhesus macaques. Our comparative studies indicate that 1) deficits in attention, memory, and learning are not unique to humans; 2) these deficits can be profoundly attenuated; 3) the early environment is extremely important to the structuring of competence; 4) computer technology can be of great assistance in rectifying these deficits; 5) stable, interactive, communicative contexts within which the subject can exer-

Preparation of this chapter was supported by grants from the National Institute for Child Health and Human Development (HD-06016) and the National Aeronautics and Space Administration (NAG2-438) to Georgia State University. Additional support was provided by the College of Arts and Sciences of Georgia State University.

cise great control over what it does is important to the rectification of these deficits; and 6) the competencies acquired by our primates both serve to instate solid attention, memory, and learning abilities *and* generalize with positive effect to conditions beyond those in which they were acquired.

The following overview considers behavior which applies to humans as well as to nonhuman primates and other animals. Following the overview, relevant research will be reviewed in greater detail.

OVERVIEW: AN ADAPTATION PERSPECTIVE OF PERCEPTION AND MEMORY IN RELATION TO LEARNING

Learning Predictive Relationships

Behavior is inextricably both enabled and proscribed by biology. *Adaptation* to the environment relies heavily upon the effective use of the time and energy budgets of behavior in relation to environmental resources and dangers. Optimal configurations assumed by behavior are those that achieve a conservative expenditure of time and energy as resources of the environment are biologically exploited and dangers are minimized. To this end, organisms are always, to some degree, sensing and interpreting energies, attending to their external environments and internal states (i.e., need states, as for food, water, warmth, exercise, rest), and responding thereto selectively.

External energy sources that index resources that might be used to attenuate internal and acquired needs are more readily perceived than others. On the other hand, other environmental energies that are either marked by their novelty and/or strength can co-opt the perceptual processes of the organism—at least for a time. Eventually, however, the processes of habituation and sensitization modulate the organism's behavior to such energies and declare them to be either "unimportant" or "important" and to be responded to accordingly, within the time and energy budgets of the organism.

Perceptions organize sensory information for interpretation and appropriate response. Perceptions based on events that span a course of time can serve to define *predictive relationships*. As a direct function of their reliability and validity, predictive relationships are more readily perceived and adaptively responded to than are those that approximate randomness.

Learning can thus be viewed as establishing and preserving predictive relationships for future use. In addition to learning instated by perception, a considerable amount of learning initially is adequately accounted for by stimulus–stimulus and stimulus–response associative models, where contingency effects are dominant. Even here, however, the affordances, biases, and constraints of biology retain the upper hand. Biological factors serve to either enhance or deter learning and do so according to whether the materials entailed in the learning context (e.g., the nature of the stimuli and consequences/reinforcers) are germane or essentially arbitrary to successful adaptation in the organism's natural ecological niche.

Even within its first few months of life, the infant primate and/or human begins to learn predictive relationships. Relationships that are very high in validity and reliability and in ecological relevance can be learned very quickly. Such learning is profoundly facilitated if the organism has a complex brain that has been optimally and appropriately developed from birth, if not before. Predictive relationships in accordance with the biologically afforded sensitivities are more readily learned than arbitrary relationships. Predictive relationships can be learned by *observations* and do not necessarily require specific overt motor responses.

Schedules of reinforcement enter into the above perspective in two ways. First, schedules inherently define the reliability of perceived/predictive relationships. Accordingly, they can either facilitate or interfere with learning to the degree that they are "rich" or "lean" in their contingencies. Second, schedules strongly influence motivation, which in this view is the organism's balance of time/energy budgets with its environment to the end that adaptation may be optimized at every point in time. Reinforcement can be part of a predictive relationship, but not all sequelae of relationships that are readily learned should be termed "reinforcers." Neither should it be assumed that learning is associated exclusively with stimuli that might be presented as "conditioned stimuli."

Brain Complexity and Plasticity

As the brains of organisms evolved in complexity, they also became more plastic—that is, "open" to early environmental patterns of stimulation and contexts for learning. For instance, as will be discussed later, we have found that chimpanzees spontaneously (e.g., without formal, structured learning/teaching) learn the meanings and appropriate use of word–lexigram symbols and come to comprehend the syntax of even novel sentences (Savage-Rumbaugh et al., 1993). With the benefit of relevant training, they can also count to at least four—and probably more (Rumbaugh, Hopkins, Washburn, & Savage-Rumbaugh, 1989). On the other hand, impoverishment of the early environment has been found to compromise cognitive capabilities in adult chimpanzees (Davenport, Rogers, & Rumbaugh, 1973; for other evidence regarding the effects of early enrichment or impoverishment, see also Greenough, Wither, & Wallace, 1990; Krech, Rosenzweig, & Bennett, 1962; Riesen, 1982).

Plasticity in brain development seemingly is optimized by key operations that call for one to 1) begin with the organism while it is very young, preferably from its birth; 2) rear it in a stable, supportive social context; 3) maintain it in an environment that affords challenges for resources that are graded with the organism's perceptual and motor competence; 4) maintain the organism in that environment, insofar as possible, as its "lifestyle," not just for an hour a day or intermittently; 5) structure the environment so that the consequences of behavior, and even those of "just perceiving," are prompt, reliable, and relevant to that behavior; and 6) extend to the organism opportunity to "control" its access to resources and its activities.

Attention

All chimpanzees reared in this manner in our research program of the past 25 years have become increasingly focused in their attention and more competent in coordinating the topics of their attention with members of their social group (e.g., joint regard). In turn, their learning of predictive relationships has become increasingly efficient, their retention of them has become more robust and increasingly time-resistant, and their ability to work tenaciously on tasks/problems has steadily increased.

Primates as Natural Models for Attention
Deficit Hyperactivity Disorder (ADHD) Research

In summary, captive-born and -reared chimpanzees are by nature *not* noted for their attentional skills, either in infancy or in adulthood. Many chimpanzees would be very appropriately classified as being hyperactive and possessing attentional deficits. As such, they are *natural* models of the attention deficit hyperactivity disorder (ADHD). Notwithstanding, through the course of being reared in accord with the key operations defined above, the chimpanzees profoundly improve.

What has been said of chimpanzees (*Pan*) as "natural" ADHD models also applies to rhesus monkeys (*Macaca*) that are captive-born and cage-reared with less than optimal social stimulation and socialization. Rhesus monkeys' brains, although complex, do not support the highly detailed language accomplishments of the chimpanzee. Notwithstanding, research with them has been highly instructive with regard to attention and how it can be cultivated to support remarkable computer-formatted task performances. Rhesus monkeys can learn to do what 40-year literature would predict that they could never do—to learn to use a joystick to master quickly a large number of very complex video-formatted tasks (e.g., Rumbaugh, Richardson, Washburn, Savage-Rumbaugh, & Hopkins, 1989). It has been our experience with several dozen monkeys that they become increasingly attentive, task-oriented, and facile in their learning as a function of training in our Language Research Center's Computerized Test System (LRC-CTS; see Figure 12.1).

The LRC-CTS is a joystick-controlled computerized learning system in which subjects come to master a wide variety of learning, memory, psychomotor, planning, vigilance, and perceptual tasks and attendant skills. Accordingly, the LRC-CTS seemingly offers great promise for supporting behavioral changes that serve to offset or attenuate ADHD in children.

To put research with rhesus monkeys in proper perspective, the reader is reminded that attention is a multifaceted construct that, for humans, incorporates the dimensions of selection, concentration, filtering, time-sharing, scanning, and

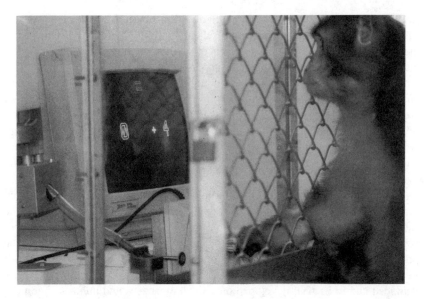

Figure 12.1.   In this Language Research Center's Computerized Test System (LRC-CTS), a rhesus macaque is controlling the movement of a cursor on the screen by use of a joystick, positioned below the monitor. (See text for details.)

vigilance. Nonhuman animals, of course, make observing responses or other overt manifestations of arousal, alertness, and orientation; these can look like, and have been interpreted to reflect, attention. However, what evidence is there that a behavioral model of attention must incorporate the findings from comparative, as well as human, investigations?

Attending to Salience   Over 40 years of literature attest to how readily the learning efficiency of rhesus monkeys can be compromised by stimulus–response spatial discontiguity. In the Wisconsin General Test Apparatus (Harlow, 1949)—the standard test device for a generation of comparative psychologists—separations of even a few centimeters between the response site and the loci of salient stimuli have consistently resulted in significant compromises in discrimination learning. Rhesus monkeys, it was concluded, sample the world in the area immediately around their fingertips and can learn only through painstaking shaping to shift their attention from the hands' loci to salient objects located at a distance.

Given these robust findings, attempts to teach rhesus monkeys to respond to computer-generated stimuli by manipulating a joystick that was located remotely seemed destined for failure. Notwithstanding this well-founded pessimism, the monkeys learned rapidly and transferred readily the joystick manipulation skills required for computer-task responding. We have reported that rhesus monkeys learned to respond in a variety of computer tasks (Rumbaugh et al., 1989), that their learning set and transfer index performance was within the range predicted on the basis of manual testing with no stimulus–response spatial discontiguity (Washburn, Hopkins, & Rumbaugh, 1989), and that these effects appear not to stem from stimulus–cursor spatial contiguity (Washburn & Rumbaugh, 1991b). Clearly, rhesus monkeys can attend to salient stimuli that are at a distance from their hands, and the oft-replicated effects of spatial discontiguity are an artifact of the Wisconsin General Test Apparatus and its procedures.

These findings are even more meaningful when one considers that the computer-generated stimuli used with the joystick-based computerized test system are planimetric. Rhesus monkeys are noted for compromised learning as a result of two-dimensional pattern versus three-dimensional object discrimination. Notwithstanding, monkeys in our test system reliably perceive the planimetric stimuli and respond to them as well (or better) than at levels reported for the manual apparatus.

The ability to learn and respond to planimetric stimuli despite large spatial discontiguities was cultivated by the training and test procedures devised for the rhesus monkeys. These same procedures appeared to enable the monkeys to become mediational or relational learners (Washburn & Rumbaugh, 1991b). In the protocol just referenced, the capacity to abstract rule-like relations—defying, if necessary, specific stimulus–response contingencies—had previously been demonstrated to be well-developed only in chimpanzees and humans. Additionally, positive transfer of training with the transfer index testing protocol (Rumbaugh & Pate, 1984), previously the exclusive domain of the great apes and humans, was also manifested by the rhesus monkeys. We conclude that the rich, structured challenges afforded by the LRC-CTS provide not only the tests for measuring complex cognition, but also the environment required to encourage the development of complex cognition in nonhuman species.

Learning How to Generalize
via Training in Diverse Contexts

It is noteworthy that training data for rhesus monkeys on our test system are quite different from the learning-and-generalization curves obtained using other techniques. For example, rhesus monkeys are trained with our system on a matching-to-sample task. The 35 monkeys trained to date on this task have reached the established criterion (70% accuracy) in only 2106 trials. At that point, performance differs significantly from chance but clearly is not asymptotic. Nonetheless, rhesus monkeys will transfer their matching skills effectively to any new set of stimuli and average 88% accuracy on the matching-to-sample task during their first postcriterion test session.

We believe the key to the animals' rapid task acquisition and seamless generalization to new stimuli lies in the *diversity* that characterizes all of our training. For the matching task, for instance, each trial uses stimuli that are randomly selected from a library of eight images. These images themselves are drawn randomly with a stimulus–production program. Every 80 trials, a new library of stimuli is generated. Stimulus position within each trial is random, and the stimuli can even be made to move whenever the joystick is manipulated. Thus, there is little opportunity for learning to become fixed on specific stimulus features, response positions, or other cues not relevant to generalized matching-to-sample. As a consequence, the monkeys acquire both the skill and the ability to generalize between contexts. An additional benefit of such training is that the introduction of new tasks (e.g., delayed matching-to-sample, sameness/difference) is facilitated.

Although the data bearing on this point are limited, we are convinced that the monkeys' training benefits both by the diversity (of stimuli, stimulus types, and positions) within a trial and the diversity of tasks introduced in training. By training the animals on a range of tasks, and frequently requiring them to generalize their training beyond specific stimulus–response boundaries, the animals both *learn* and *learn how to generalize*. This principle of providing a diverse context to support generalizable learning may have significant implications for training as well as education.

Selective Tracking The classic example of human attention is the "cocktail party phenomenon." People are capable of following an individual conversation in a crowded room of noisy interchange. Yet, a particularly interesting or salient word from one of the other, "nonattended" conversations (e.g., hearing one's name) can elicit a shift of attention. The "selective looking" experiments of Neisser and Becklen (1975) provide a visual analogue of these processes. Human subjects demonstrated proficiency at following one stimulus channel, a visual scene, despite distractor stimuli in the form of an overlapping visual scenario.

We tested human volunteers and rhesus monkeys on a selective tracking task inspired by Neisser and Becklen (1975). Subjects were required to manipulate a joystick so as to contact a moving target and subsequently to maintain unbroken contact with the target for 10 seconds. Once the target was acquired, however, two identical nontarget stimuli were also presented on the screen. The appearance and independent movements of these nontargets made it impossible to perform the pursuit tracking correctly without focusing on the appropriate target stimulus and filtering out the potential distractions of the nontargets. Humans were able to track the target amid distractors at levels significantly comparable to baseline performance (tracking without distractors) from even their first block of trials. In contrast, rhesus monkeys initially exhibited significant disruption from the nontarget stimuli and completed trials only with great difficulty and high error levels. After 1,000 trials of practice, however, the monkeys tracked the target at baseline levels even in the presence of nontarget stimuli and, in fact, exhibited performance levels rivaling those of humans.

It is clear from these data that, although rhesus monkeys had to learn the skills required for accurate selection and filtering, they were capable of focusing on a single visual stimulus and ignoring the potential distractions of other irrelevant stimuli.

Stroop Effect One of the most compelling phenomena in the attention literature is actually a demonstration of automaticity (i.e., processing *without* attention). Stroop (1935) demonstrated that subjects could not name the ink color of printed words without processing the meanings of the words. In his classic study (and in over 700 replications and extensions, reviewed by MacLeod, 1991), responding was inhibited by incongruent color-word-meaning and ink color (e.g., the word "red" printed in yellow ink, with the subject required to say "yellow") but was significantly facilitated by congruence between the dimensions (e.g., the word "yellow" printed in yellow). The Stroop effect has been used to demonstrate the automatic and compulsory nature of linguistic processing.

Stroop-like effects, assumed to be unique to humans, have been demonstrated with rhesus monkey subjects using a numerical variation of the Stroop task (inspired by Windes, 1968). We tested rhesus monkeys that had learned the relative values associated with Arabic numerals 0 to 9 (discussed below; see also Washburn & Rumbaugh, 1991a). The monkeys were presented with arrays of letters (e.g., five As versus two Bs) and learned to select the array with the most stimuli in order to receive pellets. On occasional probe trials, numerals were used instead of letters. The monkeys, like human subjects, responded significantly more slowly when the probes were incongruent (i.e., when the array with the most items contained the lesser of the two numerals, such as four 3s versus two 4s). However, both species exhibited significant response facilitation when probes were congruent (e.g., two 5s versus one 2). As with the seminal Stroop (1935) data, these data reveal automatic processing of semantic stimulus dimensions even though it is irrelevant to the response demands of the task. The present findings suggest that the processes of attention and automaticity may indeed be comparable across primate species.

Resource Allocation The resource metaphor has dominated theories of attention since the early 1970s. Although the notion of resources has weaknesses, characterizing attention as a resource-like commodity does permit discussion of topics like attentional intensity, capacity limitations, and allocation of attention to multiple, simultaneous tasks. We have studied the resource-like aspects of attention in a series of experiments on the effects of stimulus movement on learning (Washburn, 1993; Washburn et al., 1989). Humans and monkeys were found to show enhanced learning under conditions in which stimuli moved rather than remaining stationary. Numerous potential explanations for the effect were tested. It appears that learning is enhanced under conditions of stimulus movement by virtue of the increase in task difficulty that movement causes, which in turn alters the allocation policy for attention. Thus, increasing task difficulty in particular ways can elicit attention and result in improved learning or performance. This effect was found in multiple experiments both with humans and rhesus monkeys. Again, the principle of manipulating environmental stimuli to elicit the allocation and perseverance of attention has direct implications for training and education.

Dual-Task Performance The standard testing procedure within the resource theory framework is the dual-task paradigm, in which the attention allocation characteristics of one task are manipulated (e.g., by altering difficulty) to determine whether complementary changes are observed in the performance of the second, concurrent task. For example, we note that, whereas stimulus movement enhanced performance on a sameness–difference task by humans, it resulted in complementary disruption of a concurrent target detection task (i.e., relative to conditions of stationary stimuli, subjects responded significantly faster on the sameness/difference task when the stimuli moved but significantly slower on the concurrent tone detection task). Such findings are interpreted as indicative of the limited capacity of attention, as increases in allocation of attention to the primary task leave fewer attentional resources available for the concurrent task.

Humans and rhesus monkeys were tested at our laboratory on a delayed matching-to-sample task in which subjects had to remember the identity of the target stimulus while performing a concurrent pursuit tracking task (Washburn, Astur, & Raby, 1993). Performance on the memory task varied systematically for both species with manipulations of tracking difficulty. Subjects responded most accurately when no tracking was required, significantly less accurately when easy tracking conditions filled each retention interval, and significantly poorest when the intervening tracking activity was most difficult. These systematic effects for both species suggest that principles of complementarity and attentional capacity are a general feature of (at least) primate cognition and that, whereas humans may differ quantitatively from monkeys in attentional capacity, striking qualitative differences may not exist.

Sustained Performance   Attention also implies the ability to maintain one's focus across time. Rhesus monkeys have mastered a pursuit tracking task that requires unbroken contact between their computer-controlled joystick and a predictably or randomly moving target. This task requires sustained attention, as distraction or inattention will result in failure to track the target. The monkeys typically track the moving target with accuracy equal or superior to that of human subjects. The rhesus monkeys have been tested with pursuit durations of over 60 seconds; success on these trials indicates that the monkeys can focus their attention on a challenging task for relatively long periods of time.

Vigilance   A signal detection paradigm is the traditional test for vigilance, or watch-keeping. Performance on this important and demanding task reflects the ability to maintain focused attention across time. A signal detection task, in which the subject was required to manipulate a joystick upon presentation of a target stimulus but to ignore the aperiodic presentation of nontarget stimuli, was presented to the rhesus monkeys. The monkeys have never been tested for vigilance intervals longer than 2 minutes but have demonstrated the capability to monitor the screen and detect targets for up to that time.

Visual Search   Numerous investigators employ the visual search paradigm to study aspects of human attention and perception. A visual search paradigm has also been used with pigeons (e.g., Blough, 1993) and chimpanzees (Tomonaga, 1993), but in each of these cases the paradigm was a "hunt and peck" variant of matching-to-sample. We devised a go–no-go procedure for visual search that more closely resembles the procedure typically employed in cognitive investigations and tested rhesus monkeys as well as humans. Reliable set-size effects were found for both species when targets and distractor stimuli were similar (e.g., searching for an *F* embedded in *E*s), and pop-out effects were observed when targets differed from nontarget foils (e.g., searching for an *F* embedded in *C*s). Significant search asymmetries have also been reported both for humans and rhesus monkeys on our task; for example, subjects from both species were more rapidly able to locate a *C* amid 2–29 *O*s than an *O* embedded in *C*s. In general, rhesus monkeys (in contrast to pigeons; see Blough, 1993) have demonstrated pop-out effects for similar stimulus features as humans. However, rhesus monkeys and humans tend to differ with respect to serial search strategies within arrays of stimuli, as humans are more likely to employ a reading-like search pattern (top-to-bottom, back-and-forth).

THE LRC-CTS AND BATTERY OF TESTS

Because we view the training program made possible by the LRC-CTS as basic to demonstrating the uncommon skills discussed above, a review of it is in order so that it might become uniquely effective in the remediation of at least some instances of ADHD in humans.

The LRC-CTS tasks provide multiple performance measures for learning, memory, attention, perception, and psychomotor performance. Each task yields measures of response latency, response time, accuracy, topography, and number of responses. The tasks, which require subjects to respond to computer-generated stimuli by manipulating a joystick, are menu-based, with numerous parameters that can be controlled by the experimenter.

Moreover, the training curriculum is arranged so that it promotes the rapid acquisition, as well as the efficient and cumulative generalization, of each new skill to subsequent tasks. Evidence from the training of over three dozen rhesus monkeys to date corroborates the conclusion that the tasks have supported immediate generalization to new stimuli and conditions. We have not had a single monkey "drop out" because of an inability to learn. Even skills and competencies that are typically difficult to establish with nonhuman primates (e.g., matching-to-sample, sameness/difference, signal detection) have been easily trained with minimal direct intervention by experimenters.

The initial task a naive animal experiences is called SIDE (see Rumbaugh et al., 1989). The SIDE task requires the subject to manipulate a joystick to bring a cursor into contact with one border of the screen. Joystick manipulation results in movement of the cursor in isomorphic directions on the screen. Only the cursor moves on the screen, and its movements are contingent on joystick manipulation. As the subject gains skill in achieving contact with the border of the screen, the number of available target walls is decreased (from four to three, and so forth). As a consequence, the subject must discriminate which randomly selected walls of the screen are active targets. Once the subject is responding reliably to a single target wall, the size of that wall is systematically decreased across time. Thus, the animal is shaped systematically to discriminate target from nontarget areas and, across trials, to manifest increasingly precise joystick movements to bring the cursor into contact with smaller and smaller targets. This training is automatically contingent on performance, so that the SIDE task becomes more demanding as the subject becomes more skillful in joystick manipulation.

After SIDE training, a subject can reliably bring the cursor into contact with a small, stationary target. Subsequently, the animal is tested with a moving target. To date, no monkey has failed immediately to catch the moving target in this CHASE task after succeeding to learn the SIDE task. Again, no stimulus moves on the screen unless the joystick is manipulated. The monkeys learn not only to catch a moving target, but also to maintain unbroken contact with the target as it moves around the screen (PURSUIT). As with earlier training, this skill is established by titrating task demands as a function of performance. Errorless performance results in augmentation of task demands, but the task gets easier when animals struggle.

At this point, training can be adjusted along several goal-directed paths. For example, the animal can be trained to shoot at moving targets from a stationary turret (the LASER task). This task, like SIDE, CHASE, and PURSUIT, provides psychomotor performance data relevant to eye–hand coordination and target prediction. For example, we examined whether rhesus monkeys could be described, as can humans, as predictor–operators in their psychomotor responding (Washburn, 1993; Washburn & Rumbaugh, 1992b). Although humans were better at predicting the movement of a target, rhesus monkeys were also significantly more likely to respond to where a target was going than to the position actually occupied by the target in CHASE and LASER.

The LASER task also serves as the basis in training for the signal detection (DETECT) and visual search (SEARCH) tasks. The DETECT task is a go/no-go vigilance task in which subjects respond to the appearance of a target stimulus and ignore the aperiodic, sequential presentation of nontarget distractors. The SEARCH task is similar. Subjects locate as quickly as possible a target stimulus embedded in 3–100 nontargets. Rhesus monkeys tested with this task manifest set-size and pop-out effects comparable to those reported for humans.

Alternatively, one can move directly into two-choice discrimination learning using the transfer index and mediational paradigm tasks (TI and MEDIATE, respectively). These tasks provide measures of learning-to-learn (learning set), transfer-of-learning, and relational versus associative learning. The LRC-CTS rhesus monkeys were found to demonstrate the Trial 2 learning set in about 400 problems—comparable to the findings for rhesus monkeys tested with the Wisconsin General Test Apparatus using junk objects. More important, discrimination–reversal learning data from the TI and MEDIATE tasks reveal that our rhesus monkeys manifest positive transfer and relational learning—capacities previously reported only for apes and humans (Washburn & Rumbaugh, 1991b; see also Rumbaugh & Pate, 1984).

Matching-to-sample (MTS), delayed-matching (DMTS), sameness/difference (SD), and delayed-response (DR) tasks provide measures of perception and working memory. Forgetting curves for retention intervals of up to 60 seconds have been reported (Washburn et al., 1989) and can be separated for form versus spatial memory. Again, learning on MTS generalizes to introduction of DMTS, which in turn facilitates acquisition of SD concepts.

Other tasks in the battery include HOLE (another psychomotor and target–vector prediction task), DVF (a divided visual field task used to determine perceptual thresholds independently for the two cerebral hemispheres), MAZE (maze solving), and NUMBER (discussed below). All of these tasks can be administered in a menu format called SELECT (Washburn, Hopkins, & Rumbaugh, 1991). Using the SELECT procedure, the monkeys can choose what task to work on as well as when to work. The monkeys respond significantly faster and more accurately on tasks they select than on the same tasks when assigned under comparable conditions of order and variety. Not only did the monkeys learn the meanings of the icons that represented each task, but they *perceived* that they had available choices and exhibited the effects of perceived control.

Thus, the LRC-CTS has been an enabling technology in two ways. First, it has provided the tools for studying comparative cognition, revealing many similarities (e.g., target prediction, competition, relational learning, perceived control, attentional processes) and differences (e.g., search patterns, mirror-image discrimination) between human and nonhuman species. Second, we believe that it has been a critical training tool for nurturing and promoting these complex cognitive phenomena, many of which had previously been reported only for humans and apes.

Language

The *generalization* of behaviors that offset the debilitating effects of ADHD to a variety of real-world situations from the more limited contexts within which those behaviors have been instated is germane. Although much remains to be learned about the parameters of this kind of generalization, we have observed profound instances of this generalization in the research discussed above, as well as in our research on language with apes and humans.

We begin our discussion with a consideration of a bonobo, Matata (*Pan paniscus*), who lived in the forest until about 5 years of age. Matata is *not* noted for her ability to learn language and various video-formatted tasks or for her ability to generalize what she does learn in these laboratory challenges to new situations. Matata is basically a very bright bonobo; her behavior in the 55-acre forest that surrounds our laboratory strongly indicates that she is alert, clever, cunning, and resourceful. Moreover, she has excellent social skills and has readily adapted to humans interacting with her during a variety of situations that range from cleaning to feeding, playing, and birthing. However, despite extensive training and experience, Matata has been uniformly poor in learning any language skills and/or other video-formatted tasks otherwise readily mastered by other apes reared in our colony. We believe that Matata has failed because her learning was structured by her early experience in the forest and not by the electronics and methods of our laboratory.

Kanzi In striking contrast, Kanzi, Matata's adopted infant, gave evidence at the age of 2¹/₂ years that he had acquired mastery of lexigrams quite *spontaneously*. Specifically, he learned the meanings of lexigrams without any specific, food-reinforced, discrete-trial training regimens. His learning occurred through observations that had been fortuitously made available to him during his mother's daily training sessions that spanned more than 2 years.

Here it is critical to note that, by every definition, Kanzi was a *hyperactive* young male. He was by far the most "busy" ape of our experience—either spinning, running, doing somersaults, jumping on others, and so on. Kanzi was neither particularly well behaved nor an ardent observer. Nonetheless, he, and not Matata, was the one who learned and learned very well.

The first evidence of his competence with lexigrams and their meanings was seen when Matata was separated from him for purposes of breeding. It was immediately apparent that he had learned what Matata had not. He used lexigrams to request items and make comment on his activities. He also comprehended the meanings of symbols when used by others.

Comprehension of Single Words, Then Novel Sentences of Request In response to indications that Kanzi was understanding speech, controlled tests were given in which he selected either the lexigram or picture according to the word he heard over earphones. These tests revealed that he comprehended about 150 words, which surely was an underestimation of his abilities. Kanzi had received no specific training to encourage his comprehension. Rather, it had been instated by his daily experiences around those who used speech to coordinate activities.

When Kanzi was about 8 years of age, he was tested for his ability to understand the syntax of human speech. The testing included a young girl, Alia, age 2¹/₂ years. Alia's mother had worked extensively with Kanzi and worked with Alia in a similar manner from shortly after Alia's birth on a half-day basis. Thus, both Alia and Kanzi had extensive experience in a small social group in which activities were negotiated and coordinated (e.g., they determined what they would do, where they would go, what things were, etc.) through use of keyboards embossed with word–lexigrams. Although they were never required to use the keyboard, they were always encouraged to observe its use by others and to use it as they would.

The tests of comprehension included more than 400 sentences given in controlled conditions in which the experimenter was hidden from view (e.g., sitting behind a one-way mirror; Savage-Rumbaugh et al., 1993). Various sets of objects were used for these tests, with random collections/arrays of them both in front of the subject and in other areas to which Kanzi and Alia might be asked to go or retrieve certain objects (see Figure 12.2). Several different types of requests were posed; in some the subject was asked to do something to an object (e.g., "Kanzi, can you put soap on your ball?") or do something with one object relative to another (e.g., "Can you knife the onions?"), and so on.

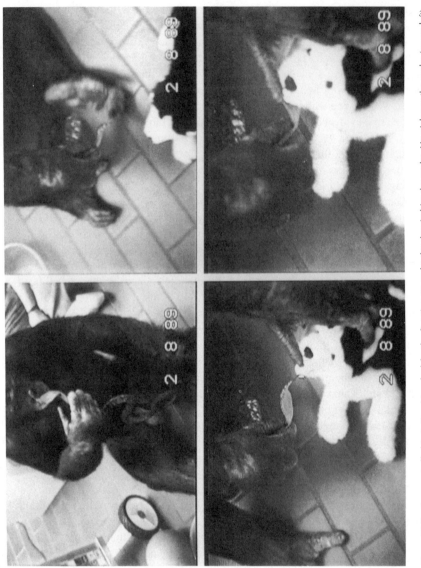

Figure 12.2. In a controlled test, Kanzi is asked for the first time to make the doggie bite the snake. He picks up the snake (upper left), brings it to the dog's mouth (upper right and lower left), and then inserts the head of the snake after opening the dog's mouth through use of his left hand and thumb (lower right).

The sentences of request presented to these two subjects were novel, unpracticed, unmodeled, and generally unusual ("Kanzi, can you get the lettuce that's in the microwave?"—where other objects as well as lettuce were to be found). Typical questions posed were, "Kanzi/Alia, can you make the doggie bite the snake?", "Go get the phone that's outdoors," "Can you tickle (agent's name) with the bunny?", and so on. Both subjects fulfilled the novel requests made of them with about 70% accuracy, where the probability of being correct by chance approximates zero, and they were far more similar than different in their achievements and mistakes.

From the perspective of language, this study was very instructive and served to document the priority of comprehension as a foundation of language as well as the spontaneous learning of both word-lexigrams and the meanings of human words and sentences spoken so as to structure world events through the course of an ape's development. For the purposes of this chapter, the study serves to document the extraordinary achievements of an ape because of 1) its early experience, 2) the attentional skills that it cultivated, and 3) the sensitivity to sounds and symbols in ways not typical of its species as a specific consequence of the patterns of experiences that characterized the conditions under which it was reared.

Concurrent with his competence for comprehension, Kanzi learned simple grammatical rules—some modeled by humans, others his own invention (Greenfield & Savage-Rumbaugh, 1991). And contrary to the claim that chimpanzees cannot make verbal statements and are limited to demands or instrumental requests, Kanzi frequently made statements of what it was that he was about to do. For instance, he would "announce" the play activity in which he was about to engage (e.g., chase, tickle, bite) or the site to which he would go next (e.g., A-frame, treehouse, hilltop). Kanzi's productive rules for ordering relations between two categories of symbols was evaluated to be that which characterizes the productive competence for grammar of 1¹/₂-year-old children.

Subsequent studies with other apes (Sevcik, 1989) have verified these important findings. Thus, the findings with Kanzi are not to be attributed to his being in our colony. Rather, the findings direct our attention to the specifics of early rearing and how they can cultivate attention and extraordinarily complex cognitive achievements and change a hyperactive, highly distractable young bonobo into a subject marked by focused attention, concentration, tenacity, and high achievement.

Pattern of Language Learning The language learning by Kanzi (Savage-Rumbaugh, 1991), and other apes as well, parallels that of the human child in that comprehension preceded productive use of language (i.e., "production" meaning speech in the child and use of lexigrams in the chimpanzee). This pattern stands in sharp contrast with the language learning by Lana, Sherman, and Austin (Rumbaugh, 1977; Savage-Rumbaugh, 1986). These subjects (all common chimpanzees, *Pan troglodytes*) received specially designed training regimens to cultivate specific skills with lexigrams (i.e., to request food and activities, to label items, etc.) on the assumption that their ability to *comprehend* would be instated as their *productive* use of lexigrams was cultivated. That assumption was, however, incorrect.

Sherman and Austin came to comprehend word–lexigram symbols (i.e., their referents) through the course of training that emphasized their coordination of social behaviors. This training taught them to attend to one another's behaviors and to give one another or the experimenter specific tools or foods (see Savage-Rumbaugh, 1986, for a complete description of procedures with an accompanying 2-hour taped documentary). After training, they began to make statements about what they were going to do or what item they were going to get from another area. They also spontaneously started to label activities (e.g., play, tickle, chase, play-bite, etc.), food and drinks, and things that they saw outdoors.

Of maximum significance is that, through the course of their specialized instruction, Sherman and Austin were able to *generalize* a limited amount of initial learning to the end that they also *categorically labeled* 17 word–lexigrams. Each lexigram was a specific food or tool learned through earlier training, and was coded as either a *food* or a *tool* in a tightly controlled test situation. In other words, when shown their lexigram for bread, they called it a *food*, when shown their lexigram for lever, they called it a *tool*, and so on. These data supported the argument that their word–lexigrams functioned representationally for them—that they were meaningful. Consequently, their performance evinced a basic capacity for *semantics*—the meaning of words.

PERCEIVED CONTROL AND THE DEVELOPMENT OF ATTENTION AND THE LEARNING OF COMPLEX SKILLS

The primitive roots of control are suggested even in the prepotent pairing that pecking and the receipt of nutrients in the crop defines for the chicken. Sterritt and Smith (1965) found that ingestive responses (e.g., pecking) of young chicks and the natural consequences thereof (e.g., the consumption of food) are synergistically effective in determining the reinforcement value of rewards in learning tasks. Chicks that had never eaten via pecking from the time of hatching learned a maze task optimally when pecking and infusion of food to their crops via a tube were temporally coupled rather than separated. By contrast, animals do not thrive in situations in which, regardless of what they do, noxious consequences are to be endured (e.g., "learned helplessness" as formulated originally by Overmier & Seligman, 1967, by Seligman & Maier, 1967, and as revised and reviewed by Abramson, Seligman & Teasdale, 1978, and by Peterson and Seligman, 1984).

When rhesus monkeys are given choice over the tasks on which they work for fruit-flavored food pellets, they do significantly better than when those tasks are either assigned arbitrarily by the experimenter or are yoked to prior choice patterns (Washburn et al., 1991). If the behavior of the rhesus monkeys were solely based on their receiving pellets, *what* task they work on would seemingly be of no consequence to them, as long as the payoff were held constant. But choice of tasks does matter. If there is no concordance between their expressed choice and the tasks that are then encountered, performance decays.

A clear implication is that *opportunities* to control activities, and even to learn, can become inherently motivating and reinforcing. The human literature on "mastery motivation" bears out this point (e.g., Harter, 1978a, b), as does our research with rhesus monkeys.

In support of this perspective, Washburn and Rumbaugh (1992a) reported that access to free food (i.e., no work required) can be a *non*preferred option for rhesus monkeys in a variant of one of their several video-formatted tasks, SELECT. As discussed earlier, it is in the SELECT task that the rhesus monkey can choose which of several tasks it will work for during the next five trials. Upon completion of those trials, the menu of icons, one to represent each task, is presented once again for the monkey to make another choice of tasks for the next five trials, and so on.

In the study at hand, the monkey could choose the option of *free food,* which resulted in the automatic delivery of five pellets distributed across time at a rate comparable to that of successful task performance (five pellets per 60 seconds). Thus, the monkeys were given a choice of *not* working but receiving food nonetheless.

Gradually, the choice of the free food option came to be preferred over all other options. It was possible, of course, that the monkeys viewed free food not as freeloading, but as a richly rewarded, single-response task. To clarify this point, a cost was introduced for exercising the free food option. Selection of the free food icon now resulted in "free" delivery of pellets (noncontingent on performance) not for one, but for 30 minutes—which meant that for 30 minutes the screen was blank and no other task option was available to them. Under these conditions, the preference for free food rapidly decayed, and the monkeys' "work ethic" returned. Thus, it would seem that the *free food* option was very attractive so long as it was an option that the rhesus monkeys could choose or not and one that did not impede the opportunity to work. But when choice of free food was at the protracted expense of choice to work on other tasks of their choice, it became a very unattractive option. Their choice of the free food option dropped to below chance (e.g., it dropped to 18% from a high of 70%). Control tests, where choice of other tasks (i.e., not "free food") was selected and continued for 30 minutes rather than for just five trials, did not result in a decreased preference for them.

Supra-Learning

If Rumbaugh and Sterritt (1986) are correct in positing inherent properties of perceived control, learning should be maximized rather than held to a bare minimum. Washburn and Rumbaugh (1991a) indicate that primates learn far more than is necessary when given the opportunity to choose between numerals 0 through 9 in a video-formatted task. When a numeral was selected, the monkey received a corresponding number of pellets. For example, on a trial in which a

"4" was paired with "7," choice of the former would result in four pellets being dispensed, whereas choice of the latter would result in the rhesus monkeys receiving seven pellets. Thus, the monkeys received pellets in accordance with the value of the numeral selected. It is important to note, however, that the rhesus monkeys did *not* have to choose the larger numeral to obtain food. They *always* got pellets, except when "0" was present and selected as a member of a pair.

The monkeys quickly came to select the larger of two numerals. They were then presented with seven novel trials in which certain numerals were paired for the first time in this particular test paradigm. In these trials, one rhesus monkey made no errors, while the second one made two errors. The rhesus monkey had learned *more* than simply how to select numerals for rewards. They learned two complex relational matrices: one matrix was between numeric symbols and numbers of pellets, and the other matrix was between numeric symbols. They treated these numeric symbols in accordance with their values and ordinal ranks where their ordinal ranks differed minimally—that is, *by one pellet*. They learned these matrices even though, to get pellets, all they had to do was to choose *any* number (other than "0"). And if they did not make the optimal choice of numerals, they had only to wait a second or so for the next trial to be presented. Thus, their learning attests to the proclivity of the primate's brain for organizing *par excellence* all information that is orderly and reliably encountered in an environment where *choice* is extended to them in a situation that has served to foster focused attention and facile learning.

In another and related situation, Sherman and Austin chimpanzees rapidly came to select whichever of *two* pairs of piles of M&M candies netted for them the greater total. They were not required to choose thusly, however, for they always got the M&Ms of whichever pair of piles they selected (Rumbaugh, Savage-Rumbaugh, & Hegel, 1987). Nonetheless, the large apes learned reliably to sum the piles of candies and to select the combination that netted even one more piece.

Thus, chimpanzees and rhesus monkeys prefer control over what they do, and they are inclined to learn more than task-minima. They are likely to learn all that they can, all that is "learnable" (regular or predictable) in the environment— bringing to bear any past experience that assists in the organization of events. That they do so is not a trivial finding or conclusion, for it holds important leads with which to possibly ameliorate the adverse consequences of attentional deficits in humans.

CONCLUSIONS

Given that the human species is unequivocally a member of the order *Primates*, to which our *non*human subjects belong, it follows that what is learned from nonhuman primates might be of value to us in coping with adaptation problems of our children. Apes and monkeys have no inherent interest in topics that characterize either the computer-formatted tasks or language studies in which they have served. Notwithstanding, their participation as subjects has cultivated their interest, attention, complex learning, and, in the apes, even substantial language skills. Their skills and learning exemplify *supra-learning*, in that they have learned far more than required of them. They have also readily generalized their skills to new tasks and to new contexts. Accordingly, we believe that our tasks and methods of rearing primates have a great deal of potential value to us in our attempts to ameliorate—but ideally to *preclude*—behavioral and learning deficits.

Research with primates at the Language Research Center has time and again been of proven value when principles derived from it have been applied to special populations, including children with pervasive language disabilities due to severe and profound mental retardation (Romski, 1989; Rumbaugh, Hopkins, Washburn, & Savage-Rumbaugh, 1991). All that has been observed and reported with our primate subjects has also been obtained in research with children with mental retardation, several of whom have come to learn representational symbolic communication so as to be able to order their own foods and drinks in restaurants and obtain gainful employment. Although not all problems are to be solved through future research with nonhuman primates, we can learn important basic principles from them and enhance the prospects of our better understanding and dealing effectively with our children's behavioral, learning, and affective disorders.

In large measure those problems come about because even the children's best efforts can be inappropriate or inadequate to their environments. Notwithstanding, the processes that supported their unfortunate, costly patterns of adaptation are one and the same as those whereby amelioration is possible. Finally, it bears emphasis that a characteristic shared by *all* of our training and rearing methods is that of *diversity*. It seems both attractive and reasonable to us that the generalization of gains made by special treatment, therapy, and learning will be heavily dependent upon 1) the degree to which diversity rather than constancy is the hallmark of the materials and contexts utilized in them and 2) the degree to which "treatment, therapy, and new learning" become new lifestyles rather than once-each-week episodes of limited duration. Problems of adaptation that are learned throughout a lifetime will not likely be modified pervasively and lastingly by brief episodic sessions in which even the best of treatment is offered.

REFERENCES

Abramson, L.Y., Seligman, M.E.P., & Teasdale, J.D. (1978). Learned helplessness in humans: Critique and reformulation. *Journal of Abnormal Psychology, 87*, 49–74.

Blough, D.S. (1993). Features of forms in pigeon perception. In W.K. Honig & J.G. Fetterman (Eds.), *Cognitive aspects of stimulus control* (pp. 263–277). Hillsdale, NJ: Lawrence Erlbaum Associates.

Davenport, R.K., Rogers, C.W., & Rumbaugh, D.M. (1973). Long-term cognitive deficits in chimpanzees associated with early impoverished rearing. *Developmental Psychology, 9*, 343–347.

Greenfield, P., & Savage-Rumbaugh, E.S. (1991). Imitation, grammatical development, and the invention of protogrammar by an ape. In N.A. Krasnegor, D.M. Rumbaugh, R.L. Schiefelbusch, & M. Studdert-Kennedy (Eds.), *Biological and behavioral determinants of language development* (pp. 235–262). Hillsdale, NJ: Lawrence Erlbaum Associates.

Greenough, W.T., Wither, G.S., & Wallace, C.S. (1990). Morphological changes in the nervous system arising from behavioral experience: What is the evidence that they are involved in learning and memory? In L.R. Squire & E. Lindenlaub (Eds.), *The Biology of memory, Symposia Medica Hoechst, 23* (pp. 159–185). New York: F.K. Schattauder Verlag.

Harlow, H.F. (1949). The formation of learning sets. *Psychological Review, 56*, 51–65.

Harter, S. (1978a). Effectance motivation reconsidered: Toward a developmental model. *Human Development, 21*, 34–64.

Harter, S. (1978b). Pleasure derived from challenge and the effects of receiving grades on children's difficulty level choices. *Child Development, 49*, 788–799.

Krech, D., Rosenzweig, M.R., & Bennett, E.L. (1962). Relations between brain chemistry and problem solving among rats raised in enriched and impoverished environments. *Journal of Comparative and Physiological Psychology, 55*, 801–808.

MacLeod, C.M. (1991). Half a century of research on the Stroop effect: An integrative review. *Psychological Bulletin, 109*, 163–203.

Neisser, U., & Becklen, R. (1975). Selective looking: Attending to visually significant events. *Cognitive Psychology, 7*, 480–494.

Overmier, J.B., & Seligman, M.E.P. (1967). Effects of inescapable shock upon subsequent escape and avoidance learning. *Journal of Comparative & Physiological Psychology, 63*, 28–33.

Peterson, C., & Seligman, M.E.P. (1984). Causal explanations as a risk factor for depression: Theory and evidence. *Psychological Review, 91*, 347–374.

Riesen, A.H. (1982). Effects of environments on development in sensory systems. In W.D. Neff (Ed.), *Contributions to sensory physiology* (Vol. 6, pp. 45–77). New York: Academic Press.

Romski, M.A. (1989). Two decades of language research with great apes. *American Speech-Language-Hearing Association, XX*, 81–83.

Rumbaugh, D.M. (1977). *Language learning by a chimpanzee: The LANA project.* New York: Academic Press.

Rumbaugh, D.M., Hopkins, W.D., Washburn, D.A., & Savage-Rumbaugh, E.S. (1989). Lana chimpanzee learns to count by "Numath": A summary of a video-taped experimental report. *Psychological Record, 39*, 459–471.

Rumbaugh, D.M., Hopkins, W.D., Washburn, D.A., & Savage-Rumbaugh, E.S. (1991). Comparative perspectives of brain, cognition, and language. In N.A. Krasnegor, D.M. Rumbaugh, R.L. Schiefelbusch, & M. Studdert-Kennedy (Eds.), *Biological and behavioral determinants of language development* (pp. 145–164). Hillsdale, NJ: Lawrence Erlbaum Associates.

Rumbaugh, D.M., & Pate, J.L. (1984). The evolution of cognition in primates: A comparative perspective. In H.L. Roitblat, T.G. Bever, and H.S. Terrace (Eds.), *Animal cognition.* (pp. 569–587). Hillsdale, NJ: Lawrence Erlbaum Associates.

Rumbaugh, D.M., Richardson, W.K., Washburn, D.A., Savage-Rumbaugh, E.S., & Hopkins, W.D. (1989). Rhesus monkeys (*Macaca mulatta*), video tasks, and implications for stimulus-response spatial contiguity. *Journal of Comparative Psychology, 103*, 32–38.

Rumbaugh, D.M., Savage-Rumbaugh, E.S., & Hegel, M.T. (1987). Summation in the chimpanzee (*Pan troglodytes*). *Journal of Experimental Psychology: Animal Behavior Processes, 13*, 107–115.

Rumbaugh, D.M., & Sterritt, G.M. (1986). Intelligence: From genes to genius in the quest for control. In W. Bechtel (Ed.), *Integrating scientific disciplines* (pp. 309–322). Dordrecht: Martinus Nijhoff Publishers.

Savage-Rumbaugh, E.S. (1986). *Ape language: From conditioned response to symbols.* New York: Columbia University Press.

Savage-Rumbaugh, E.S. (1991). Language learning in the bonobo: How and why they learn. In N.A. Krasnegor, D.M. Rumbaugh, R.L. Schiefelbusch, & M. Studdert-Kennedy (Eds.), *Biological and behavioral determinants of language development* (pp. 209–233). Hillsdale, NJ: Lawrence Erlbaum Associates.

Savage-Rumbaugh, E.S., Murphy, J., Sevcik, R.A., Brakke, K., Williams, S., & Rumbaugh, D.M. (1993). Language comprehension in ape and child. *Monographs of the Society for Research in Child Development,* Nos. 2 & 3.

Seligman, M.E.P., & Maier, S.F. (1967). Failure to escape traumatic shock. *Journal of Experimental Psychology, 74,* 1–9.

Sevcik, R.A. (1989). *A comprehensive analysis of graphic symbol acquisition and use: Evidence from an infant bonobo (Pan paniscus).* Unpublished doctoral dissertation, Georgia State University, Atlanta.

Sterritt, G.M., & Smith, M.P. (1965). Reinforcement effect of specific components of feeding in young leghorn chicks. *Journal of Comparative & Physiological Psychology, 59,* 171–175.

Stroop, J.R. (1935). Studies of interference in serial verbal reactions. *Journal of Experimental Psychology, 18,* 643–662.

Tomonaga, M. (1993). Use of multiple-alternative matching-to-sample in the study of visual search in a chimpanzee (*Pan troglodytes*). *Journal of Comparative Psychology, 107,* 75–83.

Washburn, D.A. (1993). The stimulus movement effect: Allocation of attention or artifact? *Journal of Experimental Psychology: Animal Behavior Processes, 19,* 1–10.

Washburn, D.A., Astur, R.S., & Raby, P.R. (1993, June). *Sources of forgetting in the visuospatial sketchpad of humans and monkeys.* Poster presented at the meeting of the American Psychological Society, Chicago, IL.

Washburn, D.A., Hopkins, W.D., & Rumbaugh, D.M. (1989). Video-task assessment of learning and memory in macaques: Effects of stimulus movement upon performance. *Journal of Experimental Psychology, 15,* 393–400.

Washburn, D.A., Hopkins, W.D., & Rumbaugh, D.M. (1991). Perceived control in rhesus monkeys (*Macaca mulatta*): Enhanced video-task performance. *Journal of Experimental Psychology: Animal Behavior Processes, 17,* 123–127.

Washburn, D.A., & Rumbaugh, D.M. (1991a). Ordinal judgments of numerical symbols by macaques (*Macaca mulatta*). *Psychological Science, 2*(3), 190–193.

Washburn, D.A., & Rumbaugh, D.M. (1991b). Rhesus monkey (*Macaca mulatta*) complex learning skills reassessed. *International Journal of Primatology, 12,* 377–388.

Washburn, D.A., & Rumbaugh, D.M. (1992a). Investigations of rhesus monkey video-task performance: Evidence for enrichment. *Contemporary Topics in Laboratory Animal Science, 31,* 6–10.

Washburn, D.A., & Rumbaugh, D.M. (1992b). Comparative assessment of psychomotor performance: Target prediction by humans and macaques (*Macaca mulatta*). *Journal of Experimental Psychology: General, 121*(3), 305–312.

Windes, J.D. (1968). Reaction time for numerical coding and naming of numerals. *Journal of Experimental Psychology, 78,* 318–322.

13

CONCEPTUALIZING, DESCRIBING, AND MEASURING COMPONENTS OF MEMORY

A Summary

Kimberly Boller

The measurement of memory has a long and rich history in psychology. Clearly, the overarching construct of memory is central to human learning. The early research in memory is exemplified by the work of Ebbinghaus (1885), the first experimental psychologist to study the higher mental processes of retention and forgetting. Several major contributions emerged from Ebbinghaus's research. First, his experiments on the retention and forgetting of written information provided the first quantitative picture of forgetting. Second, he invented nonsense syllables as a method to study memory for verbal information that was not contaminated by prior learning. Third, he provided an analysis of several factors that influenced memory, including the organization of the material to be remembered, the difficulty and amount of material to be remembered, and the retention interval. The puzzle of memory was explored by many who followed Ebbinghaus, including Underwood (1954), who identified the relationships between speed of learning and retention, Hebb (1949), who posited a dual route neurophysiological theory to explain short- and long-term memory, and Peterson and Peterson (1959), who pioneered experimental study of verbal short-term memory.

Within this section, Torgesen (Chapter 10), Bachevalier, Malkova, and Beauregard (Chapter 11), and Rumbaugh and Washburn (Chapter 12) have reviewed research that builds on these classic studies of memory processes. As one reviews these current contributions to the literature, it is worthwhile to ask what we have learned during the past decade about different aspects of memory. Currently, research on memory is conceptualized using theoretical orientations based upon the information processing, neuropsychological, and behavioral perspectives. Along with each of these three theoretical orientations goes the concomitant methodology used by researchers to search for answers to the memory puzzle. As we consider the question of progress in memory research, it is useful to summarize the contributions of research emanating from each of the approaches. To that end, this summary chapter reviews the current research in memory as addressed in each of the three chapters in terms of the theoretical context and model employed, the primary constructs of the model, and the manner in which the models and constructs have been operationalized. The chapter concludes with a comparison and contrast of the different perspectives and suggestions for future research.

THE INFORMATION PROCESSING PERSPECTIVE: TORGESEN

Theoretical Context and Model

The information processing model advanced by Torgesen was initially described by Baddeley (1986, 1992). In this model, information enters the system through the visual and auditory sensory stores. Visual information progresses to the visuospatial sketchpad and then can be worked on by the central executive. Auditory information travels from the auditory store to the phonological loop and then can be used by the central executive. The central executive, the visuospatial sketchpad, and the phonological loop are all parts of working memory. The central executive is conceptualized as a control system with a key role in decision making and response selection. Information can enter long-term memory from all three parts of the working memory system. In Chapter 10, Torgesen discusses one aspect of the working memory system, the phonological loop.

Primary Constructs

The primary construct required for the model described by Torgesen is working memory. The focus of his chapter is on one component of working memory, the phonological loop. In this conceptualization, the phonological loop is composed of a phonological store that serves as the depository for speech-based information. Information (referred to by Torgesen as the memory trace or coded representation) can only be maintained in the phonological store. However, information in the phonological store can be refreshed by an articulatory control process through activation of central speech motor programs.

Methodology Used to Build the Model

Torgesen reviews the methods used to construct and test the model. Four experimental effects are presented that can be explained by the functions of the phonological loop. In the first effect, aurally presented letters that sound the same are harder to recall than letters that sound different. However, when letters that physically resemble each other are presented visually, there is no evidence that the similar letters are more difficult to remember—strong support for the uniqueness of the phonological similarity effect. The evidence for the phonological similarity effect was built on methods that tested the "uniqueness" of the memory disruption for phonologically similar information against a contrast group that tested for memory disruption using similarity in another modality (the visual system). This seems to be a special case of classic memory interference in which similarity effects have been widely documented (McGeoch, 1930; McGeoch & McDonald, 1931).

In the second effect, the unattended speech effect, recall of visually presented verbal sequences is poor when background noise shares similar phonological structure with the to-be-remembered words. Recall is not disrupted if the background noise is not speech. Again, this method supports the idea that phonological similarity plays a role in and can interfere with recall.

Evidence for the articulatory process in the phonological loop was supported by the word length effect and the articulatory suppression effect. The word length effect, the third experimental effect explained by the functions of the phonological loop, refers to the finding that the spoken duration of words affects how much of a verbal sequence will be remembered. The longer the spoken duration of the words, the worse subjects do at recalling a verbal sequence. Torgesen also presents developmental evidence that suggests that articulation rate plays a role in recall: As articulation rate increases in children, performance on digit span tasks improves. The fourth experimental effect, the articulatory suppression effect—poor recall of verbal items by subjects asked to repeat a word, is also seen as interference with the articulatory control process. Subjects asked to tap on a table while the verbal items are presented display no impairment in recall.

As described, the methods used to test the model involve presenting verbal stimuli to subjects and determining whether performance on a recall task is affected by the manipulation of other information presented at the same time, or manipulation of the length of the to-be-remembered stimuli. Most of the evidence that supports the existence of the phonological loop and its two components, the phonological store and the articulatory control process, comes from contrasting the results from groups that demonstrate interference between phonological stimuli and groups that do not show interference because the verbal stimuli were presented with stimuli that were not phonologically similar.

Torgesen provides an excellent review of the types of tasks that can be used to measure the workings of the phonological loop. Correlations between the tasks and between various instantiations of the tasks for young children are also provided. The incorporation of information about how children perform on these tasks is included to prepare the reader for Torgesen's test of the model, that is, applying what is known about phonological memory to the special case of children with reading disabilities. Following a lucid review of recent data, Torgesen concludes that deficits in phonological coding efficiency are not, ". . . a powerful and unique cause of individual differences in word reading skill in young children" (pp.173–174). Torgesen also discusses the findings on the interrelationships between phonological skills. One might hypothesize that phonological memory plays a role in the development of phonological awareness over time. He concludes that current evidence does not support the idea that differences in phonological memory performance predict response to phonological awareness training. However, he briefly describes preliminary data that may support the role of the phonological loop and articulatory processes as major components in verbal short-term memory performance.

One of the limitations of Torgesen's test of the model of working memory is that the research reviewed is quite narrow in focus. Torgesen acknowledges this fact when he states that his discussion pertains only to reading. It would have been informative to know more about the similarities and differences between the phonological loop and the other side of the proposed working memory system, the visuospatial sketchpad. For example, it is not clear how visually presented verbal material (a word on a page) is processed by the visuospatial sketchpad. Is all processing of visually presented verbal material terminated once the phonological loop begins processing? If this is the case, why are we able to remember that spatial location of a particular list on a page and use that information to help us retrieve what was on the list? Exploring the interrelationships between the two "sides" of the proposed working memory model may help to further define what is unique and what is shared by both processing centers.

THE NEUROPSYCHOLOGICAL PERSPECTIVE: BACHEVALIER, MALKOVA, AND BEAUREGARD

Theoretical Context and Model

In Chapter 11, Bachevalier, Malkova, and Beauregard discuss the current trend in memory research of combining cognitive psychological theory and neurobiological mechanisms. Recent research in the area of long-term memory and learning constitutes the major topic of the discussion. The theoretical context and models proposed by Bachevalier, Malkova, and Beauregard reflect traditional neuropsychological perspectives. Hybrid techniques combine research in the area of memory loss in humans with research on the same types of memory loss induced in experimental animals. The authors frame the central theme of their chapter by noting that, "Just as neuropsychological and neurobiological evidence indicated the need to abandon the idea that memory is a unitary process, it has now been proposed that both short-term and long-term memory can be further subdivided" (p. 186).

Primary Constructs

The primary constructs required by the model described by Bachevalier and colleagues are modality-specific short-term memory stores and long-term memory. They also describe the construct of fractionation, the ability to separate different aspects of memory by demonstrating deficits in one "memory system" that leave another "memory system" intact.

Methodology Used to Build the Model

The authors review the basic tenets of the model of long-term memory fractionation. In this model, the "awareness of newly acquired information" is separable from the "acquisition of skills." The case for fractionation has been made by researchers exploring memory in patients with amnesia. The specific area of brain injury was related to the type of memory impairment displayed by the patients, with deficits in the "awareness of newly acquired information" localized to limbic system damage, and deficits in "skill acquisition" localized to "several neural systems, one of which includes the basal ganglia."

Studies that have involved experimental lesions to the brains of nonhuman primates to mimic the amnesia displayed by the human patients found strong similarities between animal and human models. Monkeys with medial temporal lobe ablations could not recognize objects they had recently seen, but they could perform tasks that required gradual and incremental learning. These results have been explained by the proposal that there are at least two memory systems and that the neural circuits that serve the two systems are independent. Bachevalier and colleagues reviewed the evidence supporting the hypothesis that the two memory systems are served by independent neural circuits. The methods used to map the neural circuits include lesioning (both physical and chemical) the critical brain areas and exploiting instances of neuropathology. Mishkin and Murray (1994) have advanced this tactic in their mapping of visual recognition memory. The neuroanatomical map for the habit system is not as clear, although evidence points to the striatum as the leading candidate.

Bachevalier and associates also review the findings that suggest that there are developmental differences in memory performance that support the existence of two memory systems. For instance, Bachevalier and Mishkin (1984) reported that monkeys did not perform the visual recognition task (their "memory" task) until 4 months of age. Adult levels of performance on the task were not seen until the monkeys were 2 years old. Bachevalier and colleagues also review analogous findings with human infants. On the other hand, Bachevalier and Mishkin (1984) also reported that 3-month-old monkeys were able to learn a concurrent object discrimination task (their "habit" task) as well as adult monkeys. The conclusion was that the medial temporal lobe structures that support visual recognition memory must be slow developing.

In subsequent studies of medial temporal lobe lesions in developing monkeys, the Bachevalier group has demonstrated that early lesions cause global and long-lasting memory deficits, but do not affect the ability to learn a concurrent object discrimination task. Thus, medial temporal lobe loss is not compensated for by other areas of the brain even when damage occurs early in development. Recent evidence supports the idea that loss of the hippocampus itself is not responsible for the memory deficit, but rather that the rhinal cortex may play the critical role in recognition memory.

Bachevalier and colleagues support their claim that the medial temporal lobe structures develop early with evidence that between 15 and 30 days of age monkeys showed a novelty preference in a preferential viewing task, but that monkeys with early or late medial temporal lobe damage did not show a novelty preference. The authors presented evidence that the association areas of the cortex (the "repositories of long-term memory") may be the "immature" areas of the brain and perhaps the cause of infantile amnesia.

The authors fail to acknowledge that the issue of multiple memory systems is still seen by some as highly controversial and problematic based upon a lack of parsimony (Spear & Riccio, 1994). Each time investigators find evidence for a dissociation between performance on one type of task and performance on another type of task, a new memory system is proposed to account for the dissociation. A litany of memory "systems" have been proposed to explain data from studies that employ the methods from all three perspectives represented in the preceding chapters (see Table 13.1). Primarily, the literature suggests that we have a definitional problem; that is, distinctions between the proposed systems are no longer clear and many researchers are using them interchangeably. Bachevalier et al. (Chapter 11) refer to visual habits as a form of procedural memory, and they refer to the formation of cognitive or representative memory as instances of declarative memory. As a researcher of memory in human infants, I have been reluctant to use the procedural/declarative distinction in describing our models because we ascribed to a literal definition of declarative memory. Infants cannot "declare" or tell an examiner the circumstances under which a piece of information was learned and remembered. What Bachevalier et al. have done is apply a broader definition of declarative to their results. This would be appropriate if you hypothesized that the ability of monkeys to perform successfully on a delayed non–matching-to-sample task is analogous to the ability of humans to successfully remember a person's name and how and when they met that person. Those who study memory in a variety of nonverbal animals (e.g., human infants, rats, rhesus monkeys, and other nonhuman primates) may feel pressured to categorize findings according to the "boxes" that have been delineated by those who study memory in human amnestics or in "normal" human adults. Although it is important to explore the parallels between work done across a variety of subjects, an unqualified adherence to the constructs described above may result in accepting assumptions that are not useful and that ultimately trivialize our results.

Table 13.1. Types of memory systems

Short-term memory	Long-term memory	Hebb (1949)
Working memory	Long-term memory	Baddeley (1986)
Episodic memory	Semantic memory	Tulving (1972, 1983)
Implicit memory	Explicit memory	Schacter (1987)
Procedural memory	Declarative memory	Cohen & Squire (1980), Squire (1992), Tulving (1983)
Working memory	Reference memory	Olton (1978)
Recognition memory	Habit memory	Mishkin, Malamut, & Bachevalier (1984)

For example, Rovee-Collier and colleagues have documented the memory abilities of 3- and 6-month-old human infants (Boller, Rovee-Collier, Borovsky, O'Connor, & Shyi, 1990; Hill, Borovsky, & Rovee-Collier, 1988; Rovee-Collier, Sullivan, Enright, Lucas, & Fagen, 1980). In the mobile conjugate reinforcement procedure, infants kick to move an overhead mobile. Infants are not learning to kick, they are learning that kicking makes the mobile move. When conditions are changed enough at test (the mobile or the context may have been changed, depending on the particular study), infants generally do not kick, "telling" us that they do not recognize/remember this novel stimulus. We do not believe that the infants are "telling" us that they do not remember how to kick. One might be tempted to categorize the above memory phenomena as implicit or procedural memory. This would be an error in the same way that Bachevalier and colleagues have made an error in describing visual habits as a form of procedural memory. Until further evidence is produced and better theoretical arguments are made that take into account data about memory and its development in a variety of species, we would be wise to resist lumping all of our results into the popular dichotomy of the day.

In addition, we should be cautious not to allow our theories to be mere descriptions of the phenomena studied. Theoretical underpinnings must be elaborated and rigorous hypothesis testing must be done to explore models of long-term memory. As researchers present their arguments in terms of the implicit–explicit memory debate, we should not forget that the best theory is the one that accounts for the data with the most "economical" model. Applying Ockham's razor (see Thorburn, 1918, for a history of the principle) to the area of memory theory and research may allow us to move beyond our current laundry list of proposed memory "systems" and on to significant theoretical and methodological progress.

THE BEHAVIORAL PERSPECTIVE: RUMBAUGH AND WASHBURN

Theoretical Context and Model

In Chapter 12, Rumbaugh and Washburn discuss the significance of the comparative behavioral approach in exploring the role of attention and memory in learning. They describe the use of novel procedures to test the cognitive skills of chimpanzees and rhesus monkeys. The authors further suggest that children with attention deficit hyperactivity disorder (ADHD) may benefit from exposure to experiences similar to those described for nonhuman primates. The authors also describe how behavioral techniques have been used to develop language comprehension and production in nonhuman primates. The comparative behavioral model described by Rumbaugh and Washburn incorporates classic behavioral theory and methods with new methods that demonstrate higher-order cognitive skills in chimpanzees and rhesus monkeys. The authors propose that the changes in attentional focus displayed by their highly trained, nonhuman subjects could serve as a model for developing treatments for ADHD in children.

Primary Constructs

The primary constructs required by the model described by Rumbaugh and Washburn are attention, learning, memory, and language. The authors describe several types of tasks and procedures that enabled them to measure these constructs in chimpanzees and rhesus monkeys. Often comparisons are made between the performance of nonhuman primates and humans on these tasks.

Methodology Used to Build the Model

The authors review the findings from two research programs in their laboratory. The first line of research focused on attention, memory, and learning. In these studies, nonhuman primates manipulated a joystick that moved a cursor on a video screen. Attending behaviors were shaped by food rewards and then developed further as the animals progressed to more challenging problems, including classic memory tasks like delayed-matching-to-sample. The animals were also given the opportunity to select which tasks they would work on at a given time. Performance was enhanced when animals chose which task they worked on at a given time.

Language was the second major focus of research discussed. The methods used to study language include intensive training of nonhuman primates on a language-based symbol system (lexigrams). In this research, behavioral techniques were used to train the subjects and reward them for remembering the association between the lexigrams and objects and concepts in the world. Rumbaugh and Washburn discuss comparative studies of the comprehension skills displayed by Kanzi, an 8-year-old bonobo, and Alia, a 2.5-year-old girl. In these studies, behavioral methods were used to strengthen memory for linguistic symbols. These methods were used to develop the System for Augmenting Language (SAL), which has been demonstrated to enhance the communication skills of youth with mental retardation and little or no functional speech (Romski, Sevcik, Robinson, & Bakeman, 1994; Romski, Sevcik, & Wilkinson, 1994).

One limitation of the proposed model is that there is no firm evidence to support the assertion that laboratory-reared nonhuman primates are analogous to children with ADHD. The calming, attention-focusing effects of attention, memory, and language training are asserted by the authors, but these effects are not supported with data that compared performance of individuals with and without training. One would expect that there are individual differences in the learning and performance of the attention and memory tasks and that these differences define the range of possible normal attending and memory behaviors in the nonhuman primates. This does not mean that change demonstrated in the attending and memory behaviors of the nonhuman primates can serve as a precise model for ADHD intervention in children. It will be interesting to see how this model is explored in further research and whether this behavioral approach to developing interventions for children with ADHD will be as successful as the interventions that were developed from the language research coming from the same laboratory.

COMPARING THE THREE APPROACHES

Given the wide range of research questions, methods, and theoretical approaches discussed in the three chapters, the task of comparing, contrasting, and synthesizing them is daunting. In all three chapters, we see the acceptance of certain constructs, methods, and theoretical approaches. The authors of all three chapters describe results from studies that use procedures that would be classified as "behavioral," including the use of verbal learning tasks with children, the use of object recognition and delayed memory tasks with monkeys, and the use of behavioral techniques in shaping and testing higher cognitive processes in children, monkeys, and other nonhuman primates.

In all three chapters, deficit models are employed to inform the reader about "normal" memory processes. That is, the authors have described research methods used by them and others that take advantage of cognitive deficits that either occur naturally in the environment (e.g., children with learning disabilities, inattentive monkeys) or that are induced by accident or in the laboratory/hospital (e.g., monkeys given physical or chemical lesions, patients who become amnestic following brain trauma or surgery to reduce other life-threatening problems). Models based on comparisons between subjects who are normal and subjects who have deficits are quite effective in helping us to develop interventions for individuals with deficits. These deficit models have also been used to map some brain systems and determine where and how brain functions might be localized. However, we should remain cautious about our reliance on deficit models as our main source of conceptualizations of normal cognitive functioning. Our models must do better at capturing the development of higher cognitive processes, especially learning and memory. Future research must grapple with the question of whether models based on individuals who have reached an adult memory proficiency and then lost that ability can adequately describe the development of memory from the fetus to the grave. Is it the same to have remembered and lost than never to have remembered at all? The answer has to be no. The brain is a remarkable organ that can compensate for devastating losses. We need more normative developmental memory research to help us build models of normal memory functioning that may or may not be analogous to the models based on the deficit approach.

The three chapters vary widely in their approach to the question of memory. The information processing approach described by Torgesen seemed the most "mature," both theoretically and methodologically. Torgesen clearly lays out his model, provides the description of the measures and methods used to examine working memory, and provides hypotheses and data that can be used to accept or reject the model. The two other chapters are not as clear in their presentation of the perspectives and models proposed. This may be because Torgesen chose to focus on one aspect of the memory system and test hypotheses about the model in a narrow area, that of reading disability. Researchers using the behavioral approach described by Rumbaugh and Washburn must face some hard questions.

The work that they outlined is largely descriptive of the behavior of nonhuman primates. Where is this research going to take us, and are there other avenues that have not been explored? We need research in memory that is both "top-down" (whole organism) and "bottom-up" (brain–behavior linkages). However, we must make sure that our "top-down" approaches stay relevant and continue to contribute to theory development and hypothesis testing.

Chapters 10, 11, and 12 summarized advances in the conceptualization and measurement of memory from the information processing, neuropsychological, and behavioral perspectives. From a historical perspective, we can see that advances made over the last 10 years are now being applied to the problem of memory development. Given new technological advances that will allow for sophisticated imaging of brain activity while subjects perform well-studied cognitive tasks, we will see the continued marriage of the techniques and methods from all three perspectives. The sharing and clarification of theoretical models and supporting methodologies among researchers working from the three perspectives will ensure that memory development research continues to thrive and make significant contributions to the understanding of cognitive development across the life span.

REFERENCES

Bachevalier, J., & Mishkin, M. (1984). An early and a late developing system for learning and retention in infant monkeys. *Behavioral Neuroscience, 98*, 770–778.

Baddeley, A.D. (1986). *Working memory.* New York: Oxford University Press.

Baddeley, A.D. (1992). Working memory. *Science, 255*, 556–559.

Boller, K., Rovee-Collier, C. Borovsky, D., O'Connor, J., & Shyi, G. (1990). Developmental changes in the time-dependent nature of memory retrieval. *Developmental Psychology, 26*, 770–779.

Cohen, N.J., & Squire, L.R. (1980). Preserved learning and retention of pattern-analyzing skill in amnesia: Dissociation of "knowing how" and "knowing that." *Science, 210*, 207–209.

Ebbinghaus, H. (1885). *Uber das Gedachtnis: Untersuchungen zur experimentelen Psychologie.* Leipzig: Duncker und Humbolt.

Hebb, D.O. (1949). *The organization of behavior.* New York: John Wiley & Sons.

Hill, W., Borovsky, D., & Rovee-Collier, C. (1988). Continuities in infant memory development. *Developmental Psychology, 8*, 33–39.

McGeoch, J.A. (1930). The influence of associative value upon the difficulty of non-sense syllable lists. *Journal of Genetic Psychology, 37*, 421–426.

McGeoch, J.A., & McDonald, W.T. (1931). Meaningful relation and retroactive inhibition. *American Journal of Psychology, 43*, 579–588.

Mishkin, M., & Murray, E.A. (1994). Stimulus recognition. *Current Opinion in Neurobiology, 4*, 200–206.

Olton, D.S. (1978). Characteristics of spatial memory. In S.H. Hulse, H. Fowler, & W.K. Honig (Eds.), *Cognitive processes in animal behavior.* Hillsdale, NJ: Lawrence Erlbaum Associates.

Peterson, L., & Peterson, M.J. (1959). Short-term retention of individual verbal items. *Journal of Experimental Psychology, 58*, 193–198.

Romski, M.A., Sevcik, R.A., Robinson, B., & Bakeman, R. (1994). Adult-directed communications of youth with mental retardation using the system for augmenting language. *Journal of Speech and Hearing Research, 37,* 617–628.

Romski, M.A., Sevcik, R.A., & Wilkinson, K.M. (1994). Peer-directed communicative interactions of augmented language learners with mental retardation. *American Journal on Mental Retardation, 98,* 527–538.

Rovee-Collier, C.K., Sullivan, M.W., Enright, M., Lucas, D., & Fagen, J.W. (1980). Reactivation of infant memory. *Science, 208,* 1159–1161.

Schacter, D. (1987). Implicit memory: History and current status. *Journal of Experimental Psychology: Learning, Memory, and Cognition, 13,* 501–518.

Spear, N.E., & Riccio, D.C. (1994). *Memory: Phenomena and principles.* Boston: Allyn and Bacon.

Squire, L.R. (1992). Memory and the hippocampus: A synthesis from findings with rats, monkeys, and humans. *Psychological Review, 99,* 195–231.

Thorburn, W.M. (1918). The myth of Occam's razor. *Mind, 27,* 345–353.

Tulving, E. (1972). Episodic and semantic memory. In E. Tulving & W. Donaldson (Eds.), *Organization of memory* (pp. 382–404). New York: Academic Press.

Tulving, E. (1983). *Elements of episodic memory.* New York: Oxford University Press.

Underwood, B.J. (1954). Speed of learning and amount retained: A consideration of methodology. *Psychological Bulletin, 51,* 276–282.

IV

EXECUTIVE FUNCTION

Executive function is a construct that is explored in detail in this section. The number of chapters devoted to the topic reflect its complexity and its associations and interactions with other constructs, such as attention and memory, as well as its resistance to a single conceptualization or definition. Consider that executive function has also been discussed widely in the literature under the rubric of metacognition or mental control processes, thus adding to the complexity of the topic. Nevertheless, executive function is viewed as a human trait that is critical to attention, memory, and learning, and it is the central importance of executive function in human development, as viewed through the lens of an information processing perspective, that is addressed by Borkowski and Burke in Chapter 14. In Chapter 15, Denckla provides a neuropsychological analysis of executive function, and Hayes and associates examine the topic from a behavioral perspective in Chapter 16. Linkages between executive function and attention are addressed by Barkley in Chapter 17, while Pennington and colleagues elucidate linkages between executive function and memory in Chapter 18. The role of instruction in the development of metacognitive instruction to enhance learning is well articulated by Graham and Harris in Chapter 19. Eslinger's excellent and informative summary of the work covered in this section is provided in Chapter 20 and is unique in its ability to synthesize the points that have been presented.

14

THEORIES, MODELS, AND MEASUREMENTS OF EXECUTIVE FUNCTIONING
An Information Processing Perspective

John G. Borkowski and Jennifer E. Burke

Perhaps the most appealing, yet least understood, aspect of cognition and metacognition is executive functioning (Weinert & Kluwe, 1987). The appeal of executive-like constructs rests in their potential for explaining the maintenance and generalization of behaviors across time and settings. For instance, executive processing seems useful in explaining the transfer of higher-level strategies across dissimilar settings and domains of expertise. It is no wonder that Belmont (1978) recognized executive functioning as the hallmark of intelligence.

Executive functioning spans the extremes of individual differences in human ability. Children who are gifted apparently have an abundance of the process (Sternberg & Davidson, 1986); children with retardation have little of it (Borkowski & Kurtz, 1987). Sternberg (1985, 1987) has argued, within the framework of his triarchic theory of intelligence, that metacomponents (i.e., processes similar to executive functioning) differentiate general giftedness from more restricted or specific forms of giftedness and distinguish students who are gifted from students with normal achievement, who are in turn differentiated from students with learning delays. Superior metacomponential functioning results in exceptionally high performance on IQ and school achievement tests. Immature development is linked with poor performance. Consider Sternberg's (1985) analysis regarding the importance of the initial role of metacomponents, figuring out the nature of a task:

> First, consider the metacomponent of defining the nature of a problem. This metacomponent is critical to those problems on intelligence tests for which the problem structure is not transparent. For example, in mathematical reasoning problems that are verbally presented, such as are found on the mathematical section of the Scholastic Aptitude Test, figuring out exactly what is being asked is critical to correct performance. Often,

distractors are purposely generated so as to be the right answers to the wrong prob-lems—that is problems that might have been asked, given the information in the prob-lem, but that weren't. Similarly, in complex abstract reasoning problems, such as Raven Progressive Matrix problems, the examinee has to figure out exactly what is being asked, and what could constitute a permissible completion of a matrix of geometric forms. (pp. 143–144)

Sternberg's (1987) claim about individual differences and the executive is complex: Metacomponents are deficient in individuals with mental retardation but are not the defining characteristics of students with learning disabilities. Sim-ilarly, superior metacomponential functioning (such as defining a problem or se-lecting a strategy) differentiates students with general giftedness from those with average talent but does not characterize giftedness confined to specific domains such as art, math, and music. Thus, metacomponents (i.e., the major processes in executive functioning) play important roles in understanding subtle differences associated with the extremes of human performance, especially on challenging, novel tasks. The concept of executive functioning also has appeal at the neu-ropsychological level, where the complexities of frontal lobe functioning are of-ten reflected in higher-order behaviors, presumably under the control of execu-tive-like processes.

This chapter attempts to clarify the role of executive functioning as used in extant psychological theories, addresses the definitional and measurement issues that seem to have hindered research progress, and presents a sampling of infor-mation-processing–based theories and promising research approaches. Finally, points of contact between executive processing, planning, and regulation and be-tween attention, memory, and executive functioning will be analyzed in order to define a research agenda.

INFORMATION PROCESSING
THEORIES OF EXECUTIVE FUNCTION

Although the major components of executive functioning are by no means agreed upon, most researchers would concur that the three components represented in Figure 14.1 are essential. The first, and perhaps most essential, component is task analysis. This aspect of the executive is critical because its proper execution is essential for the occurrence of the second essential activity—strategy selection. The third most widely studied attribute of executive processing, strategy moni-toring, has a long and substantial history in developmental, educational, and cog-nitive psychology (Borkowski, Milstead, & Hale, 1988). Another component—strategy revision—is closely linked to strategy selection and is the least understood aspect of the executive, probably because of the dearth of tasks that allow for the measurement of continuous changes in the processes that determine successful performance. We turn now to a review of several theoretical positions that relate to the interrelationships among the major components of executive functioning as well as their connections with other aspects of cognition.

Figure 14.1. Major attributes of executive functioning.

The Role of Executive Functioning in Metacognitive Theory

The central role of executive functioning in explaining higher-order behaviors, especially the generalization of newly acquired skills and strategies, is best observed in the development of metacognitive theories (Pressley, Borkowski, & Schneider, 1990; Sternberg, 1985). In an attempt to define the multiple interacting characteristics of competent information processing, Borkowski and Muthukrishna (1992) have outlined a set of behaviors that might be common to sophisticated learners. An individual who is a good information processor would possess the following skills and beliefs, most of which are related causally or correlationally to executive functioning and which help to situate the concept from a metacognitive perspective:

1. Knows a large number of learning strategies
2. Understands when, where, and why these strategies are important
3. Selects and monitors strategies wisely and is extremely reflective and planful
4. Adheres to an incremental view regarding the growth of mind
5. Believes in carefully deployed effort
6. Is intrinsically motivated and task-oriented and has mastery goals
7. Does not fear failure—in fact, realizes that failure is essential for success—hence, is not anxious about tests but sees them as learning opportunities
8. Has concrete, multiple images of "possible selves," both hoped for and feared selves in the near and distant future
9. Knows a great deal about many topics and has rapid access to that knowledge
10. Has a history of being supported in all of these characteristics by parents, schools, and society at large

Borkowski and Muthukrishna (1992) have provided a description of the development of executive functioning as it emerges from the learning of lower-level cognitive skills and becomes linked to positive motivational states. This description focuses on the events in stimulating environments that assist a child in the development of executive skills.

First, the child is taught to use a learning strategy and, with repetition, comes to learn about the attributes of that strategy (this is called specific strategy knowledge). These attributes include the effectiveness of the strategy, the range of its appropriate applications, and its proper use with a variety of tasks. Figure 14.2 shows how a simple strategy (such as repetition), in isolation from the rest of the metacognitive system, can be expected to produce an improvement in performance.

Next, the child learns other strategies and repeats them in multiple contexts. In this way, specific strategy knowledge is enlarged and enriched. Figure 14.3 presents a schematic showing the emergence of a number of specific strategies. The child comes to understand when, where, and how to deploy each strategy.

Third, the child gradually develops the capacity to select strategies appropriate for some tasks (but not others) and to fill in knowledge gaps by monitoring performance, especially when essential strategy components have not been adequately learned. At this stage, higher-order *executive processes* emerge. This is also the beginning of self-regulation, the basis for adaptive learning and thinking. Figure 14.4 shows the relationship of executive processes to specific strategies. Initially, the function of the executive is to analyze the task at hand and to select

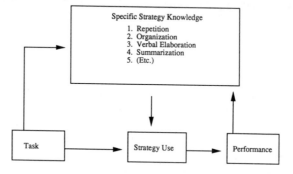

Figure 14.2. A primitive view of the strategy use-performance relationship.

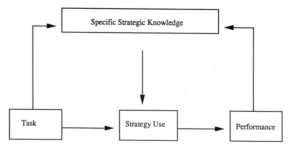

Figure 14.3. Multiple strategies and performance.

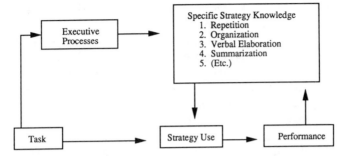

Figure 14.4. Executive functioning and strategy use.

an appropriate strategy; later during the course of learning, its role shifts to strategy monitoring and revision activities.

Fourth, as strategic and executive processes become refined, the child comes to recognize the general utility and importance of being strategic and to form beliefs about self-efficacy. Children learn to attribute successful (and unsuccessful) learning outcomes to effort expended in strategy deployment rather than to luck and to understand that mental competencies can be enhanced through self-directed actions. In this way, the metacognitive model integrates cognitive acts (in the form of strategy use) with their motivational causes and consequences. The sense of self-efficacy flows from individual strategic events and eventually returns to energize strategy selection and monitoring decisions (i.e., executive processes). Figure 14.5 suggests that, after most important cognitive acts, the child is provided with or infers feedback about the successfulness of performance and its specific cause(s). This feedback is essential for shaping

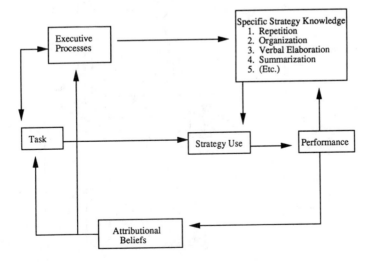

Figure 14.5. Motivational correlates and causes of strategy use.

personal–motivational states, which in turn energize the executive processes necessary for strategy selection and monitoring.

Fifth, general knowledge about the world as well as domain-specific knowledge (e.g., mathematics) accumulates. Such knowledge is often sufficient to solve problems, even without the aid of strategies. In these situations, executive processes such as strategy selection are unnecessary, although some related motivational components may remain functional and important (see Figure 14.6).

Last, crystallized visions into the future help the child form a number of "hoped-for" and "feared" possible selves (Markus & Nurius, 1986). These visions provide the impetus for achieving important short-term as well as long-term goals, such as becoming a "competent student" in order to eventually become a "successful lawyer" (cf. Day, Borkowski, Dietmeyer, Howsepian, & Saenz, 1992). In this way, the self-system takes on a futuristic perspective, providing goals and incentives that stimulate the operation of the entire metacognitive system. The complete metacognitive model, including the self-system and the domain-specific knowledge "bypass," is presented in Figure 14.6.

The absence of vivid, dynamic, and functional possible selves may inhibit the emergence of executive processing, especially in challenging, demanding situations (i.e., a failure to aspire to a college career may not only restrict the choice of college preparatory courses but also produce less reflective, deliberate

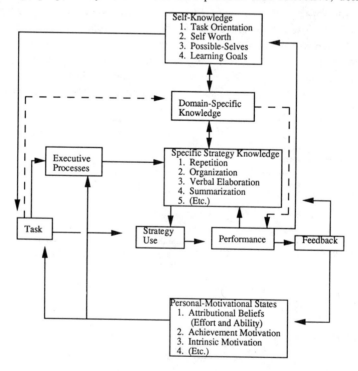

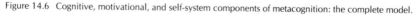

Figure 14.6 Cognitive, motivational, and self-system components of metacognition: the complete model.

decision-making activities in many academically related areas). Hence, an immature developmental connection between the emerging self and executive systems likely prolongs or exacerbates academic difficulties for students who are underachievers or have learning impairments. When viewed from this perspective, learning difficulties are often the result of insufficient maturity in the development of the executive or regulatory system.

Butterfield and Albertson's Theory of Executive Functioning

Butterfield and Albertson (1995) have developed a new theory of cognition in which executive functioning plays a central role. In their model, cognition, metacognition, and executive functioning are the three major components (see Figure 14.7). The cognitive level consists of all the knowledge and strategies that exist in long-term memory; this reservoir of information is critical for effective problem solving. The metacognitive level is aware of this level of cognition and contains models of the various cognitive processes as well as an understanding of how knowledge and strategies interconnect. Executive functioning coordinates these two levels of cognition by monitoring and controlling the use of the knowledge and strategies in concordance with the metacognitive level.

Butterfield and Albertson (1995) make use of a balance scale task as an example that helps differentiate the three concepts as well as explain their relationships. In this task a child is shown a balance scale that is latched to remain level.

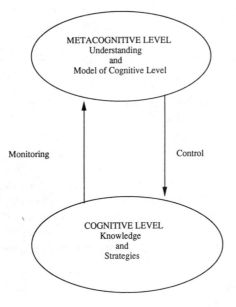

Figure 14.7 Contents of and relations between cognitive, metacognitive, and executive levels. (From Butterfield, E.C., & Albertson, L.R. [1995]. On making cognitive theory more general and developmentally pertinent. In F. Weinert & W. Schneider [Eds.], *Research on memory development* (pp. 73–99). Hillsdale, N.J.: Lawrence Erlbaum Associates; reprinted by permission.)

Various weights are placed at varied distances from the fulcrum. Before the scale is unlatched, the child is asked to predict which of the sides will go down or if the scale will remain balanced. Feedback concerning the accuracy of the prediction is then given.

Mature thinkers approach the balance beam task with the knowledge that weight and distance can be measured, torque can be calculated by multiplying weight by distance, and the side with the greater torque will be lowered. They also have the strategies necessary to measure the weights and distances, to calculate torque, to contrast these measures, and to make a prediction. Their metacognitive levels contain a model of the interaction between knowledge and strategies and an understanding of that model.

Executive functioning is shown to be crucial throughout this process because it monitors and controls all the steps necessary for a correct solution. It keeps track of the steps that have been completed and what step needs to be done next. It realizes that the goal is to predict the direction of the shift in weight and monitors the various steps along the way. It monitors processing events such as "the weights on the left have been counted, but the weights on the right have not." Finally, it notes which of the measurements was larger so that a prediction can be made. Executive functioning also manipulates knowledge and strategies to obtain the information suggested by monitoring and is important in the assessment of accuracy and utility: It can monitor and correct the measurements and calculations throughout the problem-solving process as well as assess the accuracy of predictions. Information feedback, based on incorrect predictions, often leads to the development of a more efficient strategy and a revised metacognitive model.

The concept of executive functioning allows for the suggestion of a more general theory of cognition than the previous task-specific theories. Butterfield and Albertson (1995) posit that individuals are able to create mental models about their own cognitions based on their day-to-day problem-solving activities. They believe that these models are similar to those developed by scientists through prolonged, detailed task analyses. All of these self-generated models exist in direct relation to the knowledge and strategies present at the cognitive level. In short, executive functioning integrates these two levels of cognition and coordinates the functions of the various models throughout the metacognitive level. This integration of task-specific models, made possible by executive functioning, eventually leads to a personalized (and unified) theory of cognition. The specific research program, designed by Butterfield and Albertson (1995) to address this complex theory of cognitive development, is presented in a later section of this chapter.

Bransford and Stein's Ideal Problem Solver

Bransford and Stein (1993) have incorporated aspects of executive functioning into their model of the IDEAL problem solver. The acronym IDEAL is used to symbolize the skilled components in problem solving: 1) *identify* an important problem to be solved; 2) *define* the subgoals involved in solving the problem; 3) *explore* possible approaches to the problem (that is, select a set of potential strategies); 4) *anticipate* potential outcomes before acting on the best initial approach; and 5) *look* back and learn from the entire problem-solving experience. Because these five steps are used flexibly by expert problem solvers, they do not always occur in the same fixed order, and each step is not necessary for all problem-solving tasks.

These five steps, proposed by Bransford and Stein (1993), closely resemble the components of executive functioning discussed earlier. The first steps—problem identification and definition—are a form of task analysis. The discovery and definition of an existing problem shape the next steps—exploring approaches and anticipating outcomes. In these steps, various strategies are considered and the best alternative is chosen. The last step of the IDEAL problem-solving strategy involves looking back and learning from prior efforts. In the ongoing process of problem solution, this step is at the heart of strategy monitoring and revision.

Bransford and his colleagues have incorporated aspects of the IDEAL problem solver into their video-based technology research. The Cognition and Technology Group at Vanderbilt University has developed a technology that anchors and situates instruction in shared environments, thus permitting sustained exploration by students and teachers (Bransford, Sherwood, Hassebring, Kinzer, & Williams, 1990). Students experience the value of exploring the same setting from multiple perspectives (e.g., as a scientist, historian, and mathematician). As they discover their own issues to explore in these enriched environments, they communicate their ideas to other students and presumably develop analytical skills as a result of their problem-solving activities. What are difficult to discern in the research of the Vanderbilt group are the precise sets of metacognitive skills that emerge as a result of these shared experiences. Are specific problem-solving strategies developed? Are higher-level planning, task analytical, or monitoring skills (i.e., executive-level skills) enhanced? Are specific beliefs about self-efficacy and the personal challenge to develop one's own mind explicitly fostered? For the most part, the assessment approach used by the Vanderbilt group does not allow definitive answers to these questions about how enriched environments stimulate executive development. We suspect, however, that a comprehensive video technology approach to instruction influences the emergence of planning and executive skills and also enhances positive motivational beliefs about self-efficacy.

Scholnick and Friedman's Developmental Theory of Planning

Another approach to executive processing is Scholnick and Friedman's (1993) model of the development of planning, which has incorporated several aspects of the executive necessary for planning. These include 1) problem representation, in which the problem is defined by comparing the current state with the desired end state; 2) goal selection, in which the desired end state is chosen; 3) decision to plan, in which a judgment is made to analyze rather than act; 4) strategy choice, in which a method of attack is formulated; 5) strategy execution; and 6) monitoring the effectiveness of prior actions.

Scholnick and Friedman (1993) argue that the essential components of planning, and their unique developmental sequences, depend on the task being analyzed. For instance, performance on the Tower of Hanoi task reflects representational and monitoring demands, whereas story comprehension depends more strongly on social comprehension and monitoring. Because many everyday plans, such as running errands, have prepackaged components and take place in less controllable environments, affective and attributional components likely influence the choice of goals and the strategy decisions related to planning.

MEASUREMENT ISSUES AND RESEARCH PROGRESS

Perhaps the greatest problem hindering research on executive functioning is a failure to find consensus on a general definition of the construct and then to move from the general definition to a number of operationally specific definitions. These more specific definitions would, of course, be embedded in a variety of experimental or correlational contexts and would be confined by the boundaries of the theoretical position under scrutiny.

Toward a General Definition

The lack of progress in research on executive functioning may well be due to the failure to establish shared meaning in psychological, neuropsychological, and educational realms of inquiry. This failure has led to theoretical arguments arising out of construct ambiguity and has stymied sustained research progress on the nature and dynamics of executive processing.

Since executive functioning can only be observed in terms of changes or alterations in lower-level behaviors, it likely will always be inferred as a remote, mediational process rather than observed directly. An important distinction exists here among the following information processing events: 1) performance (such as recall accuracy), 2) a process that guides successful performance (such as the use of an organizational strategy on a free recall task with category membership or a cumulative rehearsal strategy on an ordered recall task), and 3) the executive or higher-level processes that might be needed to select and monitor the strategy. Although direct measures of performance and process events can be obtained, it is difficult, perhaps experimentally impossible, to obtain on-line measures of changes in executive processing. Butterfield and Belmont (1977), however, have provided a useful general definition of the executive that might serve as a point of reference for future research efforts.

The concept of executive functioning is operationally identified as follows: "A subject spontaneously changes a control process or sequence of control processes as a reasonable response to an objective change in an information processing task" (Butterfield & Belmont, 1977, p. 284). In other words, if Strategy A is used with Task X, and if Task Y is then introduced, the subject is said to employ executive functioning if Strategy B replaces A. Or if Strategy A on Task X is found to be ineffective and hence is replaced by Strategy B during the course of problem solving, the substitution becomes an instance of executive functioning. In this sense, transfer or generalization tests indirectly measure the adequacy of the executive system in that changes in materials and/or tasks from the training to transfer phases provide an opportunity for executive processes such as strategy selection or revision to occur.

Given this broad perspective on the general definition of executive functioning, it is possible to analyze a number of experimental contexts that have been used to study the executive. Most of these examples are derived from attempts to test metacognitive theory and its interrelated components (cf. Borkowski, Milstead, & Hale, 1988; Pressley, Borkowski, & Schneider, 1990). We turn now to a series of studies on students who are gifted, have mental retardation, and have learning disabilities; these studies share a concern for identifying executive functioning, for determining its relative contribution to performance, and for locating its correlates, causes, and effects.

Executive Processes and General Giftedness

Most of the conclusions about executive functioning in students who are gifted have been inferential rather than the result of direct manipulation of higher-order processes. For instance, Borkowski and Peck (1986) hypothesized that differences in strategy generalization for students who are gifted and students with typical achievement would be due to superior executive processes in the former group. To substantiate this claim, third-grade children who differed in intelligence were presented with multiple memory tasks (paired-associate learning, sort-recall, and alphabet search) and then given different amounts of strategy instruction—complete or enriched; incomplete or partial; and no instructions. Following enriched instructions on the paired-associates task, IQ-related differences emerged only on the "far"-generalization tasks that bore little resemblance to the training tasks. It was *inferred* that the capacity to match the newly acquired interrogative strategy with a structurally dissimilar generalization task was the characteristic of executive processing that led to the superior performance of children who were gifted.

The influence of executive processing on strategy transfer was even more pronounced—but perhaps less inferential—following minimal strategy training. As hypothesized, children who were gifted realized the effectiveness of the strategy and applied it appropriately even without the aid of complete, explicit instructions. Significant metamemory-strategy use correlations were also obtained following incomplete training, suggesting that children who were gifted engaged in more metacognitive–executive processing than did children who were not gifted. Differences in strategy use were again found on a far-generalization task: As had occurred with the maximally trained strategy, children who were gifted were more successful in implementing the minimally trained strategy in the face of new task demands.

Do children who are gifted invent strategies on their own following repeated experience with a task? We suspected an indirect effect of executive processing on the untrained alphabet search task: That is, explicit strategy training on the other two tasks should have enhanced strategy selection skills and thus promoted the development of an appropriate strategy on the untrained search task. Indeed, as the untrained task was presented a second, third, and fourth time, the form of the strategy (organized recall) improved, as did accuracy. By the fifth and final session, children who were gifted had developed a highly systematic search strategy.

The data from the Borkowski and Peck (1986) study can be interpreted within metacognitive theory. Executive function was especially applicable in understanding how the experimenter-generated strategies were put to use in new learning contexts. When a child was well trained and a strategy automatic, metamemory was minimally related to performance variability, except on far-transfer tests where ability-related differences in strategy use were found. In contrast, when children received incomplete strategy training, metamemory predicted strategy use and recall differences on both maintenance and generalization tests. Children with superior metacognition generally retained the strategy, applied it without prompting on transfer tasks, and modified the strategy to meet changes in task demands on far-generalization tests. Although the concept of executive functioning is plausible in accounting for these findings, the inferences drawn require a "leap of faith." That is, metacognitively based explanations were only one of several competing theories (other possibilities include enhanced speed of processing or greater working memory capacity).

Executive Functioning in Students with Learning Impairments

There are two methodological approaches used in the direct investigation of executive processing. The first involves the explicit manipulation of the components of the executive (such as instructions in analyzing task demands, selecting a strategy, or analyzing its effectiveness). These aspects of executive functioning have usually been taught using self-instructional methods (Meichenbaum & Goodman, 1971). The second approach is to vary systematically the recall requirements of the to-be-learned task and to observe whether and when students detect small changes in task demands as evidenced by shifts in their study strategies.

Self-Instructions and Executive Processing   In order to use self-regulation routines, a student must perform some or all of the following steps: analyze task demands, select a strategy that has been successful with similar tasks in the past, accommodate the strategy to the new task, monitor its effectiveness, devise a more efficient or viable approach if necessary, and judge when the problem has been solved correctly or is unsolvable for the time being. Executive processing, which can be taught using self-instructional methods (Borkowski & Varnhagen, 1984), enables the child to approach problems in an orderly rather than a chaotic manner. The rationale behind the success of self-instructional training may be attributed to the fact that it provides internal cues to students who often do not spontaneously generate strategies while learning novel tasks (Asarnow & Meichenbaum, 1979). However, once a student learns selection and monitoring skills, he or she gains control in areas previously externally directed by others. As control is ceded from teacher to child, higher-order executive processes become internalized (Day & Hall, 1987).

As an illustration of the potential of self-instruction for developing executive skills, consider a study that was designed to promote generalization. Borkowski and Varnhagen (1984) instructed children with mental retardation to use anticipation and paraphrase strategies and then tested for generalization on a gist-recall task (cf. Brown, Campione, & Barclay, 1979). Children in the experimental conditions received training embedded in either self-instructional or didactic formats. In the self-instructional condition, they received strategy initiation and modification training. The intention of the self-instruction manipulation was to promote the development of higher-order implementation skills. Results showed that children in both experimental groups were more strategic and recalled more items on the generalization and maintenance tasks than those in the control group. Several children in the self-instruction condition also used the self-instructional strategy-implementation routine, resulting in sizable performance gains. In contrast, no children in the other two conditions reported using higher-order strategies. Thus, instructions in strategy selection and modification eventually promoted generalization for some children in the self-instructional condition (Borkowski & Varnhagen, 1984).

Similarly, Kurtz and Borkowski (1987) instructed children who were impulsive and children who were reflective in the use of executive skills in conjunction with prose-summarization strategies. Children in the two trained groups were taught a questioning strategy for use on a prose-summarization task. In addition, children in an executive group were given metacognitive information about the value of using a reflective approach to problem solving, along with training in strategy selection, monitoring, and modification. Posttraining-summarization scores showed that children in both experimental groups were more strategic than children in an uninstructed control group but that executive training provided an additional boost: Superior performance was demonstrated by children who received summarization training together with information about superordinate processing. This effect was consistent across subgroups who differed in cognitive styles. That is, children with impulsive and reflective behaviors benefited equally from a training package that integrated executive skills (taught via self-instructional methods) with specific strategies.

Changing Task Demands and Executive Skills One of the more interesting studies of executive functioning has been conducted by Belmont, Ferretti, and Mitchell (1982), who studied strategy invention in adolescents with retardation. Forty students with mild retardation and 32 students without mental retardation were given eight practice trials on a self-paced memory problem with lists of either letters or words. They were required to order their recall, first giving terminal list items, then the initial items. Subgroups of solvers and nonsolvers were identified at each IQ level on the basis of recall accuracy. Interestingly, direct measures of mnemonic activity showed that solvers, at both IQ levels, tended to fit a theoretically ideal memorization method as learning progressed. Solvers invented the "best" input strategy to meet the demands of a structured recall over trials. That is, on early trials for both groups, the correspondence (or fit) of the actual strategy to the ideal strategy was uncorrelated with recall accuracy. On late trials, however, strategy fit and recall were highly correlated at each IQ level and across levels. Poor learners, called "nonsolvers," failed to invent mature strategies. In contrast, solvers utilized a more complicated and appropriate strategy to guide their memorization efforts.

These results support a problem-solving explanation, based on executive processing, of individual differences in the memory performance of people with and without mental retardation. Some adolescents with retardation, and even more typical adolescents, were extremely successful in their use of executive skills, creating an encoding strategy sufficient to meet the demands of the recall requirements, without explicit aid from the experimenter (Belmont et al., 1982). These findings suggest that executive skills are important for efficient and effective learning because they assist in the implementation of lower-level strategies. Next, we consider an alternate and perhaps more analytical methodological approach to studying executive functioning.

Single-Subject Designs, Changing Task Demands, and Executive Processing Because it is difficult to assess the transfer of skills on multiple tasks for individuals who vary widely in skills and ability, we have begun to use single-subject designs to study the generalization of strategies (in the face of changes in task requirements) as a function of the amount of self-instructional training. The advantage of this approach is that we can systematically train strategies for each subject, manipulate the extent of self-regulating instructions, and observe changes in strategy use in close correspondence with changing recall requirements. As a control for individual differences, we selected a pair of identical twins with mild mental retardation whose learning histories and talents were highly similar. The aim was to determine the extent of strategy generalization within the domain of memory as a function of newly learned strategies and skills in self-regulation.

The training program included executive skills and specific strategies, instructed during the learning of three memory tasks. There were four training sessions for each task. One twin (S_1) received both executive and strategy training on all three tasks. The other twin (S_2) received executive skills training on the last two tasks as well as specific strategy instruction relevant to the three tasks. Both students were pretested on all tasks in Session 1; posttests were administered following training on each task (Sessions 6, 11, 16), and generalization was assessed in the final session.

Executive skills were trained in a self-instruction format in which each twin asked himself questions concerning the task. The questions were designed to assess task demands and locate an appropriate strategy. Questions included: "What should I try to remember?" "What order do I need to remember them in?" "Is this like anything I have done before?" "How have I studied problems like this one?" "How should I study this time?" The twins were trained in self-instruction in the first two sessions of each task and also during the strategy training of the third and fourth sessions of each task. As part of the self-instructions, the child suggested a way to study, which the experimenter modified as needed during strategy instruction to arrive at the appropriate strategy. The experimenter then modeled the strategy and prompted the child to use it.

This procedure was continued across three self-paced memory tasks. The tasks involved looking at seven pictures of common objects, one at a time. The first task allowed the child to look at the pictures in any order and as many times as desired. A very simple strategy was used on this task: Children were taught to check and make sure they knew all of the pictures before signaling they were ready to recall.

The second memory task required that each picture be viewed in order only once. Each child was taught to cumulatively rehearse in groups. For example, the list "comb, flag, dog, tree, bed, candle, ball," would be studied as follows: 1) comb; 2) comb, flag; 3) comb, flag, dog; 4) comb, flag, dog, tree, comb, flag, dog, and tree; 5) bed; 6) bed, candle; 7) bed, candle, ball, bed, candle, ball. The cumulative rehearsal strategy is especially useful in preventing memory losses in secondary memory (forgetting of the first few items).

The final and most complex task—circular recall—also required that each picture be viewed in order only once. During testing, items 5, 6, and 7 were to be recalled first, followed by items 1, 2, 3, and 4. The "ideal" rehearsal strategy was similar to the previous task in that items 1–4 were to be cumulatively rehearsed. However, because items 5, 6, and 7 were to be recalled first, they were to be labeled during the study period. Rehearsal should have followed this pattern: 1, 1–2, 1–3, 1–4, 5, 6, 7, a pattern referred to as cumulative rehearsal with a fast finish.

On Days 1, 6, 11, and 16, the twins were tested for strategy use on all three tasks, without instructions. The final session assessed generalization of the circular recall strategy by altering the task to require recall on items 6 and 7 followed by items 1–5. The change in recall requirements constituted an occasion that required executive processing (Butterfield & Belmont, 1977). That is, task demands changed unexpectedly. The main question was the following: On encountering a new learning situation, did either child alter his study strategy?

Study-time patterns provided us with a relatively direct measure of strategy use on each task. The most striking patterns were for Subject 1, who received three sets of self-instructions. As can be seen in Figure 14.8, Subject 1 altered his cumulative rehearsal–fast-finish strategy to meet the task demands in the general-

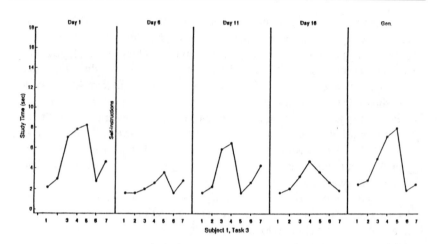

Figure 14.8 Study time patterns for Subject 1 for multiple presentations of circular recall tests, prior to and subsequent to strategy training on Day 16, as a function of three trials of self-instructional training about executive processes.

ization phase. In the circular recall task, he changed from the instructed pattern (rehearse items 1–4, label items 5–7) to a pattern reflecting the new output order (rehearse items 1–5, label items 6–7). Thus, Subject 1, who received self-instructions on all tasks, showed excellent generalization within the domain of a trained strategy. Apparently, executive processing was essential for his near-perfect generalization of the cumulative rehearsal–fast-finish strategy. It was, however, necessary to train executive processes across three tasks to produce this facilitating effect. This conclusion is based on the fact that the identical twin (Subject 2) failed to show the same generalization successes (see Figure 14.9). These results are preliminary and obviously warrant further investigation as to their replicabil-

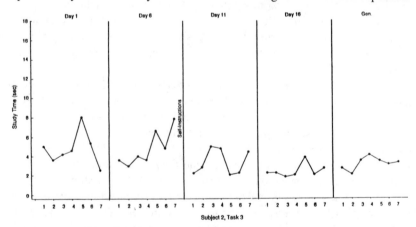

Figure 14.9 Study time patterns for Subject 2 for multiple presentations of circular recall tests, prior to and subsequent to strategy training on Day 16, as a function of two occasions of self-instructions about executive processes.

ity. They suggest, however, the efficacy of training executive process, using single-S designs and self-instructions, as well as the need for multiple instances of instruction in order to achieve generalizable skills, even within a highly restricted domain such as memory.

Executive Functions, Self-Attributions, and Beliefs About Mind

Executive functioning is a powerful determinant of strategy use. Yet, there are motivational factors that influence executive functioning and alter subsequent specific strategy use. The motivational correlates of executive functioning include positive self-esteem, an internal locus of control, and effort-related attributional beliefs about success and failure.

We have hypothesized that distinct beliefs develop as the result of each child's learning history to help the child "understand" and explain his or her own successes and failures. These beliefs include, but are not limited to, program-specific and general antecedent attributions (Reid & Borkowski, 1987). The former arise out of unique, restricted learning experiences and tend to be domain-specific at least for younger students (Marsh, 1986). The latter—historically rooted, cumulative, and transsituational—might be expected to develop over a longer period of time, in which successful learning experiences have transpired in multiple areas of learning and memory.

Based on the assumption that self-attributions are tightly woven to the use of strategies, the phenomenon of generalization should be maximized by training routines that focus not only on specific strategies but also on the executive processes necessary for their implementation and corresponding beliefs about self-efficacy. Reid and Borkowski (1987) demonstrated how these multiple types of metacognitive training could be combined to produce what appears on the surface as "spontaneous" strategy use. The study was designed to assess the effects of training specific strategy knowledge, teaching executive functioning as part of self-control training, and attributional retraining. The influence of this complex form of training on short- and long-term strategy transfer, as well as on impulsivity in classroom settings, was assessed with children with hyperactivity and learning disabilities.

Three treatment conditions were compared: self-control, self-control plus attributions, and control. In the self-control condition, the instructor modeled self-verbalization procedures (e.g., "first look to see how the problem might be solved; always stop and think before responding"). These self-control procedures were taught in the context of specific strategy instructions that focused on the use of interrogative–associative mediators appropriate for paired-associate learning and a clustering–rehearsal strategy appropriate for a recall–readiness task in which sorting was the most appropriate form of rehearsal. The most important condition—self-control plus attributions—contained the same self-control and strategy instructions as the self-control condition. In addition, children in this condition were given attributional training designed to enhance both antecedent and program-specific self-attributions. *Antecedent attribution* training took the form of a discussion that focused on pervasive beliefs about the causes of successes and failures. *Program-specific attribution* consisted of feedback about the relationship between strategic behavior (or its absence) and actual performance during paired-associate learning. That is, individual items were shown to be correct or incorrect depending upon whether the appropriate strategy had been used as instructed. The control condition received the same amount of strategy training as the experimental condition but did not receive self-control or attributional training.

Widespread strategy generalization occurred on a test conducted 3 weeks later in the self-control plus attributions condition. More important, the use of lower- and higher-level strategies was apparent at a 10-month follow-up on laboratory tests and was also observed in the classroom. Attributional beliefs, metamemory and, to some degree, impulsive behavior were significantly altered in the metacognitively complex condition. We believe the integration of executive processes and motivational beliefs were essential for producing generalized learning and problem solving, perhaps setting in motion a chain of events that enhanced learning activities beyond the confines of the experiment proper. This highly desirable chain of complex behaviors can be attributed to three factors: 1) detailed information about multiple strategies; 2) executive procedures useful for implementing those strategies; and 3) insights about the importance of effort and personal causality in leading to successful learning, memory, and problem-solving performance.

PROMISING RESEARCH APPROACHES

In the review of the research literature, a dominant methodological approach to the study of executive processing has emerged. This approach is characterized by 1) a tendency to use the instructional method, 2) an interpretative framework in which executive processing is inferred from changes in control processing rather than from changes in performance, 3) the use of transfer designs in which the novel use of previously acquired strategy serves as the basis for inferring task analytical and strategy selection skills, and 4) shifts in continuous-performance measures as signals that monitoring activities have occurred. These methodological characteristics have sometimes been used in combination, as in the Reid and Borkowski (1987) study of strategy training, attributional retraining, and executive instructions.

We now consider two more recent and promising approaches to the analysis of executive function. The first, and perhaps boldest, approach involves the transfer of higher-level control and monitoring skills across widely discrepant domains (e.g., memory, scientific inference, and analogical reasoning). The second approach—correlational in nature—involves the use of designs amenable to causal modeling techniques.

Butterfield and Albertson's Instructional Approach

As discussed earlier, Butterfield and Albertson (1995) have outlined a research proposal to examine the emergence of executive functioning and to assess how it facilitates cognitive development. They posit that the first stage of cognitive development is the learning of new knowledge and strategies. As soon as this new information becomes familiar, there is enough room in working memory for executive functioning to take place. Monitoring and control are essential in developing metacognitive understanding and models of cognition. The creation of new models likely increases the knowledge and strategies available at the cognitive level.

Butterfield and Albertson (1995) use instruction as their tool for examining in detail the mechanisms that produce cognitive change. The use of instructions helps clarify the direction of causality among the variables. In order to understand this research approach, a potential experiment—based on the instructional method—is described in some detail.

Initially, two ministudies are used to assess the ability to instruct model creation within two separate domains—memory and scientific reasoning. Each of the experiments follows the same format as that shown in Figure 14.10. First, the subjects are pretested to determine that they have the capabilities to solve all of the test problems but only lack the metacognitive models necessary to guide their problem-solving processes. Figure 14.10 depicts the procedures to be used in the memory domain: All subjects are capable of serial recall but lack the efficient use of strategy needed for circular, free, and position probe recall.

The subjects are split, with both groups learning a strategy to use in problem solving. For example, subjects would be taught a model of circular recall that involves studying the initial items with cumulative rehearsal and then rapidly reviewing the final items (i.e., a cumulative rehearsal with a fast finish strategy). In the test for circular recall, they are asked to retrieve the last few words of a string before retrieving the rest in order. The second, or executive-trained, group receives additional instructions about the rationale behind the model as well as ways to monitor and control their thought processes. In the memory domain, this metacognitive coaching would consist of the reasons why different strategies are more efficient and how to determine which kind of information needs to be rehearsed more actively. All subjects are then given a related problem that is not solvable by the previously taught model. In the memory domain experiment, the test is for a creation of a position probe recall model. In this kind of problem, a subject is given a word and asked to recall the location of that word in a previously rehearsed string. Solution to this problem provides evidence that a new model was created.

The subjects are then taught another model in order to solve a related problem (free recall); again, one group receives additional metacognitive instruction. In free recall, the words can be recalled in any order. In the final step, the subjects

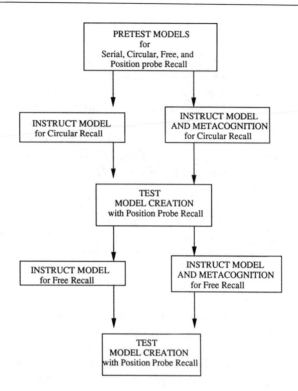

Figure 14.10 Schematic of an experiment on model creation within the memory domain. (From Butterfield, E.C., & Albertson, L.R. [1993, June]. On making cognitive theory more general and developmentally pertinent. Paper presented at a conference on Memory Development, Castle Ringberg, Germany; reprinted by permission.)

are tested for model creation using the same type of problem as before. Data analyses aim to uncover whether the supplemental instructions about understanding, monitoring, and control lead to differences in the speed or quality of model creation.

In the most complex experiment, the subjects are taught models in three different domains and tested for model creation in yet another domain. If metacognitive instructions generalize to the new domain, support for the idea of a unified cognitive theory, as mentioned earlier, is increased. The task-specific models at the metacognitive level are coordinated by executive functioning.

The format for the third experiment is similar to that of the first two. All subjects are pretested for use of models in the domains of memory, scientific reasoning, inferential reasoning, and analogical reasoning. Those subjects that have the skills but not the strategies or models for problem solution are chosen to participate in the study; none of the subjects are experienced in analogical reasoning problems.

Subjects are first instructed in the use of models in the three domains of memory, scientific reasoning, and inferential reasoning. The models used in the memory domain are similar to those validated in experiment one. The scientific reasoning models would be those necessary in the solution of balance scale, pullied train, and shadow projection models. These would be validated in a separate experiment. Letter series completion problems are used to teach a model of inferential reasoning. The order of model instruction is random for each subject. Most important, half of the subjects also receive the metacognitive instructions appropriate for each of the models. The outline of this study can be seen in Figure 14.11.

After each period of instruction, the subjects are tested for use of the models and then for model creation within the domain of analogical reasoning. Analogical reasoning was chosen as the "test domain" because of its importance for learning in the academic areas of mathematics, science, and language; it is assessed by means of problem analogies as well as classic analogies. If supplemental instructions are found to lead to model creation across domains, the data would support the idea that task-specific models can be pooled to form a unified cognitive theory. If this scenario is tenable, executive functioning will have been

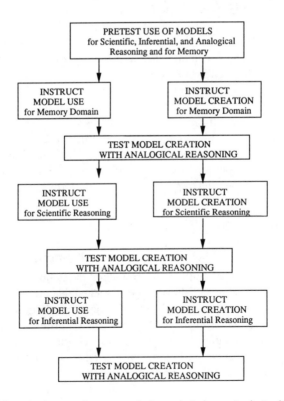

Figure 14.11   Schematic of an experiment on producing analogical reasoning by teaching model use in other domains. (From Butterfield, E.C., & Albertson, L.R. [1993, June]. On making cognitive theory more general and developmentally pertinent. Paper presented at a conference on Memory Development, Castle Ringberg, Germany; reprinted by permission.)

shown to play a critical role in cognitive development—in the form of model creation as well as in the coordination of metacognitive activity.

A Structural Modeling Approach

Structural equation modeling is a sophisticated multivariate technique that has the capacity to test two models simultaneously: a measurement model and a structural model. The measurement model focuses on the relationship between the measured, observed variables and the hypothetical, unobserved constructs the observed variables are supposed to assess. The structural model describes the interrelationships among the constructs. In doing so, the technique allows alternative theoretical positions to be compared. Although structural equation modeling does not confirm the significance of a particular theory, it does provide an indication of a theory's plausibility. Causal modeling holds potential for understanding the interrelationships among executive functioning and other constructs as well as its centrality in models of learning, transfer, and generalization.

For example, Yap and O'Neil (1994) used structural modeling to relate metacognitive knowledge and beliefs about effort and worry to mathematics achievement for 12th graders. The metacognitive construct consisted of four components of planning, self-checking, cognitive strategies, and awareness (i.e., executive skills). Using structural equation modeling, a measurement model and two structural models—one with metacognition as a second-order factor and the other with self-regulation as a third-order factor—were tested. The latter model indicated that all metacognitive components, as well as effort, were explained by this third-order factor. Self-regulation, in turn, positively affected students' academic performance in mathematics. The results further suggested that worry negatively affected students' test performance and not vice versa. Overall, the results of Yap and O'Neil imply that a small set of self-regulation measures, together with worry state, can be used to predict academic performance.

CONCLUSIONS

Executive Functioning, Self-Regulation, and Planning

Part of the terminological confusion surrounding the notion of executive functioning centers on its conceptual overlap with related, but probably distinct, constructs such as self-regulation and planning. These three concepts share a concern for goal-directed actions as instigated by the self. They differ in terms of generality versus specificity, cognitive versus motivational orientations, and frequency of usage in everyday learning and problem solving. To understand their similarities and differences, we will consider several perspectives on self-regulation and planning.

Although the bulk of this review has used the term *executive functioning* to describe the task analytic, strategy selection, and monitoring skills necessary for higher-level problem solving, occasionally we have employed the terms *planning* and *self-regulation* as synonyms for executive processing. This usage betrays the conceptual overlap among the three terms. Although planning and self-regulation have their own extensive research literatures that stretch beyond the scope of the present analysis, it is important to isolate potential points of overlap as well as the uniqueness among the three interrelated constructs—executive functioning, planning, and self-regulation—in order to augment research progress.

A Definition of Planning   Planning seems to necessitate decision making, regulation, and action. For instance, Herbert (personal communication, May 25, 1994) defines planning as follows:

> Planning is a dynamic, transactional process involving the conscious or deliberate specification of a sequence of actions aimed at achieving some problem goal, emphasizing the constantly changing relationship between plans and actions, particularly what effects completed actions have on subsequent plans, goals, and mental representation. It encompasses the choice of overarching life goals, guiding aphorisms, and long-range timetables as well as the dynamic, revisionary processes related to devising ways to attain, elaborate, maintain, monitor, update, and/or abandon these goals and schedules, in varying levels of abstraction.

A Perspective on Self-Regulation   In contrast, self-regulation, which itself is an essential component in the definition of planning, seems to involve the strategies necessary to achieve desired goal states. Furthermore, it is the more intelligent people who seem to utilize regulation more effectively. Mithaug (1993) states that "persons who consistently maximize gain across goal and choice contingencies appear to be more intelligent than those who only occasionally succeed, and . . . they feel more intelligent, too" (p. 159). Thus, intelligent behavior is represented by effective self-regulation, accompanied by a recognition of its significance.

Mithaug's theory of self-regulation has motivational (goals and expectations), cognitive (perceptions, strategies, and skills), and affective (active feedback seeking) components. Its four phases include 1) the identification of a difference between a desired goal state and the actual current state (the smaller the discrepancy between the current and the desired goal states, and the more successful past problem-solving experiences have been—that is, the person has been able to reduce the distance between states—the more likely the individual will expect the maximum gain possible toward reaching the goal); 2) choosing behaviors or strategies that will reduce actual goal discrepancies (i.e., wise choices among options produce maximum gains in performance); 3) effective and efficient resource allocation between information seeking and completing goal-directed tasks; and 4) maximizing goal attainment by optimizing all of the above activities in synchrony.

The strength of Mithaug's (1993) theory lies in its potential to detect individual impairments in the specific components of self-regulation. For instance, individuals with learning difficulties with the same IQ may differ in their identification of actual and goal states, types of choices made to resolve these discrepancies, effectiveness of these responses, or some combination of factors. The successful identification of componential differences can lead to individualized instruction and remediation.

If we compare and contrast the three views of executive functioning, planning, and self-regulation, the following points emerge: 1) Although there is a great deal of conceptual overlap among the terms, planning seems to have the greatest generality, with self-regulation and executive functioning as its major subcomponents. It is the most diverse construct, cutting across unique subject matters and domains. Given its generality, planning seems closely related to general intelligence. 2) Executive functioning, with its focus on task analysis, may be the more specific concept in that it is heavily task-dependent and hence may have greater measurement accuracy. 3) Although goal orientation is essential for both planning and regulation, motivation seems essential for understanding self-regulation and is at its definitional core. 4) The most cognitive-oriented term is executive functioning, because it guides the deployment of lower-level strategies on complex, novel tasks.

Attention, Memory, and Executive Processing

The Role of Inhibition　　The three themes of this text—attention, memory, and executive functioning—are interwoven, especially in terms of their life-span connections. One obvious connection is the limitation imposed on memory and higher-order processing by early appearing deficiencies in attention and perception (cf. Detterman, 1979). For example, deficits in perception and attention, characteristic of moderate and mild forms of mental retardation, often preclude adequate development in other aspects of the cognitive system.

A question arises as to the source of this chain of information processing deficits. One possibility is the shared role played by the inadequate emergence of inhibitory mechanisms. That is, it may be that attention, memory, and executive functioning may all be adversely affected by a failure to inhibit competing stimuli. In this scenario, a failure to learn to inhibit would work to the detriment of different psychological processes, in different ways, and at different stages of the life cycle. Clearly, more research is needed on the role of inhibition across the chain of developmental events that make up information processing during the first 5 years of life.

The Influence of Attention and Memory on the Executive　　The mature development of executive processing depends on the adequate development of early emerging, basic processes. For instance, Butterfield and Albertson (1995) claim that monitoring and control activities are limited by working memory capacity; that is, limitations in working memory imply delay or restricted development at the executive level. This notion is supported by Pressley, Cariglia-Bull, Deane, and Schneider (1987), who found that the utilization of a newly acquired imagery strategy was dependent upon working memory capacity.

Perhaps more intriguing are the dynamics through which attention might influence the development of executive processing. As suggested earlier, there is likely a direct path from attention to the formation of executive processing, perhaps linked to the development of inhibitory processes. There are also possible indirect paths from attentional processing to the quality of the environment and then back again to the formation of the executive.

A perspective on the attention–executive connection can be seen in the longitudinal model presented in Figure 14.12. In this model, immature attentional processing helps create a state of insecure attachment (perhaps through the establishment of less sensitive and responsive caregiving). In turn, insecure attachment might restrict the range of environmental enrichments necessary for the mature development of executive processing. It should be noted that the latter connections—between attachment, the instructional environment, and the teaching of executive control—have recently been given plausibility by Moss, Gosselin, Parent, and Dubeau (1993). From the viewpoint of the model in Figure 14.12, the development of executive functioning is directly dependent upon early attentional flexibility, as well as indirectly upon the quality of environments it helps create during the first few years of life.

Future Research Agenda

There is a range of important research questions on the nature and functioning of executive processing that should be addressed in order to validate and extend the concept: 1) As suggested, the connections between attention, memory, and the executive need to be determined empirically. 2) The uniqueness of executive processing vis-à-vis planning and regulation needs clarification. 3) The major components of the executive and their developmental trajectories and independence need further analysis. 4) Using the instructional approach, research should focus on training more creative and insightful learners. 5) The impact of executive training on students with learning impairments needs to be determined. That is, what gains in academic performance occur following executive training for various types of mental disabilities? Relatedly, what are the correspondences in in-

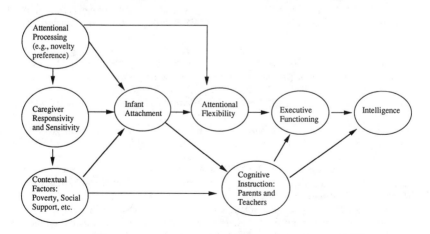

Figure 14.12 A model of attention, attachment, and the development of executive skills.

formation processing and neuropsychology when the instructional method is utilized? 6) For all of the above to transpire, greater attention needs to be given to the creation of multiple, converging measures of executive functioning on a range of tasks, both within and across domains; concern should be aimed at documenting the reliability and validity of these measures. Answers to these research questions and methodological issues should advance our understanding of the mind, brain, and pedagogy for the betterment of individuals who differ in their talents and potentials.

REFERENCES

Asarnow, J., & Meichenbaum, D. (1979). Verbal rehearsal and serial recall: The mediational training of kindergarten children. *Child Development, 50,* 1173–1177.

Belmont, J.M. (1978). Individual differences in memory: The cases of normal and retarded development. In M.M. Gruneberg & P. Morris (Eds.), *Aspects of memory* (pp. 153–185). London: Methuen.

Belmont, J.M., Ferretti, R.P., & Mitchell, D.W. (1982). Memorizing: A test of untrained retarded children's problem solving. *American Journal of Mental Deficiency, 87,* 197–210.

Borkowski, J.G., & Kurtz, B.E. (1987). Metacognition and executive control. In J.G. Borkowski & J.D. Day (Eds.), *Cognition in special children* (pp. 123–152). Norwood, N.J.: Ablex.

Borkowski, J.G., Milstead, M., & Hale, C. (1988). Components of children's metamemory: Implications for strategy generalization. In F. Weinert & M. Perlmutter (Eds.), *Memory development: Individual differences and universal changes* (pp. 73–100). Hillsdale, NJ: Lawrence Erlbaum Associates.

Borkowski, J.G., & Muthukrishna, N. (1992). Moving metacognition into the classroom: "Working models" and effective strategy teaching. In M. Pressley, K.R. Harris, & J.T. Guthrie (Eds.), *Promoting academic literacy: Cognitive research and instructional innovation* (pp. 477–501). Orlando, FL: Academic Press.

Borkowski, J.G., & Peck, V. (1986). Causes and consequences of metamemory in gifted children. In R. Sternberg & J. Davidson (Eds.), *Conceptions of giftedness* (pp. 182–200). Cambridge, England: Cambridge University Press.

Borkowski, J.G., & Varnhagen, C.K. (1984). Transfer of learning strategies: A contrast of self-instructional and traditional formats with EMR children. *American Journal of Mental Deficiency, 88,* 369–379.

Bransford, J., Sherwood, R.D., Hasselbring, T.S., Kinzer, C.K., & Williams, S.M. (1990). Anchored instruction: Why we need it and how technology can help. In D. Nix & R. Spiro (Eds.), *Cognition, education, and multi-media: Exploring ideas in high technology* (pp. 116–141). Hillsdale, NJ: Lawrence Erlbaum Associates.

Bransford, J.D., & Stein, B.S. (1993). *The ideal problem solver.* New York: W.H. Freeman.

Brown, A.L., Campione, J.C., & Barclay, C.R. (1979). Training self-checking routines for estimating test readiness: Generalizing from list learning to prose recall. *Child Development, 50,* 501–512.

Butterfield, E.C., & Albertson, L.R. (1993, June). On making cognitive theory more general and developmentally pertinent. Paper presented at a conference on Memory Development, Castle Ringberg, Germany.

Butterfield, E.C., & Albertson, L.R. (1995). On making cognitive theory more general and developmentally pertinent. In F. Weinert & W. Schneider (Eds.), *Research on memory development* (pp. 73–99). Hillsdale, NJ: Lawrence Erlbaum Associates.

Butterfield, E.C., & Belmont, J.M. (1977). Assessing and improving the executive cognitive functions of mentally retarded people. In I. Bialer & M. Sternlicht (Eds.), *Psychological issues in mental retardation* (pp. 277–318). New York: Psychological Dimensions.

Day, J.D., Borkowski, J.G., Dietmeyer, D., Howsepian, B.A., & Saenz, D.S. (1992). Possible selves and academic achievement. In L. Winegar & J. Valsiner (Eds.), *Children's development within social contexts: Metatheoretical, theoretical, and methodological issues* (pp. 181–201). Hillsdale, NJ: Lawrence Erlbaum Associates.

Day, J.D., & Hall, L.K. (1987). Cognitive assessment, intelligence and instruction. In J.D. Day & J.G. Borkowski (Eds.), *Intelligence and exceptionality* (pp. 57–80). Norwood, NJ: Ablex.

Detterman, D.K. (1979). Memory in the mentally retarded. In N.R. Ellis (Ed.), *Handbook of mental deficiency: Psychological theory and research* (2nd ed.) (pp. 727–760). Hillsdale, NJ: Lawrence Erlbaum Associates.

Kurtz, B.E., & Borkowski, J.G. (1987). Metacognition and the development of strategic skills in impulsive and reflective children. *Journal of Experimental Child Psychology, 43*, 129–148.

Markus, H., & Nurius, P. (1986). Possible selves. *American Psychologist, 41*, 954–969.

Marsh, H.W. (1986). Verbal and math self-concepts: An internal-external frame of reference model. *American Educational Research Journal, 23*, 129–150.

Meichenbaum, D., & Goodman, J. (1971). Training impulsive children to talk to themselves: A means of developing self-control. *Journal of Abnormal Psychology, 77*, 115–126.

Mithaug, D. (1993). Self-regulation theory: How optimal adjustment maximizes gain. Westport, CT: Praeger.

Moss, E., Gosselin, C., Parent, S., & Dubeau, D. (March, 1993). Does attachment influence share metaognitive experiences? Paper presented at the meeting of the Society for Research in Child Development, New Orleans.

Pressley, M., Borkowski, J.G., & Schneider, W. (1990). Good information processing: What it is and how education can promote it. *International Journal of Educational Research, 2*, 857–867.

Pressley, M., Cariglia-Bull, T., Deane, S., & Schneider, W. (1987). Short-term memory, verbal competence, and age as predictors of imagery instructional effectiveness. *Journal of Experimental Child Psychology, 43*, 194–211.

Reid, M.K., & Borkowski, J.G. (1987). Causal attributions of hyperactive children: Implications for training strategies and self-control. *Journal of Educational Psychology, 79*, 296–307.

Scholnick, E.K., & Friedman, S.L. (1993). Planning in context: Developmental and situational characteristics. *International Journal of Behavioral Development, 16*, 145–167.

Sternberg, R.J. (1985). *Beyond IQ: A triarchic theory of intelligence*. New York: Cambridge University Press.

Sternberg, R.J. (1987). A unified theory of intellectual exceptionality. In J.D. Day & J.G. Borkowski (Eds.), *Intelligence and exceptionality* (pp. 135–172). Norwood, NJ: Ablex.

Sternberg, R.J., & Davidson, J.E. (1986). *Conceptions of giftedness*. Cambridge, England: Cambridge University Press.

Weinert, F., & Kluwe, R. (1987). *Metacognition, motivation, and performance*. Hillsdale, NJ: Lawrence Erlbaum Associates.

Yap, E.G., & O'Neil, H.F. (March, 1994). A structural model of self-regulated learning in math achievement. Paper presented at the annual meeting of AERA, New Orleans.

15

A THEORY AND MODEL OF EXECUTIVE FUNCTION
A Neuropsychological Perspective

Martha Bridge Denckla

The neuropsychological perspective by definition regards executive functions as behaviors that have a specific brain basis. The context (whether or not one would properly call it "theoretical") is that the term *executive functions* has been in use in recent years in association with attempts to characterize the deficits of patients whose frontal lobes and/or frontally interconnected subcortical regions have been impaired by damage, disease, or disordered development. Anyone who admits to a neuropsychological orientation will be hard pressed to decouple the term *executive functions* (EF) from the context (physical rather than theoretical) of frontal/subcortical circuits; EF has become a useful shorthand for a set of domain-general control processes for which we need a convenient way to say that these are not domain-specific modular processing capabilities (language, perception, motor function, etc.). Unfortunately, a slippage of levels of discourse has afflicted the neuropsychological literature, so that context has too often become content; "frontal functions" (more properly, prefrontal) are spoken of as if synonymous with EF. Although this slippage does not make for clear thinking, it is undeniably a historical fact that EF has a more concrete neuroanatomical context than a purely theoretical one. As Tranel, Anderson, and Benton (1995) so aptly put it:

> It is virtually impossible to find a discussion of prefrontal lobe functions that does not make reference to disturbances of executive functions and, in parallel fashion, there is rarely a discussion of disturbances of executive functions that does not make reference to dysfunction of prefrontal brain regions . . . it must be acknowledged that the capacities subsumed by executive functions have been linked to the prefrontal region throughout the entire history of neuroscience, and to some extent, the psychology and the anatomy are inseparable.

Ideally, the levels should be kept separate; EF should not be confounded with "prefrontal" except at a hypothesis-generating level. Besides nonfrontal contributions to EF (control processes), there are functions of the prefrontal lobes that extend well beyond the list of cognitive capabilities for which EF is an umbrella. In this latter point, the analysis in this chapter diverges from Tranel et al. and restricts EF to the more "cold cognition" aspects of frontal–subcortical circuits, leaving the social–emotionality or motivational–personality aspects, more affiliated with orbital and mesial prefrontal regions, out of consideration. More difficulty exists with the other boundary circuit, that of motor control as a neighbor/fellow traveler of EF, than with the emotional control circuitry. Boundary issues are dealt with later.

The other theoretical context from which EF emanates is clinical. EF is a convenient shorthand that captures the problems of a group of patients evaluated by clinicians. Arriving with chief complaints of unexplained school underachievement, this group of patients presents itself as "bright" on standard psychometrical indices of intelligence, untroubled by any modular, domain-specific information-processing deficits, yet unable to function as "good students." Evaluation, using a neuropsychological and behavioral–neurological systems approach, reveals EF to be the weak system in this group. Some "qualify" for the DSM-III-R (American Psychiatric Association, 1987) diagnosis of attention deficit hyperactivity disorder (ADHD), some for the new DSM-IV (American Psychiatric Association, 1994) diagnosis of ADD *sans* H, but some meet no such diagnostic criteria. The EF impairment is not identical in every constituent of the domain across cases. Yet, as clinicians, we cannot escape the discriminative and predictive validity of the EF model within neuropsychological diagnosis. We might decide to abandon EF for another term (e.g., *control processes*) but would still need something of the sort to describe this group of patients with excellent psychometrical intelligence, no discrepancy-based learning disabilities, and no domain-specific modular processing deficit.

To try to make the context or model more vivid (if less theoretical), imagine an individual who is setting out to cook a certain dish, who has a well-equipped kitchen, including shelves stocked with all necessary ingredients, and who can even read the recipe in the cookbook. Now imagine, however, that this individual does not take from the shelves all the ingredients relevant to the recipe, does not turn on the oven in a timely fashion so as to have it at the proper heat when called for in the recipe, and has not defrosted the central ingredient. This individual can be observed dashing to shelves, searching for the spice next mentioned in the recipe, hurrying to defrost the meat and heat the oven out of sequence, and so forth. Despite possession of all equipment, ingredients, and recipe, this motivated but dishevelled cook is unlikely to get dinner on the table at the appointed hour. This is the picture of the patient with "pure" EF impairment: "a day late and a dollar short" in most of life's undertakings.

Finally, although closely linked to the clinical context, there is the issue of development. A great deal of the difference between child and adult resides in the unfolding of EF. Education operates on implicit expectations of increasing independence and self-generated, if externally reinforced, productivity. Here again, the surface description of the sociology of schools and the trajectory of psychological development maps well, even irresistibly, onto the protracted within-brain course of increased connectivity of prefrontal regions. On parallel descriptive levels, psychological and neuroanatomical, what develops as EF mimics the curve of frontal/nonfrontal coherence/connectivity (Thatcher, 1991). The temptation to "trespass" back and forth from psychological to neuroanatomical is just as great from the developmental as from the acquired brain damage perspective.

In summary, there are three interconnected theoretical contexts and models concerning EF. They are 1) historic linkage to prefrontal (especially dorsolateral) regions and their subcortical domain-general interconnected regions; 2) clinical convenience, the need to capture distinctive features of certain patients; and 3) developmental, in that child becomes adult largely in terms describable under the EF umbrella and isomorphic with brain circuitry dovetailing with context number one.

WHAT ARE THE PRIMARY CONSTRUCTS WITHIN THE MODEL?

Executive functions are control processes; it is not clear whether, although themselves domain-general, these are organized neurologically to connect separately with each of several modular domains (Goldman-Rakic, 1987). The most fundamental characterization of EF constructs is that these control processes involve inhibition and delay of responding. For example, executive aspects of attention involve selection, the "withdrawing from some things in order to focus on others" (James, 1890). In the simplest of visual–motor tasks, the delay implicit in the dash is a property of EF. Even a simple reaction time task involves action selection. Anticipatory set, preparedness to act, freedom from interference (the interference from previously established prepotent response tendencies), and the ability to sequence behavioral outputs are all constructs subsumed under EF. EF constructs are closest to the motor border when, as in "managerial knowledge units" (Grafman, 1989) they seem quite close to the ideational praxis concepts of 19th-century neurologists. Similarly, EF constructs hover close to the motor border when described by Heilman (1994) as aspects of the "how" and "when" of intentionality, fractionated into *initiate, sustain, inhibit/stop*, and *shift*. It may be argued that few problems or controversies would exist with respect to EF constructs if stricter adherence to their output-related or motor-affiliative aspects were emphasized to the exclusion of some of the more elusive and "exalted" constructs that have come to inhabit the space under the EF umbrella. In fact, if one backed off from the tendency to speak of EF as "supraordinate" or "higher-order" processes and remained content with designating EF as "central," one might avoid the many occasions on which neuropsychologists are accused of reinventing the *g* of general intelligence. Perhaps, following the distinguished lead of Lezak (1983), one should keep a chapter on "conceptual functions" (more akin to the *g* of IQ measurement) separate from one on "executive functions" and motor performance. Most researchers and clinicians, however, do not adhere to these lines of cleavage but rather mount the steps of a hierarchy from praxis to creativity. Almost everyone who tackles the topic, however, includes "planning" as one of EFs core constructs. Organization and integration of cognitive and output processes over time, contrasted with component linguistic or perceptual operations, capture the essence of a consensus about EF constructs.

"Time" and "planning" bring us to the distinctive future tense aspects of EF constructs; "attention to the future," "prospective memory" ("remembering to remember"), or "memory for the future" are some of the catchphrases employed. Most popular, due to the profound influence of the work of Goldman-Rakic (1987), is the term "working memory," felt by some (see Chapter 18) to be the sole key construct embodying EF. Pennington (1995) has recently collapsed his two-factor (working memory and inhibition) account of EF into a single-factor (working memory) construct, saying that "Because working memory is a limited capacity system, inhibition (or interference control) is intrinsic to its operation."

The constructs most readily susceptible to the status of central control processes are those of inhibition, delayed responding, maintenance of anticipatory set/preparedness to act, and planning of sequences of selected actions. Efficiency and productivity are observable outcomes of these constructs. Problems enter the EF construct domain when "meta" takes over, bringing (as in the analogous "metaphysics" to "physics") those higher or supraordinate elements described as "awareness of the activity of the mind," "the consciousness of being conscious," "concept formation," and "abstract reasoning." Although of great interest, these "meta" constructs threaten to overwhelm the more modest EF constructs. "Manipulation of representational systems," although still sounding fairly high-flown, at least connotes (in the term *manipulation*) the motor lineage *in the mind* of executing something. It may be of more than passing historic interest to note that Dr. Norman Geschwind trained his neurology residents and fellows to perform, as part of the bedside mental status examination, an evaluation of the patient's manipulation of old knowledge. The "manipulation of representational systems" is what goes on during the delay between stimulus and response, as in the "dash" in the word *visual–motor*, and is the "working" part of the computational arena dubbed *working memory*.

As the "meta" aspects of cognition are set aside, considerable overlaps between EF constructs and those of memory and attention remain. Obviously, what is remembered and what is here-and-now attended-to enter the "computational arena" of on-line working memory, while the EF system itself selects for attention and selects from memory. Barkley (see Chapter 17) argues that "executive function is now seen as a special case of attention," essentially with an interpolated step. Equally can one argue that working memory, so essential a construct for EF, is a special case of memory (future- rather than past-oriented). It is in the developmental trajectory that the EF constructs derive greatest utility. From the motor–praxis "boundary" to the meta–introspective "horizon," the EF domain subsumes developmentally distinctive milestones (as in Welsh, Pennington, & Groisser, 1991).

Infant and toddler developments of EF occur even earlier than is documented in the work of Welsh et al. (1991). Self-regulation, meaning the capacity for inhibition of powerful (nearly "instinctual") sensorimotor behaviors and the related capacity for delayed responding, emerges as the groundwork for later more proactive EF (Diamond & Goldman-Rakic, 1986). Delay and interpolated steps in the stimulus–response chain are fundamental properties of EF that reaffiliate the psychological constructs with what is known about prefrontostriatal pathways in primates and human beings (Diamond & Goldman-Rakic). Another early, preschool aspect of EF is inhibition of emotional responding while cognitive "calculations" are in progress; Barkley (Chapter 17) has referred to Bronowski's "separation of affect" in this regard, but this concept could well be reexpressed as another inhibitory aspect of self-regulation. The failure of Gnys and Willis (1991) to validate EF in young children resides not only in their unfortunate choice of discriminant (non-EF) tasks but in their focus within "cold cognition." Every clinician asked to diagnose ADHD and every developmentalist knows that the inhibition of emotionally driven global responses is the salient EF achievement of the preschool age group, allowing more seemingly rational, objective behavior such as conformity to the task demands (never mind the content) of school or school-like group settings.

Only with children at about 5–7 years of age can researchers clearly document the proactive filling of the interpolated interval; working memory enters here, keeping perceptions and old memories in an "on-line" computational space.

OPERATIONALIZING THE MODEL AND THE CONSTRUCTS: MEASUREMENT INSTRUMENTS, TESTS, AND PROCEDURES

In a prior publication (Denckla, 1994), I have given detailed descriptions of many clinical and research tasks oriented toward or sensitive to EF. These are listed in Tables 15.1 and 15.2. Another recent review of EF measurement is included in Tranel et al. (1995). For the current purpose and focus, however, rather than generate a catalogue of itemized descriptions of tests, procedures, and instruments, a critique of the current state-of-the-art listings is presented. Problems in the operationalization of EF arise from the confounding effects of 1) general intelligence, 2) integrity of cognitive processes (such as perception and memory) that rely on posterior brain areas but need to "feed in" to anterior brain to sustain EF, and 3) the special case of the mediating role of language in the key aspect of EF that is rule-governed behavioral regulation.

Table 15.1.   Neuropsychological measures in frequent clinical use for executive function

Stroop Color Word Test
Controlled Word Association (or Verbal Fluency) (Benton & Hamsher, 1989a, 1989b)
Rey-Osterrieth Complex Figure Copying
Go/No-Go (e.g., test of variables of attention)
California Verbal Learning Test (Clusters, intrusions, perseverations)

Table 15.2.   Neuropsychological measures developed or modified for research concerning executive function

Visual Search (e.g., Underlining or Cancellation of Targets) (Rudel, Denckla, & Broman, 1978)
Motor Sequencing (fingers or hand positions) (Denckla, 1985)
Tower of Hanoi, London, Toronto
Diamond's version of Stroop (Diamond, 1991)
Diamond's "Six Boxes"
Rey-Osterrieth Complex Figure Copying
Contingency Naming Test
Tinker Toy Test (Lezak, 1983)
Temporal Order Memory (Petrides & Milner, 1982)
Self-Ordered Pointing Task (Diamond, 1991)

General Intelligence

General intelligence must be taken into account because high IQ may mean that certain tasks for some individuals are too easy to be sensitive to their EF. Few studies concerned with frontal/nonfrontal sensitivity/specificity contrasts in adults with acquired lesions have introduced estimates of premorbid IQ as covariates in the analyses. Studies involving child development more typically raise issues of *group* differences in IQ. For example, the Wisconsin Card Sorting Test–Categories Achieved (WCST–CA) (Heaton, 1981) may correlate strongly with Verbal IQ (Reader, Harris, Schuerholz, & Denckla, in press). When reporting that a large number of frontally damaged adults perform normally on WCST–CA, the researchers do not report high IQ as a possible explanation (Anderson, Damasio, Jones, & Tranel, 1991; Grafman, Jonas, & Salazar, 1990). This is because the threshold value for EF impairment is set at a standard "cut-score," rather than the EF measure being examined in relation to some rough measure of central tendency, within-subject, of that subject's cognition (such as IQ). This is not a claim that EF is simply "old wine in new bottles" (i.e., simply neuropsychology reinventing psychometrical g), but simply a way of recognizing that there is a complex overlap between g and EF. Pennington (1995) argues that the "fluid" component of g approximates the working memory element to which he reduces EF, whereas that of g, which is regarded as crystallized intelligence, is the nonoverlapping (with respect to EF) component. It can be argued that the Performance Scale of the Wechsler IQ, PIQ, by its very title and its heavy emphasis on timed tasks, is more closely affiliated with EF than is the Verbal Scale (as in Teuber's 1964 dissociation between "knowing and doing" account of the frontal lobe "riddle": Is not verbal IQ closer to "knowing" and PIQ literally "doing"?). A finer-grained inspection of the PIQ reveals gradations of EF sensitivity; a large gap between an individual's scores on Block Design (higher) and Object Assembly (lower) suggests basic spatial ability that can operate for output in the presence of a model but is less efficient without one. This is an example of the way in which the measurement of the EF operation depends upon the expectations set both by a rough measure of general cognitive level and by a domain-specific modular measure (of perception, memory, and/or language) relevant to the output demand.

Integrity of Cognitive Processes

Operationalization of EF when there is evidence of a content-related deficit will be a difficult matter indeed. As Tranel et al. (1995) point out, many adults with nonfrontal lesions (that impair perception, memory, or language) "fail" the Wisconsin Card Sorting Test (WCST). Without error analysis as the basis for generating a distinctive pattern of failure (more than just low level of quantitative score) the WCST is declared nonspecific for either EF or frontal injury. Alternatively, error pattern may not prove discriminative (there may simply be a paucity of output), and it may be impossible to demonstrate impaired operation of EF processes if the content domain upon which the operation is expected does not provide the necessary "substrate." Perhaps it is impossible to "do" with that which you do not "know." If so, EF measurement must shift to an intact content domain (for that individual or that population). Content–domain competence sets floor and ceiling effects for the specificity and sensitivity of EF measurement. An obvious example is that of measuring the Stroop effect (Golden, 1987) (the price, in terms of time, paid for inhibition of prepotent response to read color names when required to name conflicting ink colors) in illiterates. Here, content–domain incompetence (illiteracy) makes a passing time-score on ink-color–naming an insensitive indicator of EF because great inhibitory strength would be credited to a subject of whom (due to absence of reading–response conflict) no inhibition was required. Less obvious, however, is the sensitivity-to-EF continuum represented by the interference score judged in relation to the degree of literacy of the adult subject (Cox et al., 1995). These authors have documented that unless an adult reads as fluently and automatically as would be expected for his or her IQ, that adult may not be judged with meaningful sensitivity by the usual Stroop interference algorithms.

Another example of content–domain-related issues is provided by Word Fluency; the subject with superior vocabulary who barely "passes" word fluency will represent a "false negative" for EF impairment, whereas a language-disordered subject who is failing due to lack of stored vocabulary will represent a "false positive" for EF impairment.

The Mediating Role of Language

There is a special case or instance with respect to language competence and EF measurements that begin with a verbally stated rule or verbally stated constraints. Barkley (Chapter 17) and Hayes, Gifford, and Ruckstuhl (Chapter 16) discuss this as rule-governed behavior, to them a key to EF (they consider that rules are what occupy and drive working memory). With delays between stimulus or memory and action, self-directed rules or internalized constraints initially made explicit by instructions from others permit consistent efficient behavior. Future behavior can be rule-governed, as in "don't forget to do" an action (Ceci and

Bronfenbrenner, 1985). Although it cannot be denied that some rules may be visualized "maps" or imagined schematics (this may be more true for some individuals than for others), it is nonetheless a compelling and striking probability that verbally mediated rules dominate much of working memory (and hence EF) for most human beings. Going back to Luria's treatise on the role of speech in the regulation of behavior in children as young as 3 years of age, developmentalists who not only do research but who also deal with disorders as clinicians are struck by the close connection between language and EF (Luria, 1961). The special case and first instance, then, seems to be that language weakness, in some not yet fully elucidated fashion, secondarily weakens EF, as if a crucial "conveyor belt" (possibly a verbal short-term memory circuit connecting the brain's posterior language regions with anterior EF regions) were functionally defective. This hypothesis is constructed by analogy to what is known about praxis in relation to verbal command; lesions that disconnect language (posteriorly based) from premotor/motor programming (anteriorly based) impair the output of learned motor skills. There need be no lesion directly in language or in premotor areas for this dysfunction to occur; the disconnection between them is sufficient cause.

Stepping up from praxis to EF, then, one may postulate that "between knowing and doing" (Teuber, 1964) is a connection that, if weakened or developmentally deficient, fails to keep verbally formulated rules available for the regulation of action. This would be yet another explanation of why "frontal" deficits (i.e., EF deficits) are found in cases where only nonfrontal lesions/anomalies exist. It is also a powerful explanation for the confounding effect, with respect to EF, of developmental language and language-based learning disorders in cases of ADHD (Pennington, Groisser, & Welsh, 1993; Reader et al., in press). Again, it must be emphasized that the issue is *not* confined to the extreme case of receptive language disorder that precludes comprehension of the rule; rather, the issue is one of the more subtle connections (verbal short-term memory, if you will) that provide feed-forward to the working memory system. Pennington et al. describe an adaptation of the WCST that attempts to get around this issue by providing the shift rule explicitly to the subject; if there is perseveration of a previous sorting action, then the locus of dysfunction can be more securely assigned to EF and its frontal–subcortical localization (Nelson, 1976).

Experimental approaches to EF, more typically than clinical practices, take into account the need to control for the input and output side of a putatively EF task. Conceived of as that which is central (rather than hierarchically supraordinate), EF becomes more accessible, even using clinical instruments. For instance, that most ubiquitous of clinical tests, copying forms/designs, is described as *visual–motor*; the EF lies implicit in the dash in the term *visual–motor*, in what operations (Geschwind taught us to say "manipulations") occupy the delay between perception and action. Pairing commonly available design-copying tasks with differing demands for self-generated organization reveals relevant aspects of EF. The Bender Gestalt Test (Bender, 1938) requires allocation of space within a single piece of paper to each of several designs presented on individual cards, whereas the Beery–Buktenica Test (Beery, 1989) requires copying within a boxed-off space preplaced just below the identically boxed model design (Koppitz, 1971). Even more taxing within-design problems (rather than in the spacing of designs in relation to total page and each other) are seen with the complex figure-copying test (Osterrieth, 1944; Rey, 1941; Waber and Holmes, 1985). Thus, the discrepancies within an individual in scores achieved on these three design-copying tasks constitute EF measures for that individual.

Experimentalists are more explicit in their matching and pairing of tasks designed to capture the elusive EF factor. Temporal-order memory has been paired with order-free recognition memory, so that in both instances a series of pictures is viewed. In the temporal-order condition, however, the task is to respond periodically to "which of these two pictures did you see *last*?" whereas in the control condition the probe requires response to "which of these two pictures have you *ever* seen?" (Milner, 1971). The interpolated central task in temporal order memory is to organize (possibly visualize?) on a time line in working memory the remembered pictures.

Another experimental type of pairing involves self-ordered versus fixed-ordered pointing (Petrides and Milner, 1982). Diamond (1991) has an early childhood version, "six boxes," in which opening distinctively decorated boxes, in each of which there is candy or toy rewards, substitutes for mere pointing. In the self-ordered condition, the goal is nonrepetition, with repetition negatively reinforced by the empty status of a previously opened box. Boxes are "scrambled" in lineup out of view between trials, and the score is the mean (of several trials) number of reaches to open all six reward-filled boxes. The control condition involves six fixed-position boxes that remain, trial by trial, rebaited but never scrambled out of view between trials. The control condition serves as a covariate in research design, as it controls for the subjects' perception and memory of the six distinctively decorated boxes but lacks the self-ordered task's requirement for updated working memory.

Stroop-like tasks have also been elaborated for developmental research. Gerstadt, Hong, and Diamond (1994) have a "Day/Night" test, in which the subject, when shown a white card with a sun drawn on it, is instructed to say "Night," but when shown a black card with moon and stars drawn on it is to say "Day." The control task is that of paired associate learning; when shown an abstract design A, the subject is to call it "Night," and when shown another abstract design B, the subject is to call it "Day." The EF challenge resides in the ability to inhibit the strong reaction to "sun" as "day" and "moon/stars" as "night," with the control task acting as within-subject covariate for the capacity to learn a novel visual–verbal association.

Taylor's Contingency Naming Test (Taylor, 1988) is another Stroop-like challenge to EF, utilizing no reading but progressively more elaborate rules for what aspects of the stimulus array are to be ignored in favor of other aspects to be named (Spreen & Strauss, 1991). Shifting (as in the original Stroop color-word-ink naming subtests) is a major requirement of Taylor's Contingency Naming

Test, and its control conditions are implicit in the hierarchical complexity of its shifts. The language demands (or verbal short-term memory demands) of the rules themselves are considerable, although the naming output demands are relatively elementary.

Fluency tasks (as already mentioned above) are in current use; the word fluency variety is more common in clinics, and the design fluency variety is more common in research. Because these are timed, rule-governed (constraint-limited), and self-generated, they certainly deserve their position in the EF measurement repertoire (enhancement of the sensitivity and specificity of these tasks is discussed below). Fluency tasks are sensitive to working memory for rules/constraints, freedom from repetitions or perseverations, maintenance of preparatory set, and efficiency of memory "search." Rapid response output is also necessary because of the time limits. There are many versions of word fluency tests (Benton and Hamsher, 1976; Thurstone, 1938). All require either spoken or written output within a specified time period (usually 30 or 60 seconds) of words belonging to either a specified initial-letter category ("L") or a specified semantic category ("animals"). Letter word fluency output must meet constraints such as exclusion of proper nouns, numeral names, or forms of the same word.

Design fluency was intended for research focused upon right versus left lateralization of fluency and involves the drawing of "nonsense/abstract" figures, as many different designs as possible, in a limited interval (Jones-Gotman & Milner, 1977; Vik & Ruff, 1988). Some versions provide a dot-matrix for line connection (Vik & Ruff), whereas others are entirely without any structure except that the examiner provides a piece of paper with separate boxed-off areas for the productions of the subject. Disallowed "rule breaks" are scribbles, nameable representations, and repetitions with minor embellishments. The biggest problem with design fluency is the wide variance in typical individuals' scores, much greater variance at any age level than is found with respect to word fluency.

Tower puzzles (Hanoi, London, or Toronto) require planning in order for the subject to achieve a goal, a configuration of rings or blocks that match a model, but constrained by rules specifying only certain moves and certain relationships of component pieces (Shallice, 1982). Latency to initiate the first move has also been a variable measured as a presumptive indicator of reflective planning. Critiques of Tower puzzles (Pennington, 1991; Tranel et al., 1995) admit that these require such an extensive integrated set of spatial and sequential elements that Tower tasks typically occupy a factor all their own within EF batteries (Levin et al., 1991; Welsh et al., 1991). This is both good (in terms of sensitivity) and bad (in terms of specificity), the latter because the number of subordinate cognitive processes involved increases the number of candidate interpretations of failures other than EF per se.

Go/No-Go tasks exist that are measures of the essential element of inhibition (the flip side of the coin of response preparation) within EF. There are simple bedside maneuvers that can be quantified (Trommer, Hoeppner, & Zecker, 1991).

These involve instructing the patient to raise an arm or tap a table when one signal (e.g., two raised fingers) is given by the examiner but to do nothing when another signal (e.g., one raised finger) is given. There are also available computerized tests that, although developed and marketed as continuous performance tests of attention, are actually better understood as Go/No-Go challenges with choice reaction time measured "for good measure." The Test of Variables of Attention (Greenberg, 1990) is one such computerized Go/No-Go test with capability to use two very simple geometric arrangements as the respective Go and No-Go signals, print out reaction times (and variability of reaction times) for correct responses, and hence provide useful EF information. Preoccupation with the intent of the developer and the name of the test ("Attention" in both regards) has obscured its actual properties. As for the "lowly" choice reaction time, Pennington (1995) has stated:

> Even a simple reaction time test requires action selection, hence the efficiency of working memory will affect both latency and consistency (standard deviation) of reaction time. (p. 20)

Other "lowly" motor tasks that some clinicians and researchers (often the same persons) bring to bear on the "entry level" of EF are motor sequencing (Welsh et al., 1991), quantitative counts of age-inappropriate overflow (Denckla & Roeltgen, 1992), and the antisaccade test (Guitton, Buchtel, & Douglas, 1985). This last involves instructing the patient to fixate the midline, await a peripheral visual stimulus, and look in the opposite direction (i.e., move the eyes away) from the side of the stimulus. None of these has as yet made its way into the EF literature familiar to mainstream neuropsychology, demonstrating that, despite the connotations of "executive," so compatible with Geschwind's terminology ("manipulating knowledge"), the motoric border of EF has been neglected; developmentalists are less likely to neglect this border and behavioral neurologists patrol it most regularly.

CRITERIA RECOMMENDED TO SELECT AND DEVELOP EF-SENSITIVE/SPECIFIC INSTRUMENTS, TESTS, OR PROCEDURES

The major principle to which all of the above has been leading is that of the need for content-matched control tasks for every candidate EF task. Deficits involving the language of the rules, memory for rules and constraints (the latter may be visuospatially represented), and perceptual or elementary motor functions should be controlled for on a task-by-task basis in order for any given candidate EF task to be considered for selection or development. Examples (mainly experimental) have been presented; clinical examples could be developed if scoring systems were stretched to allow quantification of intra-individual discrepancy scores, such as one that our group has already validated, "Vocabulary minus Word Fluency," using for each case that individual's z scores to generate an output discrepancy (Reader et al., in press). Within the single test, the Rey-Osterreith Complex Figure (Osterreith, 1944), the discrepancy between an organizationally oriented score (Waber and Holmes, 1985) and an item-oriented score (the 36-point score of Taylor; see Spreen & Strauss, 1991) captures an aspect of nonverbal EF. Within another single test, the California Verbal Learning Test (Delis, Kramer, Kaplan, & Oger, 1987, 1944), a ratio or a subtraction discrepancy between total correct responses across the first five trials and total responses provided in clusters across the same five trials would be an index of the memorization process in profile against the memory capability of the subject. (Levin et al. [1991] started in this direction by using "percentage of responses clustered" as an EF variable but did not relate this to level of success in memory, i.e., total correct responses). Selection and development criteria center around this dyadic approach, whereby the search is on for such content-related pairings of tasks or scorings within the same task. In each case the more EF element (anterior in terms of brain basis) demands more inhibition of prepotent automatic or overlearned response(s) and more active, on-line, rule-governed, future-oriented, goal-oriented, time-limited response preparation than does the control task. By analogy, the EF task carries out the cooking or baking procedure: The ingredients and recipe are necessary but not sufficient. How to judge EF when ingredients and/or recipe are not fully supplied is a residual difficulty, especially in the developmental context. It may be that when language, memory, perceptual, or motor "supplies" are low in a child, it will only be possible *after* the attainment of a certain threshold of remediation and/or maturation to evaluate EF. Even then, it may not be possible, on a given assessment basis, to disclose whether all along there was separate but equally important EF impairment.

It also follows from reflections on development that some tasks sensitive to EF at early stages will lose their novel character, become automatized, and move out of the EF domain. EF is time-related over the life span. Scores derived from Trails A and B (another matched pair or discrepancy dyad) may be EF-sensitive for children but reach an insensitive ceiling in adults (Tranel et al., 1994). It would be oxymoronic to expect a fixed EF battery for all age levels and/or for individual general ability levels at prime adult age levels. Another criterial cutpoint follows Lezak (1983). In order to avoid the "homunculus problem" (Pennington, 1995), the hierarchical imagery evoked by talk of "the central executive" must stick to a level playing field upon which "central" is not "higher." Lezak's separation of abstract reasoning and concept formation from "executive" appears to be a healthy decision. The central executive appears more accessible as an engineer than as a theoretical physicist or metaphysical philosopher. There is a real danger to the usefulness of EF if it is allowed to levitate to a "meta" plane; let us hope that the selection, development, and description of EF instruments, tests, and procedures remain grounded in the practical tradition.

POPULATIONS MOST RELEVANT TO
TESTING THE NEUROPSYCHOLOGICAL MODEL OF EF

Returning to the roots of the construct and model, adult-acquired lesion cases are important populations in whom the brain basis for EF must be validated. Not only frontal (more properly "prefrontal") localization, but also basal ganglia, anterior thalamus, and cerebellum, should be candidate locales for lesions producing domain-general impairments in EF.

Specific neurogenetic disorders, wherein one has the opportunity to trace the pathway from gene to brain anomaly to cognition, provide other populations in whom focal and selective "lesions" may be found, but with an added complexity: The lesions arise in and are modified by the course of development. A few examples are phenylketonuria, neurofibromatosis-1, Turner syndrome, and female fragile X. Child development and its low-severity/high-prevalence "disorders" (or are these differences?) provide large (if heterogeneous) populations in whom EF profiles may be tracked in parallel with known neuroanatomical, neurophysiological, and neurochemical changes (across development, across disorders). Mapping functional onto biological curves, even in large and untidily heterogeneous populations, may provide useful evidence that the EF domain of cognition best discriminates child from adult and best predicts the outcomes of various developmental disorders.

DISCONFIRMATORY EXPERIMENTS LEADING TO THE
ABANDONMENT OF THE EF CONSTRUCT AND MODEL

The possible abandonment of the EF model is largely a semantic issue. Pennington (1995) has already chosen to pursue working memory as his preferred substitute for EF, still associating working memory with "prefrontal cortex" (PFC) mechanisms. Barkley (Chapter 17), who only recently was prepared to abandon EF in favor of attention-bound-to-motivation, resurrects EF as a "special case of attention." Semantics aside, the core construct/model referable to delayed responding, future-oriented action-selection, and intentionality (whatever we choose to call these interpolations between stimulus and response) can and will only be disconfirmed if no persons exist for whom these variables explain their behavior. If no dissociations or discrepancies between putatively posteriorly and anteriorly based cognitive components need be invoked to characterize, understand, or remediate real people, then EF will leave the brain–behavior model. If neuroimaging fails to reveal regional sensitivity and specificity with respect to the brain mechanisms believed to underlie the EF construct, this would be, neuropsychologically, disconfirmatory experimental evidence. If, however, even a few "pure" cases, adequately studied so as to meet the above-stated criteria for adequate control over covariates, continue to provide evidence that the central organization and integration (rather than modules) can be selectively impaired, then EF will continue to have discriminative and predictive validity. Whether the neuropsychological and neuroanatomical levels will provide for each other convergent validity remains an open question (Tranel et al., 1995). There is hope, however, that if the neuropsychology of EF is construed more narrowly (central rather than meta) and constrained more fully by the content–control method and that if the neuroanatomy is construed as a more widely distributed system (not just prefrontal cortex), there is a great likelihood that the EF construct and model will not be disconfirmed.

REFERENCES

American Psychiatric Association. (1987). *Diagnostic and statistical manual of mental disorders* (3rd ed. rev.). Washington, DC: Author.

American Psychiatric Association. (1994). *Diagnostic and statistical manual of mental disorders* (4th ed.). Washington, DC: Author.

Anderson, S.W., Damasio, H., Jones, R.D., & Tranel, D. (1991). Wisconsin Card Sorting Test performance as a measure of frontal lobe damage. *Journal of Clinical and Experimental Neuropsychology, 13,* 909–922.

Beery, K.E. (1989). *Developmental Test of Visual-Motor Integration—Revised.* Chicago: Follett.

Bender, L. (1938). *A visual motor gestalt test and its clinical use.* New York: American Orthopsychiatric Association.

Benton, A.L., & Hamsher, K. (1976). *Multilingual aphasia examination.* Iowa City: AJA Associates.

Benton, A.L., & Hamsher, K. deS. (1989a). *Multilingual aphasia examination, III: Controlled word association* (2nd ed.). Iowa City, IA: AJA Associates, Inc.

Benton, A.L., & Hamsher, K. deS. (1989b). *Multilingual aphasia examination, XII: Norms for children* (2nd ed.). Iowa City, IA: AJA Associates, Inc.

Ceci, S.J., & Bronfenbrenner, U. (1985). "Don't forget to take the cupcakes out of the oven": Prospective memory, strategic time-monitoring and context. *Child Development, 56,* 152–164.

Cox, C., Chee, E., Chase, G., Schuerholz, L., Reader, M., Baumgartner, T., Mohr, J., & Denckla, M.B. (1995). *Reading proficiency modifies the psychometric properties of the Stroop Test interference score.* Manuscript in preparation.

Delis, D.C., Kramer, J., Kaplan, E., & Ober, B.A. (1987). *California verbal learning test (adult version).* San Antonio, TX: The Psychological Corporation.

Delis, D.C., Kramer, J., Kaplan, E., & Ober, B.A. (1994). *California verbal learning test (children's version).* San Antonio, TX: The Psychological Corporation.

Denckla, M.B. (1994). Measurement of executive function. In G.R. Lyon (Ed.), *Frames of reference for the assessment of learning disabilities: New views on measurement issues* (pp. 117–142). Baltimore: Paul H. Brookes Publishing Co.

Denckla, M.B. (1985). Revised neurological examination for subtle signs. *Psychopharmacology Bulletin, 21,* 733–800, 1111–1124.

Denckla, M.B., & Roeltgen, D.P. (1992). Disorders of motor function and control. In I. Rapin & S.J. Segalowitz (Vol. Eds.), *Child neuropsychology* (pp. 455–476). In F. Boller & J. Grafman (Series Eds.), *Handbook of neuropsychology.* Amsterdam: Elsevier.

Diamond, A. (1991). Guidelines for the study of brain-behavior relationships during development. In H.S. Levin, H.M. Eisenberg, & A.L. Benton (Eds.), *Frontal lobe function and dysfunction* (pp. 339–378). New York: Oxford University Press.

Diamond, A., & Goldman-Rakic, P.S. (1986). Comparative development in human infants and infant rhesus monkeys of cognitive functions that depend on prefrontal cortex. *Social and Neuroscience Abstracts, 12,* 742.

Gerstadt, C.L., Hong, Y.J., & Diamond, A. (1994). The relationship between cognition and action: Performance of 3–7-year-old children on a Stroop-like day-night test. *Journal of Cognition, 53,* 129–153.

Gnys, J.A., & Willis, W.G. (1991). Validation of executive function tasks with young children. *Developmental Neuropsychology, 7,* 487–501.

Golden, C.J. (1987). *Manual for the Stroop Color and Word Test.* Chicago: Stoetling Company.

Goldman-Rakic, P.S. (1987). Circuitry of primate prefontal cortex and regulation of behavior by representational memory. In F. Plum (Ed.), *Handbook of physiology—the nervous system: Higher function of the brain* (pp. 373–417). Bethesda, MD: American Physiology Association.

Grafman, J. (1989). Plans, actions, and mental sets: Managerial knowledge units in the frontal lobes. In E. Perecman (Ed.), *Integrating theory and practice in clinical neuropsychology* (pp. 93–138). Hillsdale, NJ: Lawrence Erlbaum Associates.

Grafman, J., Jonas, B., & Salazar, A. (1990). Wisconsin Card Sorting Test performance based on location and size of neuroanatomical lesion in Vietnam veterans with penetrating head injuries. *Perceptual and Motor Skills, 71,* 1120–1122.

Greenberg, L. (1990). *Test of Variables of Attention 5.01.* St. Paul, MN: Attention Technology, Inc.

Guitton, D., Buchtel, H.A., & Douglas, R.M. (1985). Frontal lobe lesions in man cause difficulties in suppressing reflexive glances and in generating goal-directed saccades. *Experimental Brain Research, 58,* 455–472.

Heaton, R.K. (1981). *Wisconsin Card Sorting Test manual.* Odessa, FL: Psychological Assessment Resources.

Heilman, K. (1994, January). *Intention.* Paper presented at the NICHD Conference on Attention, Memory, and Executive Function, Bethesda, MD.

James, W. (1890). *The Principles of Psychology* (pp. 403–404). New York: H. Holt and Company.

Jones-Gotman, M., & Milner, B. (1977). Design fluency: The invention of nonsense drawings after focal cortical lesions. *Neuropsychologia, 15,* 653–674.

Koppitz, E.M. (1971). *The Bender Gestalt Test for young children.* New York: Grune & Stratton.

Levin, H.S., Culhane, K.A., Hartman, J., Evankovich, K., Mattson, A.J., Harward, H., Ringholz, G., Ewing-Cobb, L., & Fletcher, J.M. (1991). Developmental changes in performance on tests of purported frontal lobe functioning. *Developmental Neuropsychology, 7,* 377–395.

Lezak, M.D. (1983). *Neuropsychological assessment* (2nd ed.). New York: Oxford University Press.

Luria, A.R. (1961). *The role of speech in the regulation of normal and abnormal behavior.* Oxford: Pergamon Press.

Milner, B. (1971). Interhemispheric differences in the localization of psychological processes in man. *British Medical Bulletin, 27,* 272–277.

Nelson, H.E. (1976). A modified card sorting test sensitive to frontal lobe defects. *Cortex, 12,* 313–324.

Osterrieth, P.A. (1944). Le test de copie d'une figure complex; contribution à l'etude de la perception et de la mémoire. *Archives de Psychologie, 30,* 286–356.

Pennington, B.F. (1991). *Diagnosing learning disabilities: A neuropsychological framework.* New York: Guilford Press.

Pennington, B.F. (1995). *Working memory and cognitive differences: The frontal lobes and intelligence revisited.* Manuscript in preparation.

Pennington, B.F., Groisser, D., & Welsh, M.C. (1993). Contrasting cognitive deficits in attention deficit hyperactivity disorder versus reading disability. *Developmental Psychology, 29,* 511–523.

Petrides, M., & Milner, B. (1982). Deficits on subject-ordered tasks after frontal and temporal lobe lesions in man. *Neuropsychologia, 20,* 249–262.

Reader, M.J., Harris, E.L., Schuerholz, L.J., & Denckla, M.B. (in press). Attention deficit hyperactivity disorder and executive dysfunction. *Developmental Neuropsychology.*

Rey, A. (1941). L'examen psychologique dans le cas d'encephalopathie traumatique. *Archives de Psychologie, 28,* 286–340.

Rudel, R.G., Denckla, M.B., & Broman, M. (1978). Rapid silent response to repeated target symbols by dyslexic and nondyslexic children. *Brain and Language, 6,* 52–62.

Shallice, T. (1982). Specific impairments of planning. *Philosophical Transactions of the Royal Society of London, Series B: Biological Sciences, 298,* 198–209.

Spreen, O., & Strauss, E. (1991). *A compendium of neuropsychological tests* (pp. 162–164). New York and Oxford: Oxford University Press.

Stroop, J.R. (1935). Studies of interference in serial verbal reaction. *Journal of Experimental Psychology, 18,* 643–662.

Taylor, H.G. (1988). Learning disabilities. In E.J. Mash (Ed.), *Behavioral assessments of childhood disorders* (2nd ed., pp. 402–405). New York: Guilford Press.

Teuber, H.L. (1964). The riddle of frontal lobe function in man. In J.M. Warren & K. Akert (Eds.), *The frontal granular cortex and behavior.* New York: McGraw-Hill.

Thatcher, R.W. (1991). Maturation of the human frontal lobes: physiological evidence for staging. *Developmental Neuropsychology, 7,* 397–419.

Thurstone, L.L. (1938). *Primary mental abilities.* Chicago: University of Chicago Press.

Tranel, D., Anderson, S.W., & Benton, A.L. (1995). Development of the concept of executive function and its relationship to the frontal lobes. In F. Boller & J. Grafman (Eds.), *Handbook of Neuropsychology* (Vol. 9, pp. 125–148). Amsterdam: Elsevier.

Trommer, B.L., Hoeppner, J.B., & Zecker, S.G. (1991). The Go–No-Go Test in attention deficit hyperactivity disorder is sensitive to methylphenidate. *Journal of Child Neurology, 6*(Suppl.), S128–S131.

Vik, P., & Ruff, R.R. (1988). Children's figural fluency performance: Development of strategy use. *Developmental Neuropsychology, 4*(1), 63–74.

Waber, D., & Holmes, J.M. (1985). Assessing children's copy productions of the Rey-Osterrieth Complex Figure. *Journal of Clinical and Experimental Neuropsychology, 7,* 264–280.

Welsh, M.C., Pennington, B.F., & Groisser, D.B. (1991). A normative developmental study of executive function: A window on prefrontal function in children. *Developmental Neuropsychology, 7,* 131–149.

16

RELATIONAL FRAME THEORY AND EXECUTIVE FUNCTION
A Behavioral Approach

Steven C. Hayes, Elizabeth V. Gifford,
and L. E. Ruckstuhl, Jr.

For a behavior analyst to write about executive function is difficult for two reasons. First, executive function is not a technical category within behavioral psychology. There is virtually no behavioral literature on executive function *per se*, although Barkley (Chapter 17) and others have drawn from that literature in their technical accounts of the area. Second, it is not at all clear what domain is covered by the term.

Our strategy in this chapter is first to examine the kinds of phenomena researchers from other traditions are terming *executive function*. We then consider what seem to be relevant literatures within basic behavior analysis and lay out a theoretical account that seems to cover these findings. Finally, we apply these analyses to executive function.

EXECUTIVE FUNCTION

The term *executive function* has been used to refer to many dimensions of human behavior. Unfortunately, the term does not just delimit a range of phenomena, however loosely—it also ties itself to particular approaches to those phenomena. Theories about the frontal lobe have been consistently associated with executive functioning, so much so that one might define some researchers' use of the term to mean "whatever function I believe might involve the frontal lobe." Furthermore, the term contains a thinly veiled reference to a homunculus-like entity that plans, chooses, decides, and otherwise engages in "higher cognitive processes."

Preparation of this chapter was supported in part by Grant DA08634 awarded by the National Institute on Drug Abuse.

Treating psychological functions as brain functions with semihuman-like properties is characteristic of some wings of modern neuroscience and cognitive psychology. It is not at all characteristic of a behavioral approach, which views psychology as the study of the interaction between whole organisms and their historical and current environments and which religiously avoids reification.

The problems of mixing phenomena with theoretical approaches to those phenomena under the rubric *executive function* are severalfold. First, we have a great deal to learn about the specific functions of the frontal lobe, and learning about these functions will require research about the very behavioral phenomena frontal lobe processes are supposed to explain. In other words, it is inconsistent to use physiologically based terms for behavioral phenomena when understanding the physiological functions will itself require this selfsame behavioral research. Second, such usage is massively premature. Third, it creates needless barriers between research traditions that all might contribute importantly to the analysis of these events.

That being said, there is a set of activities that most or all researchers refer to under the rubric of executive function. That set is both fuzzy and broad but does have recognizable outlines. It includes "self-regulation, set-maintenance, selective inhibition of verbal and nonverbal responding, cognitive flexibility, planning, prioritizing, and organizing time and space, and output-efficiency" (Harris, et al., in press). Executive function involves selecting and later monitoring and revising behavioral strategies, based on task analyses, planning, and reflectivity in decision making (Borkowski & Muthukrishna, 1992).

Executive processing is usually viewed as a component of metacognition (Borkowski, Milstead, & Hale, 1988; Brown, Bransford, Ferrara, & Campione, 1983; Flavell & Wellman, 1977; Sternberg, 1985), including such specific functions as deciding on the nature of the to-be-solved problem, selecting a set of lower-order components to help solve the problem, selecting a strategy into which to combine these components, deciding upon a mental representation upon which the components and strategy should act, allocating attentional and other resources, and monitoring the solution processes.

Approaching executive function on the basis of these terms is troublesome, however. The terms used to define executive function are themselves often vague or common-sense terms. What, precisely, do we mean by problems, strategies, planning, reflectiveness, organizing, resources, and so on? Rather than proceed from these terms, it seems useful to look at the measures people use in this area. They provide a view of the actual behaviors people are speaking about with these labels.

Tests of Executive Function

The broad range of events possibly covered by executive functioning has led to the use of many different assessment tools to measure individuals' executive function. As behavioral phenomena these tests are inherently more specific—and less theoretically contaminated—than the descriptive terms used above. As a prelude to a behavioral approach to executive function, it thus seems worthwhile to spend some time examining what are taken to be measures of executive function. We have deliberately set aside tests used with infants for reasons described later. A wide range of measures are used with children and adults.

The Stroop test (Golden, 1987) is one of the most common measures. It uses cards with the names of colors spelled out (e.g., the words *blue* or *red*) and printed in the ink of another color. Subjects are instructed to report the color of the ink rather than the word. This requires that subjects inhibit their normal tendency when reading, which is to attend to the words and ignore the color of the ink. Some memory is required because subjects must remember that the task is to name the color of the ink, but the principal ability required is inhibition. Patients with frontal cortex damage to the left hemisphere perform significantly more poorly on the task than patients with damage to other areas of the brain (Perret, 1974).

In a version of this task for children, two kinds of cards are used. The face of half of the cards is white with a brightly colored sun, to which the subject is instructed to say "night." The other cards have a face that is black with a moon and stars, to which the subject is instructed to say "day." In children age 3½–7 years, older children had a higher percentage of correct answers and a decrease in response latency (Gerstadt, Hong, & Diamond, in press).

The Wisconsin Card Sorting Test (WCST) (Heaton, Chelune, Talley, Kay, & Curtiss, 1993) has also been used as a device to measure executive functioning. For this task, four cards varying in color, shape, and number are placed in front of a subject. Subjects are given two decks of cards and asked to match the cards in the deck with one of the four "key" cards and are informed by an experimenter whether or not they have sorted a card correctly. After the subject categorizes 10 consecutive cards correctly, the sorting principle is changed without the subject's knowledge, and the experimenter gives negative feedback to the previously successful sorting strategy.

Several dependent variables can be calculated, including how many categories the subject completed, the number of errors, perseverative responses when the subject continued to use a previously correct category despite negative feedback, and the number of times the subject made five correct responses in a row but failed to sort the 10 cards necessary to complete a category. Individuals with autism show more perseverative responses than do control groups (Ozonoff, Pennington, & Rogers, 1991). Adults with damage to the dorsolateral prefrontal cortex are able to deduce the first criterion for sorting but are impaired when the experimenter changes the criterion (Milner, 1963, 1964)

The Tower of Hanoi task (Boris, Spitz, & Dorans, 1982) is thought to assess the abilities to inhibit prepotent, but irrelevant, responses and to plan and execute a sequence of moves that transforms a subject's configuration of disks to a configuration identical to the experimenter's. Two identical boards with three vertical pegs and three disks of different sizes and colors are set up, one in front of the subject and the other in front of the experimenter. Disks for the experimenter are arranged on the experimenter's right-hand peg to form a tower, with the largest disk on the bottom and the smallest disk on the top. This task has been used to assess planning capacities of typical children and adults, children and adults with retardation (Borys, Spitz, & Dorans, 1982), and adults with frontal damage (Shallice, 1982). It has also been used to discriminate children with autism from controls (Ozonoff et al., 1991).

Cole, Usher, and Cargo (1993) used a battery of tests to measure executive functioning deficits in preschoolers at risk for disruptive behavior disorders. Included in this were the Tapping Test (Becker, Isaac, & Hynd, 1987), which tests attentional control, inhibition of imitative action, and switching solutions with auditory stimuli; the Rapid-Alternating-Stimulus-Naming Test (Wolf, 1986), which measures sustained attention and ability to switch contexts rapidly during a verbal naming task; a hand movement test (Kaufman, 1983), which looks at planning and organizing functions in the nonverbal domain; a Block Sort developed by Cargo to parallel the WCST to assess ability to shift problem-solving set; and the Visual Search Test (adapted from Plude & Doussard-Roosevelt, 1989) to measure attentional control and switching motor responses. Variance in children's attentional and behavioral control could be predicted from a composite score on these measures.

Borkowski and Peck (1986) attempted to look at executive functioning in students who were gifted by presenting multiple memory tasks (paired–associate learning, sort-recall, and alphabet search) to third graders and giving different amounts of instruction (complete or enriched; incomplete or partial; and no instruction). In general, children who were gifted were able to apply strategies without prompting on transfer tasks and modify strategies to meet the demands of generalization tasks more effectively than typical children when training was incomplete or instructions were minimal. When training or instruction became more adequate, differences narrowed.

Grattan-Smith, Morris, Shores, Batchelor, and Sparks (1992) examined executive function deficits in patients with pituitary tumors. Their assessment of executive functioning consisted of three tasks. The Rey-Osterrieth complex figure required subjects to copy complex geometric figures to assess the ability to organize complex information. The Controlled Oral Word Association Tests (COWAT) required subjects to generate as many words as possible that began with a designated letter. This was used to assess the speed and ease of verbal production and the capacity to generate novel ideas. The last was a Trail Making Test (Trails B). It measured mental flexibility by having subjects link numbers and letters in an alternating, ascending sequence. Of these three measures of executive functioning, only Trails B differentiated between patients with pituitary tumors and controls.

The Core of These Tests This list of measures is hardly comprehensive— literally hundreds of different tests have been used—but it shows some of the range involved. The wide variety of assessment tools used to measure executive function point out its vague definition and lack of technical clarity in present research circles.

Although the tasks vary widely, most of these tests involve an unusual circumstance in which subjects are required to perform actions that conflict systematically with immediate and well-established sources of behavioral regulation. A fact that seems rarely noticed is that these tasks usually involve the effects of instructions, explicitly so in Borkowski and Peck's research (1986) but implicitly in almost all tests used with noninfants. Subjects are usually told what the goal is and may be instructed about how to achieve it. Often the conflict is between verbal and nonverbal sources of behavioral control. Conversely, beyond some minimal level the tasks do *not* assess previously acquired bases of knowledge, either verbal or nonverbal.

In the adult version of the Stroop test, the conflict, established by instructions (subjects are told to name the color, not the name), involves competition between semantic meaning and primary stimulus properties. The child version involves instruction-produced competition between previously trained semantic meaning and a new and opposite semantic relation. In the WCST, the conflict is between a trained (and, for verbally competent subjects, usually self-verbalized) sorting strategy and unannounced changes in task requirements. In Trails B, the competition comes from the instructed need to alternate between different sequential stimuli rather than to continue to sequence within a set as one would normally do. The Tower of Hanoi task presents, by instruction, a terminal state of affairs that can only be reached if irrelevant responses caused by immediate and habitual sources of behavioral regulation are extinguished. Similarly, the Tapping Test (Becker et al., 1987) involves the instructed need not to respond imitatively and to switch strategies; the Rapid–Alternating–Stimulus–Naming Test (Wolf, 1986) involves the instructed need to switch sources of behavioral control quickly.

In summary, on the basis of the requirements of the kinds of tests used in this area, executive function is not invoked when responses are well-practiced, smooth, or automatic. Hitting a baseball or playing the "Flight of the Bumble Bee" are not good examples of executive function. To the contrary, tests of executive function arrange situations in which immediate and habitual sources of behavioral regulation *cannot* work. Sometimes these habitual sources have been trained in the experimental situation—often they are simple behavioral functions that almost everyone brings into the test situation (e.g., the tendency to read a word or relate the sun to "day"). The habitual functions involved can be nonverbal or verbal—from preschool tests on, they seem more often to be verbal. Given that well-practiced sources of behavioral control do not work, subjects must either derive new rules that work or they must follow rules given by the experimenter and override alternative sources of behavioral control.

According to this way of looking at tests of executive function, what is at issue is the ability to derive, apply, or actually follow verbal rules when they are in conflict with other verbal or nonverbal sources of behavior. What is at issue, in short, is the flexibility and effectiveness of verbal regulation, as distinct from the adequacy of the existing set of verbal relations (i.e., the verbal "knowledge base") per se. Looking at executive function in this way puts aside for the moment purely nonverbal processes. Concepts such as *inhibition* apply equally well to verbal and nonverbal processes, and one can undoubtedly examine these phenomena in both domains. However, the psychological processes involved seem relatively distinct—a large body of literature supports the importance of distinguishing verbal from nonverbal events (some of the behavioral literature on this topic is reviewed below). This is why we did not examine tests of executive function in infants. In the absence of clear data showing that nonverbal and verbal "inhibition" or "strategies" are the same thing, a more conservative course seems to be to examine the properties of each separately, only later combining them if they can be combined.

THE NATURE OF VERBAL REGULATION

This chapter is written from within the wing of behavioral psychology represented by behavior analysis. Behavior analysis emerged from the animal learning tradition, and until the late1970s this tradition barely grappled in an empirical way with issues of human cognition (Hayes & Hayes, 1992b; Michael, 1984). Over the last 15 years, however, a research tradition has developed in the analysis of complex human behavior from a behavior analytical point of view (for several recent book-length reviews of that literature, see Hayes, 1989; Hayes & Chase, 1991; Hayes & Hayes, 1992a; Hayes, Hayes, Sato, & Ono, 1994). Behavior analysts in the area are especially focused on verbal behavior, including "that preliminary discourse called thinking" (Dewey, 1929). The work continues in the tradition of pragmatic thinkers such as Dewey, in that verbal behavior is viewed as the major substantive process in complex human behavior.

Empirical Background within the Behavioral Research Tradition

Two bodies of empirical literature set the stage for the current behavior analytical interest in verbal behavior. The first of these is the literature on rule governance. Behavioral researchers have long known that instructions often have a more significant impact than other variables in controlled laboratory settings (e.g., Kaufman, Baron, & Kopp, 1966). These effects are apparent in two areas (Ribes Inesta & Martinez Sanchez, 1990): 1) humans often do not exhibit patterns of responding typical of other animals to schedules of reinforcement (Leander, Lippman, & Meyer, 1968; Lippman & Meyer, 1967; Lowe, Harzem, & Hughes, 1978; Weiner, 1964, 1969) and 2) instructions often exert more control than direct, programmed contingencies (Galizio, 1979; Lowe, 1979; Lowe, Beasty, & Bentall, 1983; Lowe, Harzem, & Hughes, 1978; Shimoff, Catania, & Matthews, 1981). Even relatively innocuous instructions can produce a marked tendency for adults to persist in the face of strong contradictory contingencies (e.g., Hayes,

Brownstein, Haas, & Greenway, 1986; Hayes, Brownstein, Zettle, Rosenfarb, & Korn, 1986). Rules appear to be one way that humans reduce the tendency to respond automatically to immediate contingencies. These findings ultimately led behavior analysts to investigate the role of verbal rules in the differences found between humans and nonhumans.

The second relevant body of empirical literature focuses on the nature of derived stimulus relations. It originated in the early 1970s with the initial studies on stimulus equivalence (Sidman, 1971). Stimulus equivalence is usually studied using a matching-to-sample format. For example, in the presence of one of three samples, three comparisons are presented. The stimuli can be arbitrary graphical forms, sounds, or indeed any stimulus event. Selection of a particular comparison stimulus is rewarded in the presence of each particular sample: for example, in the presence of sample A1 and comparisons B1, B2, and B3, pick B1; in the presence of sample A2 and comparisons B1, B2, and B3, pick B2, and so on. Additional relations are then trained (e.g., once A–B relations are learned, a separate set of A–C relations are trained). Derived relations (i.e., relations not directly trained in the study) are then tested. The basic paradigm is shown in Figure 16.1.

There are three derived relations said to be characteristic of stimulus equivalence (Sidman & Tailby, 1982): reflexivity (e.g., A1 = A1); 2) symmetry (e.g., if A1 pick B1 is trained, then B1 pick A1 is derived); and 3) transitivity (e.g., if A1 pick B1, and B1 pick C1 are trained, then given A1 pick C1 is derived and vice versa). Stimulus equivalence has been shown with a wide variety of human subjects, using a wide variety of stimulus materials (e.g., Dixon, 1977; Dixon & Spradlin, 1976; Gast, VanBiervliet, & Spradlin, 1979; Hayes, Tilley, & Hayes, 1988; Mackay & Sidman, 1984; Sidman, 1971; Sidman, Cresson, & Willson-Morris, 1974; Sidman & Tailby, 1982; Spradlin & Dixon, 1976; VanBiervliet, 1977; Wulfert & Hayes, 1988).

The source of behavioral interest in stimulus equivalence and derived relations is twofold. First, derived stimulus relations of this kind do not emerge easily or automatically from traditional behavioral concepts. There is no obvious reason for derived symmetry; in normal behavioral chains, one cannot simply reverse the sequence and expect results. In classic conditioning preparations, backward conditioning is either absent, weak, or transient. Second, and more important, there is an apparent correspondence between the equivalence phenomena and natural language. If a child of sufficient verbal abilities is taught to point to a particular object given a particular written word, the child may point to the word given the object without specific training to do so. In an equivalence-type example, given training in the spoken word "candy" and actual candy, and between the written word CANDY and the spoken word "candy," a child will identify the written word CANDY as in an equivalence class with "candy," even though this relationship has never actually been trained. In naming tasks, symmetry and transitivity between written words, spoken words, pictures, and objects are commonplace (Dixon, 1977). Several studies on equivalence have used naming-like preparations using auditory and visual stimuli (Dixon & Spradlin, 1976; Sidman,

STIMULUS EQUIVALENCE

With this training:

A1			A2			A3		
⇓			⇓					⇓
B1	B2	B3	B1	B2	B3	B1	B2	B3

A1			A2			A3		
⇓			⇓					⇓
C1	C2	C3	C1	C2	C3	C1	C2	C3

This will emerge without additional training (i.e., will be derived):

Symmetry,   **And combinations of symmetry and**

for example: **transitivity, for example:**

B1			C1			B1		
⇓			⇓					⇓
A1	A2	A3	B1	B2	B3	C1	C2	C3

Figure 16.1. The emergence of derived relational responding in matching-to-sample paradigms.

Kirk, & Willson-Morris, 1985; Sidman & Tailby, 1982; Spradlin & Dixon, 1976; Yamamoto, 1986).

Studies have shown that deriving stimulus relations is correlated with verbal performance (Barnes, McCullagh, & Keenan, 1990; Devany, Hayes, & Nelson, 1986; Dugdale & Lowe, 1990) and that it develops over time much like early language development (Lipkens, Hayes, & Hayes, 1993). Some researchers have established successful language training or reading programs using equivalence and equivalence-like procedures exclusively (e.g., de Rose, de Souza, Rossito, & de Rose, 1992). Because of these many overlaps, some behavioral researchers have treated the stimulus equivalence phenomenon as a kind of working empirical model of semantic relations (e.g., Hayes & Hayes, 1989; Hayes, 1991).

Developing a Theoretical Account: Relational Frame Theory

Guided by the two research streams above, we start with the possibility that derived stimulus relations are a central defining feature of verbal events and that verbal regulation is based on these derived stimulus relations. To explain derived stimulus relations, however, we appeal to a simple and well-established behavioral idea: that of a learned, overarching behavioral class.

Control by stimulus relations is readily trained in nonhumans when these relations are based on formal properties of the related events. For example, animals may be taught to discriminate relationships based on formal properties such as brighter or dimmer (Reese, 1968). If it is possible to abstract such relational responding and bring it under the control of contextual cues, these relations could then be *arbitrarily applicable*. That is, stimuli could be related to each other based on a history of conventional training in deriving relations, regardless of the *form* of the related events. There is nothing about the form of *pan* that determines whether it is in an equivalence class with bread or metal containers—that relation is established by the whim of the particular social community involved.

Why would such a general behavioral class form? Much as with the behavioral account of generalized imitation (Baer, Peterson, & Sherman, 1967; Gewirtz & Stengle, 1968), we need only suppose that training with many, many exemplars of a class can lead to formation of the class. For example, training in generalized forms of symmetry may emerge from training in naming (see Figure 16.2). Names are bidirectionally related to referents. Young children are presented with thousands of instances of "given object X, say name X and not name Y," and in virtually all cases each specific direct relation predicts another relation: "Given name X, orient to object X not object Y." The reverse is also true: name–object relations predict object–name. At first both relations are trained, but ultimately in verbally mature humans training in only one direction leads to the derivation of the relation in the other direction.

With enough instances of bidirectional name–referent relations trained in both directions, the relational response becomes sufficiently abstracted to operate as an overarching class containing virtually any name–referent relation. Because the form of the relata varies, other contextual cues control the application of the relational response involved (e.g., "is" or a naming context indicates that this is a referential context). The person is said to have learned a *relational frame*.

This simple idea leads inexorably to an enormous widening of the range of phenomena that might emerge from trained relational responding. If it is possible to learn "equivalencing" as a psychological act, it should be similarly possible to learn other kinds of relational responses in the same way: difference, oppositeness, comparison, if . . . then, before-after, and so on. The general idea is shown in Figure 16.3. In testing this idea, several studies have shown that a wide variety of relational networks, not just equivalence, will emerge in arbitrary matching-to-sample training if subjects are given pretrained cues that control other forms of relational responding (e.g., Barnes & Keenan, 1993; Dymond & Barnes, 1994;

Imagined History Leading to Equivalence

[Referential context]

	Word -> Referent	Referent -> Word
1.	TRAIN	TRAIN
2.	TRAIN	TRAIN
3.	TRAIN	TRAIN

Derive a relational frame of coordination, such that

[Referential context]

	Word -> Referent	Referent -> Word
x.	TRAIN	AND GET

Figure 16.2. The emergence of derived equivalence relations in natural language environments.

Steele & Hayes, 1991). Relational frame theory suggests that an inherent component of verbal behavior, whether from the point of view of the speaker or the listener, is the learned derivation of stimulus relations based on contextual cues to do so, and not merely on the formal properties of the related events (Hayes & Hayes, 1989, 1992b). Relational frames have three defining properties.

Mutual Entailment Relations fundamentally imply bidirectionality. Any arbitrarily applicable relation must logically entail an inverse relation: Better entails worse, larger entails smaller, and so on. Mutual entailment means that, if by direct training X has relation p with Y in a given context, then by derivation Y has relation q with X in that same context. In some cases p and q are the same (e.g., sameness or similarity, difference, oppositeness), but often relations are not strictly symmetrical (e.g., comparatives, time).

Combinatorial Entailment Whereas mutual entailment describes the fundamental bidirectionality of relational responding, combinatorial entailment describes the fundamental capacity of relational responses to combine. If by direct training X has relation p with Y and Y has relation p with Z in a given context, then by derivation X has relation q with Z and Z has relation r with X in that same context. Combinatorial entailment differs from mutual entailment in both complexity and level of specificity. In mutual entailment, the level of precision in

Imagined General Relational History

[Relational context]

	Event r$_p$	Event	Event r$_q$	Event
1.	TRAIN			TRAIN
2.	TRAIN			TRAIN
3.	TRAIN			TRAIN

Derive the r$_p$ - r$_q$ relational frame such that

[Relational context]

	Event r$_p$	Event	Event r$_q$	Event
x.	TRAIN			AND GET

Figure 16.3. The emergence of derived relational responding.

the trained relation between X and Y is the same as in the derived relation between Y and X. In combinatorial entailment, the relation between X and Z and between Z and X may or may not be specified at the same level of precision as the relation between the bidirectional pairs. This can occur, for example, when the form of the relations differs between the two mutually entailed relations. Suppose X is in a relation of "more than" with Y, and Y is in a relation of "difference" with Z. There is no precise relation specified between X and Z. This lack of precision, however, is itself specified in the relation. This is part of what distinguishes a psychological from a logical or mathematical relation: A verbal relation of "no relation" is still a psychological relation because it involves responding to one event in terms of another (Hayes & Hayes, 1992b).

Transformation of Stimulus Functions The derivation of relations among events would be irrelevant in a section on "verbal regulation" were it not for this final property. If event X has a particular derived relation to event Y, and event X has a psychological function, then in a context that selects that function as relevant, event Y may acquire this psychological function, transformed in terms of the underlying derived relation. For example, if "lemon" is in an equivalence class with actual lemons in a context that selects taste as the relevant function, talking of lemons can be associated with salivation or puckering. The transformation of stimulus functions has primarily been studied with equivalence relations. Transfer through equivalence relations has been shown with conditioned reinforcing functions (Hayes, Brownstein, Devany, Kohlenberg, & Shelby, 1987; Hayes, Kohlenberg, & Hayes, 1991), discriminative functions (de Rose, McIlvane, Dube, Galpin, & Stoddard, 1988; Hayes et al., 1987), elicited conditioned emotional responses (Augustson, Dougher, & Markham, 1993), and self-discrimination responses (Dymond & Barnes, 1994), among others (e.g., Perez-Gonzalez, 1994).

This process enormously expands the sources available to regulate responding and is a primary reason why language makes a huge difference. Consider this example: Suppose "zig" is in an equivalence relation with "electric shock" and with actual electric shocks, and a person then learns that "right after zag comes zig and right after zig comes zip." Under these conditions "zag" may have emotionally arousing functions while "zip" may produce calm. "Zig" may have arousing functions based on a transfer of the functions of shock to "electric shock" and then to "zig." Zag and zip have their functions based on a transformation of stimulus functions through a temporal relational frame (see Hayes, 1992, for a discussion of temporal relations). A few trained relations, and only one direct function, could give rise to several derived relations and several transformed functions. For the same thing to happen in a nonverbal organism without these relational abilities, many, many specific relations would have to be directly trained, one at a time.

Can Relational Frames Be Learned? The term *relational frame* (Hayes, 1991; Hayes & Hayes, 1989, 1992b) thus describes a particular pattern of contextually controlled, arbitrarily applicable relational responding involving mutual entailment, combinatorial entailment, and the transformation of stimulus functions. Are relational frames learned? Behavior that is purposive and learned should have particular characteristics: It should develop, be flexible, come under stimulus control, come under consequential control, and be treatable or trainable in populations with deficits. All four properties have been shown in the empirical literature on equivalence classes and related forms of responding (see Hayes, 1994, for a review). Equivalence and similar relational responses (e.g., stimulus exclusion) develop over time in young children (e.g., Lipkens et al., 1993). Very flexible forms of relational responding can emerge given the proper form of pretraining (e.g., Dymond and Barnes, 1994; Steele & Hayes, 1991). Derived relational responding has been shown to come under both stimulus control (e.g., Steele & Hayes, 1991; Wulfert & Hayes, 1988) and consequential control (e.g., Leonhard & Hayes, 1991; Hayes, 1994).

Rule Governance

The acquisition or modification of stimulus functions through derived relational responding involves increasingly complex forms (see Hayes, 1994). These forms include the establishment of a derived relation, the modification of a preexisting relational network, or the modifications of the previously nonverbal world by the application of a relational network. The first level is that seen in the equivalence literature. The second level indicates the kind of process involved in abstract reasoning such as analogy (Lipkens et al., 1993). This second level involves both rule derivation and rule understanding. The final level is that involved in rule governance.

In our approach, rule-governed behavior is behavior under the control of antecedent stimuli that have their functions in part because they participate in relational frames (Hayes, Zettle, & Rosenfarb, 1989). To follow a rule one must understand it: In our terms, understanding is the derivation of a pattern of stimulus relations. For example, a person told that "right after zag comes zig and right after zig comes zip" may derive that right before zip comes zig and right before zig comes zag. This is the person's "understanding." If a speaker and listener "understand each other" in a verbal sense, they share a relational network in a given context. But understanding a rule and following it are two different things. Following a rule requires two additional events: the transformation of stimulus functions in terms of the underlying network of stimulus relations, and contingencies that support activity with regard to these transformed functions. A failure in either process can mean a failure in verbal regulation.

For example, suppose instead of zag, zig, and zip, an inner city youth is told, "After high school you can go to college and after college you can get a diploma." Suppose this rule has no effect on school performance. How could we account for this lack of an effect? It is unlikely that the person does not have a before–after relational frame. Rather, this frame may appear unapplicable ("No, after high school I'll probably be dead because no one makes it out of this place"); the functions of the related events may not be strong or may not transfer ("Who cares about a diploma?"); and the probability of positive consequences for following the rule itself appears to be weak because when similar rules were followed in the past nothing good happened.

Categories of Rule Following

We have identified three functional categories of rule following (Hayes et al., 1989). The first of these, pliance, is the most rudimentary level of rule following. Here responding to rules is controlled by a history of socially mediated reinforcement for a correspondence between rules and the behavior they specify. For example, suppose a child is told to sweep her room to get it clean. If she does so because Mom will praise her for doing what she was told, this is pliance. In tracking, the second functional unit of rule following, rules are followed because of a history of correspondence between rules and the actual contingencies pertaining to the form of the specified behavior. If a child told to sweep her room to get it clean does so because the room will get clean, this is tracking. Finally, augmenting is behavior due to rules that alter the capacity of specific events to function as consequences. Two types of augmentals have been identified: motivative augmentals, in which antecedent verbal stimuli temporarily alter the degree to which previously established consequences function as reinforcers or punishers, and formative augmentals, in which antecedent verbal stimuli establish new consequences as reinforcers or punishers. For example, if "being good" has developed reinforcing functions over a period of time, and "sharing" is identified as being good, then "sharing" may function as a formative augmental, as it acquires some of the functions of "being good" (Hayes & Hayes, 1994).

These three units of rule following may occur in combination with one another. It is important to bear in mind that these are *functional* units and therefore aren't defined according to formal characteristics but rather according to the history controlling the behavior of the rule follower (Hayes & Hayes, 1989, 1992b).

Evidence for these distinctions exists in several literatures. For example, social psychological research has contributed a great deal to the understanding of social influence processes relevant to pliance (e.g., Asch, 1956; Baron & Byrne, 1984; Deaux & Wrightsman, 1984; Milgram, 1969). Counterpliance or reactance may occur when rule following cannot be monitored or when the contingencies surrounding rule following are weaker than those controlling rule breaking (e.g., Bickman & Rosenbaum, 1977; Organ, 1974). Pliance itself is most likely to result when rule following can be monitored and the socially mediated contingencies surrounding rule following are strong (e.g., Brehm & Brehm, 1981; Dickenberger & Grabitz-Griech, 1972). Pliance and tracking in therapeutic interactions have also been shown. Most forms of verbal clinical interventions have, when tested, turned out to be more a matter of pliance than tracking (Hayes et al., 1985; Hayes & Wolf, 1984; Rosenfarb & Hayes, 1984; Zettle & Hayes, 1983). Finally, human operant research provides support for these distinctions as well (Barrett, Deitz, Gaydos, & Quinn, 1987; Hayes et al., 1985).

EXECUTIVE FUNCTION AS A
SUBSET OF RULE-GOVERNED BEHAVIOR

We return now to the nature of executive function, armed with a set of behavioral concepts about verbal relations and rule governance. Let us start with what executive function is not. Everyone would agree that it is not about behavior that is automatic or well-practiced. In behavioral terms, we may say that executive function is not about well-established contingency-shaped behavior. Furthermore, it is not about the extent of a person's "knowledge base." Unlike a vocabulary test or a test of the ability to form analogies, it does not assume anything beyond a minimal set of previously established verbal relations.

We argued earlier that actual tests of executive function often involve the performance of actions, usually instructed or self-instructed, that conflict systematically with immediate and well-established nonverbal and verbal sources of behavior. Some of the tests require the subject to derive rules, but the focus is not on the adequacy of the existing set of verbal relations. More often the assessments provide (e.g., Stroop test; Golden, 1987) or train (e.g., WCST) rules and then examine the effectiveness or the flexibility of these rules. The question then is this: Under what conditions do people select among available rules or generate new ones, follow rules when they are available even though they conflict with other sources of behavioral control, and change them when they no longer work? Framed this way, executive function is a subset of rule-governed behavior.

Selecting Among Available Rules or Generating New Ones

When rules are competing with behavior that is automatic and well-practiced (i.e., with well-established contingency-shaped behavior), existing behavior must be disrupted or delayed long enough for alternatives to be possible. By its very nature, smooth, contingency-shaped behavior tends to be "impulsive." Disruption of contingency-shaped behavior is one of the main and most important effects of verbal rules (Hayes, 1989).

Suppose a child is chasing a ball and the ball goes into the street. Chasing a rolling ball is the kind of behavior that is usually run off in a smooth chain—each step toward the ball leads to another slightly modified step. A change in the proximity and exact location of the ball serves both as an antecedent for the next step and as a consequence for the previous step. As the ball enters the street, the street presents a slightly different context. For the child to stop, the slight contextual modification made by the street (e.g., changes in the way the ball bounces, the color of the asphalt) must interfere with ongoing behavior. Such functions for the street could have been established through nonverbal means (e.g., the child may have been previously hit by a car in the street), but in all likelihood the street must function as a verbal stimulus or the child will not stop.

The street is a verbal stimulus in the sense that it must participate in a derived stimulus relation with "street" and have functions based on rules such as, "Don't go into the street without a grownup taking you or you might be run down by a car!" Such a rule puts a response to the street (going into it) in an if–then relation with hurt. The verbally described hurt may have aversive functions (via a transformation of stimulus functions through a derived relation), which accrue to the action via application of the underlying if–then relation. By the transformation of stimulus functions, "going into the street" predicts aversive events even though these aversive events have never been experienced directly. But "streets" and actual streets are also in a frame of coordination, and thus the *actual street* may function as a negative stimulus for going. In such a case, it is functioning as a *verbal* stimulus because its functions depend upon derived stimulus relations.

The conclusion this leads to is unexpected. Selecting among available rules depends upon the disruption of ongoing streams of behavior, which is itself largely the function of verbal rules. If this analysis is correct, in order to have time to select among rules at least some rules must already be operating. The rule may be quite general (e.g., "I've got to think about this" or "What should I do?") or quite specific (e.g., "I'm going into the street; Mommy told me not to"). It is worth noting that the idea of inhibition of ongoing streams of behavior, although not a component of most cognitive or behavior theories of problem solving (Reese, 1994), was emphasized by Dewey as an important element in his discussion of the role of reflective thinking (Dewey, 1933).

Which Rules Are Available? Once direct action has been inhibited long enough for "thinking" to take place, the other verbal functions of the current environment have a chance to participate in the regulation of current behavior. By their very nature relational networks break the environment down into elements, and without this property rule governance would not be possible. Selecting among available rules in a given situation depends upon shared elements between established rules and verbally formed elements in the current environment. It is not possible to apply rules about objects or situations until some aspect of the current environment develops its stimulus functions by virtue of its participation in a verbal class. In short, verbal formulae can control interactions with the environment because elements of the environment are members of verbal classes.

This fact is not always given due emphasis, perhaps because verbal categories can at times correspond quite closely to nonverbal stimulus classes. Balls or streets are stimulus categories that nonverbal organisms could form by direct experience; when formed they would look something like verbally established stimulus categories, except that the stimulus generalization gradients around the latter would tend to be more gradual than the step-like gradients of verbally established classes. For example, a smooth round melon is more likely to be treated as a ball by a pigeon trained to view balls as a stimulus class than it would be by a verbal adult.

Many verbal categories are unlike nonverbal categories, and in this case the division of the environment into classes is more obviously verbal. A street may be said to be "dangerous," for example. So, too, is insulting one's boss, having unprotected sex, eating raw eggs, or failing to honor God. The verbal category "dangerous" breaks the environment into elements (dangerous and nondangerous events), but while those elements involve formal properties they are not defined by formal properties. Nothing in the formal properties of cursing God or having sex is "dangerous." Rather, formal properties (the form of the curse, the presence or absence of a condom) serve as cues for the application of relational frames.

Because many, many categories can be applied to a given situation, many, many rules are potentially psychologically available in a given situation. Selecting among them depends either upon direct experience with these rules or similar rules, and the application of if–then or temporal relations to them and the construction of verbal outcomes.

Direct History of Successful Rule Governance If there is a history of successful outcomes having been produced by pliance or tracking in similar situations, and if tracks or plies are available that are similar or identical to the rules that have worked in the past, these rules may be followed quite readily. Indeed, over time they may become so well-practiced as to become almost contingency-shaped again (what we sometimes call "automatic behavior"). When we used the "Flight of the Bumble Bee" as an example of contingency-shaped behavior earlier, it was really an example of this kind: It was originally controlled by a verbal rule (i.e., the musical score) but became virtually contingency-shaped with practice.

Constructed Outcomes of Rules If direct histories of this kind are not available, a more verbal or relational approach can be used. Several rules may be reflectively considered. The person may "decide" what to do. In this case, several rules that are available by virtue of their relation to verbal categories in the environment are examined by applying an if–then relational frame to them. In other words, the person may consider the likely consequences of an action. Features of the situation will determine how successfully an if–then or before–after frame can be applied. In an ambiguous situation, when the frame is applied no certain outcome can be discerned. Even in clear situations the outcomes may be complex, containing some positive and some negative elements.

Which rule is then selected can be either a matter of applying still other verbal rules to the various verbally constructed outcomes (as when one lists all the possible pros and cons of alternative decisions) or a matter of "feel" for the consequences. In this latter case, the stimulus functions of the actual events referred to by a verbally predicted consequence, transformed through the if–then or the temporal relation, can compete with other verbal consequences associated with other courses of action and in turn alter the behavior regulatory functions of the current contextual features that participate in these various rules. In this case, selecting among courses of action is very much like selecting among alternatives that are contingency-shaped, except that the process that leads a course of action to "feel right" is indirect and relational instead of direct and experiential. For example, suppose my ball is balanced on a median strip, in between extraordinarily rapid but congested traffic. I could run after it and get it, but as I construct this relation the high likelihood of being hit by a car is obvious. The initial steps of the sequence of actions now immediately have aversive properties. I might say "even the thought of doing it gives me the willies."

Sometimes it may be possible to assign priorities to the dimensions of the verbally constructed consequences for various courses of action. It may be more important to be fast than accurate, or safe than effective, or politically correct than impactful. In this case, priorities among alternatives may be formed along qualitative as well as quantitative dimensions.

Rule Generation If, in this whole process, behavior is not at sufficiently high strength based on any of the alternatives, a process of rule generation may occur. Developing new alternatives through verbal means seems most likely when 1) the person has no directly applicable and strong contingency-shaped behavior; 2) the person has little direct and successful experience with having followed rules identical or similar to those that are psychologically available in these circumstances; or 3) the stimulus functions of verbal consequences for alternative courses of rule-governed action are weak because these outcomes seem unlikely, are mixed, or cannot be foreseen clearly in verbal terms. The axiom "necessity is the mother of invention" describes the process fairly well.

Deriving new rules in a situation seems to involve a process of 1) breaking the situation into components by applying verbal categories or responding in terms of those that are present, and 2) deriving possible rules based on the elaboration or the metaphorical application of existing relational networks. In the case of rules based upon elaboration of a relational network, derived stimulus relations that are implicit in an existing set of stimulus relations are developed, very much like what happens when a person derives an equivalence relation after having learned the underlying conditional discriminations. In this case the person "sees a connection" for the first time, but in some sense the connection was implicit already. Metaphor involves deriving a relation between one set of stimulus relations and another, and in so doing changing the derived relations that are present. A statement such as "anxiety is like quicksand" may establish an entirely new relation—in this case between anxiety and struggle with anxiety. Before application of the metaphor, struggle with anxiety may have been seen as the means by which anxiety would be removed. After application of the metaphor, struggle with anxiety may be seen as the means by which harm is done.

Mere application of existing relational networks to a new situation is not an instance of rule derivation—it involves the issue of rule availability discussed above. When a rule is applied to a new situation, there is no fundamental change in the existing network of derived stimulus relations. For example, suppose a person has learned "when you cannot open a box, take off its hinges." That same person now confronts a locked door. If opening the door by taking off its hinges occurs because the existing rule is applied to doors, no new rules have been derived. The dividing line between applying old rules and developing new ones, however, is not always clear—particularly in the case of metaphor.

Following Rules

So far we have discussed why specific rules may be developed or selected in a given situation. Whether or not particular rules are actually followed in an overt behavioral sense is another matter, but the two areas are not entirely distinct. Rule following involves rule understanding because fairly tight derived stimulus relations can make the psychological functions of consequences more available. If I really believe that x will occur if I do y, I am probably more likely to see, taste, and feel x. Conversely, if I see, taste, and feel x, I am more likely to do y. This is why lottery promoters show how winners act when they are told they have won or why sweepstakes circulars ask respondents to pick the color of the car they have an infinitesimal chance of winning: Rule following is more likely if the consequences are psychologically present, because having those functions verbally present is a motivative augmental (Hayes & Ju, 1993).

The main reason rules are followed, however, is because of a history of rule following, not of rule understanding per se. If a person grows up in a chaotic and unpredictable environment, for example, tracking is unlikely, even though the person may understand the particular rule. If a person grows up in the absence of frequent and accurate rules, rule following will also be less likely. These two factors may explain why children from low socioeconomic status backgrounds are poorer rule followers: They have been exposed to lower rates of verbal rules, and their environments are less verbally predictable. "If you study you will succeed" is inherently less reliable as a rule if you are likely to be shot, robbed, or beat up regardless of what you do. Conversely, if rule following is overemphasized or maintained by excessive negative contingencies, spontaneous contingency-shaped behavior may be undermined.

There seems to be a developmental sequence to the development of rule-governed behavior and, as a result, of human morality (Hayes & Hayes, 1994). Pliance seems to occur before other forms of rule governance. Unlike tracking, pliance adds new reinforcers and punishers to those contingencies already present. Children, for example, are told "no," and deviation from the rule is often immediately punished ("I told you no!"). This relatively tight contingency may be necessary to establish rule following in the first place. Acquiring pliance requires consistent rule givers who control and contingently deliver important reinforcers.

Tracking relies on existing consequences. The key issue is the degree to which tracks predict the actual contingencies. Acquiring a history of correspondence between the rule and the contingencies requires frequent, accurate descriptions of the world, beginning with relatively short-term and highly likely situations and gradually becoming more long term and probabilistic.

Augmenting is the most complex form of rule following, because it depends on verbal relations for reinforcement per se. Although "good boy" can be fairly tightly related to actual positive consequences and can function as a positive consequence as a result, it comes to have more than mere conditioned reinforcing functions because of the verbal relations sustained between it and other, largely verbal events ("A good boy is kind, helpful, . . . " etc.). Over time these verbal consequences become more and more abstract as individuals work to be "right" or "fair" or "honest" or "free." The development of augmenting is the form of rule following most dependent upon good verbal abilities and frequent and consistent presentations of verbal rules. Children coming from verbally impoverished environments will have the most difficulty caring about highly abstract, temporally distant, or probabilistic verbal consequences. This is important for the development of less impulsive and more thoughtful behavior, even if the child can state the verbal relation involved. "What will happen when you do well in school? Would you be more respected?" a troubled teenager is asked. "I guess so" comes the answer, but "being respected" may be nothing more than words. The rule is present, but it has no augmenting function.

Changing Rules on the Basis of Outcomes

Flexibility in rule following requires being able to test them. Rule-governed behavior tends to become inherently less flexible than contingency-shaped behavior if the consequences specified in a rule are remote or abstract or if the contingencies are concrete and maintained.

Some rules are meant to be inflexible, and they are deliberately constructed so as to be untestable. "Do good and you will go to heaven when you die" is inherently untestable (while alive) if it is treated as a track. If the verbal consequence "heaven" has strong positive stimulus functions and if the if–then relation between doing good and this consequence is strong, such a rule may support lifelong patterns of doing good things, even in the face of strong contradictory contingencies. "Do good or God will punish you" is untestable if taken as a ply, but unlike most plies it seems universally applicable. God is said to be all-seeing and all-knowing: God is a rule giver who can always monitor rule compliance.

Tests of executive function, however, often measure rule flexibility. In the WCST, a rule works for a time and then does not work. The consequence is immediate and salient: The person is told that the sorting is incorrect. If the original strategy was contingency-shaped or was rule-governed and functioning as a track, behavior should change when the consequences change. For it to change, however, the person usually must go through a process of developing or considering alternative rules (as described earlier), and the available alternatives must seem to be more effective than existing behavior. Thus, rule flexibility should increase when the person has ready alternatives to an existing rule. The rule should be tied to clear and immediately measurable outcomes and be sufficiently specific that the rule follower can know when it is not working. The consequences associated with the success or failure of rule following must be important (the person must be "interested in doing well"). The original rule following should not be merely a ply ("I guess I just need to do what she is trying to get me to do"). Finally, rules that emphasize strategies, rather than specific topographies of behavior, are likely to be followed more flexibly.

TESTS OF THE THEORY

A theory of executive function based on relational frames has two somewhat distinct components that can be tested: whether relational frame theory is a worthwhile account of human verbal behavior and verbal regulation, and whether executive function can be usefully thought of in these terms.

Relational frame theory argues that relational frames are learned and are not primitive psychological functions. We already mentioned five testable components to this claim: They should show clear developmental trends, they should be flexible, they should be under both antecedent and consequential control, and improved relational abilities should emerge from deliberate training. Supportive data exist in each these five areas, but much more remains to be done.

The last point is particularly in accord with the pragmatic assumptions of behavior analysis: The best way to test a theory or device is to see if it can lead to more effective treatment (Hayes, Nelson, & Jarrett, 1987). Training could occur with populations who have disabilities in rule generation, rule understanding, and rule following, such as children with attention deficits or hyperactivity, youth who are antisocial, and those with mental retardation. Typical youth could be given procedures designed to modify existing repertoires and accelerate their healthy development.

These five testable components of the claim that relational frames are learned also suggest ways that this key aspect of relational frame theory can be disproved. If derived stimulus relations are present in whole cloth in neonates, or emerge without training in nonhumans, the theory is disproven. If new, more subtle, or more complex stimulus relations cannot be taught to children and brought to bear on arbitrary events in a fashion envisioned by the theory, it is disproven. The theory argues that a wide variety of relations can be trained and that derived stimulus functions will be transformed by these underlying relations. The first point has some empirical support, but not yet the latter. If complex relations are merely a by-product of equivalence and nonequivalence, and if derived functions are merely transferred, not transformed, when relations such as oppositeness pertain to two stimuli, the theory is disproven. A key idea is that relational frames are a defining feature of human verbal behavior. If the behavioral functions of verbal events (e.g., self-awareness, construction of long-term futures and a resultant reduction in impulsivity, complex problem solving) do not emerge in children in a fashion that parallels developing relational abilities, the theory is disproven. If complex relational frames can be developed in nonhumans, without also seeing some of the effects produced in humans by verbal behavior, the theory is disproven.

If relational frame theory is correct, children should show increased abilities in verbal regulation as they learn to apply more complex relational frames to events (e.g., if–then, comparatives). The theory suggests that the key aspects of training are 1) increases in the number of available relational frames, 2) increases in combinatorial abilities and the resultant complexity of the derived relational networks, 3) greater sensitivity and subtlety in the contextual control of relational frames and resulting increases in both their arbitrary applicability and appropriate regulation by physical context, 4) increased ability to transform stimulus functions through derived stimulus relations and greater sensitivity and subtlety in the contextual control over this process of transformation, 5) greater ability to relate networks of relations, and 6) greater ability to alter the functions of the previously nonverbal world by including aspects of this world in relational networks. As these performances increase in children, we should see increases in self-control, reasoning, and problem solving—if not, the theory is disproven.

According to the theory, following verbal rules is a product of the ability both to apply if–then frames to events and to transform the functions of verbally constructed consequences and of experience with contingencies that support specific types of rule following, such as pliance, tracking, and augmenting. Both contentions are clearly testable. Our line of thinking also suggests that pliance usually helps establish tracking, which helps establish augmenting. It suggests that moral development and other complex forms of rule governance normally emerge in that sequence and may need to be trained in that sequence. It also suggests novel ways that deficits in rule following may occur, such as mismatches of types of rules and rule following (e.g., the tendency for persons with some histories to treat descriptions as demands and thus to show pliance or counterpliance instead of tracking in these situations).

Testing these effects of verbal rules will be difficult, but behavior analysis offers the field at large not just a theoretical approach, but also a set of methods that are highly precise and well-developed. These include refined methods of arbitrary matching-to-sample and methods for testing the effects of rules on sensitivity to changes in environmental demands. Behavior analysts have also argued for and used refined "talk aloud" methods for detecting the participation of verbal rules in problem solving (Hayes, 1986; Wulfert, Dougher, & Greenway, 1991).

CONCLUSIONS

According to our way of looking at executive function, what is at issue is the ability to derive, apply, or actually follow verbal rules in conflict with other verbal or nonverbal behavior. Although an enormous literature exists in the study of human language, it has usually emphasized the study of semantics or syntactics over the study of pragmatics. To say it another way, there has been a tendency to stay "in the head" and to de-emphasize the direct behavioral effects of verbal abilities. Executive function challenges that tendency, because it is all about the connection between human verbal abilities and actual behavioral regulation. Whether or not the relational frame approach turns out to be useful, behavioral psychologists are used to thinking about events functionally and, as a result, have something important to contribute to the development of our understanding of this area.

REFERENCES

Asch, S.E. (1956). Studies of independence and conformity: I. A minority of one against a unanimous majority. *Psychological Monographs, 70* (9, Whole No. 416).

Augustson, E.M., Dougher, M.J., & Markham, M.R. (1993, May). *The transfer of CER eliciting and extinction functions via stimulus equivalence classes*. Paper presented at the convention of the Association for Behavior Analysis, Chicago.

Baer, D.M., Peterson, R.F., & Sherman, J.A. (1967). The development of imitation by reinforcing behavioral similarity to a model. *Journal of the Experimental Analysis of Behavior, 10*, 405–416.

Barnes, D., & Keenan, M. (1993). A transfer of functions through derived arbitrary and nonarbitrary stimulus relations. *Journal of the Experimental Analysis of Behavior, 59*, 61–81.

Barnes, D., McCullagh, P.D., & Keenan, M. (1990). Stimulus equivalence in non-hearing and hearing impaired children. *The Analysis of Verbal Behavior, 8*, 19–30.

Baron, R.A., & Byrne, D. (1984). *Social psychology: Understanding human interaction* (4th ed.). Boston: Allyn & Bacon.

Barrett, D.M., Deitz, S.M., Gaydos, G.R., & Quinn, P.C. (1987). The effects of programmed contingencies and social conditions on response stereotypy with human subjects. *Psychological Record, 37*, 489–505.

Becker, M.G., Isaac, W., & Hynd, G.W. (1987). Neuropsychological development of nonverbal behaviors attributed to "frontal lobe" functioning. *Developmental Neuropsychology, 3*, 275–298.

Bickman, L., & Rosenbaum, D.P. (1977). Crime reporting as a function of bystander encouragement, surveillance, and credibility. *Journal of Personality and Social Psychology, 35*, 577–586.

Borkowski, J.G., Milstead, M., & Hale, C. (1988). Components of children's metamemory: Implications for strategy generalization. In F. Weinert & M. Perlmutter (Eds.), *Memory development: Individual differences and universal changes* (pp. 73–100). Hillsdale, NJ: Lawrence Erlbaum Associates.

Borkowski, J.G., & Muthukrishna, N. (1992) Moving metacognitions into the classroom: "Working models" and effective strategy teaching. In M. Pressley, K.R. Harris, & J.T. Guthrie (Eds.), *Promoting academic literacy: cognitive research and instructional innovations* (pp. 477–501). Orlando, FL: Orlando Academic Press.

Borkowski, J.G., & Peck, V.A. (1986). Causes and consequences of metamemory in gifted children. In R. Sternberg & J. Davidson (Eds.), *Conceptions of giftedness* (pp. 182–200). Cambridge, England: Cambridge University Press.

Borys, S.V., Spitz, H.H., & Dorans, B.A. (1982). Tower of Hanoi performance of retarded young adults and nonretarded children as a function of solution length and goal state. *Journal of Experimental Child Psychology, 33*, 87–110.

Brehm, S.S., & Brehm, J.W. (1981). *Psychological reactance: A theory of freedom and control.* New York: Academic Press.

Brown, A.L., Bransford, J.D., Ferrara, R.A., & Campione, J.C. (1983). Learning, remembering, and understanding. In J.H. Flavell & E.M. Markwen (Eds.), *Carmichael's manual of child psychology* (pp. 515–529). New York: John Wiley & Sons.

Cole, P.M., Usher, B.A., & Cargo, A.P. (1993). Cognitive risk and its association with risk for disruptive behavior disorder in preschoolers. *Journal of Clinical Child Psychology, 22*, 154–164.

Deaux, K., & Wrightsman, L.S. (1984). *Social psychology in the 80s* (4th ed.). Monterey, CA: Brooks/Cole.

de Rose, J.Y., de Souza, D.G., Rossito, A.L., & de Rose, T.M.S. (1992). Stimulus equivalence and generalization in reading after matching to sample by exclusion. In S.C. Hayes & L.J. Hayes (Eds.), *Understanding verbal relations* (pp. 69–82). Reno, NV: Context Press.

de Rose, J.T., McIlvane, W.J., Dube, W.V., Galpin, V.C., & Stoddard, L.T. (1988). Emergent simple discrimination established by indirect relation to differential consequences. *Journal of the Experimental Analysis of Behavior, 50*, 1–20.

Devany, J.M., Hayes, S.C., & Nelson, R.O. (1986). Equivalence class formation in language-able and language-disabled children. *Journal of the Experimental Analysis of Behavior, 46*, 243–257.

Dewey, J. (1929). *Experience and nature.* LaSalle, IL: Open Court.

Dewey, J. (1933). *How we think: A restatement of the relation of reflective thinking to the educative process.* Boston: D.C. Heath.

Dickenberger, D., & Grabitz-Griech, G. (1972). Restrictive conditions for the occurrence of psychological reactance: Interpersonal attraction, need for social approval, and a delay factor. *European Journal of Social Psychology, 2*, 177–198.

Dixon, L.S. (1977). The nature of control by spoken words over visual stimulus selection. *Journal of the Experimental Analysis of Behavior, 27*, 433–442.

Dixon, M.H., & Spradlin, J.E. (1976). Establishing stimulus equivalences among retarded adolescents. *Journal of Experimental Child Psychology, 21*, 144–164.

Dugdale, N., & Lowe, C.F. (1990). Naming and stimulus equivalence. In D.E. Blackman & H.Lejeune (Eds.), *Behavior analysis in theory and practice: Contributions and controversies* (pp. 115–138). Hillsdale, NJ: Lawrence Erlbaum Associates.

Dymond S., & Barnes, D. (1994). A transfer of self-discrimination response functions through equivalence relations. *Journal of the Experimental Analysis of Behavior, 62*, 251–267.

Flavell, J.H., & Wellman, H.M. (1977). Metamemory. In R.V. Kail and J.W. Hagen (Eds.), *Perspectives on the development of memory and cognition* (pp. 3–33). Hillsdale, NJ: Lawrence Erlbaum Associates.

Galizio, M. (1979). Contingency-shaped and rule-governed behavior: Instructional control of human loss avoidance. *Journal of the Experimental Analysis of Behavior, 31*, 53–70.

Gast, D., VanBiervliet, A., & Spradlin, J.E. (1979). Teaching number-word equivalences: A study of transfer. *American Journal of Mental Deficiency, 83*, 524–527.

Gerstadt, C.L., Hong, Y.J., & Diamond, A. (in press). The relationship between cognition and action: Performance of 3.5-7 year old children on a Stroop-like day-night test. *Cognition*.

Gewirtz, J.L., & Stengle, K.G. (1968). Learning of generalized imitation as the basis for identification. *Psychological Review, 5*, 374–397.

Golden, C.J. (1987). *Manual for the Stroop Color and Word Test*. Chicago: Stoelting Company.

Grattan-Smith, P.J., Morris, J.G.L., Shores, E.A., Batchelor, J., & Sparks, R.S. (1992). Neuropsychological abnormalities in patients with pituitary tumors. *Acta Neurologica Scandinavica, 86*, 626–631.

Harris, E.L., Singer, H.S., Reader, M.J., Brown, J.E., Cox, C., Mohr, J., Schuerholz, L., Chase, G.A., & Denckla, M. (in press). Executive function in children with Tourette Syndrome and/or attention deficit hyperactivity disorder. *Neuropsychology*.

Hayes, L.J., & Chase, S.C. (1991). *Dialogues on verbal behavior*. Reno, NV: Context Press.

Hayes, L.J., Tilley, K., & Hayes, S.C. (1988). Extending equivalence class membership to gustatory stimuli. *The Psychological Record, 38*, 473–482.

Hayes, S.C. (1986). The case of the silent dog: Verbal reports and the analysis of rules. A review of K. Anders Ericsson and Herbert A. Simon, "Protocol analysis: Verbal reports as data." *Journal of the Experimental Analysis of Behavior, 45*, 351–363.

Hayes, S.C. (Ed.). (1989). *Rule-governed behavior: Cognition, contingencies, and instructional control*. New York: Plenum.

Hayes, S.C. (1991). A relational control theory of stimulus equivalence. In L.J. Hayes & P.N. Chase (Eds.), *Dialogues on verbal behavior* (pp. 19–40). Reno, NV: Context Press.

Hayes, S.C. (1992). Verbal relations, time, and suicide. In S.C. Hayes & L.J. Hayes (Eds.), *Understanding verbal relations* (pp. 109–118). Reno, NV: Context Press.

Hayes, S.C. (1994). Integrating relational and direct contingency accounts of verbal behavior. In S.C. Hayes, L.J. Hayes, M. Sato, & K. Ono (Eds.), *Behavior analysis of language and cognition* (pp. 9–30). Reno, NV: Context Press.

Hayes, S.C., Brownstein, A.J., Devany, J.M., Kohlenberg, B.S., & Shelby, J. (1987). Stimulus equivalence and the symbolic control of behavior. *Mexican Journal of Behavior Analysis, 13*, 361–374.

Hayes, S.C., Brownstein, A.J., Haas, J.R., & Greenway, D.E. (1986). Instructions, multiple schedules, and extinction: Distinguishing rule-governed from schedule controlled behavior. *Journal of the Experimental Analysis of Behavior, 46*, 137–147.

Hayes, S.C., Brownstein, A.J., Zettle, R.D., Rosenfarb, I., & Korn, Z. (1986). Rule-governed behavior and sensitivity to changing consequences of responding. *Journal of the Experimental Analysis of Behavior, 45*, 237–256.

Hayes, S.C., & Hayes, G.J. (1994). Stages of moral development as stages of rule-governance. In L.J. Hayes, G.J. Hayes, S.C. Moore, & P.M. Ghezzi (Eds.), *Ethical issues in developmental disabilities* (pp. 45–68). Reno, NV: Context Press.

Hayes, S.C., & Hayes, L.J. (1989). The verbal action of the listener as a basis for rule-governance. In S.C. Hayes (Ed.), *Rule-governed behavior: Cognition, contingencies, and instructional control* (pp. 153–190). New York: Plenum.

Hayes, S.C., & Hayes, L.J. (Eds.). (1992a). *Understanding verbal relations*. Reno, NV: Context Press.

Hayes, S.C., & Hayes, L.J. (1992b). Verbal relations and the evolution of behavior analysis. *American Psychologist, 47*, 1383–1395.

Hayes, S.C., Hayes, L.J., Sato, M., & Ono, K. (Eds.). (1994). *Behavior analysis of language and cognition.* Reno, NV: Context Press.

Hayes, S.C., & Ju, W. (1993, May). *Verbal establishing stimuli and verbal reinforcers.* Paper presented at the meeting of the Association for Behavior Analysis, Chicago.

Hayes, S.C., Kohlenberg, B.K., & Hayes, L.J. (1991). The transfer of specific and general consequential functions through simple and conditional equivalence classes. *Journal of the Experimental Analysis of Behavior, 56*, 119–137.

Hayes, S.C., Nelson, R.O., & Jarrett, R. (1987). Treatment utility of assessment: A functional approach to evaluating the quality of assessment. *American Psychologist, 42*, 963–974.

Hayes, S.C., Rosenfarb, I., Wulfert, E., Munt, E., Zettle, R.D., & Korn, Z. (1985). Self-reinforcement effects: An artifact of social standard setting? *Journal of Applied Behavior Analysis, 18*, 201–214.

Hayes, S.C., & Wolf, M.R. (1984). Cues, consequences, and therapeutic talk: Effect of social context and coping statements on pain. *Behaviour Research and Therapy, 22*, 385–392.

Hayes, S.C., Zettle, R.D., & Rosenfarb, I. (1989). Rule following. In S.C. Hayes (Ed.), *Rule-governed behavior: Cognition, contingencies, and instructional control* (pp. 191–220). New York: Plenum.

Heaton, R.K., Chelune, G.J., Talley, J.L., Kay, G.G., & Curtiss, G. (1993). *Wisconsin Card Sorting Test manual. Revised and updated.* Odessa, FL: Psychological Assessment Resources.

Kaufman, A., Baron, A., & Kopp, R.E. (1966). Some effects of instructions on human operant behavior. *Psychonomic Monograph Supplements, 1*, 243–250.

Kaufman, A.S. (1983). *Kaufman Assessment Battery for Children (K-ABC).* Circle Pines, MN: American Guidance Service.

Leander, J.D., Lippman, L.G., & Meyer, M.M. (1968). Fixed interval performance as related to subjects' verbalizations of the reinforcement contingency. *The Psychological Record, 18*, 469–474.

Leonhard, C., & Hayes, S.C. (1991, May). *Prior inconsistent testing affects equivalence responding.* Paper presented at the meeting of the Association for Behavior Analysis, Atlanta.

Lipken, R. (1992). *A behavior analysis of complex human functioning: Analogical reasoning.* Unpublished doctoral dissertation, University of Nevada, Reno.

Lipkens, G., Hayes, S.C., & Hayes, L.J. (1993). Longitudinal study of derived stimulus relations in an infant. *Journal of Experimental Child Psychology, 56*, 201–239.

Lippman, L.G., & Meyer, M.M. (1967). Fixed interval performance as related to instructions and to subjects' verbalization of the contingency. *Psychonomic Science, 8*, 135–136.

Lowe, C.F. (1979). Determinants of human operant behavior. In M.D. Zeiler & P. Harzem (Eds.), *Advances in analysis of behavior: Vol. 1. Reinforcement and the organization of behavior* (pp. 159–192). Chichester, England: John Wiley & Sons.

Lowe, C.F., Beasty, A., & Bentall, R.P. (1983). The role of verbal behavior in human learning: Infant performance on fixed interval schedules. *Journal of the Experimental Analysis of Behavior, 39*, 351–361.

Lowe, C.F., Harzem, P., & Hughes, S. (1978). Determinants of operant behavior in humans: Some differences from animals. *Quarterly Journal of Experimental Psychology, 30*, 373–386.

Mackay, H.A., & Sidman, M. (1984). Teaching new behaviors via equivalence relations. In P. Brooks, R. Sperber, & C. McCauley (Eds.), *Learning and cognition in the mentally retarded* (pp. 493–513). Hillsdale, NJ: Lawrence Erlbaum Associates.

Michael, J.M. (1984). Verbal behavior. *Journal of the Experimental Analysis of Behavior, 42*, 363–376.

Milgram, S. (1969). *Obedience to authority: An experimental view*. New York: Harper & Row.

Milner, B. (1963). Effects of brain lesions on card sorting. *Archives of Neurology, 9*, 90–100.

Milner, B. (1964). Some effects of frontal lobectomy in man. In J.M. Warren and K. Akert (Eds.), *The neurosciences: Third study program* (pp. 75–89). Cambridge, MA: MIT Press.

Organ, D. (1974). Social exchange and psychological reactance in a simulated superior-subordinate relationship. *Organizational Behavior and Human Performance, 12*, 132–142.

Ozonoff, S., Pennington, B.F., & Rogers, S.J. (1991). Executive function deficits in high-functioning autistic indivduals: Relationship to theory of mind. *Journal of Child Psychology, 32*, 1081–1105.

Perez-Gonzalez, L.A. (1994). Transfer of relational stimulus control in conditional discriminations. *Journal of the Experimental Analysis of Behavior, 61*, 487–503.

Perret, E. (1974). The left frontal lobe of man and the suppression of habitual responses in verbal categorical behaviour. *Neuropsychologia, 16*, 527–537.

Plude, D.J., & Doussard-Roosevelt, J.A. (1989). Aging, selective attention, and feature integration. *Psychology and Aging, 4*, 98–105.

Reese, H.R. (1994). Cognitive and behavioral approaches to problem solving. In S.C. Hayes, L.J. Hayes, M. Sato, & K. Ono (Eds.), *Behavior analysis of language and cognition* (pp. 197–258). Reno, NV: Context Press.

Reese, H.W. (1968). *The perception of stimulus relations: Discrimination learning and transposition*. New York: Academic Press.

Ribes Inesta, E., & Martinez Sanchez, H. (1990). Interaction of contingencies and rule instructions in the performance of human subjects in conditional discrimination. *The Psychological Record, 40*, 565–586.

Rosenfarb, I., & Hayes, S.C. (1984). Social standard setting: The Achilles' heel of informational accounts of therapeutic change. *Behavior Therapy, 15*, 515–528.

Shallice, T. (1982). Specific impairments in planning. In D.E. Broadbent & L. Weiskrantz (Eds.), *The neuropsychology of cognitive function* (pp. 199–209). London: The Royal Society.

Shimoff, E., Catania, A.C., & Matthews, B.A. (1981). Uninstructed human responding: Sensitivity of low rate performance to schedule contingencies. *Journal of the Experimental Analysis of Behavior, 36*, 207–220.

Sidman, M. (1971). Reading and auditory-visual equivalences. *Journal of Speech and Hearing Research, 14*, 5–13.

Sidman, M., Cresson, O., & Willson-Morris, M. (1974). Acquisition of matching-to-sample via mediated transfer. *Journal of the Experimental Analysis of Behavior, 22*, 261–273.

Sidman, M., Kirk, B., & Willson-Morris, M. (1985). Six-member stimulus classes generated by conditional-discrimination procedures. *Journal of the Experimental Analysis of Behavior, 43*, 21–42.

Sidman, M., & Tailby, W. (1982). Conditional discrimination versus matching to sample: An expansion of the testing paradigm. *Journal of the Experimental Analysis of Behavior, 37*, 5–22.

Spradlin, J.E., & Dixon, M. (1976). Establishing a conditional discrimination without direct training: Stimulus classes and labels. *American Journal of Mental Deficiency, 80*, 555–561.

Steele, D.L., & Hayes, S.C. (1991). Stimulus equivalence and arbitrarily applicable relational responding. *Journal of the Experimental Analysis of Behavior, 56*, 519–555.

Sternberg, R. (1985). *Beyond I.Q.: A triarchic theory of intelligence*. New York: Cambridge University Press.

VanBiervliet, A. (1977). Establishing words and objects as functionally equivalent through manual sign training. *American Journal of Mental Deficiency, 82,* 178–186.

Weiner, H. (1964). Conditioning history and human fixed-interval performance. *Journal of the Experimental Analysis of Behavior, 7,* 383–385.

Weiner, H. (1969). Human behavioral persistence. *Psychological Record, 20,* 445–456.

Wolf, M. (1986). Rapid alternating stimulus naming in the developmental dyslexias. *Brain and Language, 27,* 360–379.

Wulfert, E., Dougher, M.J., & Greenway, D.E. (1991). Protocol analysis of the correspondence of verbal behavior and equivalence class formation. *Journal of the Experimental Analysis of Behavior, 50,* 125–144.

Wulfert, E., & Hayes, S.C. (1988). The transfer of conditional sequencing through conditional equivalence classes. *Journal of the Experimental Analysis of Behavior, 50,* 125–144.

Yamamoto, J. (1986). Establishing stimulus equivalence in autistic children (in Japanese with English summary). *Japanese Journal of Behavior Analysis, 1,* 1–21.

Zettle, R.D., & Hayes, S.C. (1983). Effect of social context on the impact of coping self-statements. *Psychological Reports, 52,* 391–401.

17

LINKAGES BETWEEN ATTENTION AND EXECUTIVE FUNCTIONS

Russell A. Barkley

The preceding chapters have clearly shown that the concepts of both *attention* and *executive function* are multidimensional and can be usefully considered from a number of different theoretical positions. Yet these chapters also suggest that both concepts suffer from a certain vagueness in their definitions and in the areas where they may overlap. At times, one even senses redundancy in some of their dimensions and certainly in the measures chosen to assess them. This chapter discusses these areas of overlap or linkage between the terms *attention* and *executive function*. In doing so, greater clarity of definition, perhaps, can be brought to these two terms. Without such delineation, it would not be possible to know where the linkages between them might exist.

ATTENTION BRIEFLY REVISITED

The definition of attention we offered in our earlier chapter on major trends in research on this concept may be a useful starting point for this discussion (see Chapter 4). There, attention was most broadly construed as a term describing the conditional or functional relations between environmental events and the behavior of an organism, in this case a person. Attention in this sense refers to the relationship(s) between two things and not to any specific thing itself. It does not refer only to environmental events apart from behavior; that is the principal domain of physics. Nor does it refer only to behavior or movement by a person apart from its context, which is the principal domain of ergometrics or the study of movement. Attention refers to the *relation* of behavior *to* its environment. It is important to note that environmental events as discussed here are not simply events in the external world or outside the skin. These events are any events capable of sensory detection by the individual's afferent or sensory side of the central nervous system and therefore can refer to internal sensory events, such as may occur in proprioceptive or kinesthetic sensations. Similarly, behavior as discussed here is not just the muscle movements or outward actions of the individual but also cognitive or internal actions, such as self-directed subvocal speech, of the individual. Behavior is action that occurs on the efferent side or motor system (output) of the central nervous system but need not result in muscle movement. In this sense, thinking is just as much a form of behavior as running with one's legs and feet or grasping with the hands.

From the perspective presented here, the term *attention* is the same as the statistical concept of *correlation*. *Attention* describes how one variable or set of variables, behavior in this case, changes as a function of another variable or set of variables, the environment in this case. Like a correlation, then, attention cannot be invoked as an explanatory cause of why or how the two variables relate to each other in any direct sense. The presence of one (events in the environment) seems to set the occasion for the second (response to the event). The relationship is directional or conditional in that the environmental event always immediately precedes the response to it when we use the term *attention*. These [environmental event]–[response] relations are conditional probabilities in a Bayesian sense. The probability of whether a person will attend or respond to an event is p[response]/[environmental event]. These event–behavior pairings seem to have as their principal function the alteration of the probability of an immediately subsequent consequence or set of consequences for the individual. Again, these relations are conditional in that the event–behavior pairing immediately precedes the alteration in the environment (the consequence) it seems to bring about. These consequences are described by behaviorists as contingencies of reinforcement and the control of the behavior by the event as stimulus control. The probability of the response, then, is dependent on both the probability of the environmental event and the probability of the consequences that follow that behavior. Over time, these consequences act to increase or decrease the strength of certain p[response]/[environmental event] conditional relations and create a learning history for the organism. Some of these relations, however, seem to be genetically determined, based on the phylogenetic history of the species and not just the ontogenetic history of the individual. They are not learned but are seemingly inborn or genetic. Both types of histories help to explain, in large part, why an animal attends to some things in its environment and not others.

Attention refers to functional relationships between certain qualities of environmental events (objects, actions, and their properties) and the general forms of responses to them (initiation, sustainment, inhibition, and shift). Notice that the particular topography of the response is not typically of concern in discussing attention. Instead, it is the more general form of the response, such as whether or not a response is initiated, maintained over time, or inhibited or whether a change in the nature of the response occurs (shift). The target or aspect of the event to which the organism seems to respond, or attend, may also be of interest and is often called *selective* or *focused* attention. We can now see that the latter general forms of behavior make up the most commonly accepted dimensions or components of attention discussed in the earlier chapters on this subject: *focus, initiate, sustain, inhibit, shift.* Care must be exercised in the use of the terms for these components, however, because they tend to refer to the behavior or some psychological function of the person alone. Their use may obscure their connection or relationship to certain environmental events, leading one to think that attention is actually a thing, an inner psychological act, or a response of the person when it more accurately is the *relationship* between the environmental event and the person's response to it.

The function of the attending behavior of almost all animals seems to be to produce an alteration in the probability of an immediately available consequence. Thus, attention involves [environmental event]–[response]–[environmental consequence] conditional relations that occur within the immediate context; that is, they are *temporally proximal* relations. The issue of temporal proximity among these variables is a critical feature in the conceptualization of attention that will serve us well later in distinguishing it from the concept of executive functions. Yet it is a distinction often overlooked by others attempting to scale the slippery definitional slopes of either concept. Another critical feature of attention is that the response of the person it refers to *acts upon that environment* so as to produce some consequence relative to that person. For almost all animals, attending behaviors function to produce a change in the probability of an immediately subsequent consequence (environmental event) for that animal. Both temporal proximity and change in the environmental consequence are key aspects of the concept of attention that will serve to show how executive function is distinguished from it. Attending, in short, involves behavior directed at the moment and in the immediate context for almost all animals. Although this conceptualization applies to humans in many respects, the exception to the condition of temporal proximity of the [environmental event]–[response]–[consequence] chain in attention may be found in humans and some higher primates. The exception arises because of a special case of attention, and it is this special case that is called an executive function.

EXECUTIVE FUNCTIONS REVISITED

The term *executive function* has been as elusive to define operationally as attention has been. Some have defined it simply as the actions of the frontal lobes, but this is neither wholly accurate nor helpful. It merely sidesteps the challenge of operationally defining the term by placing it in a neuroanatomical location. Others, such as Stuss and Benson (1986), have bluntly admitted that the term escapes definition at the moment but must include planning and control. They go on to state that "executive functions remain among the most significant of human frontal lobe accomplishments" (p. 205). Still others have approached the definition of executive function by referring to what actions of the individual it does and does not include. For instance, Denckla (1994) states that the term refers to "mental control processes" that are "proactive" and include interference control, effortful and flexible organization, and strategic planning, which she refers to as anticipatory, goal-oriented "preparedness to act." It may further include the concept of working memory, "highlighting as it does the delay between stimulus and response or maintenance of internal representations to guide actions" (pp. 118–119). This aspect of delay between event and response is a critical theme in understanding where an executive function may act in the event–response sequences described earlier as forming the concept of attention. The theme will recur in other efforts at definition and is addressed below. An executive function may refer to attention "not only to the present but to the future, as well as intention (preparedness to act)," Denckla argues.

Torgesen (1994; see also Chapter 10), in contrast, relies upon information processing or cognitive psychological theory to help define executive function. He claims it is equivalent to the term *metacognition* as used in cognitive and developmental psychology. Yet a greased pig by any other name is still a greased pig, and Torgesen acknowledges that the term *metacognition* may suffer from as much ambiguity of definition as does the term *executive function* for which it substitutes. Even so, Torgesen points out that definitions of metacognition have ranged from "an executive function that selects, controls, and monitors the use of cognitive strategies" (Kuhn, 1992, p. 248) to "any knowledge or cognitive activity that takes as its object, or regulates, any aspect of any cognitive enterprise" (Flavell, Miller, & Miller, 1993, p. 150). Flavell et al. seem to restrict the term *metacognition* to purely cognitive or internal actions of the individual, as when they state that its core meaning is "cognition about cognition." Yet this may be artificially and unnecessarily restrictive in its meaning, excluding as it does motor actions of the individual that can also be considered "executive." Although many executive functions may be mental actions, they need not be so to be considered "executive." Torgesen notes that developmental psychologists do subdivide the term into metacognitive knowledge and metacognitive behavior. The latter would include monitoring, planning, organizing, coordinating, and adapting knowledge and strategic resources, as well as self-regulation.

Developmental neuropsychologists, such as Welsh and Pennington (1988), have defined executive function "as the ability to maintain an appropriate problem-solving set for attainment of a future goal," consistent with the notions of Bianchi (1992) and Luria (1966). Welsh and Pennington go further to include the following components: "a) an intention to inhibit a response or to defer it to a later more appropriate time; b) a strategic plan of action sequences; and c) a mental representation of the task, including the relevant stimulus information encoded in memory and the desired future goal-state" (pp. 201–202). Again, the attempt at definition seems to focus exclusively upon mental activities instead of the broader concept of behavior as we have construed the term here.

Other neuropsychologists, such as Fuster (1989), have distinguished among three components of executive function: a) working memory, which is a temporally retrospective function; b) anticipatory set, which is a temporally prospective function; and c) an interference control that inhibits the disruption of goal-directed behavior by behavior that is incompatible with it. Fuster persuasively argues that the overarching purpose of these three components is "the cross-temporal organization of behavior" (p. 157) and the "formation of *temporal structures of behavior* with a unifying purpose or goal—in other words, the structuring of goal-directed behavior" (p. 158). The prefrontal cortex, which carries out these functions, serves to bind together temporally distal events and behaviors for the purpose of attainment of a goal. Fuster goes on to include in the concept of executive function the regulation of motivational, emotional, or other drive states in the service of goal-directed behavior. This is an important inclusion that receives scant attention in other formulations of this concept. As Fuster emphasizes, it is the delays among environmental events, behavioral responses, and their goals and attendant consequences, as well as their need for temporal structuring, which are critical to the concept of executive function and to an understanding of the role of the prefrontal cortex in primates and humans.

Critical Conditions of an Executive Function

It appears that four common themes emerge from these various attempts to define the term *executive function* that can clearly distinguish it from the concept of attention. These four themes can serve as critical conditions for establishing whether an action or function of an individual is "executive." First, the term refers to [response]–[response] conditional or functional relations rather than the [environmental event]–[response] conditional relationships included in the term *attention* as defined above. Executive functions are chains of behavior–behavior relations for which environmental events may set the occasion. More accurately, they are [environmental event]–[executive response]–[response] chains such that the second response in the chain is a function of or conditionally related to a preceding response and much less so to the environmental event. If we include cognition within the broader term of an animal's behavior as is done here, then we can see that this same point has been made by developmental psychologists like Flavell et al. (1993) when they say that metacognition is cognition about and acting upon cognition. Employing the broader term of behavior shows that executive function is, thus, behavior about and acting upon behavior. It is, in short, the organism acting upon itself.

This leads to the second emergent theme critical to defining executive function. An executive function is a response or action that functions to *alter the probability of a subsequent response of the individual*. The contrast to the term *attention* is now made obvious. That term referred to [environmental event]–[response] conditional relations that functioned to alter the probability of a subsequent *consequence* for the animal. Executive functions are [environmental event]–[response] relations that function to change the probability of *a subsequent response* of the animal. Granted, as we note below, the ultimate goal or function of such behavior–behavior relations is to alter a subsequent consequence that is distant in time from both the environmental event that set the occasion for the behavior–behavior chain and the behavior–behavior chain itself. The crucial point here is that attention involves environment–behavior relations that alter the probability of a subsequent *consequence*, whereas executive function involves environment–behavior relations that alter the probability of a subsequent *behavior*. And, although there are some examples of animal behavior that are behavior–behavior chains, they would not be considered executive in nature because they do not fulfill this condition. They do not alter the probability of the initial prepotent response to the environmental event because the behavior–behavior chains in these instances are the prepotent responses. Also, they do not fulfill the third and fourth critical conditions of an executive function described next.

The third critical theme to be considered a condition of the term *executive function* is that, in contrast to the concept of attention as applied to most other animals, the temporal proximity of the events within the chain is no longer a constraint. That is, when considering the relation of the initial response to the environmental event or to its subsequent consequence, delays between them are typical of executive functions at work. Furthermore, proximity is not a constraint between this initial response and the subsequent response, the probability of which it functions to modify. Executive functions alter the probability of both the subsequent behaviors of and their consequences to the individual distant in time from each other and from the initial [environmental event]–[executive response] chain. As Fuster (1989) so elegantly argues, an executive function is one that links environmental events, responses, and consequences that are not immediately proximal to each other in time. It serves to structure behavior and environment across lengthy time periods not possible in other animals. Executive functions provide for the cross-temporal organization of behavior relative to events and their later consequences.

To reiterate, both attention and executive function refer to conditional relations among [environmental event]–[response]–[consequence] chains. However, executive function is now seen as a special case of attention in which the initial response of the individual to an environmental event alters the probability of a subsequent response of that individual. That initial response is classified as an "executive" act or function when and only when it serves to directly modify the likelihood of another response by the individual. It only indirectly modifies the subsequent consequences to the individual through the alteration of the likelihood of the second or subsequent response. It is that second response (or series of responses) in the chain that now directly alters the probability of a subsequent consequence. In the present analysis, an "executive" response or function is a special case of an "attending" behavior of the individual. Like an attending behavior, an executive behavior ultimately functions to change the likelihood of later events (consequences) happening to the individual. It differs in two key respects, however. It changes the chances of the subsequent consequence occurring only indirectly, being at least one behavior removed from those consequences in the chain of events. It also affects both the subsequent behavior and subsequent consequences much further removed in time—that is, it permits tremendous delays to exist between each component of the [environmental event]–

[response]–[consequence] sequence involved in the term *attention* that are not possible in animals devoid of such executive functions (and, by inference, pre-frontal cortex). The sequence for an executive function can then be represented as a special case of the attention sequence noted earlier: [environmental event]–[executive act]–[response to event]–[consequence]. Or, in Bayesian probability terms, the probability of a response to an environmental event is now conditional not only upon the event itself but also upon the executive act it elicits, or p[response]/([executive response]/[environmental event]).

As most writers on the subject of executive function have noted (except for a few such as Dennis, 1991), executive functions are *inherently self-regulating* actions. This is because, by the definition applied above, they function to change the subsequent behavior of the individual. All of the processes or functions included in the concept of executive function, as used by other writers on the subject, are ways that the individual acts to alter the probability of subsequent actions by the individual. If they do not do so, they do not qualify as "executive" as that term is used here. Such actions as self-monitoring, working memory, planning, organizing, interference-prevention, and intention to act are all functions directed at the modification of the person's own behavior.

All such executive acts by the individual can also be thought of as *future-* or *goal-oriented* principally because they indirectly function to change the likelihood of future consequences for the individual, consequences often quite distant in time. Thus, an executive function is so not only because it is self-regulating but also because, as Fuster (1989) heavily emphasized, it is ultimately future-directed. As Fuster also ably described, there is nothing precluding such executive functions from being pyramidally or hierarchically organized, such that one executive act increases the probability of, or begets, a second, and that one, a third, and so on such that a chain of executive acts may exist in the sequence of environment–behavior–consequence components. This progressive chaining of ever longer, hierarchically organized, and increasingly complex chains of behavior–behavior relations is, in fact, likely to be a developmental characteristic of the maturation of executive functions, as Fuster describes.

Finally, the fourth critical theme or condition of an executive function is that the *initial executive act in the chain must be the inhibition and delay of the otherwise prepotent response* of the individual to the environmental event. This point is not made obvious by most writings on this subject, yet it is intimated in many, such as in the views of Denckla (1994) and Welsh and Pennington (1988) noted above. It is elaborated upon in the next section, but suffice it to say here that, logically, no other executive acts or functions can be imposed in the event–response chain if the initial prepotent response to the event is not delayed. This is because, even should such potentially executive acts occur following the release of the prepotent motor response, they cannot now logically serve to alter the subsequent probability of that response or its consequences. Hence, by definition, they cannot now be considered "executive." So the first executive act must be one of delay or inhibition that effectively reduces the probability of the prepotent response and permits other executive acts, if necessary, to follow. These then serve to alter directly the likelihood of the eventual response to the environmental event and, indirectly, the likelihood of future consequences related to that response.

DELAYED RESPONDING AND EXECUTIVE FUNCTIONS

A recently rediscovered theory of delayed responding may be able to provide a unifying, more coherent account of many of the myriad processes involved in executive functioning and adaptive behavior. This theory was advanced more than 25 years ago by Jacob Bronowski (1967), the late philosopher, physicist, and mathematician, and bears a striking similarity in many conceptual aspects to Fuster's (1989) more recent model of prefrontal cortical functions, developed in such a scholarly fashion in his text. This theory is also similar to more recent theories of executive functions in developmental psychology (Flavell & Wellman, 1977; Kopp, 1982; Piaget, 1954) and developmental neuropsychology (Goldman-Rakic, 1987; Welsh & Pennington, 1988). It is preferable to these because it accounts for a greater diversity of the processes many writers have referred to in describing executive functions. It also suggests new areas of deficiencies in those with prefrontal lobe injuries and developmental impairments not suggested in these other accounts. Bronowski proposed that the evolution of the capacity to inhibit a prepotent response and to impose a delay between a signal or event and the person's response to that event permitted the development of four advanced psychological processes. Such delays between stimulus and response are substantially longer than any witnessed in our closest evolutionary relatives. Bronowski reasoned that this matchless capacity for delaying a motor response to a signal formed the central feature in the evolution of human language from a system of social communication to one of personal reflection and self-regulation.

The dramatic increase in delayed responding provided the opportunity for four uniquely human capabilities to evolve that are dependent upon this delay and that distinguish human from animal languages. These capacities should be considered fundamental executive functions. They have become essential to successful daily adaptive behavior in modern human society. These four abilities are *separation of affect, prolongation, internalization,* and *reconstitution.* These four psychological processes also seem to have a remarkable similarity to many of the deficits noted in those with prefrontal lobe injuries and those with developmental impairments apparently in these same cortical areas, such as in attention deficit hyperactivity disorder (ADHD). The implications of this theory for ADHD have been discussed elsewhere (Barkley, 1994b); here, let us concentrate on its implications for a model of executive function and, therefore, of prefrontal lobe functions.

Separation of Affect

The imposition of a delay between a stimulus and the response to it permits humans to separate the message or informational content of the signal from its emotional charge for the individual. Bronowski claimed that animal responses to signals are total and must be total because they are immediate. In contrast, humans have evolved the capacity to separate the instruction from its emotional charge. This capacity permits the individual to evaluate events more objectively, rationally, and logically, as if from the standpoint of an outside, neutral witness to the event. By this process, the subsequent response of the individual is less emotionally charged, better informed, and more likely to be successful or adaptive than a more immediate, passionate, and thoughtless reaction would be. Bronowski argued that to achieve this separation the delay in responding must be used to divide the incoming signal and to distribute its components among more than one brain center for processing the content in parallel fashion, the most important property of a large brain.

Prolongation

A second function permitted by delayed responding is the ability to prolong the effect of the signal or message by symbolically fixing the event mentally. This is the concept of working memory. Thus prolonged, the fleeting quality of the real event is partially compensated by its enduring mental representation. Fuster (1989) nicely describes the kindling of patterns of sensory neural pathways involved in the real sensory event as the means by which these mental representations are kept alive. The endurance of the mental event now increases the effectiveness of that event for our adaptive functioning. This period of prolongation is used 1) to retain the event or message "on-line," 2) to provide for prolonged analysis of the event not possible with the initial sensory event alone, 3) to compare the prolonged signal to our recollection of past messages or events, and 4) to manipulate the sustained mental event as well as these recollections. From this activity, one derives both object permanence and a sense of the past. One can draw upon this information to formulate a response in the present or to propose a plan of action for a future recurrence of that event. Extending this sense of the past forward in time permits the conjecture of hypothetical futures. So long as patterns of recurrence are detected in these past events, futures can be effectively conjectured. The conjecturing of hypothetical futures brings with it the general sense of future. Prolongation, according to Bronowski (1977),

> . . . is the ability to refer backward or forward in time, and to exchange messages [with others] which propose action in the future. Human beings can interpret these messages because they have a sense of the future: that is, they can recall the past and manipulate the imagery of recall to construct hypothetical situations. In one application, this is the gift of imagination; and in another application, it forms the concept of time—both of which are effectively absent in animals. (p. 116)

Prolongation in this sense comprises the current neuropsychological concept of "working memory" as used in cognitive and neuropsychological research (Welsh & Pennington, 1988; Welsh, Pennington, & Groisser, 1991). It is the means by which a stimulus or signal is kindled, sustained, and held or symbolically fixed in mind and prolonged "on-line" while parallel processing of the content of the signal takes place (Fuster, 1989; Goldman-Rakic, 1987). The psychological retention, endurance, and reiteration of real events permits far greater powers for extraction of information from the event or signal, manipulation of its content, comparison of the signal and its content with memory, and conjecturing hypothetical future events given the results of this reference to the past. The concept of prolongation also shows some similarity to the Piagetian concepts of object permanence, conservation, and formal operational thinking (Piaget, 1954). Certainly, the notions here of working memory, hindsight, and forethought in Bronowski's model are similar to the retrospective and prospective functions of the prefrontal cortex later articulated by Fuster.

Internalization of Language

Bronowski (1977) contended that the inhibition and delay of a response permits the internalization of language. This internalization creates the most far-reaching and consequential differences between how humans and animals use language:

> When language is internalized, it ceases to be only a means of social communication, and is thereby removed from the family of animal languages. It now becomes an instrument of reflection and exploration, with which the speaker constructs hypothetical messages before he chooses one to utter. In time, the sentences that he makes for himself lose the character of messages, and become experimental arrangements of the images of past experience into new and untested projections. . . . Human beings therefore live with two languages, an inner one and an outer one. They constantly experiment with the inner language, and find arrangements which are more effective than those which have become standard in the outer language. In the inner language, these arrangements are information, that is cognitive assertions; and they are then transferred to the outer language in the form of practical instructions. (p. 118)

Bronowski's concept of internalized language has its parallel in the psychological literatures on rule-governed behavior (Hayes, 1989; Skinner, 1953) and metacognition (Flavell, 1970; Kinsbourne, 1992). For instance, rule-governed behavior deals with the stimulus control of behavior by language and posits three developmental stages in its acquisition: 1) the control of behavior by the language of others (pliance); 2) the control of behavior by self-directed public speech that ultimately becomes subvocal or private to one's self; and 3) problem solving or the novel creation of new rules. Such rules are formed from the use of questions (second-order rules; Skinner, 1953) that interrogate one's sense of the past and bring forth the novel combination of existing information within one's repertoire. Important in both Bronowski's and the behavioral conceptualizations is not just the power to reflect and create, but the capacity for practical instructions or messages formed thereby to inform the planning, execution, control, and termination of current and future motor responses. The individual's behavior is no longer under the immediate and total control of the surrounding context. It now can be governed by the individual's own hypothetical projections about the future. When these are translated into rules or practical instructions, they can initiate motor programs in keeping with those instructions. Ongoing behavior is thereby brought under the control of plans, goals, directions, and future events conjectured in the various hypothetical futures. Current behavior can now also be influenced by the wisdom gained from others' past experiences and by the propositions of others for current and future actions. A sense of the past yields a sense of the future that controls behavior in the present. This control does not arise without the imposition of the delay between signal and response (Bronowski, 1977).

Combining information from the concept of rule-governed behavior with Bronowski's concept of internalization of language seems to provide a greater understanding of the role language and rules may play in those with prefrontal lobe injuries and in ADHD. It also makes more explicit predictions about the behavior of those with such injuries or ADHD than does Bronowski's concept alone, as is shown later. For instance, Hayes (1989, 1991) has articulated a number of effects that result from internalized speech and the rule-governed behavior it permits. These include the following: 1) the variability of responses to a task is much less with rule-governed than contingency-shaped behavior; 2) the individual's behavior is less susceptible to control by immediate contingencies and their momentary and potentially spurious changes; 3) where rules and contingencies compete in a situation, the rule is typically more likely to control behavior; 4) responding under some conditions may be rigid because the rule extracted and used by the individual to control behavior is incorrect; 5) self-directed rules permit individuals to respond effectively under extreme delays in consequences; and 6) the development of rule-governed behavior will show a growth trajectory in which infants respond more like primates to conditioning paradigms but become more rule-governed and less variable in their responding with maturation. Deficits in these areas might be expected in those with prefrontal cortical injuries or in those with ADHD if they are impaired in rule-governed behavior as proposed here.

Reconstitution

According to Bronowski (1977), the internalization of language has a special structure that allows for two processes which he calls reconstitution. The first of these is analysis. It is the decomposition of the signal, now prolonged in working memory, into parts, rather than being treated as "inviolate wholes" as they are in other species. Thus, the kindled and prolonged sensory event can be repeatedly analyzed for different aspects of its properties. The second is the process of synthesis wherein these aspects or facets of the event now can be manipulated and used to construct or reconstitute entirely new messages. He states that

> ... the procedure of analysis must not be conceived as a simple breaking into parts. It is a progressive redistribution of the message, so that its cognitive content becomes more particularized, and its hortative content more generalized. ... The effect is to progressively form in man a different picture of reality from that which animals have. The physical world is pictured as made up of units that can be matched in language, and human language thereby itself shifts its vocabulary from command to description or predication. (p. 121)

Bronowski goes on to say that

> It is the procedure of reconstitution as a whole, analysis as well as synthesis, which creates the potential for original productivity in human language. By this means human beings have provided themselves individually with a vocabulary roughly a hundred times larger than the rhesus monkey, and communally another hundred times larger again. The grammatical rules for the combination of so many words . . . are themselves a conceptual description of the world as we act on it and picture it, and it is this which makes it possible for us to recognize their right use at a glance. We experiment with these units in our inner language, and make original sentences for the outer language, by a total procedure of reconstitution. (p. 123)

At its simplest and most obvious level, then, reconstitution is witnessed in our daily use of language. In analysis, it may be represented in our conversion of internal (e.g., thoughts, images, feelings) or external events into verbal or written parts of speech, such as nouns, verbs, adjectives, and adverbs, to match the objects, actions, and their properties of the outer world. The act of description or matching events in our language supports the act of analysis. This may serve to clarify the parts of signals or events and their meanings. Synthesis may be represented in our verbal fluency as the term is used in neuropsychology; it is the joining together or rapid concatenation of these parts of speech into spoken sentences to express entire thoughts, feelings, or images. For instance, in verbal fluency tasks the subject may be asked to generate as many words as possible that begin with the letter S within a brief, fixed interval of time or to explain as much as possible the events depicted in a picture. At its larger level, reconstitution can be seen to endow humans with tremendous powers of problem solving and creativity. It greatly expands the capacity to generate numerous alternative messages and, from these, numerous potential motor responses guided by those messages, as in proscriptions for action or rules. It also permits the reassembling of the parts of speech and the objects, actions, and properties they represent into new messages in a nearly infinite number of ways. We can then select among them those that may be most adaptive, not only for the moment, but also in the hypothetical future.

Note that these processes of analysis and synthesis deal with language in Bronowski's theory. They may or may not apply to nonverbal problem solving and creativity, as it is not specified that such processes are closely linked to response inhibition, as are verbal analysis and synthesis.

The Four Processes as Executive Functions

Each of these four capacities (separation of affect, prolongation, internalization, and reconstitution) resembles to some degree ideas expressed by others regarding human executive abilities or those functions subserved by the prefrontal lobes (Fuster, 1989; Luria, 1966; Stuss & Benson, 1986). Undoubtedly, each executive function can inform and interact with the others. What these processes have in common is that they serve to alter the probability of occurrence of subsequent behavioral responses of the individual to environmental events; they are deployed in the service of self-regulation, directing behavior away from the immediate context and toward the future. By initially inhibiting and delaying the response to an event or message, time is permitted for the prefrontal cortex to engage and orchestrate these executive processes. This ultimately yields information that can be used to modify or even eliminate the initial prepotent response and to substitute another more adaptive response for it. This is what defines the executive functions described above as executive in nature. Such functions act to alter the subsequent responses of the organism taking as their object of analysis not simply the events in the external world but also one's own behavior within that world.

Executive functions are distinguished from other brain functions because they are means of self-regulation: The analysis, alteration, and management of one's own behavior is their object. The ultimate goal of that object is the alteration of the probability of distal or future consequences. As Welsh and Pennington (1988) note, executive functions are goal-directed and future-oriented processes. Bronowski (1977) did not sufficiently emphasize this aspect of his theory, whereas Fuster (1989) has made such cross-temporal organization the foundation of his own theory of prefrontal functions. Although these four executive functions involve actions upon the information contained in those events or messages received by the individual, the object of such actions is ultimately the modification of the individual's own behavior in responding to those messages. Moreover, it is not just the further analysis of the outside events that is permitted by these processes that is important in appreciating their profundity but the analysis of one's own past and ongoing behavior in relation to those events as well. By applying prolongation, hindsight, and foresight to one's behavior, information also may be gleaned about one's own past behavior relative to similar events. Thus, it is not just the sense of the past and future that is yielded up in the process of prolongation, but that of self-past and self-future. Such self-knowledge can then be used to regulate subsequent responding toward goals referenced in a conjectured future.

Neuroanatomical Considerations

Bronowski asserted, and there is much evidence to show, that delayed responding is mediated by the prefrontal cortical and related limbic structures, particularly the caudate in human and primate infants, and later the orbital-frontal cortex itself (Crowe, 1992). Given that the orbital-frontal cortex seems to mediate delayed responding and object permanence (Diamond & Goldman-Rakic, 1986), it should also regulate the four consequent processes noted here, as Bronowski hypothesized. The findings of Rezai et al. (1993) that performances on neuropsychological tests of prefrontal lobe executive functions are associated with brain metabolic activity in the bilateral mesial and left dorsolateral areas of the frontal lobes lends further support to this notion. It is not unreasonable, then, to propose that prefrontal lobe injuries, and even ADHD, should involve some disturbance in these four executive processes. These processes, as Bronowski reasoned, are what make us most human. They are also what is so tragically disrupted in patients with frontal injuries and, to a lesser degree, in those with ADHD (Barkley, 1994b).

Bronowski (1977) hypothesized that human language certainly evolved from animal language but that this process had two distinct components. The first was the physiological evolution of the capacity for delayed and more complex responses: "Somewhere near the level of the primates, a number of the direct response pathways of lower animals were lengthened by being switched through the new brain . . . The effect was to delay and divide the response, and both of these are important" (p. 124). The cytoarchitecture of the orbital-frontal regions of the prefrontal lobes, their pathways to the limbic system, and their rich cortico-cortical interconnections to other brain systems would seem to provide the ideal mechanism for the lengthening of the time to respond, the referral of the signal to various brain centers for parallel processing, and the division of the response itself. The second component in the evolution of human language was the cultural selection for hindsight and foresight and the internalization of symbolism. This created a means for language to express cognitive information and not just social communication. Bronowski speculated that this second component came later in evolution but with a strong and rapid selective influence.

Developmental Considerations

Bronowski, as well as earlier and later writers on the subject of the executive functions, certainly recognized the importance of developmental stages and differential developmental trajectories among these various functions. The initially immature status of the prefrontal cortex of the infant likely permits mainly the development of the motor inhibition and delayed response pattern that serves in the model described here as the foundation to the other executive functions. The capacities for prolongation (working memory, hindsight, forethought, and sense of time) as well as separation of affect likely emerge next and overlap with the ongoing progressive development of inhibitory and delaying abilities. The internalization of language may emerge only somewhat later and again overlaps with the continued progressive development of these earlier emerging executive functions. It may then be succeeded by the developmental emergence of the capacities that comprise reconstitution which, as before, overlaps with continued development of the earlier executive functions. This is all conjectural and hinges on my own interpretation of Bronowski's brief remarks on the likely evolutionary staging of the emergence of these functions in humans.

In any event, the important points here are that the various executive functions likely emerge at different points in development, interact with each other to progressively reorganize the executive system at each new stage, and show overlapping growth trajectories with the continued development of the earlier emerging executive functions. Consequently, early developmental periods in a child with prefrontal injury or even ADHD are not likely to show the complexity of impairments in executive functions that will become manifest in later developmental periods, as these later functions emerge and blossom in typical children but remain impaired or delayed in the child with prefrontal injury or ADHD.

For instance, the young preschool child with ADHD likely shows the uninhibited, hyperactive, and impulsive behavior pattern as the predominant feature of its disorder but surely shows no more difficulties with sustained attention (sustained interference inhibition), time, internalized language, or reconstitution than do typical preschool children who have yet to develop these executive functions. Over development, however, caregivers of the child with ADHD now note deficits or delays in the more complex executive functions then emerging in typical children, such as poor sustained attention, poor cross-temporal organization of behavior, forgetfulness and slow mental computation (working memory deficits), limited self-control, hindsight, and forethought, and, eventually, limited verbal fluency, problem solving, and creativity (reconstitution). In short, the adolescent with prefrontal injury or impairment or with ADHD manifests a far more complicated clinical picture of deficient executive functions than will the preschooler with the same disorder.

Evidence for this progressive emergence and complexity of executive functions with development in typical children is already plentiful (Levin et al., 1991; Shute & Huertas, 1990; Welsh & Pennington, 1988; Welsh, Pennington, & Groisser, 1991). Some evidence is also appearing with regard to the periodic restructuring and reorganizing of the executive system as new functions appear with development (Dawson & Fischer, 1994; Thatcher, 1991). Some studies have begun to appear showing that children with ADHD seem to remain delayed in the attainment of these emerging executive functions (Barkley, Grodzinsky, & DuPaul, 1992; Grodzinsky & Diamond, 1992; Mariani & Barkley, 1994), as may be those children with early frontal lobe damage (Grattan & Eslinger, 1991).

LINKAGES BETWEEN ATTENTION AND EXECUTIVE FUNCTION

It is now possible to identify four areas of linkage between the concepts of attention and executive function: conceptual, neuropsychological, neuroanatomical, and theoretical. *Conceptually*, as noted above, an executive function can be seen to be a special case of attention. In attention, the sequence of events can be thought of as [environmental event]–[response]–[consequence]. The response of the organism and the environmental event are conditionally related and temporally proximal. The strength of this conditional relationship is, in large part, determined by the subsequent probability of a consequence to the individual. Thus, in attention, the object of the individual's response (attending) is the probability of the environmental consequence which it acts to alter. In the concept of executive function, in contrast, the sequence of events is modified to impose a response–response chain: [environmental event]–[executive response]–[response]–[consequence]. In this case, the components of the sequence are also conditionally related. In this special instance, however, the object of the executive response is the alteration of the probability of the subsequent response to the environmental event directly, whereas in attention the object is the change in the likelihood of the environmental consequence. In the executive function, this latter alteration of consequences is an indirect result of the executive response. Thus, an executive function or action is a special case of attention. It differs from most other attention (event–response) relations in that 1) it is an environment–behavior–behavior conditional relation and not just an environment–behavior relation—it is inherently self-regulating where attention need not be so; 2) it does not require temporal proximity among the components of the sequence; that is, it organizes these sequences across delays in time between the components of the sequence, thereby providing considerable cross-temporal organization to human adaptive behavior; 3) it is directed at altering the probability of consequences to the individual in the future and not the moment and, therefore, serves to maximize the future positive outcomes to the individual; and 4) it is always initiated by a delay in the prepotent response to that environmental event.

This view is, in some respects, similar to the one noted by Heilman (1994); that is, the components of attention are typically conceived of as at least these four: *initiate, sustain, inhibit,* and *shift*. Each describes a certain general form of an "attending" response or reaction that may be taken to an environmental event, although not being concerned with the specific response topography itself. Similarly, the components of executive functions may likewise comprise these same general forms (*initiate, sustain, inhibit, shift*) but refer to the actions the individual takes to modify the subsequent probability of one of these general forms of responses to the environment (the attending responses). Executive functions, then, can also be initiated, sustained, inhibited, and shifted as they are used to alter the general responses (*initiate, sustain, inhibit, shift*) of the individual to the environment. The executive system is, consequently, organized pyramidally on top of the motor or efferent system, as Fuster (1989) argues, and so it also is an efferent system in that sense but a metamotor system to be sure. The present view goes beyond Heilman's notions of executive function in articulating what the ultimate functions of such a meta-efferent system are to human adaptive behavior; these are the four distinctions of an executive function from attention noted earlier.

A second link between attention and executive function follows from the above and occurs at the *neuropsychological* or *brain functional system* level of analysis. We have previously discussed the observation that the incorporation of the three major functional axes or brain systems of sensory–motor, spatial–sequential, and inhibitory–excitatory systems (Barkley, 1994a) is important in understanding the components of attention and their measurement. We can now see that the executive system provides a fourth functional system that is cross-temporal in nature and acts to govern or subordinate these other systems in the service of future-oriented, goal-directed behavior. As Denckla (1994), Fuster (1989), Luria (1966), Stuss & Benson (1986), and Torgesen (1994), among others, have all noted (see above), it is a top-down system, with the executive system situated above the others in this functional hierarchy. Thus, the executive system is, in one sense, a special case of a more general system of attention (responsiveness to the world) and, in another, a governor over it. As a result, the attention system permits the individual to be responsive to or under the control of three-dimensional space, whereas the executive system within and above it makes the individual attentive and responsive to the more subtle yet equally important fourth dimension of the physical world he or she must inhabit: *time*.

A third link that can be seen between these two concepts comes at the *neuroanatomical* level, as could be deduced from the foregoing two other levels of linkage. Attention arises as a result of the dynamic interaction of the brain stem arousal/alertness systems with the limbic system drive, motivational, and emotional centers, and these two regions with the sensory–motor and premotor zones of the cortex, and tertiary posterior cortical areas related to spatial–sequential processing and movement. The prefrontal cortex, housing the executive system, links up neuroanatomically with all of these brain regions and regulates them, as needed, in the service of self-regulated, goal-directed, and future-oriented behavior. Located just anterior to the tertiary motor, premotor, and sensory–motor strips, it is ideally situated to impose a delay between environmental event (stimulus) and the prepotent motor response to it. Richly connected to the posterior cortical sensory analyzers, the prefrontal executive cortex can redirect the event to these tertiary spatial–sequential systems for further parallel processing, the obvious advantage of a large brain. Seated above and apparently evolving out of the lower limbic system, the prefrontal cortex is similarly suited to receive, regulate, and even reciprocally kindle limbic motivational, drive, and emotional states to subserve goal-directed behavior. All of these interconnections are eloquently described in Fuster's (1989) text.

Finally, it seems that the conceptualization of attention and executive function provided here may provide *theoretical* linkages as well. Differences among theories or schools of thought seem to have stemmed in part from terminological ambiguity and in part from an emphasis on internal or external actions of the individual to the relative de-emphasis of the other. Where behavioral theorists have historically concentrated on observable behaviors and their functional relations to stimuli and response contingencies (the external relations), cognitive, developmental, and neuropsychological theorists have concentrated more on the internal or mental actions of the individual in defining their views of these two concepts. Yet, it appears that if the behavior or actions of the individual are broadly construed as both internal and external actions of the nervous system incorporating both cognitive and motor acts, then there are few contradictions among these theories. All of these theorists have been exploring their respective pieces of the elephant, which seem to be converging to some extent on a common body of empirical truths about these aspects of human behavior. The convergence is readily seen in the fact that behavioral scientists are now seeking to measure and incorporate "cognitive" or internal events such as rule-governed behavior and self-directed speech into their paradigm (see Chapters 7 and 16). Meanwhile cognitive, developmental, and neuropsychological theorists have had to make room in their conceptual models for the important role of motivational (reinforcement) variables and the learning, ontogenetic, and phylogenetic histories of the individual they seek to model. There is much reason to rejoice in these increasing convergences of literatures and models in research on attention and executive function.

REFERENCES

Barkley, R.A. (1994a). The assessment of attention. In G.R. Lyon (Ed.), *Frames of reference for the assessment of learning disabilities: New views on measurement issues* (pp. 69–102). Baltimore: Paul H. Brookes Publishing Co.

Barkley, R.A. (1994b). Delayed responding and response inhibition: Toward a unified theory of attention deficit hyperactivity disorder. In D.K. Routh (Ed.), *Disruptive behavior disorders in children: Essays in honor of Herbert Quay* (pp. 11–57). New York: Plenum.

Barkley, R.A., Grodzinsky, G.M., & DuPaul, G.J. (1992). Frontal lobe functions in attention deficit disorder with and without hyperactivity: A review and research report. *Journal of Abnormal Child Psychology, 20*, 163–188.

Bianchi, L. (1992). *The mechanism of the brain and the function of the frontal lobes*. Edinburgh: Livingstone.

Bronowski, J. (1967). *Human and animal languages: To honor Roman Jakobson* (Vol. 1). The Hague: Mouton & Co.

Bronowski, J. (1977). *Human and animal languages: A sense of the future* (pp. 104–131). Cambridge, MA: MIT Press.

Crowe, S.F. (1992). Dissociation of two frontal lobe syndromes by a test of verbal fluency. *Journal of Clinical and Experimental Neuropsychology, 14*, 327–339.

Dawson, G., & Fischer, K. (1994). *Human behavior and the developing brain*. New York: Guilford Press.

Denckla, M.B. (1994). Measurement of executive function. In G.R. Lyon (Ed.), *Frames of reference for the assessment of learning disabilities: New views on measurement issues* (pp. 117–142). Baltimore: Paul H. Brookes Publishing Co.

Dennis, M. (1991). Frontal lobe function in childhood and adolescence: A heuristic for assessing attention regulation, executive control, and the intentional states important for social discourse. *Developmental Neuropsychology, 7*, 327–358.

Diamond, A., & Goldman-Rakic, P.S. (1986). Comparative development in human infants and infant rhesus monkeys of cognitive functions that depend on prefrontal cortex. *Social and Neuroscience Abstracts, 12*, 742.

Flavell, J.H. (1970). Developmental studies of mediated memory. In H.W. Reese & L.P. Lipsett (Eds.), *Advances in child development and behavior* (pp. 181–211). New York: Academic Press.

Flavell, J.H., Miller, P.H., & Miller, S.A. (1993). *Cognitive development*. Englewood Cliffs, NJ: Prentice Hall.

Flavell, J., & Wellman, H. (1977). Metamemory. In R.V. Kail & J. Hagen (Eds.), *Perspectives on the development of memory and cognition* (pp. 3–33). Hillsdale, NJ: Lawrence Erlbaum Associates.

Fuster, J.M. (1989). *The prefrontal cortex* (2nd ed.). New York: Raven Press.

Goldman-Rakic, P.S. (1987). Development of cortical circuitry and cognitive function. *Child Development, 58*, 601–622.

Grattan, L.M., & Eslinger, P.J. (1991). Frontal lobe damage in children and adults: A comparative review. *Developmental Neuropsychology, 7*, 283–326.

Grodzinsky, G.M., & Diamond, R. (1992). Frontal lobe functioning in boys with attention-deficit hyperactivity disorder. *Developmental Neuropsychology, 8*, 427–445.

Hayes, S. (1989). *Rule-governed behavior.* New York: Plenum.

Hayes, S. (1991, November). *Rule-governed behavior.* Invited address for the Association for the Advancement of Behavior Therapy, New York.

Heilman, K. (1994, January). *Intention.* Paper presented at the NICHD Conference on Attention, Memory, and Executive Function, Bethesda, MD.

Kinsbourne, M. (1992). Development of attention and metacognition. In S.J. Segalowitz & I. Rapin (Eds.), *Handbook of neuropsychology* (Vol. 7, pp. 261–278). New York: Elsevier.

Kopp, C.B. (1982). Antecedents of self-regulation: A developmental perspective. *Developmental Psychology, 18*, 199–214.

Kuhn, D. (1992). Cognitive development. In M.H. Bornstein & M.E. Lamb (Eds.), *Developmental psychology: An advanced textbook* (3rd ed., pp. 211–272). Hillsdale, NJ: Lawrence Erlbaum Associates.

Levin, H.S., Culhane, K.A., Hartmann, J., Evankovich, K., Mattson, A.J., Harward, H., Ringholtz, G., Ewing-Cobbs, L., & Fletcher, J.M. (1991). Developmental changes in performance on tests of purported frontal lobe functioning. *Developmental Neuropsychology, 7*, 377–396.

Luria, A.R. (1966). *Higher cortical functions in man.* New York: Basic Books.

Mariani, M.R., & Barkley, R.A. (1994, June). *Cognitive and academic functioning in preschool boys with attention deficit hyperactivity disorder.* Paper presented at the Society for Research in Child and Adolescent Psychopathology, London.

Piaget, J. (1954). *The construction of reality in the child.* New York: Basic Books.

Rezai, K., Andreasen, N.C., Alliger, R., Cohen, G., Swaze, V., & O'Leary, D.S. (1993). The neuropsychology of the prefrontal cortex. *Archives of Neurology, 50*, 636–642.

Shute, G.E., & Huertas, V. (1990). Developmental variability in frontal lobe function. *Developmental Neuropsychology, 6*, 1–11.

Skinner, B.F. (1953). *Science and human behavior.* New York: Macmillan.

Stuss, D.T., & Benson, D.F. (1986). *The frontal lobes.* New York: Raven Press.

Thatcher, R.W. (1991). Maturation of the human frontal lobes: Physiological evidence for staging. *Developmental Neuropsychology, 7*, 397–419.

Torgesen, J.K. (1994). Issues in the assessment of executive function: An information-processing perspective. In G.R. Lyon (Ed.), *Frames of reference for the assessment of learning disabilities: New views on measurement issues* (pp. 143–162). Baltimore: Paul H. Brookes Publishing Co.

Welsh, M.C., & Pennington, B.F. (1988). Assessing frontal lobe functioning in children: Views from developmental psychology. *Developmental Neuropsychology, 4*, 199–230.

Welsh, M.C., Pennington, B.F., & Groisser, D.B. (1991). A normative-developmental study of executive function: A window on prefrontal functions in children. *Developmental Neuropsychology, 7*, 131–149.

18

EXECUTIVE FUNCTIONS AND WORKING MEMORY
Theoretical and Measurement Issues

Bruce F. Pennington, Loisa Bennetto,
Owen McAleer, and Ralph J. Roberts, Jr.

In this chapter, we 1) consider the discriminant validity problem posed by the fact that executive function (EF) deficits are found in many complex behavioral disorders; 2) identify theoretical and measurement problems with current molar EF tasks, using the Wisconsin Card Sorting Test (WCST) (Heaton, Chelune, Talley, Kay, & Curtiss, 1993) as a case example; 3) lay out the beginnings of a new theoretical framework for understanding the functions of the prefrontal cortex (PFC), based on the construct of working memory (WM); and 4) illustrate two measurement approaches that derive from this new framework. It is hoped that new measurement approaches such as these will help solve the discriminant validity problem.

At the outset, it is important to acknowledge that the term *executive function* is provisional and general. In an earlier work, Welsh and Pennington (1988) defined executive function as "the ability to maintain an appropriate problem-solving set for attainment of a future goal" (p. 201) and further said that executive function included inhibition, planning, and mental representation of tasks and goals. The term has also been used as an umbrella term for the functions of the PFC. Of course, this dual meaning of the term increases the chance that not all executive functions are prefrontally mediated, or not all functions of the PFC are executive, or both. When we speak of "EF tasks" here, we mean tasks that fit the cognitive definition given above and for which there is evidence that they are prefrontally mediated in human or nonhuman primates. The number and diver-

The work reported in this chapter was supported by three National Institute of Mental Health (NIMH) grants: MH00419 (RSDA), MH38820 (MERIT award), and MH45916, as well as by a National Institute of Child Health and Human Development (NICHD) Center Grant (HD 27802). Loisa Bennetto was supported in part by NIMH grant MH10470 (NRSA).

Special thanks to Sally Ozonoff for sharing data presented here.

sity of tasks that fit these twin constraints are still great; therefore, more theoretical and methodological work is needed to define executive function.

Impairment on EF tasks, as defined in the previous paragraph, is found across a broad range of neuropsychiatric and developmental disorders. With respect to developmental disorders, EF deficits relative to IQ-matched controls have been found in the following disorders: early-treated phenylketonuria (PKU), autism, attention deficit hyperactivity disorder (ADHD), and fragile X syndrome in females. As shown in the second column in Table 18.1, impairments have been found across a range of tasks purported to assess EFs.

Thus, EF deficits are at least a correlate and possibly a cause of the disruptions in complex behavior seen in these disorders, implying that all the disorders involve PFC dysfunction. Although interesting, these findings raise two difficult and related questions: 1) How can symptomatically different complex behavior disorders all be due to the same cognitive and/or neural dysfunction? and 2) What is a more precise cognitive characterization of executive functions? The first question refers to the discriminant validity problem. The second question highlights the fact that our theoretical models for executive functions are much less satisfactorily developed than is the case in other domains of cognition, such as attention or memory.

THE DISCRIMINANT VALIDITY PROBLEM

The goal in neuropsychological studies of developmental disorders has been to find the primary neurocognitive deficit in each disorder. Primary means that the deficit is universal, specific, and necessary and sufficient to cause the symptoms of the disorder. In other words, the primary deficit is the proximal cognitive cause of the behavioral symptoms of the disorder (Morton & Frith, in press). So, by definition, it would appear that an executive deficit, at least as currently operationalized (i.e., impaired performance on clinical EF tasks such as the WCST or the Tower of Hanoi [Welsh, Pennington, & Grossier, 1991]), *cannot* be primary in any of these disorders because such a broadly defined executive deficit lacks specificity. That is, if these molar tasks are detecting the same underlying neurocognitive deficit in each disorder, then that deficit cannot be necessary and sufficient for more than one distinct disorder. Of course, because these are molar tasks, each one may tap multiple executive functions, and each clinical group may perform poorly on these tasks in different ways and/or to different degrees. This possibility has not been systematically explored.

What are some other possibilities? Some of the less interesting ones are that EF deficits might be artifactual (e.g., due to clinical ascertainment) or that they might just be a nonspecific, secondary effect of growing up with some developmental disorders. There are data that counter both of these possibilities, although we cannot entirely exclude the second one without longitudinal studies that begin before the onset of the disorder in question. There are more interesting possibilities, where "interesting" means that the finding of EF deficits tells us about primary neuropsychological dysfunction in the disorder. We will consider six possi-

Table 18.1. EF deficits in developmental disorders

Disorder	EF tasks used	Representative studies
Early treated PKU	Tower of Hanoi	Welsh et al. (1990)
	Verbal Fluency (Milner, 1964)	Diamond et al. (1994)
	Visual Search (Rudel, Denckla, & Broman, 1978)	
	Stroop test	
	Six Boxes (Diamond, 1991)	
	Corsi Test and other tasks (Milner, 1971)	
Autism	WCST	Rumsey (1985)
	Tower of Hanoi	Ozonoff, Pennington, & Rogers (1991)
	Trail Making Test B (Reitan & Davidson, 1974)	
	Milner Maze (Prior & Hoffman, 1990)	Russell et al. (1991)
	Rey-Osterreith Complex Figure Copying (Osterreith, 1944)	
	Windows Task (Hughes & Russell, 1993)	
ADHD	WCST	Grodzinsky & Diamond (1992)
	Tower of Hanoi	Shue & Douglas (1992)
	MFFT (Kagan, Rosman, Day, Albert, & Phillips, 1964)	Pennington, Groisser, & Welsh (1993)
	CPT (Rosvold, Mirsky, Sarason, Bransome, & Beck, 1956)	
	Stroop test	
	Trail Making Test B	
	Porteus Maze (Porteus, 1965)	
	Self-Ordered Pointing Task (Diamond, 1991)	
	Rey-Osterreith Complex Figure Copying	
	Go/No-Go Task (Greenberg, 1990)	
	Conflicting Motor Response (Shue & Douglas, 1992)	
	Gordon Vigilance Task (Gordon, McClure, & Post, 1986)	
Fragile X in women	WCST	Mazzocco et al. (1992)
	Tower of Hanoi	
	Contingency Naming Test (Taylor, 1988)	

EF, executive functions; PKU, phenylketonuria; ADHD, attention deficit hyperactivity disorder; WCST, Wisconsin Card Sorting Test; MFFT, Matching Familiar Figures Test; CPT, Continuous Performance Test.

bilities in which there are different brain changes across the disorder, all of which lead to EF deficits.

The first five possibilities all involve localized changes in brain development, and the first two are restricted to the PFC. Let us consider the first possibility—severity differences. Conceivably, since the PFC is a complex system, differences in severity of a change in brain development could, by itself, produce both quantitative and qualitative differences in executive functions and hence different syndromal patterns, all with a common core. Just restricting ourselves to the four disorders listed in Table 18.1, we could hypothesize that these disorders all involve varying degrees of dopamine depletion in the PFC, with the rank order of increasing depletion being PKU, ADHD, fragile X syndrome in females, and autism. In fact, there is evidence of dopamine depletion in three of these four disorders (i.e., PKU, ADHD, and autism), although some studies have failed to find dopamine depletion in ADHD and autism. If true, this hypothesis would provide a very parsimonious, unified account of four seemingly disparate disorders.

The second possibility involves the well-known principle that the effects of a change in brain development depend on when the change occurs. This hypothesis is unlikely to help us explain the differences among the four disorders listed in Table 18.1 because each is usually present early in life. Nonetheless, subtle timing differences, both prenatally and in infancy, could produce significant differences in behavioral development. Larger timing differences might help explain the similarities and differences between autism and schizophrenia, two disorders with prominent EF deficits that have very different ages of onset (e.g., Frith & Frith, 1991).

The third possibility involves changes in brain regions closely connected to the PFC. This possibility moves us beyond the PFC but retains the notion of a localized change in brain development. The PFC has extensive reciprocal connections to many areas of brain, including the basal ganglia, the limbic system, the thalamus, and the posterior cortex. It is well known that among adult neurological disorders causing EF deficits only some involve neuropathology within the PFC, whereas others involve neuropathology outside the PFC but in brain systems that are closely interconnected to the PFC. Weinberger (1992) distinguishes these two kinds of disorders as intrinsic and extrinsic "frontal" disorders. An intrinsic disorder is caused by neuropathology within the PFC, whereas an extrinsic disorder is caused by neuropathology outside the PFC. Both Parkinson's and Huntington's diseases are examples of extrinsic "frontal" disorders. Both involve basal ganglia rather than PFC pathology, yet both produce EF deficits, presumably because of close connections between the PFC and the basal ganglia. So, neuropathology outside of the PFC appears to be able to produce dysfunction in the PFC because the PFC is part of a complex system. Both Parkinson's and Huntington's diseases are "frontal" disorders in which EF deficits occur and are important for understanding the clinical symptoms. Nonetheless, each is a distinct disorder in terms of etiology, the exact nature of the neuropathology within the basal ganglia, behavioral symptoms, and course. Are EF deficits primary in either disorder? This presents a quandary.

On the one hand, EF deficits appear to be universal in both disorders. Moreover, because of the close reciprocal connections between the basal ganglia and the PFC, localizing symptoms to one or the other structure may be problematic.

In a real sense, there appears to be primary PFC dysfunction in each disorder. On the other hand, EF deficits are not specific to either disorder, nor are they necessary and sufficient to produce the symptoms of each. Hence, the EF deficits in these two disorders do not meet all the criteria for being primary, but they are not merely correlated or secondary deficits either.

Thus, different developmental disorders that produce EF deficits could be caused by changes in different parts of the distributed neural system of the PFC and closely connected structures. Some would be intrinsic to PFC; for instance, the dopamine depletion that produces EF deficits in PKU appears to be fairly restricted to the PFC (Diamond, Ciaramitaro, Donner, Djali, & Robinson, 1994). Others would be extrinsic; for instance, some converging evidence implicates the basal ganglia in ADHD (Hynd et al., 1993; Lou, Henriksen, Bruhn, Borner, & Nielson, 1989; Schacter, 1987; Zametkin et al., 1990). At a gross level, these different lesions would all produce deficits on molar EF tasks, but we would expect finer-grained analyses to reveal different profiles of executive problems in each.

The fourth possibility also involves single, localized brain changes, specifically different single brain changes *within* the PFC. Since the PFC is a large and cytoarchitectonically heterogeneous part of the neocortex, it is reasonable to expect that altering different parts of it would have different behavioral effects, even though there might be an overall "family resemblance" among these different symptoms. Lesions in different parts of the PFC that are acquired in adulthood have different behavioral effects (Fuster, 1989; Kolb & Whishaw, 1990).

The last two possibilities to be considered do not involve single changes. The fifth possibility envisions two localized changes in brain development—one in the PFC system, which produces other EF deficits, and one outside the PFC system, which produces behavioral effects specific to a given disorder. Although quite possible, this is not an appealing alternative from the point of view of parsimony.

Finally, the sixth possibility does not involve a localized change. Instead, the changes are diffuse ones, either structural or metabolic. In thinking about developmental disorders, it is important not to be too fixated on the localization approach that has dominated adult neuropsychology. Many developmental disorders may result from a general change in some aspect of brain development such as neuronal number, structure, connectivity, neurochemistry, or metabolism. Nonetheless, such a general change could have a differential impact across different domains of cognition, with more complex aspects of cognition such as EFs being most vulnerable and other aspects being less vulnerable. The nature, severity, and relative distribution of the general change could lead to different behavioral phenotypes, each sharing some degree of executive impairment.

The possibilities considered here are hardly exhaustive; one can generate other possibilities by combining ones from this list (e.g., a local plus a diffuse change). The point of the discussion is to demonstrate that there are plausible neuropsychological solutions to the discriminant validity problem.

At this point, our neurobiological understanding of most developmental disorders is so preliminary that it does not allow us to distinguish among these five hypotheses (although what we do know cautions us against expecting single, local brain changes). To take autism or fragile X syndrome as examples, we cannot confidently exclude any one of these hypotheses for either disorder.

MEASUREMENT PROBLEMS OF CURRENT EF TASKS

Moreover, before we can rigorously test these alternative hypotheses, we have to deal with the poor measurement properties of existing EF tasks, some of which may contribute to the apparent problem of discriminant validity. To the extent that an EF task is a complex, molar task that assesses many interacting component processes, performance on it can be disrupted in many different ways. A similar complexity of components underlies the simultaneous weakness and strength of existing IQ measures. Because of this complexity, IQ measures capture a wide range of meaningful variance. However, because they are not specified theoretically or measured analytically, we do not know which underlying cognitive components are responsible for a given score.

Similarly, EF tasks like the WCST or Tower of Hanoi appear to tap functions that are theoretically central to the PFC—perhaps tapping too many executive functions. Unfortunately, they may tap multiple functions of the PFC as well as nonexecutive components that are unlikely to be specific to the PFC. Thus, these tasks may be poor at differentiating among different types of PFC deficits (e.g., deficits in different aspects of working memory). They may also be poor at differentiating PFC deficits from non-PFC deficits. For instance, knowledge and salience of the category of number would affect performance on the WCST; a child without a category of number could only sort to color and form and would thus be likely to perseverate to these categories. Spatial cognition may affect performance on the Tower of Hanoi. Both of these tasks are also relatively unconstrained problem-solving situations. On the WCST, the experimenter deceives the subject by changing the sorting rule without warning. Some antisocial or paranoid patients react angrily to this deception. One can wonder if other aspects of social processing, such as the understanding of deception itself, might affect performance on the WCST. Ozonoff (in review) conducted a study to examine whether computer versus in-person administration affects the performance of children with autism on the WCST. She found that computer administration attenuated but did not eliminate their deficit.

Second, differences in cognitive style or strategy that are unrelated to PFC function may contribute to variance on the WCST. For example, it is not uncommon to have a bright, intact subject achieve few categories on the WCST because the subject is testing very complicated sorting rules (Nelson, 1976). Although such a subject would not necessarily make an excessive number of perseverative responses, his or her performance would not look entirely normal. Hence, the WCST has a potential problem with specificity; it may not always distinguish intact from impaired subjects.

The WCST also has a specificity problem among patients with different kinds of brain damage. In several studies it has failed to discriminate patients with focal frontal damage from patients with diffuse damage (see Heaton, Chelune, Talley, Kay, & Curtiss, 1993, for a review). It has even failed to discriminate patients with focal frontal damage from patients with focal nonfrontal damage (Anderson, Damasio, Jones, & Tranel, 1991; Grafman, Jones, & Salazar, 1990).

Finally, the WCST also has a sensitivity problem. Some patients with documented frontal lesions and dramatic "frontal" problems in everyday life perform completely normally on the WCST (Damasio, Tranel, & Damasio, 1991; Shallice & Burgess, 1991).

However, we do not conclude from all this that there is no relation between what the WCST measures and the functions of the PFC, only that the WCST has significant measurement problems. The findings from the positron emission tomographic (PET) scan studies of Weinberger, Berman, Gold, and Goldberg (1994) indicate that performing the WCST activates the PFC somewhat selectively in both typical subjects and subjects with schizophrenia and that there is less PFC activation in subjects with schizophrenia, which might help explain their poor WCST performance. Even more telling is the result that there is still PFC activation in typical adults who have already mastered the task; this contrasts with the result in PET studies of other tasks in which PFC activation drops out once the task is no longer novel. Even after a subject knows that the WCST involves set shifting, he or she still needs working memory to integrate information across trials in order to shift to the correct set.

The poor measurement properties of the WCST may help explain one puzzling finding from the studies reported by Weinberger et al. (1994), namely that degree of frontal activation in typical subjects did not correlate with WCST performance. As we will see shortly, there are questions about what produces variance within the normal range on this task.

As part of our research program, we have begun to examine the measurement properties of the WCST. This effort was spurred mainly by the failure to find expected levels of monozygotic (MZ) correlation on the WCST in a twin study. As seen in Table 18.2, MZ correlations were significant only for total errors, and even these MZ correlations were much lower than what is typically found for cognitive measures (e.g., .86 for IQ, Bouchard & McGue, 1981).

A low MZ correlation means either that the reliability of the measure is low or that a substantial portion of the variance of the task is due to the nonshared environment. One must reject the first hypothesis to provide indirect support for the second. Consequently, we began by examining the reliability of the WCST. In typical samples and samples with less impairment, the reliabilities are sometimes unsatisfactorily low. The most recent manual for the WCST (Heaton et al., 1993) reports a one-month test–retest reliability study using child subjects across a broad age range. This study found an acceptable reliability of .71 for total errors. However, for percent of perseverative response, a measure from the WCST com-

Table 18.2. Twin correlations for the WCST

	N (Pairs)	Mean age	Total errors	Perseverative response	% Perseverative response
Control					
MZ	20	10.8 (8–16)	.46*	.32**	.26
DZ	30	10.7 (7–16)	.17	.26**	−.05
RD					
MZ	43	10.9 (8–18)	.33*	.15	−.06
DZ	80	10.5 (8–17)	.36*	.14	−.13

Note: WCST, Wisconsin Card Sorting Test; MZ, monozygotic; DZ, dizygotic; RD, reading disabled.
*$p<.05$; **$p<.10$.

monly used in research studies, the reliability was only .39. We conducted a small test–retest reliability study of the WCST with child subjects drawn from a narrower age range. As can be seen in the second line of Table 18.3, the reliabilities were lower than those reported in the WCST manual, possibly because the exclusion of younger child subjects restricted the range of scores. (Another possibility is small sample size.) Of course, ideally, we would like to have test–retest reliabilities for each age considered separately.

In contrast, in two clinical samples, one of subjects with autism and one of controls with learning disorders, Ozonoff (personal communication, November 15, 1993) found very impressive test–retest reliabilities over more than a 2-year interval. The subjects with autism as a group were markedly impaired on the WCST, and there was considerable variance within the group. The controls with learning disorders performed significantly better than the subjects with autism but still somewhat below normative expectations, so there was not a markedly restricted range of scores.

One straightforward explanation of these different reliability results is a ceiling effect producing a skewed distribution of scores. We examined data from a large twin study in which we are examining the relation between reading disability and ADHD and executive functions. The subjects were school-age twin pairs, about half of which were ascertained for reading disability (RD) in at least one member of the pair, and the rest were control pairs in which neither member of the pair had RD. As we can see in Figure 18.1, we found a markedly skewed distribution on the WCST in this sample; moreover, this skewness and kurtosis was found on all the WCST scores, not just the one displayed here. Furthermore, these various scores are moderately to highly correlated with each other, so there is unlikely to be some score on the WCST that is not affected by skewness and kurtosis. Second, both the fact that this is a twin sample and the fact that some of the twins had RD introduced slight biases toward worse EF performance. It is im-

Table 18.3. Test–retest reliability of the WCST

Representative studies	N	Interval	Mean age	Total errors	Perseverative response	% Perseverative response
Heaton et al. (1993)	46	1 mo	13.1 (6.5–17)	.71[a]	.61[a]	.39[a]
Pennington et al. (1993)	15	1 yr	10.7 (9–14)	.33	.24	.35
Ozonoff (personal communication, November 15, 1993) Control Ss	17	2.7 yr	13.4 (8.6–21.2)	.82*	.90*	.91*
Ozonoff (in review) Autistic Ss	17	2.4 yr	14.3 (8.1–23.3)	.88*	.87*	.86*

Ss, subjects; WCST, Wisconsin Card Sorting Test.

[a]These test–retest reliabilities were computed using a generalizability theory approach, which estimates multiple sources of variation (in this case, subject, time, and error). The reliabilities shown here are the ratio of subject variance to the total of subject plus error variance. According to Heaton et al. (1993), values greater than .60 are considered to indicate good scale reliability.

*$p < .001$.

portant to note that this is a conservative bias. In a nontwin, typical sample of children of the same age, there would be even *more* skew than exhibited in Figure 18.1.

Because these distributional problems can inflate or deflate Pearson's product–moment correlations, we decided to examine Spearman's rank correlations, which are not inflated by outliers and are less deflated by kurtosis. Tables 18.4 and 18.5 compare the Pearson's and Spearman's values. As can be seen, the more extreme Pearson values become less extreme, but the poor reliability among essentially typical samples remains. In contrast, the reliability for groups with lower scores, especially the group with autism, remains quite good. We interpret these results to mean that the WCST is a bit like a pathognomonic sign: a good indicator of pathology, but a poor measure of normal variation. These results also suggest that there could be a threshold amount of some EFs (e.g., working memory) needed to perform the WCST; beyond that threshold, other less interesting sources of variation affect performance. Hence, the WCST detects abnormal variation in EFs but may not be sensitive to less extreme variation in EFs.

To conclude, we have identified four measurement problems with some molar EF tasks. Specifically, these tasks 1) are not theoretically well-specified, 2) do not allow us to identify component processes, 3) are not always reliable and normally distributed, and 4) do not appear to be sensitive to the same underlying processes across the range of performance. The first two problems are largely theoretical, whereas the latter two are methodological and could be solved without making any theoretical advances. To tackle the discriminant validity problem,

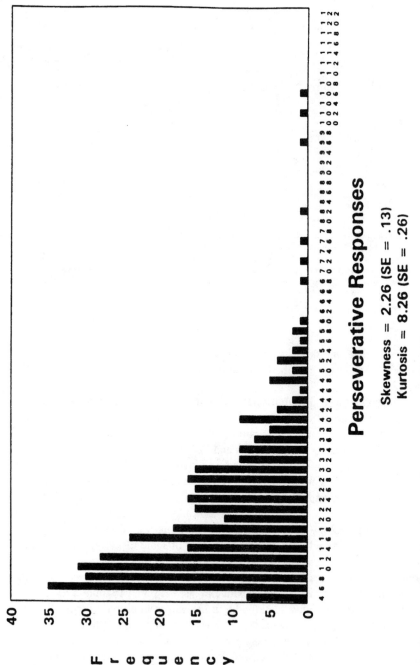

Figure 18.1. Wisconsin Card Sorting Test—frequency of perseverative responses (N = 349).

Table 18.4. Twin correlations for the WCST

	N (Pairs)	Mean age	Total errors	Perseverative response	% Perseverative response
Control					
MZ	20	10.8	.46**	.32*	.26
		(8–16)	**.60*****	**.49****	**.45****
DZ	30	10.7	.17	.26*	−.05
		(7-16)	**.16**	**.21**	**.21**
RD					
MZ	43	10.9	.33**	.15	−.06
		(8–18)	**.32****	**.27****	**.23***
DZ	80	10.5	.36**	.14	−.13
		(8–17)	**.36****	**.26****	**.20****

WCST, Wisconsin Card Sorting Test; MZ, monozygotic; DZ, dizygotic; RD, reading disabled.
Values in boldface are Spearman's rank correlations.
*$p<.10$; **$p<.05$; ***$p<.01$.

we need to develop better EF measures by dealing with all four of these measurement problems. We next turn to the beginnings of a theoretical framework that may help address some of the measurement problems outlined above.

A THEORETICAL FRAMEWORK FOR WORKING MEMORY

At first, providing a unified theoretical account of tasks measuring EFs seems like an impossible task because of the heterogeneity of their surface characteris-

Table 18.5. Test–retest reliability of the WCST

	N	Interval	Mean age	Total errors	Perseverative response	% Perseverative response
Heaton et al. (1993)	46	1 mo	13.1 (6.5–17)	.71[a] —	.61[a] —	.39[a] —
Pennington et al. (1993)	15	1 yr	10.7 (9–14)	.33 **.55***	.24 **.34**	.35 **−.02**
Ozonoff (personal communication, November 15, 1993) Controls	17	2.7 yr	13.4 (8.6–21.2)	.82*** **.80*****	.90*** **.69****	.91*** **.67****
Ozonoff (in review) Autistics	17	2.4 yr	14.3 (8.1–23.3)	.88*** .78***	.87*** .75***	.86*** .77***

WCST, Wisconsin Card Sorting Test.
[a]These test–retest reliabilities were computed using a generalizability theory approach, which estimates multiple sources of variation (in this case, subject, time, and error). The reliabilities shown here are the ratio of subject variance to the total of subject plus error variance. According to Heaton et al. (1993), values greater than .60 are considered to indicate good scale reliability.
[b]Values in boldface are Spearman's rank correlations.
*$p<.05$; **$p<.01$; ***$p<.001$.

tics. However, important theoretical insights about the commonalities across such tasks have been provided by several neuroscientists studying the functions of the primate PFC (e.g., Fuster, 1989; Goldman-Rakic, 1987a, 1987b; Luria, 1966). Although each researcher has developed a distinct theoretical position, some commonalities among their theories emerge: Tasks or behaviors that are sensitive to PFC dysfunction require planning or programming future actions, holding those plans or programs on-line until executed, and inhibiting irrelevant actions.

More recently, several computational modeling studies (Cohen & Servan-Schreiber; 1992; Dehaene & Changeux, 1991; Kimberg & Farah, 1993; Levine, Leven, & Prueitt, 1992) have provided a more formal analysis of the components of molar EF tasks. All but the Cohen and Servan-Schreiber simulation modeled the WCST. In the two most recent studies (Cohen & Servan-Schreiber; Kimberg & Farah), the authors used a common architecture to model performance across several EF tasks. What is most striking in these two studies is that the same change in the model across tasks produced performance on each task very similar to that observed in adult patients with PFC dysfunction. In other words, molar EF tasks with very different surface characteristics could be modeled with a common architecture and disrupted by the same "lesion" to that architecture.

In the Cohen and Servan-Schreiber (1992) simulations, the network for each task included context that represented units; selectively weakening sensitivity of the threshold function (i.e., gain parameter) for these context units produced executive deficits. Descriptively, one can say that this manipulation weakened the working memory (WM) representation of the current task context, thereby allowing other prepotent, but inaccurate, response tendencies to prevail.

In the Kimberg and Farah (1993) simulations, a production system architecture was used in which a production was more likely to fire again if it had recently fired (this is called "priming activation"). However, selection of a production was determined mainly through the interaction of elements in WM. The result of this interaction could override the priming activation advantage of a particular production, allowing a different new production to fire. However, weakening the connection strengths among WM elements allowed priming activation to prevail in selecting the next production. As a result, when the connections among WM elements were weakened, there was increased perseverative responding across all four of the tasks modeled, just as is observed in patients with PFC lesions.

Both of these simulation studies make it clear that the operation of WM may help to override prepotent but inaccurate responses. A similar account of the functions of the PFC has been emphasized by Goldman-Rakic for some time (e.g., Goldman-Rakic, 1987a, 1987b). Cohen and Servan-Schreiber (1992) identified these same two dimensions as being critical for understanding various EF tasks: WM demand and demand for inhibition (see Figure 18.2). Tasks that require both are more likely to tax the PFC, although tasks that have a very high demand for either are also hypothesized to be prefrontal tasks.

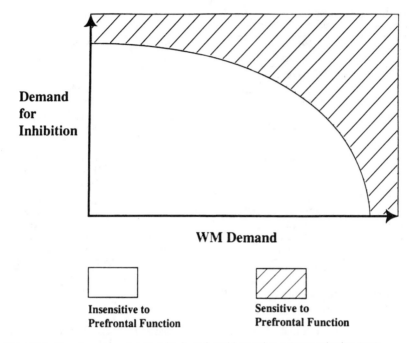

Figure 18.2. Two dimensions of prefrontal tasks. (Adapted from Cohen & Serran-Schreiber, 1992).

Roberts, Hager, and Heron (1994) similarly conceptualize the cognitive processes required for many prefrontal tasks as involving an interaction between the strength of an incorrect prepotent response and the WM requirements for carrying out the correct response(s). They show how these two task dimensions are present in a variety of prefrontal tasks that vary considerably in their surface-level characteristics (see Table 18.6). Although inhibition and WM can be viewed as independent processes, they do not necessarily need to be mediated by separate cognitive mechanisms (Goldman-Rakic, 1987a). In the computational models discussed earlier, inhibition is an intrinsic property of a WM system (e.g., Cohen & Servan-Schreiber, 1992; Kimberg & Farah, 1993). Increased activation of WM processes inhibit the activations required for competing response outcomes. More generally, competitive dynamics in the WM system and in its connections with other systems determine which response will be selected: one that best fits the current context or one that is prepotent but a poor fit. In the final sections, we describe research examining some properties of the interaction between WM and inhibitory processes.

In summary, WM appears to be critical for understanding what various executive tasks have in common and for understanding the functions of the PFC. But what exactly is WM? How does it relate to other memory constructs and systems? How does it relate to attention? Do we need a separate construct of working memory? We, as well as others, have attempted to answer some of these

Table 18.6. Prepotent responses, alternative responses, and working memory demands for several prefrontal tasks

Task	Prepotent response	Alternative response	Working-memory demand
Wisconsin Card Sorting Test	Sort by previously successful category	Sort by new category	Use feedback to determine possible correct category
Antisaccade Task	Saccade to flashed cue	Saccade in opposite direction of cue	Keep task instruction active, apply to current context
Stroop test	Read the word	Say the ink color	Keep task instruction active, apply to current context
A–Not-B Task	Search where previously found	Search where hidden	Keep last seen location in mind over a delay
Delayed Alternation Task	Search where previously searched	Search in location opposite to where previously searched	Keep last location reached in mind, apply "opposite" rule

Adapted from Roberts et al. (1994).

questions (Bennetto, Pennington, & Rogers, 1994; Pennington, 1994; Roberts et al., 1994). Pennington (1994) defines WM as follows:

> Working memory is a limited capacity computational arena. Its key characteristics are 1) *action selection,* which operates through dynamic process of 2) *constraint satisfaction,* which must necessarily be 3) *context-specific* and *transient.* (p. 248)

The WM system allows an organism to temporarily hold on-line constraints relevant to the current context so that the interaction of those constraints can lead to adaptive action selection, even in a novel context. Constraints can include attributes of the current environment, the organism's current motivational state, goals and plans retrieved from long-term memory (LTM), as well as other information retrieved from LTM.

To understand the relation between WM and other memory systems, it is helpful to think of two dimensions: prospective versus retrospective and transient versus archival. These relations are illustrated in Figure 18.3.

Even though WM interacts with both short-term memory (STM) and LTM, they are conceptually distinguishable systems. In a later section, we present evidence from an autism study that supports this theoretical distinction of WM from both STM and LTM.

In summary, we would argue that in the domain of memory there is a definite need for a separate construct of WM. There has been very little theoretical or empirical work relating EFs or WM to attention. However, both selective attention and the anterior attentional system would appear to overlap with EFs and WM as we are defining them.

In thinking further about WM, we have realized that its function can be influenced by a number of different factors. Several factors are listed in Table 18.7 and are illustrated in Figure 18.4. Each factor is discussed in turn.

	Transient	Archival
Prospective	WM	
Retrospective	STM	LTM

Figure 18.3. Relation of working memory (WM) to short-term memory (STM) and long-term memory (LTM).

Traditional conceptions of WM have often emphasized capacity, the number of bits or chunks that can be held on-line at once. In Figure 18.4, capacity is illustrated by the number of circles in the central hexagon.

However, since WM is a computational arena, much more than passive storage of bits or chunks is involved. The relations among elements in WM are also very important. The next three factors shown in Table 18.7 address these relations. "Connectivity" refers to connections between the PFC and other networks in the brain. These are shown to be bidirectional, as it is known that the extensive connections between the PFC and other parts of the brain are reciprocal. In this model, constraints are generated in other parts of the brain (e.g., through perceptual processing in the posterior cortex) and then held on-line in WM by means of

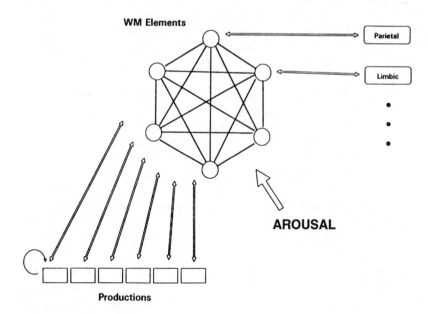

Figure 18.4. A model of working memory (WM).

Table 18.7.   Factors influencing working memory

1. Capacity: number of WMEs that can be active at once
2. Connectivity: relation between WM and other networks
3. Interconnectivity: number of connections among WMEs
4. Complexity: appropriate weights on connections
5. Maintenance: decay rate of WMEs
6. Priming: arousal of a WME or production from prior firing
7. Arousal: nonspecific activation level of all WMEs

WME, working memory element.

the reciprocal connections with the PFC. Failure of this connectivity to develop, or its loss through damage, would affect WM performance even without a direct lesion in the PFC.

Interconnectivity refers to connections among WM elements (the neural analogue here is less clear). Interconnectivity is represented in Figure 18.4 by the lines connecting the WM elements (circles) in the central hexagon. Kimberg and Farah's model (1993) emphasizes the importance of the strength of the connections among WM elements; weakening these connections in their model lessened the interaction of competing constraints, allowing a previously selected but now inappropriate production to be reselected.

The third aspect of the relations among WM elements is complexity. Even if all other factors listed in Table 18.7 were equal, two different sets of constraints could tax WM differentially because of the complexity of their relations and the computations needed to solve the constraint satisfaction problem. As we implied earlier, contexts with conflicting constraints pose particular problems for the operation of WM. So conflict among constraints is one dimension of complexity, but there are obviously others. Complexity could be represented, in part, by the pattern of signs (+ or −) on the connections among the memory elements in Figure 18.4.

The next three factors refer to the activity level of units in the network and how easily that activity is maintained over time. Because WM is transient, the decay rate of WM elements is obviously important. Constraints cannot interact unless they are maintained on-line simultaneously for a period sufficient to find the best fit among them. Likewise, it is important that constraints not remain too long in WM. Decay rate is not explicitly represented in Figure 18.4.

Next we consider priming activation. In Table 18.7, we have extended priming to include both productions, as discussed earlier, and the WM elements themselves. We are proposing that a WM element that was recently activated would be easier to reactivate and maintain than one that was less recently activated.

Finally, nonspecific arousal of the entire WM system will obviously affect its operation, with too much or too little arousal leading to problems. In the real brain, the arousal level of the PFC appears to be modulated by dopaminergic fibers originating in brain stem nuclei. Dopamine depletion or excess is well known to affect PFC functioning (Goldman-Rakic, 1987a, 1987b). In a model like that in Figure 18.4, nonspecific arousal could be simulated by adding or subtracting a constant amount of activation to each unit.

In summary, the functioning of WM can be influenced by several different factors. A number of these can be manipulated experimentally, thus leading both to refinements in how we measure WM and to a more differentiated understanding of different disorders with molar EF deficits. However, what we have sketched out here is not a full theoretical model, and more work is needed before this framework can be fully applied to the task of differentiating EF disorders. In the final section, we briefly present some current research that moves beyond global assessments of EF deficits by focusing on processes of WM and response inhibition.

NEW MEASUREMENT APPROACHES

Consistent with the computational models described earlier, Roberts et al. (1994) examined the hypothesis that the ability to inhibit an incorrect but prepotent response on prefrontal tasks is a dynamic interaction between the strength of the prepotency, the current functioning of WM processes, and the WM requirements for determining the correct response. Three studies tested nonpatient adults on various versions of the Antisaccade task (AST), a task that is highly sensitive to prefrontal functioning (Guitton, Buchtel, & Douglas, 1985). In the task subjects foveate on a center fixation point on a computer monitor. At an undetermined moment, a cue flashes on the left or right side of the screen. The subject's task is to make an eye movement to the *opposite* side of the screen. Although this may seem relatively simple, there is a strong reflexive-like tendency to saccade to abrupt visual onsets in the periphery. Even normal adults make incorrect reflexive saccades to the cue about 30% of the time (thus there is no ceiling with normal adults, as there appears to be on the WCST).

To examine the interaction between WM and inhibition, subjects performed the AST while carrying out concurrent secondary tasks that placed varying demands on WM. It was hypothesized that increasingly taxing WM resources would result in increased difficulty inhibiting reflexive saccades. In an arithmetic-load condition, subjects heard single digits and had to add the current number to a running total. In a shadowing-load condition, subjects heard digits but only needed to repeat the last digit. Thus, the arithmetic secondary task placed a greater demand on WM than the shadow task. Increasing WM load was expected to worsen inhibitory processes on the AST.

As shown in Figure 18.5, the findings supported this hypothesis. The graph in Figure 18.5(a) shows that reflexive responding increased as concurrent WM load increased. Figure 18.5(b) shows that latency to make correct antisaccades was significantly increased in the arithmetic condition, but that latency to make the relatively automatic reflexive saccades was unaffected by WM load. Additionally, it was found that these WM loads did *not* affect performance on a Prosaccade task where subjects made saccades directly to the cue. The Prosac-

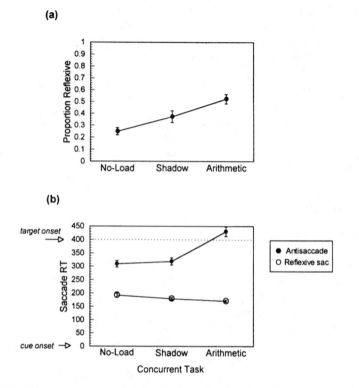

Figure 18.5 Performance on Prosaccade task and antisaccade tasks with or without concurrent tasks. RT = reaction time. (From Roberts, R.J., Hager, L., & Heron, C. (1994). Prefrontal cognitive processes: Working memory and inhibition in the antisaccade task. *Journal of Experimental Psychology: General, 123,* 374–393; reprinted with permission of the author.)

cade task is not sensitive to prefrontal functioning (Guitton et al., 1985) and was hypothesized not to heavily utilize WM resources.

It is worth noting that the degree of decrement in the AST in both inhibiting reflexive saccades and in the slowing of correct antisaccades under the arithmetic load closely resembled the performance of patients with prefrontal lesions. Thus, the findings suggest more of a continuum between normal and abnormal functioning than is often presented in the literature, as in the case of the WCST. More generally, the findings suggest that WM processes are involved in selecting appropriate action alternatives as well as inhibiting inappropriate ones.

The second approach looks to existing tasks in other areas of neuropsychology. If we assume that WM is the underlying or critical cognitive component of molar EF tasks, then we would expect to see this WM deficit in other areas of cognitive functioning. Bennetto et al. (in revision) used this approach to further test the validity of an executive dysfunction theory of autism.

Memory theorists distinguish several different types of memory, have developed experimental tasks for each type (and its components), and have demonstrated different profiles of memory impairment across patient groups with different etiologies and lesion locations (Squire, 1987). Frontal lobe pathology is associated with a specific profile of memory dysfunction, which is distinct from the pattern of deficits associated with damage to the medial temporal lobes or diencephalic midline. In particular, patients with frontal lobe deficits have shown impairment on tasks of memory for temporal order, source memory, and free recall (Schacter, 1987). These kinds of tasks utilize a memory system that allows an individual to access, organize, and manipulate memories, thus allowing consideration of their spatial, temporal, or semantic contexts. Therefore, these tasks place strong demands on WM.

In contrast, patients with frontal lobe deficits are typically not impaired on learning new information, cued recall, or recognition memory, which rely primarily on effective storage and consolidation of declarative information and place relatively few demands on a WM system. Considerable empirical evidence suggests a dissociation between these two memory systems in both human and animal subjects (see Schacter, 1987, for a review).

Using these theoretical and empirical advances in the field of memory, Bennetto et al. (1994) demonstrated that individuals with autism showed memory deficits similar to those exhibited by patients with frontal lesions, thus providing further support for a frontal dysfunction theory of autism. Furthermore, this study demonstrated a dissociation between performance on tasks that required WM and tasks that tapped only STM or LTM.

CONCLUSIONS

Traditional EF measures, such as the WCST, have detected cognitive deficits in various developmental disorders. The cognitive deficits in these developmental disorders are often much less evident on other cognitive measures, such as traditional IQ tests, or on more standard memory or attention tests. Nonetheless, the construct of executive functions has the potential to explain a wide range of symptoms in each of these disorders. However, to understand fully what these findings mean, we need to solve fundamental measurement problems, which include better theoretical and empirical specification of what executive functions are. We have sketched out the beginnings of a WM theoretical framework and illustrated two measurement approaches that derive from this framework. Use of such measurement may help solve the discriminant validity problem posed by the fact that several symptomatically different disorders all exhibit deficits on molar EF tasks.

REFERENCES

Anderson, S.W., Damasio, H., Jones, R.D., & Tranel, D. (1991). Wisconsin Card Sorting Test performance as a measure of frontal lobe damage. *Journal of Clinical and Experimental Neuropsychology, 13,* 909–992.

Bennetto, L., Pennington, B.F., & Rogers, S.J. (in revision). Intact and impaired memory functions in autism: A working memory model. *Child Development.*

Bouchard, T.J., Jr., & McGue, M. (1981). Familial studies of intelligence: A review. *Science, 212,* 1053–1059.

Cohen, J.D., & Servan-Schreiber, D. (1992). Context, cortex, and dopamine: A connectionist approach to behavior and biology in schizophrenia. *Psychological Review, 99,* 45–77.

Damasio, A.R., Tranel, D., & Damasio, H.C. (1991). Somatic markers and the guidance of behavior: Theory and preliminary testing. In H.S. Levin, H.M. Eisenberg, & A.L. Benton (Eds.), *Frontal lobe function and dysfunction* (pp. 217–229). New York: Oxford University Press.

Dehaene, S., & Changeux, J.P. (1991). The Wisconsin Card Sorting Test: Theoretical analysis and modeling in a neuronal network. *Cerebral Cortex, 1,* 62–79.

Diamond, A. (1991). Guidelines for the study of brain-behavior relationships during development. In H.S. Levin, H.M. Eisenberg, & A.L. Benton (Eds.), *Frontal lobe function and dysfunction* (pp. 339–378). New York: Oxford University Press.

Diamond, A., Ciaramitaro, V., Donner, E., Djali, S., & Robinson, M. (1994). An animal model of early-treated PKU. *Journal of Neuroscience, 14,* 3072–3082.

Frith, C.D., & Frith, U. (1991). Elective affinities in schizophrenia and autism. In P.E. Bebbington (Ed.), *Social psychiatry: Theory, methodology and practice* (pp. 65–68). New Brunswick, NJ: Transaction.

Fuster, J.M. (1989). *The prefrontal cortex: Anatomy, physiology and neuropsychology of the frontal lobe* (2nd ed.). New York: Raven Press.

Golden, C.J. (1987). *Manual for the Stroop Color and Word Test.* Chicago: Stoelting Company.

Goldman-Rakic, P.S. (1987a). Circuitry of primate prefrontal cortex and regulation of behavior by representational memory. In F. Plum (Ed.), *Handbook of physiology. The nervous system: Higher functions of the brain* (pp. 373–417). Bethesda, MD: American Physiology Association.

Goldman-Rakic, P. (1987b). Development of cortical circuitry and cognitive function. *Child Development, 58,* 601–622.

Gordon, M., McClure, F.D., & Post, E.M. (1986). *Gordon diagnostic system.* New York: Gordon System, Inc.

Grafman, J., Jones, B., & Salazar, A. (1990). Wisconsin Card Sorting Test performance based on location and size of neuroanatomical lesion in Vietnam veterans with penetrating head injury. *Perceptual and Motor Skills, 71,* 1120–1122.

Greenberg, L. (1990). *Test of Variables of Attention 5.01.* St. Paul, MN: Attention Technology, Inc.

Grodzinsky, G.M., & Diamond, R. (1992). Frontal lobe functioning in boys with attention-deficit hyperactivity disorder. *Developmental Neuropsychology, 8,* 427–445.

Guitton, D., Buchtel, H.A., & Douglas, R.M. (1985). Frontal lobe lesions in man cause difficulties in suppressing reflexive glances and in generating goal-directed saccades. *Experimental Brain Research, 58,* 455–472.

Heaton, R.K., Chelune, G.J., Talley, J.L., Kay, G.G., & Curtiss, G. (1993). *Wisconsin card sorting test manual: Revised and expanded.* Odessa, FL: Psychological Assessment Resources.

Hughes, C., & Russell, J. (1993). Autistic children's difficulty with mental disengagement from an object: Its implications for theories of autism. *Developmental Psychology, 29,* 498–510.

Hynd, G.W., Hern, K.L., Novey, E.S., Eliopulos, R.T., Marshall, R., Gonzalez, J.J., & Voeller, K.K. (1993). Attention deficit-hyperactivity disorder and asymmetry of the caudate nucleus. *Journal of Child Neurology, 8,* 339–347.

Kagan, J., Rosman, B.L., Day, L., Albert, J., & Phillips, W. (1964). Information processing in the child: Significance of analytic and reflective attitudes. *Psychological Monographs, 78,* N. 578.

Kimberg, D.Y., & Farah, M.J. (1993). A unified account of cognitive impairments following frontal lobe damage: The role of working memory in complex, organized behavior. *Journal of Experimental Psychology: General, 122,* 411–428.

Kolb, B., & Whishaw, I.Q. (1990). *Fundamentals of human neuropsychology.* New York: W.H. Freeman.

Levine, D.S., Leven, S.J., & Prueitt, P.S. (1992). Integration, disintegration, and the frontal lobes. In D.S. Levine and S.J. Leven (Eds.), pp. 301–305. *Motivation, emotion, and goal direction in neural networks.* Hillsdale, NJ: Lawrence Erlbaum Associates.

Lou, H.C., Henriksen, L., Bruhn, P., Borner, H., & Nielson, J.B. (1989). Striatal dysfunction in attention deficit and hyperkinetic disorder. *Archives of Neurology, 46,* 48–52.

Luria, A. (1966). *Higher cortical functions in man.* New York: Basic Books.

Mazzocco, M.M.M., Hagerman, R.J., Cronister-Silverman, A., & Pennington, B.F. (1992). Specific frontal lobe deficits among women with the fragile X gene. *The American Academy of Child and Adolescent Psychiatry, 31,* 1141–1148.

Milner, B. (1964). Some effects of frontal lobectomy in man. In J. Warren & K. Akert (Eds.), *The frontal granular cortex and behavior.* New York: McGraw Hill.

Milner, B. (1971). Interhemispheric differences in the localization of psychological processes in man. *British Medical Bulletin, 27,* 272–277.

Morton, J., & Frith, U. (in press). Causal modelling: A structural approach to developmental psychopathology.

Nelson, H.E. (1976). A modified card sorting test sensitive to frontal lobe defects. *Cortex, 12,* 313–324.

Osterreith, P.A. (1944). Le test de copie d'une figure complex: Contribution à l'étude de la perception et de la mémoire. *Archives de Psychologie, 30,* 286–356.

Ozonoff, S. (in review). Reliability and validity of WCST in studies of autism, *Neuropsychology.*

Ozonoff, S., Pennington, B.F., & Rogers, S. (1991). Executive function deficits in high functioning autistic children: Relationship to theory of mind. *Journal of Child Psychology and Psychiatry, 32(7),* 1081–1105.

Pennington, B.F. (1994). The working memory function of the prefrontal cortices: Implications for developmental and individual differences in cognition. In M.M. Haith, J. Benson, R. Roberts, & B.F. Pennington (Eds.), *The development of future oriented processes* (pp. 243–289). Chicago: University of Chicago Press.

Pennington, B.F., Groisser, D., & Welsh, M.C. (1993). Contrasting deficits in attention deficit hyperactivity disorder versus reading disability. *Developmental Psychology, 29,* 511–523.

Porteus, S.D. (1965). *Porteus Mazes.* San Antonio, TX: Psychological Corporation.

Prior, N., & Hoffman, W. (1990). Neuropsychological testing of autistic children through an exploration with frontal lobe tests. *Journal of Autism and Developmental Disorders, 20,* 581–590.

Reitan, R.M., & Davidson, L.A. (1974). *Clinical neuropsychology: Current status and applications.* Washington, DC: V.H. Winston & Sons.

Roberts, R.J., Hager, L., & Heron, C. (1994). Prefrontal cognitive processes: Working memory and inhibition in the Antisaccade task. *Journal of Experimental Psychology: General, 123,* 374–393.

Rosvold, H.E., Mirsky, A.F., Sarason, I., Bransome, E.D., Jr., & Beck, L.H. (1956). A continuous performance test of brain damage. *Journal of Consulting Psychology, 20,* 343–350.

Rudel, R.G., Denckla, M.B., & Broman, M. (1978). Rapid silent response to repeated target symbols by dyslexic and nondyslexic children. *Brain and Language, 6,* 52–62.

Rumsey, J.M. (1985). Conceptual problem-solving in highly verbal, nonretarded autistic men. *Journal of Autism and Developmental Disorders, 15,* 23–36.

Russell, J., Mauther, N., Sharpe, S., & Tidswell, T. (1991). The "windows task" as a measure of strategic deception in preschoolers and autistic subjects. *British Journal of Developmental Psychology, 9,* 331–349.

Schacter, D.L. (1987). Memory, amnesia, and frontal lobe dysfunction. *Psychobiology, 15,* 21–36.

Shallice, T., & Burgess, P. (1991). Higher-order cognitive impairments and frontal lobe lesions in man. In H.S. Levin, H.M. Eisenberg, & A.L. Benton (Eds.), *Frontal lobe function and dysfunction* (pp.125–138). New York: Oxford University Press.

Shue, K.L., & Douglas, V.I. (1992). Attention deficit hyperactivity disorder and the frontal lobe syndrome. *Brain and Cognition, 20,* 104–124.

Squire, L.R. (1987). *Memory and brain.* New York: Oxford University Press.

Taylor, H.G. (1988). Learning disabilities. In E.J. Mash (Ed.), *Behavioral assessments of childhood disorders* (2nd ed.) (pp. 402–405). New York: Guilford Press.

Weinberger, D.R. (1992, May). *A neural systems approach to the frontal lobes.* Paper presented at the American Academy of Neurology, San Diego.

Weinberger, D.R., Berman, K.F., Gold, J., & Goldberg, T. (1994). Neural mechanisms of future oriented processes: In vivo physiological studies of humans. In M.M. Haith, J. Benson, R. Roberts, & B.F. Pennington (Eds.), *The development of future-oriented processes* (pp. 221–242). Chicago: University of Chicago Press.

Welsh, M.C., & Pennington, B.F. (1988). Assessing frontal lobe functioning in children: Views from developmental psychology. *Developmental Neuropsychology, 4,* 199–230.

Welsh, M.C., Pennington, B.F., Ozonoff, S., Rouse, B., & McCabe, E.R.B. (1990). Neuropsychology of early-treated phenylketonuria: Specific executive function deficits. *Child Development, 61,* 1697–1713.

Zametkin, A.J., Nordahl, T.E., Gross, M., King, A.C., Semple, W.E., Rumsey, J., Hamburger, S., & Cohen, R.M. (1990). Cerebral glucose metabolism in adults with hyperactivity of childhood onset. *The New England Journal of Medicine, 323,* 1361–1366.

19

Addressing Problems in Attention, Memory, and Executive Functioning

An Example from Self-Regulated Strategy Development

Steve Graham and Karen R. Harris

Although children with learning problems represent a heterogeneous population, the significant difficulties they face are typically the result of multiple factors. Recent research indicates that one contributor to these students' academic difficulties may be difficulties in the self-regulation of organized strategic behaviors, behaviors they can acquire and use given appropriate scaffolded instruction (Bjorklund, 1990; Harris, 1990; Hughes & Hall, 1989). For example, they may experience difficulty in using verbalizations to guide their behavior or establishing correspondence between saying and doing (Harris, 1990). They may also have difficulty in understanding the demands of the task, spontaneously producing appropriate strategies to accomplish the task, or using these strategies to mediate performance (Hallahan, Lloyd, Kauffman, & Loper, 1983).

In addition to problems with self-regulation, students with learning problems may possess other cognitive characteristics that impede their performance, including impulsivity, lack of problem-solving skills, and difficulties with memory and other aspects of information processing such as attention (Harris, 1982). Many of these students also exhibit maladaptive attitudes and emotions, including negative task orientations and low levels of motivation, that may further undermine their academic success (Licht, 1983). The situation is further complicated by the situational, educational, cultural, and systems network of which the child is a part (Harris, Graham, & Pressley, 1992; Turkewitz, 1984).

The frequency of multiple, interrelated problems of an affective, behavioral, and cognitive nature among students with learning disabilities has led us to recommend the use of multicomponent, integrative interventions with this population of students (Harris & Graham, 1992a; Harris & Graham, 1994). In this chapter, we present a model of strategy instruction, self-regulated strategy development (SRSD), that can be used to address the behavioral, cognitive, affective, social, and ecological aspects of learning. In line with the purpose of this book, the components of the model that focus on attention, memory, and executive functioning are highlighted. SRSD provides an example of *one* approach for addressing these processes conjointly in the context of meaningful academic instruction (cf. Harris & Graham, 1994). Readers interested in examining other examples of multicomponent approaches for teaching strategies to children with learning difficulties are referred to the work of Borkowski and Muthukrishna (1992), Deshler and Schumaker (1986), Englert et al. (1991), Gaskins, Cunicelli, and Satlow (1992), Palinscar and Brown (1984), and Pressley, Goodchild, Fleet, Zajchowski, and Evans (1989).

SELF-REGULATED STRATEGY DEVELOPMENT

SRSD was designed to help students 1) master the higher-level cognitive processes and strategies underlying effective performance in a variety of academic areas; 2) develop autonomous, reflective, self-regulated use of these processes and strategies; and 3) form positive attitudes about themselves and their academic capabilities. Students learn specific strategies important to successfully engaging in academic tasks in conjunction with procedures for regulating or controlling the use of these strategies, the task, and undesirable behaviors (e.g., impulsivity or negative self-talk) that may impede performance. Although SRSD has been used to teach strategies and self-regulation procedures in both reading and mathematics (Bednarczyk & Harris, 1992; Case, Harris, & Graham, 1992; Johnson & Graham, 1994), most of our work has involved writing (see Graham & Harris, 1993; Graham, Harris, MacArthur, & Schwartz, 1991). The example of the model presented here, therefore, draws upon our work in the area of writing.

Components, Stages, and Characteristics of SRSD

Over a decade ago, four sources played a prominent role in designing the SRSD model: Meichenbaum's (1977) development of cognitive behavior modification; the work of Soviet theorists and researchers, especially Vygotsky (1962), Luria (1961), and Sokolov (1972) on verbal self-regulation and the social origins of self-control; the concept of self-control instruction offered by Brown, Campione, and Day (1981); and the development of the learning strategies model by Deshler and Schumaker (1986). Since that time, multiple theoretical and instructional works have continued to influence our work with SRSD (see Harris & Graham, 1992b, for a more detailed discussion of these influences).

Components The foundations for the model (Harris & Graham, 1985) began with the three components generally considered essential in effective strategy instruction: skillful use of strategies; understanding of the use, significance, and limitations of those strategies (metastrategy information); and self-regulation of strategic performance (including any combination of goal setting, self-monitoring, self-instructions, and self-reinforcement).

Stages Seven instructional stages, designed to be flexible and recursive, provide the frame for operationalizing these basic components. These stages and the description presented below provide a "metascript" for the SRSD model. We encourage teachers and other service providers to individualize and modify the approach to meet their and their students' needs. Students generally progress through these stages in the following manner:

1. The teacher helps students acquire any preskills necessary to understanding, acquiring, or executing the target strategy that have not already been mastered (*preskill development*); this stage generally occurs in conjunction with the second stage.

2. The teacher and students examine and discuss prior performance and the methods students presently use to accomplish a given task (*initial conference: instructional goals and significance*). The benefits and significance of the proposed program are also discussed, and each student is asked to make a commitment to learn the strategy and participate as a collaborative partner during instruction. Negative or ineffective self-statements that students currently use may also be discussed at this time.

3. The teacher and students discuss the strategy, its purposes, and how and when to use it (*discussion of the strategy*).

4. The teacher (or a trained peer) models how the strategy is used along with appropriate self-instructions (*modeling of the strategy and self-instructions*). Self-instructions typically include problem definition, planning, strategy use, self-evaluation, coping and error correction, and self-reinforcement statements. After discussing the model's performance, teacher and students may collaborate on how to change the strategy to make it more effective or efficient. Each student also develops and records personal self-statements he or she plans to use.

5. Students memorize the agreed upon strategy steps (and any accompanying mnemonic); paraphrasing is allowed as long as the original meaning is maintained (*memorization of the strategy*).

6. Students practice using the strategy and self-instructions with the teacher acting as a coach or guide until the instructional objectives for use of the strategy are met (*collaborative practice*). Both the teacher and students continue to evaluate the effectiveness of the strategy, making any needed adjustments. Self-regulation procedures, including goal-setting and self-assessment, may be introduced at this point (or earlier).

7. Students are encouraged to use the strategy and accompanying self-instructions independently and covertly (*independent practice*). The teacher and students may decide to start fading out any self-regulation procedures (e.g., self-assessment) currently in use.

Procedures for promoting maintenance and generalization are incorporated throughout instruction. These include but are not limited to 1) the teacher and students discussing opportunities to use and the results of using the strategy and self-instructions with other tasks and in other settings, 2) asking other teachers as well as parents to comment on students' success in using the strategy, and 3) working with other teachers to prompt or reinforce the use of the strategy in their classrooms.

Characteristics There are seven characteristics crucial to the effective implementation of SRSD. First, explicit teaching of strategies and self-regulation procedures is emphasized in the SRSD model. Students with learning difficulties often profit from initial teacher direction and structure during learning (Hallahan et al., 1983; Harris & Pressley, 1991) and may require more extensive and explicit instruction to master skills and processes that other students acquire more easily (Reeve & Brown, 1985). The level of explicitness and structure provided, however, should be adjusted to student needs (Harris & Graham, 1992b; Harris & Pressley, 1991). For example, SRSD procedures can be used to explicitly teach single or complex strategies, or they can be modified to guide students in the discovery of a predetermined strategy or assist them in creating their own strategy. Whether students are taught or guided to discover strategies, however, they should be encouraged to *make the strategies their own* by personalizing them. Resulting changes should be carefully monitored to ensure that students do not change strategies in ways that make them less effective.

A second key characteristic of SRSD is individualization. The strategies and skills targeted for instruction are tailored to students' individual needs and capabilities. In some instances, this means helping a student "upgrade" current strategies. In other situations, new strategies may need to be mastered. In either case, the strategies and accompanying skills to be learned should be based on a thorough understanding of the student as well as the task. Some students will not require full-blown SRSD to master the target strategy and accompanying skills (Harris & Pressley, 1991; Pressley & Harris, 1990). Modeling, explaining, or facilitating discovery of a strategy may be all that some students need. Even when the strategies to be learned are appropriate for a group of students and the basic components of instruction are the same, specific aspects of instruction are still individualized (feedback and reinforcement, the amount and type of assistance provided, the nature and content of self-instructions, etc.).

Third, collaborative learning between the teacher and students is emphasized throughout the SRSD model. Much of this collaboration occurs as students learn to use independently the targeted strategies and self-regulation procedures. At first, students are provided whatever degree of support is needed in order to successfully apply the strategy. As students become more adept in applying the strategy and accompanying self-regulation procedures on their own, this scaffolding is gradually withdrawn. Students also act as collaborators in determining the goals of instruction (students do best when their participation is voluntary); completing the task; and implementing, evaluating, and modifying the strategy, strategy acquisition procedures, and self-regulation procedures. Collaboration is further kindled through the use of Socratic dialogue, a give-and-take exchange where the teacher asks students how they would do the task and then provides feedback and builds on that advice.

Fourth, working with students with learning problems can be a demanding and challenging task. An important part of SRSD, therefore, is anticipating difficulties that may arise. This helps the instructor avoid or be ready for problems as they occur. We have found that it is particularly helpful to consider issues concerning the promotion of strategy maintenance and generalization. In addition, students are also encouraged to anticipate difficulties in using what they have been taught and to develop appropriate solutions to counter anticipated problems.

Fifth, instruction is criterion based rather than time based. We believe that students should move through the instructional process at their own pace and should not proceed to later stages until they have met at least initial criteria for doing so. For instance, preskill development is an early stage in our model where unmastered prerequisite skills necessary to understanding, acquiring, or executing the target strategy are presented. Although students may not need to fully master all prerequisite skills before going on to the next stages of instruction, they will need to do so before proceeding to the later stages, such as collaborative or independent practice.

Sixth, SRSD is meant to be an ongoing process in which new strategies are introduced and previously taught strategies are upgraded. For instance, in the area of spelling, students might initially be introduced to the strategy of invented spelling, but this strategy may later be upgraded to include the generation of several possible spellings in order to try to identify the correct spelling. Students' repertoire of spelling strategies might further be expanded to include thinking of words that "you already know" that sound the same (e.g., same–frame) or have similar meanings (e.g., metal–metallic) as an aid to spelling unknown words (Harris, Graham, Zutell, & Gentry, 1994).

Finally, it is important to realize that SRSD, and other strategy instructional models as well, demands a great deal of teachers, including enthusiastic, responsive teaching. Teachers need to establish the credibility of strategies and serve as models of "good strategy use" (Pressley et al., 1989). A great deal of individualization and student support is necessary as well. Given these demands, it is not surprising that teachers who support one another in using strategy instruction are more successful in implementing and sustaining approaches such as SRSD. Working together with other teachers not only makes the job easier, but provides an opportunity for teachers to collaborate and consult with each other.

An Example Involving a Report Writing Strategy

To better illustrate the SRSD model, we next examine the use of this approach to teach a report writing strategy in a class of 25 fifth-grade students. The class included four students with learning disabilities and was team-taught by a special and regular education teacher. Writing instruction followed a Writers' Workshop format (Atwell, 1987). Students consulted with their peers when planning and revising their work, conferenced regularly with the teachers about their work, shared their completed and in-progress work with classmates, selected pieces for publication, and reflected on their accomplishments and challenges in a journal. Although students typically choose the topics for their papers, the genre was often specified by the teachers. This was in accordance with a countywide curriculum that specified the types of genres that were to be covered at each grade level.

Most of the students in this fifth-grade class had already been taught at least one writing strategy and accompanying self-regulation procedures using the SRSD model (Danoff, Harris, & Graham, 1993). This strategy involved brainstorming ideas to use in a story. A series of questions, pertaining to the basic parts of a story, were used to focus the brainstorming process, and students used goal setting, self-monitoring, and self-instructions to regulate the strategy and the writing process.

The report writing strategy was primarily taught by the special education teacher, Barbara Danoff, with the regular classroom teacher providing support as needed. The regular education teacher and other teachers from the school planned to implement the strategy in their other classes after observing and conferencing with Ms. Danoff about the process. This same pattern had been followed when the story writing strategy was first implemented. Furthermore, Ms. Danoff met and talked with special education teachers from three other county schools who were also helping students develop the report writing strategy (MacArthur, Schwartz, Graham, Molloy, & Harris, 1994).

When teaching the story writing strategy, instruction had primarily occurred as a series of mini-lessons during Writers' Workshop (Danoff et al., 1993). Because the report writing strategy was much more complicated and time consuming, the Workshop was temporarily suspended during the initial stages of instruction. As will be seen shortly, a number of cooperative learning procedures were incorporated into the strategy instruction; students were experienced in these procedures. Once collaborative practice started, the Workshop returned to its previous format.

Before deciding to teach the report writing strategy to the fifth-grade class, Ms. Danoff carefully considered what she knew about her students, the writing task, and the types of assignments students were expected to complete now and in the near future. Students currently wrote reports for their social studies class, and it was anticipated that the demands for this type of writing would increase dramatically when they entered middle school in the fall. Furthermore, the teachers' assessments indicated that students in the fifth-grade class were not particularly adept at report writing. Report writing requires the ability to generate and organize information from multiple sources (background knowledge, information from other written sources, etc.). Although the students were reasonably skilled at brainstorming their ideas, their facility in organizing collected information (through webs, outlines, or other organizational aids) varied considerably, and they had little experience in reading to locate expository information for writing. The teacher also thought that some of the students, including the four students with learning disabilities, would have difficulty effectively regulating and monitoring a task of this complexity. For these students, and several others in the class as well, it would be important to include instructional components that would help them stay on task, compensate for difficulties in retrieving and remembering information, and help establish an "I can do this" attitude.

In describing Ms. Danoff's instruction, we primarily focus on the four students with learning disabilities. While these students were taught the strategy along with their regularly achieving peers, they were provided additional time to learn the strategy, as Ms. Danoff scheduled time to work with them separately. In addition, during collaborative practice and independent performance, Ms. Danoff focused her attention mostly on students who needed greater support to learn the strategy; this included the four students with learning disabilities and a few other students. The regular class teacher assisted the other students in the class.

Ms. Danoff held a conference with each of the students with learning disabilities to discuss the goals of instruction (*initial conference*). (She decided to do the *initial conference* before *preskill development,* and *memorization of the strategy* before *modeling of the strategy and self-instructions.*) They discussed the student's approach to writing an earlier report (either writing solely from prior knowledge or mostly copying verbatim facts from reading material), and Ms. Danoff indicated that she thought the student would profit from learning a strategy for report writing (their reports would become more informative and better organized as well as more fun for others to read). She briefly described the report writing strategy and indicated that the procedures used to learn the story grammar strategy would again be used to learn this strategy. She further stressed the student's role as a collaborator and the importance of effort in strategy mastery. Each of the students with learning disabilities indicated a willingness to learn the report writing strategy.

In a session with the whole class, Ms. Danoff next focused on the characteristics of a good report (*preskill development*). After the class brainstormed ideas on how people work together cooperatively (e.g., using nice words, staying on topic, looking at the speaker), cooperative groups were formed and students brainstormed and discussed what makes a good report and why it is important to write good reports. Each of the groups shared their ideas with the class as a whole.

The next day, all the students were assigned to groups of three (a reader, a writer, and a manager) and given an example of a good report. They were asked to identify what made it a good report. When the groups shared their ideas, Ms. Danoff webbed them on the board. She also asked students to note any weaknesses they identified. She then asked them to refer back to the ideas they had brainstormed in the previous section to see how well their prior knowledge and current knowledge matched. An uncompleted web was then passed out, and each of the groups was asked to use it to organize the information in the report.

By involving the students in activities (brainstorming and semantic webbing) central to the report writing strategy, Ms. Danoff was not only able to make sure students understood the purpose of report writing and the characteristics of a good report—she was further able to assess their facility in using these strategies. This assessment informed the ongoing instruction (for discussion of the forms and roles of assessment in SRSD, see Harris, 1985; Harris & Graham, 1992a, 1992b). At this point, students were also asked to assess their progress (self-monitoring) by keeping a log in their journal on what they were learning.

During the next class session, Ms. Danoff described in detail the report writing strategy to small groups of students (*discussion of the strategy*); each student received a small chart listing the strategy steps. The strategy included these six steps: 1) choose a topic; 2) brainstorm all you know and would like to know about the topic; 3) organize your ideas by main points and detail on a web; 4) read to find new information and verify the accuracy of already generated material (add, delete, and modify information on the web as necessary); 5) write your report using information from the web, but continue planning as you write; and 6) check to be sure you used everything you wanted to from the web.

Ms. Danoff first asked students what they thought the reason for each step might be. They then discussed how and when to use the strategy, making linkages to social studies and other writing assignments. As a homework assignment, students were asked to memorize the steps of the strategy, using the following key words as reminders: topic, brainstorm, organize, read, write and say more, check (*memorization of the strategy*). The regular class teacher encouraged students to make up a silly sentence (mnemonic) to help them remember the steps. Most of the students memorized the steps easily. The students with learning disabilities, however, required some additional practice rehearsing the steps of the strategy.

In several subsequent sessions, Ms. Danoff modeled (while "thinking out loud") how to use the strategy to write a report (*modeling*). She and the students collaboratively planned, wrote, and revised a report. While composing, Ms. Danoff modeled a variety of self-instructions including problem definition, planning, self-evaluation, self-reinforcement, and coping. Once the report was finished, students were asked to volunteer personal self-statements they had previously developed to help them regulate their behavior, particularly when learning the story writing strategy. A discussion also ensued on the importance of what we say to ourselves, and the class identified the functions and types of self-statements used by Ms. Danoff when modeling the strategy. Students then generated and recorded their own self-statements to help them regulate their use of the report writing strategy and the writing process. Statements generated and later used by the students with learning disabilities included, "I can do it," "Am I doing it right?" "I did a good job," and "I need to reread my paper." Finally, Ms. Danoff asked for recommendations on how the strategy steps and mnemonic might be made more effective. The only change made at this point was to cross out brainstormed items as they were transferred to the semantic web.

Students now began to use the strategy to write their own reports, receiving assistance from Ms. Danoff or the other teacher as needed (*collaborative practice*). During individual conferences, students were encouraged to use a writing checklist (introduced earlier in the year) to evaluate their written product and make decisions about needed revisions. Students continued to reflect on what they were learning in their journals. Use of these self-regulation procedures as well as the personalized self-statements was prompted as needed. As students became more proficient in using the strategy, reliance on the teacher and instructional materials (charts with strategy steps and personalized self-statements) was faded, and Ms. Danoff began encouraging students to use their self-statements covertly. Although most of the students were ready for the final stage of instruction, *independent performance*, after only two or three collaborative experiences, it took the students with learning disabilities more time to learn to use the strategy. Accordingly, additional instructional time was provided for these students.

Finally, during collaborative practice and independent performance, the students shared their opinions on how to make the strategy better: Do brainstorming and webbing together; do not brainstorm for unfamiliar topics; and number on the web what will appear first in the report, second, third, and so forth. Some of the students personalized the strategy by following one or more of these suggestions. Discussion also occurred on how to encourage continued use of the strategy. The students identified opportunities they might have for using the strategy in the near future and identified problems that might occur and how they could be addressed. They further set a goal for using the strategy in their social studies class and agreed to participate in a review and booster session to help promote maintenance and generalization.

How SRSD Addresses Problems in Attention, Memory, and Executive Functioning

Although the constructs of memory, attention, and executive functioning overlap, we consider separately how each was dealt with in the example of SRSD just presented. This is not an exhaustive review but provides a representative sample of some of the more common instructional procedures used to attend to these functions in the SRSD model.

Attention Three aspects of attention addressed by Ms. Danoff when teaching the report writing strategy included *focus/execute, sustained attention*, and *attentional shift*. At the general task level, the strategy helped students focus on the writing process, emphasizing specific strategies for successfully completing the task. For students with learning difficulties, this represents an important shift in how the task is approached, as they overemphasize product variables, such as handwriting and spelling, when writing (Graham, Schwartz, & MacArthur, 1993) and may fail to execute appropriate writing processes, like brainstorming, even though they have mastered such strategies. This increased focus on process was reinforced through the use of the cue cards containing the strategy steps as well as prompts and cues from the teachers (and in some instances from other students) to execute these processes. Furthermore, during modeling, Ms. Danoff repeatedly cued herself to check if she was doing each of the strategy steps, and several of the students in the class developed similar personalized self-statements.

At a more local level, instructional procedures focused students' attention on the mechanisms for completing specific steps of the strategy and selected aspects of their writing. For instance, the modification by students to check off brainstormed items as they were completed highlighted items that still needed attention. During collaborative and independent practice, reinstatement of the writing checklist fixed students' attention on specific qualities and features of their written products. Comments by teachers or students during conferences or sharing further sharpened this focus. This may be beneficial to students' future writing as some of the criteria included in the checklist or underlying teacher or student comments may become internalized, influencing how subsequent papers are written (Graham & Harris, 1994).

Ms. Danoff used multiple procedures to address problems of sustained attention and the lack of active task engagement that frequently characterizes the performance of many students with learning difficulties (Harris, 1982). Right at the start, students made a commitment to learn the strategy. Goal setting can boost motivation and result in increased persistency (Graham & Harris, 1994). Other methods designed to strengthen motivation and persistence included emphasizing the collaborative nature of instruction, encouraging student choice (e.g., topic selection, personalization of the strategy), working collaboratively with peers, creating a supportive environment, stressing the role of effort in strategy learning, reinforcing students for their efforts, making the benefits of instruction clear at the outset, asking students to assess their progress (again emphasizing the benefits of instruction), and providing students with an effective and meaningful method for accomplishing the assigned tasks. In addition, when a student had difficulty sustaining attention, the teachers and sometimes other students prompted him or her to remain on task. Some students also used personalized self-statements, such as "I can do it," to prompt themselves to stay on-task. If a problem in sustaining attention persisted, Ms. Danoff typically held private "pep" talks with the students involved, reminding them of their commitment, reviewing the importance of what they were learning, and reemphasizing their progress.

Attentional shifts at the general task level were facilitated by clearly defined transitional markers. For each step of the strategy, key words were developed and displayed prominently in the classroom and on students' individual cue cards. Furthermore, teachers and sometimes other students provided prompts and cues when a child was having difficulty shifting attention.

Memory Ms. Danoff used multiple techniques to help students memorize important information, extend their internal memory through prosthetic and orthotic devices, and facilitate retrospective and prospective memory. To help students remember the strategy steps, students were asked to rehearse the steps by themselves or with another person (e.g., a parent). The process of memorizing the strategy was simplified by providing students with key words for each step, and students were encouraged to develop their own silly sentence, using the key words, as a memory aid. They were already familiar with how to construct such mnemonics. For students who had difficulty remembering the strategy steps, additional practice was provided over several school days (spaced practice). Students were further assisted in remembering the strategy steps or their personalized statements through the use of cue cards as well as prompting and cuing by teachers and sometimes other students during collaborative and independent practice. Practice in using the strategy undoubtedly facilitated the memory process as well. Finally, students participated in a booster session designed to ensure that they remembered the strategy steps and how to use it.

We would like to further highlight a memory aid, visual imagery, not used in the current example. In an SRSD study by Graham and Harris (1989a), students were encouraged to visualize a tree when trying to remember three steps of a four-step strategy for planning and writing an opinion essay. First, they were told that the *topic* sentence is like the trunk of a tree—everything is attached to it. Second, the *reasons* to support the topic sentences are like the roots of a tree—they hold the tree up. Third, just as it is important to *examine* the health of the roots of a tree, it is necessary to examine the strength of the supporting reasons—if they are strong, then the essay is strong. Furthermore, the mnemonic used to help students remember the steps of the strategy was *TREE: T*opic sentence, *Re*asons to support topic sentence, *E*xamine if a reader will believe each reason, and add an *E*nding sentence.

To return to the current example, students' retrospective memory, memory for past information, was facilitated by encouraging them to use the brainstorming strategy. Additionally, as students read for information about their writing topic, other past memories were likely stimulated. One student also developed a personalized self-statement—"I can think of more"—to help him as he brainstormed what he already knew.

Ms. Danoff helped students extend their internal memory through the use of notes, the semantic web, cue cards, and the checklist. Notes from brainstorming and the semantic web provided easy and organized (in the case of the web) access to the information already generated. The cue cards and checklist provided external reminders to execute a particular action; that is, do a particular step or evaluate the writing product in terms of specific attributes.

While the cue cards and checklist served to remind students to execute a certain action while writing, Ms. Danoff put into place several procedures to facilitate prospective memory—remembering to take a plan of action at some future point in time. Students identified situations where the strategy might be used and set a goal for using the strategy in a particular situation (social studies). Another instructional option for promoting prospective memory not applied by Ms. Danoff, but used by other teachers, involved helping students identify cues that signal strategy use.

Executive Functioning   Important components of executive functioning are students' metacognitive knowledge of the task, the strategies they can apply to accomplish the task, and their capabilities as learners. Ms. Danoff attended to strengthening each of these cognitive resources while teaching the report writing strategy. Knowledge of the *task* was increased during preskill development by specifying the components of a good report. This was further strengthened during modeling and collaborative and independent practice as students received help writing reports that attempted to meet these standards. Students' knowledge of *how* to write a good report increased as a result of examining the basic strategies underlying this endeavor, discussing when and how to use them (metastrategy information), seeing them applied by a competent other (modeling), and putting them into operation themselves. Students clarified and enlarged their own internal visions of their *capabilities* as writers by evaluating what they were learning (journal), using the checklist to evaluate their written products, and receiving feedback from teachers and peers concerning their use of the strategy and the quality of their writing products. This appeared to be an important aspect of the learning process for many of the participating students, as evaluative self-statements were common.

A key feature of Ms. Danoff's instruction was providing students with a strategic plan of action for writing a report. This action plan was meant to be flexible, and students were encouraged to personalize it in useful ways. A central ingredient in the action plan was the report writing strategy. It provided the participating students with a powerful form of support—it helped them structure and organize their behavior and cognitive resources. This is especially helpful for students with learning problems, who often approach academic tasks in an inefficient or ineffective manner (Harris, 1982).

Additional support in recruiting and executing an effective action plan was provided via the instructional processes used to teach the report writing strategy. Ms. Danoff and the regular class teacher provided students with temporary and adjusted assistance and guidance (or scaffolding) in carrying out the action plan during controlled and independent practice. This support was aimed at helping students learn to do independently what they previously were able to do only with the help of a competent other. At first, the teachers provided students with considerable help in implementing and using the action plan—modeling, explaining, and assisting whenever necessary. Gradually, this help was withdrawn as students became increasingly adept at using the strategy.

In addition to scaffolding, the teachers used several traditional self-regulation procedures to help students become better equipped at regulating the action plan and the writing process. Self-control processes, such as goal setting, monitoring, and planning, were facilitated through the various self-assessment procedures implemented by the teachers (journal, checklist, etc.) and the personalized self-statements developed by students.

In some instances, the personalized self-statements were used to help control interference, a common component in definitions of executive functioning (see Chapter 17). One student, who was impulsive, developed a personalized self-statement to "go slow." Interference control was also addressed by discussing with students difficulties they might have in applying the strategy and considering appropriate solutions to these difficulties.

INVESTIGATIONS EVALUATING SRSD

In this section, the basic findings from over 10 years of research on SRSD are summarized. The students participating in our studies were primarily students with learning disabilities in grades 4 through 8. Although SRSD has been used effectively with students without learning problems (Danoff et al., 1993), this summary focuses on the findings from students with learning problems. Major findings in the area of writing are summarized first, as most of our research has concentrated on this area.

Writing

Across a variety of writing genres, SRSD has proven to be an effective and efficient approach for teaching writing strategies to students with learning problems. These students have successfully learned to use writing strategies involving brainstorming (Harris & Graham, 1985); semantic webbing (MacArthur et al., 1994); text structure prompts for generating and organizing possible writing content (Danoff et al., 1993; Graham & Harris, 1989a, 1989b; Sawyer, Graham, & Harris, 1992); goal setting (Graham, MacArthur, Schwartz, & Voth, 1992); monitoring written output (Harris, Graham, Reid, McElroy, & Hamby, 1994); peer response in revising (MacArthur, Graham, & Schwartz, 1991); and revising for both mechanics and substance (Graham & MacArthur, 1988). In general, students with learning problems were able to use the target strategies independently and in a constructive manner after only five to eight 40-minute sessions.

In terms of the writing product, the quality and usually the length and structure of compositions produced by students with learning problems improve significantly after learning a writing strategy and the accompanying self-regulation procedures via SRSD (Graham & Harris, 1993). The "effect sizes" for quality and schematic structure typically range from 1.0 to 5.12; effect sizes of +.40 or greater are usually considered educationally significant. Particularly promising are the findings from one group of studies, where writing improvement was so pronounced after learning a planning strategy that the schematic structure of stories written by students with learning problems was equivalent to that of their typically achieving classmates (Graham & Harris, 1989b; Sawyer et al., 1992).

We have further found that writing gains were maintained over time and generalized across settings and persons (Graham et al., 1991). Students' skills at adapting specific strategies to different writing genres (e.g., from expository to narrative writing) following SRSD, however, have been less constant. Although some students with learning problems were able to adapt a strategy across genres without additional teacher assistance, others needed direct and assisted practice in order to accomplish such transfer. Consequently, we recommend that such assistance be routinely provided.

The positive impact of SRSD on students' writing performance has recently been independently replicated by other investigators. In a study by Collins (1992), the length and quality of stories written by 11- to 13-year-old children with learning disabilities improved as a result of teaching a story writing strategy (the one taught to Ms. Danoff's students earlier) via SRSD within the context of a whole language classroom. We have also found that integrating SRSD into whole language classrooms can positively affect students' writing (Danoff et al., 1993; MacArthur, Schwartz, & Graham, 1991). In a second study, Tanhouser (1994) found that the length and quality of essays written by 17- and 18-year-old students with learning disabilities improved as a result of teaching the TREE strategy presented earlier.

We have also observed that SRSD influences students' persistence, metacognitive knowledge, approach to composing, and self-efficacy (Graham et al., 1991). In a recent single-subject design study, for example, four students with learning problems were taught a goal-setting strategy for writing (Graham et al., 1992). The strategy involved these steps: 1) do *PLANS* (*P*ick goals, *L*ist ways to meet goals, *A*nd, make *N*otes, *S*equence notes); 2) write and say more (use your plan while writing, and continue to plan); 3) test goals (assess to see if goals were met). Goals were selected from a predetermined list and focused on the purpose, structure, and length of the composition.

All of the students increased the amount of time (persistence) they spent composing. For three students, conceptualizations of good writing shifted from a concentration on the mechanical aspects of text production to an emphasis on process following SRSD instruction. The number of planning strategies students were familiar with increased as well, and their perceptions of competence (self-efficacy) became more accurate following instruction. In addition, the students in this study initially did no planning in advance but after learning the "goal-setting" strategy reliably developed plans and ideas prior to writing.

SRSD has consistently received positive evaluations in follow-up interviews with students and teachers (Graham et al., 1991). Students who received SRSD instruction have indicated they would recommend teaching others the strategies they were taught, as well as the procedures used to teach them. Finally, the findings from several studies generally support the use of the full SRSD model when teaching writing strategies to students with learning disabilities (cf. Danoff et al., 1993; Harris & Graham, 1992b; Sawyer et al., 1992).

Reading and Mathematics

Although we have conducted only three studies examining the effectiveness of SRSD in the areas of reading and mathematics, the results generally parallel the findings for writing. Case et al. (1992) found that elementary-age students' performance in correctly answering word problems involving addition and subtraction improved as a result of learning a problem-solving strategy via SRSD. Similarly, SRSD studies by Bednarczyk and Harris (1992) and Johnson and Graham (1994) found that elementary-age students with learning disabilities recalled more information from stories after learning a strategy that focused their attention on the major parts of stories, the setting and major episodes.

CONCLUSIONS

In our opinion, a major strength of SRSD is that it draws upon multiple theoretical positions and instructional procedures, making it possible to simultaneously address a number of factors at once, including issues involving attention, memory, and executive control. It is important to keep in mind, however, that an approach such as SRSD does not provide a cure-all for educational problems. No single instructional approach can affect all aspects of reading, writing, or mathematics or fully address the complex nature of learning or learning difficulties (Harris & Pressley, 1991). Used appropriately, however, SRSD is a significant contribution to the repertoires of both regular and special education teachers.

For those who are interested in additional examples of the application of SRSD or greater detail on how to implement the model, we refer you to a recent book (Harris & Graham, 1992a). All of the writing strategies field-tested to date, with the exception of the report writing strategy described here, are presented along with recommendations on how to use the SRSD model. Example lesson plans can also be obtained from Graham and Harris (1990).

REFERENCES

Atwell, N. (1987). *In the middle: Reading, writing, and learning from adolescents.* Portsmouth, NH: Heinmann.

Bednarczyk, A., & Harris, K.R. (1992). [Story grammar instruction to improve reading comprehension]. Unpublished raw data.

Bjorklund, D. (1990). *Children's strategies: Contemporary views of cognitive development.* Hillsdale, NJ: Lawrence Erlbaum Associates.

Borkowski, J., & Muthukrishna, N. (1992). Moving metacognition into the classroom: "Working models" and effective strategy teaching. In M. Pressley, K.R. Harris, & J. Guthrie (Eds.), *Promoting academic competency and literacy in school* (pp. 477–501). San Diego: Academic Press.

Brown, A.L., Campione, J.C., & Day, J.D. (1981). Learning to learn: On training students to learn from texts. *Educational Researcher, 10,* 14–21.

Case, L., Harris, K.R., & Graham, S. (1992). Improving the mathematical problem solving skills of students with learning disabilities: Self-regulated strategy development. *Journal of Special Education, 26,* 1–19.

Collins, R. (1992). *Narrative writing of option II students: The effects of combining whole-language techniques, writing process approach and strategy training.* Unpublished thesis, State University of New York, Buffalo.

Danoff, B., Harris, K.R., & Graham, S. (1993). Incorporating strategy instruction within the writing process in the regular classroom. *Journal of Reading Behavior, 25,* 295–322.

Deshler, D.D., & Schumaker, J.B. (1986). Learning strategies: An instructional alternative for low-achieving adolescents. *Exceptional Children, 52,* 583–590.

Englert, C., Raphael, T., Anderson, L., Anthony, H., Stevens, D., & Fear, K. (1991). Making writing strategies and self-talk visible: Cognitive strategy instruction in writing in regular and special education classrooms. *American Educational Research Journal, 28,* 337–373.

Gaskins, I., Cunicelli, E., & Satlow, E. (1992). Implementing an across-the curriculum strategies program: Teachers' reaction to change. In M. Pressley, K.R. Harris, & J.

Guthrie (Eds.), *Promoting academic competency and literacy in school* (pp. 407–426). San Diego: Academic Press.

Graham, S., & Harris, K.R. (1989a). Improving learning disabled students' skills at composing essays: Self-instructional strategy training. *Exceptional Children, 56,* 201–214.

Graham, S., & Harris, K.R. (1989b). A components analysis of cognitive strategy instruction: Effects on learning disabled students' compositions and self-efficacy. *Journal of Educational Psychology, 81,* 353–361.

Graham, S., & Harris, K.R. (1990). Self-instructional strategy development. *LD Forum, 16,* 15–22.

Graham, S., & Harris, K.R. (1993). Self-regulated strategy development: Helping students with learning problems develop as writers. *Elementary School Journal, 94,* 169–181.

Graham, S., & Harris, K.R. (1994). The role and development of self-regulation in the writing process. In D. Schunk and B. Zimmerman (Eds.), *Self-regulation of learning and performance: Issues and educational applications* (pp. 203–228). New York: Lawrence Erlbaum Associates.

Graham, S., Harris, K.R., MacArthur, C., & Schwartz, S. (1991). Writing and writing instruction with students with learning disabilities: A review of a program of research. *Learning Disability Quarterly, 14,* 89–114.

Graham, S., & MacArthur, C. (1988). Improving learning disabled students' skills at revising essays produced on a word processor: Self-instructional strategy training. *Journal of Special Education, 22,* 133–152.

Graham, S., MacArthur, C., Schwartz, S., & Voth, T. (1992). Improving the compositions of students with learning disabilities using a strategy involving product and process goal setting. *Exceptional Children, 58,* 322–335.

Graham, S., Schwartz, S., & MacArthur, C. (1993). Learning disabled and normally achieving students' knowledge of the writing and the composing process, attitude toward writing, and self-efficacy. *Journal of Learning Disabilities, 26,* 237–249.

Hallahan, D., Lloyd, J., Kauffman, J., & Loper, A. (1983). Academic problems. In R. Morris & T. Kratochwill (Eds.), *Practice of child therapy: A textbook of methods* (pp. 113–141). New York: Pergamon.

Harris, K.R. (1982). Cognitive-behavior modification: Application with exceptional students. *Focus on Exceptional Children, 15,* 1–16.

Harris, K.R. (1985). Conceptual, methodological, and clinical issues in cognitive-behavioral assessment. *Journal of Abnormal Child Psychology, 13,* 373–390.

Harris, K.R. (1990). Developing self-regulated learners: The role of private speech and self-instructions. *Educational Psychologist, 25,* 35–50.

Harris, K.R., & Graham, S. (1985). Improving learning disabled students' composition skills: Self-control strategy training. *Learning Disability Quarterly, 8,* 27–36.

Harris, K.R., & Graham, S. (1992a). *Helping young writers master the craft: Strategy instruction and self-regulation in the writing process.* Cambridge, MA: Brookline.

Harris, K.R., & Graham, S. (1992b). Self-regulated strategy development: A part of the writing process. In M. Pressley, K. Harris, & J. Guthrie (Eds.), *Promoting academic competence and literacy in school.* San Diego: Academic Press.

Harris, K.R., & Graham, S. (1994). Constructivism: Principles, paradigms, and integration. *Journal of Special Education, 28,* 233–247.

Harris, K.R., Graham, S., & Pressley, M. (1992). Cognitive behavioral approaches in reading and written language: Developing self-regulated learners. In N.N. Singh & I.L. Beale (Eds.), *Current perspectives in learning disabilities: Nature, theory, and treatment* (pp. 415–451). New York: Springer-Verlag.

Harris, K.R., Graham, S., Reid, R., McElroy, K., & Hamby, R. (1994). Self-monitoring of attention versus self-monitoring of performance: Replication and cross-task comparison studies. *Learning Disability Quarterly, 17,* 121–139.

Harris, K.R., Graham, S., Zutell, J., & Gentry, R. (1994). *Spell it—Write.* Columbus, OH: Zaner-Bloser.

Harris, K.R., & Pressley, M. (1991). The nature of cognitive strategy instruction: Interactive strategy construction. *Exceptional Children, 57,* 392–404.

Hughes, J., & Hall, R. (1989). *Cognitive behavioral psychology in the schools: A comprehensive handbook.* New York: Guilford Press.

Johnson, L., & Graham, S. (1994). [The effects of goal setting and self-instructions on the acquisition, maintenance, and generalization of a reading comprehension strategy.] Unpublished raw data.

Licht, B. (1983). Cognitive-motivational factors that contribute to the achievement of learning-disabled children. *Journal of Learning Disabilities, 16,* 483–490.

Luria, A. (1961). *The role of speech in the regulation of normal and abnormal behavior* (trans. J. Tizard). New York: Liveright.

MacArthur, C., Graham, S., & Schwartz, S. (1991). Knowledge of revision and revising behavior among learning disabled students. *Learning Disability Quarterly, 14,* 61–73.

MacArthur, C., Schwartz, S., & Graham, S. (1991). Effects of a reciprocal peer revision strategy in special education classrooms. *Learning Disabilities Research and Practice, 6,* 201–210.

MacArthur, C., Schwartz, S., Graham, S., Molloy, D., & Harris, K. (1994). [Case studies of classroom instruction in a semantic webbing strategy]. Unpublished raw data.

Meichenbaum, D. (1977). *Cognitive behavior modification: An integrative approach.* New York: Plenum.

Palinscar, A., & Brown, A. (1984). Reciprocal teaching of comprehension-fostering and comprehension-monitoring activities. *Cognition and Instruction, 1,* 117–175.

Pressley, M., Goodchild, F., Fleet, J., Zajchowski, R., & Evans, E. (1989). The challenges of classroom strategy instruction. *Elementary School Journal, 89,* 301–342.

Pressley, M., & Harris, K.R. (1990). What is really known about cognitive strategy instruction. *Educational Leadership, 48,* 31–34.

Reeve, R., & Brown, A. (1985). Metacognition reconsidered: Implications for intervention research. *Journal of Abnormal Child Psychology, 13,* 343–356.

Sawyer, R., Graham, S., & Harris, K.R. (1992). Direct teaching, strategy instruction, and strategy instruction with explicit self-regulation: Effects on learning disabled students' compositions and self-efficacy. *Journal of Educational Psychology, 84,* 340–352.

Sokolov, A. (1972). *Inner speech and thought* (trans. G. Onischenko). New York: Plenum.

Tanhouser, S. (1994). *Function over form: The relative efficacy of self-instructional strategy training alone and with procedural facilitation for adolescents with learning disabilities.* Unpublished doctoral dissertation, Johns Hopkins University, Baltimore.

Turkewitz, H. (1984). Family systems: Conceptualizing child problems within the family context. In A. Meyers & E. Craighead (Eds.), *Cognitive behavior therapy with children* (pp. 69–98). New York: Plenum.

Vygotsky, L. (1962). *Thought and language.* Cambridge, MA: MIT Press.

20

CONCEPTUALIZING, DESCRIBING, AND MEASURING COMPONENTS OF EXECUTIVE FUNCTION
A Summary

Paul J. Eslinger

In Section IV there are six chapters that comprise varied perspectives and approaches to executive functions. Each chapter deals in some way with the following critical issues and questions about executive functions:

- What theoretical context and theoretical model guide each conceptual view of executive function and its relationship to attention and memory?
- What are the primary constructs within the model of executive functions?
- How can the model and the constructs be operationalized, specifically:
    - What instruments, tests, or procedures are used to measure the model and the constructs of executive function?
    - What criteria are used to select and/or develop the instruments, tests, or procedures for executive function?
    - What populations are most relevant in testing the model?
- What are a series of testable hypotheses that provide an opportunity for disconfirmation of the executive function model? What experimental designs and experiments would be applied and conducted?

These questions underscore not only conceptual advances, but also experimental rigor, with an emphasis on definition, measurement, and specific hypotheses to be tested. Therefore, the organization of this chapter is centered around these guiding questions. After a note on the importance of executive function for human development, each approach is briefly summarized. Specifically, the definition and measurement of executive function as well as future research directions of each approach are covered, with subsequent discussion of their commonalities and differences, relationship to neurobiological and neuropsychological aspects of typical and altered brain development, and new research directions in this area.

THE IMPORTANCE OF EXECUTIVE FUNCTIONS FOR HUMAN DEVELOPMENT AND ADAPTATION

Executive functions are considered by many scientists to be one of the crowning achievements of human development. They underlie many seemingly unique realms of adaptive human behavior, including the wonders of being able to think about ourselves, our social relationships, and what the future may bring. Executive functions allow us to be guided by our personal goals and to act despite long delays in rewards. Although we may wish everyone to fully develop and share in those intriguing psychological processes, many people do not develop adequate executive functions for diverse reasons, and we have incredibly little understanding of what these marvelous functions are and what fosters their development.

Denckla (Chapter 15) succinctly describes that "the difference between child and adult resides in the unfolding of executive function" (p. 264). This difference can include notions such as increasing independence, maturation of self-regulation, and development of self-generated productivity. Executive functions also manage emotional influences on behavior so that rational thought and adaptive social responses can occur. Borkowski and Burke (Chapter 14) suggest that the concept of executive function has the "potential for explaining the maintenance and generalization of behaviors across time and settings" (p. 235). From a clinical standpoint, Pennington, Bennetto, McAleer, and Roberts (Chapter 18) state that the "construct of executive function has the potential to explain a wide range of symptoms in each of these disorders" (p. 345). Among those persons with learning difficulties, deficiencies in self-regulation and executive control processes are often found. Their remediation may hold an important key to improved adaptation as students learn to "structure and organize their behavior and cognitive resources" (Graham & Harris, Chapter 19, p. 360).

With the many perspectives on the importance of executive functions in the preceding chapters, it appears that a valid and crucial scientific dialogue about executive functions is beginning to emerge. In the entire field of developmental neuroscience, few challenges loom as large as how cognitive processes and emotions come to be organized and lead to intelligent, adaptive behavior that benefits the individual, family, and other persons, as well as society at large. However, this need does not give license to treat executive functions in a nonscientific manner. In fact, it underscores the great importance of scientific analysis in this area. One of the important goals of this book is to advance such conceptualization, model development, measurement, and hypotheses testing.

The six chapters represent different but not entirely orthogonal approaches. A brief descriptor of each chapter's approach is presented in Figure 20.1. These are organized in a somewhat arbitrary manner, being placed around the central concept of executive function. Chapter 14 emphasizes an information processing

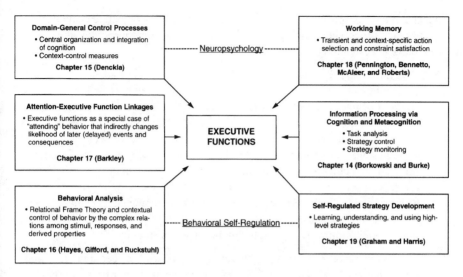

Figure 20.1. Summary of theoretical and empirical approaches to executive functions represented in the six chapters of Section IV.

approach and the distinctions between cognition and metacognition. Chapters 15 (Denckla) and 18 (Pennington et al.) represent overlapping neuropsychological views, though the respective clinical neuropsychological (Chapter 18) and behavioral neurological (Chapter 15) orientations create distinctive approaches. The other clearly overlapping chapters are the behavioral approaches of Chapters 16 (more theoretically oriented) and 19 (more applied and focused on implementation of interventions). Finally, Chapter 17 offers an integrative behavioral and neuropsychological focus on attention and executive functions. Each chapter's definition, measurement, and research directions for executive functions follows.

INFORMATION PROCESSING APPROACH: BORKOWSKI AND BURKE

The information processing view described by Borkowski and Burke (Chapter 14) emphasizes the necessity of executive functions for successful learning, academic achievement, self-image, and future-oriented thoughts and goals. It "enables the child to approach problems in an orderly rather than a chaotic manner" (pp. 246–247). Executive functions have also been key to the emergence of metacognitive theories; that is, awareness, beliefs, and knowledge about one's self, including abilities, weaknesses, knowledge, skills, and personal history.

Definition of Executive Function

Borkowski and Burke have chosen an operational definition of executive function that was articulated by Butterfield and Belmont in 1977. Executive function is indicated when "a subject spontaneously changes a control process or sequence of control processes as a reasonable response to an objective change in an information processing task" (p. 244). Three essential components underlie such flexibility of responding:

1. Task analysis: The analysis geared to "sizing up" the problem; that is, understanding not only the literal information presented in the task but also possibilities of interpretation, its logical basis, and possible task outcomes
2. Strategy control: a) selection and utilization of possible strategies in solving the tasks (this presupposes knowledge about specific strategies as well as attributes and even beliefs about these strategies), and b) revision of strategy selection and utilization that permits continuous change in the process of performance for the purpose of solving the task and achieving the goal
3. Strategy monitoring: the analytical process of perceiving and evaluating effectiveness of the selected strategy that underlies sustained action, modification, or inhibition with shifting to another selected strategy if necessary.

The information processing approach distinguishes between cognitive and metacognitive levels. Cognitive levels refer to perceptual abilities and domains of knowledge, accumulated developmentally and comprising the specific skills, actions, and strategies that can be employed in various responses. Metacognition refers to awareness and knowledge about skills and strategy attributes, including patterns of utilization and prior successes and failures. Butterfield and Albertson (1994) have further defined executive function as the *coordinator* of cognitive and metacognitive processes that acts through monitoring and controlling the use of knowledge and strategies in accordance with metacognitive processes. Executive functions may, in a sense, provide a reservoir of "internal cues" when an individual does not or cannot spontaneously generate adaptive skills and strategies for specific situations.

Measurement of Executive Function

Borkowski and Burke indicate that measures of *transfer* and *generalization* of learning may expose executive functions, albeit indirectly. Specifically, changes in stimulus materials or task parameters from training to transfer phases of learning may provide opportunities for empirical observation of executive function, as revealed by measuring strategy selection, strategy usage, and revision. Two types of experimental manipulations are possible: 1) direct and explicit modification of executive components (the instructions for analyzing task demands, selection of a strategy, etc.), and 2) variance of the response requirements in the to-be-learned task and observation to see if such changes are detected and whether strategies are modified to meet new demands. These approaches have been employed in samples of gifted and typical students, students with mental retardation, and students with learning disabilities. In addition to group designs, Borkowski and Burke also advocate the importance of within-subject analyses, including single-subject experimental designs, in order to evaluate strategy use, generalization, and shifts during multiple tasks. This approach may help counter the difficulty of assessing strategy manipulation in samples where there is a wide diversity of skills and abilities and hence avoid masking potentially important effects in certain students.

Research Directions

Future research in executive function from an information processing perspective will need to apply a number of clear methodologies in typical students, gifted students, and students with learning disabilities. The methods include

- Provision and manipulation of instructional designs (self-learned and experimenter-provided strategies)
- Use of transfer designs to infer task analytical and strategy selection skills
- Measurement of executive function from changes in control processing rather than from change in performance
- Measurement of shifts in continuous performance as an indication of strategy monitoring and revision

These methods have the ultimate goal of identifying the most effective training parameters for fostering creative and insightful learners whose individual talents and weaknesses can be reliably examined with valid psychological measures. Hypotheses revolve around the effect of specific strategy interventions to improve adaptive behavioral responses, namely those that lead to problem solving and goal attainment.

NEUROPSYCHOLOGICAL APPROACH:
PENNINGTON, BENNETTO, McALEER, AND ROBERTS

In their neuropsychological approach, Pennington et al. (Chapter 18) begin with a critical problem: How is it that symptomatically different behavior disorders with different neurobiological etiologies can show similar manifestations of executive function defects? These disorders include early treated phenylketonuria, attention deficit hyperactivity disorder (ADHD), autism, and fragile X in females; the problem involved is referred to as a *discriminant validity problem*. A possible answer is that there are multiple forms of neurological pathophysiology that affect the emergence and development of executive functions. These can include different types of alterations in the frontal cortex and its related neural networks (e.g., structural damage, neurochemical deficiencies and excesses, neurophysiological changes). A second major question is whether more precise cognitive characterization of executive functions is possible, because of several methodological problems with current measures that include inadequate sensitivity, specificity, and reliability.

Definition of Executive Function

Pennington et al. defined executive function as "the ability to maintain an appropriate problem-solving set for attainment of a future goal" (Welsh & Pennington,

1988, p. 201). Some of its mechanisms include inhibition, planning, and mental representation of tasks and goals. Common parameters to this and several other neuropsychological approaches (e.g., Fuster, 1989; Goldman-Rakic, 1988; Luria, 1966; Shallice, 1988) focus on three critical types of mechanisms: 1) planning or programming of future actions, 2) maintaining such plans and programs in mind (or "on-line") until implemented, and 3) inhibition of other actions. An evolving and important construct in these events is *working memory*, which is conceptualized by Pennington et al. as a computational arena for prospectively maintaining the various constraints relevant to the current context of the organism, so that action selection processes can occur to satisfy those constraints and hence lead to problem solving and goal attainment, even in entirely novel contexts.

Measurement of Executive Function

Executive function tasks can be defined by two component dimensions: *working memory demand* and *demand for inhibition*. These provide a basis for overriding prepotent (e.g., automatic, obvious, literal, primed) responses by inhibiting their activation. In turn, inhibition provides an opportunity to shift to an alternative response or strategy. A specific example of such an executive function measure is the antisaccade task, which has been shown to be sensitive to frontal cortex lesions in adults (Guitton, Buchtel, & Douglas, 1985). In this paradigm, subjects are visually fixating on a central stimulus during presentation of lateralized flashing cues. They are instructed to make eye movements to the side opposite the presented cues, thus pitting the instruction held in working memory against the strong tendency to naturally (even reflexively) saccade to the lateralized cue flashes. This is a difficult task even for control subjects, with about a 70% correct response rate. However, when control subjects had to complete a concurrent working memory task (serial addition of running numbers) during the antisaccade task, their accuracy declined in comparison to shadowing and repeat concurrent tasks, as errors doubled and reaction time increased (Roberts, Hager, & Heron, 1994). These results resembled those generated by the adult patients with frontal lobe lesions for the antisaccade task alone (Guitton et al., 1985) and support Pennington et al.'s supposition that working memory is tied into action selection and inhibition of prepotent responses. A second approach to measurement is to utilize existing paradigms and tasks but empirically separate the component of working memory in contrast to those processes not dependent on working memory. An example is the distinction of manipulating memory stores (e.g., ascertaining a particular temporal order of presentation) versus memory storage itself.

Research Directions

The neuropsychological approach of Pennington et al. places a strong emphasis on developing the conceptual and measurement aspects of working memory. Hence, future studies in executive function would necessarily incorporate working memory measures such as the antisaccade task and organizational–manipulation aspects of memory. The experimental rigor of this approach is sound, as there is clear, empirical measurement of behavior that is hypothesized to reflect executive functions, and clear control measures to assess nonexecutive aspects of the task. Furthermore, these methods are applicable to a variety of control and clinical populations, including those with traumatic brain injury, learning disabilities, and other developmental disorders. This approach has the long-term goal of solving the discriminant validity problem of executive impairments in numerous developmental disorders by identifying and empirically measuring specific components of executive function.

NEUROPSYCHOLOGICAL APPROACH: DENCKLA

The neuropsychological perspective of Denckla (Chapter 15) is anchored in three conceptual models: 1) the historic linkage of executive functions to the prefrontal cortex and its interconnected subcortical regions, 2) the diverse clinical presentations of executive dysfunction in childhood neurological disorders, and 3) the critical role of executive processes and its associated neural circuitry in psychological development from childhood to adulthood. Although executive processes and prefrontal–subcortical circuits have been inextricably bound in neuropsychological models, this does not give license to use the terms interchangeably. In fact, equating executive functions with the prefrontal lobe may be scientifically counterproductive except at the hypothesis-generating level.

Definition of Executive Function

Denckla broadly defines executive function as "a set of domain-general control processes . . . . that involve inhibition and delay of responding" (pp. 263, 265) for the goal of "organization and integration of cognitive and output processes over time" (p. 260). Executive functions have "distinctive future tense aspects" (p. 266) and include such processes as anticipatory set, preparedness to act, freedom from interference of prepotent response tendencies, and sequencing behavioral responses. Her model addresses primarily cognition, and not social, emotional, motivational, or personality aspects of executive functions. Particularly important, she advocates a move away from hierarchical models of executive function (i.e., executive functions as "higher" or "supraordinate" processes) and favors its conceptualization as *central* to diverse cognitive operations. This leaves a very strong overlap between executive functions, attention, and memory that is theoretically and clinically useful as one tackles models of development. From a life-span perspective, Denckla views the process of psychological development from childhood to adulthood as the "unfolding of executive functions" (p. 264).

Measurement of Executive Function

Operationalized measures of executive functions can be confounded by 1) general cognitive level (such as high or low IQ, so that executive function tasks would be too easy or too hard to be specific and sensitive); and 2) domain-specific competencies (such as high or low spatial ability) that provide perceptual, cognitive, and other data for a specific (e.g., spatial) executive measure. Such domain- or content-specific competency creates the range of fundamental processing that executive functions can tap (not unlike a rate-limiting step in a chemical equation). An example of a limiting effect would be reading illiteracy and the Stroop test (Stroop, 1935). Finally, 3) there is a special case to be made for the relation between language competence and executive function measures that require verbal processing. That is, verbal formulations of rule-governed behavior are a powerful aspect of both working memory and executive functions. Deficient language processing (not just aphasia but a range of "feed-forward" language difficulties to working memory) may, therefore, have a pervasive, deleterious effect on maturation of executive functions.

Solutions to these confounding variables are possible. Denckla proposes, for example, that "pairing commonly available design-copying tasks with differing demands for self-generated organization reveals relevant aspects of executive function" (p. 270). Thus, matching and pairing tasks that overlap in content- or domain-specific competence but do not overlap in the self-organizational or working memory aspects of the tasks is a viable method for measuring executive function. Another dyadic comparison is the pairing of temporal order memory tasks with order-free recognition memory tasks, the only difference being the temporal order condition. Other examples include self-ordered versus fixed-ordered pointing and word associative fluency versus vocabulary tasks. In each paradigm, the executive function elements must center around "inhibition of prepotent automatic or overlearned response(s) and more active, on-line, rule-governed, future-oriented, goal-oriented, time-limited response preparation than . . . the control task" (p. 274).

Research Directions

As with the three conceptual models driving Denckla's neuropsychological perspective on executive functions, future research is suggested in neurobiological, clinical, and developmental aspects. There is a great need to examine the proposed constructs and operationalized measures in samples with well-defined pathophysiology (e.g., phenylketonuria, neurofibromatosis-1, Turner syndrome, female fragile X) and in normative samples via functional neuroimaging as well as neurophysiological profiles. This is expected to advance not only understanding of executive functions with typical and altered neural states, but also the management and possible behavioral treatment of developmental disorders. In the clinical domain, the method of content-controlled neuropsychological examination may reveal more sensitive, specific, and reliable patterns of executive dysfunction, important to diagnosis and management of patients as well as characterization of subjects subsequently studied with specific intervention protocols. Finally, developmental research must address the need for age-appropriate executive function tasks. Sensitivity and specificity of executive function tasks will change according to the neurobiological maturation of the organism and its executive function operations.

BEHAVIORAL APPROACH: HAYES, GIFFORD, AND RUCKSTUHL

Hayes et al. (Chapter 16) begin their chapter on a behavioral approach to executive function with a number of interesting observations:

- "There is virtually no behavioral literature on 'executive function' per se" (p. 279).
- "The term does not just delimit a range of phenomena . . . it also ties itself to particular approaches to those phenomena" (p. 279).
- "Treating psychological functions as brain functions with semihuman-like properties . . . is not at all characteristic of a behavioral approach" (p. 280).
- A behavioral approach . . . "views psychology as the study of the interaction between whole organisms and their historical and current environments" (p. 280).
- "Activities that most or all researchers refer to under the rubric of executive function . . . is both fuzzy and broad but does have recognizable outlines" (p. 280).

The behavioral approach described by Hayes et al. focuses on "the actual behaviors people are speaking about with these terms" (p. 280). Their orientation is positioned within the *behavioral analytical* view of complex human behavior that reaches back to the animal learning tradition that was at one time a dominant focus of experimental psychology. Contrary to those approaches that stay "in the head," the behavioral analytical approach is functionally oriented and is interested in the vital connection between verbal abilities and behavioral regulation within specific contexts.

Definition of Executive Function

Hayes et al. begin by analyzing the behavioral aspects of several tasks commonly associated with executive function (e.g., the Stroop test [Stroop, 1935], the Wisconsin Card Sorting Test [Heaton, 1981], Tower of Hanoi [Borys, Spitz & Dorans, 1982], Controlled Oral Word Association [Benton & Hamsher, 1989]) and hence offer some definitional elements in behavioral terms. For example, executive function tasks "arrange situations in which immediate and habitual sources of behavioral regulation *cannot* work." Hence, "subjects must either derive new rules that work or they must follow rules given by the experimenter and override alternative sources of behavioral control." In many instances, these parameters distill down to "flexibility and effectiveness of verbal regulation." Hayes et al. clearly focus on verbal self-regulation as a key process underlying *rule-governed behavior*. Verbal self-regulation refers to thinking about and guiding one's behavioral responses by specific verbal mediation. Hayes et al. link verbal behavior to relational frame theory, which describes how behavioral responding can come to be contextually controlled by the complex relationships among stimuli, responses, and their many derived properties (Hayes & Hayes, 1992). Such a process theoretically provides complex and rich associations that verbal self-regulation can mediate, including relations of stimulus equivalence (e.g., reflexivity, symmetry, and transitivity), mutual entailment, combinatorial entailment, and transformation of stimulus functions.

Measurement of Executive Function

In the behavioral analytical view, tests of executive function often measure rule flexibility, particularly when there are conflicting stimulus situations. Therefore, it is necessary to identify and measure components of rule derivation, rule application, and rule following. The behavioral analytical methods described in Chapter 16 have an almost complete emphasis on verbal mediation of relational frames and their utilization in verbal self-regulation. Examples are the application of "if . . . then" frames to events, and testing what effects particular verbal cues have on sensitivity to stimulus changes. It may also be possible to use "talk aloud" methods as an empirical approach to assessing how and when verbal rules are employed in problem-solving situations (Hayes, 1986).

Research Directions

Hayes et al. advocate testing "whether relational frame theory is a worthwhile account of human verbal behavior and verbal regulation, and whether executive function can be usefully thought of in these terms" (p. 298). The hypotheses to be tested are as follows: 1) there are developmental trends in learning relational frames, 2) relational frames provide flexibility in responding, 3) relational frames are under antecedent stimulus control, 4) relational frames are under consequential control, and 5) improved relational abilities result from specific training. Clinical populations that have developmental or acquired difficulties in rule generation, rule understanding, and rule following are appropriate for study of effective interventions. Subjects can include those with attention deficit disorder, antisocial behavior, mental retardation and control populations of different ages. Empirically establishing that relational frames are learned, and learned according to developmental and antecedent–consequential parameters, would provide an important impetus to evaluating relational frame training as a key element for emergence of flexible, adaptive responding to complex stimulus configurations—processes that comprise an important part of executive function.

SELF-REGULATED STRATEGY
DEVELOPMENT: GRAHAM AND HARRIS

The approach of Graham and Harris (Chapter 19) to executive function emphasizes a multifactorial, integrative model of instruction and activity for *learning*, *understanding*, and *strategically using* various high-level strategies to support and enhance problem solving, academic achievement, and subsequent self-image. They term the model *self-regulated strategy development* (SRSD) and view it as one approach to the behavioral, cognitive, affective, social, and ecological aspects of learning. It emerged from the converging influences of 1) Meichenbaum's (1977) cognitive approach to behavior modification, 2) the emphasis of Soviet scientists (e.g., Vygotsky, Luria, Sokolov) on verbal self-regulation and the social origins of self-control, 3) the concept of self-control instruction (Brown, Campione, & Day, 1981), and 4) Deshler and Schumaker's (1986) articulation of the learning strategies model.

Definition of Executive Function

Graham and Harris do not offer a formal definition of executive function. However, their writing suggests several constructs that overlap with those of Borkowski and Burke, Hayes et al., and even Pennington et al. If the SRSD model can be used to infer their definition of executive function, it might include the following elements:

- Metacognitive knowledge about tasks, strategies, and one's own capabilities
- Specific action plans
- Strategic (skillful, flexible) use of strategies
- Verbal self-regulation of behavior
- Attentional and memory processes that guide the above elements (i.e., working memory)
- Combined explicit and implicit learning
- Self-control processes (goal setting, monitoring, planning, interference control)

However, Graham and Harris do not view executive function as an isolated domain for intervention, as their samples with learning disabilities typically show attentional, memory, language, and executive function impairments. Hence, their treatment of executive function impairments is embedded within a model and instructional protocol that addresses attention, memory, and other psychological domains as well.

Measurement of Executive Function

Graham and Harris describe the process by which SRSD can be implemented, beginning with seven instructional stages:

1. Preskill development
2. Initial conference: instructional goals and significance
3. Discussion of strategy
4. Modeling of the strategy and self-instructions
5. Memorization of the strategy
6. Collaborative practice
7. Independent practice

The measurement of executive functions during this process appears to be indirect and inferred from progress students make in the various stages, each with its own criteria. The overall goal in teaching writing strategies, for example, is the writing product (specifically its length, schematic structure, and overall quality) as well as students' behavior around the task (e.g., time spent composing, development of plans and ideas prior to writing, number of planning strategies they can identify, accuracy of their competency perceptions). Experimental design emphasizes within-subject analyses (single-subject and multisubject), comparing baseline (preinstruction) to posttreatment (postinstruction) levels.

Research Directions

Since the SRSD model relies upon different theoretical ideas and instructional strategies around learning and effective problem solving, its range of potential application is wide. However, it has to date been used in limited samples of typical students and students with learning disabilities. Presumably, students with various neural developmental disorders, head injuries, and poor academic achievement would benefit from this approach. Another strength of this approach is that it provides a model within which multiple cognitive and behavioral domains can be addressed in an integrative manner, including attention, memory, self-regulation, and self-monitoring. Its effectiveness, however, requires motivated students who are committed to learning, and it must be viewed as only part of the overall intervention program for students with learning disabilities. Some of its new directions would appear to include both empirical studies with well-defined clinical populations and derivation of testable hypotheses about the effectiveness of specific instructional methods for learning and applying specific strategies.

ATTENTION AND EXECUTIVE FUNCTION: BARKLEY

Barkley's perspective on executive function (Chapter 17) is formed in large part by the relationship between constructs of attention and executive function. By identifying what is similar and different about these psychological domains, "greater clarity of definition" (p. 307) may be possible. Attention is defined in terms of "the relation of behavior to its environment" (p. 307) (with environment broadly construed as external and internal sensory events). Attention is metaphorically compared to statistical correlation; that is, it "describes how one variable or set of variables, behavior in this case, changes as a function of another variable or set of variables, the environment in this case" (p. 308). Such pairings are noteworthy because of the possible alterations or effects they imply for the immediate context. However, when alterations are not tied to the immediate context but to future or delayed contexts, an executive function may be identified.

Definition of Executive Function

Barkley argues that "an 'executive' response or function is a special case of an 'attending' behavior . . . an executive behavior ultimately functions to change the likelihood of later events (consequences) happening to the individual" (p. 312). But this must occur *indirectly* (i.e., "at least one behavior removed from those consequences in the chain of events"; p. 312) and must affect "both the subsequent behavior and subsequent consequences much further removed in time" (p. 312). Such a process would permit various delays between components to occur.

There are four critical themes or criteria that must be met for identification of executive behaviors:

- The behavior must be part of a chain of behavior–behavior relations (as opposed to environment–behavior relations as in attention).
- The behavior must cause an alteration in the probability of a subsequent response.
- Delays between events, actions, and consequences are typical.
- The initiation of an executive behavior necessarily involves inhibition and delay of prepotent responses.

Measurement of Executive Function

In this model, there are four fundamental executive functions or capacities that require study with empirical methods, suggested by the seminal work of Bronowski (1967). They all revolve about delayed responding processes.

1. *Separation of affect:* The capacity to delay responding to immediate environmental events permits a separation of "informational" content from "emotional charge" and hence a broader range of cognitive and emotional processing that requires time, even reflection.
2. *Prolongation:* Capacities that establish an enduring mental representation of events (i.e., possibly related to working memory) are critical for information analysis, manipulation, and planning.
3. *Internalization of language:* Delay of responding also permits language to develop as a means of self-regulation (e.g., rule-governed behavior) and even development of mental models that can be defined, articulated, and modified on a verbal basis. Complex configurations can be broken down to component features on the basis of language.
4. *Reconstitution:* This capacity refers to synthesis, construction, and manipulation of events and knowledge held through delayed responding. Reconstitution is dependent on prolongation and language as forms of mental representation (and possibly other nonverbal forms of representation). Reconstitution permits generation of possibilities, alternatives, and what might be considered original or creative solutions and formulations.

Research Directions

An overriding theme of Barkley's chapter is the need for empirical testing of the hypotheses generated in this model of executive functions. The clinical populations that can be studied include many with developmental and acquired neurological conditions (e.g., attention deficit, head injury), as well as other populations with executive impairments or deficiencies. There is a clear need to develop further measures of executive function to test these hypotheses, such as measures of hindsight and foresight.

DISCUSSION OF CHAPTERS

There are a number of commonalities and differences in conceptualizing, describing, and measuring components of executive function in the six chapters of this section.

Definition of Executive Functions

There is no universal definition of executive functions. At the conference sponsored by the National Institute of Child Health and Human Development in January 1994, an informal survey was taken of what behaviors were indicated by the term *executive function*. The 10 respondents in the working group on executive functions generated 33 terms. Those terms for which there was general agreement were surprisingly few. The following six terms had a 40% or greater agreement rate: 1) self-regulation, 2) sequencing of behavior, 3) flexibility, 4) response inhibition, 5) planning, and 6) organization of behavior. These are not easy or straightforward aspects of behavior to observe, measure, and empirically define, which was one of the decisive reasons for the conference and for scientific dialogue in this area.

The definitions offered by the authors in this section emphasize the following elements:

- Orderly approach to problems (Borkowski and Burke)
- Maintenance of problem-solving set for future goals (Pennington et al.)
- Control processes for organization of behavior over time (Denckla)
- Flexibility and effectiveness of verbal self-regulation (Hayes et al.)
- Skillful use of strategies (Graham and Harris)
- Behaviors that alter likelihood of later events and behaviors (Barkley)

In arriving at a common definition of executive function, it must first be recognized that there are multiple levels of analysis that are scientifically legitimate and informative. Hence, depending on the magnification setting for one's telescopic view of executive functions, the definition can be highly restrictive (e.g., the action potential of a cell when a stimulus signaling placement of pending reward is removed) or formulated in more general terms in order to capture its diverse elements (e.g., flexibility of responding in multiple situations). The processes uncovered by such levels of analysis may or may not be interrelated, but the possibility of dialogue across these approaches is critical for addressing agreement and disagreements. With this foundation in mind, the following definition of executive functions is formulated to encompass several elements from the preceding chapters.

Executive functions are defined as psychological processes that have the purpose of

- Controlling implementation of activation–inhibition response sequences . . .
- that is guided by diverse neural representations (verbal rules, biological needs, somatic states, emotions, goals, mental models) . . .
- for the purpose of meeting a balance of immediate situational, short-term, and long-term future goals . . .
- that span physical-environmental, cognitive, behavioral, emotional, and social spheres.

All chapter authors would agree, I believe, with at least a part of each of these four elements. However, elucidating the development of these elements, their coordinated organization, as well as the psychological and neural mechanisms that underlie them, remains a formidable challenge to investigators.

Measurement of Executive Functions

A major aim of the chapters in this section was to address the measurement of executive functions within a scientific framework, including criteria for development of such tasks and instruments. Phenomena amenable to scientific investigation must, by definition, be *observable, measurable, repeatable*, and formulated within a *hypothesis-testing* format that permits direct test of the null hypothesis. If these criteria are not met, other forms of inquiry can be used, but the purpose of these chapters was to address the scientific analysis of executive functions.

The concept of executive functions has been most identified with the psychology literature and, for purposes of this discussion, the construct of metacognition from the information processing and behavioral branches of psychology is included under the rubric of executive functions. Psychology has steadfastly held to the need for a scientific approach to human behavior, even through the transition from behaviorism to cognitivism. Therefore, the question must be raised whether study and understanding of executive function is possible in scientific terms and within a psychological framework. All chapters would seem to agree that scientific study of executive functions is not only possible but highly important to understanding adaptive human behavior.

There are at least three measurable elements to tasks of executive functions: 1) representation and holding of diverse information, 2) abilities to integrate and manipulate new representations (such as situational constraints) with respect to knowledge and prior experiences, and 3) powerful access to control of the motor system. These elements encompass two mechanisms for executive functions described in the preceding chapters: inhibition and working memory. These mechanisms necessarily imply *stopping* of motor activation and *holding* of information to guide subsequent actions—both over some period of time. Although these mechanisms may not be the crux of problem solving, skillful use of strategies, or flexibility, they are the *gatekeepers* that open the possibilities for responses, processes, and reactions to occur other than what has occurred before. In addition to gatekeeping functions, the working memory mechanism mentally defines the field of play so that actions can be memory-guided rather than sensory-guided. Both types of mechanisms—inhibition and working memory—are amenable to scientific study with a variety of neuropsychological measures that deserve further development and application. Examples include delayed responding and delayed alternation tasks, conflicting stimulus paradigms (e.g., Go/No Go, Stroop, antisaccade tests), and other working memory tasks (e.g., temporal ordering, frequency estimates, sentence span, dot counting, Wisconsin Card Sorting Test, and Paced Auditory Serial Addition test [Gronwall, 1977]).

Neuropsychological approaches focus in part on identifying aspects of cognition that indicate control of responding and manipulation of knowledge for the purpose of attaining goals. Executive functions are invoked, for example, in solving nonroutine problems of a verbal and nonverbal nature, maintaining goal-directed behavior in the face of distraction and delay, learning strategies, and control of responding in order to modify and influence subsequent actions and situations. The criteria for such tests and instructions are discussed by Pennington et al., Denckla, and Barkley in their respective chapters. New sources of ideas have included a much greater emphasis on identifying *how* persons with brain injuries and developmental disabilities fail in problem solving, learning, and goal attainment and on increasing the dialogue with cognitive scientists, developmental psychologists, and linguists in order to adapt reliable and valid paradigms from normative research. The suggestions of Dennis (1991) have been particularly important for expanding the empirical assessment of executive processes and social discourse. By-products of these exchanges will be more effective diagnostic tools for a variety of clinical populations and more interventions that emphasize process variables and their relation to goal attainment.

The executive processes that occur after inhibition, delay of responding, and registration of situational parameters and goals become much more vague. That is, once a prepotent response is stopped and the constraints of the current situation are registered, what happens? This problem has invited a diversity of ideas. The information-processing and behavioral approaches would suggest that buying such time allows for search and activation of other response strategies that may be effective. This is not unlike the suggestion of Duncan (1986) that registered goals have the force of a comparative operation; that is, determining a match or mismatch between the current situation and selected goals. Duncan theorizes that there is a "store of actions" that is available to the organism and that this store is interviewed for the purpose of choosing actions that will reduce the mismatch to zero. Another way of describing this comparative operation is to place it in terms of "skillful use of strategies," flexibility, and effectiveness of verbal self-regulation and rule-governed behavior, which all of the authors in this section would include in their models. Experimental measures in these approaches have focused on strategy derivation and learning and strategy choice, application, following, monitoring, and revision. Reliable tests of these aspects of executive processes potentially provide a wealth of measurable data that are highly relevant to both educational and psychological interventions and programs. Borkowski and Burke, as well as Hayes et al., offer specific guidelines and criteria for such measures in their chapters. However, what occurs in tasks for which no strategy has been taught and for which a person must generate a ready flow of ideas and answers? Examples include word associative fluency (generating words beginning with a particular letter of the alphabet), alternative uses of objects (e.g., other uses for a newspaper than reading), and design fluency (e.g., generating drawings that all have four lines and are not verbalizable). These divergent production tasks require bypassing the more automatic or common strategies for knowledge retrieval and formulating a novel strategy on the spot, often under a time constraint. Here, a store of actions or strategies may not be available. How do people create and implement such strategies under these circumstances? This aspect of executive functions requires much greater definition and borders on research into creativity, imagination, foresight, and inventiveness. Such definition, however, becomes developmentally important only if inhibition and working memory processes are intact.

Working Memory Construct for Executive Function

The construct of working memory has assumed a prominent role in models of executive function during the past 10 years. Five of the six chapters in this section either directly or indirectly include such a construct in their models. Pennington et al. place working memory in a central position in their model of executive functions. They define it as a computational arena for prospectively maintaining the various constraints or situational variables relevant to the current context of the organism. The effect of this process is to define the parameters along which action selection processes can occur in order to satisfy those constraints and hence lead to problem solving and goal attainment, even in novel situations. Denckla emphasizes the importance of working memory when she describes executive function as involving "on-line" response preparation. Barkley invokes a construct that may arise from working memory when he discusses Bronowski's (1967) description of prolongation, which refers to capacities that establish an enduring mental representation of events that are critical for information analysis, manipulation, and planning. Working memory processes are implied in the models of Borkowski and Burke as well as Graham and Harris, presumably in the stages of strategy selection, monitoring, and revision in specific situations. Working memory would also appear to be a necessary underpinning in the relational frame theory described by Hayes et al., but this is not well delineated.

The construct of working memory implies that certain information remains at the forefront of cognition despite distraction and hence active in the nervous system for the purpose of guiding appropriate responses, even when the stimulus configurations that gave rise to that information are no longer present. Working memory differs from other forms of information representation in the nervous system (e.g., memory for familiar faces of family members, word meanings) in that it is highly transient, situation-specific, and powerful enough to guide the impending responses of the organism. It is prospective rather than retrospective in function. It is reasonable to ask if there are data suggesting that such information can remain temporarily "on-line" or "in mind" and in a position to guide or influence motor responses. Supportive data have been described by Bates and Goldman-Rakic (1993), Fuster (1991), and Sawaguchi and Goldman-Rakic (1994).

It may be hard to grasp the disabling effect of an impaired working memory system, but a clinical example may help illuminate it. Patients with acquired injury to the frontal lobe as well as to the thalamus have been described as showing "utilization behavior" (Brazzelli, Colombo, DellaSala, & Spinnler, 1994; Eslinger, Warner, Grattan, & Easton, 1991; Lhermitte, 1983, 1986; Shallice, Burgess, Schon, & Baxter, 1989). That is, as these patients encounter various circumstances, they respond to them in a highly instrumental and concrete way, with failure to inhibit or guide their behavior according to anything but the most literal aspects of the circumstances. As an example, when patients with utilization behavior encounter an orange and a knife on a tabletop, they immediately begin to peel the orange, quite appropriately and accurately, thereafter leaving it on the table without any intention of eating it or offering it to anyone else. The same type of response may be seen when a patient encounters an envelope, piece of paper, and pencil on a tabletop, whereupon he or she will take the pencil and write a brief note on the paper, placing it in an envelope, sealing it, and even addressing the letter. However, there is no identifiable purpose or intention behind this sequence of behaviors besides using these materials in the most automatic and routine fashion. Hence, processes of perception, learned motor responses, sequencing of even complex behavioral acts, and attaining a literal goal associated with these environmental materials are all executed quite accurately and succinctly. But, for what purpose? One might infer that there is no goal or plan that is "in mind" beyond the most immediate and literal aspects of the situation. Therefore, although the apparent constraints of the situation are met, they do not necessarily imply an adaptive response that is of benefit to the organism. Lhermitte (1986) conceptualizes this defect as a form of environmental dependency and as loss of personal autonomy. Shallice (1988) has described this impairment as loss of the supervisory system.

If utilization behavior reflects a loss of working memory, an interesting question arises about the role and influence of working memory in executive functions.

That is, working memory is by definition a process that "temporarily holds on line constraints relevant to the current context" (Pennington et al., p. 340). However, executive functions importantly include diverse goal-directed behaviors over a period of time that extends beyond a few minutes and even to different spatial settings. For example, completing a graduate degree requires constant vigilance to both short-term and long-term goals. Development and maintenance of important social relationships, such as those encountered in family units, also requires persistent attention to immediate, short-term, and long-term goals. This type of *prospective archival memory* is not well defined in current models, either psychologically or neurobiologically. It qualifies as a type of working memory because it implies prospective memory-guided responding rather than sensory-guided responding. It is frequently changing yet enduring over a long period of time. Does the influence of future goals reside in some form of long-term working memory that is kept active by daily activities such as the behaviors that alter future consequences, as described by Barkley? It would seem necessary to postulate some mechanism to maintain the driving force of these goals. A likely candidate is the multiple forms of partial reinforcement that produce a consistent and high level of responding in relation to goals. Grafman (1989), among others, has argued that there are long-term, enduring representations that are processed and stored within the frontal lobe and may represent complex knowledge such as event structures and sequences, as might be expected with mental models. That is, after formulating a mental model of what is required for a graduate degree, such representation may come to guide many aspects of day-to-day behavior by providing a larger framework to the task, the behaviors, and the small advances that reinforce and maintain an extended phase of productivity and vocational maturation. It must include multiple branch points for alternative scenarios and response options increasing the flexibility of behavior. This view of long-term goals and how they influence our everyday behavior is not specifically formulated in any of the chapters of Section IV, yet may be a critical feature of executive function development. As one might expect, it is extremely difficult to empirically or experimentally evaluate given the constraints of current methods of cognitive and neuropsychological studies. However, there are certain experimental paradigms that may tap into measurement of how a person goes about achieving both short-term and long-term goals, such as simulation-based assessment of managerial competence (Streufert, Pogash, & Piasecki, 1988).

Developmental Vulnerability of Executive Functions

From a psychological perspective, it seems fair to conclude that development of executive functions is different from attention and memory. That is, it is critically dependent on a wide (possibly the widest) variety of other psychological processes. For example, Borkowski and Burke suggest that the cognition level must develop before metacognition can emerge. Denckla posits that content- or domain-specific competencies are needed before domain-general control processes can evolve. Graham and Harris identify "preskill development" as the first stage for instruction and utilization of higher order strategies. From a different perspective, Barkley argues that executive function requires behavior influencing other behaviors (rather than the environment). Hence, one must have prepotent or routine behaviors before modification and shifting can take place.

There is strong agreement among all authors of this section that executive functions do not refer to elementary cognitive processes, such as sensation, perception, motor activation, attention, and even memory. Development of nonexecutive psychological processes, furthermore, are highly dependent on neurobiological maturation as well as environmental exposures, particularly in development of the senses (Greenough, Black, & Wallace, 1993). Hence, executive functions can be thought of as several steps removed from (yet highly influenced developmentally by) fundamental psychological development. This places the emergence of executive functions in a highly vulnerable position, which can be altered and compromised by a variety of factors such as inborn errors of metabolism, neuronal migration and maturation patterns, environmental deprivation, and other causes of poor psychological development. The frequency of executive function impairments in diverse neurodevelopmental disorders should not, perhaps, be surprising and may fit with the idea of a final common pathway that can be altered by a wide variety of factors. This is also reflected in greater discussion about strategy deficits and metacognitive weaknesses in students with learning impairments (Torgeson, 1994). However, the type and degree of executive function alteration in different neurodevelopmental disorders are probably more specific than indicated by current measures.

From a neurological perspective, maturation of brain systems that are thought to mediate executive functions (particularly the prefrontal cortex and its extended networks) has the most prolonged course of postnatal development. Myelination can be used as one index of development, reflecting the growth and integrity of the fatty sheath encasing axons and hence separating activation/inhibition of one neuron from another, which is critical to development of specific pathways. This process continues in the prefrontal lobe well into adolescence and early childhood (St. James-Roberts, 1979; Yakelov & Lecours, 1967). Neurophysiological measures from EEG coherence patterns also indicate that typical development of the prefrontal region follows a persistent although irregular series of changes that are correlated with cognitive development (Pribram, in press; Thatcher, 1991) and continue into adulthood. There are a variety of other important neurobiological parameters that also need to be considered, including programmed cell death, neuronal density, synaptogenesis, and synaptic density (Bourgeois, Goldman-Rakic, & Rakic, 1994; Huttenlocher, 1990; Rakic, Bourgeois, Zecevik, Eckenhoff, & Goldman-Rakic, 1986).

Another way to conceptualize development of executive functions in relation to neurobiological dynamics is that *differentiation* of functions must precede and then synchronize with *integration* of functions (Grattan & Eslinger, 1991a). The development of connections of the prefrontal cortex with other brain areas presumably provides a structural basis on which cognitive or content-specific competencies can feed-forward fundamental processing to cortical executive networks. However, there is a point at which the development of cognition and content-specific competencies can be affected by early injury or alterations to the neural substrate of executive processing as demands for complexity increase. For example, damage to the frontal lobe with executive function impairment in the early years does appear to have a constraining effect on general intelligence measures to a moderate degree (10–25 points), whereas similar damage to the frontal lobe in adults does not appear to lower IQ (Benton, 1991; Grattan & Eslinger, 1991a). This discrepancy is probably related to the consequent limitations in working memory, attentional control, and organizational abilities caused by early frontal lobe damage. The so-called "Kennard Effect," named for the experimental work of the neuroscientist Margaret Kennard, refers to the observation that greater recovery of function can occur after early cerebral injury than after later cerebral injury, at least for motor and sensory functions. What type of recovery or compensation is possible after early damage or developmental alterations to the neural substrate for executive functions? This question leads to the next section on the course of development after early executive function impairments.

Natural Course of Executive Function Impairments Over the Life Span

Executive function impairments have a particularly insidious effect on child, adolescent, and even adult development and may underlie difficulties in many poor learners and workers as well as poorly adjusted parents and citizens. Throughout life phases, there is increasing demand for complexity and organization of psychological processing, as well as control of powerful emotions and potentially destructive behaviors. With development, most settings also provide only partial information pertinent to long-term goals and require greater inhibition of prepotent responses and longer delays before rewards are to occur. Hence, unlike content-specific deficiencies in reading and spelling, developmental executive function impairments are much more difficult to observe, identify, and manage. Clear documentation of this pattern was first provided in the observations of case JP by Ackerly and Benton (1947) and more recently in the case report of patient DT who suffered a localized injury to the left prefrontal lobe at 7 years of age and was studied 26 years later (Eslinger, Grattan, Damasio, & Damasio, 1992). DT displayed completely normal social, cognitive, and emotional development until 7 years of age, when she suffered a spontaneous intraparenchymal hemorrhage that required surgical evacuation. With the exception of a well-controlled seizure disorder, her recovery was considered complete. She returned to school and her usual activities without incident for approximately 3–4 years, although a decrease in learning abilities was noted. In late childhood and early adolescence, there was a progressive upsurge in behavioral difficulties as social, cognitive, and emotional demands began to increase. Her grades declined and she eventually maintained only one friend, having alienated herself from others through noncooperative and argumentative behavior and an inability to follow through on plans and contribute to social relationships. While she was passed through high school, her academic achievement levels remained at approximately a third-grade level. Her overall IQ as an adult was measured at 80 (ninth percentile), which is approximately 20 points below that expected for someone of her educational and family background. Memory, language, and visual perception were also within the low-normal range, but measures of executive function were markedly impaired. DT became pregnant soon after high school by the first man whom she dated and was quickly married. However, she proved unable to anticipate and meet her child's needs, such as planning meals, changing clothing, and providing nurturance and comfort. After her divorce and loss of child custody, her life became more unstructured and volatile. Promiscuity increased with numerous antisocial and unsavory characters, with frequent conflicts and abnormal sexual activity. Yet DT can profess great religiosity and morality as dictated by the Bible. Her friendships are transient and unstable because of the unreasonable demands she put on others and her lack of reciprocity. In the vocational domain, her performance has also been erratic, impulsive, and marked by poor follow-through on required tasks, failure to learn from mistakes, and very negative reactions to criticism. Her current vocational plan is to open a religious bookstore in the West because a friend reported there were no such stores there. Further study of her personality and social development has indicated very limited capacity for empathic understanding, inadequate identity development, difficulties in vocational adjustment, and a concrete level of moral reasoning (Grattan & Eslinger, 1992). These findings suggest that there may be important interrelationships between psychosocial development and executive processes (Table 20.1). That is, executive processes may have a critical role not only in developing the behavioral and cognitive tools for goal attainment, but also in psychosocial development that encompasses cognitive, emotional, and social domains. The recent case report of Marlowe (1992) also supports the important interrelationship of executive and psychosocial processes in development. In adults with focal frontal lobe lesions, the interrelationship between executive and psychosocial impairments depends on the specific location of damage (Grattan, Bloomer, Archambault, & Eslinger, 1994). This is not yet established for childhood cases.

DT's natural history since the time of her childhood frontal lobe injury indicates how profound and devastating the lack of executive functions can be in an individual with otherwise no motor or sensory impairments and a broadly normal range of intellectual performance, perceptual abilities, language, and memory. Her level of psychosocial development remains at approximately 12 years of age even though she is in her mid-30s. As Denckla's clinical impressions have suggested, it is in the developmental trajectory from childhood to adulthood when the executive function construct has its greatest utility and where the pervasive, disruptive effects of its impairment are most powerfully observed. The case of DT also indicates that the effects of executive function impairments do not lie simply in the cognitive or problem-solving domain but extend broadly into social behavior, emotional regulation, empathy, vocational maturation, and even moral

Table 20.1. Salient cognitive prerequisites (executive functions) associated with selected psychosocial skills

Psychosocial skills	Cognitive prerequisites
Empathic understanding	Cognitive flexibility, perspective-taking ability
Identity formation	Impulse control, temporal integration, synthesis of multiple pieces of information
Moral maturity	Symbolic thinking, consideration of a wide range of possibilities, anticipating consequences among alternatives
Vocational maturity	Planfulness, time perspective, decision making, reality orientation

From Grattan, L.M., & Eslinger, P.J. (1992). Long-term psychological consequences of childhood frontal lobe lesion in patient DT. *Brain and Cognition, 20,* 185–195; reprinted by permission.

maturity. Therefore, early executive function impairments may have profound effects on adjustment and adaptation throughout the life span. By way of comparison, we have made the observation that similar injury in adulthood may also have long-term consequences but of a different presentation and variety. That is, adults who acquire frontal lobe lesions have previously developed a number of adaptation and adjustment strategies that continue to serve them in limited contexts that are predictable and familiar (Eslinger & Damasio, 1985; Grattan & Eslinger, 1991a). However, their capacities to learn from experience and even develop "wisdom" appears to be limited, as their stage of psychosocial maturation may remain fixed to the time of their lesion (Grattan & Eslinger, 1991b). It is our view, in fact, that continuing maturation of executive functions (and continuing maturation in the prefrontal lobe and its neuronal networks) provides a critical psychological substrate for adaptation and adjustment throughout the life span.

Social Aspects of Executive Function

The most striking case examples of impaired executive function in the neurological and neuropsychological literatures have shown not only cognitive difficulties but also alterations in social behavior and personality. In fact, the social disability of these patients, whether children or adults, is frequently their most distinctive characteristic (Ackerly & Benton, 1947; Eslinger & Damasio, 1985; Eslinger et al., 1992; Marlowe, 1992). Although the models of executive function discussed in this section have focused primarily on cognitive aspects and specific learning and problem-solving paradigms, the construct of executive function may also encompass a powerful influence on social behavior. Yet there is no comprehensive model of executive function that addresses the interrelationship of cognitive and social aspects of behavior, including the various types of impairments that can occur. An initial step in this direction is to begin developing a working taxonomy for the types of social-behavioral impairments that can occur with alterations in executive functions. One source of such entities are the cases of impaired executive function after frontal lobe damage. The expression of social impairments in these patients can be diverse and include the following:

- Demanding and self-centered behavior
- Lack of social tact and restraint
- Impulsive speech and actions
- Disinhibition
- Apathy and indifference
- Lack of empathy

To address these problems, we have proposed a preliminary model for social impairments that is based on the concept of the "social executor." As with cognitive systems that are geared toward perceiving and acting on objects and physical features of the environment, there are also social cognitive systems that very likely have an executive function role. That is, social executors organize, integrate, and influence perceptions, emotions, and responses to other persons across time and space to meet the needs and goals of the organism. After reviewing the available literature, Grattan (see Eslinger, Grattan, & Geder, 1995, for more details) has identified four aspects of social and interpersonal behavior that appear to have strong executive features, as follows:

1. *Social self-regulation:* Processes necessary to manage the initiation, rate, intensity, and duration of interaction with others. Impairment of this social executor may cause reduced initiation and volition in social settings, limited appreciation for interpersonal boundaries, and difficulty inhibiting responses in social contexts.

2. *Social self-awareness:* Knowledge and insight about oneself in social settings, involving perception of emotions, managing emotions, perceiving the impact of one's behavior on others, and general interpersonal effectiveness. Impairment of this social executor may be shown by patients who underestimate or overestimate their social and emotional effectiveness compared to reports of others. Reduced social self-awareness may be associated with denial of social difficulties and hence reduced motivation for modifying these behaviors.

3. *Social sensitivity:* This social executor resembles the construct of cognitively based empathy and refers to the ability to understand another's perspective, point of view, or emotional state. Impairment may be shown by superficial and unusually self-centered behavior as well as by insensitivity to others.

4. *Social salience:* This construct subsumes a variety of cognitive, autonomic, and visceral processes that regulate somatic and emotional states and impart a sense of meaningfulness to social situations and to specific individuals within those situations. Impaired social salience may also be thought of as a disruption in affectively based empathy or the ability to share the emotional experiences of another. When all persons and environmental stimuli have similar social salience, patients are unable to organize their environments into any hierarchy of meaningfulness or relevance.

The social executors interact with a number of moderating variables, developmental and pathophysiological, that affect their expression (Figure 20.2). Premorbid variables include personality traits, educational background, cognitive capacities, and the patient's particular social system, among other variables. Postmorbid variables that result from acquired injury to the nervous system and developmental alterations include certain severe neuropsychiatric and reactive psychological states (e.g., depression, posttraumatic stress) as well as cognitive and executive function deficits.

Although social and interpersonal behaviors have not been the main focus of neuropsychological, information-processing, and behavioral approaches in this section, they are critically important to any model of executive function. Although many aspects of social executors do have a strong cognitive basis, the influences of other neural systems will also need to be considered, such as the hypothalamic–pituitary axis, emotional processing, autonomic, and other somatic systems.

Executive Functions and the Frontal Lobe

In the neuropsychological literature, data supporting an association between impaired executive functions and frontal lobe damage date back to the early reports of Harlowe (1868), who described the crowbar case of Phineas Gage. Many subsequent studies have strongly supported this neural–behavioral association, and

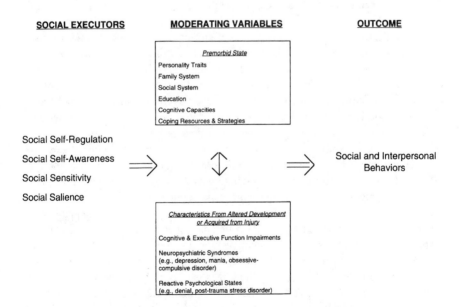

Figure 20.2. Grattan's proposed model of social executors and their interaction with developmental and pathophysiological factors.

the terms *executive function* and *frontal lobe function* have sometimes been used interchangeably. Although this has a certain clinical and didactic value, it has become increasingly clear that the terms are not interchangeable and that the neural substrate of executive functions includes but is not limited to the prefrontal cortex. For example, the Wisconsin Card Sorting Test requires working memory and shifting of response set, yet can be impaired by lesions not only to the frontal lobe but also nonfrontal cortices and the basal ganglia (Anderson, Damasio, Jones, & Tranel, 1991; Eslinger and Grattan, 1993; Grafman, Jones, & Salazar, 1990). In a study of survivors of severe closed head injury, Goldenberg, Oder, Spatt, and Podreka (1992) reported that tests of executive functions correlated more strongly with cerebral blood flow measures in the thalamus than the frontal lobe. Functional magnetic resonance imaging studies of control subjects performing working memory tasks have indicated a component of frontal lobe activation, but also temporal and parietal lobe activation. The neural substrate of executive functions, therefore, is more accurately conceptualized as a neural network that involves synchronized activation of multiple cerebral regions, cortical and subcortical. Equipotentiality of these regions is unlikely, for they are designed to interact with each other in complementary ways. Therefore, although the importance of the prefrontal cortex for executive functions is not lost, its role is placed within a broader neurological model.

Relationship of Memory, Attention, and Executive Functions

All chapters in this section agree that memory, attention, and executive functions are interrelated. Executive functions would not be able to emerge if memory systems could not operate to register, store, and make available diverse forms of knowledge and experience. Similarly, attention is critical to operation of executive functions because of the focused, sustained, and divided forms of attention that permit sensory and perceptual processing of both environmental and somatic events. Metaphorically, memory, attention, and executive functions may be interrelated as past, present, and future are interrelated. Short-term and long-term declarative memory systems are geared toward registering and maintaining what was: specific episodes of one's life, general knowledge, or decisions one has made. Attentional systems are necessary to keep certain information in the forefront of ongoing information processing, as well as to process new information and illuminate particular parts of memory, perception, and other cognitive activities. Executive functions, however, are almost entirely future-oriented and are organized for behavioral expressions whose consequences may occur in far-distant spatial and temporal settings. Executive functions perhaps make possible many of the goals that we live for and permit ways to identify and achieve those goals. However, to know where one is going, it is necessary to know where you have been and where you are. In this sense, development and elaboration of executive functions are critically dependent on memory and attention and, when built upon that foundation, can provide a basis for continuing adaptation, adjustment, and achievement throughout the life span.

REFERENCES

Ackerly, S.S., & Benton, A.L. (1947). Report of a case of bilateral frontal lobe defect. *Research Publications of the Association for Research in Nervous and Mental Disease, 27,* 479–504.

Anderson, S.W., Damasio, H., Jones, R.D., & Tranel, D. (1991). Wisconsin Card Sorting performance as a measure of frontal lobe damage. *Journal of Clinical and Experimental Neuropsychology, 13,* 926–939.

Bates, J.F., & Goldman-Rakic, P.S. (1993). Prefrontal connections of medial motor areas in the rhesus monkey. *Journal of Comparative Neurology, 336,* 211–228.

Benton, A.L. (1991). Prefrontal injury and behavior in children. *Developmental Neuropsychology, 7,* 275–281.

Benton, A.L., & Hamsher, K.deS. (1989). *Multilingual Aphasia Examination* (2nd Ed.). Iowa City, IA: AJA Associates Inc.

Borys, S.V., Spitz, H.H., & Dorans, B.A. (1982). Tower of Hanoi performance of retarded young adults and nonretarded children as a function of solution length and goal state. *Journal of Experimental Child Psychology, 33,* 87–110.

Bourgeois, J.-P., Goldman-Rakic, P.S., & Rakic, P. (1994). Synaptogenesis in the prefrontal cortex of rhesus monkeys. *Cerebral Cortex, 4,* 78–96.

Brazzelli, M., Colombo, N., DellaSala, S., & Spinnler, H. (1994). Spared and impaired cognitive abilities after bilateral frontal lobe damage. *Cortex, 30,* 27–51.

Bronowski, J. (1967). *Human and animal languages: To honor Roman Jakobson* (Vol. 1). The Hague: Mouton and Company.

Brown, A.L., Campione, J.C., & Day, J.D. (1981). Learning to learn: On training students to learn from texts. *Educational Researcher, 10,* 14–21.

Butterfield, E.C., & Albertson, L.R. (1994). On making cognitive theory more general and developmentally pertinent. In F. Weinert & W. Schneider (Eds.), *Research on memory development* (pp. 73–99). Hillsdale, NJ: Lawrence Erlbaum Associates.

Butterfield, E.C., & Belmont, J.M. (1977). Assessing and improving the executive cognitive functions of mentally retarded people. In I. Bialer & M. Sternlicht (Eds.), *Psychological issues in mental retardation* (pp. 277–318). New York: Psychological Dimensions.

Dennis, M. (1991). Frontal lobe function in childhood and adolescence: A heuristic for assessing attention regulation, executive control, and the intentional states important for social discourse. *Developmental Neuropsychology, 7,* 327–358.

Deshler, D.D., & Schumaker, J.B. (1986). Learning strategies: An instructional alternative for low-achieving adolescents. *Exceptional Children, 52,* 583–590.

Duncan, J. (1986). Disorganization of behavior after frontal lobe damage. *Cognitive Neuropsychology, 3,* 271–290.

Eslinger, P.J., & Damasio, A.R. (1985). Severe disturbance of higher cognition after bilateral frontal lobe ablation. *Neurology, 35,* 1731–1741.

Eslinger, P.J., & Grattan, L.M. (1993). Frontal lobe and frontal-striatal substrates for different forms of human cognitive flexibility. *Neuropsychologia, 31,* 17–28.

Eslinger, P.J., Grattan, L.M., Damasio, H., & Damasio, A.R. (1992). Developmental consequences of childhood frontal lobe damage. *Archives of Neurology, 49,* 764–769.

Eslinger, P.J., Grattan, L.M., & Geder, L. (1995). Impact of frontal lobe lesions on rehabilitation and recovery from acute brain injury. *NeuroRehabilitation, 5,* 161–182.

Eslinger, P.J., Warner, G., Grattan, L.M., & Easton, J.D. (1991). Frontal lobe utilization behavior after bilateral paramedian thalamic infarction. *Neurology, 41,* 450–452.

Fuster, J.M. (1989). *The prefrontal cortex: Anatomy, physiology and neuropsychology of the frontal lobe.* New York: Raven Press.

Fuster, J.M. (1991). Role of prefrontal cortex in delay tasks: Evidence from reversible lesion and unit recording in the monkey. In H.S. Levin, H.M. Eisenberg, & A.L. Benton

(Eds.), *Frontal lobe function and dysfunction* (pp. 59–71). New York: Oxford University Press.

Goldenberg, G., Oder, W., Spatt, J., & Podreka, I. (1992). Cerebral correlates of disturbed executive function and memory in survivors of severe closed head injury: A SPECT study. *Journal of Neurology, Neurosurgery and Psychiatry, 55*, 362–368.

Goldman-Rakic, P.S. (1988). Circuitry of primate prefrontal cortex and regulation of behavior by representational memory. In F. Plum, (Ed.), *Handbook of physiology, The nervous system V* (pp. 373–417). Bethesda, MD: American Physiological Society.

Grafman, J. (1989). Plans, actions and mental sets: Managerial knowledge units in the frontal lobes. In E. Perecman (Ed.), *Integrating theory and practice in clinical neuropsychology* (pp. 93–138). Hillsdale, NJ: Lawrence Erlbaum Associates.

Grafman, J., Jones, B., & Salazar, A. (1990). Wisconsin Card Sorting Test performance based on location and size of neuroanatomic lesion in Vietnam veterans with penetrating head injury. *Perception and Motor Skills, 74*, 1120–1122.

Grattan, L.M., Bloomer, R., Archambault, F.X., & Eslinger, P.J. (1994). Cognitive flexibility and empathy after frontal lobe lesion. *Neuropsychiatry, Neuropsychology and Behavioral Neurology, 7*, 251–259.

Grattan, L.M., & Eslinger, P.J. (1991a). Characteristics of favorable recovery from frontal lobe damage. *Neurology, 41*, 266.

Grattan, L.M., & Eslinger, P.J. (1991b). Frontal lobe damage in children and adults: A comparative review. *Developmental Neuropsychology, 7*, 283–326.

Grattan, L.M., & Eslinger, P.J. (1992). Long-term psychological consequences of childhood frontal lobe lesion in patient DT. *Brain and Cognition, 20*, 185–195.

Greenough, W.T., Black, J.E., & Wallace, C.S. (1993). Experience and brain development. In M.H. Johnson (Ed.), *Brain development and cognition* (pp. 290–322). Oxford: Blackwell.

Gronwall, D. (1977). Paced Auditory Serial-Addition Task: A measure of recovery from concussion. *Perceptual and Motor Skills, 44*, 367–373.

Guitton, D., Buchtel, H.A., & Douglas, R.M. (1985). Frontal lobe lesions in man cause difficulties in suppressing reflexive glances and in generating goal-directed saccades. *Experimental Brain Research, 58*, 455–472.

Harlowe, J.M. (1868). Recovery after severe injury to the head. *Publication of the Massachusetts Medical Society, 2*, 327–346.

Hayes, S.C. (1986). The case of the silent dog: Verbal reports and the analysis of rules. A review of K. Anders Ericsson and Herbert A. Simon, "Protocol analysis: Verbal reports as data." *Journal of Experimental Analysis of Behavior, 45*, 351–363.

Hayes, S.C., & Hayes, L.J. (1992). Verbal relations and the evolution of behavior analysis. *American Psychologist, 47*, 1383–1395.

Heaton, R.K. (1981). *The Wisconsin Card Sorting Test Manual.* Odessa, FL: Psychological Assessment Resources.

Huttenlocher, P.R. (1990). Morphometric study of human cerebral cortex development. *Neuropsychologia, 28*, 517–527.

Lhermitte, F. (1983). "Utilization behavior" and its relation to lesions in the frontal lobes. *Brain, 106*, 237–255.

Lhermitte, F. (1986). Human autonomy and the frontal lobes. Part II: Patient behavior in complex and social situations: The "environmental dependency" syndrome. *Annals of Neurology, 19*, 335–343.

Luria, A.R. (1966). *Higher cortical functions in man.* New York: Basic Books.

Marlowe, W. (1992). The impact of right prefrontal lesion on the developing brain. *Brain and Cognition, 20*, 205–213.

Meichenbaum, D. (1977). *Cognitive behavior modification: An integrative approach.* New York: Plenum.

Pribram, K.H. (in press). The work in working memory: Implications for development. In N.A. Krasnegor, G.R. Lyon, & P.S. Goldman-Rakic (Eds.), *Development of prefrontal cortex: Evolution, neurobiology, and behavior.* Baltimore: Paul H. Brookes Publishing Co.

Rakic, P., Bourgeois, J.P., Zecevic, N., Eckenhoff, M.F., & Goldman-Rakic, P.S. (1986). Isochronic overproduction of synapses in diverse regions of the primate cerebral cortex. *Science, 232,* 232–235.

Roberts, R.J., Hager, L.D., & Heron, C. (1994). Prefrontal cognitive processes: Working memory and inhibition in the antisaccade task. *Journal of Experimental Psychology: General, 123,* 374–393.

St. James-Roberts, I. (1979). Neurological plasticity, recovery from brain insult, and child development. *Advances in Child Development and Behavior, 14,* 253–319.

Sawaguchi, T., & Goldman-Rakic, P.S. (1994). The role of D1-dopamine receptor in working memory: Local injections of dopamine antagonists into the prefrontal cortex of rhesus monkeys performing an oculomotor delayed-response task. *Journal of Neurophysiology, 71,* 515–528.

Shallice, T. (1988). *From neuropsychology to mental structure.* Cambridge: Cambridge University Press.

Shallice, T., Burgess, P.W., Schon, F., & Baxter, D.M. (1989). The origins of utilization behavior. *Brain, 112,* 1587–1598.

Streufert, S., Pogash, R. & Piasecki, M. (1988). Simulation-based assessment of managerial competence: Reliability and validity. *Personnel Psychology, 41,* 537–557.

Stroop, J.R. (1935). Studies of interference in serial verbal reactions. *Journal of Experimental Psychology, 18,* 643–662.

Thatcher, R. (1991). Maturation of the human frontal lobes: Physiological evidence for staging. *Developmental Neuropsychology, 7,* 397–419.

Torgeson, J.K. (1994). Issues in the assessment of executive function: An information-processing perspective. In G.R. Lyon (Ed.), *Frames of reference for the assessment of learning disabilities* (pp. 143–162). Baltimore: Paul H. Brookes Publishing Co.

Welsh, M.D., & Pennington, B.F. (1988). Assessing frontal lobe functioning in children: Views from developmental psychology. *Developmental Neuropsychology, 4,* 199–230.

Yakelov, P.I., & Lecours, A.R. (1967). The myelogenetic cycles of regional maturation of the brain. In A. Minkiniwski (Ed.), *Regional development of the brain in early life* (pp. 1–25). Oxford: Blackwell.

V

SUMMARY AND CONCLUSIONS

This book reflects an attempt to consolidate and present current knowledge that is relevant to the relationship between attention, memory, and executive function on the one hand and human cognition, learning, and behavior on the other. Because the literature addressing each of these constructs is so vast, we employed a strategy that helped to organize the research according to three paradigms—namely, research information was organized according to an information processing paradigm, a neuropsychological paradigm, and a behavioral analytical paradigm. Within this context, H. Gerry Taylor's task in this section was to review the major points raised about attention, memory, and executive function within each of the three overarching paradigms, to evaluate the state of past and present research, and to provide a vision of future scientific endeavors in these domains. In Chapter 21, Taylor accomplishes this objective. He provides us with a well-thought-out and well-organized summary of the most current information on the theoretical, conceptual, and measurement issues that are critical to our understanding of attention, memory, and executive function and on the deficits and disorders that are associated with each of these clinical and research domains.

21

CRITICAL ISSUES AND FUTURE DIRECTIONS IN THE DEVELOPMENT OF THEORIES, MODELS, AND MEASUREMENTS FOR ATTENTION, MEMORY, AND EXECUTIVE FUNCTION

H. Gerry Taylor

Tests of cognitive ability play a central role in clinical neuropsychology. Cognitive ability testing is also critical in investigating research hypotheses with regard to brain–behavior relationships and human information processing. Although the procedures used to assess cognitive abilities vary considerably in both practice and research applications, most measures of cognitive ability fall into one of several distinct test domains. The consensus of opinion among neuropsychologists is that these domains include the three types of abilities that are the topic of the present volume—that is, attention, memory, and executive function. Additional cognitive domains include general intelligence, language, spatial-constructional skills, sensorimotor and perceptual motor abilities, and reasoning and concept formation (Fletcher, Taylor, Levin, & Satz, 1995; Levin, Soukup, Benton, Fletcher, & Satz, 1995; Lezak, 1983; Lyon, 1994).

Special interest in tests of attention, memory, and executive function stems partly from the fact that impairments in these areas are frequently observed in association with outright brain disease or injury, as well as with a wide array of developmental conditions (see Pennington, Bennetto, McAleer, & Roberts, Chapter 18). Deficits in one or more of these domains are common in individuals with traumatic brain injury, learning disabilities, attention deficit hyperactivity disorder (ADHD), and autism (Fletcher et al., 1995; Graham & Harris, Chapter 19; Pennington, 1991; Stanovich, 1986; Taylor, Schatschneider, Petrill, Barry, &

Owens, in press). In many instances, these deficits occur in relative isolation and cannot be readily accounted for in terms of global mental deficiency or weaknesses in other areas of neuropsychological assessment. Problems in memory, attention, or executive function, moreover, can be found in individuals who do not meet diagnostic criteria for a disorder but who nonetheless are having significant problems meeting the expectations of others. Executive dysfunctions, for example, are sometimes discovered in children who have difficulties at school yet who may not meet strict criteria for either learning disabilities or ADHD (Denckla, 1989).

PURPOSES OF COGNITIVE ASSESSMENT: THE BIOBEHAVIORAL SYSTEMS APPROACH

The major goals of administering tests of attention, memory, and executive function are not so much to make formal diagnoses as to understand reasons for the individual's behavioral or learning problems and to make recommendations for treatment based on this understanding (Taylor & Fletcher, 1990). It is important to emphasize, however, that neuropsychological assessment does not consist of test administration alone. Additional factors considered in the overall evaluation include 1) the nature and severity of the problems for which the child or adult is referred, such as the type of behavioral disturbance or learning disability; 2) potential biological or "state" influences on the presenting problems, such as a previous history of neurological insult or disorder, genetic heritability, current health and medication status, and developmental status; and 3) environmental variables, such as the individual's previous experiential and reinforcement history, as well as the more immediate stimulus context and contingencies in place in testing the individual.

Conceiving of the assessment process in accordance with a broader, "biobehavioral systems" approach (Fletcher & Taylor, 1984; Taylor & Fletcher, 1990) has two major advantages for our understanding of tests and what they measure. First, this approach implies that scientific inquiry can take place at several levels. Study of a given cognitive ability may involve investigation of the relationships of that ability to other cognitive or behavioral traits, indices of brain status, or environmental variables. Each of these relationships represents a legitimate area of inquiry. Study of each relationship adds different information with regard to meaningfulness of the ability under investigation. The perspectives of the three research paradigms contributing to the present volume—neuropsychology, information processing or cognitive psychology, and behavior analysis—can, in this way, each be viewed as making a unique and complementary contribution to the study of cognitive abilities. Neuropsychological studies to date have focused most on relationships between brain status and abilities and between these abilities and measures of learning or behavior. Information processing studies have concentrated most on cognitively testing per se, or on the constituent skills that contribute to test performance. And the methods of behavior analysis have been applied primarily to study associations of behavioral measures with environmental context and response contingencies.

A second advantage of the biobehavioral systems approach is that measurable behavior traits, whether consisting of test performance or of more ecologically meaningful measures of learning and behavior, are viewed as combined products of nature and nurture. Consistent with the scientific structure of psychology (Kimble, 1989), the direct effects of brain status on cognitive abilities or of cognitive abilities on learning and behavior can never be studied. The individual's experiences and learning history, together with more immediate stimulus conditions and individual motivational states, constitute additional influences on performance both inside and outside of the examining room. Although some types of performance may be more subject to deviations of brain status than others (Fletcher & Taylor, 1984; Taylor & Schatschneider, 1992), extraneurological factors must always be considered as moderating influences. Seen from this perspective, the disciplines of neuropsychology, information processing, and behavior analysis are inextricably linked. Although these three disciplines have distinct foci of interest, the findings that emerge from these approaches have clear relevance for the understanding of cognitive function and dysfunction.

NICHD CONFERENCE ON ATTENTION, MEMORY, AND EXECUTIVE FUNCTION

The NICHD Conference on Attention, Memory, and Executive Function, which took place January 1–3, 1994, provided a rare opportunity for researchers from these three theoretical perspectives to discuss commonalities and differences in theory and measurement of attention, memory, and executive function. The major rationale for the meeting, as described by the conference convener and organizer (Lyon, see Chapter 1), was to promote research methods that would further understanding of these three ability domains and their relationship to learning and behavior. Arguments supporting the need for this conference and the present volume summarizing it were essentially twofold. First, research to date suggests that the cognitive domains of attention, memory, and executive function are distinct from other neuropsychological domains and of critical importance in understanding development and developmental disabilities. Second, current knowledge with regard to these cognitive functions is highly limited, even more so for children than for adults. Neuropsychologists tend to interpret test results within these domains on the basis of what they believe the tests measure (content validity) rather than on empirical studies of construct validity (Morris, Chapter 2; Taylor et al., in press). A related issue is the tendency to assume that performances on different tests within a given domain measure similar capacities when, in fact, a test domain may be composed of a number of dissociable skills. A further and more profound limitation is that performances on tests of these abilities generally have not been considered within a broader conceptual framework, such as the biobehavioral systems approach. The latter limitation clearly justifies inclusion of multiple theoretical orientations.

Review of the preceding chapters suggests that the interdisciplinary exchange was indeed effective. Neuropsychologists, information processing researchers, and behavior analysts are discovering common interests. As evident from the papers contained in this volume, investigators from each of these disciplines have made a number of noteworthy advancements in theory and measurement of memory, attention, and executive function. The present chapters demonstrate an increasing awareness of the need to study these test domains more critically than has been the case in the past and to link cognitive constructs to behavior and learning, brain status, and environmental factors. More specifically, there are six distinct themes that emerge in review of these chapters, each of which marks significant scientific progress in the study of cognitive functions. These several themes are reviewed below both to summarize the contents of this volume and to emphasize areas of recent advancement in research methods and conceptualization. Related research directions are also discussed.

EMERGING THEMES IN CURRENT RESEARCH
ON MEMORY, ATTENTION, AND EXECUTIVE FUNCTION

The Need for Theoretical
Formulations and Study of Construct Validity

Whether acknowledged or not, all research is theory driven (Pedhazur & Schmelking, 1991). Our choice of test procedures and the manner in which we interpret test performance are based on preconceived notions, even if just hunches, as to the processes we are measuring or the relationships we expect to discover. A limitation of many current applications of cognitive testing, at least by neuropsychologists, is that there have been few attempts to formalize our theories and test constructs, especially as pertains to the domains of attention and executive function.

Several of the chapters in the current volume have addressed this need head on. In Chapter 18, for example, Pennington and associates (see also Pennington, in press) develop a model of working memory that involves a number of interrelated subprocesses and that helps to account for performance on diverse tests of executive function. Additional examples of comprehensive theoretical formulations of test constructs include Sergeant's cognitive-energetic model of information processing (Chapter 5), Mirsky's multidimensional model of attention (Chapter 6), and the distinctions between declarative memory and procedure learning drawn by Bachevalier, Malkova, and Beauregard (Chapter 11) and Boller (Chapter 13). Further illustrations are provided by Barkley's proposal (Chapter 17) that deficits in response inhibition and delayed responding are the basis for impaired executive function and his notion that "response-response" chains are central to the cross-temporal organization of behavior.

Discussions by the authors of the essential attributes of the three test domains under consideration also aid in theory formulation. Emphasis is placed on the fact that attention, memory, and executive function are overlapping multidimensional constructs, and careful analysis is provided regarding the hypothesized nature of these constructs. Several of the authors, for example, identify what they view as key features of executive function, including set maintenance and inhibition of prepotent responses, planning and the cross-temporal organization of behavior, and self-regulation and self-monitoring (Chapters 14–18). Viewed from this perspective, attention might be best regarded as a subset of the more wide-ranging executive function domain. Many of these same authors also provide helpful analyses of the demands of specific tests of executive function.

At the same time, both Denckla (Chapter 15) and Pennington et al. (Chapter 18) urge us to resist the temptation to view the construct of executive function too broadly, lest it lose some of its explanatory power. For these authors, executive function, although central to many types of human performance (see also Barkley, Chapter 17), is described as distinct from conceptual abilities and short- and long-term information stores. Boller (Chapter 13) and Wagner (Chapter 9) register similar cautions in discussing memory constructs.

In more general terms, the chapters in this volume provide excellent illustrations of the two major approaches to construct validation, referred to by Embretson (1983) as "construct representation" and "nomothetic span." The focus of the former approach is on decomposition of tasks and manipulation of task demands as a means of exploring the processes contributing to performance. Manipulations hypothesized by Sergeant (Chapter 5) to influence the encoding, central processing, and response organization stages of the information processing model exemplify this approach. Additional examples include the effects of changes in task demands on transfer and generalization of problem-solving strategies (Borkowski & Burke, Chapter 14), the relationship between variations in demands for inhibition and working memory on tests of executive function (Pennington et al., Chapter 18), and the influences on attentional performances of alterations in task complexity and length (Halperin, Chapter 8). The essential feature of this method of construct validation is a focus on variability across tasks rather than across subjects. Constructs validated in this manner are then applicable to the study of individual differences. As discussed by Halperin (Chapter 8), variations in task demands are hypothesized to affect both clinical and normal groups, but in different ways.

The nomothetic span approach, in contrast, examines the network of associations between a given test performance and other measures. This includes relationships of test performance to performances on alternative measures of the same response trait, as well as associations and dissociations of the test with other measurements (i.e., criterion-related and discriminant validity). The latter approach to construct validity is richly illustrated in the present volume by the work of Fletcher et al. (Chapter 3), Mirsky (Chapter 6), and Torgesen (Chapter 10).

Fletcher and his colleagues (Chapter 3) place special emphasis on the virtues of confirmatory factor analysis. Constructs defined by this method can be simultaneously related to other variables, such as academic achievement, in testing the fit of data to hypothetical structural models (Francis, 1988). Evaluating measurement models (i.e., test constructs) in this way allows the investigator to summarize individual tests in terms of a smaller set of theoretically meaningful test composites, with resultant elimination of test redundancy and greater statistical power.

Using structural equation models, Torgesen (Chapter 10) investigated reasons for individual differences in reading acquisition, as well as reciprocal relationships between verbal skills and reading during the early school years. Data from his studies suggest that the relationship between verbal short-term memory skills and word reading ability is due in large part to the phonological processing components of the memory tasks. These results, which are of substantial theoretical interest, exemplify the virtues of the latent construct method.

More recent research by de Jong and Das-Smaal (1995) demonstrates that it is also possible to combine the nomothetic span and construct representation approaches. In the latter study, item response modeling was used to examine the relationship between task demands and performance on an attentional measure referred to as the Star Counting Task. Confirmatory factor analyses were then used to test hypotheses regarding the relationship of test performance to other tests of attention and memory, mental speed, fluid intelligence, and school achievement. Results from the latter analyses supported a model in which the Star Counting Task, together with tasks of immediate verbal memory and paced serial addition, formed a working memory factor. This factor was distinct, although highly associated with both fluid intelligence and school achievement.

Analysis of Task Demands and Measurement Properties

A second theme to emerge from the foregoing chapters is the need for both careful analysis of task demands and study of the measurement properties of the tests we employ. Understanding of task requirements and a focus on psychometric issues is important not only in making theoretical distinctions between test constructs, but also in interpreting test results.

One pitfall in designing and interpreting psychological tests relates to the fact that these procedures are inherently molar. As Denckla so cogently points out (Chapter 15), tests of any given ability assume that other abilities of less immediate interest to the examiner are held constant, or at least have minimal impact on test performance. This assumption is frequently unwarranted. Because multiple abilities are typically required, there may be several alternative interpretations for a deficit in test performance (Morris, Chapter 2). Many tests of executive function, for example, place considerable demands on spatial analysis or concept formation. Another type of confound is introduced when highly competent individuals find ways to compensate for inherent weaknesses in structured test settings; or when individuals with disorders in areas such as language or perceptual-motor skills perform poorly due to the latter limitations rather than, say, to difficulties in attention or executive function.

Denckla advocates for further research on the relationship of such confounding variables to test performance. She suggests that "intra-individual" discrepancies be examined as a means for assessing one skill relative to another. She also provides several useful examples of how this approach can be implemented (e.g., by comparing performance on tasks that place heavy demands on executive functions to performance on tasks of similar content but with lesser executive requirements).

The probing analysis by Pennington et al. (Chapter 18) of the Wisconsin Card Sorting Test highlights other potential problems in developing our assessment procedures. Pennington and colleagues found that scores on this test, although accurate in identifying more obvious disability, are likely to be of limited value in measuring variations in skill within the normal range. Additional measurement issues include limitations in test sensitivity as a function of age or previous exposure to test procedures (Welsh & Pennington, 1988). Measures having greatest potential to advance our knowledge of a given ability construct are those with good reliability and sensitivity to interindividual differences. It is also essential that stimulus materials, response requirements, and procedures for administration be carefully designed and theoretically based.

Investigation of Central Nervous System Substrates

The chapters of this volume also place considerable emphasis on the neural systems that subserve test performance. Knowledge regarding the brain mechanisms underlying higher-order cognitive functions has increased dramatically in recent years. Results from studies of human neuroanatomy and neurophysiology, together with animal research, suggest that cognitive performances are mediated by neural networks, rather than by discrete areas of the brain (Alexander, DeLong, & Strick, 1986; Cummings, 1993; Goldman-Rakic, 1988; Krasnegor, Lyon, & Goldman-Rakic, in press; Zola-Morgan & Squire, 1993). Executive dysfunctions originally attributed to abnormalities in the prefrontal cortex are now linked to a more widely distributed neural system involving, in addition to the prefrontal cortex, the basal ganglia, limbic system, thalamus, and posterior cortex (Eslinger, Chapter 20; Pennington, et al., Chapter 18). Damage or dysfunction in any part of this circuit may lead to executive problems, but with perhaps somewhat different effects depending on the nature and location of the abnormality.

Neural networks for attention and memory have also been hypothesized (Bachevalier et al., Chapter 11; Halperin, Chapter 8; Mirsky, Chapter 6; Posner & Petersen, 1990). A major advantage of these networks is their potential to account for distinctions between component attentional and memory skills. Bachevalier et al. (Chapter 11), for instance, provide evidence for separate neural bases for "declarative or explicit" memory and "procedural learning" in animals. The former ability is subserved by the rhinal cortex and related medial temporal and diencephalic areas, while the latter function is mediated primarily by corticostriatal systems. Similar brain–behavior correlations are discussed by Mirsky (Chapter 6) and Halperin (Chapter 8).

Investigation of the central nervous system correlates of human cognition takes essentially two forms. One method involves study of the effects of alterations in brain status on test performance. This method is exemplified by a spate of recent studies examining the effects of neurological conditions or lesion sites on specific aspects of memory, attention, and executive function (Denckla, Chapter 15; Levin et al., 1993, 1994; Mirsky, Chapter 6; Taylor et al., in press; Yeates, Blumenstein, Patterson, & Delis, 1995; Yeates, Enrile, Loss, Blumenstein, & Delis, in press). Investigations of patterns of hereditability of cognitive functions also fall into this category (Mirsky, Chapter 6). A second method is to study patterns of cortical and subcortical "activation" during cognitive tasks, by means of techniques such as positron emission tomography and functional magnetic resonance imaging (Pardo, Fox, & Raichle, 1991; Rezai et al., 1993). A unique advantage of this latter method is the capacity to time-link brain and behavioral functions. Problems in drawing inferences about normal cortical processes based on the study of persons with brain insults are also avoided.

Applications to the Study of Clinical Disorders

Another common theme is that test performance has the potential to enhance our understanding of a variety of clinical disorders. According to a wealth of research summarized throughout this book, measures of attention, memory, and executive function generally have proved useful in discriminating persons with brain disease or developmental disabilities from nonaffected individuals. Although testing is by no means a substitute for clinical diagnosis (Barkley, 1991), test performance may serve as corroborating evidence for or against the presence of a given clinical disorder (Pennington, 1991).

Cognitive assessment also permits investigation of hypotheses regarding the nature of clinical disorders. To illustrate, Brouwers and Poplack (1990) found evidence to suggest that attentional deficits were to some extent responsible for the short-term memory problems observed in children treated for acute lymphoblastic leukemia. Another example is provided by a study by Hooks, Milich, and Lorch (1994), who found that boys with ADHD performed more poorly than a control sample on tests of sustained attention and efficiency of processing, but not on a measure of selective attention. Manipulations in task demands and analyses of symptom patterns (e.g., memory requirements, error types, response time variability) have also been fruitful in developing more refined clinical classifications and in assessing medication effects (Barkley, Chapter 4; Barkley, Grodzinsky, & DuPaul, 1992; Halperin, Chapter 8; Morris & Fletcher, 1988; Pennington et al., Chapter 18; Sergeant, Chapter 5; Tannock, Schachar, & Logan, 1995).

Other clinical applications of cognitive testing include use of test results to sort out primary from secondary or co-morbid symptoms (e.g., Pennington, Groisser, & Welsh, 1993; Yeates & Bornstein, 1994) and the case study approach

(Shallice, 1979). The latter approach involves detailed study of individuals with distinct types of neurological insults. Examination of associations and dissociations of skills, referred to as "fractionation" of ability structures, enables the researcher to identify discrete cognitive subsystems. The most notable example of the latter method is the discovery, in patient H.M., of a dissociation between immediate and long-term memory (Bachevalier et al., Chapter 11).

Researchers need be wary, however, in drawing conclusions with respect to causal relationships between cognitive impairments and clinical disorders (Fletcher & Taylor, 1984). Cognitive impairments, even if present, need not constitute a necessary condition for the disorder. The cognitive deficit may merely exist in parallel with the disorder. Alternatively, the cognitive deficit and clinical disorder may have reciprocal influences on one another. The discovery by Torgesen (Chapter 10) of reciprocal influences over time between phonological processing skills and word reading in young children illustrates the latter possibility.

Study of Cognitive Development

A further common link between the chapters in this book is an interest in developmental differences. Research summarized in this volume substantiates the fact that young children demonstrate many of the same attentional skills and executive functions as older children or adults (Mirsky, Chapter 6). However, there are clear age-related changes in skill levels, with different skills developing on different growth trajectories. According to the primate literature summarized by Bachevalier et al. (Chapter 11), object discrimination matures prior to visual recognition memory. Similarly, studies by Halperin and colleagues (see Chapter 8) suggest that focused attention matures at an earlier age in children than either sustained attention or response organization. Several other investigations have documented similar task-dependent growth patterns (Becker, Isaac, & Hynd, 1987; Passler, Isaac, & Hynd, 1985; Levin et al., 1991; Welsh, Pennington, & Groisser, 1991). The latter findings indicate that, while attention and executive function can be examined across a wide age range, it may also be important to examine some developmental changes within relatively restricted age spans (Welsh & Pennington, 1988).

The mechanisms responsible for these changes are largely unknown but of substantial relevance to the study of both normal and abnormal development. Developmental changes in executive function may be related to protracted cortical maturation, especially in the tertiary association areas (Eslinger, Chapter 20; Stuss, 1992; Thatcher, 1991). At the level of psychological constructs, age-related improvements in these skills may also reflect more extended planning prior to motor output, more complex language or other representational codes, or greater automatization of lower-level skills (Barkley, Chapter 17; Borkowski & Burke, Chapter 14; Denckla, Chapter 15; Eslinger, Chapter 20; Hayes, Gifford, & Ruckstuhl, Chapter 16). Whatever the mechanism, cognitive deficits early in life pose risks for the later-developing skills. For children with ADHD or early brain injuries, deficits tend to change over time, with some problems not apparent until later childhood or adolescence (Barkley, Chapter 17; Eslinger, Chapter 20; Grattan & Eslinger, 1991).

Awareness of Environmental Influences on Cognition

A final collective message of the present volume is that there are important environmental influences on test performance. Relatively little is known about environmental effects on cognitive abilities other than IQ (Carroll & Maxwell, 1979). However, all tests are subject to these influences; hence, environmental factors always must be considered in interpreting test results (Lyon, Chapter 1; Taylor & Schatschneider, 1992).

Environmental factors are relevant to test performance in several ways. To begin with, stimulus conditions and response contingencies constitute essential elements of all test procedures (McIlvane, Dube, & Callahan, Chapter 7). Minor alterations in instructions, preparatory set, or stimulus conditions sometimes can have marked effects on test outcomes (Barkley, Chapter 4). Test interpretation is likewise threatened if instructional sets are inadequately established or if customary social reinforcers are insufficient to ensure compliance. A related issue is that the stimulus conditions and response contingencies in place during formal testing typically differ from those present at home or school. This mismatch may be one reason for the well-known insensitivity of some clinical tests to deficits in attention or executive function among individuals with ADHD or frontal lobe lesions (Barkley, 1991; Shallice & Burgess, 1991).

An individual's previous learning history is also likely to have some bearing on cognitive performance. Rumbaugh and Washburn (Chapter 12) report dramatic effects of carefully sequenced, computer-based activities on the laboratory performances of chimpanzees. Their findings, which have clear implications for human development, indicate that learning is facilitated by stable social environments that provide for graded behavioral challenges, prompt and reliable response consequences, diverse skill applications, and some degree of self-control over activities. Links between early attachment patterns and later self-regulatory behaviors also suggest effects of early experiences on cognitive abilities (Borkowski & Dukewich, in press).

The success of methods for training attentional skills and executive functioning in individuals with developmental disabilities constitutes a third type of evidence for environmental influences (Borkowski & Burke, Chapter 14; Graham & Harris, Chapter 19; McIlvane et al., Chapter 7). Assessment of responsiveness to training is an alternative to more traditional psychological testing and may yield information on higher-level information-processing capacities (i.e., "learning to learn" skills) not tapped by tests of already acquired skills (Brown & Ferrara, 1985). Training procedures based on the principles of applied behavior analysis have also proved useful in evaluating persons with limited verbal abilities (McIlvane et al., Chapter 7; Rumbaugh & Washburn, Chapter 12).

CONCLUSIONS AND FUTURE DIRECTIONS

As evident from this overview, the study of attention, memory, and executive function has expanded considerably in recent years. Investigators from the diverse disciplines represented in this book share a common interest in these ability domains. There is increasing recognition that attention, memory, and executive function are distinct from other aspects of mental functioning and that research in this area is critical to an understanding of learning and behavior disorders. There is also a consensus of opinion favoring more careful analysis of component processes within each of these domains, more highly specified theoretical formulations, and greater attention to construct validity and measurement issues. Although consistent with the principles of psychological science (Kimble, 1989), this consensus represents a significant conceptual advance over previous approaches to research in this area. Additional areas of interdisciplinary convergence evident in this volume include interests in the brain mechanisms underlying test performance, associated clinical disorders and developmental processes, and environmental influences.

Despite their differing methods and orientation, the disciplines of neuropsychology, information processing or cognitive psychology, and behavior analysis have a good deal to learn from one another. Contributions from each discipline are best viewed as complementary or mutually reinforcing. Judging from the present chapters, there is a clear trend for cross-disciplinary exchanges of methods and for recognition of commonalities in concepts. Examples of this trend include adaptations of information processing paradigms by neuropsychologists (Halperin, Chapter 8), applications of behavioral analytical methods in the study of neurological disorders (McIlvane et al., Chapter 7), and the attention that both neuropsychologists and behavior analysts have given to the critical role of verbal mediation and "rule-governed" behavior in executive functioning (Barkley, Chapter 17; Denckla, Chapter 15; Hayes et al., Chapter 16). Studies of linkages between cognitive and neurophysiological substrates, via techniques such as positron emission tomography and functional magnetic resonance imaging, is a further example of the benefits of interdisciplinary cross-fertilization. Integration of methods and knowledge across disciplines also better serve the broader goals of research in this area, as outlined by the biobehavioral systems framework described earlier.

Future research directions are likely to entail a continued emphasis on this more integrated approach. One specific need is for further inquiry into the construct validity of component cognitive processes. Both latent variable modeling and task analysis will be useful in this regard (Embretson, 1983; Fletcher et al., Chapter 3; Taylor et al., in press). We also need to enhance our understanding of the cognitive underpinnings of more complex behavior disorders. Impairments in knowledge application, planning, self-awareness, pragmatic language, and social behavior associated with frontal lobe lesions are cases in point (Dennis, 1991; Borkowski & Burke, Chapter 14; Grattan & Eslinger, 1991; Shallice & Burgess, 1991; Stuss, 1992). Other worthwhile research endeavors include more detailed studies of developmental change, especially in association with early brain insults or developmental disabilities, design of "process-sensitive" assessment techniques, and investigations of environmental influences on cognitive function and of cognitive modifiability. The prospects for significant advances are excellent.

REFERENCES

Alexander, G.E., DeLong, M.R., & Strick, P.L. (1986). Parallel organization of functionally segregated circuits linking basal ganglia to cortex. *Annual Review of Neuroscience, 9*, 357–381.

Barkley, R.A. (1991). The ecological validity of laboratory and analogue assessment methods of ADHD symptoms. *Journal of Abnormal Child Psychology, 19*, 149–178.

Barkley, R.A., Grodzinsky, G., & DuPaul, G. (1992). Frontal lobe functions in attention deficit disorder with and without hyperactivity: A review and research report. *Journal of Abnormal Child Psychology, 20*, 163–188.

Becker, M.G., Isaac, W., & Hynd, G.W. (1987). Neuropsychological development of nonverbal behaviors attributed to "frontal lobe" functioning. *Developmental Neuropsychology, 3*, 275–298.

Borkowski, J.G., & Dukewich, T.L. (in press). Environmental covariations and intelligence: How attachment influences self-regulation. In D.K. Detterman (Ed.), *Current topics in human intelligence*. Norwood, NJ: Ablex.

Brouwers, P., & Poplack, D. (1990). Memory and learning sequelae in long-term survivors of acute lymphoblastic leukemia: Association with attention deficits. *The American Journal of Pediatric Hematology/Oncology, 12*, 174–181.

Brown, A.L., & Ferrara, R.A. (1985). Diagnosing zones of proximal development. In J.V. Wertsch (Ed.), *Culture, communication, and cognition: Vygotskian perspectives* (pp. 273–305). New York: Cambridge University Press.

Carroll, J.B., & Maxwell, S.E. (1979). Individual differences in cognitive abilities. *Annual Review of Psychology, 30*, 603–640.

Cummings, J.L. (1993). Frontal-subcortical circuits and human behavior. *Archives of Neurology, 50*, 873–880.

de Jong, P.F., & Das-Smaal, E.A. (1995). Attention and intelligence: The validity of the Star Counting Test. *Journal of Educational Psychology, 87*, 80–92.

Denckla, M.B. (1989). Executive function, the overlap zone between attention deficit hyperactivity disorder and learning disabilities. *International Pediatrics, 4*, 155–160.

Dennis, M. (1991). Frontal lobe function in childhood and adolescence: A heuristic for assessing attention regulation, executive control, and the intentional states important for social discourse. *Developmental Neuropsychology, 7*, 327–358.

Embretson, S. (1983). Construct validity: Construct representation versus nomothetic span. *Psychological Bulletin, 93*, 179–197.

Fletcher, J.M., & Taylor, H.G. (1984). Neuropsychological approaches to children: Towards a developmental neuropsychology. *Journal of Clinical Neuropsychology, 6*, 24–37.

Fletcher, J.M., Taylor, H.G., Levin, H.S., & Satz, P. (1995). Neuropsychological and intellectual assessment of children. In H.I. Kaplan & B.J. Sadock (Eds.), *Comprehensive textbook of psychiatry/VI* (pp. 581–601). Baltimore: Williams & Wilkins.

Francis, D.J. (1988). An introduction to structural equation models. *Journal of Clinical and Experimental Neuropsychology, 10*, 623–639.

Goldman-Rakic, P.S. (1988). Topography of cognition: Parallel distributed networks in primate association cortex. *Annual Review of Neuroscience, 11*, 137–156.

Grattan, L.M., & Eslinger, P.J. (1991). Frontal lobe damage in children and adults: A comparative review. *Developmental Neuropsychology, 7*, 283–326.

Hooks, K., Milich, R., & Lorch, E.P. (1994). Sustained and selective attention in boys with attention deficit hyperactivity disorder. *Journal of Clinical Child Psychology, 23*, 69–77.

Kimble, G.A. (1989). Psychology from the standpoint of a generalist. *American Psychologist, 44*, 491–499.

Krasnegor, N.A., Lyon, G.A., & Goldman-Rakic, P.S. (Eds.). (in press). *Development of the prefrontal cortex: Evolution, neurology, and behavior.* Baltimore: Paul H. Brookes Publishing Co.

Levin, H.S., Culhane, D.A., Hartmann, J., Evankovich, K., Mattson, A.J., Harward, H., Ringholz, G., Ewing-Cobbs, L., & Fletcher, J.M. (1991). Developmental changes in performance on tests of purported frontal lobe functioning. *Developmental Neuropsychology, 7*, 377–395.

Levin, H.S., Culhane, K.A., Mendelsohn, D., Lilly, M.A., Bruce, D., Fletcher, J.M., Chapman, S.B., Harward, H., & Eisenberg, H.M. (1993). Cognition in relation to magnetic resonance imaging in head-injured children and adolescents. *Archives of Neurology, 50*, 897–905.

Levin, H.S., Mendelsohn, D., Lilly, M.A., Fletcher, J.M., Culhane, K.A., Chapman, S.B., Harward, H., Kusnerik, L., Bruce, D., & Eisenberg, H.M. (1994). Tower of London performance in relation to magnetic resonance imaging following closed head injury in children. *Neuropsychology, 8*, 171–179.

Levin, H.S., Soukup, V.M., Benton, A.L., Fletcher, J.M., & Satz, P. (1995). Neuropsychological and intellectual assessment of adults. In H.I. Kaplan & B.J. Sadock (Eds.), *Comprehensive textbook of psychiatry/VI* (pp. 562–581). Baltimore: Williams & Wilkins.

Lezak, M. (1983). *Neuropsychological assessment* (2nd ed.). New York: Oxford.

Lyon, G.R. (Ed.). (1994). *Frames of reference for the assessment of learning disabilities: New views on measurement issues.* Baltimore: Paul H. Brookes Publishing Co.

Morris, R.D., & Fletcher, J.M. (1988). Classification in neuropsychology: A theoretical framework and research paradigm. *Journal of Clinical and Experimental Neuropsychology, 10*, 640–658.

Pardo, J.V., Fox, P.T., & Raichle, M.E. (1991). Localization of a human system for sustained attention by positron emission tomography. *Nature, 349*, 61–63.

Passler, M.A., Isaac, W., & Hynd, G.W. (1985). Neuropsychological development of behavior attributed to frontal lobe functioning in children. *Developmental Neuropsychology, 1*, 349–370.

Pedhazur, E.J., & Schmelking, L.P. (1991). *Measurement, design, and analysis: An integrative approach.* Hillsdale, NJ: Lawrence Erlbaum Associates.

Pennington, B.F. (1991). *Diagnosing learning disorders: A neuropsychological framework.* New York: Guilford.

Pennington, B.F. (in press). The working memory function of the prefrontal cortices: Implications for developmental and individual differences in cognition. In M.M. Haith, J. Benson, R. Roberts, & B.F. Pennington (Eds.), *Future oriented processes in development.* Chicago: University of Chicago Press.

Pennington, B.F., Groisser, D., & Welsh, M.C. (1993). Contrasting cognitive deficits in attention deficit hyperactivity disorder versus reading disability. *Developmental Psychology, 29*, 511–523.

Posner, M.I., & Petersen, S.E. (1990). The attention system of the human brain. *Annual Review of Neuroscience, 13*, 25–42.

Rezai, K., Andreasen, N., Alliger, R., Cohen, G., Swayze, V., & O'Leary, D.S. (1993). The neuropsychology of the prefrontal cortex. *Archives of Neurology, 50*, 636–642.

Shallice, T. (1979). The case study approach in neuropsychological research. *Journal of Clinical Neuropsychology, 1*, 183–211.

Shallice, T., & Burgess, P.W. (1991). Deficits in strategy application following frontal lobe damage in man. *Brain, 114*, 727–741.

Stanovich, K.E. (1986). Cognitive process and the reading problems of learning disabled children: Evaluating the assumption of specificity. In J.K. Torgesen & B.L. Wong (Eds.), *Psychological and educational perspectives on reading disabilities* (pp. 87–131). New York: Academic Press.

Stuss, D.T. (1992). Biological and psychological development of executive functions. *Brain and Cognition, 20*, 8–23.

Tannock, R., Schachar, R., & Logan, G. (1995). Methylphenidate and cognitive flexibility: Dissociated dose effects in hyperactive children. *Journal of Abnormal Child Psychology, 23*, 235–266.

Taylor, H.G., & Fletcher, J.M. (1990). Neuropsychological assessment of children. In M. Hersen & G. Goldstein (Eds.), *Handbook of psychological assessment* (2nd ed., pp. 228–255). New York: Plenum Press.

Taylor, H.G., & Schatschneider, C. (1992). Child neuropsychological assessment: A test of basic assumptions. *The Clinical Neuropsychologist, 6*, 259–275.

Taylor, H.G., Schatschneider, C., Petrill, S., Barry, C.T., & Owens, C. (in press). Executive dysfunction in children with early brain disease: Outcomes post *Haemophilus influenzae* meningitis. *Developmental Neuropsychology*.

Thatcher, R.W. (1991). Maturation of the human frontal lobes: Physiological evidence for staging. *Developmental Neuropsychology, 7*, 397–419.

Welsh, M.C., & Pennington, B.F. (1988). Assessing frontal lobe functioning in children: Views from developmental psychology. *Developmental Neuropsychology, 4*, 199–230.

Welsh, M.C., Pennington, B.F., & Groisser, D.B. (1991). A normative-developmental study of executive function: A window on prefrontal function in children. *Developmental Neuropsychology, 7*, 131–149.

Yeates, K.O., Blumenstein, E., Patterson, C.M., & Delis, D.C. (1995). Verbal learning and memory following pediatric closed-head injury. *Journal of the International Neuropsychological Society, 1*, 78–87.

Yeates, K.O., & Bornstein, R.A. (1994). Attention deficit disorder and neuropsychological functioning in children with Tourette's syndrome. *Neuropsychology, 8*, 65–74.

Yeates, K.O., Enrile, B.G., Loss, N., Blumenstein, E., & Delis, D.C. (in press). Verbal learning and memory in children with myelomeningocele. *Journal of Pediatric Psychology*.

Zola-Morgan, S., & Squire, L.R. (1993). Neuroanatomy of memory. *Annual Review of Neuroscience, 16*, 547–563.

INDEX

Page numbers followed by "t" or "f" indicate tables or figures, respectively.

Absence attacks, 71, 85
Activation, 64
Adaptation to environment, 200
Additive factor method (AFM), 58–61, 119
ADHD, *see* Attention deficit hyperactivity disorder
Affect, separation of, 314–315, 379
Affective problems, 349
AFM, *see* Additive factor method
Alcohol exposure, fetal, 78, 88–89, 89t, 92
Amnesia
  in brain-injured persons, 142–143, 145–147, 186–187, 189, 192–193, 225
  global anterograde, 186–187
  infantile, 192
Amphetamines, 65
Antecedent attribution training, 251–252
Antisaccade task (AST), 343–344, 382
Arithmetic Test, 82, 83t–84t
Arousal, 64, 126, 342–343
Articulatory control process, 161
Articulatory loop, *see* Phonological loop
Articulatory suppression effect, 162, 223
Asphyxia neonatorum, 78
Assessment, *see* Measurement tools
AST, *see* Antisaccade task
Attention, 43–133
  behavioral analytical approach to, 97–115, 122–123
    see also Stimulus control
  comparison of approaches to, 45, 123–125
  components of, 125–127, 308–309
  concentration and, 61–62
  converging trends in research on, 46, 52–54
  definitions of, 47–49, 97, 307–308

  development and, 14–15, 65–67, 120, 129–130
  drug effects and, 65
  encoding and, 59–60, 60t, 64, 78
  evolutionary perspective on, 72–74, 72f–73f, 120–121
  experimental analysis of, 98
  four- and five-factor models of, 76–77, 78t, 121
  functions of, 309
  genetic contributions to, 53–54
  history of theories of, 47–50, 57–59
  impact on learning and behavior, 1–2, 202
    see also Learning
  importance of, 1–2
  information processing (cognitive) approach to, 57–67, 119–120
  instructional control of, 112–114, 113t
  involuntary aspects of, 48
  limitations of theories of, 50
  linkages between executive function and, 14, 39, 46, 57, 258–259, 259f, 307–324, 392
    conceptual, 321–322
    differentiating conditions, 311–314
    neuroanatomical, 323
    neuropsychological, 322–323
    theoretical, 323–324
  localization of attention functions in brain, 75–76, 76f
  models of brain's attention system, 78–81
    Heilman et al./Mesulam model, 80, 81f
    Mirsky et al. model, 14, 39, 47, 80–81, 121–122, 402
    Posner and Petersen model, 79–80
    Pribram and McGuiness model, 78–79

Attention—*continued*
  motivation and, 47, 48
  neuropsychological approach to, 53, 59,
    71–93, 120–122, 130–131,
    322–323
  operationalizations of, 59–61, 60*t*
    additive factor method, 58–61, 60*t*
    cognitive energetics, 63–65
    selective attention, 61–63
    sustained attention, 63
  passive, active, and voluntary, 47
  relationship with memory and executive
    function, 14, 39, 46, 57, 258–259,
    259*f*, 307–324, 392
  selective (focused), 57, 61–63, 122–123,
    126–127, 308
    additive factor method and, 61
    dual task methodology, 62
    priority allocation and control, 62
    resource model of, 61–62
    theories of, 58, 61
  self-regulated strategy development for
    problems with, 357–358
  sensorial versus intellectual, 47
  shift of, 77, 121, 357
  stability of, 78, 121
  statistical concept of correlation and,
    308
  studies in epilepsy, 71–72, 74–75, 75*f*
  subject factors influencing, 53
  sustained, 18, 47, 57, 63, 76–77,
    122–123, 126–127, 207, 357
    developmental differences in, 129–130
Attention deficit hyperactivity disorder
  (ADHD), 1, 78, 264
  executive function deficits in, 321, 328,
    329*t*, 330, 371, 399–400, 406
  impulse control and, 46
  inheritance of, 53–54
  internalization of language in, 317
  measures of attention in children with,
    50–52
  P300 studies in, 85
  primates as natural models for, 202–204,
    227–228
    attending to salience, 203–204
  reading disability and, 30, 334
  theories of, 46–47
  types of attention deficits in, 132
Attention disorders, 131–133, 399–400
  childhood conditions associated with,
    78, 79*t*

  clinical diagnosis and, 131–133
  due to selective vs. focused deficits, 61
  interventions for, 132
    behavior analytical procedures,
      132–133
    stimulants, 132
  theories of etiology in children, 78
Attention measurement, 11–14, 81–91,
  123–125, 127–129
  application in clinical research, 85–91
    attention profiles in seizure disorders,
      85–86, 86*f*–87*f*
    fetal alcohol exposure, 88–89, 89*t*
    Johns Hopkins–NIMH Epidemiologi-
      cal Study, 89–91, 90*t*, 91*f*–92*f*
    prediction of schizophrenia spectrum
      disorders, 86–88, 88*f*
  behavioral analytical approach to, 124
  cognitive approach to, 123–124
  criteria for selection or development of,
    82, 83*t*–84*t*, 128–129
  limitations of tests for, 54, 127–128
  neuropsychological approach to,
    124–125
  psychophysiological methods for, 83–85
  subjective behavioral observations for,
    54, 127–128
  tools to measure Mirsky model and con-
    structs, 81–82
  trends in, 50–52
"Attentional set," 58
Attitudinal problems, 349
Auditory Analysis Test, 35*t*, 38*t*
Auditory Discrimination in Depth, 176
Augmenting, 291–292, 297, 316
Autism, 328, 329*t*, 330, 371, 399

Balance-beam task, 241–242
Barbiturates, 65
Beery-Buktenica Test, 271
Behavioral approach, 3
  to attention, 97–115, 122–123
    see also Stimulus control
  to executive function, 279–300,
    309–310, 375–376
  to memory, 199–217, 227–228
    see also Learning
Behavioral checklists, 13
Behavioral psychologies, 97
Bender-Gestalt Test, 270
Block Sort task, 282

"Bootstraps effect," 18, 19
Boston Naming Test, 34, 35*t*, 38*t*
Brain, 405–406
  centrencephalic system of, 74, 75
  complexity and plasticity of, 201–202
  electrical activity of, 53, 83–85
  evolutionary perspective of, 72–74,
    72*f*–73*f*, 120–121
  localization of attention functions in,
    75–76, 76*f*
  locus of word priming in, 153
  models of attention system of, 78–81,
    130–131
  neural circuits for memories and habits,
    188–190, 188*f*
  prefrontal lobe function, 52, 263–264,
    319–320, 327–331
    see also Executive function
  timing of developmental changes in,
    330, 386
  "triune brain" concept, 72–73, 72*f*
Brain and Language, 13
Brain lesion, 399
  attention and, 53, 130–131
  executive function and, 263–264, 275
  Kennard Effect and, 386
  memory and, 142–143, 145–147,
    186–187, 189, 192–193
Brown-Peterson task, 144

California Achievement Test (CAT), 91, 92
California Verbal Learning Test, 267*t*, 274
Cancellation tests, 13, 268*t*
CAT, *see* California Achievement Test
Central executive, 158*f*, 159–160, 222
Central nervous system
  brain evolution, 72–74, 72*f*–73*f*, 120–121
  centrencephalic system, 74, 75*f*
  levels of differentiation or integration of
    functioning of, 74
  localization of attention functions in
    brain, 75–76, 76*f*, 130–131
  neural circuits for memories and habits,
    188*f*, 188–190
Central-incidental learning tasks, 13
Cerebral blood flow studies, 53, 391
Child Development, 13
Chunking strategy, 163
CNV, *see* Contingent Negative Variation
"Cocktail party phenomenon," 205
Coding Test, 13, 83*t*–84*t*, 90

Cognition
  development of, 407–408
  domains of, 399
  environmental influences on, 408
Cognitive assessment, 399
  biobehavioral systems approach to,
    400–401
  clinical applications of, 406–407
  limitations of, 402
    see also Measurement tools
Cognitive energetics, 61, 63–65, 120, 402
Combinatorial entailment, 288–289
Concentration, 61–62
  shyness or aggessiveness and, 90, 91*f*
Confirmatory factor analysis, 22–25, 404
  advantages of, 23, 25, 39
  compared with exploratory common
    factor methods, 24–25, 39
  definition of, 22–23
  errors of measurement in, 25
  estimating factor scores in, 29
  flexibility of, 25
  steps in, 25–29, 26*t*
  used in Yale Center for Learning and
    Attention Disorders study, 29–37
Conflicting Motor Response, 329*t*
Consensual validation, 20
Conservation, 316
Construct representation, 403–404
Construct validity, 17–19, 403–404
  aspects of, 20
  "bootstraps effect" and, 18–19
  construct underrepresentation and, 18
  definition of, 17
  evaluation of, 22–29
    data reduction, 23
    exploratory versus confirmatory
      methods, 23–25
    redundancy, 23
  insufficient attention to, 20
  latent variables and, 18
  "mono-operation bias" and, 19
  relation to internal validity of study,
    18–19
  scaling issues and, 22
  steps in, 21*t*, 21–22
  surplus construct irrelevancies and, 18
Contingency analysis, 98–99
  procedures for establishing by three-
    term contingencies, 108–109
  three-term, 105–108, 106*f*–108*f*, 123
  two-term, 104–105, 105*f*

Contingency Naming Test, 268*t*, 271, 329*t*
Contingent Negative Variation (CNV), 84
Continuous performance tasks, 13, 50
  effect of setting on, 52
  effect of stimulus parameters on, 51
  types of errors on, 51
  variations in response formats for,
    51–52
Continuous Performance Test (CPT), 82,
    83*t*–84*t*, 90, 90*t*, 92, 329*t*
  for children with fetal alcohol exposure,
    89, 89*t*
  for persons with seizure disorders, 86,
    87*f*
Controlled Oral Word Association, 267*t*,
    282, 375
Corsi Blocks, 35*t*, 38*t*, 329*t*
Cumulative rehearsal strategy, 163

Data reduction, 23, 28–29
"Day/Night" Test, 271
Decision making, 60, 160
Decision-time test, 13
Decoding Skills Test–Real Words, 33*t*
Delayed nonmatching-to-sample task,
    190–191, 193
Delayed responding, 46–47, 52, 314–321,
    379, 381, 402
  capacities necessary for, 314, 379
    as executive functions, 318–319
    internalization of language, 316–317
    prolongation, 315–316
    reconstitution, 317–318
    separation of affect, 314–315
  development and, 320–321
  neuroanatomical mediation of, 319–320
  theory of, 314
    see also Stimulus control
Delayed S+ procedure, 110, 111*f*
Derived stimulus relations, 285–286, 286*f*
Development, 14–15
  attention and, 65–67, 120, 129–130
  delayed responding and, 320–321
  executive function and, 264–265,
    320–321, 385–387
  memory and, 190–192
  rule governance and, 297
Developmental psychology, 46, 52–53
Developmental Test of Visual-Motor
    Integration–Revised, 36*t* 38*t*
Dichotic listening tasks, 13

Digit Cancellation Test, 83*t*–84*t*, 90*t*
Digit Span Test, 13, 82, 83*t*–84*t*
  in brain-injured persons, 142, 146
  cognitive strategies to enhance perfor-
    mance on, 163
  factors affecting performance on,
    162–163
  long-term memory and, 144
Digit Symbol Substitution Test, 82
Discriminant validity, 21, 328–332, 371
Discrimination, 48
Dopamine depletion disorders, 330–331
Dual-task performance, 206–207

Economy of processing, 62
Educational Psychology, 13
Effort, 63–64
Embedded Figures Test, 13, 36*t*, 38*t*
Embedded Phonemes Test, 36*t*, 38*t*
Emotional problems, 349
Encoding, 59–60, 60*t*, 64, 77, 121
Environmental influences on cognition,
    408
Epilepsy, 71–72, 74–75, 75*f*, 85–86,
    86*f*–87*f*
Equivalence, 48
Errors of measurement, 25
Event-related potentials, 13, 84–85, 153
Executive function, 233–392
  attention, memory, and, 14, 39, 46, 57,
    258–259, 259*f*, 307–324, 378–379,
    392
    conceptual linkages, 321–322
    neuroanatomical linkages, 323
    neuropsychological linkages, 322–323
    theoretical linkages, 323–324
  behavioral approach to, 279–300,
    309–310, 375–376
    nature of verbal regulation, 284–292,
      see also Verbal regulation
    relational frame theory, 287–290, *see
      also* Relational frame theory
    rule governance, 292–298, 316–317,
      see also Rule governance
    testing of, 298–300
  Bransford and Stein's IDEAL problem
    solver and, 242–243
  Butterfield and Albertson's theory of,
    241–242, 241*f*
  comparison of theories of, 309–311,
    368–369, 369*f*, 403

conditions associated with impairment
of, 264, 328, 329*t*, 330, 371
critical conditions differentiating attention from, 311–314
deficits in attention deficit hyperactivity disorder, 321, 328, 329*t*, 330, 371
definitions of, 244–245, 279–280, 292, 309–310, 327–328, 369–373, 375, 378–379
comparison of, 380–381
delayed responding and, 314–321, 379, *see also* Delayed responding
development and, 14–15, 264–265, 320–321, 385–387
future research directions related to, 259–260, 371–374, 376, 378–379
general giftedness and, 235–236, 245–246
impairments of, 399–400
importance of, 1–2, 363–364
information processing approach to, 235–260, 310, 369–371
intelligence and, 235–236, 257
major components of, 236, 237*f*, 403
motivational correlates of, 251
natural course of impairments over life span, 387–388, 389*t*
neuropsychological approach to, 263–276, 310–311, 322–323, 371–374
discriminant validity problem with, 328–332, 371
populations most relevant to testing of, 275
primary constructs of, 265–267
studies leading to abandonment of, 275–276
prefrontal lobe and, 391–392, *see also* Prefrontal lobe function
prefrontal lobe function and, 263–264
problems in operationalization of, 267
promising research approaches to, 252–256
Butterfield and Albertson's instructional approach, 253–256, 254*f*–255*f*
structural modeling approach, 256
role in metacognitive theory, 237–241, 238*f*–240*f*
Scholnick and Friedman's developmental theory of planning and, 243–244
self-attributions and, 251–252

self-regulated strategy development for problems with, 359–360
self-regulation, planning and, 256–258
social aspects of, 389–390, 391*f*
in students with learning disabilities, 246–251
changing task demands and executive skills, 247–248
self-instructions and executive processing, 246–247
single-subject designs, changing task demands, and executive processing, 248–251, 250*f*
working memory construct for, 327–345, 383–385, *see also* Memory, working
Executive function measurement, 11–14, 267–274, 280–284, 372
behavioral approach to, 376
commonly used instruments for, 267*t*–268*t*
comparison of approaches to, 381–383
core of, 282–284
criteria for selection and development of tests for, 273–274, 381
general intelligence, 268–269, 332
information processing approach to, 370–371
integrity of cognitive processes, 269
measurable elements of tasks for, 381
mediating role of language, 269–273
neuropsychological approach to, 372–374
new approaches to, 343–345
problems with, 332–337, 345
self-regulated strategy development and, 377–378
Exploratory factor analysis, 22–24, 39

Fetal alcohol exposure, 78, 88–89, 89*t*, 92
Focusing of consciousness, 47, 48, 76, 121, *see also* Attention
Formal operational thinking, 316
Formal Reading Inventory (FRI), 33*t*
Fragile X syndrome in females, 275, 328, 329*t*, 330, 371
FRI, *see* Formal Reading Inventory
Frontal lobe function, *see* Executive function; Prefrontal lobe function

Galvanic skin response (GSR), 53

Generalization of learning, 204–208, 210, 251–252, 370
Genetic influences, 91–92
  in attention deficit hyperactivity disorder, 53–54, 78
Giftedness, 235–236, 245–246
Goal orientation, 258
Go/No-Go Task, 267t, 272f–273f, 329t, 381
Gordon Vigilance Task, 329t
GORT, see Gray Oral Reading Test
Gray Oral Reading Test–Revised (GORT), 33t

Halstead-Reitan Scale, 82
Huntington's disease, 330

IDEAL problem solver model, 242–243
Impulsivity, 349, 350
Information processing approach, 3, 49, 51, 59
  to attention, 57–67, 119–120
  controlled vs. automatic processing, 61, 63
  to executive function, 235–260, 310, 369–371
  to memory, 157–180, 222–224
Inhibition, 258, 284, 316, 327, 381
  working memory and, 343
  see also Delayed responding; Stimulus control
Intelligence, 37
  executive processes and, 235–236, 245–246
  frontal lobe damage and, 386
  self-regulation and, 257
  tests of, 268–269, 332
Internal validity, 18–19
Internalization of language, 316–317, 379
Item coding, 160
Item response theory, 22, 404

Johns Hopkins–NIMH Epidemiological Study, 89–91, 90t, 91f–92f
Journal of Clinical and Consulting Neuropsychology, 13
Judgment of Line Orientation, 35t, 38t

Kennard Effect, 386

Language
  analysis of, 317–318, 379
  internalization of, 316–317, 379
  learning of, 210–214, 228
  mediating role of, 269–273
  processing of, 142, 145
  reconstitution of, 317–318, 379
  synthesis of, 317–318
  verbal regulation, 284–292
  see also Verbal regulation
Language Research Center's Computerized Test System (LRC-CTS), 202, 203f, 208–210
  benefits of, 210
  description of tasks of, 208–210
  training curriculum using, 208
Lead poisoning, 78, 92
"Learned helplessness," 214
Learning, 199–217, 227–228
  adaptation perspective of perception and memory in relation to, 200–208
  attention and, 1–2, 202
    primates as natural models for attention deficit hyperactivity disorder, 202–204, 227f–228f
  brain complexity and plasticity and, 201–202
  generalization of, 204–208, 210, 251–252, 370
  how to generalize via training in diverse contexts, 204–208
    dual-task performance, 206–207
    resource allocation, 206
    selective tracking, 205
    Stroop effect, 205–206
    sustained performance, 207
    vigilance, 207
    visual search, 207–208
  of language, 210–214, 212f, 228
  Language Research Center's Computerized Test System for, 202, 203f, 208–210
  nonword, 165
  one-trial discrimination learning, 110–112
  perceived control and, 214–215
  of predictive relationships, 200–201
  primate research on, 199–217, 227–228
  procedural, 402, 405
  schedules of reinforcement for, 201
  supra-learning, 215–216
Learning disabilities, 399–400

Learning Disability Quarterly, 13
Lexical decision task, 152
LISREL VII, 27–29, 32, 34
Locus coeruleus, 130–131

Magnetic resonance imaging, 53, 391
Malnutrition, 78
Matching Familiar Figures Test, 13, 329*t*
Maternal alcohol consumption, 78, 88–89, 89*t*, 92
Mathematics disability, 30
  self-regulated strategy development for, 362
Measurement tools, 11–14
  analysis of component behaviors required for completion of, 13–14
  analysis of task demands and properties of, 404–405
  for attention, 50–52, 81–91, 123–125, 127–129
  construct validation of, 17–22, 403–404
  evaluation of, 22–29
  for executive function, 267*t*–268*t*, 267–274, 280–284, 370–371
  lack of community standards for, 12
  limitations of, 11
  literature review of, 13
  for memory, 151–154, 221, 343–345
  need for test-derived measures, 12
  overlap among, 13
  purposes of, 400–401
Medications, 65
Memory, 137–230
  behavioral approach to, 199–217, 227–228
  see also Learning
  in brain-injured persons, 142–143, 145–147, 186–187, 189, 192–193
  comparing approaches to, 229–230
  converging evidence from brain-behavior studies of, 152–153
  declarative (explicit), 186, 192, 402, 405
  development and, 14–15, 190–192
  echoic, 158
  episodic, 226*t*
  functions of, 157–158, 158*f*
  iconic, 158
  impairments of, 399–400
  importance of, 1–2
  information processing approach to, 157–180, 222–224

interdisciplinary studies of, 139, 151, 154
long-term, 140, 141, 151, 154, 158*f*, 159, 185–186
  fractionation of, 186–188, 224–227
  multiple systems of, 185–186, 224–227, 226*t*
  neural circuits for habits and, 188*f* 188–190
  neuropsychological approach to, 139–140, 154, 185–193, 224–227
  procedural (implicit), 186, 192, 226*t*
  prospective archival, 384
  recognition, 226*t*
  relationship with attention and executive function, 14, 39, 57, 258–259, 392
  self-regulated strategy development for problems with, 358–359
short-term, 139–151, 185–186, 226*t*
  auditory, 158, 160, 186
  capacity for, 148, 150
  changes in traditional concept of, 140
  contemporary conceptualization of, 148–151
  definition of, 148
  demise of modal view of, 140, 143–147
  functions of, 148
  modal view of, 140–143
  recency effect in free recall, 141, 143–144
  role in language processing, 142, 145
  structure of, 149, 149*f*, 151
  visual, 158
working, 48, 149–151, 154, 158*f*, 159, 186, 222, 226*t*, 275, 381, 402
  capacity of, 341
  central executive and slave systems, 159–160, 222
  concept of prolongation and, 315–316
  decay rate of, 342
  definition of, 159, 340, 384
  executive function and, 327–345, 383–385
  factors influencing function of, 340, 341*f*, 342*t*
  function of, 340
  interaction with inhibition, 343
  interconnectivity among elements of, 342
  model of, 341*f*
  new approaches to measurement of, 343–345

Memory—*continued*
   nonspecific arousal of, 342–343
   phonological loop, 149, 154,
      160–180, 222*f*
     see also Phonological loop
   priming activation of, 148–149, 152,
      338, 342
   relation to short-term and long-term
      memory, 340, 341*f*
   theoretical framework for, 337–343
   utilization behavior as loss of, 384
   visuospatial sketchpad, 159–160, 222
Memory measurement, 11–14, 151–154,
   221
   difficulties in, 153–154
   new approaches to, 343–345
   working memory during reading,
      150–151
   in young children, 153
Mental retardation, 235–236
Metabolic disorders, 78
Metacognition
   definition of, 310, 370
   theory of, 237–241, 238*f*–240*f*, 280
   training of, 251–252
Metacomponential functioning, 235–236
Methylphenidate, 85
Milner Maze, 329*t*
Morphological Awareness Test, 35*t*, 38*t*
Motivation
   attention and, 47, 48
   executive function and, 239*f*, 240, 251
   lack of, 349
Motor decision time, 60
Motor sequencing tests, 268*t*, 273
Mutual entailment, 288

National Institute of Child Health and
      Human Development (NICHD), 2
   Conference on Attention, Memory, and
      Executive Function, 2–3, 401–402
Neurofibromatosis-1, 275
Neuroimaging studies, 53, 152–153, 275,
   391
Neuropsychological approach, 3
   to attention, 59, 71–93, 120–122,
      130–131, 322–323
   to executive function, 263–276,
      310–311, 322–323, 371–374
   goal of, 328
   to memory, 139–140, 154, 185–193,
      224–227

NICHD, *see* National Institute of Child
      Health and Human Development
Nomothetic span, 403–404

Object permanence, 316
Objective of book, 6
One-trial discrimination learning (OTDL),
   110–112
Organization of book, 4–6
Orienting response, 126
OTDL, *see* One-trial discrimination
     learning

P300 studies, 85
Paced Auditory Serial Addition Test, 13, 382
Parasitic infection, 78
Parkinson's disease, 330
Peabody Picture Vocabulary Test–Revised,
   34, 35*t*, 38*t*, 83*t*
Perceived control, 214–215
Perceptions, 200
Perceptual processing, 158, 158*f*
Perceptual sensitivity, 63
PET, *see* Positron emission tomography
Phenylketonuria (PKU), 78, 92, 275, 328,
   329*t*, 330, 371
Phonological awareness, 153, 175, 223–224
   definition of, 153
   factors affecting development of,
      175–176
   impairments in, 30
   measures of, 19, 21, 153
   training in, 176–178, 177*t*
Phonological loop, 149, 154, 160–180, 222
   articulatory suppression effect and, 162,
      223
   components of, 160–161
     articulatory control process, 161
     phonological store, 160–161
   function of, 160
   item coding, 160
   measuring functional capacity of,
      162–165, 223
     forward digit span, 164
     forward digit span with visual
       presentation, 164
     forward word span, 164
     nonword repetition, 164–165
     repeated trials, nonword learning, and
       free recall, 165
     sentence repetition, 165

phonological memory problems in children with reading disabilities, 165–174
  causal relationship of, 168–174, 169*f*, 172*t*–173*t*, 174*f*, 175*t*, 178–179
  conceptualization of, 165–168, 167*f*
  phonological similarity effect and, 161, 222–223
  relationships among phonological variables, 175–178, 176*t*–177*t*
  unattended speech effect and, 161, 223
  word length effect and, 161–162, 223
PKU, *see* Phenylketonuria
Planning, 256–258, 327
  see also Executive function
Pliance, 291–292, 297, 316
Pop-out effects, 207–208
Porteus Maze, 53, 329*t*
Positron emission tomography (PET), 152–153
Praxis, 270
Predictive relationships, 200–201
Predictive validity, 21
Prefrontal lobe function, 52, 263–264, 319–320, 327–331
  connectivity with other networks in brain, 341–342, 386
  dimensions of prefrontal tasks, 338–339, 339*t*
  executive function and, 391–392
  new approaches to measurement of, 343–345
  problems with tests of, 332–337, 345
  see also Executive function
Prepset task, 112–114, 113*f*
Priming activation, 148–149, 152, 338, 342
Principal component analysis (PCA), 23–24
Problem-solving skills, lack of, 349
Processing load, 60
Program-specific attribution training, 252
Prolongation, 46, 315–316, 379
Prosaccade Task, 343–344, 344*f*
Psychophysiological measurement of attention, 83–85

Rapid Naming tests, 35*t*–36*t*, 38*t*
Rapid-Alternating-Stimulus-Naming Test, 282–283
Reaction time tasks, 13, 51–52, 58, 120, 127
Reading decoding ability, 19
Reading disabilities

attention deficit hyperactivity disorder and, 30, 334
phonological memory problems and, 165–174
  causal relationship of, 168–174, 169*f*, 172*t*–173*t*, 174*f*, 175*t*, 178–179
  conceptualization of, 165–168, 167*f*
selective attention deficits and, 132
self-regulated strategy development for, 362
Yale Center for Learning and Attention Disorders study of, 29–37
Recency effect in free recall, 141, 143–144
Receptive vocabulary skills, 21
Reconstitution processes, 317–318, 379
Redundancy, 23
Relational frame theory, 287–290, 288*f*–289*f*, 376
  combinatorial entailment, 288–289
  learning of relational frames, 290
  mutual entailment, 288
  testing of, 298–300
  transformation of stimulus functions, 289–290
Report writing strategy, 353–357
Research themes, 402–410
  analysis of task demands and measurement properties, 404–405
  applications to study of clinical disorders, 406–407
  environmental influences on cognition, 408
  future directions of, 409–410
  investigation of central nervous system substrates, 405–406
  need for theoretical formulations and study of construct validity, 402–404
  study of cognitive development, 407–408
Resource allocation, 206
Response bias, 63
Response inhibition, 46–47, 51, 402
Response preparation, 60
Response selection, 60
Rey-Osterrieth Complex Figure Copying, 267*t*, 268*t*, 271, 274, 282, 329*t*
Rule governance, 284–285, 290–291, 316–317, 375–376
  categories of rule following, 291–292, 297, 316
    augmenting, 291–292
    pliance, 291–292
    tracking, 291–292

Rule governance—*continued*
    developmental sequence to, 297
    executive function as subset of, 292–298
        changing rules on basis of outcomes, 297–298
        following rules, 296–297
        selecting among available rules or generating new ones, 293–296

Salience, social, 390
Scaling, 22
Schizophrenia spectrum disorders, 86–88, 88*f*
Seizure disorders, 71–72, 74–75, 75*f*, 85–86, 86*f*–87*f*
Selective tracking, 205
Self-attributions, 251–252
Self-awareness, social, 390
Self-efficacy, 239, 251
Self-esteem, 251
Self-Ordered Pointing Task, 268*t*, 271, 329*t*
Self-regulated strategy development (SRSD), 349–363, 376–378
    anticipating difficulties during process of, 353
    for attention problems, 357–358
    benefits and limitations of, 363
    characteristics of, 352–353
    collaborative learning and, 352–353
    components of, 350–351
    criterion-based instruction for, 353
    definition of executive function, 377
    demands on teachers of, 353
    designing model for, 350, 376–377
    evaluation of, 361–362
        reading and mathematics, 362
        writing, 361–362
    example of report writing strategy, 353–357
    for executive function problems, 359–360
    individualization of, 352
    measurement of executive function during, 377–378
    for memory problems, 358–359
    purposes of, 350
    research directions for, 378
    stages of, 351–352, 377
Self-regulation, 46, 53, 238, 251, 256–258, 314, 319, 349
    social, 389–390, 391*f*
        see also Delayed responding; Executive function; Stimulus control; Verbal regulation
Self-verbalization procedures, 251
Sensitivity, social, 390
Sentence Repetition, 36*t*, 38*t*
Separation of affect, 314–315, 379
Signal detection paradigm, 207
Single photon emission tomography, 53
Six Boxes, 268*t*, 329*t*
Social executors, 389–390, 391*f*
Specific strategy knowledge, 238, 238*f*–240*f*
Speech rate, 144
Speed of Articulation, 35*t*, 38*t*
Spelling strategies, 353
SRSD, *see* Self-regulated strategy development
Star Counting Task, 404
Statistical approaches, 22
Stimulant drugs, 85, 132
Stimulus control, 48, 97–112, 122–123
    attention and, 97, 98
    contingency analysis of, 98–99, 123
        three-term contingencies, 105–108, 106*f*–108*f*
        two-term contingencies, 104–105, 105*f*
    evaluating behavior analytical assumptions about, 103–104
    malleability of, 102, 123
    procedures for establishing by three-term contingencies, 108–109
    shaping of, 102, 109*f*, 109–112
        delayed S+ procedure, 110, 111*f*
        one-trial discrimination learning, 110–112
    source of new forms of, 102
    theoretical analysis of, 99*t*, 99–103
        assumptions specific to antecedent stimulus control, 100–103
        general assumptions, 100, 101*f*
    topographies of, 102
    variables affecting development of, 98–99, 99*f*
        see also Delayed responding
Stimulus equivalence, 285–286, 286*f*
Stimulus-response compatibility, 60
Strategy monitoring, 236, 237*f*, 239, 370
Strategy revision, 236, 237*f*, 370
Strategy selection, 236, 237*f*, 238, 370

Strategy use-performance relationship, 238, 238*f*
Stroop effect, 205–206
Stroop test, 13, 39, 82, 103, 267*t*, 271, 281, 283, 292, 329*t*, 375, 381
Structural equations analysis, 23, 39, 404
Subtractive method, 58
Sustained performance, 207
  see also Attention, sustained

Talland Letter Cancellation Test, 82, 87, 89*t*
Tapping Test, 282–283
Task analysis, 236, 237*f*, 370
Task variables, 59–61, 60*t*
Temporal Order Memory test, 268*t*, 271
Test of Written Spelling, 33*t*
Theoretical formulations, 402–404
Tinker Toy Test, 268*t*
Tongue Twisters, 35*t*, 38*t*
Tower of Hanoi, 268*t*, 272, 281–282, 328, 329*t*, 332, 375
Tower of London, 53, 268*t*, 272
Tower of Toronto, 268*t*, 272
Tracking, 291–292, 297, 316
Trail Making Test, 13, 82, 282, 329*t*
Transfer of learning, 370. *See also* Generalization of learning
"Triune brain" concept, 72*f*, 72–73
Turner syndrome, 275
Types I and II errors, 23

Unattended speech effect, 161, 223
Underlining tests, 35*t*, 38*t*, 268*t*
Utilization behavior, 384

Verbal fluency tests, 269, 272, 329*t*
Verbal regulation, 284–292, 375–376
  categories of rule following, 291–292
  derived stimulus relations, 285
  empirical background within behavioral research tradition, 284–286
  relational frame theory, 287–290, 288*f*–289*f*
    combinatorial entailment, 288–289
    learning of relational frames, 290
    mutual entailment, 288
    testing of, 298–300

transformation of stimulus functions, 289–290
  rule governance, 284–285, 290–291, 316–317
    executive function as subset of, 292–298
  see also Rule governance
Vigilance, 207
Visual habit formation, 188–190, 188*f*
Visual imagery, 359
Visual recognition memory development, 190–192
Visual Search Test, 207–208, 268*t*, 282, 329*t*
Visuospatial sketchpad, 159–160, 222, 224

WAIS–R, *see* Wechsler Adult Intelligence Scale–Revised
WCST, *see* Wisconsin Card Sorting Test
Wechsler Adult Intelligence Scale–Revised (WAIS-R), 82, 268
Wechsler Intelligence Scale for Children–Revised (WISC-R), 13, 30, 35*t*, 36*t*, 38*t*, 90, 90*t*, 163
"What is it?" reflex, 48
Wide Range Achievement Test (WRAT), 33*t*
Windows Task, 329*t*
WISC-R, *see* Wechsler Intelligence Scale for Children–Revised
Wisconsin Card Sorting Test (WCST), 53, 82, 83*t*–84*t*, 103, 121, 268–270, 281, 283, 292, 298, 327, 329*t*, 375, 382, 391, 405
  frequency of perseverative responses on, 334, 336*f*
  problems with, 332–335
  reliability of, 333–335, 335*t*, 337*t*
  sensitivity of, 333
  specificity of, 332–333
  twin correlations for, 333–335, 334*t*, 337*t*
Wisconsin General Test Apparatus, 203, 204
Woodcock-Johnson Test, 33*t*
Word length effect, 161–162, 223
Word String Recall, 35*t*, 36*t*, 38*t*
Writing disability, self-regulated strategy development for, 353–357, 361–362

Yale Center for Learning and Attention
    Disorders study of reading disabil-
    ity, 29–37
  confirmatory factor analysis model for,
    31–32
  correlations of factors in, 33, 34, 34*t*, 39*t*

factor loadings for, 32, 33*t*, 34, 35*t*–36*t*,
    38*t*
  Levels I and II test batteries for, 30
  model fit statistics for, 32–33, 33*t*, 34,
    37*t*
  population selection for, 30